Making Empire

This is the dramatic story of the colonial encounter and the construction of empire in southern Africa in the nineteenth century. What did the British make of the Xhosa and how did they make sense of their politics and culture? How did the British establish and then explain their dominion, especially when it ran counter to the cultural values they believed themselves to represent? Richard Price answers these questions by looking at the ways in which individual missionaries, officials and politicians interacted with the Xhosa. He describes how those encounters changed and shaped the culture of imperial rule in southern Africa. He charts how an imperial regime developed both in the minds of the colonizers and in the everyday practice of power and how the British imperial presence was entangled in and shaped by the encounter with the Xhosa from the very moment of their first meeting.

RICHARD PRICE is a Professor and the Chair of the Department of History, University of Maryland, College Park. His previous publications include *Labour in British Society 1780–1980* (1986) and *British Society 1680–1880: Dynamism, Containment and Change* (1999).

D1453212

Making Empire

Colonial Encounters and the Creation of Imperial Rule in Nineteenth-Century Africa

Richard Price

University of Maryland, College Park

CAMBRIDGE UNIVERSITY PRESS
Cambridge, New York, Melbourne, Madrid, Cape Town, Singapore, São Paulo, Delhi

Cambridge University Press
The Edinburgh Building, Cambridge CB2 8RU, UK

Published in the United States of America by Cambridge University Press,
New York

www.cambridge.org
Information on this title: www.cambridge.org/9780521718196

First published 2008

Printed in the United Kingdom at the University Press, Cambridge

A catalogue record for this publication is available from the British Library

Library of Congress Cataloguing in Publication data
Price, Richard, 1941–
Making empire: colonial encounters and the creation of imperial rule in
nineteenth-century Africa / Richard Price.
    p.   cm.
Includes bibliographical references.
ISBN 978-0-521-88968-1
1. Xhosa (African people) – History – 19th century.   2. Xhosa (African people) –
Colonization – South Africa – Cape of Good Hope.   3. Xhosa (African people) –
Missions.   4. British – South Africa – History – 19th century.   5. Kaffraria –
History – 19th century.   6. Cape of Good Hope (South Africa) – History –
1795–1872.   7. Great Britain – Colonies – Africa – History – 19th century.
8. Imperialism – History – 19th century – Case studies.   I. Title.
DT1768.X57P75   2008
968′.004963985–dc22
                                                                2008018713

ISBN 978-0-521-88968-1 hardback
ISBN 978-0-521-71819-6 paperback

To the memory of Kathleen Price and Lilian Chedgey

Contents

Figures

Plates to be found between pages 189 and 190.

Missionaries

1. Reverend Henry Calderwood. South African National Library, Cape Town.
2. Reverend William Shaw. South African National Library, Cape Town.
3. Reverend Richard Birt. South African National Library, Cape Town.

Xhosa chiefs

4. Sandile. South African National Library, Cape Town.
5. Sandile and his counselors. South African National Library, Cape Town.
6. Maqoma. South African National Library, Cape Town.
7. Xhoxho. Western Cape Provincial Archives, Cape Town, Photo Collection.

Meetings

8. Meeting between Governor Janssens and Chief Ngqika, 1803. South African National Library, Cape Town.
9. Meeting with Xhosa chiefs at Charles Brownlee's residence. Western Cape Provincial Archives, Cape Town, Photo Collection.

Officials

10. Sir Harry Smith. Photo by Hulton Archive/Getty Images.
11. George Grey © Bettmann/Corbis.
12. Charles Lennox Stretch, frontier official. Western Cape Provincial Archives, Cape Town, Photo Collection.
13. Lt. General Sir George Pomeroy Colley. South African National Library, Cape Town.

Chiefs and prophetesses

Maps

Preface: Intentions and purposes

In early January 2000 I found myself standing in the small, old-fashioned catalogue room of the Cape Archives in Cape Town, South Africa, leafing through the binders that contain the depository's finding lists. I had come to Cape Town on a scholarly whim. It was a luxury that I had given myself during a sabbatical year – an alternative to a scholarly lifetime of making the trek across the north Atlantic to the comfortable familiarity of the British Library. After many years working in British social history, I was searching for a new research project. I had spent the previous ten years working on a book that was a synthesis of pre-existing scholarship and I knew that I wanted to get back into historical archives again after a long absence. Cape Town was not, perhaps, an obvious place to satisfy this need, although it would certainly be warmer and more beautiful than anywhere I knew in Britain. But, of course, this trip was not entirely an indulgent caprice. My interest in South Africa had longer and more complicated roots.

I grew up in Britain in the 1950s. It was a childhood that I remember as being dominated by two major political themes. There was the question of empire and there was the question of class. Both were a constant presence in the culture and politics and both were inextricably bound up with what it meant to be British. It was impossible to escape the issues of class and empire. The seeming propensity of the male British worker to go on strike and the growing nationalist movements in the empire were seldom out of the public eye. It is no surprise that my own scholarly career has been dominated by those two themes.

My early interest in history was kindled by an old four-volume set of *Cassell's History of England* given to me by my grandfather, which presented an imperial version of British history. I early developed the habit of browsing the history shelves of the local public library, which seemed to be crammed with books on empire. It was the history of the empire that first made me want to be a historian. At university, I was lucky enough to be taught by Ranajit Guha, who mentored me as an undergraduate and as a graduate student. I wrote a thesis which later became a book on the culture of empire and the working classes, using the case of the South African War of 1899–1902. After that, I went in a different scholarly direction, although I never lost interest in the question of empire and always regarded the imperial experience as essential to a full understanding of Britain's history.

By 2000, however, these influences of empire had been reawakened by personal circumstances. A few years before, I had traveled to South Africa on personal business. I was struck by the beauty of the place and, of course, by the exciting political changes that were associated with the transition to a democratic nation. That visit in 1996 also rekindled the interest in empire that had been my starting point as a historian. So I began to scheme in my head for ways to return to the Cape more regularly, as something slightly more than a tourist.

My inclination was reinforced as I watched how empire had recently become important again in my own field of modern British history and beyond. The publication of Edward Said's *Orientalism* in 1978 may be said to have initiated this renewed interest in empire, and following his lead, post-colonial theory moved the focus of attention in empire studies away from its traditional concentration on politics and economics and towards culture. In the past, historians had treated empire almost entirely from the standpoint of political economy, so the shift that Said initiated was quite a departure. But there were other sources, too, for the renewed attention to empire in scholarly consciousness. In Indian history, for example, the Subaltern Studies project sought to place the colonial subject at the center of the imperial experience. Elsewhere, the disciplinary lines were constantly being breached. Indeed, some of the most important work on colonial relations was being done by anthropologists who possessed a historical bent, such as Greg Dening for the south Pacific, Anne Stoler for the Dutch empire, and John and Jean Comaroff in southern Africa.

I watched this scholarly turn to empire from the sidelines. I was impressed with its vitality and appeal. In British history the scholarly turn to empire focused on the way empire had been central to the making of Britain's history and had permeated deeply into its culture. I was in sympathy with this move. But I was somewhat reserved as to the degree to which one could reduce British history to the imperial connection. Other contexts also seemed important – such as Europe, or even class. More interesting to me was the question raised by the Indian scholar Ashis Nandy in a wonderful book, published in 1983, which he titled *The Intimate Enemy: Loss and Recovery of Self under Colonialism*. One of Nandy's major themes was precisely the way empire damaged and distorted British culture; so that ultimately, perhaps, this damage was greater to the colonizer than it was to the colonized. And personal conversation with Ranajit Guha helped keep that question in my head. My scholarly inclination, therefore, drew me more and more away from Britain itself. I thought it might be useful to go *to* the empire and see what happened to British culture there, at the frontier of empire. This book is about what I found when I made that journey.

It was these vague and unformed intentions that I carried to Cape Town in January of 2000. There, I did what historians do when they are not quite sure where they are going: I began to rummage through the archives, testing various ideas against what the sources revealed. On the morning in question I opened a binder whose title page read: "List of British Kaffraria Records." A distant memory stirred in my mind. I had heard the name "British Kaffraria" many years before in some long-forgotten school lesson, or perhaps from one of those old books in my home town public library. The "Kaffir Wars" were frontier and land conflicts on the eastern Cape frontier in the middle years of the nineteenth century; some of Queen Victoria's *little* wars; wars which hardly rippled the tides of British public opinion; wars which did not figure in most histories of colonial warfare, and occasioned little notice in contemporary politics. I called up some of the volumes in the finding list, opened the large books into which the material was bound, and knew almost instantly that I had found my project.

The material handed me was often disorganized and eccentrically classified. But it electrified me. Among the first things I examined were reports of British colonial officials – they were variously termed diplomatic or resident agents – who lived with the Xhosa tribes in the 1830s. It was immediately evident that this was amazing stuff – especially to a British historian. Imperial states are obsessed with recording, watching and surveilling, and the compulsion to inform and log was evident in these reports and letters. The volumes contained records of what the early imperial administrators were doing and thinking. Stories of encounter, observation and of the struggle to understand the culture and politics of the Xhosa tribes were all to be found in these volumes. It was a rich collection which allowed me insight into the mentality of people who were constructing the empire on the ground in the context of their encounter with the Xhosa. This was the empire as it was experienced at the frontier, not as it was imagined to be back home.

The book that has resulted from my encounter with this colonial archive has been the most enjoyable of all the books I have researched and written. It was impossible not to be hooked by the stories that I found in the Cape Archives and elsewhere. As the reader who persists will discover, the archives that have provided the key source material for this book – that is, the missionary archives and the records of the imperial administration – are packed with stories detailing the nitty-gritty of the encounter between the British and the Xhosa. This turned the book into a very personal project. Inevitably, I found myself fascinated by the personalities that were my daily companions in the sources. This was particularly true of the Xhosa chiefs who will appear throughout the whole narrative. But it was true also of figures like Sir Harry Smith and Sir George Grey on the British side. My engagement with these and other luminaries was a determining influence on the way I wanted to shape the book. It is therefore appropriate to explain why the book takes the shape that it does, to declare its historical logic and to deal with other housekeeping matters that will enhance the reader's understanding of the narrative.

When I sat down to write this book, I was very conscious of those historians who had explored this frontier of empire before me. The story of how the Xhosa came to be part of the British empire has been told before – although it has received relatively little attention in imperial history. My own excursion into this corner of African and imperial history has depended entirely upon the work of others, particularly those colleagues working in the area of South African history. South African history is a lively field and at many points this book bumps up against the debates and controversies that animate the field. The book also touches on histories that are often distant from imperial historiography, such as the history of African religion; and it draws upon scholarship in fields other than history, such as historical anthropology.

But while I wanted to properly acknowledge my considerable debt to other specialists, I did not want to write a book whose narrative was constantly interrupted by the need to address this or that historical controversy, or comment on how my argument contrasts with the theoretical framework of other historians. I have drawn upon other scholars where I feel they help me understand and illuminate the historical processes I am describing. And I have taken issue with the way other historians have treated particular events where I felt it would help the reader better understand the historical story I wanted to tell. But I did not want to frame this book around engagements with other historians or historiographies. I have not aspired to write a book whose principal aim is to displace, contest or confirm the work of other historians. And the reason for this is very simple. The story that I have to tell is too dramatic and too important for that. I do not want readers to be diverted away from the rich and engaging stories that are told between the covers of this book. Although the book was partly inspired by the "imperial turn" in British history it has not been written either within that school of history or as a counterpoint to it. It is, rather, a study of how colonial encounter produced a culture of imperial rule.

I use the word "culture" a lot in what follows, and this is a good place to describe what I have in mind by that term. By "culture" in this context I am speaking of how a culture of difference, power and domination emerged out of the dynamics of the encounter between the British and the Xhosa. The argument tracks the growth of an imperial culture that enabled, explained and rationalized why the British should establish dominion over the Xhosa. I am concerned principally with the practices, modes of behavior, mindsets, values and ideologies that shaped the way relationships between the British and Xhosa played out. I am less concerned with the institutional forms of this imperial culture – with the structures of imperial administration, for example – than I am with how the ideologies of that culture evolved and worked.

By the same token, I have not intended to track the debates and divisions within imperial culture itself. That is, I do not focus on the differences within the various segments of the cultural processes I describe. I am aware, of course, that cultural forms are not monolithic, either in ideology or in political practice. In the present case, for example, doctrinal differences between the various missionary groups influenced their attitudes to racial politics. Within the apparatus of imperial administration, the competing priorities of the frontier officials, the provincial administration at Cape Town, and the metropolitan authority of London are mainstays of imperial historiography. Such divisions are important. But to highlight the internal histories of the cultural formations would shift the focus of the book more toward the cultural institution itself. I have wanted to put the behavior of individuals at the center of my story; to use the experience of individual stories to explain what happened when British culture met Xhosa culture and politics.

Finally, a word about nomenclature. The nomenclature of African history is, of course, inevitably inflected with the experience of colonialism. Africanists are still sorting out what are the most appropriate spellings to describe indigenous peoples and cultures. When I have used the word "Kaffir," for example, it is either because it is in the historical sources, or because it refers to a particular epoch when the historiography used that disparaging term. In other cases, such as the word Khoesan for Khoisan (what an earlier generation would have referred to as "Hottentot"), I have tried to use the word most widely accepted at the present day. Xhosa spelling presents special difficulties because when the British encountered the Xhosa there was no dictionary or orthography they could use to understand the Xhosa language. They had to make these aids for themselves. As a consequence Xhosa names and words appear in the sources in a variety of different spellings. The chief Maqomo, for example, was recorded as Maqoma, Mocomo, Macoma, and even MacKomer! Except when I am quoting from an original source, I have tried to achieve a consistent spelling throughout which uses the form that is accepted as most reflective of Xhosa grammar itself. For guidance in these matters, I have consulted Africanists and I have noted the usages in books by other scholars.

Acknowledgments

In this book I have wandered into new and fascinating scholarly places. I had no background in African history, a little in South African history, and somewhat more in imperial history. The willing help I have received from colleagues in these areas of history has been one of the real pleasures of working on this book. It is only proper, then, that they take pride of place in this list of professional colleagues to whom I owe thanks.

My colleagues Paul Landau and David Gordon (now at Bowdoin College), expert Africanists themselves, were tolerant and helpful critics. They answered my questions and responded helpfully to them. Paul Landau is an important scholar of African religion and his work touches directly on the themes of this book. But he has always been mindful of my agenda, and in his readings and critiques he kept that in mind. He was generous enough to read the whole manuscript and provided an astute and very helpful reading. Elizabeth Elbourne was kind enough to read and comment on early parts of the manuscript. Elizabeth is one of the pre-eminent imperial historians of her generation. She has been most generous in sharing her knowledge and giving me her reflections on the early chapters, as well as being a sharp but gentle critic of various scholarly papers I have presented. Likewise, I was flattered that Robert Ross, another pre-eminent historian in the field, also took time to read the manuscript. His comments were particularly welcome since they allowed me to correct some errors of fact and detail. Another colleague of mine at Maryland, Arthur Eckstein, is not an Africanist, but a distinguished historian of Ancient Rome. He is also a widely read historian and he has a special interest in empire that almost makes him a specialist in the field. He read the whole manuscript and his comments were most helpful.

In Cape Town itself, I had the great pleasure of getting to know Bill Nasson, of the Department of History at University of Cape Town. Bill was extremely helpful in being a ready listener for my interests and speculations, particularly when the project was in its early stages. He (and his wife, Anne) were generous with their time and were very welcoming to two strangers who wandered into their world. The staff of the Cape

Archive and of the Cory Library, Rhodes University, Grahamstown, were unfailing in their help. At the Cory Library, in particular I would like to thank Zweliyanykima Vena for his assistance in digging out collections from the obscure corners of the library. Timothy Stapleton and Roger Levine deserve notice for help with Xhosa spelling. Roger Levine generously shared with me his important work on Jan Tzatzoe.

In the United States and the United Kingdom this book has been a way of adding new professional friends. In Washington, I am fortunate to have Dane Kennedy, a leading historian of empire, as a colleague at nearby George Washington University. Dane listened to the ideas of this project from its beginning and read the whole manuscript as it neared its final draft. His commentary at every stage was unfailingly helpful. Likewise, Philippa Levine at the University of Southern California has followed the project from its early formulation to the final drafts. At every stage she willingly read and made useful comments. Alison Twells, of Sheffield Hallam University, likewise interrupted her busy schedule to read large chunks of the manuscript. Alison is a scholar of missionary culture in Britain and I was most grateful to receive her reflections on my arguments about missionary culture. Susan Thorne helped me formulate the project by reading and commenting upon an early position paper. My friend Philip Hare is not a historian, but he is South African, and he knows a lot about the racial politics of the place and its history. He read the whole manuscript in draft form and had intelligent things to say about it. My conversations with him have taught me a lot about South Africa itself and recent South African history.

My good friend John Belchem of the University of Liverpool, as always, was helpful and supportive. He facilitated a presentation to the Department of History research seminar and a lecture in the Victorian Studies Lecture Series at Liverpool that gave me the opportunity to talk about this project. I have delivered parts of the project to a variety of scholarly gatherings and have always come away both pleased and stimulated by the quality of the discussion that it evoked. In particular, I would like to mention the Rethinking British History Seminar at the Institute of Historical Research, London, which Catherine Hall kindly invited me to attend; the British Worlds Conference in 2000 at Cape Town and at Bristol in 2007 where John Mackenzie, Jeffrey Cox and Saul Dubow among others made helpful remarks; the Center for European History, Harvard University, where Jim Cronin invited me to present an early version of this project; the European Social Science History Conference at Amsterdam in 2006; Martin Weiner was kind enough to invite me to talk about this project to an African Studies group and a student seminar at Rice University; I gave an early version of the project in the History honors lecture series at George Washington University. My own colleagues at Maryland responded most generously to an early description of the project I delivered to the Nathan and Jeannette Miller Center for Historical Studies in the Department of History. Barbara Weinstein, Ira Berlin, Jeannie Rutenberg, Paul Landau and David Gordon were particularly helpful and encouraging. Various parts of the book were presented at the North American Conference on British Studies in Philadelphia 2005 and Denver 2006, at the American Historical Association in Atlanta in 2007, and at the lecture series on British History at Stanford University in May 2007, where David Como and Priya Satia were kind enough to invite me to lecture. My thanks to all participants in those gatherings.

Ranajit Guha has been a major intellectual influence in my life. This is true not only of his scholarly work but also of his commitment to scholarly values and to the life of the mind. He was my graduate supervisor many years ago. And although I have worked in very different areas of history and in different ways, I have never ceased to learn from him. The deep origins of this book lie in my early studies on imperialism as an undergraduate with Ranajit Guha, and its more recent formulation flowed from conversation and discussion I had with Ranajit in New York in early 2000 as I was casting around for a new scholarly focus.

I must also acknowledge the general support I have received from my institution, the University of Maryland. The Dean of Arts and Humanities, James Harris, awarded me a semester of supported research leave in academic year 2000 and a sabbatical leave in the same year. I received a Distinguished Research Fellowship in 2003–4, and the Chair of my Department, Gary Gerstle (now of Vanderbilt University) generously gave me a reduced teaching and service load to enable me to write a nearly final draft of the book. Without that support the research for this book could not have been done, nor could the writing have been so expeditiously completed. Courtenay Lanier has helped me by using her technical skills with the computer to good effect. Michael Watson, my Cambridge editor, and several anonymous readers also deserve my thanks. The readers led me to clarify some arguments and revise others. Michael pushed for several changes that were both improving and necessary. I also wish to thank Howard and Marilyn Simler and Derek and Judy Simler for their hospitality during several research sojourns in London.

Finally, I want to recognize the two most important people in my life, my son Marshall and my wife Adele. Marshall contributed to this book by just being there and affording me the pleasure of watching him as he grew into a fine young professional in his own right. Adele's contribution was more varied and labor-intensive. Adele introduced me to South Africa in the first place; and it was from that introduction that I got the idea to work there. More than that, she brings light into my life; her presence sustains and supports me, and provides the energy and inspiration to do projects like this book. She also assisted me by performing a real labor of love. She spent many hours reading and editing the manuscript for flow and consistency, giving the best sort of editorial advice. Any literary qualities this book may possess are due largely to her work. Obviously, any flaws the book contains are not the responsibility of Adele nor of anyone else mentioned here; they are mine alone.

Cast of characters

AYLIFF, JOHN 1797–1862; Methodist missionary associated particularly with Mfengu; 1820 settler; established Healdtown school and settlement for Mfengu 1854.

BENNIE, JOHN 1796–1869; GMS missionary; the earliest serious student of Xhosa; author of many published works on Xhosa orthography; 1820 settler; founder of Lovedale with John Ross in 1824; left missionary work to concentrate on teaching in 1853 after a squabble with GMS.

BROWNLEE, CHARLES 1821–90; one of the first British "experts" on Xhosa; son of John Brownlee, missionary founder of King William's Town; interpreter for American missionaries in Natal with Dingane and nearby when Boer trekkers massacred; Commissioner to the Nqgika 1849–66; Resident Magistrate, Somerset East 1866–72; first Secretary for Native Affairs, Cape Colony 1872–78; considered a leading authority on native law and customs; created system of "native administration" for the Transkei that was modeled elsewhere; 1878 chief magistrate Griqualand east.

BOYCE, WILLIAM BINNINGTON 1803–89; Methodist missionary; established Buntingville 1830; worked at Mt. Coke, Wesleyville, Newtondale and Grahamstown before returning to England in 1843; compiled the first printed grammar of Xhosa in 1834; discovered the euphonic concord; adviser to D'Urban in sixth frontier war and modified D'Urban's original intention to expel Xhosa.

CALDERWOOD, HENRY 1808–65; LMS missionary; was already a minister in Kendal when in 1838 accepted by LMS; married to Eliza Taylor by whom he had five sons and a daughter; published in Zulu 1844 and was proficient in it; left ministry in 1846; associated particularly with resettlement of Mfengu on new frontier in 1848 and the establishment of military villages; author of several reports on education policy towards the Mfengu.

CHALMERS, JOHN AITKEN 1837–88; GMS missionary; son of William Chalmers, who arrived at Tyhumie in 1827; spoke fluent Xhosa and was considered an expert on the Xhosa; educated at Glasgow University and at the College of the United Presbyterian Church; attended medical classes at Edinburgh; composed Xhosa hymns.

CATHCART, LIEUTENANT GENERAL, SIR GEORGE 1794–1854; ADC to Wellington at Waterloo and a member of Wellington's Horse Guards clique, even though he was generally unknown to the public; Wellington responsible for his appointment as Governor of the Cape Colony 1852–53, where he brought the eighth frontier war to an end; killed in the Crimean War.

CURRIE, SIR WALTER 1819–72; 1820 settler family; frontier official; served in 1846 and 1850–3 wars; commandant of FAMP 1855; advocate of policy of annexing Sarhili's territory and of punitive expeditions into Independent Kaffraria; given a KCB for role in Prince Alfred's 1860 visit; played large role in establishment of Griqualand east; effected the transfer of 40,000 Mfengu from their "overcrowded colonial locations" to Transkei.

GREY, SIR GEORGE 1812–98; Colonial governor and leading representative of Liberal imperialism; earned initial fame as an early explorer of Australia, which led to his appointment as Governor of South Australia 1841–5; achieved national standing as Governor of New Zealand 1845–53, where he also attained status as an "native expert"; Governor of Cape Colony 1854–61; New Zealand again 1861–8, when he was fired by the Colonial Office; remained in New Zealand to become a leading politican, and Prime Minister 1877–9 before returning to England shortly before his death.

HINTSA 1790–1835; grandson of Gceleka the last undisputed chief of all the Xhosa; thus, Hintsa was the Xhosa paramount but his real power extended only over the Gceleka branch; his relations were particularly tense with the Rharhabe Xhosa; recognized to be a benevolent ruler and not a tyrant; never imposed death penalty, effectively abolishing it within Xhosa law; known for his welcoming attitude to white travelers; accused by British of complicity in sixth frontier war and was killed in a celebrated incident trying to escape from his British captors.

MACLEAN, JOHN 1810–74; leading frontier administrator; army captain who arrived at Cape in 1835 to serve under Smith in the sixth frontier war; appointed Resident Agent at Fort Peddie in 1845; Commissioner to Ndlambe's Xhosa; Chief Commissioner of British Kaffraria 1852 and made Lieutenant Governor 1860; knighted and appointed Lt. Governor to Natal on absorption of British Kaffraria into the Cape Colony 1866.

MAQOMA 1799–1872; son of Ngqika and elder half-brother of Sandile; for much of this period, generally recognized as the most respected, militarily expert and politically powerful of the Xhosa chiefs.

MHALA? –1875; son of Ndlambe, on whose death the tribe split into three parts with Mhala leading the most important group; achieved chiefly status due to his own political skills, rather than being recognized as Ndlambe's legitimate successor; known as "wild cat" because of his cunning; the most resistant of all the chiefs to British control and, after Maqoma, the most able of the Chiefs.

NDLAMBE 1740–1828; Rharhabe Xhosa, grandson of Phalo and father of Mhala; and uncle, guardian and then rival to Ngqika, with whom he contested for leadership of the Rharhabe Xhosa; cuckolded by Nqgika, who started an affair with Ndlambe's mistress, Suthu, whom he married; even though Ndlambe defeated Ngqika for supremacy over the Rharhabe, Ngqika outmaneuvered him by securing British support.

NGQIKA 1775–1829; chief of the Rharhabe Xhosa, thanks largely to support of British, who continued to treat him as a paramount even though he rapidly lost his power after his alliance with them in 1819–20. The British commonly referred to him as Gaika, and to his tribe as the Gaika Xhosa.

ROSS, JOHN 1799–1878; the first GMS missionary ordained specifically for service in South Africa; Xhosa linguist; graduate of Glasgow University; a scholarly man; printed the first Xhosa booklet in 1824 and the first book of Xhosa hymns; spent the entire period of his mission at Pirie, even though he was burned out of his mission four times due to war.

SARHILI 1814–92; son of Hintsa, and thus formal paramount of Xhosa and chief of Gceleka; managed to escape British rule until the annexation of the Transkei after the last frontier war in 1878.

SMITH, SIR HENRY GEORGE WAKELYN, LT. GENERAL 1787–1860; served in South America, 1806–7, in the Peninsular War 1809–12; chief of intelligence in the war of 1812, present at the burning of the White House and lifted one of James Madison's jackets as a souvenir; Battle of Waterloo 1815; Military Secretary at the Cape, 1828–40 and frontier commandant 1835–6; India 1840–7, victor of Aliwal in the Sikh

War 1845–6, for which he was knighted; Governor of Cape Colony 1847–52; Commandant of Western District 1853–60.

SOGA, TIYO 1829–71; the first Xhosa missionary, son of "Old Soga"; educated in Glasgow in the late 1840s and 1850s and ordained there after attending classes at Glasgow University; married Janet Burnside, by whom he had several childen and founded the first generation of Xhosa intellectuals; arrived in eastern Cape to take up full-time mission work in 1858; died of consumption 1871.

SHAW, WILLIAM 1798–1872; Methodist missionary; 1820 settler; super-intendant of WMMS in the eastern Cape; active in support of Mfengu; in 1846 war was leading adviser to Governor Peregrine Maitland; implemented policy of a string of Methodist mission stations into Natal; returned to England in 1857, where he served as President of the Methodist General Assembly.

Abbreviations

BK	British Kaffraria
CA	Cape Archives
CAD	Cape Archives Depot
CO	Colonial Office
CL	Cory Library
CWM	Council on World Missions
f(f).	folio(s)
FAMP	Frontier Armed Mounted Police
GH	Government House
GMS	Glasgow Missionary Society
LG	Lieutenant Governor
LMS	London Missionary Society
MSB	The Grey Collection, NLSA (CT)
NA	National Archives, Kew, formerly the Public Record Office
NLSA (CT)	National Library of South Africa, Cape Town
SPCK	Society for the Propagation of [now: for Promoting] Christian Knowledge
WMMS	Wesleyan Methodist Missionary Society

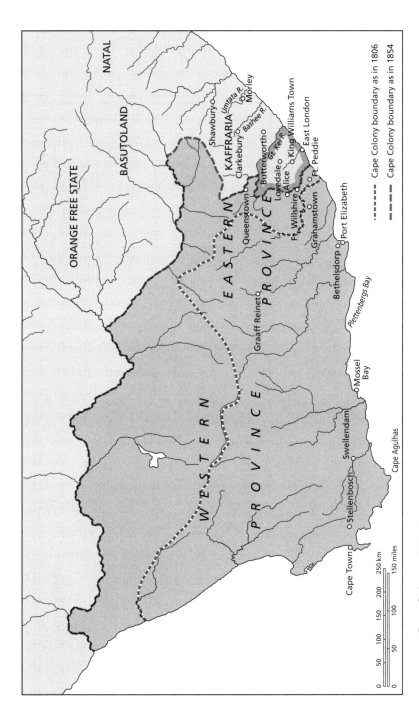

NATAL

BASUTOLAND

ORANGE FREE STATE

KAFFRARIA

Shawbury

Umtata R.
Clarkebury
Morley
Bashee R.

Butterworth
Gt. Kei R.
Lovedale
Alice
King Williams Town
Ft. Willshire
East London
Grahamstown
Ft. Peddie
Queenstown

EASTERN PROVINCE

WESTERN PROVINCE

Graaff Reinet

Bethelsdorp
Port Elizabeth

Plettenbergs Bay

Mossel Bay

Swellendam

Cape Agulhas

Stellenbosch

Cape Town

Cape Colony boundary as in 1806
Cape Colony boundary as in 1854

0 50 100 150 200 250 km
0   50   100   150 miles

1. Cape Colony 1806–65

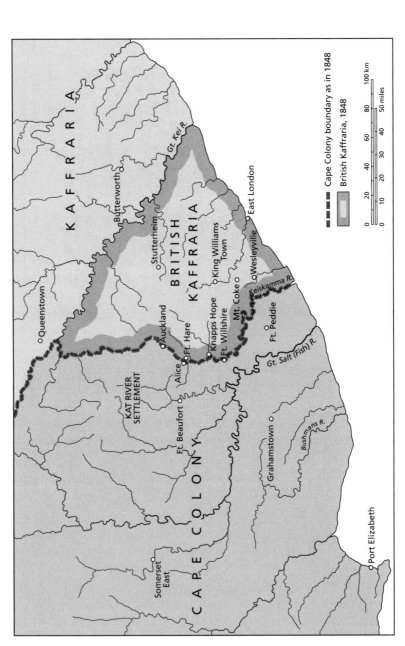

2. The eastern frontier 1795–1858

Cape Colony boundary as in 1848

British Kaffraria, 1848

| 0 | 20 | 40 | 60 | 80 | 100 km |
| 0 | 10 | 20 | 30 | 40 | 50 miles |

KAFFRARIA

BRITISH KAFFRARIA

CAPE COLONY

Butterworth

Gt. Kei R.

Stutterheim

King Williams Town

East London

Queenstown

Wesleyville

Mt. Coke

Keiskamma R.

Auckland

Knapps Hope

Ft. Hare

Ft. Willshire

Ft. Peddie

Alice

Gt. Salt (Fish) R.

KAT RIVER
SETTLEMENT

Ft. Beaufort

Grahamstown

Bushmans R.

Somerset
East

Port Elizabeth

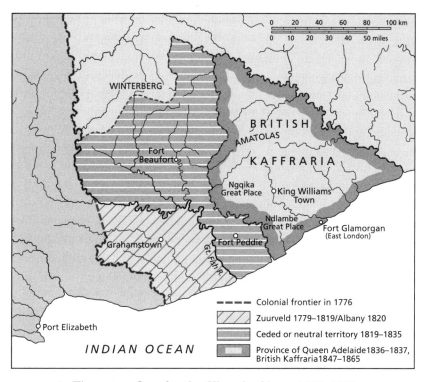

3. The eastern Cape frontier: Xhosa land losses 1779–1850

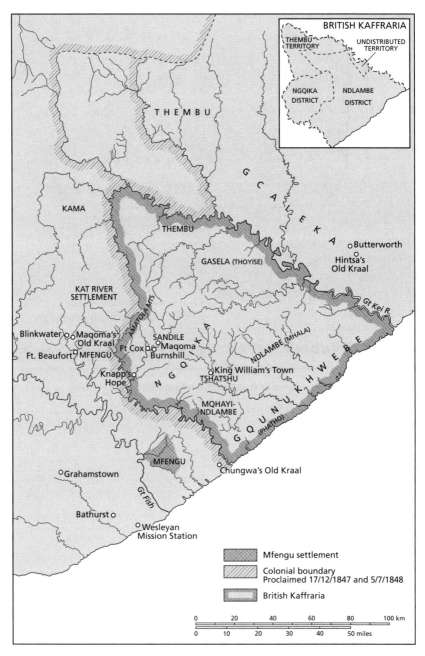

4. The eastern Cape frontier area 1847–50

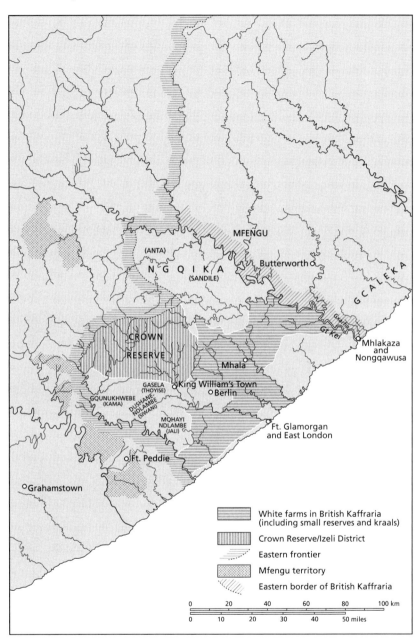

5. The eastern Cape frontier area 1858–66

1   Encounters in empire

I have called this book *Making Empire* because it tells how the British came to create a culture of imperial rule in Southern Africa in the first half of the nineteenth century. And the first words of its subtitle, *Colonial Encounters*, express the centrality in this process of the interaction between the British and the Xhosa peoples who occupied the eastern Cape frontier in that period. Indeed, the main narrative of the book flows from many stories of what happened when individual Britishers – missionaries, military men, frontier officials and others – had to deal with Xhosa people and Xhosa society. I have used these stories to enter into the imperial mind. What did the British make of the Xhosa as they struggled to figure out who the Xhosa were and what their relationship with the British empire should be? How did a culture of imperial rule emerge out of the encounter between the British presence and the indigenous people? How did the British develop a knowledge system about the Xhosa that enabled them to make sense of their politics and culture? By what means did the British actually establish their dominion over these African people? How did they explain this dominion, especially when it ran counter to the cultural values they believed themselves to represent? How was the belief that Britain's empire was a "liberal" empire, an empire of freedom, reconciled with the very dark things that accompanied the creation of this empire in the early nineteenth century? And, finally, (and only lightly touched on in this book), what does all this suggest about the relationship between empire and British culture?

In the early nineteenth century the eastern region of Cape Colony was a distant frontier of empire. It was difficult to get to and it was not a place where fame and recognition were likely to be won. Indeed, more often it was a place where careers foundered and remained stuck. The principal town in the eastern Cape, Grahamstown, was over 500 miles from Cape Town and accessible only over difficult roads or by the equally difficult sea voyage to Port Elizabeth. Perhaps it is for this reason that the eastern Cape has not featured very large in the historiography of the British empire. Yet there are reasons to suggest that this absence is unwarranted.[1]

For one thing, Britain had the tie of kith and kin with the eastern Cape. It was part of British rather than Dutch southern Africa; and it remained so into the modern day. Even today, to see the layout of the main street of Grahamstown, with Rhodes University at one end and a grand Anglican cathedral at the other, is to be reminded of pastoral southern English country towns. The reason for this Britishness was that in 1820 the British government had sponsored an emigration scheme that sent 4,000 settlers to the eastern Cape to establish a new colony that was to be called "Albany." The idea was to create a replica of British pastoral and aristo- cratic society in the colony. Many of the settlers were grouped into "parties" headed by a sponsor who was to become the local landowning aristocrat, accompanied by a panoply of agricultural workers and artisans who would cluster around his patronage. This delightful little fantasy soon fell apart once the settlers hit the ground and discovered that their flimsy tents were no protection against the fierce weather of the region, that their seeds failed to take root, leaving them facing the threat of imminent starvation, and, to cap it all, that they were in the middle of a war zone between competing branches of the Xhosa polity.[2]

Thus, even though the strategic priority for colonial policy-makers in London was the Cape itself, the eastern frontier continued to intrude itself rudely into their line of vision. The problem was that the eastern Cape was the place where relentless white expansion finally met the deep resistance of the Xhosa peoples. The frontier was in a state of perpetual unrest. The British settlers chafed under the restraints of official policy which tried to maintain a line between British and Xhosa spheres of influence. There was tension between the British settlers and the Xhosa over cattle-rustling, in which each side was probably as bad as the other. The Xhosa were eternally disaffected with the progressive dispossession of their "ancestral" lands, as well they might be. Thus, for 100 years the frontier remained an unstable zone of contact. Nine wars were fought from 1779 to 1879, first against the Dutch and then against the British, before the final resistance of the Xhosa people to white domination was crushed.[3]

In this context it is rather surprising that the Xhosa remain relatively unknown to the British. Yet Nelson Mandela is a Xhosa, as is Thabo Mbeke; and the ANC is a Xhosa-dominated party. But it is not the Xhosa who represent black South Africans in the British imagination.[4] It is the Zulu. The Zulu captured the British imagination from the very beginning of imperial contact. Unlike the Xhosa, the Zulu had the fortune to be observed by a small group of traders at Port Natal (what was to become Durban) in the early 1820s. For a variety of reasons these adventurers sent reports back to Cape Town of a fearsome, martial race ruled by a powerful, tyrannical leader, Shaka, who was busy using his military prowess to create a powerful state. This image of the Zulus as a warrior race in the process of nation-building appealed to the British. As a conquering race themselves, they appreciated the qualities of military prowess and nation-building. It was an image that was confirmed by later engagements, such as when in 1838 the Zulu king Dingaan murdered Piet Retief's party of Boer trekkers while parlaying under (what they thought) was a flag of truce; or, most famously, of course, when a British army was overwhelmed by the Zulu *impis* at Isandlwana in 1879. There is nothing like military defeat at the hands of uncivilized natives to raise their estimation in the mind of the imperialist. And from then on the Zulus were Britain's favorite Africans.[5]

But the predominance of the Zulu in the British imagination was purely a metropolitan construction. For most of the nineteenth century, the Zulu offered little trouble to the British. The British were much more preoccupied with the Xhosa than they were with the Zulu. They fought three serious wars against them, in 1834–5, 1846–7 and 1850–3, each of which stretched the local capacity of the British army almost to breaking point. Unlike the Zulu, the Xhosa were an enemy who did not fight in the way the British thought fitting. They quickly learnt to avoid the set-piece battles that were common to both European and Zulu military strategy. They were among the first guerrilla fighters in Africa, and as such they inflicted many a setback to British arms. But since such calamities were not admitted as defeats – as all the world could see Isandlwana was – they did not get registered in British culture or history as the debacles they often were.[6]

This relative neglect of the British encounter with the Xhosa is surprising for another reason, too: *the Xhosa were the first African people whom the British had to decide how to rule.* The eastern Cape was the place where the foundations of Britain's modern African empire were laid. The Xhosa were quite obviously not the first Africans to feel the cold steel of British power, or the fervent importuning of its missionaries. But the Xhosa *were* the first to experience the full panoply of British civilization arrayed before them – its missionaries, settlers and soldiers, imperial governors and politicans – each offering different promises and threats. The history of how the British came to decide to rule the Xhosa was tortured and complicated. But if we are interested in asking how and by what processes a culture of imperial rule is developed out of British culture, the encounter with the Xhosa on the eastern Cape frontier in the first half of the nineteenth century is a good place to take up scholarly residence.

For much of the period under consideration, the British preferred to try to control the Xhosa at arm's length. The underlying strategic concept the British employed was the notion of a buffer zone that would separate the zone of British settlement from the Xhosa. This was a familiar imperial ploy. Van Riebeeck had planted a hedge around the early Cape settlement in an attempt to keep the Dutch community and the local Khoesan people apart – parts of the hedge can still be seen in Kirstenbosch Botanical Gardens in Cape Town. The British had tried similar policies in Ireland and North America with equally little success. But ideas die hard in imperial culture, and the notion of separation and distinct development of both colonists and indigenes was an inspiration for the conception of British Kaffraria as a solution to the unstable frontier of the eastern Cape. It was the records of this effort to establish British Kaffraria that had caught my eye that January day in the Cape Archives building.

An initial attempt was made in 1835 to create a homeland for the Xhosa that would stabilize the frontier and allow the British to keep a watch on their movements. Following the end of the sixth frontier war in August 1835, Sir Harry Smith and Benjamin D'Urban established Queen Adelaide Province. This venture lasted nine months, killed by the opposition of the Colonial Office. And until 1847 the main aim of frontier policy was to maintain the peace by a system of mediation between the British and the chiefs using resident agents whom the British appointed to sit with the tribes. But in 1847 the idea of such a territory was revived and British Kaffraria was created. British Kaffraria was designed as a security buffer. As a political entity it lasted until 1866, when it was absorbed into the Cape Colony. British Kaffraria occupied a peculiar constitutional status. The governor of the Cape possessed virtually unlimited and undefined power as High Commissioner of British Kaffraria. He was the sole and virtual ruler of the territory. He was responsible only to the British Government, and they were thousands of miles and many months away. He did not even have to listen to the rowdy voices of the Grahamstown political public if he chose not to, and they certainly felt unattended to in this regard.

But British Kaffraria was not solely designed as a security buffer zone. It had other purposes, which allow us to observe in close detail how a culture of imperial rule grows. The eastern Cape was one of the main sites of the great missionary evangelizing effort of the early nineteenth century. The Wesleyans, the Congregationalists and the Presbyterians were all there by the 1820s. The Wesleyans had arrived with the 1820 settlers and rapidly became associated with settler culture. But in the early years the Wesleyan Methodist Missionary Society shared a lot of the same values and experiences as the leading missionary group in the Cape Colony, the London Missionary Society. Indeed, for the latter society the region was second only to Polynesia for the effort that it expended in seeking out the Christian potential of the heathen in order to civilize them through conversion. The missionary presence in the eastern Cape was important for the encounter between British culture and the Xhosa. Until the later 1850s, the only representatives of British culture permitted to have close contact with the Xhosa were those who embodied its highest humanitarian virtues. That meant missionaries and representatives of the imperial state. White settlers were not permitted beyond the colonial boundary for fear of contaminating the Xhosa with the less desirable attributes of western civilization. Thus, British Kaffraria was a place where missionaries resided with the tribes, along with various agents of the imperial state and the odd trader.

The missionary interest in the Cape was one link in an important imperial network that tied together metropole and colony. Indeed, in the early part of the century, the missionary interest in South Africa played a major role in determining the course of evangelical politics in Britain itself. What happened in the Cape fed directly into humanitarian politics in Britain. This was largely thanks to the part played by Dr. John Philip, who from 1817 until his retirement in 1850 served as the superintendent of the London Missionary Society missions in the Cape. Philip was an organizer rather than a missionary himself. After bringing order to the early London Missionary Society effort in the Cape, Philip set about influencing the course of the missionary discourse in British politics. He had an unmatched access to key members of the anti-slavery lobby in London, the Buxtons and Gurneys in particular, and he used that access to influence humanitarian politics and metropolitan policies. His book, *Researches in South Africa* (1828), for example, was published to influence an important debate in Britain about frontier policy and to project a view of missionary work and influence that confirmed the claims of humanitarian politics.[7]

Although the focus of this book is on how the British responded to the encounter with the Xhosa, it is obviously impossible to tell this story simply from the British side. By its very nature, the colonial encounter was a place of inter-relationships and hybridity where each participant was conditioned in some way by the behavior of the other. Although the Xhosa left behind no archives to match those of the colonial archive, their imprint is stamped on almost every page of the records of the colonizer. This was not just a matter of a record of what the Xhosa were seen to be doing – their cultural customs, or their response to particular British initiatives. The Xhosa imprinted themselves in the minds of the British as they struggled to make *sense* of what they observed and encountered. This was true of missionaries who went to the eastern Cape expecting to find embryonic black Christians in waiting. It was true also of the soldier Sir Harry Smith, who believed that all it would take to make the Xhosa into proper Englishmen was the strength of his own personality, but who found himself mired in a complex game of evasion and negotiation that he could not begin to understand. It was less true (or true in different ways) of Sir George Grey, the governor from 1855 to 1861, who went to South Africa with a plan of action already in mind. But it remained true for the imperial officers on the frontier who were tasked with carrying out Grey's policies.

The heart of this book, then, is an exploration of the dynamics of the encounter between the Xhosa and the British. The encounter was an experiential process, composed of countless instances for each party. But these moments reveal larger themes which I have come to see as describing the phenomenon of empire more generally, and which have informed my treatment of the colonial encounter. These were themes that leapt from the pages of the records of the British occupation of the eastern Cape and Xhosaland. The reader will find them running through many parts of this book, so it is as well to identify and describe them at this point.

First, empire was and is a utopian project. It rests on a series of assumptions that involve enormous leaps of faith, hope and sheer invention. The idea that a colonizer can know what is best for another people – that he or she can create a program of change which the colonized can then be persuaded to accept – involves a breathtaking vision. In the case of Britain's relationship with the Xhosa, this utopian dream was very close to the surface of the British actors in the drama. It was to be found at its most ecstatic among the missionaries, until they encountered Xhosa reality. But it was part, also, of the more hard-headed mentality of imperial officers, like Charles Brownlee and Sir Harry Smith, who will figure large in the subsequent pages.

Because of exaggerated expectations about what empire can achieve – that it can ignore, for example, the history of those it rules and bring them immediately into the orbit of the imperial culture – empire is inherently fragile. Indeed, as I worked through the records of Britain's adventures and misadventures in the eastern Cape, one of the first things that struck me was just how *fragile* this whole enterprise was. I have already alluded to the ambiguities that underlay the success of British arms. But the social, cultural and even the psychological fragilities that ran through imperial culture equally impressed me. We shall see how empire constantly *destabilized* those who claimed its territory; how the conditions of existence and the content of the encounters with the Xhosa were not navigated with the assurance and ease that the cultural superiority of the colonist had led them to expect.

It is true that the agents of British culture came armed with coherent and complete discourses and programs about how they could influence and interact with the Xhosa. But these knowledge systems were quickly

undermined and even displaced by the experience. This was true sometimes at the personal level where all sorts of conventions and boundaries
crumbled under the conditions of the frontier. More importantly, it was
true also at the level of empire as a system. This frontier of empire was a
place where hegemony was constantly being negotiated and defended,
and, in the case of the eastern Cape, where it was ultimately secured only
by the accidental intervention of a cattle plague and the ruthless violence
of Sir George Grey. Empire was *constantly* problematic for those who were
attempting to maintain it; empire could never be assumed to be a hegem-
onic formation. Only in the metropole itself could the idea of empire as a
hegemony be real – and even then, there were times when the Colonial
Office at least was aware of its fractures and fragilities.[8]

And it was the subalterns of empire, its subjects, who were the principal
agents of this fragility, not because they necessarily possessed an opposi-
tional political consciousness, but because of the presence of their own
deep-rooted cultural practices and values. I have already suggested what a
large part the Xhosa will play in this story. It is important to emphasize
here what will become obvious very soon, that their relationship with the
British was a complicated and tangled knot. The Xhosa interacted with
the British at many levels. Their relationship with the British was mutual
and reciprocal; cooperative as well as contentious. These bonds of
mutuality served to erode the separate autonomy of Xhosa society as
much as the physical assaults of the British. The Xhosa had joined with
the British from the moment they appeared on the horizon. Their chiefs
made alliances with the British against their own internal enemies; they
sought the presence of missionaries; they allowed the British to think that
they accepted their sovereignty; they took gifts; they asked for tools; they
accepted money from the imperial state. All of these things may have had
different valences for the Xhosa, but taken together they wove a web of
mutuality that contributed to their ultimate demise.

From the British side, the Xhosa posed a never-ending series of riddles.
They blew hot and cold on the message of Christianity. They were evasive
when it came to settling disputes. They talked endlessly when they were
negotiating, and were so effective in argument that the British very quickly
came to regard them as characterologically lawyer-like. They were not a
martial race like the Sikhs or the Maori, although they fought persistently
and with cunning. They were not masculine, therefore, but neither were
they feminine. Yet the British needed to find a place for the Xhosa within
the terms of their own cultural framework. This led them to create a
knowledge system about the Xhosa that served to resolve and settle all
the contradictory evidence about the Xhosa that the British saw around
them. This was a knowledge system that settled those contradictions, that

squashed them and reconciled them into a set of precepts that made sense for the British, and which, in addition, provided a secure basis of information they could use to rule the Xhosa.

I see this knowledge system as flowing as much from the dynamic of the encounter itself as from the cultural baggage that the British brought with them from the metropole. In other words, I do not see imperial culture as simply another kind of "orientalism" that is invented in the metropole and then carted out to empire to prove a ready-made do-it-yourself handbook on to how to rule the natives. It was not something that was predetermined the moment the first representative of British culture crossed the frontier to meet the Xhosa. Indeed, such a knowledge system could be constructed only after the ideas and values that the British missionaries (in particular) had brought with them were destabilized by the Xhosa encounter.

But the creation of an imperial knowledge system is complicated. What was the colonizer to do with the evidence of Xhosa humanity and civilization, for example? How were they to accommodate within their frame of reference evidence that the Xhosa possessed an intelligence that could match and perhaps surpass their own? They could navigate these mental turns only by strategies that may be described as *colonial reasoning*; that is, ways of thinking and reconciling cognitive contradictions that allow the imperialists to maintain their belief in their own supremacy and superiority. A central feature of colonial reasoning is *reversal* of logic. It was very common in discussions of the Xhosa for the power equation between the British and the Xhosa to be inverted. Everyone knew that the British were, in fact, much more powerful than the Xhosa; everyone saw that even if they did not have enough soldiers in place at a particular moment, they could eventually mobilize their resources to bring overwhelming power to bear. But in discussing the condition of the British interest in the eastern Cape, and even the Cape Colony, it was quite common for the British to tag themselves as the weak victim and the Xhosa as the strong aggressor.[9]

The reversals of colonial reasoning extended also to reconciling the sharp disjunctions that empire posed for a "civilized" culture like the British. It was a way of allowing the contradictions between the rhetorical claims of empire and the dark realities to be explained. The claim of empire (and not only in southern Africa, of course) was that it brought progress and civilization. Its proponents still make that claim.[10] But even if we were to grant its legitimacy (and it is, of course, a claim that *entirely* misses the point about empire), the reality was that too often the methods of despotism were used to bring about those gains. The British quite shamelessly manipulated their own standards of law and due process to pack weakened and desperate men off to Robben Island. To these men, British law was an instrument of repression and tyranny, not the harbinger of progressive civilization. And how were those who were in the business of implementing the law to explain the tension between their own values and their political acts? The answer to that question was complicated, and operated at many levels. But it remains a critically important question if we wish to understand how Britain developed an ideology that portrayed its empire as a "liberal empire," as a humanitarian "trust" and not as a brutal instrument of domination.

Over the course of the late eighteenth century to the last third or so of the nineteenth century, the image of empire changed in British culture and politics. It morphed from a problematic construct to a benign concept; the notion of empire was purified. Questions about the morality and justice of imperial rule in Ireland, North America and India dominated British politics into the later eighteenth century. But the French Revolution swept them away. The period covered by this book (c. 1820–60) is a transition period when the notion of empire as morally problematic gives way to the idea that the British empire was a force for liberal progressivism around the globe. How this happened is a huge question for British historiography. It must be said as an aside that this is a question that has not received the kind of concentrated attention that it deserves. But it is clear that by the middle part of the nineteenth century, doubts about the morality of empire had been resolved. When the morality of empire was raised, as it was by Gladstone around the "Bulgarian agitation" and the election of 1880, it was not to question the idea of empire, but rather to question its methods and purposes.[11]

One reason why it was possible for the British empire to be categorized as a liberal empire in the later nineteenth century was through another device of colonial reasoning: silence and denial. Not long into the research for this book, I began to gather a file of evidence of brutalities and atrocities that marked the history of Britain's relations with the Xhosa. These incidents ranged from the small-scale humiliations that could be visited on Xhosa of all ranks, to the scandal that surrounded the death of Chief Hintsa in May 1835. The frontier wars in particular were marked by pretty rough tactics on the British side. But such histories do not figure much in the imperial historiography. Yet, judging by the history of British–Xhosa relations, the failure to enter the various strategies of violence that were in the culture of empire is a serious absence. It perpetuates the image of the British empire as a liberal and progressive empire.[12]

The idea of British imperialism as a "liberal" empire does not necessarily describe the reality of empire, although it may have some purchase at the more rarified levels of policy. The idea of the liberal empire is important as a description of the ideology that underlay imperial culture in the metropole and that served to depict the empire in public discourse in Britain. Of course, the empire contained some of the more comforting practices of liberalism. But the real question about the "liberal" empire is how the values of liberalism were reconciled with the darker arts that were also prevalent in empire. In this respect, it is of particular importance to recognize that the image of empire that prevailed in British culture was an ideological construct that had to be maintained and fostered. The empire as it was imagined in Britain was not the same empire that was to be found at the frontier of imperial power.

This book is about the latter, not the former. It is more about what happened to British culture in the empire than about what happened to the empire in British culture. The role the empire played in shaping the course of British history has long been recognized. Empire has been particularly constitutive of that history in the realms of political economy and of politics (at certain times), and in international relations.[13] Likwise, traces of the empire may be seen in the culture of Britain at all times in its modern history, from the self-fashioning of the eighteenth-century collector of Indian artefacts, to the advertising themes of the later nineteenth century, to the nostalgia for the end of empire at the close of the twentieth century. But it is important that we remain sensitive to the different valance of empire at different time periods and to the *relative* weight of empire as against other determinants within the culture such as class. In particular, when we speak of empire in the national culture of Britain, we need not only to attend to the traces of empire that were deposited – the curries, the bungalows, the definitions of feminism, the interconnections with scientific development, the imperial heroes and the like – but also to ask *how* the culture of empire was constructed and broadcast in Britain, and by what means and for what purposes the images of empire were left in British culture. In writing this book, I have been impressed time and again with the huge gulf that separated the empire as it was experienced at the frontier and the empire as it was represented in British culture. We know, for example, that missionary literature in Britain tended to gloss over the tensions the imperial encounter created for missionary culture. The model of the missionary project that existed in Britain was tailored to serve the purposes of missionary subculture within Britain. And to that extent it was a home-grown project whose connections with empire were structured to serve the purposes of a *domestic* culture of empire.[14]

The most important group on the British side to interact with the Xhosa in the early years were the missionaries. They also left behind the richest archive of the encounter. Thus, the first part of the book is an extended study of what happened to missionary culture as it met the Xhosa people.

The following few chapters will discuss how missionaries equipped themselves for their work among the Xhosa, what happened to them when they got there, how they responded to Xhosa cultural practices and how their world view was destabilized by their encounter with the Xhosa. I shall pay particular attention to the missionaries' relationships with the Xhosa chiefs because they occupied a key place in the evangelical strategy for conversion and were often the Xhosa whom the missionaries came to know best of all. What happened to the missionary belief system as a result of their relationship with the Xhosa was important in creating a colonial knowledge system about the Xhosa in the middle years of the nineteenth century. I discuss the creation of this colonial knowledge system in Chapter 6, and this chapter is the pivot of the book, connecting the earlier emphasis on the missionaries with the later emphasis on the state.

In the second part, I discuss how the imperial state interacted with the Xhosa. This is where the story of British Kaffraria enters the picture. I open this section with a description of the kinds of strategies that were developed to impress British power upon the Xhosa at a time when no formal machinery (or mandate, for that matter) existed to express and enforce the will of the imperial state. I then move to the pattern of the state's relationship to the chiefs. Like the missionaries, the state hoped to use the chiefs as the channel to influence and guide the tribes in the interests of imperial policy. In this, I argue, we may see the origins of the strategy of indirect rule in Africa. But in this interaction, the chiefs came to be seen as obstacles to the spread of British civilization and progress. In response, the language of liberal progress was appropriated by the imperial administration. The view began to be expressed by the imperial administration that the empire represented liberation and freedom from the political and cultural tyrannies of the chiefs. Thus I conclude with a discussion of how liberalism was combined with and reconciled to empire and became an instrument of imperial rule.

And this leads to the final part of the book, where I will take a close-in view of how the Xhosa polity was destroyed both by the intervention of the cattle plague and cattle killings – which undermined the wealth of Xhosa society – and by the deliberate policies of Sir George Grey. I shall focus on the way this story illustrates how empire inverted the values and institutions that in metropolitan Britain represented freedom and democracy, and turned them into instruments of coercion and tyranny. This part of the story is not only about what the empire did to Britain; it is most dramatically about what it did to the Xhosa. It is therefore appropriate that I bring the book to a close with a discussion of the way in which these events of the 1850s ended one phase of British–Xhosa relations but were also a transition to a new phase in Xhosa history.

British rule over the Xhosa of the eastern Cape was not accomplished by military victory; it was achieved by clever administrative moves and the ruthless exploitation of Xhosa vulnerabilities. Once that had been concluded, the British (and British history) forgot about the Xhosa and their leaders. They forgot the names of chiefs such as Sandile and Maqoma and Sarhili, and nobody noticed a minor Thembu chief named Mandela. In the long run – which empire neither remembers nor can afford to remember – this was to prove something of an error.[15]

NOTES

1. The eastern Cape region got more attention in the older historiography of empire than it has in more recent works. Thus, see J. Holland Rose, A. P Newton and E. A. Benians (eds.), *The Cambridge History of the British Empire*, vol. VIII: *South Africa, Rhodesia and the Protectorates* (Cambridge, 1936), esp. chs. 9 and 13. By contrast, Andrew Porter (ed.), *The Oxford History of the British Empire*, vol. III: *The Nineteenth Century* (Oxford, 1999), has one short chapter covering the period 1795–1910. The most notable exception to the absence of the eastern Cape from British imperial historiography is Alan Lester's important book, *Imperial Networks: Creating Identities in Nineteenth-Century South Africa and Britain* (London, 2001). Lester's main focus is to explore the relationships and intersections between the three dominant discourses of colonialism at this point: those of the missionary, the settler and the imperial state.

2. The story of the 1820 settlers has been of considerable importance to white South African identity formation in the past. It has been largely ignored by British history, although it is a fascinating story that brings together some important themes of the early nineteenth century. It reflected the Malthusian fear of overpopulation, Owenite social engineering, and the enduring significance of paternal impulses in British social relations. The only work from the British side that I know of is Isobel Eirlys Edwards, *The 1820 Settlers in South Africa: A Study in British Colonial Policy* (London, 1934).

3. My own excursion into South African history is entirely dependent upon the work of others. I cannot mention them all here; the extent of my debt will become apparent, I hope, in the notes. But the key works that have informed the South African side of this story include Noel Mostert, *Frontiers: The Epic Story of South Africa's Creation and the Tragedy of the Xhosa People* (London, 1992); J. B. Peires, *The House of Phalo: A History of the Xhosa People in the Days of their Independence* (Johannesburg, 1981); Timothy Keegan, *Colonial South Africa and the Origins of the Racial Order* (Cape Town, 1996); Elizabeth Elbourne, *Blood Ground: Colonialism, Missions, and the Contest for Christianity in the Cape Colony and Britain, 1799–1853* (Kingston, Ont., 2002); and Clifton Crais, *White Supremacy and Black Resistance in Pre-Industrial South Africa: The Making of the Colonial Order in the Eastern Cape, 1770–1865* (Cambridge, 1992). Among the many works by Robert Ross, I would cite *Beyond the Pale: Essays on the Colonial History of South Africa* (Hanover, CT, 1993); *Status and*

Respectability in the Cape Colony, 1750–1870: A Tragedy of Manners (Cambridge, 1999); *Adam Kok's Griquas: A Study in the Development of Stratification in South Africa* (New York, 1976); Christopher Saunders (ed.), *Black Leaders in Southern African History* (London, 1988); and Timothy Stapleton, *Maqoma: Xhosa Resistance to Colonial Advance 1798–1873* (Johannesburg, 1994). Alan Lester's work on British Kaffraria has been very important for my thinking; see particularly his *Imperial Networks: Creating Identities in Nineteenth-Century South Africa and Britain* (Cambridge, 2001).

4. European–Xhosa contact goes back to the early modern period, however, mainly through the shipwrecks that littered the shores of the eastern Cape from ships plying to and from India. There were famous stories of heroic marches of survivors down the coast to civilization and of beached Europeans who married into the local societies to form distinct groups of their own. There are two clans still living on the Transkei coast who trace their origins to survivors of shipwrecks. But apart from these Robinson Crusoe-type experiences, the land of the Xhosa remained closed to the British until around the beginning of the nineteenth century, when a stream of observers began to visit them and record their impressions. For an interesting story of a shipwreck off the coast of the eastern Cape in the 1780s and the fate of the survivors see Stephen Taylor, *Caliban's Shore* (London, 2002).

5. For the invention of the Shaka image see Carolyn Hamilton, *Terrific Majesty: The Powers of Shaka Zulu and the Limits of Historical Invention* (Cape Town and Johannesburg, 1998); Jeff Guy, "Shaka KaSenzangakhona – A Reassessment," *Journal of Natal and Zulu History* 16 (1996), pp. 1–29. For an older but still important history of the making of the Zulu kingdom, see J. D. Omer-Cooper, *The Zulu Aftermath: A Nineteenth Century Revolution in Bantu Africa* (Evanston, 1966). A more recent history of the Zulu people which is worth reading is John Leband, *Rope of Sand: The Rise and Fall of the Zulu Kingdom in the Nineteenth Century* (Johannesburg, 1995).

6. The best account of these wars until 1853, and much more besides, is Mostert, *Frontiers*. There is no published history of the last of the frontier wars, 1877–8.

7. The best information on John Philip is in William Miller Macmillan, *Bantu, Boer and Briton: The Making of the South African Native Problem*, rev. edn. (Oxford, 1963), although the perspective is decidedly dated. But see also Andrew Ross, *John Philip 1775–1851: Missions, Race and Politics in South Africa* (Aberdeen, 1986). Philip's papers were destroyed in a fire at the University of Witswatersrand library. Very significant theological and socio-political differences were to emerge as important between the Wesleyans and the GMS and LMS. Their doctrinal differences are not my concern.

8. Thus Ranajit Guha's aptly formulated notion of dominance without hegemony; see his *Dominance without Hegemony: History and Power in Colonial India* (Cambridge, MA, 1997).

9. For examples of this see Reverend Francis Fleming, *Kaffraria and its Inhabitants* (London, 1853), p. 17; Cape Archives [CA], LCA 21, *Appendix to the Minutes of Legislative Council, Volume I, 1848*, f. 21; LCA 33, *Masters and Servants Committee, Replies to Questionnaire 1848*; CCP 1216, Cape Colony Parliamentary Papers, *House of Assembly Papers for 1859*, Cd. A-26, ae59,

"Petition from certain inhabitants of the Field-cornetcy Fish River, District of Somerset." My notion of reversal in colonial reasoning focuses on the mind of the colonizer, not the colonized. More typically, reversal is applied to the way subaltern consciousness is created through the power of the colonial power as, for example, in Ranajit Guha's *Elementary Aspects of Peasant Insurgency in Colonial India* (Dehli, 1983).

10. Thus see Niall Ferguson, *Empire: The Rise and Demise of the British World Order and the Lessons for Global Power* (New York, 2002), pp. xxv–xxix.

11. For a very important study of the emergence of liberal imperialism see Jennifer Pitts, *A Turn to Empire: The Rise of Imperial Liberalism in Britain and France* (Princeton, 2005). For another perspective, see C. A. Bayly, *Imperial Meridian: The British Empire and the World 1780–1830* (London, 1989).

12. The theme of silence is beginning to be recognized as important as an explanation for the *absences* of empire in British culture. See Catherine Hall, "At Home with History: Macaulay and the *History of England*," in Catherine Hall and Sonya Rose (eds.), *At Home with the Empire: Metropolitan Culture and the Imperial World* (Cambridge, 2006), pp. 32–52.

13. It is very important not to ignore the political economy of empire. The most recent formulation of this relationship is, of course, the magisterial work by P. J. Cain and Anthony Hopkin, *British Imperialism 1688–2000* (New York, 2002). Empire has always figured in the histories of domestic Britain; see for example the work of John Pocock, who, as befitted a colonial expatriate academic, made empire central to his discussions of the proper limits of "British" history; see his "The Limits and Divisions of British History: In Search of an Unknown Subject," *American Historical Review* 87.2 (1982), pp. 311–36. Similarly, Eric Hobsbawm, *Industry and Empire: The Making of Modern English Society from 1750 to the Present Day* (London, 1968).

14. For a fuller discussion of my estimation of what has been called a "new imperial history" in British history, see my "One Big Thing: Britain and its Empire," *Journal of British Studies* 45.3 (2006). For a very balanced and informed assessment of this scholarship, especially its post-colonial dimensions, see Dane Kennedy, "Imperial History and Post-Colonial Theory," *Journal of Imperial and Commonwealth History* 24.3 (1996), pp. 345–63. Bernard Porter, *The Absent-Minded Imperialists: Empire, Society and Culture in Britain* (Oxford, 2004), is the most effective critique of this scholarly trend. The following are among the books that I feel to be the best examples of the idea that empire is determinant in the culture and practices of the metropole (the list is limited to those relating to British history): Catherine Hall, *Civilising Subjects: Colony and Metropole in the English Imagination 1830–1867* (Oxford, 2002); Hall and Rose, *At Home with Empire*; Kathleen Wilson, *The Island Race: Englishness, Gender and Empire in the Eighteenth Century* (London, 2002); Wilson (ed.), *A New Imperial History: Culture Identity and Modernity in Britain 1660–1840*; Antoinette Burton, *Burdens of Empire: British Feminists, Indian Women and Imperial Culture 1865–1915* (Chapel Hill, NC, 1994); Burton (ed.), *After the Imperial Turn: thinking with and through the nation* (Durham, NC, 2003); Maya Jasanoff, *At the Edge of Empire* (New York, 2005); Philippa Levine, *Prostitution, Race and Politics: Policing Venereal Disease in the British Empire* (New York, 2003); Levine (ed.),

Gender and Empire (Oxford, 2002); David Armitage, *The Ideological Origins of the British Empire* (Cambridge, 1999); David Armitage and Michael Braddock, *The British Atlantic World, 1500–1800* (New York, 2002); Christine Daniels and Michael Kennedy (eds.), *Negotiated Empires: Centers and Peripheries in the Americas 1500–1820* (London, 2002); Norman Etherington, *Missions and Empire* (Oxford, 2005); Anna Johnston, *Missionary Writing and Empire 1800–1860* (Cambridge, 2003); Susan Thorne, *Congregational Missions and the Making of an Imperial Culture in Nineteenth England* (Stanford, 1999); Alison Twells, "'Children of a larger growth': The South Pacific and the English Missionary Public in the 1820s to 1840s," in Twells, *The Civilizing Mission and the English Middle Class, 1792–1857* (New York, 2009).
15. Anthony Sampson, *Mandela: The Authorized Biography* (New York, 1999), p. 8.

2 The making of missionary culture

The missionary world

The early missionaries to South Africa encountered a world that was harsh and alien. The story of how David Livingstone sacrificed the health of his wife Mary, and in effect abandoned his family in pursuit of his exploring and evangelizing career, is well enough known not to need repeating. But compared to an earlier generation of missionary wives Mary Livingstone was in fact quite comfortably off. When she married David, Mary had a real house to live in and did not have to survive in one of the wattle and daub huts that were the standard accommodation for new arrivals.[1]

The missionary encounter with the world of the Xhosa posed physical challenges as much as the cultural and mental ones that I shall explore in more detail in other chapters. In the early years of the nineteenth century, missionaries frequently set off into the wilderness with virtually no provision for the necessities of life. They were too busy digging for water, looking for animals to hunt and kill for food, trying to catch fish, dealing with truculent servants, and guessing whether the natives they encountered were dangerous or not for there to be much time to preach the word of God.[2]

By the third decade of the century, a truly pioneering experience was less common, at least on the eastern Cape. A community of sorts existed that served to welcome and socialize the new arrivals from Glasgow or London. But illness and accidents were ever-present hazards of missionary life. Missionaries were seldom murdered – only five died in this way between 1823 and 1856. Waggon accidents, rhumatoid arthritis, and, for women, death during childbirth, were the typical dangers that faced missionary families. Women were particularly vulnerable, of course, primarily because of their role as child-bearers. And it might be well to say a few words about women in the missionary effort here, because in this period they are virtually absent from the main body of missionary records. We know they were not absent from the frontier itself. Indeed, after the early part of the century, being a missionary wife became something of a profession when it was realized that, in the absence of white British women, missionary men would form attachments with native women.

By this time the London Missionary Society had observed the near collapse of the missionary effort in the South Pacific thanks to sexual mixing. Securing a mate was an important qualification for being a missionary. The German missionary Friedrich Kayser was told by the London Missionary Society in 1826 to find a wife. And so, while he was waiting in London for a posting, Kayser looked around the circle of available missionary women until he identified a woman with the right qualifications. She had been vetted by the London Missionary Society to be a "missionary sister" in New Zealand. Friedrich's charms were stronger than the Antipodes, and she married him to share his long and hard life on the Cape frontier.[3]

Obviously, there were more reasons to get a wife than simply to have someone to do the cooking and provide sexual services. And once they were ensconced in southern Africa, the engagement of women was often as intense as their husbands, even if it was directed in slightly different directions. The London Missionary Society mission to the Cape was effectively run jointly by Jane and John Philip, although it was John, the superintendent of the society in southern Africa, who appears in the historical record. At a more dramatic level, when the Xhosa swept into British Kaffraria in December 1850, Mary Chalmers, the widow of pioneer missionary J. A. Chalmers, took the initiative in protecting the station at Igqibiri when the male missionaries had either fled or felt it more prudent to stay out of sight. At one time about a thousand Xhosa were camped at the mission, and she took an active role in negotiating with them and bringing some order to the chaos that surrounded her.[4]

Thus, long before the imperial woman was registered in feminist discourse in domestic culture, women were fully occupied as teachers and instructors for Xhosa children and women. A formal sphere for women in mission work began with the creation of the Society for the Promotion of Female Education in 1834. But fundraising "ladies' committees" appear earlier. Local missionary societies also sponsored single women workers in the mission field. There was a women's auxiliary of the Glasgow Missionary Society as early as 1839 and a Miss McLaren was sent out to Igqibiri in 1841. Lovedale, the most famous of the missionary schools in the eastern Cape, established in 1841, had a girls' department run by an Isabella Smith, and there were other cases of schools that were organized and run by single women, such as the redoubtable Miss Hannah Harding, sent out to Block Drift to promote female education in connection with the Scottish Free Church mission there. She taught the Xhosa girls the usual domestic arts of sewing and other housekeeping skills, but she also ran a boarding school and supported the effort by cultivating a piece of land to grow food.[5]

We know very little about how women negotiated the missionary encounter in the early nineteenth century. Some women clearly reveled in the opportunity for self-fulfillment that missionary work provided. When the missionary Joseph Williams died in 1818, for example, his wife Elizabeth had to be strongly dissuaded from staying on with her two children to continue his work. From the 1870s, it is possible to speak of a feminization of missionary work.[6] But in our period, there was quite likely a sharp divide between the formal definition of women's place in missionary culture and the realities of life on the frontier. Formally, women were supposed to represent the domesticity of British civilization. This was a role that the women involved accepted and did their best to fulfill. But there was always a tension between the ideology and the reality. It was not just a matter of women becoming unacknowledged partners in the missionary enterprise. Women like Bessie Price, the daughter of Robert Moffat, were explicit about their role being to support their husband and represent the standards of "civilization" in the kind of home that was kept. In this respect Bessie Price prefigured the role that women generally were to assume in the imperial enterprise as guardians of domestic "civilization." But at this point in time the range of activities that this covered included much that fell outside of the accepted definition of "women's work." One missionary wife described her life as that of a "busy farmer." And Bessie Price herself, for example, was quite accustomed to taking command of the mission when her husband was away itinerating. And she was not above lending a hand at repairing wagons or buildings when needed.[7]

Missionaries, therefore, faced a series of challenges as they settled on the frontier. It is important to keep in mind the physical and social challenges that were part of the missionary experience. But the missionary world was not simply a world of missionaries. It was predominantly a world wherein missionaries encountered an alien and different people and culture. How well prepared were the missionaries for the physical and cultural encounters they were destined to meet? What kind of ideology accompanied the decision to become a missionary, and what were the theological and intellectual assumptions about their chosen work? How well equipped mentally and culturally were missionaries to face physical challenges? These questions are important to answer if we are to follow the main story of missionary interaction and encounter with the cultural and political worlds of the Xhosa.

Missionary training

The preparation of the candidate for mission work was almost entirely personal and spiritual. From the 1830s a rudimentary system of academies was established to provide what passed for formal training. But the curriculum remained biased toward classical learning and did not incorporate the practical lessons that had been learnt from the prior thirty years of missionary experience. Greek was regarded by some authorities as an essential qualification. The qualities that were prized had to do with spirituality and strength of character. Approved candidates for the mission field were those who demonstrated "zeal," "piety," "steadfastness of purpose," and "good native sense."[8]

Missionaries were largely a self-selected group who for one reason or another felt the calling and made application to local committees that were looking to support missionary work. What is striking about how missionaries prepared themselves for their life work is how divorced it was from practical or worldly designs. When they recounted the process they underwent to become a missionary, there was no suggestion of social or cultural dimensions. The focus was entirely upon their preparation to commune with God. When John Cumming decided after a long period of personal struggle and reflection that he did in fact possess the calling to be a missionary, he made application to the directors of the Glasgow Missionary Society. Their interview tested his abilities by asking him to preach a sermon, after which he was pronounced fit enough to face the rigors of the eastern Cape.[9]

The first ship load of missionaries sent off to the South Seas were not trained in any sense of the term; they were just put on a boat and expected to preach the Gospel. It was hardly surprising that the mission had very mixed results, with many of the missionaries backsliding straight into the arms of Polynesian maidens. Likewise, William Carey, the founder of the Baptist missionary effort and a pioneer missionary in India, sailed off to India with his wife and one colleague with literally no preparation. Carey had not even traveled out of Britain before! His colleague, John Thomas, had been in India as a surgeon. But this was of little use to Carey, because the good doctor went mad soon after their arrival in Bengal.[10]

The emphasis on spiritual and personal qualities in missionary candidates meant that piety and spiritual purity were privileged over intellect and learning. Many missionaries were smart people, but there was a definite bias toward the uneducated as against those who were intellectually well trained. The early London Missionary Society preferred plain men from forge or farm, well read in the Bible and full of faith, over university-educated men. This reflected the cultural bias within society about missionary work. The uneducated were regarded as suitable carriers of British culture to uncivilized natives. Indeed, the low state of intellectual standing of some of the missionaries is quite astounding. Here is a piece of a paper written by one candidate to the London Missionary Society as part of the examination of his suitability for missionary work:

> I am more than usual made to think that the dispensation of Providence has something of a dark appearance and when judgments are begun at the house of God such persons as of that have been so long at ease in Zion may have gloomy apprehensions where it shall end, yet trust as the sun of righteousness is begun to arise the clouds intervene and that shall intervene will make that even an object of greater desire and in the moral world more conspicuously glorious and when cunning mischief is devised.[11]

This candidate was judged suitable for the work. He was John Brownlee; he was a pioneer London Missionary Society missionary in Xhosaland; he founded King William's Town – the future capital of British Kaffraria – and he was a revered figure in the missionary world of southern Africa.

The fullest account of the preparation that was considered necessary for missionary work is contained in a series of lectures delivered by David Bogue, a minister at the Gosport Academy. Bogue was active in the formation of the London Missionary Society, and these classes were developed by him sometime in the late 1790s or early 1800s. Bogue's lectures tell us how the challenges and prospects that faced missionaries were understood; they provide an insight into the missionary mind at the beginning of the century.[12]

David Bogue's course of lectures made some gesture toward the practicalities of missionary life. He recommended that missionaries learn native languages, for example. But he immediately qualified this recommendation with the comforting assurance that past experience had shown that good conversion results could be gained by communicating through interpreters. Indeed, Bogue was not entirely prepared to dismiss the possibility that the missionaries might discover the gift of tongues as had the apostles on the first day of Pentecost. But he advised them not to count on this! On the other hand, he recognized that the missionaries would need to know how to deal with native cultures and intellect. He devoted one lecture on how to reason with the heathen about religion, and several classes on how to structure sermons in order to most effectively convey the ideas of Christianity to peoples who had little understanding of it. Likewise he spent several lectures identifying the obstacles missionaries would face from the existing rulers and their priests, although he had little to offer in the way of how to combat this except to point to the necessity to "keep up a suitable frame of heart for the work." There was little else Bogue could recommend except to draw attention to the need of the missionary to fortify himself against the many difficulties he would face.

Bogue was very wide of the mark in his advice on how to negotiate with the politics of the indigenous cultures. He recommended showing respect for civil authority and obeying the law, except where it offended God's law; he urged missionaries to avoid meddling with existing political arrangements, and even suggested that they basically ignore local politics. Yet from the very first day of their engagement with the Xhosa, missionaries would find it impossible not to tangle with local politics. On the other hand, there was enough evidence to hand to lead Bogue to recognize that missionaries required very deep psychological resources. The final lecture in his series was about the need to persevere in a mission even if it seemed fruitless: "missionaries," he wrote, "are sometimes apt to be discouraged and to think they ought not to persevere in a mission when no success appears." Indeed, this question of how missionaries could remain optimistic about their mission was to lie at the heart of their dynamic of their cultural encounter with the Xhosa.

The emphasis on the power of the personal qualities of the missionary is not surprising. Missionary recruits came straight out of the culture of eighteenth-century evangelicalism, which placed at the center of its religious and social thought the power of individual salvation. The beliefs and attitudes of the missionaries had their roots in one of the most important sociocultural events of British history: the evangelical revival of the eighteenth century. In order to understand the missionary mentality as it encountered the Xhosa, it is therefore necessary to understand the culture of the evangelicalism that the missionaries carried with them to southern Africa.

The evangelical roots of missionary culture

Although much of the interest that British historians have displayed in the evangelical revival has been focused on their impact on the domestic culture and society, the missionary project was an integral part of the evangelical revival. It was particularly associated with the late eighteenth-century phase of that movement which spawned the political crusade to abolish the slave trade and then slavery itself. This was the moment when missionary culture came to occupy its key place at the center of the wider culture of nineteenth-century Britain. The representation of missionary evangelizing in the heathen world became an important part of national identity, and especially a site for urban middle-class elites to express their class and cultural identity.[13]

The idea of the *mission* had been present from the moment of the Great Awakening in the 1730s and 1740s. John Wesley's own evangelizing career had been inspired by the figure of David Brainerd, who had attained heroic status within missionary culture for the sacrifice of his (short) life to converting the Indians of north America. Foreign missionary work remained somewhat controversial, however, since it was not obvious that energies were best spent converting the heathen abroad instead of the heathen at home. The young William Carey, who almost single-handedly founded the Baptist Missionary Society, was severely rebuked by the older John Rylands when he advocated missions to foreign lands. Rylands's objection followed from his notion that the heathen would be converted when God was good and ready, and Carey had no business trying to interfere with the mechanics of divine providence. By this time, however (1785), Rylands's interpretation of scriptural authority was increasingly old-fashioned. Rylands's gloomy pessimism that pagan peoples were so depraved that it was useless to preach at them was no longer fashionable. By the 1790s a more optimistic theology was predominant. This held that salvation was possible for all individuals, and was dependent only upon receiving God. Divine grace, the atonement of man's wickedness by Christ's sacrifice, could be accessed by all. Indeed, it was a significant reflection of this shift to a more optimistic grounding for missionary work that Rylands's son was a strong supporter of Baptist missionary effort.[14]

By the end of the eighteenth century, then, the theological answer to the question whether foreign evangelizing was worth the effort was decidedly in the affirmative. The clinching argument in favor of foreign missions was a moral one, just as it was for the question of slavery. How could one justify *not* sharing the beauties of God's grace and the possibility of salvation if one knew this to be available to all mankind? How could one justify leaving in a state of ignorance the millions of souls who had been untouched by Christianity? The result is well known. There was a flurry of activity in the 1790s that led to the creation of a Protestant missionary establishment in Britain, from which was launched the missionary offensive of the early nineteenth century.

The Baptist Missionary Society was the first, created in 1792. Its energies were directed toward India and Asia. The London Missionary Society, formed in 1795, made southern Africa a main focus of its attention, as did the Wesleyan Methodist Missionary Society when it was established in 1818. Scottish evangelicals were also very prominent in southern Africa, and an interdenominational committee of Glasgow and Edinburgh Presbyterians in 1796 marked the beginning of their foreign mission.[15]

In order to understand how the missionaries behaved when they encountered the indigenous culture of the Xhosa, it is useful to identify the features of evangelical religion that shaped the cultural and mental assumptions that missionaries carried with them to southern Africa. There were seven such elements, as follows: the emphasis in evangelical culture on *personal* conversion and experience; the belief in the power of preaching the direct word of God; the millenarianism within evangelicalism; the activism of the evangelical creed; the optimism of the evangelical revival; the emotional and intellectual fragility that was bequeathed to missionary culture by evangelicalism; and finally the notion of a universal humanity of mankind.

Evangelical culture privileged the individual and the experiences of the individual. The narrative of missionary experience revolved essentially around the stories of heroic individuals who had wandered into heathen societies with no large-scale resources at their disposal and won significant numbers of converts for Christ. These men were seen as replicating the tradition of the apostles, who, it was claimed, had converted half of mankind by following Christ's command to go and preach to every living being. Evangelical religion asserted that this practice had been lost, although there was no evidence that the original injunction had lapsed. This view of the history of Christianity projected an idea that the apostles' work had been accomplished with relative ease. If this was the case, it was argued, how much more opportunity there was at the present day! Surely missionaries would quickly find success among the sea of heathen who for centuries had been eagerly awaiting the message of the word?[16]

But this personal focus within missionary culture reflected the key place of individual salvation within evangelical religion. Indeed, for evangelicals the key division in the world did not run along class or race or national lines; it ran along the divide between Christian and pagan. The world of the saved Christian could be open to all who experienced personal conversion and acceptance of the word of God. In its emphatic conviction that anyone could be saved whatever the prior state of his or her soul, evangelicalism was a profoundly liberating doctrine. But this freedom was not unqualified. Indeed, it was undercut and constrained by other doctrinal tendencies which served to complicate the belief and values that shaped the life and culture of the evangelical missionary.[17]

There remained, for example, the doctrine of providentialism. Providentialism held that man could do nothing without the permission of God. If God was active everywhere, then attempts to artificially interfere with his decisions were not only futile, but dangerous. It was such reasoning that provided the neat trick of reconciling what made economic sense – free trade – with the idea that divine intervention was still the hidden hand of economic and social progress. So it was with evangelical missionary culture. "God's providence must be *followed*, not *anticipated*. We must wait for his motion," intoned the Reverend John Venn at a sermon to proclaim the foundation of the Church Missionary Society. It was only through the will of God that success could be achieved in the missionary endeavor, as in others.[18]

But how was providentialism to be reconciled with the emphasis upon the individual that was *also* a central tenet of evangelicalism? The answer was that it was not, and the end result was that evangelicalism created a mental framework that pulled in two very different directions. On the one hand, evangelicalism gloried in the individual's potential for salvation. But, on the other hand, it postulated a form of divine determinism to explain individual and other actions. How was the believer to know whether what was happening to him was part of God's will for the world, or whether it was brought on by some action of his own which deserved and was receiving punishment from God? Thus, there was a considerable potential within missionary culture for schizoid reactions to personal dilemmas and tribulations.

The personal character of evangelical belief was further complicated by the doctrine of reparation. The doctrine of reparation referred to the awareness of sin and corruption that were believed to mark the character of mankind, and therefore demanded that mankind make restitution by doing Christ's work on earth. Salvation was through the grace of God, not from any inherent goodness within the body of the saved. Evangelicals had a very highly tuned sense of the dangers of backsliding, of succumbing to the ever-present temptations that Satan threw in the way of the godly. The doctrine of reparation instilled in missionaries, therefore, a strong sense that unworthiness and sin were inherent and ever-present perils. Thus, an unstable soul-searching was a profoundly important part of the everyday life of the missionary. Missionaries were always checking on themselves and on the meaning of what was happening to them. Were they submitting themselves enough to God's will, or were they claiming too much self-pride for themselves? Was their fate the result of God's design, or were they being punished for some transgression they had committed? It was not enough that the physical challenges of missionary life were daunting and difficult. Missionaries also brought with them an evangelical culture that contained a volatile mix of beliefs and induced a high degree of emotional fragility.[19]

A second tenet that the evangelical revival contributed to missionary culture was the belief in the power of the word of God. Evangelical culture possessed an astoundingly simplistic conception of how the heathen would be converted. It boiled down to the assumption that God's intention was so powerful that *all* that needed to happen was for the scripture to be revealed. The key to conversion was the truth of the scriptures. The missionary was merely the interlocutor between the Bible and those who had not had the benefit of receiving its wisdom. He was the carrier of the message, and all that was needed for conversions to happen, and for the word of God to spread and take hold, was for him to preach effectively. Preaching was therefore the most important thing that missionaries did. The (fairly short) catalogue of successful conversion campaigns that was always trotted out by evangelicals as evidence of the rich harvest of souls just waiting in foreign lands to receive the missionary message was essentially a catalogue of effective preachers. As Thomas Haweis put it at the organizational meeting of the London Missionary Society in 1795, the missionary must preach "just the Gospel, the pure unadulterated Gospel ... if Christ be preached – only preached – always preached – then shall we see the power of his death and resurrection, and the Lord will add again daily to his church of such as shall be saved."[20]

There were several implications of this surrender to a godly determinism that was recommended by evangelical culture. For one thing, it betokened a profound otherworldliness. The charismatic Edward Irving, for example, in a sermon of 1826, went so far as to argue that organization-building should not be part of missionary activity, but that the latter should be totally separate from all worldly expedients and focus only on preaching God's word. Such an extreme – not to say, bizarre – conception of missionary work, of course, was absurd. But its sentiments were no caricature of missionary culture which *did* imagine its strategy of conversion as quite simply an individual missionary, tramping across a foreign landscape, clutching his Bible. These kinds of images describe quite well the mind of missionaries as they determined to become missionaries. Indeed, the celebrated Robert Moffat was inspired to mission work by the dream of just leaving Britain and landing on some distant shore to begin preaching to the natives. Neither Irving nor others seemed to realize that the conception of the missionary armed only with the all-powerful word of God was bound to slam up against inconvenient realities at the frontier of empire.[21]

A further implication of the central place of preaching the word of God in evangelical culture was the belief that conversion to Christianity would (and should) precede the introduction of the more material benefits of British culture. The issue of conversion versus civilization had been the subject of a considerable theological debate during the eighteenth century. Was it possible to preach the Gospel and to save souls if they existed within various states of barbarism and savagery? Was it not necessary, first of all, to bring the attributes of a civilized society to them, to educate them, for example, before they were then exposed to the truths of Christianity?

By the end of the century, an uneasy consensus had been reached, however, that "the preaching of Christ crucified, *ipso facto*, would effect the transformation of primitive society to civilised society." Indeed, it tended to be argued, conversion not only could precede civilization, but was a necessary precondition for it. Missionaries believed that the Xhosa should be Christianized before they could be civilized.[22]

The belief in the power of the word of God through preaching was reinforced by a further element of the evangelical revival that stimulated missionary enterprise: the sense that this was an era of millenarian events. From the Great Awakening of the 1740s there was a strong tendency to interpret events as signs that Providence was stirring and world-changing events were about to unfold. Such beliefs were fed by achievements like the opening of the Pacific, which revealed large new populations available for evangelizing, by political events such as the break with America, or by the French Revolution, which betokened a political world turned upside down. These events suggested that the time was now ripe for a concerted push to spread Protestant religion around the world. Evangelicals believed their era to be premillennial. It is not surprising, then, that the announcment of the formation of the London Missionary Society in January 1795 talked explicitly about how "the knowledge of the Lord would soon cover the earth" and registered the "apprehension that the Lord is about to produce some great event."[23]

The notion that the second coming was imminent imparted a sense of urgency into the evangelical revival. Evangelicalism was an *active* religion. Numbers were all-important to the evangelical revival. One Methodist minister claimed to have led 90,000 souls to Christ at his meetings. Henry Venn claimed 900 conversions during his three years at Huddersfield. With standards like this going the rounds, it is hardly surprising that the missionaries who trucked off to the South Seas or to southern Africa saw in their mind's eye an endless sea of imminent Christians. Although, by the 1820s, there were plenty of suggestions that Xhosaland was not Huddersfield, it was not until the 1850s that missionaries in the eastern Cape began to come to terms with that difference.[24]

But activism had another dimension. Activism fitted well with the emphasis on the *personal* within missionary culture. It reinforced the privileging of internal spirituality *over* the acquisition of practical skills that would fortify the missionary for the trials to come. Enthusiasm, energy and spiritual preparedness were the key qualities that selection boards looked for when assessing missionary candidates. The possibility of the missionary being tested by adversity and unfamiliar conditions was not discounted, but its possible implications were disregarded. The qualities that made the perfect missionary were solely internal. At one level this was appropriate and admirable. For one thing, it was very democratic. If the empire was a vast system of out relief for the unemployed sons of the British aristocracy, missionary culture was the early nineteenth century's affirmative action plan for the sons of the upper working and lower middle classes.

The image that was drawn was that of the apostles. Twelve apostles had changed the world. Why, it was asked, should the conversion of the heathen be any more difficult than the conversion of Israel by the apostles, or the subsequent Christianization of Europe? For evangelicals, then, there was every reason to expect the current phase of evangelical conversions to proceed easily and rapidly. And this was particularly so because of all the signs that could be read of divine Providence gathering its energies for a possible second coming. Thus, young William Carey recorded how history was full of evidence that, if the spirit was willing and the time was right, conversions could be made with surprising ease. It was indeed the general assumption that the natives were a mass of humanity waiting only to *hear* the word of God, and that they would respond to it immediately. Such evidence as Carey presented might not impress us much with its rigor or credibility, but it was pretty clear that he and others were willing to act on it.[25]

Thus, a further quality the evangelical revival bequeathed to missionary culture was a deep sense of *optimism*. Optimism flowed from the evangelical beliefs in the perfectibility of man, in the doctrinal certainty that God was in control of the world, and in the fact that the second coming was probably about to occur. Practical considerations were relegated to the minor league of issues that missionaries would have to face. Thus William Carey explained

that the right kind of person must take every opportunity of doing them [i.e. the natives] good and labouring and travelling they must instruct, exhort and rebuke with all long suffering and anxious desire for them, and above all, must be instant in prayer for the effusion of the Holy Spirit upon the people of their charge. Let but missionaries of the above description engage in the work, and we shall see that it is not impracticable.

Carey glided easily over such issues as where to procure the necessities of life. He blithely argued that missionaries could live off the land, eating the same food as the natives did! Nor was language a problem. If interpreters were not available, "it is well known to require no very extraordinary talents to learn in the space of a year or two at most the language of any people upon earth, so much of it at least as to be able to convey any sentiments we wish to their understandings."[26]

The setbacks and opposition that missionaries might encounter were conceptualized as challenges to faith and seriousness that could be overcome by spiritual effort. Furthermore, when a serious obstacle was glimpsed it was always possible to fall back on the comforting thought that it was God, after all, who was going to do this work, not the missionaries who would merely be the instrument of his will. It was very soon evident that this prescription was going to be much needed. Three weeks after William Carey had arrived in India, the gilt of his optimism had begun to wear a bit thin as he began to note the tenacity of Hindu cultural practices. Optimism began to give way to pessimism. Within six months Carey was confiding to his journal that his hopes of rapid conversions looked about to be denied. Carey's oscillation between naive optimism and darker pessimism was a pattern that was to become typical of missionary culture in southern Africa.[27]

Carey's experience, then, suggests a sixth element to evangelical culture that was to be of critical importance to the missionary experience. *It was an inherently unstable ideological formulation which fostered an equally unsteady mental frame of mind.* There was a fragility and volatility at the heart of missionary culture that made it vulnerable to disruption, especially as it encountered the intransigence of indigenous cultures. This volatile mix was not simply a product of the imperial encounter. It was a function of the theology of evangelicalism that attributed so much to the hand of Providence and thus allowed missionary culture to blithely ignore the importance of cultural difference. An unusual and interesting source allows us to gain entry to the inner workings of the missionary mind in this respect. The diaries of John Forbes Cumming provide a revealing insight into this aspect of missionary culture. They allow us to observe the inner workings of the missionary mind as it struggled with the demons that evangelical culture implanted in its consciousness.

Cumming was sent out to southern Africa by the Glasgow Missionary Society in 1840. He remained an active missionary until his death in the 1890s. He was a remarkably successful worker in the mission field. But as he passed from lowland Scotland to the eastern Cape in the early 1840s, he was frequently in deep inner turmoil. In the precise trajectory of his experiences Cumming is an example only of himself. But from cryptic references in other sources, it is clear that Cumming's experience was not that unusual.[28]

Cumming's fragile state of mind reflected the common evangelical tendency toward self-examination and self-reflection. Long before he decided to become a missionary Cumming had struggled with his inability to judge the worth of his life in relation to God's plan for him. He was tormented by inner conflicts that he did not understand, and which were made worse by the sense that he was not reading properly God's purpose for his life. He resolved this particular crisis in the late 1830s by persuading himself that God was calling him to missionary work. Yet this determination brought no lasting peace or conviction. The bouts of "agony and doubt" returned. He experienced sleepless nights ruminating on his suitability for the ministry, and became discouraged and full of doubt, even to the extent of making him wish for death.[29]

It is important to note two things about these moods. The first is that they were governed entirely by the role assigned to God in Cumming's cosmology. Every mood was interpreted as a judgment sign from God on his behavior or worth. The large part that God played for these evangelical missionaries cannot be overestimated. The second point follows naturally from the imminence of God in Cumming's worldview: how easily shifts in Cumming's mood were triggered. Evangelicals were accustomed to scanning about them for small signs of wonder in their own world. Quite trivial events were capable of provoking Cumming to extensive self-flagellation as to wretchedness and sin. But this mood just as easily lifted once he felt that God had restored him to his favor. The evangelical mindset was programmed to be highly volatile, with mood swings that switched easily between optimism and pessimism. This was to be a key feature of the dynamic of the missionary encounter with the Xhosa.[30]

Having been accepted by the Glasgow Missionary Society for their Caffrarian Mission, Cumming arrived in London in early 1840 to prepare for his voyage to southern Africa. There he experienced the most tumultuous bout of agonizing turmoil to date, which seems to have been related to a romantic relationship that had developed in Glasgow. An intense month had been spent together and an arrangement had been come to; lockets of hair had been exchanged, for example. Then, on top of this, a series of mishaps meant that Cumming had trouble getting away from England. He missed two boats. When he did get aboard, contrary winds kept the boat from entering the Bay of Biscay, where it would catch the southwesters to carry them into the Atlantic.[31]

This ignited the deepest and most agonizing crisis in Cumming's mind. He read these difficulties as a sign that God did not intend him to be a missionary. The conviction that he should not go to Africa, but "return to my native country," became fixed in his mind even after the ship did make it into the Atlantic and they were on their way to Cape Town. It was a conviction that remained with him for some years. It was a reflection of his mental turmoil that in the same diary entry he could express three different feelings as he struggled at one and the same time to match God's will for him with his own desire and sense of free will: "If Jesus carries me thither I go because I wish to have my will confirmed to his." But "Why does he take me against my will, [for] if my heart is against going I can attribute it only to the arrangement of his own Providence." And, then, "I will pray with all my heart Lord Jesus does not take *me out to Africa* [these words are deleted] [and] do permit me to return to Scotland if it be thy will." His bouts of spiritual and personal self-doubt were joined by physical symptoms that convinced him he suffered from heart disease or consumption. These feelings were to continue over the next year or so, as he faced the realities of life on the frontier. The diary entries of Cumming's initial months on the frontier suggest a lonely, miserable man who feared he was seriously ill, and who found missionary society deeply disappointing in its petty jealousies. At the beginning of 1841, he remarked in his diary that he would "either be in heaven or Scotland" in a few years.[32]

By the spring of 1841 Cumming had begun to settle in. He was kept busy finding a place to live and he also recorded some successes, such as a first sermon in Xhosa in July 1841. The bouts of depression came less regularly, and when they did they were contextualized against Xhosa cultural practices. In January 1842, for example, only three people turned up for a Sunday prayer service, and he was once again thrown into despair. But this time his distress was not turned inward at himself for his own inadequacies; rather, it was directed at the difficulties of accessing the Xhosa mind and culture and the compromises he was called upon to make in his interactions with them. This marked a crucial distancing between himself and the results of the work that he was doing, and was the survival strategy he developed to cope with the disappointments and difficulties that faced him in the missionary world. But unfortunately we cannot know how his state of mind evolved because at this very moment the diaries dry up as an entry into the mind of this particular missionary. Occasional eruptions of the old kind of spiritual crises are recorded. But they are few and far between. The entries are largely concerned with the growing mission and the observation of and engagement with Xhosa cultural practices that were the characteristic mode of missionary culture during these years.[33]

A final attribute that the evangelical revival contributed to missionary culture was the commitment to universal humanity. The evangelical idea that all were available to receive God's word had several implications. Most significantly it infused evangelicalism with a democratic tone. It was the Christian/non-Christian divide that was the key social distinction for evangelicals; and it was culture rather than race that explained racial differences. It is obviously important to realize the ideological limitations of evangelical humanitarianism. The idea of a universal humanity hardly implied the absence of hierarchies. Evangelical certainty about their God and religion provided missionary culture with an "imperial" sense of superiority. It was also the case that the idea of a universal humanity derived from one common origin (the idea of monogenesis) never held an unchallenged dominance in the discourse of eighteenth-century racial hierarchies. But the evangelical insistence that all were open to salvation irrespective of class or color was the dominant vocabulary of cultural and racial difference during the period from the later eighteenth century to the end of the 1840s.[34]

For the moment, however, it is important to appreciate the place that the idea of a universal humanity occupied in missionary culture. It was a bedrock notion which lay in the heads of the missionaries as they encountered indigenous cultures and peoples such as the Xhosa. As with the other elements of missionary culture, it was entirely a creation of metropolitan culture. Long before William Carey had actually seen any Indians, he was quite fixed in his belief that, although they were barbarous, "these poor heathens are as capable of knowledge as we are; and in many places at least ... have uncommon genius." Ignorance, he pointed out, was not the property only of the heathen. Plenty of Christians, too, existed in a state of ignorance. Even those evangelicals who saw savage lands and peoples as darker repositories of Satan's work did not see their savagery as essentialized, but as something that was capable of reformation with the right words and the right preaching.[35]

And these were ideas that were not displaced or refuted even after initial encounters had suggested the possibility of revision. Of course, adaptations were made to fit the evidence with the expectations. Once it was clear that conversions were not going to be spontaneous, the timeline for their achievement began to be stretched out. But well into the 1830s, the possibilities of the conversion of Africans were being compared favorably with the conversion of people in other countries. Thus, the official statement of missionary humanitarianism in southern Africa, John Philip's *Researches in South Africa*, published in 1828, was an extended assertion of the principle of universal humanity and the responsibility of government to allow missionaries to work to spread the values of civilization through Christian conversion.[36]

Conclusion

The most striking feature of the culture we have described here was the entire focus on the spiritual senses of the individual. The cultural assumptions that surrounded missionary recruitment, their training, such as it was, and the expectations of their mission were all directed to the spiritual purity and strength of the inner soul. Missionaries certainly needed to have a strong sense of spiritual commitment. Yet the focus of missionary evangelicalism entirely on the internal state of the individual, and the concomitant absence of anything more practical than this, is, from another angle, astounding. In what ways did it equip missionaries for their encounters with indigenous societies like the Xhosa? How did it equip them for the rigors and arduous realities of life on the frontier of empire? And what guidance did it provide for their interactions with indigenous peoples? Missionaries were simply advised to "cultivate a friendly intercourse with the natives, and by living among them in habits of friendship, adopt the most prudent means of leading them to a gradual acquaintance with the glorious truths of Revelation." The next few chapters will demonstrate how incomplete and inadequate such advice turned out to be.[37]

NOTES

1. See Andrew Ross, *David Livingstone: Mission and Empire* (London, 2002), pp. 50–2. It was standard practice for missionaries to live in Xhosa huts or tents while they built their houses. Early missionaries were often accompanied by artisan carpenters for precisely this reason. George Barker recorded in 1816 how he constructed a plastered house, complete with a lock on the door, but with windows covered with sheepskin since he had no glass. George Barker, *Journal 1815–1828*, June 1816, CL.

2. The material for the story of the Namaqualand mission is to be found in CWM, LMS, *South Africa Journals 1798–1810*, ff. 6, 10, 11. The account of Johannes van der Kemp's expedition to Nqgika is taken from LMS, *Transactions of the Missionary Society from its Institution in the Year 1795 to the End of the Year 1802*, vol. I (London, 1804). This consists largely of van der Kemp's journal of this time in Xhosaland.

3. E. Neville Sparks, *The Kayser Missionaries and their Descendants* (Port Elizabeth, 1973), p. 3.

4. Virtually the only reference that Stephen Kay made to his wife in his account of his missionary work, for example, was to tell the story of his being away preaching and her receiving rumors of his death! See Stephen Kay, *Travels and Researches in Caffraria: Describing the Character, Customs, and Moral Condition of the Tribes Inhabiting that portion of Southern Africa* (London, 1833), p. 292. See Natasha Erlank, "Jane and John Philip: Partnership, Usefulness and Sexuality in the Service of God," in John De Gruchy (ed.), *The London Missionary Society in South Africa, 1799–1999: Historical Essays in Celebration of the Bicentenary of the LMS in South Africa* (Athens, OH, 2000), pp. 82–98. The American mission to Natal seems to have been more interested in keeping records of women involved in missionary work, although this is for a slightly later period. See Norman Etherington, "Gender Issues in South-East African Missions, 1835–1885," in Henry Bredekamp and Robert Ross (eds.), *Missions and Christianity in South African History* (Johannesburg, 1995), pp. 134–52; George Brown, *Personal Adventures in South Africa* (London, 1855), pp. 273, 297, 305. There are obviously other ways of reading gender into the story of missionary culture during this period than just by looking for women in the records.

5. On the involvement of women in evangelical missionary culture, see the very informative article by Clare Midgley, "Can Women Be Missionaries? Envisioning Female Agency in the Early Nineteenth Century British Empire," *Journal of British Studies* 45.2 (2006), pp. 335–58; and R. H. W. Shepherd, *Lovedale: South Africa 1824–1955* (Lovedale, 1971), p. 18. Miss Harding's building was pulled down to accommodate a fort, so she pursued the imperial administration for compensation and was granted land and money by Sir Harry Smith. The next sighting we have of Miss Harding is several years later, when she is reported to be returning to the eastern Cape from Scotland, where she had recruited her sister to come and help her, and raised the money to transport an iron cottage for their accommodation. CA, GH 8/46, *Letters of the Reverend Henry Calderwood*, Memorial from Miss Harding, 8 December 1847, Reply from Smith, 1 January 1848; United Presbyterian Church, *Missionary Record*, October 1855, p. 182, where she is reported as headed for the Peelton mission.

6. Roger Levine, "Diplomat and Intellectual," in *Sable Son of Africa* (unpublished MS), p. 53; Deborah Gaitskell, "Rethinking Gender Roles: The Field Experience of Women Missionaries in South Africa," in Andrew Porter (ed.), *The Imperial Horizons of British Protestant Missions 1880–1914* (Grand Rapids, 2003), p. 141; Jane Haggis, "'A heart that has felt the love of God and longs for others to know it': Conventions of Gender, Tensions of Self and Constructions of Difference in Offering to be a Lady Missionary," *Women's History Review* 7.2 (1998), pp. 171–92.

7. Gaitskell, "Rethinking Gender Roles," pp. 134–5.

8. Neil Gunson, *Messengers of Grace: Evangelical Mission in the South Seas 1797–1860* (Melbourne, 1978), pp. 71–82; CWM, LMS, *Home Odds*, Box 8, 1833–99, Folder 1, D. G. Bishop to LMS, 19 June 1832; [?] Smith to LMS, 21 June 1833; Ralph Wardlow to Rev. John Arundell, 7 October 1833; Report of J. Whitehouse, 7 November 1875. The emphasis on character remained the main requirement into the 1860s and 1870s, when it began to be joined by a more practical curriculum.

9. Cumming, *Diary*, vol. I, 11, 12 and 18 November 1837, and 16 July 1838 for a description of the interview; John V. B. Shrewsbury, *Memorials of the Rev. William J. Shrewsbury*, 4th edn. (London, 1869), pp. 28–9. See also Sara Potter, "The Making of Missionaries in the Nineteenth Century," *The Sociological Yearbook of Religion in Britain* (London, 1974), pp. 111–12. For a similar pattern among Baptists, see Catherine Hall, *Civilizing Subjects: Metropole and Colony in the English Imagination 1830–1867* (Oxford, 2002), pp. 90–1.

10. Brian Stanley, *The History of the Baptist Missionary Society 1792–1992* (Edinburgh, 1992), pp. 16–17; William Carey, *An Enquiry into the Obligations of Christians to Use Means for the Conversion of the Heathens* (London, 1891), p. xiv. For the first missionaries to the South Pacific, see Rod Edmond, "Missionaries in Tahiti, 1797–1840," in Alex Calder, Jonathan Lamb and Bridget Orr (eds.), *Voyages and Beaches: Pacific Encounters, 1769–1840* (Honolulu, 1999), pp. 226–40. Not all missionaries left with such little preparation. The Dutch LMS missionary Johannes van der Kemp gave

himself survival training. He learnt brick-making and other practical trades. He purchased large quantities of gardening equipment and several guns. See Ido Enklaar, *The Life and Work of Dr. J. Th. Van Der Kemp 1747–1811* (Cape Town and Rotterdam, 1988), p. 64.

11. Cited in Potter, "The Making of Missionaries," p. 113. For the preference of the uneducated over the educated, see LMS, *Sermons Preached in London at the Formation of the Missionary Society* (London, 1795), sermon of Thomas Haweis, 22 September 1795, pp. 14–15. On the lower-class social background of missionaries see Stuart Piggin, *Making Evangelical Missionaries 1789–1858: The Social Background, Motives and Training of British Missionaries to India* (Sutton Courtenay, 1984).

12. We know about these lectures because Robert Moffat kept a full set of notes. We do not know how who else attended them, although at least one unnamed missionary in Xhosaland was reported as having heard them. Basil Holt, *Joseph Williams* (Lovedale, 1954), p. 10. Moffat's notes of Bogue's lectures are to be found in CWM, LMS *Home Odds*, Box 25. Why Gosport for Bogue's academy is a bit of a mystery; Portsmouth, however, was a frequent port of embarkation for missionaries.

13. The pattern of focusing on the domestic impact of the evangelical revival was set by Elie Halevy's masterly *England in 1815*, 2nd. edn. (New York, 1961), and continued by such standard works as Ford Madox Ford, *Fathers of the Victorians* (Cambridge, 1962). E. P. Thompson's classic *The Making of the English Working Class* (New York, 1963) ignored England's imperial role, even though his famous dissection of the psychology of Methodism is of considerable relevance to missionary culture. Indeed, this emphasis is somewhat justified. Only two of the 360 subjects that were discussed in John H. Pratt (ed.), *The Thought of the Evangelical Leaders: Notes of the Discussions of the Eclectic Society, London, during the years 1798–1814* (London, 1856) related to missionaries. The foreign missionaries in our period numbered only in the hundreds. Missionary work was just one subset of an evangelical culture that was hydra-headed in its reach and included such worthy causes as societies for moral improvement, ragged schools and temperance societies. For the missionary project in domestic evangelical culture, see Susan Thorne, *Congregational Missions and the Making of an Imperial Culture in Nineteenth-Century England* (Stanford, 1999); Catherine Hall, *Civilising Subjects: Metropole and Colony in the English Imagination 1830–1867* (Cambridge, 2002); and Alison Twells, *The Civilizing Mission and the English Middle Class, 1792–1857* (New York, 2009).

14. The best analysis of the relationship of the evangelical revival to missionary culture is contained in Elizabeth Elbourne, *Blood Ground: Colonialism, Missions, and the Contest for Christianity in the Cape Colony and Britain, 1799–1853* (Kingston, Ont., 2002), ch. 1. Much of what follows in this chapter draws heavily upon her analysis. Other useful overviews include Bebbington, *Evangelicalism in Modern Britain;* Andrew Porter, *Religion versus Empire? British Protestant Missionaries and Overseas Expansion 1700–1914* (Manchester, 2004); and Bradley, *The Call to Seriousness: The Evangelical Impact on the Victorians* (New York, 1976). Catherine Hall's *Civilising*

Subjects focuses on the work of the Baptist missionaries in the West Indies. On the Anglo-American background to missionary culture – which was very important in southern Africa – see Andrew Porter, "North American Experience and British Missionary Encounters in Africa and the Pacific, *c.* 1800–50," in Martin Daunton and Rick Halpern (eds.), *Empire and Others: British Encounters with Indigenous Peoples, 1600–1850* (Philadelphia, 1999), pp. 345–63. For the Baptists see Stanley, *History of the Baptist Missionary Society*, pp. 5–7, 9.

15. Porter, *Religion versus Empire?*, pp. 56–7; Elbourne, *Blood Ground*, p. 62; for the CMS see Elbourne, "The Foundation of the Church Missionary Society: The Anglican Missionary Impulse," in John Walsh, Colin Haydon and Stephen Taylor (eds.), *The Church of England c. 1689–c. 1833: From Toleration to Tractarianism* (Cambridge, 1993), pp. 247–64; Richard Lovett, *The History of the London Missionary Society 1795–1895* (London, 1899).

16. Carey, *Enquiry*, pp. 7, 31; LMS, *Sermons Preached*, p. xiv.

17. Porter, *Religion versus Empire?*, pp. 32–3; Gunson, *Messengers of Grace*, p. 49; Carey, *Enquiry*, p. xiv. Enklaar, *Life and Work of Dr. J. Th. Van Der Kemp*, pp. 27–35. Van der Kemp was exceptional in terms of his age and maturity when he converted, being well into his forties.

18. Boyd Hilton has shown how the idea of providential determination was a central underpinning of Victorian modernity. Boyd Hilton, *The Age of Atonement: The Influence of Evangelicalism on Social and Economic Thought 1785–1865* (Oxford, 1988); Bebbington, *Evangelicalism in Modern Britain*, pp. 60–3; Pratt, *Thought of the Evangelical Leaders*, pp. 95–8.

19. Gunson, *Messengers of Grace*, pp. 49–50, 150–4, for the doctrine of reparation in missionary culture. We may note in passing that this combination of beliefs provided some grounds for the accusation that evangelicalism was part of Britain's imperial identity. Evangelicals *were* convinced that God had providentially determined on the conversion of the heathen and that all missionaries had to do was to introduce his word. If the Gospel was thus presented "with all its gracious calls, invitations and promises, and received with faith and love, it will most certainly prove the gospel of their salvation." The logical flaw was obvious; it assumed only one reading which would be so obvious that even a neophyte could see it. But what would happen to the reasoning of the missionary if the obvious reading was not regurgitated by the Xhosa reader? See LMS, *Sermons* (London, 1795), sermon by Robert Balfour, "The Salvation of the Heathen Necessary and Certain," pp. 10–11, 29–30, 34; and Doug Stuart, "Converts or Convicts? The Gospel of Liberation and Subordination in Early Nineteenth-Century South Africa," in Holger Bernt and Twaddle Hansen (eds.), *Christian Missionaries and the State in the Third World* (Oxford and Athens, OH, 2002), pp. 66–75.

20. LMS, *Sermons*, sermon by Thomas Haweis, 22 September 1795, pp. 16–17, 19. And this was echoed by others: preaching alone could "convince the sinner of his need of Christ ... the simple declaration of the love of God in sending his Son is the one grand instrument of converting the world." See Pratt, *Thought of the Evangelical Leaders*, pp. 95–8. The success of the Danish missionaries in Greenland provided a model that was much admired and was

taken to confirm the evangelical belief in the sheer power of the word. David Crantz, *The History of Greenland including an Account of the Mission Carried on by the United Brethren in That Country* (London, 1820). This mindset was not just a feature of this particular phase of missionary activity, although it was at its most unqualified at this time, before the actual experiences in Africa and elsewhere revealed that things would not work quite so smoothly. But for similar assumptions in the late nineteenth-century missionary world, see T. O. Beidelman, *Colonial Evangelism: A Socio-Historical Study of an East African Mission at the Grassroots* (Bloomington, IN, 1982), pp. 100–4.

21. Bebbington, *Evangelicalism in Modern Britain*, pp. 76–7; Stuart, "Converts or Convicts?," p. 69.

22. Andrew Ross, "Christian Missions and the Mid-Nineteenth Century Change in Attitudes to Race: The African Experience," in Porter, *Imperial Horizons*, pp. 85–7. John Philip in 1828 cited the cases of prominent conversions of Africans to illustrate how the preaching of the Gospel could quickly raise individuals up the scale of civilization. For the way this prioritizing of conversion over civilization is reversed by the mid-century see Chapter 6 below.

23. There is, of course, a large literature on millenarianism in this period; see, for example, J. F. C. Harrison, *The Second Coming: Popular Millenarianism, 1780–1850* (New Bruswick, NJ, 1979); Bebbington, *Evangelicalism in Modern Britain*, p. 62; Porter, *Religion versus Empire?*, pp 33, 59. LMS, *Sermons*, pp. xxi, xiv, xvi.

24. Bebbington, *Evangelicalism in Modern Britain*, pp. 10–11.

25. Carey, *Enquiry*, p. 31, where he tells of "one Frumentius [in the time of Constantine] who was sent to preach to the Indians, and met with great success. A young women who was a Christian, being taken captive by the Iberians or Georgians, near the Caspian Sea, informed them of the truths of Christianity, and was so much regarded that they sent to Constantine for ministers to come and preach the word to them." See also LMS, *Sermons*, especially sermons by George Burden, 27 September 1795, p. 27, and Robert Balfour, "The Salvation of the Heathen Necessary and Certain," p. 35.

26. Bebbington, *Evangelicalism in Modern Britain*, pp. 60–3; Rev. Thomas Haweis, *An Impartial and Succinct History of the Revival and Progress of the Church of Christ from the Reformation to the Present Time* (Worcester, MA, 1803), pp. 385; Carey, *Enquiry*, pp. 71–4, 75–6.

27. LMS, *Sermons*, sermon of David Bogue, 24 September 1795, pp. 123–6; Stanley, *History of the Baptist Missionary Society*, pp. 36–7, 43–7.

28. Ten years before Cumming, Friedrich Kayser, *en route* to southern Africa, experienced a similar crisis of doubt and self-confidence that led him to question whether he was worthy or able to face the challenges that awaited him. And at the same time his wife also experienced what seems to have been an emotional illness that she attributed to God's testing of her resolve. CWM, *South Africa Journals 1824–1897*, f. 96, F. G. Kayser, Journal, 15 April and 21 June 1827. And for a similar experience, see Rev. William Impey, *Journal 1838–1847*, 27 October and 7 November 1838, CL, MS 15109.

29. Cumming, *Diary*, 31 December 1836; 5, 12, 22 January; 18, 21 February; 12, 19 March 1837; 11, 12, 18 November 1838.

30. Ibid., 30 November 1839.
31. It seems likely that the woman played a large role in his mind as he struggled through the series of spiritual crises of the next few months, because in September 1840, as part of a disquisition on why he is convinced that Africa is not his intended destiny, he notes that "I know full well that she [her name was Margaret] does not possess that strength which is requisite to live amongst the people amongst which I probably will dwell for sometime. Although she [would] come out with cheerfulness it would be cruel in me to ask her." See ibid., 20 September 1840.
32. Ibid., 9 August and 13 December 1840; 25 and 28 January 1841.
33. Ibid., 15 July 1841; 5 and 20 January 1842. See entries of 5 and 10 May and 26 June 1843 for recurrences of the old kind of spiritual crises. The change in tone of the diary entries and the shifting direction of Cumming's attribution of responsibility for difficulties are surely not coincidental. By the early 1850s his diaries are merely a catalogue of doings, with no reflective entries on his state of mind or mentality. This change in the quality of such evidence was reflected in other sources, too, and reflected wider changes in missionary culture that we shall discuss in Chapter 5.
34. This is a huge and complicated topic, of course, which I shall discuss in more detail as it is relevant to missionary culture in southern Africa in Chapter 6. For a recent discussion of racial theory in the eighteenth century with which I do not entirely agree, see Roxanne Wheeler, *The Complexion of Race: Categories of Difference in Eighteenth Century British Culture* (Philadelphia, 2000).
35. Carey, *Enquiry*, p. 63; LMS, *Sermons*, sermons of George Burden, pp. 35–7, and of Samuel Greathed, pp. 56–7.
36. Stanley, *History of the Baptist Missionary Society*, pp. 36–7; William J. Shrewsbury, *Sermons Preached on Several Occasions on the Island of Barbados* (London, 1825), p. 352: "I have seen that Christ is able to convert Africans by the same word of truth that converts men of other countries." Philip, of course, was also concerned to *defend* the missionary discourse on race against the history of white settler treatment of the indigenous peoples. Indeed, like most other missionary analysts at this moment, he regarded this treatment as a major reason for the degraded state of the indigenes. See, for example, Philip, *Researches in South Africa*, vol. I, p. 362; vol. II, pp. 203, 315–17. For the way missionary culture in the metropole adapted to the failures of its expectations in the empire see Alison Twells, *The Civilizing Mission and the English Middle Class, 1792–1857* (New York, 2009).
37. Lovett, *History of the London Missionary Society*, p. 23. It was, of course, true that individual missionaries probably tried to educate themselves in preparation for their missions, as the example of van der Kemp illustrates. We do not know how typical this was. Van der Kemp, it should be remembered, was an older and more mature man than the average missionary, who tended to be just out of his or her teens. See Enklaar, *Life and Work of Dr. J. Th. Van Der Kemp*, p. 64. There is a wonderful story that Elizabeth Elbourne has recovered, which illustrates the thoughtlessness that underlay the missionary initiative at this time. In 1802, seeking to spread God's word, the Edinburgh Missionary Society looked at a map of the world and their attention was drawn

to the Caucasus, populated by "numerous tribes of men, all sunk in the deepest ignorance and depravity." Here was a succulent opportunity for an outlay of missionary enterprise! Their actual knowledge of the area was negligible, but this hardly mattered. All that mattered was the field of opportunity offered for missionary zeal by the hordes of depraved savages. And so they raised the money to send a mission of three hapless Britons, namely the former chaplain of Sierra Leone, a British artisan and an "African youth," deep into the interior of Asia minor. Elbourne, *Blood Ground*, p. 34.

Observation

In February 1801 Johannes van der Kemp, the pioneer missionary to southern Africa, sent a long report to the London Missionary Society of the religion, cultural practices and government of the Xhosa. The report is some nineteen pages long, and in parts almost impossible to decipher. It is the earliest such report from a missionary, and it provides a detailed account of what van der Kemp had observed and learnt about Xhosa society during his fairly short sojourn with Ngqika, one of the most important Xhosa chieftains. Between June 1799 and January 1801, van der Kemp lived in close physical and social proximity to Ngqika and his people. He watched from close up the struggle for power between Ngqika and his uncle, Ndlambe. And he spent a lot of time negotiating and worrying about his personal safety, since Ngqika was also keeping a wary eye on him, fearing that he was an agent of the British imperial state, which had recently replaced the Dutch presence at the Cape.

Whatever the immediate motivation, van der Kemp was intellectually engaged with Xhosa society. He packed a great deal of information into his report to the London Missionary Society. He described the nature of chiefly power, the cooking methods of the Xhosa, their clothing, their various cultural and marriage customs, the way their laws worked, their labor practices, their burial practices, and the nature of their religious beliefs. He even compiled a list of Xhosa words. We do not know what he knew about the Xhosa when he went out to southern Africa. But even allowing for some information and impressions that he brought with him, what he learnt during his time on the eastern frontier was quite impressive. The analogy comes to mind of the young child soaking up and categorizing data from the world around him or her.[1]

What struck me as important when I first encountered this document was the intense level of *observation and engagement* that was revealed on both sides of the relationship. Van der Kemp was watching the Xhosa, and they were watching him. This sense was reinforced when I realized that van der Kemp was not peculiar in this regard. Even though he was not representative of the typical missionary sent to southern Africa – he was, after all, a highly educated man – his style of engagement with the Xhosa was not unusual. Indeed, it was a style that was quite characteristic of missionary culture until the middle of the century. The early generations of missionaries encountered the Xhosa in close and intimate ways. It was a mode of engagement in which the missionaries followed van der Kemp's precedent of observing and entangling and being entanged *with* Xhosa society.[2]

Until the early 1850s the missionary records of the LMS vivdly convey the enthusiasm of the proselytizing evangelical. They record the work of people who are not only deeply committed, but also engaged in a vital and lively interaction with the Xhosa. The tone of this interaction was self-confident, and to that extent it was the tone of an "imperial eye." But it was also a tone that was fully aware that there was another culture involved, a culture that must be contended with and engaged. To that extent, and this is critically important, *it was a tone that implied an open mind rather than the obverse.* The quality of these missionary archives, then, for this early period, is quite remarkable. They not only disclose what the missionaries were doing as they encountered Xhosa culture; they also reveal what they thought about what they were doing.

But in the early 1850s, the nature of these records changes quite radically. It is as if a different purpose, a different intention, had announced itself. The content of those same records dries up; they become perfunctory. They cease to describe the nature of their engagement with the Xhosa. Detailed descriptions of chiefs' behavior disappear; missionary struggles against polygamy, witchcraft or circumcision drop out of sight. One giant absence captures the essence of this change – something that should have flooded the records, but which did not. The great cattle-killing of 1856–7 was hardly referred to. Yet this was the moment when Xhosa society imploded, committed social suicide. It was impossible to imagine missionaries like van der Kemp being so disengaged from the Xhosa world around them. What had happened to cause this disengagement? Behind this simple question lies the complex story of what happened to missionary subjectivities during this period of initial encounter.[3]

Engagement

At this moment in its history, evangelicalism was an activist and optimistic faith. The missionaries of the early part of the nineteenth century, who emerged from the evangelical revival, possessed an open and hopeful attitude towards the Xhosa, an attitude that welcomed engagement with them since they were sure that it presaged conversion. To illustrate this, I want to open with the example of the Reverend William Shrewsbury, a Wesleyan Methodist missionary who served in southern Africa from 1825 to 1835. Shrewsbury's experiences provide a rich source for the dynamics of the missionary encounter with the Xhosa. His personal story encapsulates in vivid detail the course of missionary culture over the period 1820–50, and in the next chapter I shall return to him in this context. Since we shall meet Shrewsbury again, a few brief biographical facts are in order here.[4]

Shrewsbury came from that stratum of society that hovered between the poor working class and the slightly less poor lower middle class. His grandfather had been a pilot in the port of Deal, Kent – a position that in the Cinque Port town traditionally carried a certain status. His father was a grocer, and his mother had been a servant before her marriage. Born in 1796, Shrewsbury left school at age ten, so he was largely self-educated. But his theological education was wide, if eclectic, and he had aspirations to biblical scholarship. In later life, he produced a multi-volume commentary on the Old Testament, some of which appeared in print. He had an aptitude for languages; he taught himself Greek and Hebrew and successfully learnt Xhosa.

Shrewsbury was driven and intelligent. Like most evangelicals he got the "call" at an early age and as a teenager preached in the local Methodist circuit in east Kent. By 1815 the Methodists of Canterbury had selected him as suitable material for a missionary career, and he departed for the West Indies, where he married a Creole woman from Barbados and remained until 1824 before being transfered to the Cape. After returning home from southern Africa in 1835, he spent a year in Boulogne, France, before moving on to Rochester, Kent, and finally Bacup, Lancashire, where he remained until his death in the mid-1860s.[5]

In the West Indies, Shrewsbury was a loud advocate of cultural relativism. He preached the equality of all cultures before God's eyes, and the equal availability to God of white or black persons. He challenged the morals of the planter class, and condemned their treatment of their slaves. When he arrived in southern Africa he threw himself into the work of the itinerant, engaged and observant missionary, and his first comments on Xhosa society and its leaders suggest an openness to cultural difference; he was eager to observe and engage with Xhosa culture as a necessary preliminary to entering the hearts of the people.[6]

Thus, his residences at the Butterworth and then Mt. Coke mission stations were recorded in great detail. His diary entries burst with intelligent and accurate observations about Xhosa culture. They suggest a high level of engagement with the local community, and a fine eye for observing the habits and customs of the people. He did not discount the magnitude of the task facing him; he fearlessly confronted cultural practices that epitomized the hold of witchcraft. He did not hesitate to challenge witch-doctor divinations. He wrote long and detailed accounts of various cultural practices, such as the licentious marriage feasts which, he claimed, turned the countryside into a land "filled with fornication, whoredom and all uncleanliness." Shrewsbury was never starry-eyed about Xhosa society. He recognized that there were "*many, many* facts of a very painful and *discouraging* nature." Nevertheless, in these early years he remained committed to the idea of a universal humanity, and his attitude towards the Xhosa was balanced and open. In a long report to London in February 1828 he told of the signs he had seen among the Xhosa that confirmed the predictions of evangelical discourse – signs that revealed evidence that the Spirit of God was working among the people. There is at least the suggestion that he was willing to turn a blind eye in certain cases to baptizing converts who were also in polygamous relationships – a position that horrified the missionary authorities in London. He pointed out that an absolute prohibition could not possibly meet all circumstances, and he was willing to alter the baptism service to accommodate native custom and usage.[7]

Shrewsbury's discussion of the prophet Nxele (also known as Makana) provides insight into his attitude towards the Xhosa. Nxele was one of the first in a line of Xhosa prophets who were to combine a religious sensibility with a political purpose. Nxele had inspired the attack on Grahamstown in the war of 1819–20, which had come within reach of overrunning the settlement. Nxele was also a boundary-crosser, however. He was a Xhosa diviner, but his contact with early London Missionary Society missionaries had led him to absorb aspects of Christianity. He believed he was a relative of Christ and he gained a following of thousands. He presented a confusing and threatening spectacle to the British. When he surrendered in 1820, he was rushed away from the frontier zone and imprisoned in (where else?) Robben Island, from which he tried to escape in a small boat, which capsized, drowning him and his companions.[8]

Nxele was therefore an interesting character for Shrewsbury to comment on. By this time Nxele was a hero to the Xhosa, who refused to believe in his death. As late as the 1850s he was believed to be still alive. Shrewsbury's comment is somewhat tortured, reflecting his own internal struggle to come to grips with what he did believe. But its most salient character is its attempt to present a balanced view of Nxele. This alone is noteworthy. On the one hand, Nxele possessed the immoral attributes common to Xhosa culture; but he was also " a sort of mixed character ... influenced by a sort of ambition ... [to be] the means of scattering some rays of light in this land of darkness." In other words, even in this prophet who had escaped the missionary net, and who had led a serious rebellion against the British, Shrewsbury found signs of humanity.[9]

Shrewsbury's mode of encounter with the Xhosa was not unusual. Let us turn now to the case of the Reverend James Laing. Laing arrived in the eastern Cape shortly after Shrewsbury, in 1831, and he remained there until his death in the early 1870s. He established himself at Burnside mission in 1832, where he stayed until 1843, when he moved for twelve years to Lovedale before being transferred back to Burnside for the rest of his life. Like many of the early missionaries, he suffered his fair share of physical hardship and personal loss. But the dominant fact of his early years was Laing's deep immersion in Xhosa society. His *Journal* for the first few years is crammed full of the details of that engagement and of its implications for the conversion of the Xhosa. In Laing's case, however, his engagement with the Xhosa was not entirely of his own making.[10]

Laing arrived at Burnside bursting with enthusiasm to take on the Xhosa. He settled into his wattle and daub hut, with his artisan companion Alexander McDairmird, and set about trying to preach in his pidgin Xhosa, ignoring the laughter this provoked from the local people. Within weeks of his arrival, however, he was drawn into the quick sands of local Xhosa politics, and he spent the next four years mired in this engagement. The occasion was the pending conversion to Christianity of Matwa, a lesser son of Chief Ngqika. Matwa's connection with the leading chiefly family among the Xhosa made his commitment to Christianity more than just an affair of individual conscience. There was considerable ambivalence in the royal kraal – to put it at its mildest – about Matwa's interest in the missionary cause, especially as he seemed so eager to adopt the ways of the British. He started to dress in European clothes and to build a European-style cottage. And although it is quite clear that the politics of the case were Byzantine, the essence of it boiled down to a power struggle for the possession of Matwa's commitment.

Laing soon discovered that cultural practices like witchcraft were weapons in the struggle for Matwa's body. When Matwa got sick, for example, word spread that he had been bewitched by the missionaries. When Laing and his associate challenged this, they were immediately engaged in debate by three women witchdoctors, which ended with their being told that "it is our way, you have your way, but this is ours." Over the following month Laing was drawn deeper and deeper into the world of Xhosa witchcraft. Along the way he acquired an understanding of the political dimensions of the issue thanks to the interlocution of Charles Henry, a Khoi convert who served as the mission's intermediary and translator.

Charles Henry became a target for the anti-mission faction among the Xhosa and he was accused of being the agent who had bewitched Matwa. Charles Henry became so frightened that on Christmas Eve he fled the mission.

Laing struggled to understand what was going on. He found himself caught in conflicting sensations as to what to believe. Should he accept Charles Henry's judgment when he claimed that Laing should not believe the signs of friendship that the Xhosa were giving out on one occasion? The interpreter claimed that the Xhosa were merely trying to lull the missionaries into a false sense of security. But Laing could not understand the reasons for Charles Henry's fears. Neither Laing nor McDairmid (his fellow missionary) could see the danger, and he was left wondering whether in fact Charles Henry had some hidden motive in wanting to leave the mission.[11]

Indeed, at this very moment Laing's engagement with the Xhosa seemed to belie any danger to him or the mission. No threatening moves were made against the missionaries. On the contrary, the Xhosa were more than usually friendly. Maqoma and Suthu – the Queen Regent – visited on the Sabbath. Several widows of Ngqika began to attend services, along with followers of Matwa. In February, Laing had an encouraging exchange with Maqoma about witchcraft, in which the chief insisted that he wanted to abolish the practice, and looked to missionaries for instruction as to how to do it. On the other hand, Charles Henry was insistent enough about the danger to send for his wife and children on 5 January and to remain away until April 1832, thus depriving Laing of his essential interlocutor. And then there were reports of a Mfengu man, accused of bewitching Matwa, being tortured to confess.[12]

By May things had settled down considerably. Charles Henry had returned, one of the witchdoctors appeared at services, and Matwa attended church, dined with the missionaries and talked again of building a European-style house. It seemed as if Matwa were about to commit and convert. But this did not happen, and Charles Henry took off again in July, not to return until the end of the year. Matwa did eventually come over to the mission side. But he proved a disappointing convert. He was perpetually backsliding, getting drunk and taking part in various rainmaking ceremonies, abusing his wives and committing adultery. Throughout this opening period of Laing's mission to the Xhosa, therefore, he was closely engaged with the cultural and political practices of Xhosa society. During one of Matwa's backsliding episodes Laing attended a rainmaking ceremony and confronted the rainmaker. A few months later he was involved in a similar struggle with a witchdoctor; he intervened in a "smelling out" and described in detail the ritual that he had fruitlessly tried to stop.[13]

It was common practice for these missionaries to insert themselves into the public ceremonies and rituals of the Xhosa if they were seen as witchcraft or if they involved perceived moral lasciviousness. Nor were missionaries reticent about confronting powerful chiefs. Maqoma was constantly admonished by missionaries who were stationed near him, and even the great Hintsa was upbraided by Shrewsbury for a catalogue of bad practices, including working on Sundays and, of course, permitting witchcraft. When Sandile, the young heir to Ngqika's position as chief of the Rharhabe Xhosa, had his circumcision ceremony, the Glasgow missionaries from the Burnside mission did not hesitate to condemn the various ceremonies around the ritual, such as dancing on the Sabbath, and to protest to Suthu (Sandile's mother) about allowing such evils. In this case, the missionaries were motivated in part by the split loyalties of the mission natives, many of whom participated in the ceremonies. And although they received short shrift from Suthu, some kind of compromise was worked out that allowed the ceremony to proceed without requiring the presence of the mission Christians.[14]

Reading the reports and letters from missionaries in these early days of their contact with the Xhosa is often like reading an eclectic collection of ethnographic descriptions. Missionaries were committed to establishing a relationship with Xhosa culture, as a necessary part of their project of changing it. This led them to operate first and foremost as activists, almost as participant observers in the various rites and ceremonies of Xhosa society. Each body of archives they left behind in this period is steeped in descriptions and explanations of what they saw and how they responded. Missionaries were hungry for information about the Xhosa, and tended to seek it wherever they could. John Bennie, for example, a missionary of the Glasgow Missionary Society, used one of his native interlocutors to tutor him in the history of the Xhosa. Mostly, they were led to seek out what they could see and experience directly. William Shaw, the leading Methodist missionary on the frontier from the mid-1820s to the mid-1850s, attended a smelling-out ceremony with a group of native Christians; this was an invitation-only event put on precisely to impress him with the power of the practice. The chief ordered the people to make way for the mission natives, so that they could see there was no trickery involved in the discovery of the bewitching material (the *ubuti*).[15]

When confronted with what they categorized as witchcraft or other superstitions, missionaries sometimes had to struggle to retain the idea of Xhosa humanity. But they continued to retain a vision of the Xhosa grounded in the assumption that the deficits in Xhosa society were no different from those of heathen souls anywhere. They were deficits that were cultural, not racial, and they could be redeemed once a way was found into their hearts. In this respect, the state of indigenous peoples was analogous to that of the working classes at home rather than their being racial others. They possessed the same capacity for salvation, and needed only to have their eyes opened for the truth to enter their hearts. Commenting on the murder of the missionary William Threlfall and two native preachers, the Methodist missionary Stephen Kay was at pains to combat the idea that the Xhosa possessed an essentialized savagery. Such catastrophes "are much less frequent than might be expected among uncivilized nations" and he reported feeling quite safe living with his wife and children among the Xhosa.[16]

Missionaries were staunchly monogenesist in their conception of the racial hierarchy. A clear insight into missionary culture's predominant view on racial difference may be gained from a lengthy reflection that J. F. Cumming committed to his diary as he was *en route* to southern Africa in 1840. The significance of this passage is enhanced because, as we have noted, at this time Cumming was in a state of perpetual emotional turmoil. It is not a particularly profound passage. Indeed, it is typical of the plodding and ponderous intelligence of the auto-didact. Yet, as an articulation of ideological belief, it possesses a powerful sincerity. In his musing, Cumming puts forth reasons why he believes in the possibility of African salvation. It is clear that he knew the arguments that were mounted *against* the mongenesis view of human development. But he rejected them on the basis of biblical authority. Thus, he reasoned that if blacks and whites are both descended from the same individual – Adam – then the covenant of grace that Adam was allowed to enter after his fall was a covenant that must apply to all his descendants.[17]

A more fully developed analysis of how missionary culture saw the Xhosa is to be found in an obscure pamphlet written by Robert Niven, also a missionary of the Glasgow Missionary Society. By the time Cumming arrived in the Cape, Niven was a stalwart of the mission community. He remained there for about twenty years until he ran foul of the military authorities in the eighth frontier war (1850–3) and was expelled. In the 1830s, his humanitarian sentiments were more consonant with official policy, however, and he was close to a group of frontier officials who shared his views. Niven's pamphlet was drawn from an extended letter to one of those officials, and it laid out the governing conceptions that missionaries held about Xhosa character and the possibilities for their salvation.[18]

Niven's statement reflected mainstream evangelical humanitarianism. He rejected the view of the Xhosa as "irredeemably wicked" and unreformable, which had been expressed by Sir Benjamin D'Urban when he was Governor in 1835 and which was now fast gaining ground in settler consciousness. By the same token, Niven was at pains to reject the view that he attributed to metropolitan humanitarianism that the Xhosa were innocent and docile. Rather, Niven proclaimed, the Xhosa was a person "of like passions with ourselves guided by the same laws and influenced by the same passions as the most polished of our race." It was Xhosa culture that molded their character. It was interesting that Niven did not regard such practices as witchcraft or polygamy as particularly important vices in the catalogue of Xhosa depravity. These cultural practices were at the center of much missionary struggle and they were to occupy a prominent place in the ultimate bill of indictment that the British created about Xhosa culture. But Niven's explanation for Xhosa character was at bottom *cultural*. The individual psychologies of the Xhosa were a product of cultural conditioning. For Niven, the road to reforming the Xhosa's character and culture was education, which would drain him of "all the peculiarities which render him an object of dread or of sympathy to his detractors or panegyrists."

What was it within the culture that shaped behavior? In this respect Niven pointed to social and economic forces such as the division of labor, which assigned women to the most active economic agency and encouraged men to indolence and to polygamy. In addition, within Xhosa culture the powerful claims of *community* ownership over the claims of *individual* property rights served to discourage enterprise and initiative. Thus, what the missionaries saw as debilitating cultural practices that defined Xhosa society were a function not of an inherently deficient sensibility, but of a political and social practice that it was dangerous for enterprising persons to challenge. Niven cited the case of a cultivator who produced a surplus of grain, only to find himself surrounded by family and friends pleading for handouts. It was impossible for him to resist this pressure if only because of what would happen to him should he fall on bad times. It was this kind of social and political practice that eroded the moral fiber of the culture, Niven claimed. In such a case, the virtues of ownership and possession were inverted, encouraging deceit and lying about what one possessed in order to stave off importuning demands. In this way, Niven argued, the nation was "converted into a race of liars." It was similarly the case with livestock, the major currency in Xhosaland. Since livestock was used to pay taxes and fines, owners understated their real wealth, often dividing their herds and sending them off to board with friends or relatives elsewhere in order to reduce their holdings, and they "will deny the fact fifty times every day." Niven thus had a *social* and a *cultural* explanation for the British assertion that the Xhosa were a nation of liars, claiming that what at first glance may seem like beggary or thieving "is in fact not that."

Niven's analysis of Xhosa society and Xhosa character, therefore, was resolutely *materialist*, rather than moralistic. It represented a curious departure from the largely spiritual and unworldly evangelical culture that provided the backdrop for missionary enterprise in British society. To that extent Niven's explanation of Xhosa character may be seen as the kind of adaptation that evolved as missionaries faced the practical matter of going about their business. But Niven's understanding of Xhosa culture was also consonant with evangelicalism. His materialist evaluation of the Xhosa implied an essentially *optimistic* view of the encounter. It meant that there were no intractable impediments to reaching into Xhosa hearts and opening them for salvation. The right tools would do it; a combination of inspired preaching and plows would dislodge the cultural obstacles that settlers and others attributed to the savagery of Xhosa hearts. Niven's statement is useful, then, as illustrating the ways in which this discourse of optimism was translated and formulated by missionaries on the ground, and how it formed an integral part of the culture of his generation of missionaries as they entered into the encounter with the Xhosa.

Optimism

Missionary activity at *all* times must possess a heavy does of utopian hope. And to that extent the optimism of the evangelical culture of the late eighteenth and early nineteenth centuries was a generic feature of missionary activity *tout court*. The place of optimism in the missionary culture of the early nineteenth century, therefore, does not possess a historical peculiarity. But it does possess historical specificity in at least one sense: during the early nineteenth century, missionary culture was less troubled by challenges to the discourse of evangelical humanitarianism than it had been before or was to be later. For this brief moment, the discourse of the missionary program and agenda in Britain and that in specifically southern Africa were synchronous; the program and agenda in both were dominated by the discourse that we have described as missionary evangelicalism.[19]

The first thing to note about the optimism of early nineteenth-century missionary culture is that it was for a long time resistant to contrary evidence. After the shaky start of missionary evangelicalism in the South Seas, it should have been apparent that expectations were not likely to be matched in the real world of missionary work. Yet the rhetoric of expectation continued to thrive. The experience of Joseph Williams is relevant here. Williams was the first London Missionary Society missionary to follow in van der Kemp's footsteps, in 1816, fifteen years after the Dutchman had fled the dangers of Ngqika's kraal. He was the first missionary to settle permanently in Xhosaland and was the forerunner of successive waves of missionaries throughout the 1850s, who all exhibit the same patterns of optimism we shall describe here.

Williams traveled with his wife and child from Bethelsdorp, the Khoesan mission settlement that van der Kemp and James Read had established. He was accompanied by Jan Tzatzoe, the celebrated Xhosa "chief" whom Philip paraded before the missionary public in Britain during the hearings of the Select Committee on Aborigines, 1836–7. Tzatzoe served as companion and interpreter and brought along a strong party of six Khoesan men and their families. Presumably it was these people who built the reed house, planted the garden and the cornfield and built the dam that were all established in the first year. Since this was beyond the colonial frontier, Williams could get permission from the authorities to cross the frontier only if he would agree to keep a watch on Ngqika. In spite of this, Williams was well received by the Xhosa and was initially very successful. He reported that within six days of arrival he and his wife had opened a school that attracted fifty children; within a year, the mission had attracted 150 inhabitants, and he and Tzatzoe offered four services on Sunday. The first year was an encouraging success, although no one had been baptized. Mrs. Williams wrote home in glowing terms about the Xhosa, how "their perseverance is remarkable, they listen attentively in service, they never seem weary and are always willing to help. I feel much pleasure in living with them." If this was the success that could be expected, then no wonder the wave of waiting missionaries set off with high expectations.[20]

But then the enterprise fell apart. Ngqika was engaged in yet another struggle with Ndlambe for supremacy over the Rharhabe Xhosa. He was decisively defeated at the battle of Amalinde in October 1818, and driven into dependence upon the British. Williams was caught in the middle of this, and because the British tried to use him as an intermediary his credibility with both Xhosa factions was destroyed. At the same time, Tzatzoe left the mission under a cloud of womanizing. Williams sank into a deep depression at the collapse of his good work, describing himself as sick and worn out, and reporting that "I have been more tried these last two years than in all my life." At just that moment, in an appropriately dramatic flourish, he caught a fever, and died in August 1818, leaving his wife to bury him and arrange the closure of the mission.[21]

William's experience, however, did not undermine the optimistic aspirations of the succeeding generations of missionaries that historical time could be foreshortened and the Xhosa rapidly introduced to British civilization. Each wave of missionaries to arrive in southern Africa until the 1850s imbibed the same nectar of evangelical expectations. Individual triumphs were taken to substantiate the hope that large shifts in the spiritual direction of native life were possible. Thus, as he left the Clarkebury mission in June 1837 to return home, W. J. Davis, a Methodist missionary, admitted that he could point to only twelve conversions. Nevertheless, he claimed to have changed behavior. He noted that his preaching was always treated with respect and that he had no trouble attracting congregations. He believed that he had lifted darkness from Xhosa society and implanted the concepts of God and Jesus and of eternal reward and punishment. And he assured the Directors that he had observed signs of God moving in the Xhosa, citing the evidence of one woman who "spoke of feeling the joy of God in her."[22]

At this stage of missionary culture, optimism was a renewable commodity. It served to reconcile the predictions of evangelical culture for missionary work with the patent evidence of small measurable results. In these early years, such claims were common. Hope sprang eternal. The claims that were made for Robert Moffat's ministry in Bechuanaland were that it had brought peace and civilization. Such large achievements were broadcast mainly for public consumption, although sympathetic border officials also perpetuated this optimistic discourse. In the 1840s, Charles Stretch wrote to the Lieutenant Governor of the eastern frontier describing how missionary work had greatly diminished superstitious beliefs among the Xhosa. Optimism proved to be a very hardy quality. Even though expectations had to be modified almost from the first encounter, each group of missionaries who arrived between 1820 and the 1850s possessed the same expectations of great things. Some continued to pursue the same pipe dreams for over thirty years. Until the later 1840s and the beginning of the 1850s, this kind of renewable optimism was a core value of missionary culture. As late as 1862, when John Chalmers, after eleven years in England, returned to the Emgwali mission station which his father had established, he too revealed a similar kind of wondrous optimism that was reminiscent of that expressed by W. J. Davis, mentioned above. He spoke of the rapid progress he was making against the witchdoctors and the dark cultural practices of the Xhosa, and of the promising signs for the future.[23]

The ability of missionary culture to remain optimistic about its project depended upon its ability to interpret the results of its observation and engagement within a context that was consonant with their theology and their knowledge of conversion practices at home. If they did not experience mass conversions on the scale of the Great Awakening, this made them all the more attuned to the many small signs that the humanity of the Xhosa was both real and open to God's presence. In this period of engagement and observation, then, optimism was sustained and maintained by what we might call (with apologies to Homi Bhaba) small signs taken for wonders. Missionaries were ever on the lookout for token indications that God was working his way through them. The small signs they detected enabled them to reconcile faith with experience. Such signs spoke to the missionaries as evidence that the indigenous peoples of the area possessed the same spiritual wiring and responses as those in Britain. In this phase of the encounter, missionaries were listening and watching intently for signs that they were touching on the right nerves to open the Xhosa to the grace of the Lord.

Missionaries read the responses to their preaching by direct reference to their British experience. In Namaqualand, the early missionary J. H. Schmelen saw the Spirit of the Lord moving directly in the natives when his preaching moved them to tears or produced other signs that, at home, were evidence of God's presence. These signs convinced him of "a sincere desire of many of them to be instructed on the way of salvation," even though they do not know it. He recorded conversations in which he posed questions designed to elicit evidence of a hidden, suppressed belief in God. He reported hearing from a woman how prayer had helped cure her of a paralysis and of an adulterous relationship. It was no wonder, then, that Schmelen felt that "the Lord is doing wonders among the nations."[24]

George Barker, part of the second wave of missionaries to enter southern Africa, long behind the pioneers van der Kemp and Read, arrived in Bethelsdorp in 1815. His first journal entries reflect his belief that the light of God was waiting to be lit among the natives. In February 1816 he wrote a long account about a shepherd who had never heard a sermon, and had no knowledge of God, but had heard people calling him at night, and received a vision of "some person lying in a manger." When the person arose, "his whole body was covered with wounds and ... nails were driven through his hands and feet ... and [he] commanded me to follow him." In the vision, the shepherd followed the man over rivers and mountains, and came across a large glass house in which people were reading and singing and which he wanted to enter. A few days later, the shepherd came again, and reported another vision in which the man he had followed – who Barker had decided was Christ – led him to a stream, at which he knelt and had water poured over his head amid a weeping multitude.[25]

Likewise, William Shrewsbury found evidence of God's Spirit in the trembling and weeping that his sermons produced. He described an encounter similar to that recorded by George Barker, which suggests that these kinds of stories were not unusual among the missionaries of this generation. They tended to read great things into such experiences. William Shaw, the leading Methodist missionary on the frontier, recorded, for example, how William Shepstone had heard reports of a discussion of Christianity in a kraal 50 miles away, in which the skeptics were silenced by a native who had attended a sermon at Wesleyville. This was taken as proof that the Gospel excited attention among the people and as an example of the discrete ways in which the missionary message could take hold in the land.[26]

What the missionaries did not reckon with was that, even in the remotest parts of the Cape Colony, cultural contact was capable of introducing such ideas without a direct missionary presence. Indigenes had their own circuits that transmitted information and knowledge. But missionaries were not particularly aware of the pathways of contact that tended to tie even areas like Namaqualand into affiliation with the wider world. Indeed, they were always surprised when they came across evidence that their message could spread without them. They read this as evidence that God was everywhere and that the Xhosa were ripe to receive his message. Missionary culture possessed little sense of prior historical contacts or context.

Joseph Williams's inital success, for example, owed much to the presence of Ntsikana. Ntsikana was one of the founders of a specifically African Christianity. He preached a syncretic mix of Christianity and traditional Xhosa belief. Ntsikana had been influenced by van der Kemp when the latter had visited Ngqika in 1801, and he took further lessons in Christianity from Williams. In fact, after Williams died, Ntsikana seems to have inherited his congregation. But Williams was not likely to have contextualized his early success within this history of contact and transmission whereby it was conditioned by the Xhosa themselves. This was certainly not the message that was projected back home in Britain of what was happening to the missionary project. And to judge by their writings, few missionaries seemed to notice the process of syncretization of religious belief that they were part of. They were much too fixated on the originality of their effort and message.[27]

Even as late as 1863 the longstanding missionary Friedrich Kayser recorded how he believed that "the good seed of the Gospel had been sown ... and [we] are patiently waiting in hopes for the outpouring of his Spirit and the fulfillment of his ever true promises." Friedrich Kayser had been on the frontier since 1827. He was one of those missionaries who remained true to the original intent he possessed on his first arrival in the 1820s. Indeed, by the 1860s, his voice of missionary culture was the voice of the past; this was the language of missionary culture as it had emerged from the evangelical revival of the late eighteenth century. It was not the language most missionaries were speaking by the 1860s.[28]

Conclusion

The engagement and the optimism that fueled and drove the missionary project from its inception in southern Africa was not to survive its encounter with Xhosa culture. Our discussion of missionary culture in the early part of the century has so far been presented in a one-dimensional way. But, of course, missionary culture did not exist in a static and one-dimensional world. On the contrary, it was surrounded by a world of the Xhosa and it existed in a context of cultural encounter. It is to that aspect of the missionary experience – the dynamic aspect – that we must now turn.

NOTES

1. For van der Kemp's report see CWM, LMS, South Africa, *Incoming Correspondence*, 1797–1801, Box 1, folder 4. See also LMS, *Transactions*, vol. I, 1804, pp. 430–505, for a chapter by van der Kemp on "Religion, Customs, Population, Government, History and Natural Productions of Caffraria."
2. Others might read the document as an example of the "imperial eye." See Mary Louise Pratt, *Imperial Eyes: Travel Writing and Transculturation* (London, 1992). I shall return to this question in Chapter 6. Early missionaries like van der Kemp and James Read established intimate personal relationships also, although mainly, it would seem, with the Khoesan. Both van der Kemp and his protégé, the young James Read, scandalized Cape and missionary society by their cross-race marital and extramarital liaisons. For sexual boundary-crossing see Elizabeth Elbourne, *Blood Ground: Colonialism, Missions, and the contest for Christianity in the Cape Colony and Britain, 1799–1853* (Kingston, Ont., 2002), pp. 217–19, 227–31; Karel Schoeman, "The Wife of Dr. van der Kemp: The Life of Sara Janse (1792–1861)," *Quarterly Bulletin of the South African Library*, 49.4 (1995), pp. 189–98.
3. This characteristic of the evidence is found in other archives, too, which reinforces the distinctiveness of the encounter of the period *c.* 1820–*c.* 1850. The same is true of the Wesleyan Methodist Missionary Archive, although the quality of this archive diminishes much earlier than that of the London Missionary Society due to the decision of the Wesleyans to concentrate their pastoral work among the English settlers in the eastern Cape. It is true, also, of primary collections of individual missionaries, such as J. F. Cumming's *Diary*, referred to earlier, or the *Journals* of the Reverend James Laing, which in this case may be illustrated quantitatively by the two volumes of diaries that cover the first fifteen years, 1830–44, and the two that cover the last twenty-seven years, 1845–71, of Laing's work in the Cape. The Laing *Journals* are in the Cory Library, Rhodes University. The Wesleyan Mission Society's journal, *The South African Christian Watchman and Wesleyan Church and School Record* for 1855–8, was similarly blind to the cattle-killing, although other periodicals did talk about it. It may be that an initial phase of engagement is common in this period of empire. The process that I am describing has broad similarities to the early years of British and native Australian relations as recounted by Inga Clendinnen, *Dancing with Strangers* (Cambridge, 2005). There was the same pattern of openness, of observation, of *attempts* to understand, and of an ultimate breakdown of these, not from any prior determination on either side, but because of the intransigence of a system of *mis*communication. But in Australia that phase of positive engagement lasted only about three years.
4. Shrewsbury is not unknown to historians. His story has been told in various forms before. See Alan Lester and David Lambert, "Missionary Politics and the Captive Audience: William Shrewsbury in the Caribbean and the Cape Colony," in David Lambert and Alan Lester (eds.), *Colonial Lives Across the*

British Empire: Imperial Careering in the Long Nineteenth Century (Cambridge, 2006), pp. 88–112. He also gets some attention in Andrew Porter, Religion versus Empire? British Protestant Missionaries and Overseas Expansion 1700–1914 (Manchester, 2004), esp. 136–9. Shrewsbury's journal and letters are also gathered in a very good edition by Hildegarde Fast, The Journal and Selected Letters of Rev. William J. Shrewsbury 1826–1835 (Johannesburg, 1994). Fast's edition is unusual among such editions of missionary letters because it treats them as most valuably read as a record of the cultural encounter between Shrewsbury and the Xhosa. Subsequent references are to this edition.

5. Shrewsbury, Journal and Selected Letters, p. 5; John V. B. Shrewsbury, Memorials of the Rev. William J. Shrewsbury (4th. edn., London, 1869) for his background.
6. See Rev. William J. Shrewsbury, Sermons Preached on Several Occasions in the Island of Barbados (London, 1825), p. 225.
7. Shrewsbury, Journal and Selected Letters, pp. 138, 149–50, 152–8, 73–4, 70. He was particularly distressed by the licentiousness and nudity of the people.
8. Ibid., pp. 73–4, 78–81 for the polygamy issue. For Nxele see J. B. Peires, The House of Phalo: A History of the Xhosa People in the Days of Their Independence (Johannesburg, 1981), pp. 66–71; Janet Hodgson, "A Battle for Sacred Power: Christian Beginnings among the Xhosa," in Richard Elphick and Rodney Davenport (eds.), Christianity in South Africa: A Political, Cultural and Social History (Berkeley, 1997), pp. 71–2; Elbourne, Blood Ground; Hildegarde Fast, "'In at one ear and out at the other': African Response to the Wesleyan Message in Xhosaland 1825–1835," Journal of Religion in Africa 23.2 (1993), pp. 147–74.
9. WMMS, South Africa, Incoming Correspondence, fiche 52, Shrewsbury to James Townley, 31 December 1826; Shrewsbury, Journal and Selected Letters, p. 48.
10. Rev. William Govan, Memorials of the Missionary Career of Reverend James Laing (Glasgow, 1875), which is based largely on Laing's Journals. Shrewsbury lost his wife and young child, and Laing's wife died in 1837.
11. Rev. James Laing, Journals 1830–1871, vol. I, 22, 24 and 19 December 1831.
12. Ibid., 22, 23, 24, 26 December 1831, 17 February 1832.
13. Ibid., 4 and 24 April, 24 and 19 May, and 18 June 1832; 13, 15 and 18 February, 30 October and 1 November 1833. GMS, Minutes of the Presbytery of Kaffraria, 5 July 1832; 3 January 1833; 13 and 15 February and 23 June 1833. Govan, Memorials of ... Laing, p. 59. Charles Henry himself also turned out to be something of a problem. He was suspected of disloyalty in the 1835 war, was found with stolen cattle afterwards, engaged in various Xhosa cultural practices, and was suspended from the congregation several times. Charles Henry is an example of that interesting phenomenon of the boundary-crosser. Others at this time and place include Robert Balfour and Jan Tzatzoe. Laing's Journals possess the same feature we noted as characteristic of these kinds of missionary sources. By the end of the 1830s, the quality of information reported in detail in his journals drops off. Occasionally there are entries which suggest that the old cultural practices continued. But there is a sense of a far lower level of contest and confrontation with Xhosa culture. Laing had not given up on his calling; he remained an active and successful missionary for another thirty years. His mode of engagement with the Xhosa changed from an intense and intimate encounter to something more remote and routine.

14. Shrewsbury, *Journals and Selected Letters*, pp. 138, 149–50, 71; GMS, *Minutes of the Presbytery of Kaffraria*, 1 April 1840.

15. John Ayliff, for example, wrote a long paper to the Directors of the WMMS in 1834 on the "superstitions" of the Xhosa, identifying ancestor worship and belief in witchcraft as the two key delusions, with the latter being the most powerful and important. WMMS, South Africa, *Incoming Correspondence*, fiche 91, 1 July 1834; GMS, *Minutes of the Presbytery of Kaffraria*, 5 April 1832; William Shaw, *The Journal of William Shaw*, ed. W. D. Hammond-Tooke (Cape Town, 1972), pp. 106–9. Subsequent references are to this edition. For another example of a Methodist missionary encounter with witchcraft of this type, see WMMS, South Africa, *Incoming Correspondence*, fiche 51, Kay Journal, 1 April 1826.

16. WMMS, South Africa, *Incoming Correspondence*, fiche 52, Kay Journal, 20 June 1826.

17. Cumming, *Diary*, 11 July 1840. "if Blacks are not the lineal descendants of Adam the same as Whites, then they have no rights to any of the blessing that were agreed upon in the Covenant … But the Gospel has been preached to Blacks as well as Whites and many of them have received it as cordially and have given as strong evidence that their heart have been influenced by its dictates as ever was manifested by the Whites. If they were not included in the original covenant, is it reasonable to suppose that the Holy Ghost would have been bestowed upon them equally with others who were included? … What does all this amount to, but that as they have received the blessing God agreed to bestow upon only the descendants of Adam, therefore they must be his descendants." Samuel Young, another Methodist missionary, who returned home on the death of his wife, delivered a lecture in Canterbury sometime in the 1840s that asserted the common origins of all mankind and that racial hierarchy reflected cultural diversions from this original beginning. Even as late as 1850, Methodist missionaries (and the Methodists were the most overtly imperial of all the missionaries) may be found repeating the belief that the Xhosa were inherently "capable of the highest achievements of man" if only they could be "freed from the chains of superstition." See Elbourne, *Blood Ground* pp. 102–8, 152 for a good statement of the assumptions of missionaries before they left Britain. Rev. Thornley Smith, *South Africa Delineated* (London, 1850), pp. 80–2. WMMS, *Special Series*, Box 9, *Journal of Samuel Young*, f. 363.

18. The pamphlet was published as Reverend. R. Niven, *An Impartial Analysis of the Kaffir Character in a letter from Rev. Robert Niven to Mr. Stretch* (Graham's Town, 1840).

19. For similar optimism in the late nineteenth-century Church Missionary Society work in east Africa, but without the accompanying belief in the universal humanity of the indigenes, see T. O. Beidelman, *Colonial Evangelism*: A Socio-Historical study of an East African Mission at the Grassroots (Bloomington, IN, 1982), pp. 110–4, 128–33. For a description of contemporary evangelical missionary culture see Daniel Bergner, "The Post-Colonial Missionary: What in God's Name American Evangelicals are Doing in Africa," *The New York Times Magazine*, 29 January 2006.

20. Basil Holt, *Joseph Williams* (Lovedale, 1954), pp. 43–6. There is a very good description of Williams's mission and Tzatzoe's key role in it in

Roger Levine, "Diplomat and Intellectual," in *Sable Son of Africa* (unpublished MS).

21. Holt, *Joseph Williams*, pp. 32, 39, 43–6, 79–87.

22. For the promise suggested by individual conversions, see Philip, *Researches in South Africa*, pp. 215–21. For a similar argument at the same time, about the speed with which the Griqua were converted, see Andrew Steedman, *Wanderings and Adventures in the Interior of Southern Africa*, 2 vols. (London, 1835). WMMS, South Africa, *Incoming Correspondence*, fiche 105, Davis to Directors, 19 June 1837.

23. LMS, *Reports*, pp. 52–4. CA, LG 402, *Letters Received from the Diplomatic Agent of Caffraria, 1844*, Stretch to Hare, 14 January 1844. United Presbyterian Church, *Missionary Record*, 1 March 1862, pp. 38–9. WMMS, *Report for 1847*, p. 71, and pp. 51–2 for an example of the optimism that a chief – in this case, Sarhili – was showing signs of opening himself to missionary influence. As an example of optimism being developmental rather than generational at this time, we can note the case of Bishop Colenso, who, after ten weeks of visiting his new diocese in Natal in 1854, spoke grandly of his plans for grammar and boarding schools for boys and girls, orphans' homes, infant schools and perhaps a "theological Institution ... wherein young men both white and coloured might be trained with a view to Holy Orders." Needless to say, little, if any, of this came to pass and Colenso had to measure his influence also in small quantities. See John Colenso, *Ten Weeks in Natal* (London, 1855), p. 206.

24. CWM, LMS, *South Africa Journals 1810–16*, Box 2, f. 50, Journal of J. H. Schmelen, 1815. Such calculations commonly appear in the missionary record at this period. See the examples cited by William Corner at Griqua Town and of Albrecht and Siedenfaden, two other missionaries in Namaqualand. Ibid., ff. 50; 5, 20, 21 and 16 March; 8, 11, 14, 15, 22 and 23 May 1815.

25. George Barker, *Journal of George Barker 1815–1828*, 3, 4 and 10 February 1816, MS 14258, CL.

26. Shrewsbury, *Journal and Selected Letters*, pp. 70–3. Shrewsbury recorded a dream told to him by a Xhosa in which God appeared and urged him to preach the word of God. He awoke weeping and "began to call on the name of the Lord," obsessed with his recollection of sin, but no longer afraid to die, and with the urge to preach for the salvation of Hintsa and an end to polygamy and witchcraft. Shrewsbury was ecstatic. How could he not have been? His faith and belief in the process of missionary work had received seemingly objective validation. "With this extraordinary account from a man who now for the first time saw a missionary and before I had spoken a sentence on divine things exceedingly astonished me." Hammond-Tooke, *Journal of William Shaw*, pp. 146–7. It is important to note, however (as Elizabeth Elbourne has pointed out to me in private correspondence) that dreams were frequently associated with conversion experiences for Africans. Such tales may therefore have been meaningful gestures.

27. Holt, *Joseph Williams*, pp. 105, 112. On Ntsikana see Hodgson, "A Battle for Sacred Power."

28. CWM, LMS, South Africa, *Incoming Correspondence*, Box 33, folder 2, 24 December 1863, Report from Knapps Hope.

4   Cultural encounters: the destabilization of missionary culture

Failure in empire

The imperialist project is always heavily contoured by optimism and hope. Empire carries with it a prescription for change that must be conveyed with self-confidence and certainty. The audacious claim of empire is that it *knows* in advance what kind of modifications its subjects need to make for them to gain access to the secrets of civilization. Yet the projects of empire are continually blocked, compromised and altered as they encounter the realities of the frontiers of empire. The history of empire is seldom written as the history of upset and disappointment. But empire is invariably a place of disenchantment. This does not mean that empire is without its successes. But it does mean that even at times when empire seems to be the natural order of history, failure and fragility lie embedded at the heart of those very successes.[1]

Missionary culture was destabilized by Xhosa culture and politics. Missionaries were the victims of culture shock. Measured by the standards of what evangelical culture *expected* from its missionary outreach, the effort in southern Africa was an astounding failure. The challenge that missionary culture faced over the period *c.* 1820 to *c.* 1850 was how to respond to the evidence that its optimistic expectations about its ability to reach into Xhosa hearts and change Xhosa culture were thwarted at every turn. What was it to do when it discovered that native culture did not respond as expected and predicted? How was it to explain and understand this failure? The narrative of the missionary experience in the early nineteenth century revolved around these questions. The end result was that missionary culture was drained of the optimism which it had inherited from the evangelical revival, and the consequences of this were to deplete missionary politics of its ability to defend the "humanitarian" perspective against shifting tides of cultural power in southern Africa and in the metropole. How this happened may be tracked through a series of personal vignettes which reveal the inner, psychological dynamics of the cultural encounter between missionaries and Xhosa.[2]

Such vignettes show how the encounter with the Xhosa upended the core beliefs and assumptions of missionary culture. They show how painfully the missionaries struggled with the implications of the encounter; how they sought to reconcile the precepts of their culture with their experience of interaction with the Xhosa. Ultimately, they were unable to achieve this reconciliation, with the result, as I shall describe in Chapter 6, that the missionary mind moved from a mode of open engagement with Xhosa culture to a mode that was closed and hostile to Xhosa culture. But this was not a straightforward process, nor was it a response that was predetermined.

Although the engagement between the missionaries and the Xhosa ended with the "closing of the missionary mind," it is not particularly useful to see this as implicit from the very beginning of the encounter. Indeed, to do so denies the possibility of understanding the process by which the missionaries moved from the phase of engagement that marked these early years of the encounter, to the withdrawal into the closed culture that had emerged by the 1850s. In a similar vein, it is quite clearly wrong to see missionaries as determining the conditions of the cultural encounter by establishing a hegemony over the *discourse* of the cultural exchange and encounter. This was most certainly not the case in the eastern Cape. Indeed, it was the *absence* of missionary control that was the problem. Time and again, it was the Xhosa who controlled the terms of the encounter, and the missionaries who were caught left-footed, desperately dancing to respond. It is too simple to regard the Xhosa as suffering from a colonization of their minds by missionary (or imperial) culture. In this respect, the Xhosa were *hybridized*. But this hybridization was a process regulated largely by the Xhosa themselves. Indeed, they demonstrated considerable ingenuity and open minds in picking through the cultural baggage of the missionaries and taking what best fitted their own indigenous beliefs, to produce, for example, a syncretic religion out of Christian offerings and Xhosa traditions.[3]

In this chapter and the next, I am concerned to explore the question: what happened when the missionaries encountered the cultural practices and the political-social world of the Xhosa? Here I shall concentrate upon the dynamics of the cultural encounter; in the next chapter I shall turn to the history of the missionaries' relationship with the chiefs. These were two sides of one coin. Missionaries came to see a strong link between the cultural practices they so deplored and the system of chiefly power. And the chiefs occupied a special place in the perceptions of the missionaries.

In what follows, I shall emphasize the interactive relationship between the Xhosa and missionary culture. I will discuss the various signals that from the beginning made it unlikely that missionary expectations would be fulfilled. I will address the increasing recognition by missionaries that Xhosa cultural practices were not being moderated or abandoned by their admonitions, and were, perhaps, impermeable to their influence. I will consider examples of the more active response of the Xhosa to missionary culture, in the form of their challenges and engagement with its assumptions. And finally I will consider the various strategies of missionary response to these features of the encounter with the Xhosa. Those strategies included attempts to establish communication with Xhosa culture through hybridized forms and missionary magic. But the dominant response of the missionaries was their own personal struggle to retain a psychic balance of optimism over pessimism, a balance that would allow them to retain intact the ideologies they had inherited from the evangelical interpretation of racial hierarchy.

Converts and culture

Conversion was the ultimate hope of the missionaries; it was the single most important part of their work. There was a widespread belief in evangelical circles that the millennium would be ushered in by the conversion of the heathen. Yet from the very beginning it was clear that fulfilling that expectation was going to be problematic. Although subsequent missionary ideology and history have tended to downplay the significance of this failure, this generation of missionaries experienced serious anguish and soul-searching over the meager fruits their strenuous efforts harvested. And when this was piled on top of the other failures of their anticipated game plan, it was no small factor in the subsequent devolution of missionary culture away from the beliefs of the evangelical revival.[4]

The early reports of the London Missionary Society missionaries brimmed with optimism about the prospects for conversion. Even though the actual numbers reported as converted were always small, the expectations were that success could not be long delayed. But, of course, the real story behind the pattern of conversion in this period was very different, and this was implicitly recognized almost from the beginning. Missionary reports quickly shift gear towards emphasizing the small signs we have noted and individual cases. Missionaries were willing to count as converts anyone who told a story, however obscure, that could conceivably be made to fit a Christian religious experience. But what is equally surprising is how *little* there is on the conversion experience in some important missionary accounts. Robert Moffatt's *Missionary Labours and Scenes in Southern Africa* – one of the standard accounts of the missionary enterprise at this time – is an example. But then his numbers of converts, like everyone else's, were very small. The church that was eventually built at Kuruman could never be filled. The same was true of James Laing's church at Burnside, which in the 1830s could hold 200 people. Normally, not more than forty to fifty people were scattered in its ample spaces, and Laing baptized only six people in as many years. It filled only when he prayed successfully for rain during a drought. And Friederich Kayser, after nearly thirty years on the frontier, could count only forty-six in his congregation in 1856.[5]

In addition, when conversion did take place, it was typically partial, uncertain and fluctuating. Not only did the mass exodus from heathenism into Christianity fail to materialize, but converts moved casually in and out of the Christian sphere. Missionaries did not quite know what to make of this. Ultimately, they came to see it as reflecting the spiritual void of Xhosa culture and personality. They failed to realize that it reflected political and social pressures rather than the weakness of Xhosa spirituality.[6]

Attendance at mission services could suddenly fall away for any number of reasons. The appearance of a new Xhosa prophet was followed by an immediate hemorrhage from the church. And, infuriatingly, the prophet would often be heard spouting some bastardized version of the Gospel! An especial danger for the missionaries was to lose the favor of the chiefs. This often happened very suddenly for no ostensible reason. Once it had happened, those Xhosa who had been attending services dropped right away. As early as the 1820s, it was noted how converts would flee the mission stations at the first sign of a chief's hostility. When Nqgika visited the Thyumie mission in 1825, the native Christians "stopped work, put on their kaross and walked about as if they were mere onlookers." When Suthu ceased to attend Kayser's services, everyone else from her kraal followed suit. Those few who resisted were forced by family or peer pressure to reject Christianity symbolically by smearing themselves with the red clay in an outward acceptance of Xhosa tradition. By this time in his career, Kayser was experienced enough in the ways of the mission work to be used to such variations. Indeed, he was considered wise enough for Henry Calderwood, a recent arrival, to call him in as a consultant. Calderwood had just lost one group of potential converts, but had acquired another lot and wanted to get Kayser to give him a reality check on their sincerity, confessing that "it is generally difficult fully to understand the state of the native mind."[7]

Those who *were* converted and accepted often proved prone to serious backsliding. Particularly disappointing in this respect was the split loyalty of the native teachers. Native teachers played key roles as intermediaries between the mission and the local society. Indeed, by the 1840s much of the itinerancy fell on their shoulders. One such native preacher, Thomas Fortune, for example, was reported to have been away preaching for fifty days at a stretch in 1842. The two leading intermediaries for the Glasgow Missionary Society, Robert Balfour (his Xhosa name was Noyi) and Charles Henry, had been baptized at Lovedale in 1826. Both had been followers of Ntsikana, who, it will be recalled, had assisted Joseph Williams in his mission and was a preacher in his own right who integrated Christian principles with Xhosa traditional beliefs.[8]

Such intermediaries tended to keep a foot in both cultural camps. If they followed Ntsikana's teachings they would have been practicing a hybridized religion anyway. This remains hidden in the missionary records. But missionaries could not ignore the continued attachment to Xhosa cultural practices, which neither Balfour nor Henry abandoned. Charles Henry was suspended from the Burnshill congregation in 1839 for employing a Xhosa healing rite for an eye infection. Balfour, too, was expelled for some time from the Lovedale community for an unspecified "gross act of injustice and extortion perpetrated by aid of a chief, under colour of law, such that even the heathen Kafirs pointed to it as glaringly inconsistent with the Christian profession." But they were too valuable to the missionaries to cut off entirely, and both continued to proselytize during periods when they were under a cloud.[9]

Politically, too, Balfour and Charles Henry proved unreliable. In the mid-1840s both Balfour and Henry were involved with the missionary leadership at Burnside in an open dispute that had clear racial overtones. Balfour and Henry led a religious strike in which they failed to turn up for church and kept the presbytery waiting five hours when summoned to a meeting. At one point Balfour said that although the teachers might have a lot to say to them, "they [the Xhosa] too had much to say to the Teachers." Robert Balfour was one of the first to steal away from Burnside on Christmas Eve in 1834 and join the Xhosa in the sixth frontier war. Charles Henry had somehow come into possession of stolen colonial cattle during the conflict, and the suspicion was that he was either involved in the theft or the knowing recipient of stolen goods.[10]

Indeed, these cross-over figures turned out to be serious disappointments to their missionary sponsors. The best-known boundary-crosser of the period was Jan Tzatzoe. Tzatzoe was one of the first Xhosa converts and came from a family of Xhosa intermediaries. His father had taken up residence at the mission settlement of Bethelsdorp in 1804, and Jan had been baptized there. But as early as 1814 there were complaints about his propensity to idleness. Nevertheless, in May 1818 he preached with George Barker at Theopolis, another missionary settlement, and in 1824 he joined Brownlee at King William's Town, where again he was reported as allowing his children to "follow the customs of the heathen." He worked with other missionaries, including William Shaw and Friedrich Kayser, throughout the 1820s, introducing them to Xhosa society. In 1829, however, the suspicion of backsliding was attached to him when his son was accused of using a Xhosa witchdoctor to treat his consumption. Indeed, it was reported that his father had engaged in witchcraft ritual to find the cause of Jan's illness in 1829, and "smelt out" a witch who was then burned at the stake. In spite of this somewhat checkered past, Read and Philip selected him (over Maqoma) in 1834 to travel to Britain as part of their campaign before the Select Committee on Aborigines, where he made a convincing appearance as the stereotyped "converted" Xhosa chieftain, a promise of future Xhosa modernity.[11]

In fact, Tzatzoe was a very minor chief and his chiefly status was always under question within the tribe. A few years after his visit to England, the missionaries had begun to turn sour on Tzatzoe. It was noted that he was attending entirely to affairs of the tribe, and had given up preaching. He was accused of taking part in the attack on Fort Peddie during the war of 1847, and although that was never proved, it is certain that most of his tribe joined in the assault on British positions. In December of that year the London Missionary Society decided that he had moved beyond their pale and he was suspended from his salaried position as a preacher for the Society. By this time, too, it was reported that he was addicted to alcohol. In the war of 1850–3, his loyalties were firmly identified with the Xhosa. His people were the main spy network that kept tabs on British troop movements for Maqoma. And it was believed that he had sold ammunition to Maqoma. Tzatzoe only just escaped the prosecutorial net of the imperial administration after the war, and he was lucky not to have ended up on Robben Island. In the event, Governor Cathcart granted him some land as part of the settlement at the end of the war.[12]

The obstacles that the missionary conversion project faced were merely one part of a wider foundering on the rocks of Xhosa traditional cultural practices. From the very beginning, missionaries were confronted with the strength of Xhosa traditional culture. In principle, missionaries wanted to insist that any Xhosa who entered into Christian communion abandon all their traditional cultural practices. In reality, if missionaries wanted Christianity to have *any* place in Xhosa society, they not only had to live with these practices; they also had to compromise actively with their presence.

The case of circumcision rituals provides a good illustration of this. Circumcision customs played a significant role in the missionary encounter with Xhosa culture. It was a practice that fed into the way missionary culture absorbed and processed the implications of its relationship to the Xhosa. Circumcision ceremonies were one of a cluster of traditional practices, like polygamy and witchcraft, which missionaries quickly identified as serious obstacles to conversion and civilizing influences. Missionaries seldom mentioned circumcision without discomfort and disgust. Circumcision was associated with the coming of male sexuality and with the licentiousness that they believed described Xhosa sexual relations generally. Circumcision rites announced that Xhosa boys had now become men. Male bonding was an important part of the rites; the initiates went away from the kraal for some period of time, and missionaries identified this as the moment when the gendered division of labor in Xhosa society was formalized. They could therefore represent circumcision both as marking the beginning of sexual awareness and as a way of perpetuating the heavily gendered division of labor, whereby women were perceived as doing the heavy work while men controlled the cattle wealth. More generally, of course, the rituals spoke of the inaccessibility of Xhosa cultural practices to the missionaries and the obstacle that was presented to the spread of the "civilizing" culture of the missionaries. A rite such as circumcision was not only a sign of barbarism; it was also a sign of Xhosa control over the definition of masculinity and the denial of a Christian definition of masculinity. Circumcision, it was proclaimed in 1858, "was not so much sinful as useless and pernicious because of the cult of manhood it inspires. It is a badge of manhood and impossible to displace."[13]

Missionaries could not escape contact with these rituals; they intruded into the lives of the mission even when they were not avidly sought out by missionaries to combat. Church attendance dropped away during every circumcision season. John Ayliff initially tried to insist that all who embraced Christianity abandon the circumcision ritual. But early on, he discovered three of his mission boys creeping away in secret to prepare for the circumcision ceremony. When he protested to them, they cheerfully assured him that they would continue to pray while they were ensconced in the bush during the phase of the ceremony when they spent time isolated from the tribe in the company of their fellow initiates. And they asked him to continue to send them their lessons. Ayliff was not much amused by this admirably open attitude to his teaching. But there was little he could do, for the boys' families were prepared to leave the mission in order for their sons to go through this ritual.[14]

Ayliff's experience was the norm. A crisis in the congregation at Emgwali in 1862 was caused in part by the participation of "some of our most hopeful youths, sons of members of the Church," in the "heathen rite of circumcision." They "went about in their blankets and painted their bodies with white clay which showed that they wished to approach as nearly as possible to the observance of all the ceremonies." As this suggests, it took very unusual circumstances for the parents of Xhosa boys to refuse to allow the participation of their children in this important traditional cultural practice. And those that did often compromised the issue by allowing some sons to participate while holding others back. Missionaries were left no choice by to tolerate the custom.[15]

Intense pressure was brought to bear on the young Sandile, heir to Ngqika's chiefship, in 1840, when it was time for his circumcision rites. Local missionaries mounted a major campaign against the dances and feasting that were part of the ceremonies, believing that it was at those moments that sexual innocence was lost. They were successful to the extent that the Xhosa agreed not to hold dances on the Sabbath! But they failed in their attempt to prevent local mission girls being recruited for the dances and other "debasing purposes." When they approached Sandile's mother, Suthu, about the matter, she "appeared irritated at being spoken to on such a subject, said that the people in the station were her people, that she would persist in calling them out to aid in that work, and abruptly withdrew without allowing the matter to be fully stated." But it seems that she did put a stop to females being called away from the mission to participate in the event.[16]

When the Xhosa seemed to want to avoid confronting the missionaries directly, they resorted to all sorts of subterfuges to secure freedom from the prying eyes and moralizing rants of the ministers of God. In the mid-1840s it was noted at Lovedale that the local people were engaged in much festivity and dancing "for the purposes they explained of washing away the smallpox." But it had been two years since a smallpox epidemic had swept through the region. The missionaries were understandably suspicious that this was not the real reason. They were right; it was a Xhosa way for the local people to control access to a round of ceremonies that they knew would meet the opposition of the missionaries. Indeed, this was a most interesting and disturbing event for the missionaries, who found that giving thanks for the end of the smallpox – ostensibly a bow towards Christian Providence – was being turned into a way of reinforcing traditional customs. Here was hybridization with a vengeance. It was an excuse for large gatherings to revive practices that missionaries thought they had eliminated – such as festivity and dancing and slaughtering of cows on the occasion of a betrothal.[17]

What were missionaries to do when confronted with the evidence of the persistence of such practices? In the final analysis, not much. Just as Ayliff decided in 1833 that he could either keep the circumcised mission boys or lose them, so William Shaw also came to the same conclusion that they were so committed to the rite that it was impossible for him to resist. But it continued to be an issue of some anguish throughout this period. In the 1840s the missionaries at Burnside debated what to do about their boys' participating in circumcision rituals. They decided that they could only exert moral pressure. Threatening excommunication would do no good. So they turned to the native teachers to impress upon the youths the "duty of Christians to set themselves in opposition to it [i.e. circumcision]."[18]

Although some early missionaries were quickly led to despair by the strength of these cultural practices, the general tendency in the early years was optimistically to assume the future demise of these customs. There were frequent announcements that practices like circumcision were fast diminishing, that the commitment of the Xhosa to their heathenish customs was eroding. Such optimism was but a momentary fantasy. There was a considerable distance between the real record of missionaries' encounter with such practices and the one they presented for public consumption, where they tended to remain silent about the degree of backsliding and the impossibility of weaning even mission youths away from participating in circumcision rituals.[19]

After the 1850s a new mood of resignation and acceptance may be glimpsed among the missionaries. William Govan, one of the most enlightened missionaries in Xhosaland, explained the persistence of traditional cultural practices as reflecting the deep resistance of the Xhosa to the missionary message: "they have been determined to preserve their own customs and culture," he wrote in the 1870s, "even when they have not been hostile or antagonistic to missionaries … they have for the most part pretended to be willing to receive their instruction. But … it is true that from the first public opinion has been decidedly opposed to it." And another churchman in the 1880s explained that after "eight years in Kaffraria" he concluded that it was futile to try to stop it, and the best solution was to ensure that it was carried out under Christian supervision, since it could then be drained of its association with "impure customs." In effect, by the turn of the century a virtual toleration of circumcision (along with other traditional practices) had been forced upon the missionaries.[20]

Xhosa engagement, missionary response

The Xhosa–missionary relationship was interactive. It is not particularly helpful to see the missionary–Xhosa relationship purely in terms of missionary offensive and Xhosa resistance. Those qualities were frequently present. On at least one occasion, for example, missionaries were told in no uncertain terms that they should live and let live on the question of cultural practices. But it is more useful to see the relationship of this encounter as fluid and open. Missionaries were not only "imperial eyes." They were also participant observers. In these early years the Xhosa were everywhere in the missionary gaze. What stands out is the way the Xhosa entered into a dialogic interaction with missionary culture. To their credit, missionaries were open enough and optimistic enough about their mission that they were able to record much of this dialogic interaction. They were unwitting witnesses to the challenge they were to face from the Xhosa response to their culture. This is not to say that they correctly read Xhosa culture; they did not. They gained very little understanding of Xhosa cosmologies of the world. Miscommunication was endemic in such encounters. But for our purposes, the important point is how they responded to the Xhosa reaction to *their* culture. And it is such a perspective that I want to follow through here as we try to get a sense of how the dynamic of the encounter between the Xhosa and the missionaries actually worked.[21]

Just as the missionaries were eager to engage with the Xhosa, so the Xhosa were willing to engage with them. Missionaries were surprised by the extent, the nature and the quality of Xhosa engagement and reaction to their presence. But this is a common feature of colonial peoples, who, by necessity, must know much more about their rulers than their rulers need to know about them. For the Xhosa, as for others, it was a complicated matter, since far more was at stake (their very way of life) for them than for the missionaries. The general character of the interaction from the Xhosa side was remarkable openness to cross-cultural exchange and hybridization. From the very first moment when the missionaries crossed the frontier into Xhosaland, the Xhosa reached out to register Christianity and absorb it into their existing worldview.

Thus, the two prophets Ntsikana and Nxele, whom we have met before, emerged straightaway in the second decade of the nineteenth century. Although these prophets represented different strains and traditions, they each absorbed Christian ideas and fused them with indigenous Xhosa religious ideas. Both preached like missionaries, used biblical themes and claimed to have had visions of Christ. Nxele had grown up on a Boer farm in the Zuurveld, and Ntsikana was the son of a counselor to Ngqika and, as we have noted, picked up his Christian ideas from Johannes van der Kemp. But both were also rooted firmly in Xhosa culture and identity. Nxele also had a reputation as a diviner, and Ntsikana was a renowned singer and storyteller in the Xhosa tradition. It is not surprising that Ntsikana established the Xhosa hymnal tradition. His Great Hymn, written in 1814, was sung at virtually all Xhosa Christian meetings. It was adopted by some missionaries, such as J. A. Chalmers at the Tyhume mission station. Indeed, it was sometimes sung at ceremonial occasions when imperial officials wished to emphasize cross-cultural communication and reciprocity. But it was a hymn drawn from a Xhosa wedding song. Its words resembled the form of a praise poem and it was sung in traditional Xhosa cadences. Missionaries later westernized it; its original form remained buried, out of sight, in Xhosa culture, and was only rediscovered by musicologists in the 1960s.[22]

The religious differences between Ntsikana and Nxele were relatively insignificant. The differences between them lay more in their different political paths. From the turmoil that enveloped the Xhosa from the 1820s, Ntsikana established a tradition of pacific response. Ntsikana represented the voice of conciliation between the Xhosa and the British. His following was quite small. After his death in 1821 he left behind some influential followers. Most notable of these was "Old Soga," a counselor to Sandile and the founder of a dynasty of ministers and professionals that was to remain a prominent Xhosa family of intellectuals into the early twentieth century. Nxele's vision, by contrast, presaged nationalist rebellion. He saw the colonial contact as a war between competing gods. In his theology, "Thixo," the God of the blacks, was destined to punish the whites for their murder of Christ, the son of their God. Nxele stood for a nineteenth-century version of liberation theology; he was the leading ideologue behind the Xhosa in the war of 1819. It is not surprising that he ended his days on Robben Island. Nxele was not alone in integrating the language and worldviews of the Christian missionaries into a Xhosa political discourse. At times of political tension it became a common practice among the Xhosa prophets to speak against witchcraft, for example, while also standing against British domination.

The Xhosa were insistently curious about some of the finer points of missionary cultural practice. And they were not reluctant to interrogate these points, or to exchange ideas. When the wife of Methodist missionary Samuel Young died in the summer of 1830, for example, local Xhosa used the opportunity to query him about Christian ideas of marriage and death. They used her death to point out to him the advantages of polygamy! More intently, they wanted to question him about the circumstances of her death. Young's wife had died an intensely "evangelical" death. Young described her as eagerly leaving him and embracing death because she was going to Christ. The Xhosa heard of this and were, understandably, curious about it. They wanted to know how she could tell where she was going before her death; how was she able to talk of the place before she had actually been there? They conceded that they could see some advantages in knowing of this place before death, because although they knew they must die, they were scattered all over the country and it would be a great advantage for them to know that there was a place where they might all be reunited. Young was buoyed by this conversation, since it was another small sign that suggested that they were learning his message. What he did not realize was that it was an example of Xhosa hybridization, an interrogation of his worldview as part of their process of selection and filtering in the construction of their own version of Christianity.[23]

Xhosa curiosity about missionary belief systems frequently engaged the missionaries in discussions that went to the very heart of the logical weaknesses of Christianity. William Shrewsbury was honest enough to record some of these occasions. He got involved in a long discussion with the Xhosa about the power of God. They wanted to know why God did not use his great power to solve the problem of sin by cutting off its source and destroying Satan. This was a common Xhosa query; John Cumming records being asked the same question in 1844, and he was clearly stumped for an answer, since he records in his diary that only much later did a good answer occur to him. In the course of the Xhosa–Shrewsbury exchange, however, Shrewsbury was also asked if trees or cattle struck by lightning had displeased God and were being punished by him. On another occasion he was interrogated about the idea of an afterlife in a way which challenged the superiority of his cognitive epistemology. The Xhosa pointed out that they *knew* where their dead went. They were left out to be eaten by wolves, so how could they possibly go to heaven? Other Xhosa wanted to know how the words got into the Bible; how did the first man who wrote them know them? Was the soul of a good man in heaven the same soul that he had on earth? Would we know one another in a future world? Similarly, Shrewsbury was asked to describe God. What sort of man was he? Did he have a wife? And when Shrewsbury reproved his interrogator for his frivolousness, he was told that "he [i.e. the Xhosa person] had too much wisdom to ask idle questions, but being ignorant he wished to learn." In this one exchange the superiority of Xhosa intellect is dramatically revealed.[24]

Such interrogations were not likely to destabilize the worldview of tough, intelligent characters like Shrewsbury. One has to wonder, though, how the half-educated auto-didacts from the working class, who composed the majority of these missionaries, coped with such sophistication. Some were clearly not up to the strains imposed by the social and cultural challenges of the encounter. When faced with audiences that were disrespectful, unruly or indifferent, missionary James Cameron wrote how he "became so confused that I could scarcely proceed … the perspiration burst from every pore of my body … sometimes I am so discouraged as to fly from the work of the Lord, and bury myself in oblivion." And one has to assume that at least some of those missionaries who returned home in this period did so because they could not take the intellectual stresses and strains of the encounter.[25]

The missionaries of this generation found themselves in a dilemma that they had not anticipated. Their whole intellectual posture obliged them to enter into a variety of interactions with the Xhosa. They sought engagement; it was a *sine qua non* of their evangelical activism. But this raises the question: what was the impact of the engagement with the Xhosa on missionary minds and missionary culture? How did they respond to the range of responses they received from a people whom one described as "an acute and inquisitive people, and peculiarly evidencing a natural tendency to scepticism." What did the encounter do to the strategies, beliefs and minds of the missionaries?[26]

Missionary attempts at intercultural communication

Let us start with the strategies. Missionaries needed to establish means and methods of dialogue and communication with the Xhosa. Indeed, their response to the Xhosa was more varied than we have so far allowed. There were tendencies to hybridizing even among missionary culture. There were experiments with using Christian magic to connect with the Xhosa, as well as better-known early attempts, by men like Johannes van der Kemp and James Read, to cross racial and ethnic lines through marriage and sexual relations.

Both William Shaw and William Shrewsbury, for example, were willing to make compromises with polygamy. Soon after the arrival of the missionaries, it became obvious that a strict prohibition on converts who were in polygamous relationships would crimp the potential pool of congregants. In the 1820s, when Shaw and Shrewsbury were grappling with this issue, there was considerable ambivalence on the part of commentators on the Xhosa about the effects of polygamy. Some early observers had described it in a non-moralistic way, and had pointed out that it was quite compatible with domestic harmony. One of William Shaw's first dispatches as the Wesleyan Methodist Superintendent of missions was to suggest that the prohibition on the admission of polygamists to the Society be relaxed.

Shaw argued that the Xhosa were not comparable to slaves in the Caribbean, where the rule against polygamy in the Wesleyan Methodist Missionary Society had originated. For the Xhosa, to surrender their polygamous status would put them into a state of illegality among their own people. At the very least, they would be expected to pay fines and return dowry cattle to fathers of the wives they were forced to abandon. Then there was the question of the wives themselves. Who was going to decide which wives got thrown out of the household? What was the morality of the breakup of families that this implied? Shaw was clearly uneasy about the social and familial consequences of the rule against multiple marriages, and in his recommendations to the home committee he was groping toward an early nineteenth-century version of cultural diversity. He recommended that converts not be obliged to abandon polygamous marriages made prior to their acceptance of Christianity, although men would be permitted to marry only one woman in a Christian ceremony.[27]

We cannot be exactly sure what happened next, since most of the correspondence has disappeared. The London authorities seem to have initially responded with some caution, perhaps even granting the local missionaries the right to "exercise ... some degree of discretion to meet the ever varying circumstances of the cases which should come before him." Shaw clearly hoped that the right to interpret the rules flexibly would remain with the missionaries on the frontier, for he urged that "you may I think repose confidence in us in this matter that we shall not go far astray." But it was an issue that was very sensitive and contentious even among the frontier missionaries, who were "not all perfectly agreed in any one clear view of the subject." William Shrewsbury, however, was one who was willing to bend on the issue. He clearly understood that there were cases of polygamists which no rule could meet. And he seems to have admitted to conversion at least one case where it was necessary to change the ceremony in order to walk the line between interfering with established customs and maintaining the general principle against admission of polygamy into the Society. Exactly how he did that is not clear. In any case, this avenue of compromise was soon closed off. At some point, the home committee exerted its control and forbad any tampering with the rule barring any polygamist from membership in the Society.[28]

By 1834 there is the edifying spectacle of John Ayliff insisting that potential converts must put aside all wives but one. It is worth contemplating his account of this incident for a moment. It illustrates the inversions of logic and culture that imperial culture involved. When he was asked what the rejected wives should be told, he replied with the logic of the rationalist that "they must call them together and tell them that they could lie no longer in such a state and request them to return to the place of their father and if they thought well to marry" someone else. The next day he went to speak to one of the convert's wives, "telling her that she must not be angry, because her husband wished to keep God's word. It was not because he was displeased with her, that he wished to put her away, but because he wished to save his soul." When it all worked out as he wanted – the women left, sorrowful, but accepting God's word that it must be so, according to the missionary – Ayliff sighed a huge sigh of relief, urged the people to remember what they had seen, prayed with them, sang a hymn and returned home smug, "thanking God and taking courage for this proof of his blessing on his Word." So, how do we deconstruct this little piece of gross hypocrisy? In the course of a few short moments, Ayliff had condoned bigamy, and broken up families with children, and sent several wives packing back to their father's kraals to face highly uncertain prospects. Such women were not likely to find other husbands, but this counted for little, for Ayliff's view of the Xhosa was that they were inherently licentious anyway. He had destroyed a domestic setting in order to create his own version of domesticity.[29]

But if polygamy was too incendiary an issue around which to build a hybridized avenue of religio-cultural communication, there were more promising affinities between missionary magic and Xhosa magic. Missionaries were understandably coy and reticent about parading their own magical forms. But they could not escape the analogies between Xhosa appeals to divine intervention and their own, especially since Providence played such a large role in their own mentality. Indeed, the Xhosa tended to confront them with the suggestion that their claims regarding the Christian faith were as magical as the Xhosa cultural practices that missionaries condemned. This was the import behind Maqoma's claim to Laing, in the early 1840s, that perhaps they should each live and let live in regards to different cultural practices. Certainly, the missionaries were not keen to let the impression seep back to the folks at home that they were engaged in a competition with the Xhosa over whose magic was superior. Nor were they eager to leave the impression that they were letting the Xhosa *think* that they were practicing better magic when their prayers had the desired result. Yet the reality was that missionary magic was never far below the surface of the missionary interaction with the Xhosa. And some were prepared to defend it.

The potential advantage of missionary magic for the Xhosa was present from the very first moment of the encounter. Xhosa were curious to test the validity of missionary claims of how God could be accessed. Van der Kemp was asked by Ngqika to pray for rain, and after somewhat weakly resisting this request, he did so. The results were quite astounding, and may in fact have left a more profound impression on the Xhosa than van der Kemp could have realized. The day after he had offered up a prayer for rain, it began to rain ceaselessly. Indeed, it rained so much that Nqgika's kraal was washed away, and he had to beg van der Kemp to intercede with Thiko (God) "that he might hear no more such tremendous thunder claps." James Laing was equally endowed with magical powers. At the opening of his new church at Burnside in 1837, during a particularly heavy drought, Laing prayed for rain. And right on cue, the rains came. This impressed the Xhosa, and the following Sunday Laing's congregation had jumped to over 200, with an overspill of 30 outside. Naturally, this attendance failed to last, and in the later retelling of the story, it became an example of Xhosa incredulity. Yet from our perspective, it is a nice example of the kinds of compromises missionaries found themselves drawn into.[30]

For the missionary, requests from the Xhosa to exercise their powers of intercession were not a straightforward matter. On the one hand, they did not want to lead the Xhosa to believe that God was in fact receptive to this kind of supplication, or that the missionaries actually had the power to call on him for favors. On the other hand, they were entitled to give thanks for a good harvest, for example. And they were anxious to impress upon the Xhosa the power of prayer. Making the fine distinction to the Xhosa that prayer *might* gain results, but only if God was inclined to grant the wish, was a problem. In any case, it seems likely that they were often prepared to let the Xhosa *think* that they were exercising a magic that the Xhosa could understand.

Samuel Young, the Methodist missionary whose wife's death we recounted earlier, noted an incident that demonstrates the ambiguities surrounding this issue for the missionaries. A relative of Chief Khama, a Christian chief, was to be married to a Christian convert in the tribe. Khama urged the celebrants to drop the customary dances in the celebration – dances that, missionaries claimed, encouraged "lewd" and "licentious" behavior. The celebrants refused, led by one young chief, in particular, who rejected the entreaties of the mission party and insisted on following traditional practices. During one of the dances the young chief collapsed and died. This caused enormous consternation among the Xhosa. Phato, brother of Khama, was impressed enough to disappear for several days into the bush to pray that the young man would revive. All sorts of traditional remedies were employed to bring the victim back to life. None was successful. The brother of the young man turned up at Young's house to ask for a spade to bury him. This was significant, because the Xhosa did not usually bury their dead in the Christian manner, and it was therefore an implicit recognition of the power of missionary magic. Young was quite happy to allow him to take this lesson from the episode, and seized "the opportunity of reproving him and shewing him the consequences of obstinately persisting in their evil ways."[31]

For their part, the Xhosa were prepared to hedge their bets on the possibility that missionary magic might be more powerful than their own traditions. Knowing that the missionaries believed in certain kinds of magical forms made it easier at times for the Xhosa to explain things to the missionaries. Tiyo Soga's father, who practiced a deeply hybridized cultural lifestyle, was confronted by William Chalmers when he called in a witchdoctor to attend to a sick daughter. Soga replied that although he knew the word of God and wished to serve him, his family was being struck with sickness because "he does not obey the word of God." He therefore had no option but to follow another course. At about the same time, it was noted that a lack of rain was followed by an increased attendance at church services as some Xhosa sought to "obtain rain by prayer to the true God." But others, including Suthu, the powerful Queen Regent, were also using Xhosa diviners in an attempt to achieve the same objective. So the Xhosa were wisely hedging their bets.[32]

Some missionaries, however, were prepared to go further and defend the theological purity of intercessionary prayer. In a sermon that Henry Calderwood preached in Cape Town in 1843, he listed a series of biblical authorities to support instances when the use of public prayer had been answered, including the prophet Elijah praying for rain; and he cited a captive narrative in which a prisoner of the Turks had successfully prayed for the death of his captor. Thornley Smith, a Methodist missionary who spent seven years in Xhosaland, successfully prayed for rain and asked whether it was not so wrong "to recognise in such occurrences the hand divine?" After all, he pointed out, this could be God working in mysterious ways to impress his power on the heathen. Although it was not the aim of "the Christian missionary to foster superstitious views in heathen minds," neither was it appropriate for him to "deny the power of prayer, or to interpret such events as the above on the cold principles of rationalism."[33]

But perhaps the most interesting aspect of missionary magic, for our purposes, was its use by the missionaries themselves to understand aspects of their encounter with the Xhosa. Magic was useful as a way of understanding what precisely they were observing as they watched and participated in their encounters with the Xhosa. A very good example of this aspect of the cultural encounter is provided by the protracted struggle that Laing conducted with the Xhosa hierarchy at Burnside over who was to own the loyalties of Matwa. At one point in this struggle, which has been discussed above, his interpreter and interlocutor, Charles Henry, became the target of intimidatory witchcraft accusations and feared for the security of his life and property enough to flee the mission. Laing could not see the threat, for on the surface everything had calmed down and seemed to be returning to normal. Here was a case where observation failed him. Laing was at a loss, and where else did he have to go for understanding in this case but to God? "I may be mistaken, so may C. H., but we only owe our preservation to God, if we are preserved. Even then we do not see danger. He preserves us. Twelve men with assegais are now passing but they have not called at our house, nor made any stay at the place ... Should the Kaffers be so disposed they could easily take all we have."[34]

Laing's experience is a nicely documented example of a general feature of the missionary encounter with the Xhosa: their failure to feel confidant that they *understood* what was going on around them. Indeed, given the opaque nature of their cultural encounters, they must have felt entirely befuddled a lot of the time. If we read carefully the accounts of missionaries as they tried to make sense of their encounters with the Xhosa, we can only conclude that the missionary mind of these years was filled with a high degree of cognitive dissonance. And this, of course, raised the ultimate question for missionary culture and for the viability of the missionary project. How were they to understand the dissonance between what they believed should be happening in their encounter with the Xhosa, and what actually *was* happening? How was their knowledge system to process and absorb their experiences?

The volatilities of missionary culture

The cognitive dissonance that was provoked in missionary minds by the encounter with the Xhosa had one extremely important consequence. It triggered volatilities that lay embedded within the very marrow of missionary culture. Missionary culture contained an unstable mix of values. A naive expectation that the world could be moved by individuals inspired by the word of God was yoked with a recognition of the helplessness of the individual before Providence. We have seen how for J. F. Cumming these values instilled an obsession with evaluating how consonant his movements were with God's will. The result was a violent syncopation between optimism that he was in tune with what God wanted for him and deep pessimism that he was not following God's message and that his labors were useless and to no avail. The violent mood swings between optimism and pessimism that marked Cumming's introduction to southern Africa were not merely a function of personal psychology. That pattern was also a social phenomenon, part of the social psychology of the encounter between the missionaries and the Xhosa.

The tension between optimism and pessimism was inherent in the culture of evangelicalism. But it was a stress that was triggered as missionaries faced the crumbling of expectations among the Xhosa. Missionary culture strained to hold on to its foundational beliefs and expectations and at the same time to *explain* failures that could not be shunted away. At times the records allow us to see individual missionaries mentally casting about for ways to bring the world around them into line with their conceptual beliefs and assumptions. The first place they tended to land in their search for the source of failure was *themselves.* This was hardly surprising, given what we know of the mental world of their faith.

Ultimately, of course, they moved beyond blaming themselves, and came to blame Xhosa culture for their own failures. But they moved only gradually and reluctantly in this direction.

The fragile state of missionary mentality was not helped, of course, by the arduous physical conditions and hardships they faced. These were often enough to test the strongest missionary faith. Samuel Young had a difficult time cleaving to his faith in God when his wife and unborn child died, hard on the heels of another child. Joseph Williams, who had gotten off to such an optimistic start, confessed himself to be out of spiritual resources by April 1818, when Tzatzoe left, taking with him the Khoe helpers. He wrote despairingly of being alone, abandoned, sick, weary and worn out.[35]

From the very beginning of the enterprise the mental state of missionaries on the frontier was liable to volatile mood swings, one moment buoyed to optimism, the next plunged into varying degrees of pessimism.[36] This volatility was ever near the surface. When George Impey, a Wesleyan missionary newly arrived at the eastern Cape, greeted the new year of 1839 in his journal, his mood was ecstatic with evangelical joy. He looked forward "with lively emotions of joy [to] the great honour that has been put upon me by my Lord and Master." But a few days later, and without warning, things changed. He suspected that Satan was getting hold of him. "I know not how, nor why, but suddenly my spirit is cast down unto the ground, my heart becomes cold and feels no delight in approaching unto God." Then, again, suddenly his optimism reappeared, his faith was renewed and "my spirit rejoices in the Lord."[37]

Similarly, William Shrewsbury, after just a few weeks in southern Africa, was already on the edge of a roller-coaster of emotion. He noted how encouraged he was by the numbers in his congregation, yet hoped he could retain his faith "without fainting *and without doubting* although I should not see *one* heathen converted unto God." Unfortunately, he was not to be so blessed. By January 1831, having trouble finding a suitable interpreter and facing small congregations, he wondered: "How can I go on throughout the week in the various services and duties connected with my work?" Shrewsbury's sense of the imminence of God imposed a heavy burden upon him. Missionaries were subjected entirely to his determination. They were therefore highly susceptible to the signs of God's will, which could include signs of displeasure as well as approval.[38]

The same shock of the encounter reawakened John Cumming's intense self-doubt once he had reached the frontier. Finding a place to build his mission, encountering the "mortifying sight" of Xhosa cultural practices, and the frustrations of negotiating with the local chief, all contributed to a sense that he was wasting his time. His struggle with depression was so bad that he persuaded Robert Niven to bleed him, in the hope that it would "have a good effect on my system." Things got a bit better for him after that. He found a place and began to build a Xhosa hut. But by the beginning of 1842, he was again in despair about the continual compromises he was forced to make in order to secure even a hearing from the local Xhosa. In one instance he decided not to confront the chief about a Xhosa dance ceremony that was about to be held because he was not sure he could explain "exactly wherin they are wrong" – an interesting confession of how Xhosa culture had disrupted his mental and intellectual worldview.[39]

The kind of volatility of mood and frustration that Cumming experienced was by no means unusual. A joint letter from Friederich Kayser, John Brownlee and Richard Birt in April 1841 speaks in the same register. Birt was relative newcomer to the frontier, but Kayser and Brownlee were of longstanding residence. All admitted to having to grapple hard to hang on to the faith in what they were doing. "There is much to discourage and try in Caffreland," but there were also grounds for hope. So they ended with the belief that although "the clouds are not yet chased away, we can distinctly see the break in the clouds cheering us onward by reminding us of the promise and faithfulness of God." Yet the sense one gets from this is that it was written largely to convince themselves, rather than as an accurate assessment of the sociology of their missionary work.[40]

This last extract suggests another feature of the missionary experience during this period: the efforts to reconcile their evangelical worldview with the very different evidence of their own experience on the ground. In their reports to the home authorities, this is an issue that is frequently raised. Few were able to grapple with it coherently. More often, these reports were shaped by logical confusions, reasoning that tapered off as it reached the end of its explanatory power, or observations that ranged loosely over a wide area as if scouring the data for some meaningful pattern. Stephen Kay, a Methodist missionary who wanted to be sympathetic to the Xhosa, tried to explain why his message seemed to fall on deaf ears in spite of the intelligence and sophistication he recognized among the Xhosa in other ways. But as he got deeper and deeper into his description, and approached trying to explain in sociological terms the varied reception he had received, his efforts at analysis failed him. Ultimately he fell back on an explanation that he knew well, an explanation that provided a way of reconciling the contradictions that his attempt at a reasoned explanation had exposed. He retreated to the comforting notion that Satan had established a hold over Xhosa culture, so complete as to degrade and distort their spirit and character.[41]

Similarly, from the other end of the missionary spectrum, we can note a confused report from John Ross, a missionary with the Glasgow Missionary Society. In attempting to explain the sluggish response to the missionary preaching of the word of God, Ross began to make the link between the continued strength of traditional cultural practices and the deliberate *refusal* by the Xhosa to accept God's word. But he was very reluctant to follow this thought. We can well understand why. To do so would be to throw into doubt one of the basic premises of missionary culture: that the Xhosa were open to receiving God's word. His argument then became painfully convoluted as he struggled with this conundrum. What he found particularly disturbing was that God had recently showed his goodness to the Xhosa by showering them with rain (had he called for this?) and had saved their crops from a threatened drought. Yet the Xhosa did not respond to this beneficence with the gratitude he had expected. They were not brought any closer to accepting God's presence or word by this gift of rain. On the contrary, the Xhosa continued to deny him and to reject his "Word of Grace and Truth." Instead of thanking God, they immediately set about feasting and dancing. Ross's world was, in a way, turned upside down. In a perverse way God's goodness was being used to reinforce traditional cultural practices rather than to weaken them.[42]

There was one missionary, however, who did lay out his thinking on the quandary of how to explain the gap between expectation and reality in this regard. We have already encountered the Reverend William J. Shrewsbury in this book. But it is now time to focus on him more closely. For the history of Shrewsbury's missionary sojourn in southern Africa reveals in close detail the challenge that missionary culture faced in its encounter with the Xhosa. It is a history that also provides a fast-forward preview of what was to be the main features of the missionary story from the 1830s to the 1850s.

The apostasy of William J. Shrewsbury

When Shrewsbury went to southern Africa his credentials as an evangelical humanitarian were unassailable. In the West Indies his notoriety lay in his support of the slave population and his excoriating sermons against the white planters. As a missionary in the West Indies in the 1820s his theology followed the evangelical humanitarianism line on the question of race and redemption. As a consequence he incurred the wrath of the planter class. But if we have cited Shrewsbury earlier as an example of the openness with which missionaries encountered the Xhosa, he was also an example of the way in which that openness could turn into closure, and cultural relativism could be transformed into racism. It is this side of Shrewsbury that I want to concentrate on here.

For by 1835 a different Shrewsbury had emerged. This Shrewsbury was a supporter of the punitive frontier policy of Governor Sir Benjamin

D'Urban and Harry Smith, the frontier commander. He was an advocate of the harshest of measures against the Xhosa, and he articulated a theory of racial difference that attributed the difference of the Xhosa to the essential incorrigibility of their characters. Shrewsbury's story captures the main narrative of the challenges that faced missionary culture over this period of initial encounter with the Xhosa. How William Shrewsbury worked his way through those challenges between the time he first confronted Xhosa culture to the time he was sent away from southern Africa in disgrace in 1835 reveals something of the psycho-cultural dynamic that ran through missionary culture in this period.

Given Shrewsbury's history, it was not surprising that the Wesleyan Methodist Missionary Society decided to ship him off to southern Africa. Here, they must have thought, was land well suited to the drive, determination and toughness of the Reverend William J. Shrewsbury. The Wesleyans were committed to the vision of a string of Methodist mission stations stretching from the eastern Cape through Kaffraria and Pondoland to Natal. The promise of a rapid progress in opening African hearts to God was believed to be very great. This was a place that needed spiritually hardy men. And so Shrewsbury was sent to join a powerful group of Methodist missionaries already in place among the Xhosa. For the first five years or so, it seemed that this was the right decision. But ultimately, southern Africa drained the strength out of Shrewsbury. In the West Indies, Shrewsbury had disturbed the white settler plantation class with his attacks on their moral turpitude as slave-owners and whoremongers. In southern Africa, Shrewsbury lost his power to shock and in his turn found that *his* belief system was destabilized by the Xhosa. The man who had come to southern Africa as a cultural relativist left South Africa as a hardened racist who rejected the possibility of their salvation without their coercive subjugation.

How did this happen? It was not a predetermined passage for Shrewsbury. In the beginning, he retained a positive view of the Xhosa and his humanitarian ideology remained intact. He arrived in southern Africa disposed to favor the Xhosa over the white settlers. When digging started to build the chapel at Butterworth in December 1827, he chose one representative from each group to unite in laying the foundation stone in the hope that it would "help us ... abolish from the face of the earth those vile distinctions arising from case or the colour of the skin, and which ought to have no existence in the Church of Christ." He remarked on their good order and the complete sense of safety he felt. Nor was he put off by Xhosa spiritual beliefs: "idolatry is wholly unknown among them," and although it was true that they were unlike other people in being devoid of either true or false religion, they were not without some sense of a supreme being. Thus the way was open to his ministrations.[43]

He spoke favorably of the chiefs; he was impressed by their dignity and bearing. He recognized Hintsa as a wily and able politician. He viewed with tolerant amusement the verbal sparring between his missionary party (himself, William Shaw and George Shepstone) and the chiefs of the Gqunkhwebe Xhosa, who thanked them for the present of the "word" but wondered if they had any cloth to give them also. After a lengthy conversation he left this meeting convinced that he and his missionary companions had established a trust relationship and had begun to persuade them of the truth of revelation. Indeed, perhaps he had, since all three chiefs were to become loyal allies of the British, and one of them, Khama, was to be the only committed Christian chief in Xhosaland.[44]

Such attitudes did not last. Towards the end of 1830 a new tone appeared in his reports home. It was a tone of growing confusion and frustration, and it marked the closing down of Shrewsbury's humanitarian evangelical spirit. It was as if the enormity of the task was now less a stimulating challenge and more a mounting tidal wave that threatened to overwhelm him. He shifted into a more embattled mode where he constantly struggled to retain belief in himself *and* in the ideological and practical dimensions of his worldview. The core problem that sparked this tortured reappraisal was the Xhosa resistance to receiving the word of God. This was, of course, a common problem that all missionaries had to face, and we shall return again to the consequences of their engagement with it. But in Shrewsbury we have a seldom granted opportunity to observe closely the challenge that it posed to the basic assumptions of a missionary's humanitarian culture.

In September 1830 he reported that since the start of his mission four years ago, only ten persons had "awakened to sense of their sinfulness." Two years earlier he had proclaimed his strength to continue even if he convinced only *one* heathen; now he was not sure that he could hold to such optimism. "The difficulties are immense which oppose themselves to the general instruction and conversion of the people. It is hardly possible to dwell on them without sinking under discouragement; the heart would be quite overwhelmed with them were it not for faith in those promises of holy writ which relate to the salvation of the heathen." Two years later, in June 1832, he was still struggling with this pessimism. But now a new element had been introduced: an *intellectual* confusion in his mind about how to reconcile the certainty of his belief in the wisdom of God's words with the failure to find a hearing among the Xhosa. "Where shall I look for flourishing congregations? Where for a rapidly increasing society? Where are the triumphs of the everlasting Gospel in the conversion and salvation of immortal souls? Such inquiries as these have frequently occupied my mind."[45]

Where did the problem underlying this poor rate of return lie? In coming to grips with this question, Shrewsbury entered a years-long struggle to suppress the demons that had been roused by his encounter with the Xhosa. It was both an emotional and an intellectual struggle, for the stake was no less than the creed of evangelical humanitarianism that he had previously lived by. Not until the spring of 1834 do we have direct evidence that he had settled the debate within himself and, in the process, had come to a new position on the problems of converting the Xhosa, a position that transferred responsibility for those problems on to the inherent character of the Xhosa themselves. Although one can see that this ultimate resolution was *implicit* in his earlier distress at the obduracy of Xhosa cultural practices, it is noteworthy that he did not immediately leap to that analysis. Rather, he conducted what amounted to an intellectual inquiry, interrogating the various tenets of his belief and the possible causes for the disjuncture he perceived between the power of God's word and the failure of it to penetrate into Xhosa minds. He searched for the reasons for his failure in various places: in the conditions of the mission, in his own lack of worth, and finally in the Xhosa themselves.[46]

From the end of 1830, a new volatility is manifest in his reports home. Nothing in Shrewsbury's past history suggested that he lacked self-confidence. Indeed, he was known as a rigid and self-righteous individual.[47] But his reports now began to exhibit the familiar evangelical instability, as they swung wildly between optimism and despair. In September 1830 he ended his dispatch by looking for a miracle as the solution to the dilemma. Eighteen months later, faced with an upturn in the number of converts, he resolved the same conundrum more optimistically, concluding that "the work that has been wrought proves the existence of a divine agency with us." In the same period, he moved back and forth between the three prescriptions of blaming variously himself, the mission enterprise and the Xhosa, before finally settling on the last to provide an explanation. It was through this process of interrogation and agonizing that Shrewsbury learnt a new way of thinking about race.

Thus, in this same dispatch in September 1830 he explained the low rates of conversion in material and cultural terms that suggested the need to take it out of the realm of morality and theology. Neither the conditions of the mission effort, nor the circumstances of Xhosa life, he argued, were conducive to their properly hearing the word he was preaching. The Xhosa were without learning or books; and this was something he noted that even the apostles did not have to confront. Under such circumstances, he asked, "How shall they be made to understand?" In addition, the circumstances of the missionary project presented enormous obstacles to getting the word of God across. The challenge of communication was difficult enough. Scripture needed to be translated first into Dutch and then into Xhosa, by which time who knew what meaning was being conveyed to the listeners? And if the word of the Bible was thus shielded from the Xhosa, how was it possible to combat such obstacles to Christian civilization as barbarous cultural practices like circumcision?[48]

Indeed, in what is perhaps the most powerful evidence of the intellectual debate he was conducting with himself, a few months later he extended this analysis of why Christianity was not working among the Xhosa by suggesting that perhaps it lay in the different signification of words. Here he came very close to suggesting that different words possessed different meanings within the contexts of different worldviews. Although the Xhosa had words for God, they did not have a theology that associated God with creation. It was therefore difficult to convey to them the proper idea of creation according to Christian doctrine.

What would have happened if Shrewsbury had continued with this line of reasoning? Just to pose that question is to reveal the sharp dilemma he faced. For to continue along that logical road would have led him to a reaffirmation of his original belief in a universal humanity. But then, what would *that* have implied but the accommodation of cultural practices and beliefs that he (in common with others) had tagged as the major obstacles to the spread of Christianity? He would have found himself in the position of endorsing polygamy, witchcraft, licentious practices and the like. In his quest to understand the failure of his message to move the Xhosa, Shrewsbury's mental and intellectual world was in danger of coming apart. He was bumping up against the limits of his own mental worldview. He was moving was very close to undermining the common evangelical assumption that the power of the word of God was enough to convert and alter Xhosa culture. Small wonder his mind was in turmoil.[49]

But if the conditions of the missionary enterprise were deeply problematic, Shrewsbury was also led to consider his own internal qualities as a missionary. The fact that Shrewsbury was willing to entertain the possibility that somehow *he* was to blame for the failure of his efforts is a reflection of the depth of his interrogation of this dilemma. But as we have had occasion to note before, it was also a reflection of the fragility of the evangelical mindset. It was not an unusual experience for missionaries at the first sign of trouble to turn back upon themselves, as if they were not up to the task that God had set them. Thus, as part of his inquiry into why he was finding it so difficult to secure a hearing for God's truth, he was led to attribute these poor results to himself, wondering whether it did not reflect an unworthy self-pride in wanting to be the agent of a conversion "that was more properly God's to bestow." "It becomes me rather to pray for the conversion of sinners, than that I should be the instrument of producing that glorious change."[50]

And, finally, there was the question of Xhosa responsibility. The possibility that the fault lay with the Xhosa themselves was present from the beginning of his ruminations in September 1830. "They do not manifest much concern about salvation," he wrote then. But still at this stage the main diagnosis pointed to the material conditions of the culture and the inadequate strategies available to the missionaries. By the spring of 1831, however, a shift has occurred. Satan had ruled unchallenged for so long, he claimed, that the power of preaching the scriptures through oratory was not enough to dislodge the depths of depravity that had been embedded in Xhosa culture. Indeed, so complete had been Satan's reign that it had been naturalized by the Xhosa, who had come to "love that darkness rather than light." But if this could still be taken to at least partially exonerate the Xhosa from self-responsibility for their failure to receive Shrewsbury's worldview, there was another factor that *was* more personal.

Shrewsbury had come to see the Xhosa as characterologically deceitful. Ironically, he was led to this by a recognition of Xhosa worldliness. In his dealings with the chiefs, Shrewsbury had taken full note of their political sophistication. He quickly grasped how the chiefs' interest in missionaries lay in the latter's usefulness as political assets in tribal politics and in relations with the imperial power. Similarly, in a quite remarkable insight, he recognized signs of spirituality within Xhosa culture. He noted, for example, that they had three words for "deity," which was "a very striking and singular fact not to be met with in the history of other pagan nations."[51]

Shrewsbury recognized that he was not dealing with savage minds, even if they did practice savage customs. And it was this intellectuality that set up the final and most telling cognitive dissonance for Shrewsbury. For these signs suggested that the Xhosa *should* be ready for God's word; that they did in fact have the mental and perhaps spiritual equipment to receive it. But how were these signs to be reconciled with the Xhosa's obdurate evasion when it came to accepting the word of God? How was this to be explained? Ultimately, Shrewsbury could explain it only by attributing to the Xhosa a characterological deceit. Thus, he noted, "it is not uncommon with this people to acknowledge the excellence of the Truth when they wish to avoid its further application to the conscience." Here we come to the heart of the transition that Shrewsbury had been struggling both to avoid and to undertake. It was a transition that ended up dumping on to the Xhosa themselves the missionary failure to persuade them of the truth of this – the most humanitarian – side of British culture. "It is not Error merely that we have to encounter but sin and not merely vicious practices but *deeply rooted depravity in the heart*; for in every man we meet with, of all those tribes it is evident to us that the heart is utterly corrupt and that every imagination of its thoughts are evil."[52] It was now mentally and intellectually possible for Shrewsbury to make the move that led to his disgrace.

By 1835 he was in Grahamstown, ministering to the settler community of that frontier town. At this time Grahamstown was a well-established, small and enclosed world whose British community was just beginning to mount an organized challenge to the dominant humanitarian view of race relations. Shrewsbury's move there a year or so earlier had been influenced by the personal hardship he had experienced. His own health was bad and from the autumn of 1834 he began to request a return to England. His wife and youngest child were to die soon after his move to Grahamstown. But beyond these personal circumstances, his move to the capital of the eastern Cape was also a reflection of his disillusionment with the possibilities of the Xhosa mission.[53]

And then came the final blow. At the end of 1834 the sixth frontier war broke out, the mission stations were burned and Grahamstown was once again besieged by the Xhosa tribes. In a stroke, all the work that the missionaries had expended in the frontier zone was put at risk. In the midst of this crisis, Shrewsbury wrote to the Directors expressing what was the official settler line on the war: "The Hordes of Kafirs are murdering the scattered setters in their solitary habitations daily, plundering them of all their prospect and taking their flocks of sheep and cattle." Then, in a letter of 15 January 1835, he explained how he had been persuaded by Colonel Harry Smith, commandant of the frontier forces, to "put on paper a few thoughts concerning the mode of conducting the Kafir war." Although he was mindful of the official policy to keep mission separate from politics, "I did not think I should be justified in declining this service." He also explained that he had read the articles to his colleagues, who thought them just fine.[54]

Shrewsbury had no idea just how controversial this was to become. He claimed that he quickly composed his memorandum, kept no copy and sent it off to Harry Smith, who passed it along to the Governor, Sir Benjamin D'Urban. No further discussion about it took place, and Shrewsbury soon left Grahamstown to return to London. It is true that the document itself bears more the character of a series of jottings than of a formal memorandum. Still, by the time Shrewsbury was back in London, his recommendations had reached the hands of the Directors of the Wesleyan Methodist Missionary Society, who could barely conceal their horror.

What did Shrewsbury recommend to Smith? In sum, his recommendations endorsed the harsh, indeed brutal, policy against the Xhosa that D'Urban himself had proclaimed at the beginning of the war when he described them as "irredeemable savages." This was a notorious and controversial statement at the time, since it directly contradicted both the dominant assumption of missionary culture and the official "humanitarian" policy of the British government. Shrewsbury's recommendations included summary execution of those who had murdered British subjects (presumably without the benefit of trial to establish the fact), and thorough dispossession of arms and property from the chiefs. All Xhosa were be registered and to wear identity tags around their necks (the latter reminiscent, of course, of slave collars); neutral chiefs who allowed those at war to quarter cattle with them to be treated as enemies (this was justified because of the "duplicity of character of the Kafir chiefs"), and Xhosa offenders – presumably warriors – were to be employed as forced labor on the roads; finally, the "neutral territory" that separated the Cape Colony from Xhosaland should be occupied.[55]

The Committee of the WMMS received a copy of the memo from the Colonial Office, and although they were obviously concerned about any political fallout that could result, there was no mistaking their dismay. At its meeting of 30 December 1835, they expressed their "most entire and unqualified disapproval of the step unhappily taken by Mr. Shrewsbury," asserting that his recommendations were "most unwarrantable and revolting against the principles and feelings of humanity and religion; that it was unbecoming of [his] station and character as a missionary that he should take part in such discussions with the military."[56]

And with this the Reverend William Shrewsbury fades from our story, temporarily exiled to the ministrations of the Methodist community of Boulogne, France. But before he goes, we should note a sermon he preached and published in 1854 during the Crimean War. Its subject was "War, as a means of Advancing the Kingdom of Christ," and it surely marked the terminus to the intellectual journey that Shrewsbury had begun in southern Africa. It opened by drawing upon his African experience to explain how African culture had nothing of Jesus in it, was "directly antagonistic to Christ," and was given over to the most degrading customs, whose fruits were "envy, lust, rapine, misery, murder, death, hell." This formidable list of attributes presented an "impenetrable barrier to the admission of the truth" of the Gospel. It was war, and war alone, that "must throw that barrier down," just as war in India under Robert Clive had destroyed paganism and opened the way to the spread of Christian light. War, Shrewsbury explained, in this context was all part of God's design, and although it was not to be undertaken by missionaries, it was the only answer to the "internal darkness and cruelty" that characterized the African paganism, degenerate Islam and even the corrupt Orthodox Church of Greece.[57]

Conclusion: the need to make new sense of the Xhosa

The importance of Shrewsbury's story lies in what it reveals about the dynamic of the encounter between the missionaries and the Xhosa in this initial period of engagement. His story exposes in stark contours how it was in the process and details of encounter that missionary subjectivities changed and missionary culture shifted away from it original moorings. Shrewsbury moved fairly rapidly along a spectrum from cultural relativist to racial essentialist. He made the journey to a new racial discourse before most others within the religious and political communities. The encounter with the Xhosa destabilized missionary culture and undermined the understanding of the Xhosa that missionary culture had carried with it from Britain. A new understanding of the Xhosa was called for. But before we can fully approach that part of our story, it is necessary first to address another aspect of the missionary encounter with the Xhosa: the record of their relationship with Xhosa politics.

NOTES

1. This contradiction is best illustrated at the personal level. For an interesting example of the challenge empire posed to subjectivities of identity and how empire experiences could end badly, see Nicholas Thomas and Richard Eves, *Bad Colonists: The South Seas Letters of Vernon Lee Walker and Louis Becke* (Durham, NC, 1999), esp. pp. 58–9, 60–7, 72, 104–7, 133–8.
2. There is, of course, a paradox here. It does not follow that the importance of the missionary presence has been exaggerated, or its impact on the future course of southern African history overstated, by the large amount of attention it has received from historians. The contribution of missionary culture to the liberal political discourse of the nineteenth century and beyond, and the fertile interaction between evangelical religion and indigenous African religions, were legacies enough of the missionary project. See Richard Elphick and Rodney Davenport (eds.), *Christianity in South Africa: A Political, Social and Cultural History* (Berkeley, CA, 1997); Henry Bredekamp and Robert Ross (eds.), *Missions and Christianity in South African History* (Johannesburg, 1995).
3. Jean and John Comaroff, *Of Revelation and Revolution: Christianity, Colonialism and Consciousness in South Africa*, vol. I (Chicago, 1991), for missionary control over the cultural discourse. For a critique of the Comaroffs on this very point see Paul Landau, "Hegemony and History in Jean and John L. Comaroff's *Of Revelation and Revolution*," *Africa* 70.3 (2000), pp. 501–9. For an introduction to some of the themes of African religion, see Hodgson, "A Battle for Sacred Power: Christian Beginnings among the Xhosa," in Richard Elphick and Rodney Davenport, *Christianity in South Africa: A Political, Cultural and Social History* (Berkeley, 1997), pp. 68–89, and also Hodgson's *The God of the Xhosa* (Cape Town, 1986); Paul Landau, "Nineteenth Century Transformations in Consciousness," in Robert Ross, Carolyn Hamiton, Bill Nasson and Bernard

Mbenga, *The Cambridge History of South Africa*, vol. I (Cambridge, forthcoming), ch. 8, and Landau, *The Realm of the Word: Language, Gender and Christianity in a Southern African Kingdom* (Portsmouth, NH, 1995), are important studies of this aspect of African religion.

4. David Bebbington, *Evangelicalism in Modern Britain: A History from the 1730s to the 1980s* (London, 1989), pp. 5–7, 62; Comaroff, *Revolution and Revelation*, pp. 117–18. There was some debate also as to whether the millennium would have to wait for the conversion of the Jews; see Reverend James Laing, *Journals 1830–1871*, MS 16579, CL, Laing to Falconer, 11 October 1830, a letter written just as Laing was about to embark for southern Africa, in which he added that although he did not believe there would be a general conversion "until Israel shall be saved," he did not consider "Hindoo or Kaffir souls any less important." For the Indian experience in this respect, see Jeffrey Cox, *Imperial Faultlines: Christianity and Colonial Power in India, 1818–1940* (Stanford, CA, 2002), pp. 122, 130–1.

5. For some examples of early optimism regarding conversion, see CWM, LMS, *South Africa Journals 1810–1816*, Box 2, folder 50, Journal of J. H. Schmelen, 5, 20 and 21 February; 16 March; 8 and 11 May; 12 and 27 September 1815; also folder 53, Journal of Anderson and Helm, 24 and 26 May 1815. WMMS, South Africa, *Incoming Correspondence 1825–30*, Box 2, fiche 52, Journal of Stephen Kay, January 1827. See Natasha Erlank, "Re-examining Initial Encounters between Christian Missionaries and the Xhosa, 1820–1850: The Scottish Case," *Kleio* 31 (1999), pp. 23–30, for a good discussion on the meaning of conversion for the Xhosa. For Cumming, see United Presbyterian Church, *Missionary Record*, May 1849, p. 72. See Glasgow African Missionary Society, *Caffrarian Messenger*, February 1845, pp. 248–50, for a witchdoctor who also "insensibly converted" and who was put to death "with the word of the Lord on his lips" for refusing to pray for rain. See also a similar account in Moffat, *Missionary Labours and Scenes in Southern Africa* (London, 1842), pp. 572–5. As late as 1874 the LMS missionary at King William's Town cited the case of a man who gradually shed the red clay and kaross of the Xhosa and replaced them with a suit of European clothes, as a polygamist debated with Harper, the missionary, which wife he should give up. CWM, LMS, *Report for 1874*, pp. 49–50. Similar stories dot the archives throughout the whole period. See CA, A 80(2), Rev. John Ayliff, *Journal of Rev. John Ayliff 1832–1850*, 5 March 1835, for a typical story taken as a sign of Christian wonder. Rev. William Govan, *Memorials of the Missionary Career of Reverend James Laing* (Glasgow, 1875), pp. 15–16, 62, 64, 67–8. In CWM, LMS, South Africa, *Incoming Correspondence*, Box 30, folder 2, Kayser to Tidman, Annual Report, October 1856, Kayser is till hopeful: "my confidential trust is to our almighty Lord, that he, for his holy name and truth's sake, will let have his holy truth the victory over the cuning [*sic*] lies, which the old enemy of souls – who will not leave up, until he is bound by the prince of peace – has sown again among the Kaffir tribes by anorther [*sic*] falsh [*sic*] prophet and filled the mind of this superstitious proud race to surprising actions."

6. Consider Frederick Kayser's experience in the 1830s. In 1836, Kayser's reports, for example, he described how Sunday services held at Maqoma's

kraal sometimes attracted 100 people. A year later, however, he reported that he had lost his influence over Maqoma to a rain-maker. Prayers had been discontinued at the kraal. Nine months later, he reported that there were about thirty in the congregation and around ten children in the Sunday school. The following year, things had turned around again. Maqoma was once again welcoming, and Sutu, Sandile's mother, was showing signs of being moved by the Spirit of God. A couple of years later Kayser was telling a different story. He had been planning to build a new church because the attendance had shot up. But then Tyhali (Maqoma's brother) and some of the younger chiefs put it about that the people "must not only go and pray but make them also red with their red clay and follow their chiefs to the dance and show that they love their chiefs." CWM, *Africa and Madagascar Committee*, Minutes of Home Committee on Africa, 1836–68, 30 November 1836; 16 June 1837; 21 May 1838. LMS, South Africa, *Incoming Correspondence*, Box 16, folder 1, 7 August 1838, Kayser to Ellis; see also Brownlee to Ellis, 16 October 1838. Box 17, folder 1, Kayser to Board of Directors, 12 February 1840.

7. LMS, South Africa, *Incoming Correspondence*, Box 18, folder 1, Calderwood to Directors, 18 May 1841; Natasha Erlank, "Gendered Reactions to Social Dislocation and Missionary Activity in Xhosaland, 1836–1847," *African Studies* 59.2 (2000), p. 215.

8. GMS, *Minutes of the Presbytery of Kaffraria*, 6 April 1842; Donovan Williams, *When Races Meet: The Life and Times of William Ritchie Thomson, Glasgow Society Missionary, Government Agent and Dutch Reformed Church Minister 1794–1891* (Johannesburg, 1967), p. 99. Hildegarde H. Fast, "'In at one ear and out at the other': African Response to the Wesleyan Message in Xhosaland 1825–1835," *Journal of Religion in South Africa* 23.2 (1993), pp. 147–74.

9. GMS, *Minutes of the Caffrarian Presbytery*, 4 January 1837; 17 April 1838; 29 December 1839; 23 January 1842; Anthonie Eduard DuToit, "The Cape Frontier: A Study of Native Policy with Special Reference to the Years 1847–1866," D.Phil. thesis, University of Pretoria, 1949, p. 394.

10. GMS, *Minutes of the Presbytery of Kaffraria*, 1 December 1842; 4 January 1843; Govan, *Memorials of … Laing*, pp. 88–9. These intermediaries were often politically unreliable in other ways, too. Charles Henry threw in his lot with the Xhosa prophet Mlanjeni, who had called for the war of 1850–3. In spite of all the time and investment in Charles Henry by the missionaries, he ultimately returned to Xhosa culture. There is a somewhat poignant letter from John Laing in the mid-1850s pleading with Colonel Maclean, the frontier administrator, to allow the ailing Charles Henry to join his son in the Royal Reserve, in spite of his transgressions. Maclean was not moved, and Charles Henry's request to move to be taken care of by his son was refused. See CA, BK 90, *Missions: Correspondence Between Chief Commissioner, British Kaffraria and Missionaries, 1848–56*, Laing to Maclean, 6 October 1856.

11. Barker, *Journal*, 11 May 1818; CWM, LMS, South Africa, *Journals 1824–1892*, Box 4, f. 99, Kayser journals from the Buffalo River, 1828–9; *South African Odds*, Box 9, Brownlow to Tidman, 27 December 1844.

12. CA, BK 89, *Reports from Special Magistrate King William's Town, Superintendent of Fingoes, Magistrate with Toise, Native Police, Secret Information, 1844–65,* Maclean to Mackinnon, 9 June 1852; BK 437, *Letters from Hlambie Commissioner,* 14 June 1851; BK 1, *Letters of High Commissioner, 1847–1856,* Cathcart to Mackinnon, 15 June 1852; CWM, LMS, *Africa, Odds,* Box 9, Brownlow Letters, Brownlow to Tidman, 27 December 1844; *Africa, Southern Outgoing Letters 1847–52,* Ellis to Brownlee, 15 December 1847.

13. See CWM, LMS, South Africa, *Incoming Correspondence,* Box 18, folder 1, Birt to Directors, 3 May 1841 for the moral depravity that was associated with circumcision; Celia Sadler (compiler), *Never a Young Man: Extracts from the Letters and Journals of William Shaw* (Cape Town, 1967), p. 134; United Presbyterian Church, *Missionary Record,* 2 August 1858.

14. The prominence of circumcision in African culture was one of the things that led to the fairly common assumption that there was an affinity between the Xhosa and Zulus on the one hand and Jews or Arabs on the other. Thus, Eliza Fielden in *My African Home; or, Bush Life in Natal When a Young Colony [1852–1857]* (London, 1887), p. 137; and the Free Church of Scotland, *Home and Foreign Record,* May 1855, pp. 254–58. Ayliff, *Journal 1830–1852,* 26 March 1833 and 2 March 1834. His encounter with the ritual did provide him the opportunity to describe it in great detail, however.

15. Ironically, the complainant in Emgwali was Tiyo Soga, the first Xhosa ordinand and someone who had not been circumcised, although his brothers had. Rev. H. T. Cousins, *Tiyo Soga: The Model Kaffir Missionary* (London, 1897), pp. 104–5. GMS, *Minutes of the Presbytery of Kaffraria,* 1 July and 7 October 1840; Ayliff, *Journal 1832–1850,* 26 March 1833.

16. GMS, *Minutes of the Presbytery of Kaffraria,* 1 April 1840.

17. Ibid., 3 January 1844. The missionary position on circumcision was not necessarily supported by the imperial state. The imperial administration closely watched the preparations for Sandile's ceremony and implicitly condoned it by sending presents of sheep, cattle and a suit of clothes, including a blue stock coat, trousers and a waistcoat. The lead frontier official assured Sandile of the government's "desire to pay him all due respect on the occasion of his circumcision." See CA, LG 398, *Letters Received from the Resident Agent in Caffraria 1838–1840,* Hudson to Stretch, 7 January 1840.

18. Sadler, *Never a Young Man,* p. 134; GMS, *Minutes of the Presbytery of Kaffraria,* 3 January 1844. The teachers effectively took control of this issue and not only agreed to exercise their influence against the practice, but promised to not allow their sons or relatives to participate in circumcision rituals. The presbytery responded with gratitude to this sentiment and especially because the "meeting alluded to and all its proceedings originated entirely with the native Christians themselves, without the slightest suggestion from any of the Missionaries."

19. For a missionary who soon concluded that practices like circumcision posed an insurmountable obstacle to conversion, see Rev. William J. Shrewsbury, *The Journal and Selected Letters of Rev. William J. Shrewsbury.* 1826–1835, ed. Hildegarde Fast (Johannesburg, 1994), pp. 128–30, report of 30 September 1830. For examples of optimistic expectations see CA, GH 8/45, *Letters of*

Captain Maclean, pp. 36–52, "Report from Maclean on the T'Slambi district and the chiefs," no date, but the late 1840s – a report on the Fort Peddie Mfengu settlement, where "circumcision has altogether ceased and the desire for European clothes is general." The tendency to remain silent over the intensity of the struggles against traditional practices can be seen by comparing the internal source of the GMS, *Minutes of the Presbytery of Kaffraria*, with the published source, the *Caffrarian Messenger*, of the same Society. The former is full of their struggle and lack of success, with a growing despair about success; this tends not to be reflected in the pages of the latter.

20. Alan Gibson, *Eight Years in Kaffraria* (New York, 1891), pp. 171–2; Govan, *Memorials of ... Laing*, p. 12. For this *modus vivendi* in the late nineteenth century, at least in East Africa, where similar struggles against traditional practices were common, with the same very mixed results, see T. O. Beidelman, *Colonial Evangelism: A Socio-Historical Study of an East African Mission at the Grassroots* (Bloomington, IN, 1982), pp. 135–6. Wallace G. Mills, "The Taylor Revival of 1866 and the Roots of African Nationalism in the Cape Colony," *Journal of Religion in Africa* 8.2 (1976), p. 118; and Mills, "Missionaries, Xhosa Clergy and the Suppression of Traditional Customs," in Bredekamp and Ross, *Missions and Christianity in South African History*, pp. 153–67.

21. GMS, *Minutes of the Presbytery of Kaffraria*, 13 February 1833, reported that "Maqoma ... thinks that we ought to let the kaffers have our approbation of their services, as they do of ours. At least we ought to let them go on without annoyance, as they don't annoy us in our worship." For the nature of communication and miscommunication in such encounters, see the essays in Stuart B. Schwartz (ed.), *Implicit Understandings: Observing, Reporting and Reflecting on the Encounters Between Europeans and Other Peoples in the Early Modern Era* (Cambridge, 1994), esp. Wyatt MacGaffey, "Dialogues of the Deaf: Europeans on the Atlantic Coast of Africa," pp. 249–67. And, of course, Greg Dening, *Islands and Beaches: Discourse on a Silent Land: Marquesas 1774–1880* (Honolulu, 1980); and Dening, *The Death of William Gooch: A History's Anthropology* (Honolulu, 1994). Ian G. Barber, "Early Contact Ethnography and Understanding: An Evaluation of the Cook Expeditionary Accounts of the Grass Cove Conflict," in Alex Calder, Jonathan Lamb and Bridget Orr, *Voyages and Beaches: Pacific Encounters* (Hololulu, 1999), pp. 156–79. Anne Salmond, *Two Worlds: First Meetings between Maori and Europeans, 1642–1772* (New York, 1992). Isabel Hofmeyr, *The Portable Bunyan: A Transnational History of The Pilgrim's Progress* (Princeton, 2004).

22. My sources for this and the next few paragraphs are Hodgson, "A Battle for Sacred Power"; Hodgson, "Soga and Dukwana: The Christian Struggle for Liberation in Mid Nineteenth Century South Africa," *Journal of Religion in Africa* 16.3 (1986), pp. 186–208; David Dargie, "Christian Music among Africans," in Elphick and Davenport, *Christianity in South Africa*, pp. 68–88, 319–27; and J. B. Peires, "Nexele, Ntsikana, and the Origins of the Xhosa Religious Reaction," *Journal of African History* 20.1 (1979), pp. 51–61. For a study of the different appropriations of a core missionary text by Africans see Isabel Hofmeyr, *The Portable Bunyan: A Transnational History of The Pilgrim's Progress* (Princeton, 2004).

23. WMMS, *Special Series*, Box 9, *Journal of Samuel Young*, ff. 104–8 for the description of his wife's death, and ff. 113–14 for the exchange with the Xhosa.

24. On another occasion John Ayliff was asked where those African ancestors who had not heard about God went after death: could they still go to heaven? It is not surprising that Ayliff found himself stumped by this question, for it remains a matter of dispute between theologians. Fast, "'In at one ear and out at the other,'" pp. 34–5, 161, 166. Cumming, *Diaries*, 6 June 1844.

25. Landau, "Nineteenth-Century Transformations," p. 18.

26. Shrewsbury, *Letters and Selected Journals*, p. 34.

27. WMMS, South Africa, *Incoming Correspondence 1825–30*, Box 2, fiche 1, Shaw to Secretaries, 5 May 1825.

28. Ibid., Box 1, fiche 52, Shaw to Moseley, 11 August 1827. From the internal evidence of this correspondence it is obvious that other letters were exchanged on the issue, but I have been unable to locate them. See also Shrewsbury, *Journals and Selected Letters*, pp. 78–81, 197 n. 108.

29. Ayliff, *Journal*, 8–9 January 1834. Of course, we have no knowledge of the Xhosa calculations that were involved in this exchange. But our concern is not with them; it is with the logic of this cultural maneuver from the missionary side. It is important to note that polygamy was one of those issues that Xhosa prophets like Ntsikana preached against. See Peires, "Nexele, Ntsikana, and the Origins of the Xhosa Religious Reaction," pp. 51–61.

30. LMS, *Transactions of the Missionary Society from Its Institution in the Year 1795 to the End of the Year 1802*, vol. I (1804), p. 427; Govan, *Memorials of … Laing*, pp. 67–8.

31. WMMS, South Africa, *Incoming Correspondence 1830–57*, Journal of Samuel Young, f. 152, 10 June 1832. Not that it had much effect. A day later the dancing started again, although some people came to Young to ask for the talisman of the Xhosa hymn to ward off attacks by evil spirits as a result.

32. GMS, *Minutes of the Presbytery of Kaffraria*, 6 April 1842.

33. Henry Calderwood, *Prayer: The Christian's Stronghold and Means of Triumph* (Cape Town, 1842), pp. 23–5; Rev. Thornley Smith, *South Africa Delineated* (London, 1850), p. 129.

34. Laing, *Journals* 23–24 December 1831. This whole episode is fraught with fascinating possibilities. It is likely that all this was orchestrated by the Xhosa, who were masters of this form of psychological warfare. The time of the year, for example, was significant. Maqoma and the others would have known that to ratchet up the tension at Christmas would disturb the missionaries. Part of Laing's distress may have been a reluctance to lose Charles Henry at all, but especially at this time of the year.

35. WMMS, Special Series, Box 9, *Journal of Samuel Young*, f. 117; Basil Holt, *Joseph Williams* (Lovedale, 1954), pp. 79–82.

36. We can only imagine how much worse this must have been for missionary wives. Few traces of *their* mental state remain in the records that I have consulted. An unusual confession of this kind of despair – which was probably overlain by more personal troubles, however – occurs in a letter from Margaret Anderson to Elizabeth Williams, which speaks of how the "zeal that animated my heart when I left my native country, which had burned in

my breast from childhood, no longer exists and everything is become a toil and a burden." See Karel Schoeman, *"A Thorn Bush that Grows in the Path": The Missionary Career of Ann Hamilton, 1815–1823* (Cape Town, 1995), p. 58.

37. Rev. William Impey, *Journal 1838–1847*, 1, 3, 6 January 1839, CL, MS 15109. These moods must have posed serious difficulties in a place like the eastern Cape, on the very edge of the world and without access to much therapy of the sort one could seek in Britain, with family and friends, for example.

38. Shrewsbury, *Journal and Selected Letters*, pp. 75–6, 133. There is a mystery as to why successive waves of missionary recruits, at least to the eastern Cape into the 1850s, continued to fall into this pattern. Each one had to learn to limit and restrain his or her expectations. I think that it was only after the 1850–3 war that this began to change.

39. CWM, LMS, South Africa, *Incoming Correspondence*, Box 19, folder 2, Calderwood to Tildman, 12 June 1843; Cumming, *Diaries*, 13 December 1840; 25 January 1841; 4 December 1840; 3 June 1841; 20, 30 January 1842; 5 May 1843. But after this, things seemed to improve for Cumming; at least he ceased to complain. Perhaps it was the company he got. He was joined by Alexander Campbell in early 1843, and at some point he married and started a family. By mid-1843 he had clearly come to some stoical resolution of his lot: "I began to think of my situation and my difficulties and took courage from the thought that no good object is to be gained by inscribing difficulties – resolved to persevere."

40. CWM, LMS, South Africa, *Incoming Correspondence*, Box 18, folder 1, Kayser, Brownlee and Birt to Directors, 12 April 1841.

41. WMMS, South Africa, *Incoming Correspondence 1825–30*, Box 2, fiche 64, Kay to Secretaries, 3 March 1830. In this letter Kay provides a much fuller account of what he saw as the degradation of Xhosa culture than he provided in his pamphlet *A Succinct Statement of the Kaffir's Case* (London, 1837).

42. GMS, *Minutes of the Presbytery of Kaffraria*, 3 January 1844. He observed the same pattern during a recent relief from the smallpox epidemic.

43. Shrewsbury, *Journal and Selected Letters*, pp. 6, 34, 47, 67; WMMS, South Africa, *Incoming Correspondence 1825–30*, Box 2, fiche 52, Shrewsbury to Townley, 31 December 1826. He remarked how they (i.e. blacks) "are far less …tyrannical towards us, than we are towards them."

44. Shrewsbury, *Journal and Selected Letters*, p. 30; Peter Hinchliff (ed.), *The Journal of John Ayliff*, vol. I: *1821–1830* (Cape Town, 1971), p. 64.

45. WMMS, South Africa, *Incoming Correspondence 1825–1830*, Box 3, fiche 76, Shrewsbury to Directors, 30 September 1830.

46. WMMS, South Africa, *Incoming Correspondence 1830–1857*, Box 3, fiche 90, Shrewsbury to Directors, 11 April 1834, when he speaks of the work of conversion as taking generations and asserts that the "ignorance" of the Xhosa was ingrained and not likely to change even with their children. By this time he is in Grahamstown, ministering to the settler community.

47. Shrewsbury was tough and prickly. Before he sailed for South Africa, the WMMS wrote ahead to William Shaw to warn him of Shrewsbury's difficult temperament. Even his son admitted that his father was rigid, that he tended to discount secular comfort because of his concern for spiritual

well-being, and that he was given to "excessive strictness in the management of the family." Hardly a fond endorsement; more the portrait of a real-life Theobald from Samuel Butler's *The Way of All Flesh*. See WMMS, South Africa, *Incoming Correspondence 1825–1830*, Box 2, fiche 52, Shaw to Directors, 24 August 1826; John V. B. Shrewsbury, *Memorials of the Rev. William J. Shrewsbury*, 4th edn. (London, 1869) pp. 470, 485.

48. WMMS, South Africa, *Incoming Correspondence 1830–1857*, Box 3, fiche 76, Shrewsbury to Directors, 30 September 1830.

49. Ibid., fiche 78, Shrewsbury to Directors, 30 June 1831; reprinted in Shrewsbury, *Journals and Selected Letters*, pp., 142–44. Shrewsbury was not the only missionary to recognize this problem; see Cumming, *Diary*, 5 January 1842: "one great difficulty in speaking to the people is a consciousness that they have no foundation on which my words may be built. When I tell of Christ they know nothing of who he is they do not even know there is a God and what am I to do? … May the spirit of truth lead me into the proper way to reach their hearts."

50. WMMS, South Africa, *Incoming Correspondence 1830–1857*, Box 3, fiche 81, Shrewsbury to Directors, 30 June 1832.

51. Ibid., fiche 78, Shrewsbury to Directors, 30 June 1831.

52. Ibid., fiche 77, Shrewsbury to Directors, 31 March 1831, emphasis added. Again, this was a common perception by missionaries and others that we will consider more fully later on. Clearly, there are better ways of reading this habit of evasion than to attribute it to inherent deceit. But these other ways were not easily available to missionaries like Shrewsbury, because to admit, for example, that Xhosa evasion reflected a reluctance to accept the grip of British religion would be to challenge the very *raison d'être* of British imperial culture.

53. Ibid., fiche 93, Shrewsbury to Directors, 15 January 1835, in which he refers to a letter of 23 September 1834 requesting a return home. I could not find that letter in the collection.

54. Ibid., fiche 93, Shrewsbury, Haddy and Young to Directors, 15 January 1835; Shrewsbury to Directors, 15 January 1835. Note that Smith's request to Shrewsbury for advice was not unprecedented. W. B. Boyce, another Methodist missionary, had earlier been asked for advice by D'Urban, the Governor. See ibid., fiche 89, copy of Boyce to D'Urban, 31 March 1834. Boyce later became an authority on the Xhosa, publishing his *Notes on South African Affairs 1834–1838* (Grahamstown, 1838), an important work in the projection of a settler view of frontier affairs to challenge and displace the missionary view.

55. Shrewsbury, *Memorials*, pp. 408–12, where his son admits the harshness of the recommendations. The memo is to be found undated in GH28/12/1, *Enclosures to Despatches 1833–1838*. See also Shrewsbury, *Journal and Selected Letters*, pp. 173–6.

56. WMMS, extract from minutes of Committee meeting 30 December 1835, which include a copy of a letter from Shrewsbury to the Committee, 24 December 1835, defending his memo. See also Shrewsbury, *Journal and Selected Letters*, pp. 173–6, 215.

57. William J. Shrewsbury, *War, A Means of Advancing the Kingdom of Christ: A Sermon* (London, 1854).

5 Missionaries encounter the chiefs: the growth of colonial reasoning

The chief in missionary culture

On 21 December 1834, between 12,000 and 15,000 Xhosa warriors swept down from the Winterberg mountains across the Kat river, heading to Grahamstown and then through the village of Salem to the sea. The sixth frontier war had begun. When news reached the London Missionary Society missionary Friedrich Kayser that war had broken out, he immediately understood how it threatened missionary dreams. At considerable personal risk, he ventured out into the bush to find Chief Maqoma, whose forces were at that moment beseiging Fort Willshire. Kayser was beside himself, crying and begging Maqoma to return home. It was useless, Maqoma replied, hinting that even if he wanted peace, his younger chiefs would not allow it. When Kayser turned to Maqoma's retinue and urged them to go home, they laughed at him. "*Ilizwe, lifile,*" they cried, "The land is dead." Like all the missions on the frontier, Kayser's was burned; he and his family took refuge in Grahamstown, and, once peace was declared, they had to start all over again.[1]

Kayser knew Maqoma well. All the missionaries knew Maqoma; he was the most talented of Ngqika's many sons. But then the missionaries knew most of the chiefs; often, they were in daily or weekly contact with them. This was not happenstance. The chiefs occupied a very special place in the missionary game plan for Christianizing the Xhosa. They were the gateway for missionary access to Xhosa society and culture, and afforded the most intimate viewings of Xhosa character. The relationship between the chiefs and the missionaries was a key aspect of the cultural and political encounter.

Missionaries had expected to find Xhosa culture shocking. What they found in their experience with the chiefs was, in a sense, more startling. They found minds that were astute, supple, evasive and relentlessly political. In their dealings with the chiefs, missionaries discovered that they neither controlled the terms of the engagement nor determined the negotiating strategy of the relationship. Such a challenge was liable to ignite the psychic volatility that was embedded within missionary culture. But it did more than that. Missionaries had the uncomfortable experience of being bested intellectually and politically by the Xhosa chiefs. Confronting evidence of Xhosa intellectuality, even perhaps Xhosa intellectual superiority, challenged the missionaries' intellectual framework. It undermined the cultural assumption that the Xhosa would not be able to mount much of a challenge to their offer of the Gospel. And in its turn this suggested the need for a new view of the Xhosa in order to understand how this could be so. How did this happen and how did the missionaries respond to this evidence of Xhosa humanity? These are the fundamental questions that this chapter is intended to answer.

What the missionaries knew or thought about the chiefs before they ventured into Xhosaland is not clear. But David Bogue's lectures, which we have referred to previously, probably represent the best general guide to what was in missionaries' heads as they trundled across the bush to their meetings with Xhosa chiefs. Bogue devoted only one lecture to this matter. Significantly, he folded it into a lecture that addressed the *opposition* that missionaries could be expected to face. Bogue possessed the traditional dissenting suspicion of civil rulers whose tendencies were to bolster their own power and constrain liberty. He believed that indigenous rulers would be resentful of a new religion, but if missionaries were likely to arouse the hostility of the civil power, they should do nothing to provoke it. They must obey the laws of the country and not meddle in the political arrangements, and they must stay clear of any political disputes in the tribe. Still, this respect for civil authority went only so far. If the civil order went against God's law, missionaries were obliged to challenge it. And where politics impacted on the mission, it was acknowledged that they could not be avoided.[2]

Bogue's prescriptions were not only contradictory; they were to prove totally unrealistic. They evaded the essential truth that soon became patently obvious to any practicing missionary: the mere presence of the mission was a political fact. Was a mission convert to follow the chief's orders and participate in a circumcision or other cultural ceremony? Was that same convert to follow his chief's orders and report for battle duty? And what about marriage ceremonies? Was the mission native to respond to pressure from the civil society to follow Xhosa custom? These were the kinds of conflicts that missionaries faced on an almost daily basis during this period of their work in the eastern Cape.

Most of all, of course, Bogue's knowledge was not based upon any reliable understanding of the particular local circumstances of Xhosa chieftainship. By the time the missionaries arrived at the eastern Cape, Xhosa society was split into three main groupings. The dominant group were the Rharhabe Xhosa, headed by Ngqika, whose sons were the chiefs we shall meet most often in this book. The next group were the Gceleka Xhosa, whose chiefs were generally regarded as the paramount chiefs among the Xhosa – in our period these were Hintsa and his son Sarhili. And the smallest grouping were the Gqunukhwebe, who were the most concerned of all the units to stay on good terms with the British. The chiefs of all these groups traced their lineage back to Tshawe, who had founded the Xhosa polity sometime in the mid-seventeenth century, although it was Phalo, who ruled from perhaps 1715 to 1775, who produced the sons who then split the tribe into its three main groups.[3]

As this suggests, chieftainship among the Xhosa was hereditary in the sense that their position flowed from their place in a particular lineage and the seniority of their position within a particular clan network. But there was little else about chieftainship that was settled. The relationship between the chief and the people was based upon complex and shifting clan relationships, political loyalties and social reciprocities. The Xhosa polity was never based upon ethnic or geographical belonging; it was a political unit. All who accepted the rule of a descendant of Tshawe were Xhosa. Furthermore, because of intermarriage, and particularly marriage alliances by the chiefs, groups like the Thembu – formally a separate grouping – could at times be brought within the Xhosa polity.

Chiefs were not able, therefore, to count upon loyalty simply because of their chiefly lineage. The political allegiances within the Xhosa were complicated and shifting. Chiefly authority was not precisely or clearly defined, although the respect owed to clan leaders because of their seniority was well established. The chief operated within a well-established system of law and custom. But his power rested ultimately upon the numbers of people who were willing to accept his rule, and this in its turn rested upon his ability to retain their loyalty. A chief who was unable to protect his people or who tried to establish a tyrannical dominion would soon lose that loyalty. In this case, the commoners would vote with their feet and either form a new grouping or transfer their allegiance to a rival chief.

Thus, the Xhosa polity was always inherently unstable. Chiefdoms were in constant motion. There were possibly nine Xhosa chiefdoms by 1800; the Thembu were about to split into two in the 1850s before they were brought under colonial rule. Rivalry between brothers and half-brothers was endemic. Indeed, such tension was built into the Xhosa conception of chiefship. It was the tradition that the eldest son of the chief's great wife would be his heir. But the great wife was usually the last wife the chief took before he died. Thus, the heir would not only likely be one of the youngest sons; he would also be surrounded by half-brothers jostling for their position. Some of these would go off and form their own groupings. But some, like the notorious Chief Mhala, would stay around their father's kraal and become a focus for intrigue and opposition.

The power of the Xhosa state was therefore inherently weak. The more it expanded through splits, the weaker it became, and the more opportunities were created for tense rivalries. This tendency to fissiparousness was particularly acute from the beginning of the nineteenth century. Ngqika, for example, fell into a serious power struggle with his uncle Ndlambe, which was made worse by his seduction of Ndlambe's young wife. Just at the moment when the centrifugal divisions within the Xhosa were at their strongest, the British presence was to pose the greatest threat to their independence. It was a terribly important context for this confrontation that Xhosa society was cross-hatched with divisions and tensions. The response of the Xhosa chiefs to the British was, therefore, variable and changing. It depended not only upon the relative position of the clan or grouping within the larger Xhosa polity, but also upon the changing politics of competition within the polity. Unity was impossible, even though some valiant efforts were made to achieve it. Each group would make their own accommodation or otherwise with the British. Of course, this suited the British just fine.

None of this was obvious to the missionaries as they arrived in south Africa. It was not part of what the British knew about the Xhosa. Indeed, the chaotic complexity of Xhosa politics was a major reason why the British found the Xhosa so difficult to deal with. Nevertheless, from the very beginning the missionaries had a great deal invested in their relationship with the chiefs. They were dependent on the chiefs for their living space and for the basic necessities of life. They needed the chief's support for access to the tribe. The hopes for rapidly converting the Xhosa rested in large part on evangelizing the chiefs. They believed that if they could convert individual chiefs, the tribes would follow. This, however, was not necessarily true. Those few chiefs who did convert merely added a new element of difficulty and instability into their tribal politics. The problem for the missionaries, then, was that their relationships with the chiefs were anything but straightforward. Following the tensions that surrounded the chiefs in their Xhosa polities, the missionaries' relationships with the chiefs were complex, contingent and ambiguous.[4]

A complex and ambiguous relationship

There were four major flashpoints in the relationship between missionaries and the chiefs: the tangled relationship of the missionaries to tribal politics; the way the missionaries' presence and programs disrupted internal lines of authority within the tribe; the status of the missionaries with the imperial state; and finally the constantly changing balance of advantage and disadvantage that missionaries presented in the internal and external politics of the tribe.

Although the social theory of missionary culture prescribed avoiding politics, it was impossible for missionaries to escape tribal politics, or to clearly define their relationship with the imperial state. Johannes van der Kemp spent most of his time with Ngqika in 1800 trying to manage the cloud of political suspicion that surrounded his sudden appearance on the scene. Van der Kemp's timing was unfortunate. Ngqika was in the middle of a power struggle with Ndlambe, and he was not sure of the British position. So he was naturally suspicious that van der Kemp was a British spy, especially because soon after the missionary arrived a frontier official turned up at Ngqika's kraal with a message from the British that the Governor wanted a meeting to settle border frictions.[5]

Van der Kemp was probably the last person the imperial administration would be willing to entrust with official agency. But no responsible chief could afford *not* to be suspicious of the missionaries. And they had good cause. Missionaries were not conscious agents of empire, but they were an available resource the imperial state could use to slake its growing thirst for insight into what the Xhosa were doing. In the 1820s the commander of the frontier forces, Colonel Lord Henry Somerset, built a network of contacts and informants among the missionaries. John Brownlee, one of the first London Missionary Society missionaries, had served for a while as a government agent. Later, several prominent missionaries became full-time government agents. And Thomas Jenkins, a Methodist missionary with the Pondo Chief Faku (who throughout this whole period remained outside of formal British control) from 1838 to 1868, was deeply involved in the politics of Pondoland, and also the principal conduit of information and exchange between the chief and the imperial authorities. Missionaries had constant contact with the frontier officials, and they were expected to offer advice and pass along information as required. So the chiefs never quite knew for certain where they were with the missionaries.[6]

By contrast, tribal politics was disrupted by the missionary presence. Missionaries challenged the established system of authority in the tribe in a variety of ways. Their mission stations were refuges for the disaffected and deviants of the tribe, aside from those, like Mtawa, who seemed ready to throw in their lot with missionary culture. And since the cultural practices that the missionaries disliked were inseparable from the structures of civil authority in the tribe, their social proselytizing could easily turn into a direct attack on the authority of the chiefs. Nor was this simply a matter of high political principle; it extended into the very intimacies of family relations.[7]

Gender and sexual lines of authority were especially vulnerable to missionary influence. Christianity was particularly attractive to Xhosa women, and the kinds of difficulty this posed for the chiefs were illustrated by the case of Vena, a Christian daughter of a counselor to Sandile. On the occasion of her marriage in 1844, she expressed a wish to follow Christian marriage practices rather than those of the Xhosa, even though she was marrying a non-Christian. The missionaries, of course, were fully in favor of this and appealed to the imperial state to intervene with the chief and to press him to allow his daughter to abandon Xhosa practice. Sandile's reply to the sympathetic diplomatic agent, Charles Stretch, pointed out the difficulty this created for him. He was committed to having missions in his country, and he wanted to protect them, but it had to be acknowledged how this kind of issue exposed the limits of the chief's power. There was a strong sentiment among his people to "follow the customs of their fathers"; furthermore, Sandile revealingly explained, the chief was not like "your Governor," who, "if he speaks he is obeyed." Ultimately, Vena had her way, but only after a meeting of the chiefs' counselors approved her returning to the mission.[8]

Conversion to Christianity created competing loyalties. The boundaries of tribal identity were always porous and unstable. Tribes frequently changed their composition and allegiance, splitting and dividing into new groups. Chiefs therefore were very sensitive to the possibilities of secession, since it was the principal way populations expressed their displeasure with a particular polity. The chiefs had a far more realistic appreciation of the complexities of the relationship with the missionaries than the missionaries themselves, who saw it through a simplified prism of the degree of acceptance of Christian culture. In most cases missionaries ignored or did not allow for the inherent complexities of the relationship. As they preached against the cultural customs integral to the system of social and political authority of the tribes, the missionaries subverted the systems of chiefly power. The missionaries threatened to split the tribe by providing refuge for those who were at odds with tribal authority, or who associated themselves with the mission presence and therefore posed an implicit ideological and political pole of opposition and difference. Who knew where the loyalties of the missionaries really lay? Whenever war threatened or broke out, most missionaries packed up and rushed into Grahamstown, even though it was unusual for their persons to be threatened. Still, if all this was the downside of the missionary presence, there were some advantages for the tribal chiefs.[9]

Missionaries could be used as intermediaries and as protectors. At least they might enable chiefs to better understand the enigmas of the imperial state. Joseph Williams accompanied a nervous Ngqika to meet Governor Somerset at the Kat river in 1817. Ngqika crossed the river clinging to Williams's arm as they advanced to meet the imperial party. Similarly, in the early 1830s, when Maqoma was dragged by a drunken and abusive sergeant from the Kat river settlement, where he had come at James Read's invitation to address a meeting, he begged Read to accompany him to Fort Hare for fear of being killed by the soldiery. Just having a missionary station in one's territory was a way of demonstrating that the chief was not unfriendly to the British presence. It also served the useful purpose of having an interlocutor on hand to deal with imperial officials and others when needed. In the early days of their relationship in the late 1830s, Maqoma always went to Henry Calderwood when he had trouble with the Colony. And even though Calderwood was at pains to tell Maqoma that he had nothing to do with the Government, and was there only to preach the word of God, Maqoma would cleverly ask who else he could go to, and who better than a servant of a God, who had one heart for all men.[10]

Missionaries were always part of the official events that the imperial state staged to declare a new frontier policy, to negotiate some adjustment to the frontier line, or to address the persistent problem of stock theft and rustling. Missionaries were therefore endowed with a certain prestige and status, and it was perfectly rational for the Xhosa to view with skepticism their claims to be independent of the state. Furthermore, having a missionary attached to the kraal possessed certain status advantages. Bhotomane told Richard Birt, for example, that "all the chiefs who have missionaries are made great men and do not go about in a kaross." It marked you out as a chief worth visiting and converting, and it also held the promise of lubricating relations with the imperial state.[11]

Navigating evasion and learning colonial reasoning

The missionaries first encountered the chiefs as negotiators. It was not a happy experience. Negotiating to settle in a chief's territory and begin to evangelize was seldom a simple matter. Missionaries found the chiefs evasive and elusive negotiators. Why should we care much about this? Surely it could be seen as just another chore for the burdened missionary as he lugged his baggage across the bush to find a place where he could build a weatherproof shelter with suitable access to water and a food supply chain to feed his party? The reason this is an interesting matter is that it allows us to glimpse the missionary's cognitive responses to the Xhosa. We can access the *reasoning* processes that were ignited in the missionary minds by this kind of encounter, how they absorbed the challenges the chiefs presented to them, and how they then came to conclusions about what kind of people the Xhosa *really* were. The experience of negotiating a settlement was one of the roots of the notion that the Xhosa were inherently evasive and deceitful. *It was an example of how colonial reasoning was* _produced_. It is therefore a matter of considerable historical interest and importance.

Navigating the evasiveness of the chiefs was a problem from the beginning. James Read and Joseph Williams had trouble bringing Ngqika to the table to negotiate a place to settle. Ultimately, he was driven to accept them only by the sense that if he turned them down, they would go to his arch-rival Ndlamble. In any case, this pattern repeated itself a few years later, in 1827, when William Shaw decided to set up a mission at the great place of Hintsa, chief of the Gceleka Xhosa.[12]

William Shaw was the Superintendent of the Wesleyan Methodist Missionary Society missions in the eastern Cape. He spent many years in Grahamstown, where the local Methodist chapel in the main street still bears his name. He had originally been sent out to minister to the 1820 British settlers, but he had quickly decided that the Xhosa were in greater need of his ministrations. This was a most debatable proposition. Nevertheless, in 1823 he set off with his wife to live with the Gqunukhwebe Xhosa (Phato and Khama's people), who occupied the land between the Keiskamma and Buffalo rivers. He made a promising start here by converting Khama and his wife; the latter was also Ngqika's sister.[13]

Shaw was an ambitious man. He formulated the dream of a string of Methodist missions stretching into Pondoland and beyond. The big prize in this project was Hintsa, the most important chief of the Xhosa on the frontier. Winning him over would open the way to the rest. In 1827 Shaw took advantage of the recent arrival of William Shrewsbury to approach Hintsa with the idea of a mission. His account of the subsequent events is the fullest description of the process of negotiating with the chiefs. It is therefore worth following in some detail. His account illustrates the complexities of the missionary encounter with the chiefs. It throws light on how difficult it was for missionaries to accommodate this experience.[14]

Shaw had been pressing Hintsa for some time to accept a missionary. He had visited him for the first time in April 1825, and then again on the occasion of Hintsa's marriage to wife number eight in December 1826. Each time, Hintsa put him off. In December 1826, he told him that he needed to consult with Ngqika, Phato and Ndlamble. In March 1827, Shaw tried to short-circuit Hintsa's evasions by taking Shrewsbury with him on a visit to Ngqika, figuring that if he approved, this would clear the way with Hintsa. But they received no satisfaction from Ngqika either. Shaw and Shrewsbury were kept waiting for several days, and when he did grant an interview, he was "unwilling to say much on the subject." Even worse, when he did deign to speak, it was to throw the decision back to his counselors and chiefs, saying that he needed their advice because of the importance of the issue. But since this meeting could not take place for two weeks, Shaw and Shrewsbury decided not to stay around, and left.

It is pretty clear that Ngqika was giving them the run-around. A month after they had left they were summoned back again. Rushing up to Ngqika's great place, they were horrified to find a circumcision ceremony in progress. Surely this was no accident. Ngqika's next move was an obvious insult. He requested that they write to William IV requesting that he send Ngqika a "handsome white woman for a wife." One can only imagine the shock that Shaw and Shrewsbury registered at this unconventional request (though it was not the last time that such a solicitation was to be made by a chief). But they recovered enough to launch a diatribe against polygamy before Ngqika was called away on business.

Shaw and Shrewsbury were then called to a meeting of chiefs and counselors, who questioned them as to what they had heard from Hintsa. A debate ensued. The missionaries found this all very tiresome, and at the end Ngqika summed up the discussion by announcing that he would send a messenger to Hintsa. Although he would always welcome missionaries, he would not formally advise Hintsa to receive the missionaries. It was the job of the missionaries themselves to "go to that Chief, and let Hintsa say, from his own heart, whether he [the missionary] must remain or go away." To add insult to injury, Shaw was then approached by Ngqika with a request for beads and brandy. When Shaw refused both, Ngqika got enraged.

The missionaries were getting nowhere using the methods of consultation and diplomacy. Chaffing under these circumstances, the brash and forceful Shrewsbury decided to take matters into his own hands. It was agreed that he would go into Hintsa's territory and set up camp at Butterworth, Hintsa's great place. He and Shaw set out, probably in the middle of May. But their journey was not an easy one. Their wagons kept breaking down. More seriously, their reception from the Xhosa was hardly reassuring. The first time they had trekked to visit Hintsa, they had traveled through empty countryside, all the people avoiding contact. This time, the landscape was full of people, but they were hardly welcoming. The missionaries were constantly surrounded, almost jostled all the way, and when they tried to preach they were laughed at and derided. The turbulence of their reception was such that they appealed to the various chiefs along the way to keep their people in order.

Fighting their way through these unsettling throngs, they arrived at Hintsa's place to find him gone. One of his counselors told them that he would not give them permission to build until the great men of the tribe advised him to accept them. They then had a meeting with his counselors, who questioned them closely about God and resurrection. Hintsa still did not appear. Nevertheless, it must have been apparent that no active opposition would be mounted to their presence, and after a week or so Shaw left and Shrewsbury started to build. By the end of June, Hintsa had still not appeared or sent word, but work proceeded unhindered, and William Shepstone – a member of another family of 1820 settlers – was sent to lend a hand to Shrewsbury.

Hintsa finally recognized the mission in October of 1827, two years after it had first been broached. And he did so because the politics of the frontier were heating up again. There was internal tension within the Xhosa polity, there was instability on the northern boundaries with Pondoland (what used to be called the *mfecane*), and a large body of imperial troops had appeared on the border in case the disturbances reached into the Colony.[15] Hintsa clearly felt it a wise moment to do something that might appease the imperial administration, while affording him a degree of protection. Still, this was the breakthrough that Shaw and the other Methodists had been working for. Hintsa's acceptance cleared the way for the other chiefs. By October, Shrewsbury had already made contact with a Thembu chief over 100 miles away, and the string of stations that Shaw envisioned was about to become reality.[16]

What precisely did William Shaw make of all this? What conclusions did he draw from this long, protracted negotiation? The simple answer is that he did not know *what* to make of it. Beyond the most superficial level, he found it difficult to mold these events into a coherent narrative of understanding. At one point he recounted how he had tried to mobilize the lesser chiefs to signify their approval to Hintsa of his request. But he found they were unwilling to declare themselves, and referred him to statements that Hintsa had made to the Landdrost several years ago indicating that he was willing to receive missionaries. When Shaw prevailed upon Phato and Ndlambe to send messengers to Ngqika signifying their willingness to give Hintsa their approval, he was shocked to find Ngqika (who had requested the message) refusing to receive the messengers for purely frivolous reasons.

This led Shaw to his one moment of reflection as to what was going on. In his mind he could only process the Xhosa behavior as mere guile and wile. He could only wonder that among such a people "in the rudest state of society" there was so much "craft and policy." And how did he resolve the contradiction that stared him in the face – the contradiction, that is, between the truth that the Xhosa were successfully tangling him up in negotiating knots and the "fact" of their rude state of society? He resolved it against all the logic of what he saw, and even against the logic of what he wrote. He resolved it with a collection of incompatible and illogical statements about the government of Xhosa society. He explained to himself that his negotiating experience flowed from the "arbitrary and despotic" character of Xhosa government, where "all parties from the highest to the lowest are usually cautious [lest] they incur responsibility." It was a reflection of Shaw's mental confusion that he did not seem to recognize the logical difficulty of his explanation. How could a society with such a high degree of consultation be at the same time arbitrary and despotic?

What Shaw had *really* received was a lesson in Xhosa civics. In particular, part of what he had been privileged to observe was the democratic nature of Xhosa government. He had watched attempts by the various parties to find a consensus agreement. It is not clear why that had proved so difficult. But whatever the reason, Shaw had been treated to the *complexity* of Xhosa politics. Yet Shaw did not allow that to inform his conclusion about the event. Everything was reduced to the categories of "despotism," "arbitrariness," "deceit," and the disordered state of Xhosa society.[17]

This vision, of course, was reinforced by his response to the cultural practices that he observed while visiting Ngqika's place, and his outrage at being asked to arrange for a white wife. He did not ask himself *why* the Xhosa were giving him such a run-around; he did not consider the implications of his demand for a mission to the internal and external politics of Xhosa society. Once again, a glance around him could have led him to appreciate that in the time of turmoil that surrounded the Xhosa – with the *mfecane* to the north of them, and the British to the south; with rivalries between Ngqika and Ndlambe – it was not at all clear to the Xhosa that the missionaries would be an advantage sitting at Butterworth. Could the missionary presence add yet another level of instability into an already unstable political environment?

All of these were alternative questions Shaw could have asked in order to process his experience. *But the point is that he did not ask them.* His reasoning was a nice example of colonial reasoning – in this case, the inability of Shaw to imagine an autonomous world of the Xhosa outside of his own narrow terms of reference. Shaw's experience with Hintsa and the rest was not unique. Nor was the way his encounter with these Xhosa chiefs disturbed the missionary mind. It is worth taking a close look at another event which demonstrates how the etiology of colonial reasoning was triggered, taken, this time, from the missionaries of the Glasgow Missionary Society.

Sometime in 1828, the Thembu chief, Vusani, expressed an interest in having a missionary attached to his tribe. In late 1829, John Ross and Alexander McDiarmid, two Glasgow missionaries at Burnside, were sent to negotiate with him. By then Vusani's interest had faded, perhaps because the threat from the *mfecane* had dissipated, perhaps because the politics of the tribe had shifted. In any case, when Ross and McDiarmid arrived, they were met with a barrage of reasons from Vusani as to why it would *not* be a good idea for them to settle with him. They would be robbed of their cattle;

he could not go on commando raids if they were with him; he could not protect them and then he would get a bad name. He was by turn surly, evasive and welcoming. But at every point he managed to block or to disrupt Ross's argumentation.[18]

He somehow maneuvered Ross into the position of agreeing that the missionaries would help him with his enemies. Although it is not clear what was meant by that, its implications could be serious. It was not unknown for missionaries to take an active role in supporting their chief and tribe, even to the extent of seeking to obtain guns for them to defend themselves. Moffat had done as much to help the Tswana against the Boers. But Vusani then turned this around against Ross, to suggest the worthlessness of missionary protection. He asked how it was that other chiefs who had accepted God's word continued to be harassed by military commandos. Ross's reply can hardly have comforted him; Ross answered that perhaps those other chiefs had not really accepted God in their hearts! What must Vusani have made of this piece of specious reasoning? Then McDiarmid made a serious strategic error. He tried to put an end to all this backing and forthing, to cut through the verbiage to ask if they could not just start to build their mission and resolve these difficulties later. Ross immediately recognized the mistake McDiarmid had made and he tried to retrieve the situation. But it was too late. Vusani was being forced to choose. He said no and told them to go home.

Two things are interesting about this exchange, as it was recorded by the missionaries. The first is that the missionaries were clearly bested by the chief in negotiation, and by the chief and his counselors in argumentation. Ross recounted a meeting with the tribal council at which they were challenged on religious matters. He admitted that they were effectively interrogated by questions "some of them very pertinent, others not [but] all of them however apparently intended to draw me off from the subject." Whether pertinent or diversionary, we have here the specter of two British missionaries struggling to keep up in debate with some Xhosa "savages." This kind of intellectual challenge was not an unusual occurrence in the world of the missionary–Xhosa encounter. Nor were the cognitive effects on the missionaries unique. Ross's internal mental gyroscope was thrown off course by this exchange.

Ross's account of this confrontation is notable for its befuddlement and confusion. It is marked by a failure of internal logic similar to that of Shaw's attempt to explain his dealings with Hintsa. Like Shaw, Ross's report is marked by disjuncture and inconsistency. On the one hand, the rough ride the missionaries received at the meeting of counselors exposed the sharp internal debate in the tribe about a possible missionary presence. Ross could not ignore the political pressures on Vusani. At one point he noted that Vusani appeared to be afraid of the disapproval of his counselors, which suggests that the missionary understood very clearly how the chief was restrained by hostile public opinion in the tribe. But Ross did not reason from these perceptions. When he finally came to offer an explanation of why the negotiations collapsed and he and McDiarmid were forced to withdraw to Lovedale, however, Ross failed to draw the logical conclusion: that the chief was not a free actor in this decision, that he *was* subject to an internal democracy in the tribe. Instead, the chief's explanation for his decision to turn the missionaries away – that public opposition made anything else impossible – became for Ross a subterfuge, an artifice that exposed Vusani's inherent deceitfulness. And to satisfy himself that this was indeed true, Ross used *his* logic to expose Vusani's deceit. Thus, as the missionaries prepared to leave, he asked Vusani point blank exactly *when* his people decided against the missionaries. Vusani replied that it was at the time of Somerset and Dundas. Both names were associated in Xhosa memory with aggressive frontier policies. Ross, however, seems not to have appreciated the subtlety behind this reply. He probably did not know the history; why should he? Using *his* logic, it merely proved the point that Vusani was arguing speciously, and Ross refuted it with the remark: "But you asked for Teachers after that time." To which Vusani replied with silence.[19]

Experiences like this left the missionaries in a quandary. As both these episodes suggest, it was not within the scope of missionary culture or reasoning to allow the possibility that Xhosa politics governed the shifting tides of the chiefs' interactions with the missionary project. They were therefore left with the conclusion that the chiefs' behavior was a mirror of Xhosa culture and character. In that mirror, the missionaries saw only deceit and deception. Ironically, any further interactions with the chiefs that demonstrated their intellectuality and cleverness served only to reinforce missionary perceptions of the Xhosa personality as dark and cunning. The stories of John Weir's experiences with Chief Mhala and of Henry Calderwood's ordeal with Chief Maqoma provide stark examples of how this worked.

Mhala and Weir

John Weir was a Glasgow Missionary Society missionary who had been assigned to evangelize Mhala's tribe. Weir was another one of those earnest, self-educated Scottish artisan missionaries who were so prominent in missionary endeavors in this period. His attempts to establish himself with Mhala in the early 1840s were frustrated by the chief's clever hostility, and he was eventually driven out. Thanks to the interest the imperial state took in Mhala, we know much more about him than we do about John Weir. And it is worth saying a few words about Mhala here because he will figure prominently at a later stage in our story of the encounter between the British and the Xhosa.

Mhala was a son of Ndlambe, Ngqika's great rival. Unsurprisingly, Mhala always had uneasy relations with Sandile, Maqoma and the other Xhosa chiefs who were from Ngqika's blood line. Even within his own branch of the Rharhabe Xhosa, Mhala's own legitimacy to chieftainship was always contested. It was rumored that he was not really Ndlambe's son.[20] But using a combination of ruthlessness and talent, he climbed the greasy pole of Xhosa politics and established himself as a power to be reckoned with. "Mhala" means "wild cat," and his elusiveness and cunning gave substance to his name. Of all the chiefs, he was the least willing to ingratiate himself with the imperial state. Mhala got away with a studied insolence that no other Xhosa chief could manage. He made sexual advances to a white woman with an offer to purchase her; and he had the reputation of a master stock thief. By these standards, stifling the hapless J. Weir was child's play. Ironically enough – although with this chief, one suspects that there was no irony involved, but rather deliberate artifice – the issue he used to paw Weir around was horse theft.

The prologue to the story is unknown, and the sources do not reveal exactly how Weir had come to settle in Mhala's territory. But in October 1841, Weir's horse was stolen. Weir sought assistance from Mhala, as was commonplace in such cases. What would typically happen next was that the chief would either offer compensation or put the word out for the return of the horse. But Weir received no cooperation from Mhala. And thus began a six-month saga orchestrated by Mhala with the clear intent of sabotaging Weir's ability to function as a missionary. Mhala's tactics were designed to disorient Weir. Instead of treating him in a straightforward, consistent way, Mhala subjected Weir to a shifting and arbitrary series of contradictory responses and actions. He refused to deal with Weir, using the excuse of fear of the smallpox that had recently been raging through the district. Then, when the horse was spotted being ridden by one of Mhala's brothers, he refused to assist in the search for the horse. Indeed, he demanded a ransom for arranging the return of the horse. Then he claimed that he had found the horse at a Mfengu bar, then that the horse was lost again. In February he sent Weir a horse with the demand that Weir stop accusing Mhala of having stolen the horse. Weir had never accused Mhala of doing this, and he refused to accept the horse Mhala was offering under these conditions. But Mhala would not let that go. He continually returned to it as a demand for the return of the horse. Mhala had succeeded in placing Weir in the role of culprit rather than victim.[21]

Weir was already seriously out of his depth. And his narrative now became less and less coherent. Mhala was messing with Weir's head and succeeding in destabilizing the worthy missionary. And then the cycle of evasion and obfuscation began all over again. At one point Mhala reported that the horse was found. When Weir went to get it, he found it was not his horse, and in response Mhala again accused Weir of branding him as a thief. Then a thief was produced, who verified that the horse was the one he had stolen from Weir. Mhala offered Weir the horse, but Weir rejected the offer, denying that the horse was his. A few days later, Mhala sent a delegation to Weir demanding to know if Weir had told one of his men that Mhala had given his horse away. Weir denied that he had said any such thing. But the delegation accused him of having called Mhala a thief and demanded payment of a fine. When he refused, they warned him that the surrounding people knew where his cattle were, with the obvious threat that they would take some.

At this point, Weir made his way to Burnside by way of Mhala's kraal, where a tremendous altercation took place about Weir's right to be in that part of the country. Mhala also told him he could not leave without paying a fine – although it is not clear what the fine was for: perhaps to settle the charge that he had accused the chief of being a thief. Intellectually and emotionally, Weir was on his last legs, and when a Xhosa commando stopped by his house the next day, he paid the fine. He was then told that the case was finished. Weir threw in the towel and returned to Burnside, confessing that he could remain no longer at his station. Mhala had driven Weir away. He had done so in a way that made it difficult for the imperial administration to accuse him of anything, since he had effectively turned the tables on Weir, accusing him of being the cause of all the turmoil.[22]

This was not quite the end of the matter, however. The presbytery took the question up with Sandile, Mhala's nominal paramount. A committee was appointed to deal with Sandile, and they spent many months trying to get a meeting with him and then trying to get him to do something about Mhala's behavior. This went on at least through April 1843, when the matter disappears completely from the records. The likelihood is that it was quietly dropped. Xhosa tactics of evasion and counter-offensive had effectively outworn missionary persistence.

Indeed, after this event a new tone appears in the minutes of the Kaffrarian presbytery when they comment on the Xhosa. It is a tone which reflects a wave of pessimism washing over them about the missionary project among the Xhosa. And its most significant theme is a tendency to blame the Xhosa for the failures of the missionary. Thus, juxtaposed to the entry in which it was admitted that "Mr. Weir having been compelled by the tyrannical conduct of Umhala to leave the Kwelehra," it was also noted how the Xhosa existed in a sterile moral desert, refusing the word of God. A few months later, in an entry that recorded Sandile's failure to respond to their pleas for help with Mhala, it was reported how, in spite of the evidence of God's displeasure, the Xhosa maintained "an undiminished indifference respecting the revelation which God makes of himself and of his will in his works and in His word; *and they have continued practically to declare that they will not come to Christ that they may have life.*"[23]

Maqoma and Calderwood

At about the same time, another missionary was coming to exactly the same conclusion as he struggled to understand the nature of his encounter with a Xhosa chief. This missionary was the Reverend Henry Calderwood and the chief was Maqoma. The answer Calderwood came to was the answer Shrewsbury had anticipated in 1835. But whereas Shrewsbury was marginalized and disgraced for his answer, Calderwood went on to become a frontier policy-maker. By the mid-1840s, missionary culture was in the process of shifting and the Calderwood–Maqoma encounter was a key event in that process. It is also an event that provides a further example of how the missionary mentality was disturbed by evidence of Xhosa intellectuality.

Like Mhala, Maqoma is a chief who will appear many times in this book. Some facts of his life are, therefore, in order. Maqoma was Ngqika's eldest son, born in 1798, which made him twenty years older than his half-brother Sandile. Maqoma was not the paramount, however, since Sandile had been born to Ngqika's great wife, Suthu. This was one reason why relations between Maqoma and Sandile were always wary. But there were others. Maqoma was regarded as the natural leader of the Xhosa. He was the chief the British feared the most. In part this was because of his abilities as a military leader, first demonstrated in the war of 1834–5. But it was also because of his recognized intellect and bearing. Maqoma was the chief the British took the most seriously. They recognized his leadership potential and his personal abilities at a time when they still had the capacity to respect the Xhosa.[24]

Virtually all the testimony one can find on Maqoma pays tribute to the power of his presence, and to his strength of intellect and mind. He was exactly the sort of chief the missionaries had to snare if they were to convert the Xhosa. If Maqoma would convert, then the example would be a compelling sign of the power of missionary magic to the rest of the Xhosa people. For forty years the missionaries made their best efforts. Their hopes for his conversion died only with his final exile to Robben Island in the 1870s. All the missionaries who worked closely with

Maqoma (and they included some of the leading missionaries on the frontier) experienced the same pattern of signs of hope followed by disillusionment. Maqoma always successfully evaded the avid wooings of his missionary suitors.[25]

What Henry Calderwood was to experience, then, was part of a longer-term pattern. The importance of the story I am about to tell, however, extends beyond that. It provides a further example of the way the dynamics of the missionary–Xhosa encounter rather quickly spiraled out of the political and mental control of the missionaries. But its central significance is that it reveals how the missionary *intellect* could be destabilized by the encounter with the Xhosa chiefs. Just as the Mhala–Weir confrontation illustrates the ability of a chief to politically outmanuever a missionary, so the Maqoma–Calderwood encounter reveals how one Xhosa chief could intellectually best a British missionary. Indeed, as a result of his experience with Maqoma, Calderwood was plunged into a crisis that eventually led him to abandon the belief in a universal humanitarianism that he had brought with him from Scotland, and to embrace an essentialized racism.

Let us turn, then to the events as we know them. Calderwood had arrived at the eastern Cape in 1838 with the latest batch of London Missionary Society missionaries. He was a cut above the average missionary recruit. A graduate of the University of Edinburgh, he had pretensions to theological scholarship that led him to publish a disquisition on the role of prayer. He had other pretensions, too. It was reported that he turned up on the frontier with enormous amounts of baggage, which suggested a somewhat unseemly love of things. Certainly, he soon began to look longingly toward the urban sophistication of Cape Town, for within a few years he seized the opportunity to take a position at the Union Chapel and only reluctantly answered the call to return to his frontier mission.

On his initial arrival at the frontier, however, in 1838, Calderwood established himself at Blinkwater, near to Maqoma, and began to send home reports that overflowed with self-confident schemes and dreams. He settled in, looked around and quickly saw what he needed to do. He had been on the station only a few weeks before he was ready to comment authoritatively on frontier policy and on the Xhosa. He recognized immediately the impossibility of maintaining the distinction between religion and politics, and baldly stated his intention to "stand between the oppressor [i.e. the British] and the oppressed" (i.e. the Xhosa). He had bold plans to found a network of six schools, and to train up a cadre of native teachers, whom he would supervise as they spread out to take the word of God to open the minds of the Xhosa. He had infinite confidence in the power of prayer as sufficient to remove all the obstacles that were presented to Christianization in Africa.[26]

Most of all, he was sure of his growing relationship with Maqoma. He had sized up Maqoma, making inquiry as to how he was regarded, and assessed his political importance both to the British and to the Xhosa. The portrait that he drew of Maqoma was basically favorable. It was consistent with other descriptions – such as those given by Harry Smith in the 1830s – and confirmed that this Xhosa chief was a complex and impressive individual. Calderwood judged him as a human being with the same attributes and potential as Calderwood himself. He described him as thoughtful, with a decided intellect and good sense. Indeed, like Shrewsbury in a different context, he was able to compare him favorably to many of the "white men with whom he comes into contact and who think themselves so superior." He was confident that he could make a difference with this important chief: "there is no man in Caffreland who could do more good, if the grace of God were in his heart. And he is not beyond reach of that grace." Almost immediately he was involved in mediating between Maqoma and the frontier officials, defusing some tension that had arisen over Maqoma's treatment by the court at Fort Beaufort which had fined him some cattle. And he believed that he was reaching Maqoma, who is described as frequently weeping "aloud in public and private when I preached." At this point Calderwood's perspective was consistent with the view of evangelical culture on the essential humanity of this Xhosa chief.[27]

A few months later, the tone of Calderwood's assessment began to change. The occasion was the first serious encounter he had with Maqoma over cultural practices and the first time he felt the full power of this chief's intellect. Calderwood discovered that Maqoma had ordered the infanticide of a child believed to have been conceived by one of his wives from an adulterous relationship. On hearing this, Calderwood steamed up to Maqoma's kraal and publicly condemned him for this crime. What surprised Calderwood was the aftermath. Instead of just taking this condemnation, Maqoma turned it against Calderwood himself. He pursued him back to the mission station, bringing his ten wives with him, and demanded that Calderwood identify his accuser. He denied the charge. Most surprising of all, however, he engaged Calderwood in a long argument, and gave as good as he got. When Calderwood repeated the biblical arguments against adultery and murder, Maqoma replied that Calderwood was defending bad behavior by his wives. Calderwood's account at the time and his recounting of the story twenty years later suggest the deep impact that the episode had upon him.

At the time, he admitted that "we had a long argument [in which] he [Maqoma] made some hard and truly Caffrelike efforts to throw me on my back ... but he did not succeed." In fact, Calderwood's reporting reflected the intellectual confusion we have seen before when missionaries were confronted by intellectually powerful chiefs. His reports to the London Missionary Society were dominated by a defensive and split tone that suggest that Maqoma had succeeded in doing *something*. In one and the same place, Calderwood reported that the trouble with Maqoma was so serious that he might be required to leave Xhosaland. But then he reassured the Secretary of the Society that Maqoma was regaining faith in Calderwood as a friend, and "he appears to have implicit confidence in me and he said he will take no important step without consulting me." And he went on to repeat that there was much that was favorable in Maqoma: he was reassured by an address the chief had given to the Lieutenant Governor at Fort Beaufort, where he "praised the word of God and showed his great respect for the truth of the gospel."[28]

This was not the first time that Calderwood had experienced Xhosa intellect and what the British referred to as the lawyer-like abilities of the Xhosa to argue a point to exhaustion. When he first arrived on the frontier, for example, he reported being engaged in long debates by Maqoma's counselors, who challenged him in argument in ways he had not antici-pated.[29] But after the encounter with Maqoma, something snapped in Calderwood. His description of the encounter in his autobiography (pub-lished in 1858) was consistent with the private letters he wrote at the time to the London Missionary Society. Both accounts reveal how upsetting he found the event. The first thing to note about his account is how the ostensible cause of the conflict – the infanticide – soon dropped out of a central place in the narrative. Indeed, the purported infanticide was largely a rhetorical device. Calderwood either made up the incident, or was acting on rumor. In either case, the root cause of this confrontation came from his mind, not Maqoma's. Still, such an issue served to establish Maqoma's savagery, and highlighted the point that Calderwood ultimately wanted to make about how heathenism was deeply ingrained in the Xhosa. Contextualizing this struggle around such an event was a particularly useful device for public consumption, since it confirmed what was already known about the missionary project.[30]

It was not the horror of such cultural practices that provided the main theme of Calderwood's account. It was rather the matching of these two intellects and Calderwood's insistence that *he* won that formed the center-piece of the narrative. Yet it is quite clear that he did *not* win; or at least he did not win entirely. His unsteady presentation of this incident provides more than a clue to what was truly disturbing about the episode: Calderwood was brought face to face with the Xhosa intellect and the realization that this intellect was not to be moved by the power of his rhetoric.

Calderwood described the contention with Maqoma as "a long, tedious argument [which] it was no easy matter to conduct … in the peculiar circumstances. He is a clever man and his intellect on this occasion seemed whetted for the discussion." Twenty years later he recounted how events such as this reflected "the wit, shrewdness and observation of Maqomo [while also] present[ing] him in the lowest moral aspect." He described himself as feeling weak and faint from the rigors of the encounter. Indeed, he was so weakened by the argument that he found it necessary to call out silently to God for help in meeting Maqoma's arguments. God did not fail him: "I was enabled to be perfectly calm, and sometimes had an answer for him which I felt was not supplied by my own skill or ingenuity." Now here was a remarkable confession. What is Calderwood saying here? That he, a graduate from Edinburgh University, a man of considerable initiative and intelligence himself, had to be furnished by God with arguments about adultery, infanticide and murder with a Xhosa chief![31]

If this was the extent to which Maqoma out-argued him, it was not surprising that Calderwood now began to behave differently. He slipped into the familiar missionary mentality of volatile mood changes, swinging between optimism and pessimism. In August 1840, he confessed how the last year had seen him "cast down, but not destroyed." His initial optimism was now singed with pessimism. "A missionary life is now entirely stripped of its extrinsick [sic] charms to us. [He is referring for the first time in his record to his wife]. The Heathen appears less lovely or inviting than at a distance. But I trust that my dear partner and myself can say with truth that we have a much stronger desire than ever to seek the salvation of man." If this sounded a little forced, it was. Calderwood now entered a period of emotional turmoil, perhaps real clinical depression. He was no longer the self-assured missionary who had arrived on the frontier a year or so earlier. He began to express anguish and doubt about the possibility of missionary work among the Xhosa. He described how he was frequently overcome with "a deep, depressing crushing sense of my utter powerlessness in attempting to reach the heart of the people among whom I laboured," and how at those times the only thing that revived him was to go with his wife out into the bush, where they would pour out their hearts to God amid the mimosa bushes.[32]

Calderwood's judgments became more volatile and erratic. In his correspondence to the home authorities, we may watch his self-confidence draining away. There were moments of optimism and glimpses of the belief in universal humanitarianism that he brought with him on the boat from London. In March 1843, he noted approvingly a sermon by a native teacher which preached that distinctions between people lay in the quality of their souls, not in the color of their skins. But such moments were followed by withdrawal into contemplative pessimism. Thus in the same letter he signaled a retreat from his previously unqualified support for native agency, noting that it "requires to be handled with great care ... it would be very easy to do more harm than good."[33]

Most revealingly, Calderwood's attitude towards Maqoma changed. He began to speak of the chief in far less favorable and less promising terms. After his initial attempt to reassure the London Missionary Society that his relationship with Maqoma had been strengthened by the blow-up, a more qualified tone enters his reports, which signifies that Calderwood was reassigning Maqoma's place on the scale of humanity. Maqoma now began to be seen as irredeemable, while Calderwood occupied a place of moral superiority. Maqoma's drinking began to be highlighted, combined at times with expressions of pity. Thus, Calderwood referred to him as "poor man, intemperate as ever," who was ashamed to meet Calderwood's eyes. But drunk or not, Maqoma still remained capable of turning Calderwood's own logic against him. In response to Calderwood's claim that drink was killing him, Maqoma retorted that British hypocrisy led them to drink privately and secretly behind their lace curtains, and that even people who did not drink got sick and died too! Then, Calderwood began to categorize Maqoma as dishonest and untrustworthy. "His public word is with us. His character and I sometimes fear his private word is against us." Two years later, "I have ceased to hope" for him and ceased to believe in him. By 1846, the transition of Maqoma from honorable man to dishonorable, shifty and untrustworthy native was complete: "I do not place confidence in him myself." A few months later he wrote to the Secretary of the London Missionary Society about Maqoma, saying that "a Caffer sometimes does not mean all that his words convey."[34]

By this time, Calderwood was no longer the enthusiastic young missionary of 1838. Like the other missionaries, Calderwood failed in his attempts to convert Maqoma or to smother the cultural practices he found so abhorrent. Unlike most of the other missionaries, however, he gave up on Maqoma and the Xhosa altogether. In 1846 he left missionary work to join the imperial administration as a tribal commissioner. In that role he was a loud exponent of tough measures and coercive policies. The encounter with Maqoma was the moment when Calderwood began to rethink his position on the Xhosa.[35]

So by the time he came to summarize and explain his missionary experiences to the British public in the 1850s, Calderwood's view of the Xhosa had settled into a set of new certainties. As he explained in his book *Caffres and Caffre Missions*, the liberal attitudes he had held when he arrived in southern Africa had not survived his encounter with the Xhosa. He had once believed in the oppression of the Xhosa and the evils of British control. Now he believed in the necessity of extending British control. He used to believe in the innocence of the Xhosa in causing the frontier wars. He now believed that the reason for the continuing series of wars was that the Xhosa had been insufficiently punished and never properly subjugated.

But the main lesson he had learnt had to do with the character of the Xhosa. They were, he argued, "the very incarnation of selfishness"; they had few scruples, and predatory habits. The heart of his position was that the Xhosa *had* no hearts. Contrary to what he had believed in 1839, their souls were not in fact waiting to receive the word of God. Indeed, their characters were insensate, which explained their cunning and deceitful evasion of missionary efforts to save them for Christ. Their behavior was incorrigible. They were therefore inherently closed to the possibilities of the kind of Gospel message he had brought with him from Britain in 1839. As he put it, in what is the most revealing comment of all, they "may be said to have *refused* the gospel." It was the experience with Maqoma that started this train of thought: "soon after I went to reside near Maqomo, I was painfully made to understand some of the worse features of the social state of Caffraria."[36]

In simple terms Calderwood had become a modern racist. He now saw the Xhosa as *essentially* different. Once the scales had fallen from his eyes about Maqoma, he could realize how Xhosa culture was constructed around deceit and duplicity. Once he had reached that insight, he could understand the difficulties that he and other missionaries had faced in Xhosaland, particularly their failure to convert the Xhosa on the scale they had originally expected. For Calderwood, this could now be explained by the machinations of chiefs like Maqoma – their deceptive cunning and trickery – and by the inherent nature of Xhosa culture and character. Calderwood was thus able to project responsibility for his own depression in the mid-1840s onto the Xhosa. And it was but a small step from here to concluding that the Gospel could not prevail among the Xhosa "while Caffre institutions remain entire." Xhosa culture and custom, the political manipulations and evasions of chiefs like Maqoma, were impermeable to persuasion. The logic of Calderwood's position was that Xhosa institutions and culture needed to be changed by main force. It was a logic he enthusiastically accepted.

Maqoma, Old Soga and the Reverend George Brown

We may end this discussion of missionary encounters with chiefs with another story that featured Maqoma. It is a story that confirms many things we have already suggested about Maqoma himself, and about how missionary culture was destabilized by encounters with chiefly intellects. It is also a story that occurred in the very different conditions of wartime, specifically the eighth frontier war of 1850–3, when Maqoma led the

Xhosa out of their mountain fastness of the Amatolas with the aim of driving the British into the sea. I shall return to the lessons of this war later on. But for now let us focus on the story of how the Reverend George Brown processed his encounters with Maqoma and other Xhosa.

Brown arrived in Xhosaland in July 1849 with the latest team of missionaries from the Glasgow Missionary Society. Brown's arrival had been much anticipated, and a big ceremony was held at the Tyhume mission to welcome him. At first everything went well. The usual pattern of missionary encounter fell into place. Brown was optimistic that the Xhosa could meet his high expectations. He wrote of the Xhosa in a patronizing but not disrespectful way. He testified that they possessed "vigorous intellects and are keen observers and able to reason shrewdly from what they see." He wrote approvingly of a minor chief, Xayimpi, later to become notorious for his role in the murder of British military settlers at the beginning of the war of 1850–3, who engaged him a lively argument. He paid tribute to Xhosa independence of mind, and was willing to excuse their reputation for thievery. He denied that they were barbarians or savages and was optimistic about the prospects of conversion.[37]

But all this was not to last. Brown soon got at cross-purposes with his colleagues. And with good reason. In February 1850, Brown impregnated Janet Chalmers, the daughter of the senior missionary family in the area. They were married in August and a baby boy appeared on 30 November. This was an interesting illustration of the fragilities that existed at the frontier of empire. As can be imagined, however, it caused a mighty row within the missionary community. Brown was exiled to Igqibiri, about 20 miles from Tyhume, and the Glasgow directors sent the Reverend Robert Renton to investigate the affairs of the mission. Brown was already in a difficult position, then, when war broke out in December 1850. As the Xhosa streamed across the border and the mission stations were surrounded by a sea of seething warriors, Brown found himself away from home and cut off from his wife. While trying to catch up with her, he found himself unexpectedly brought before Maqoma.[38]

This seems to have been a contrived meeting at which Maqoma was concerned to humiliate Brown intellectually, for when Brown was brought before him the chief began to interrogate him on the contradictions in missionary behavior. He pointed out how their claims to be men of peace were belied in many cases. "I am doubtful whether any of you be men of peace; Read, I think he is; but look at Calderwood; what have you to say about him – did he not come as a teacher? Now he is a magistrate, one of those who make war."[39] By contrast, Maqoma pointed out, no missionary had died in earlier wars. But this one was different; the feeling on the Xhosa side was so strong that there was sentiment for just killing them all. By his own admission, Brown was very scared by all of this. Even as he was writing a scorching indictment of Xhosa culture four years later, he had this to say about Maqoma: "Naked barbarian though he be, Macomo has a intellectual character, that well entitles him to the consideration of any one capable of estimating man; by this standard he can both give and understand a reason."[40]

In his account of these events, Brown (like Calderwood) kept returning to the enigma of Maqoma. It is as if he was aware that Maqoma did not fit his developing image of the Xhosa as savage and was seeking to understand just where he could fit him into his hierarchy of civilized and barbaric. Like most of the others who came into contact with Maqoma, Brown recognized that he had a strong intellect and a sense of honor, that he despised flattery and wanted people to tell him the truth, and that he was a good judge of character. Brown had a deep view of Maqoma. But this sophistication faltered when it came to explaining Maqoma. He treated the vices that he discerned in Maqoma as canceling out the virtues, rather than as revealing a complicated person caught in a complex situation. He noted that Maqoma had always professed respect for missionary religion as a source of good for his people; yet he also upheld "the customs of heathenism." Ultimately Brown could explain the mass of contradictions in Maqoma only as reflective of the inherent character of the Xhosa.[41]

Brown's experience with Maqoma was a major reason why he was able to rid himself of a "vapid, or rather unnatural sentimentality" about the "poor native," and to understand that Xhosa culture was in reality one of the "dark places of the earth … full of the habitations of cruelty." His experiences during the war of 1850–3 were particularly important in this respect. Like many on the eastern frontier in 1850, Brown was taken by surprise at the outbreak of hostilities. He blamed the Xhosa for his massive ignorance about what was stirring around him in the last months of 1850. His local chief, Stock, had "assured me in the most positive terms that none of the chiefs had any thoughts of war," and urged him to stay on the mission station. Once the war had started, Brown was disoriented by the hostility that he experienced from those he felt he had known. When he returned home to find his wife and child gone, he could get no information even from those who had known her family for thirty years. Other humiliations followed. He watched members of the kraal use his plundered household goods, or take and cook his oxen. Incidents such as these convinced Brown that "deceit appears to be the very basis of the Caffre character, and cupidity the almost only motive under which he is capable of being prompted to action. He cannot live by honesty."[42]

This then became the prism through which Brown now viewed the Xhosa. It is worth listening to Brown's voice because it was ultimately the voice that the colonial encounter fostered within imperial culture. Like Calderwood, Brown was driven to explain his experiences as the result of Xhosa character. The failures of missionaries to secure the kinds of conversions that their universal humanitarianism anticipated was not a failure of missionary culture. It was not a failure, for example, of missionaries to find the right language of communication. It was rather a *deliberate refusal* of the Xhosa to accept God. Both Brown and Calderwood attributed this to their character. "I believe no people have so obstinately refused to embrace the Gospel."[43]

Missionary culture was unable to grasp and understand complexity among the Xhosa. Brown was deeply confused by Maqoma. But he was confused also by other Xhosa who presented similarly challenging personalities. Another example was the father of Tiyo Soga, a man known as "Old Soga." Brown's attitude to Old Soga revealed the inability of missionary culture ultimately to cope with the complexities that the encounter produced both for the missionaries themselves and for the Xhosa.

Soga came from a family of counselors to the Rharhabe paramount. His father had died fighting for Ngqika at the battle of Amalinde in 1818. But the son who became known as Old Soga was a hybrid product of the colonial encounter. On the one hand he fathered the first line of westernized Xhosa intellectuals and, on the other hand, he remained rooted in traditional aspects of Xhosa culture. His life and his circumstances were produced by the tensions, opportunities and contradictions of the colonial encounter. Yet he was more than just a transitional figure. He was an example of the hybridity contained within the colonial encounter, and his life attempted to fuse both cultures, Xhosa and British, without being swamped by either.[44]

Old Soga was a model of Xhosa modernity. He was the first Xhosa to adopt western agricultural methods. He developed an irrigation system for his land, produced goods for the colonial market and paid his workers a wage. He opposed the great Xhosa cattle-killing of 1856–7. And he maintained good relations with certain imperial officials, such as Charles Stretch, Resident Agent with Sandile in the 1830s, and after him Charles Brownlee, the long-time Commissioner with Sandile's tribe.[45]

Soga also professed a Xhosa Christianity. He was a follower of Ntsikana. Although Soga's kraal was placed near to the Emgwali mission, he resisted the attempts of the missionaries to incorporate him into their culture. He refused to attend their mission services, but held his own, at which only the hymns of Ntsikana were sung. To the frustration of the missionaries, he continued to practice traditional Xhosa customs. He was a polygamist, worshiped ancestors, and consulted diviners and witchdoctors at times of personal crisis. On the death of a daughter, and the sickness of a son, he accused a wife and one of his sons of witchcraft just at the moment when the mother was seeking baptism. By the same token, missionary Christianity ran through his family. Two of his sons, Tiyo and Festiri, were educated by missionaries and gravitated into their cultural orbit – although there is some evidence that he was ambivalent about this move. Indeed, Tiyo was educated in Glasgow, married a white Glaswegian, Janet Burnside, and was the first ordained Xhosa minister.[46]

Soga was under no illusions about the brutal side of imperial culture, however. During the 1835 war he did not join the Xhosa, and protected the local mission from attack, even though the missionaries had fled to the protection of military camps. He received no reciprocal courtesy. His kraal was attacked and destroyed, even though (he complained to the missionary William Chalmers) it contained a school and was a place where "I prayed to God and sang praises to God every day." Indeed, in a fine display of Christian charity, Chalmers refused to support Soga's claim for compensation for these losses, because of his religious independence. Old Soga learnt his lesson and in future wars he deliberately kept channels of communication open with the Xhosa. This was especially true in 1850–3, when he served as adviser to Sandile and facilitated a meeting between Sandile and the Reverend Robert Renton, of the Glasgow Missionary Society, at which Sandile made an impassioned critique of imperial policy.[47]

Old Soga remained on the fence in the 1850–3 war. Ultimately, however, he was unable to continue this balance. He opposed the war of 1877–8, surely knowing how it would end, and he remained a non-combatant. But he refused to leave Sandile, as he was pursued by Britain's Mfengu and, like Sandile, he was murdered by them. At that very moment, his grandson, John Henderson Soga, one of the first Xhosa academics in South Africa, was in Glasgow preparing to enter Edinburgh University.[48] So here we have a picture of a man who tried to navigate between the two worlds that defined social, cultural and political existence on the eastern frontier. Like Maqoma, Soga was a man of intelligence and resource. In a way, he was the kind of man whom the missionaries might have expected to find among the Xhosa, for surely, like Maqoma, he confirmed the idea of a universal humanity.

How did George Brown read Old Soga's attempts at a cross-cultural, hybrid existence? The central theme of Brown's account of Old Soga was its failure to acknowledge the complexity that surrounded this man's life or circumstances. Soga's attempts to span the competing worlds and tensions of the frontier were reduced in Brown's account simply to the categories of "guile," "deceit" and "hypocrisy." Now it is, of course, impossible to make an accurate assessment of exactly what Old Soga was doing during this time. Brown described him as playing a double game. But in the context of his whole history, it is likely to have been more complicated than that. And it is exactly those complications that are missing from Brown's report.

Thus, we can note Brown's account of Sandile's visit to the mission in January 1851, when he met Renton and attempted to recruit the mission Christians for his cause. For Sandile, as he made plain in the exchange with Renton on that occasion, this was an issue that went to the heart of the interaction between missionaries and chiefs. It was a matter of political loyalty. What did the missionaries do, Sandile asked, but "come here to take my people from me … [and] teach men they were not to fight, even although their Chief be in danger?" For Soga, too, this question of loyalty was important. At this point he seemed to be playing the role of intermediary between Sandile and the missionaries, and between Sandile and the mission Christians. Thus, Brown described Soga as "wanting to prove his importance" by acting as a go-between. Even though much of the description that Brown provided could be read as evidence for the ambiguities of Soga's role, this was not allowed to qualify the simple terms used to describe him. In recounting an outburst from Soga that challenged the missionaries' claim to a monopoly on the word of God, Brown could put it down only to the hypocrisy of a man "upon whose lips was the name of God so often found when it suited his purpose to assume the character of a man who honoured God." Thus, he wrote about a conversation in which Soga regretted the foolishness of the Xhosa in provoking war. Brown treats this as pure deception: "Language like this in the mouth of Soga, could excite only the disgust and suspicion in the mind of everyone that knew him. He was assuming his favourite, though vilest of characters – hypocrisy and more, not only studying to deceive, but also to draw into some snare the party to whom he addressed himself."[49]

What is notable about these descriptions of Old Soga is that Brown could explain his behavior only by simplifying Soga's character and assigning a bottomless degree of deceit and cunning to it. In the final analysis this was all that was needed to understand Soga or his situation. Brown expressed the direction in which missionary and imperial culture generally was moving in their assessments of Xhosa culture. This was a view that at one and the same time reduced that culture to a series of simple formulations which enabled it to be easily known, but also attributed to it a depth of darkness that could *not* be known.

Conclusion

The encounter with Xhosa cultural practices and Xhosa intelligence triggered a volatility in missionary culture that suggested a displacement of its internal gyroscope. As a consequence, these encounters brought home to the missionaries the need to reassess what exactly it was that they were doing and how they were doing it. At the very least, they needed to reassess how they could secure access to Xhosa culture and the reasons for their failure to penetrate its boundaries. They needed to understand the ability of the Xhosa chiefs to block and best them politically and argumentatively. How did they respond to those experiences? They reasoned through a two-step process which began with their inability to allow these challenges to question their own cultural and ideological beliefs and concluded with the necessity to *project on to the Xhosa* the blame and reasons for the failures of their own worldview. It was the Xhosa who were to blame, because, as Shrewsbury had anticipated, as Calderwood had explained and as Brown concurred, Xhosa hearts had *refused* the gospel.

Let us conclude with a statement by Henry Calderwood at the time of the outbreak of the frontier war of 1846. He recounts here how disillusioned he was at the Xhosa responsibility for the war:

The extent of my disappointment I cannot express ... I bestowed great labour on the station, and experienced no common anxiety; my prospects of usefulness were most inviting; and my heart, full of hope, was set upon that place as likely to be the spiritual birthplace of many. But all these hopes are dashed to the ground in a moment by the ruthless hand of the poor savage. The Lord have mercy upon them and change their hearts. They have inflicted a deep wound on my feelings. Miserable men; they are the greatest sufferers.

What is the psychology that is revealed by this explanation? It is the psychology of wounded narcissism. Calderwood saw Xhosa action as a *personal* affront and insult to him and to the worthiness of his work. Calderwood's narcissism was surely real enough; here he comes close to comparing himself with the sacrifice of Christ. But this kind of narcissistic wound was a characteristic theme of colonial culture. It allowed the responsibility for what went so wrong with the colonial project to be projected firmly upon the colonized. It was the intellectual trick that permits a series of reversals in reality and perception to excuse and justify the imperial project. It is they, the Xhosa, who are not wise enough to see the offerings that Calderwood and his like are bringing to them. *They* are not free enough from their heathenish practices, or from Satan, to be able to open their hearts to God. *They* are responsible for the anger of the colonialist because they are impermeable to colonial reason.[50]

The process that Calderwood was confessing here was at one level a description of a personal failure, a failure of his knowledge system to encompass his own experience. But Calderwood was also testifying to the implosion of missionary culture, which is perhaps why it was accompanied in his case by such personal anguish – calling on God for help, for example, or going into the bush to pray. But if blame for this failure was to be loaded on to the Xhosa, another consequence followed. And this was the need to rethink the discourse of evangelical missionary culture, to reorient it in such a way that it could accommodate what was being experienced. To accomplish this, a new knowledge system about the Xhosa was needed, one that took into account the fact that they refused the missionary message. It is to those questions that we must now turn in the next two chapters.

NOTES

1. For a thorough and detailed narrative of the war see Noel Mostert, *Frontiers: The Epic Story of South Africa's creation and the Tragedy of the Xhosa People* (London, 1992), pp. 655–761. Although there was no single cause of war, it was triggered by the shooting of Xhoxho, a minor son of Nqgika by a British patrol. Xhoxho was not killed, only wounded, but the incident epitomized the disregard the frontier forces had for the chiefs. He was the third in a decade to be shot, and the only one to survive.
2. CWM, LMS, *Home Odds*, Box No. 25, lecture on "Behaviour of Missionaries to Different Classes of People."
3. My account of the nature of chieftainship is taken from Monica Wilson, "The Nguni People," in Leonard Thompson and Monica Wilson (eds.), *The Oxford History of South Africa*, vol. I: *South Africa to 1870* (Oxford, 1969), pp. 116–24; J. B. Peires, *The House of Phalo: A History of the Xhosa People in the Days of Their Independence* (Johannesburg, 1981), chs. 2–4; and John Henderson Soga, *The South-Eastern Bantu* (Johannesburg, 1930), which was the first attempt to write a history of the Xhosa.
4. Cumming, *Diary*, 5 January 1842, for debate with himself as to where to settle; CWM, LMS, South Africa, *Incoming Correspondence*, Box 17, folder 1, Kayser to Board of Directors, 12 February 1840, for the importance of settling next to a chief.
5. LMS, *Transactions*, vol. I, pp. 395–427.
6. See Timothy Stapleton's very informative biography, *Faku: Rulership and Colonialism in the Mpondo Kingdom (c. 1780–1867)* (Waterloo, Ont., 2001).
7. Natasha Erlank, "Re-examining Initial Encounters between Christian Missionaries and the Xhosa, 1820–1850: The Scottish Case," *Kleio* 31 (1999), pp. 14–17, 20–2.
8. CA, GH14/2, *Papers Received from Native Tribes, Diplomatic Agents and Government Officials, 1844–1845*, Stretch to Montague (secretary to the Governor) 20 and 23 December 1844. For the gender implications of missionary intervention in the tribes, see Natasha Erlank, "Gendered Reactions to Social Dislocation and Missionary Activity in Xhosaland, 1836–1847," *African Studies* 59.2 (2000), pp. 205–27.
9. See CWM, LMS, South Africa, *Incoming Correspondence*, Box 29, folder 2, Birt to Thompson, 31 August 1854, for an example of the tensions set up between a convert and his tribe. This was an example from 1840 which Birt included in this document. Some missionaries did appreciate the complexities; Stephen Kay was one; see Rev. William J. Shrewsbury, *The Journal and Selected Letters of*

Rev. William J. Shrewsbury 1826–1835, ed. Hildegarde Fast (Johannesburg, 1994), p. 9, for a citation that illustrates this. See also Donovan Williams, *Umfundisi* (Lovedale, 1979), p. 83; Monica Hunter [Monica Wilson], *Reactions to Conquest: Effects of Contacts with Europeans on the Pondo of South Africa*, 2nd edn. (London, 1961), p. 428. W. D. Hammond-Tooke, *The Journal of William Shaw* (Cape Town, 1972), pp. 82–3, for the example of Phato being offended because a woman he wanted as a wife was married in a Christian ceremony by Shaw, who also took the opportunity to preach against polygamy.

10. Basil Holt, *Joseph Williams* (Lovedale, 1954), pp. 57–60; for the Calderwood–Maqoma exchange see CWM, LMS, *South Africa Correspondence*, Box 17, folder 1, Annual Report from Blinkwater, 1840; Timothy Stapleton, *Maqoma: Xhosa Resistance to Colonial Advance 1798–1873* (Johannesburg, 1994), pp. 73–4.

11. Celia Sadler (compiler), *Never a Young Man: Extracts from the Letters and Journals of William Shaw* (Cape Town, 1967), pp. 56–60; WMMS, *Special Series 1827–55*, Box 9, Journal of Samuel Young, f. 145, 21 March 1831, for meeting; CWM, LMS, South Africa, *Incoming Correspondence*, Box 16, folder 3, Birt to Directors, 29 October 1839, for Bhotomane; Box 23, folder 5, Read to Tidman, 21 January 1848, for an example of a meeting.

12. Holt, *Joseph Williams*, pp. 29–32; Erlank, "Re-examining Initial Encounters between Christian Missionaries and the Xhosa," p. 12. This was not Shaw's first experience of negotiating with chiefs, however. Several years before, he had successfully, and seemingly without the same difficulties, negotiated a place with Phato and his brothers. See [William Bennington Boyce,] *Memoir of the Rev. William Shaw, Late General Superintendent of the Wesleyan Missions in South-Eastern Africa* (London: Wesleyan Conference, 1874), pp. 99–107.

13. William Shaw, *The Story of My Mission in South-Eastern Africa: Comprising Some Account of the European Colonists, with Extended Notices of the Kaffir and Other Native Tribes* (London, 1860), pp. 96, 348–65, 374.

14. This account is taken from the very full description given by Shaw and published in Hammond-Tooke, *Journal of William Shaw*, pp. 71–85. See Johannes Du Plessis, *A History of Christian Missions in South Africa* (London, 1911), pp. 173–4, for the general history of Methodist missions at this point.

15. The *mfecane* refers to the name given to the political disruption throughout southeast Africa that was believed to have come from the creation of a strong centralized Zulu kingdom under Shaka. The idea was that a ripple effect moved displaced people and political instability outward across the high veld and down the coast. There is some controversy around this notion which is beyond my competence to judge. What is clear, however, is that the frontier zone at this period was rent with instability that was both internal to the Xhosa and external, and in which the British state was a major contributor. I shall continue to use the word as a synonym for the instability that came from the north. On this whole question, see J. D. Omer-Cooper, *The Zulu Aftermath: A Nineteenth Century Revolution in Bantu Africa* (London, 1966); Carolyn Hamilton (ed.), *The Mfecane Aftermath: Reconstructive Debates in South African History* (Johannesburg, 1995); Norman Etherington, *The Great Treks: The Transformation of Southern Africa, 1815–1854* (Harlow, 2001).

16. But it is worth noting that Hintsa was still capable of pulling away from the missionary presence. There was a crisis in September 1834 when Hintsa made plans to move his kraal away from Butterworth. By this time the missionary was John Ayliff, who tried to stop him with the argument that he (Ayliff) could not just move his home. But Hintsa replied, obviously disingenously, that he could come with him and build a new house where he settled. Ayliff figured that Hintsa's intended move was designed to escape missionary influence. It could just as likely have been designed to escape missionary surveillance as tensions on the frontier mounted to the war that broke out in December. See CA, A80(2), *Ayliff Journal*, 3 and 7 September 1834.

17. Hammond-Tooke, *Journal of William Shaw*, pp. 74–5, for this rumination.

18. This account is taken from GMS, *Minutes of the Presbytery of Kaffraria*, 3 December 1829.

19. It is not obvious who Vusani was referring to here. There were several Dundases associated with the Cape, going back to William Pitt's main strategist on empire matters. But Robert Ross has pointed out to me that it was likely a reference to William Dundas, a frontier official in the mid-1820s. "Somerset" could have referred to the Governor (who left in 1826) or to his son, the frontier commandant who was still there. But whatever the context, it certainly revealed a sense of history and a long memory.

20. On Ndlambe's death in 1828, his tribe split into three, with his sons Mhala, Mdushane and Mqhayi (whom the British called Umhala, Dushane and Umkye respectively) becoming separate chiefs. See Hammond-Tooke, *Journal of William Shaw*, p. 100; Soga, *South-Eastern Bantu*, p. 225.

21. It is important to note, however, that much of the negotiating between Weir and Mhala was carried out by Thomas Fortune, a Khoe member of the mission. His role illustrates once again the importance of such persons as intermediaries. Obviously, his place in the story adds an element of uncertainty to Weir's account of his dealings with Mhala. But there is enough consistency on this issue with other evidence on Mhala's behavior to make the main outline of Weir's account entirely credible.

22. GMS, *Minutes of the Presbytery of Kaffraria*, 6 April and 6 July 1842.

23. Ibid., 6 July and 5 October 1842; 4 January and 5 April 1843; emphasis added.

24. There is an excellent biography of this great man by Timothy Stapleton, *Maqoma: Xhosa Resistance to Colonial Advance 1798–1873*. I have drawn freely on this book for these few paragraphs. See also Mostert, *Frontiers*, for very detailed accounts of Maqoma's military exploits. There were persistent doubts among the Xhosa as to whether or not Ngqika was really Sandile's father. See Mostert, *Frontiers*, p. 566; Lumley Graham, *Journal 1853*, Africanea Collection, Rhodes House Library, 21 June 1853, p. 63: "According to Kafir scandal, Sandilli is not Gaika's son, but of Tsatsoe's father with whom it appears Mrs. Sutu went wrong. Brownlee says there is a strong likeness between Jan Tsatsoe and Sandili." For a description of Maqoma that recognizes his talents, while contextualizing him in a stereotyped view of the Xhosa, see Alfred W. Cole, *The Cape and the Kafirs: Or Notes of Five Years' Residence in South Africa* (London, 1852), pp. 174–7; and Robert Wilmot, *A Cape Traveller's Diary, 1856* (London, 1857), p. 63.

25. CWM, LMS, South Africa, *Incoming Correspondence*, Box 14, folder 1, Ellis to Directors, 8 July 1834; *South African Journals 1824–1892*, f. 109, Kayser to Directors, 8 December 1834, on Maqoma visiting Kayser in European clothes; Laing, *Journals*, 16 September 1833; CA, A80(2), Ayliff, *Journal 1832–1850*, who also gave evidence that he was somewhat battered intellectually by an encounter with Maqoma: "I desire to be thankful to God for the words he gave me to speak which repeatedly confounded the Chief and all his counsellors."

26. Much of the following few paragraphs is based on part of a very long report that Calderwood wrote to the London Secretary of the LMS; see CWM, LMS, South Africa, *Incoming Correspondence*, Box 16, folder 3, Calderwood to Ellis, 28 June 1839. See also Basil Le Cordeur and Christopher Saunders, *The Kitchingman Papers* (Johannesburg, 1976), p. 209; Henry Calderwood, *Prayer: The Christian's Stronghold and Means of Triumph* (Cape Town, 1842), p. 100. This latter book is interesting because it was written while Calderwood was in Cape Town for a year, serving as pastor of the Union Chapel – a time when he was already beginning to rethink his intellectual approach to the Xhosa, but still retained a commitment to the humanitarianism of the evangelical project.

27. CWM, LMS, South Africa, *Incoming Correspondence*, Box 16, folder 3, Calderwood to Ellis, 30 December 1839.

28. Ibid., Calderwood to Ellis, 30 December 1839, 14 January 1840.

29. Calderwood, *Caffres and Caffre Missions* (London, 1858), pp. 37–42, 85–6. He also described a case where some Xhosa counselors of Maqoma skillfully destroyed the testimony of three mission Khoi regarding the theft of cattle from the station. Maqoma was reported by Calderwood as summing up "shrewdly and with a great deal of waggery ... that the teachers's party had evidently not made a story, for they did not tell the same story." Note in this account, though, that Calderwood saves the day by intervening to ensure that the culprit was properly identified, and by shaming Maqoma into accepting that and punishing him.

30. Infanticide was not a common practice among the Xhosa; it never features as evidence of their cultural practices. And when it was mentioned to Suthu by Barrow in the early part of the century, she expressed horror. Sir John Barrow, *Travels Into the Interior of Southern Africa in the Years 1797 and 1798* (London, 1801), p. 204. Indeed, the British thought the Xhosa were too soft on their children, coddling and spoiling them. So infanticide was not a likely occurrence. Adultery, however, was a serious crime, and assault on a chief's wife was punishable by death. Calderwood dealt with those awkward facts by blithely asserting that adultery was common among the licentious Xhosa, and this certainly would resonate with the missionary public, used to being fed salacious hints about what went on during marriage ceremonies, firstfruit ceremonies and the rest. Maqoma himself, of course, was accused of being one of the most enthusiastic adulterers, but the evidence allows us only to say that he practiced polygamy.

31. We may speculate that Maqoma reacted so strongly toward Calderwood because the issue went to the heart of the challenge to Xhosa civil authority systems and the chief's authority that was posed by the missionary presence.

Calderwood later confessed that he had got his information from a spy in Maqoma's kraal, presumably one of his wives. See Calderwood, *Caffres and Caffre Missions*, pp. 65–72, for this whole episode.

32. CWM, LMS, South Africa, *Incoming Correspondence*, Box 17, folder 1, Annual Report from Blinkwater, 28 August 1840. Calderwood, *Caffres and Caffre Missions*, p. 99.

33. CWM, LMS, South Africa, *Incoming Correspondence*, Box 19, folder 1, Calderwood to Tidman, 13 March 1843; folder 2, 12 June 1843; Calderwood, *Caffres and Caffre Missions*, p. 99.

34. CWM, LMS, South Africa, *Incoming Correspondence*, Box 18, folder 1, Calderwood to Directors, 18 May 1841; Box 19, folder 1, Calderwood to Tidman, 13 March 1843; Box 22, folder 1, Calderwood to Tidman, 2 March 1846; Box 22, folder 2, Calderwood to Tidman, 8 October 1846.

35. After the struggle with Maqoma, Calderwood's relationship with his missionary colleagues also deteriorated. He distanced himself from the LMS culture of racial equality and intimacy. By 1844 he was in open conflict with his colleagues over questions of racial equality, especially over the issue of racially mixed congregations. In early 1845, for no apparent reason, he precipitated a nasty smear campaign against the venerable James Read and his mixed-race son, which revolved around their treatment of their colored congregation as "brethren" and equals. It is important to note, though, that Calderwood had support from the other frontier missionaries in his campaign against the Reads. For this see Le Cordeur and Saunders, *Kitchingman Papers*, pp. 243–54; CWM, LMS, South Africa, *Incoming Correspondence*, Box 21, folder 1, Philip to Directors, 8 February 1845; Cumming to Philip, 10 February 1845; Philip to Directors, 25 March 1845; Box 22, folder 1, James Read Sr. to Directors, 31 March 1846. Robert Ross, "Congregations, Missionaries and the Grahamstown Schism of 1842–3," and Elizabeth Elbourne, "Whose Gospel? Conflict in the LMS in the Early 1840s," in John de Gruchy (ed.), *The London Missionary Society in South Africa: Historical Essays in Celebration of the Bicentenary of the LMS in Southern Africa 1799–1999* (Cape Town, 1999), pp. 120–131 and 132–55, describe the split within the Grahamstown ministers on mixed congregations. On Calderwood's attitude toward missionary sentimentalism, which had developed as part of his ruminations on the Maqoma experience, see Calderwood, *Prayer*, pp. 88–90.

36. Calderwood, *Caffres and Caffre Missions*, pp. 49, 55, 56, 60–2, 65, 96, 103.

37. See United Presbyterian Church, *Missionary Record*, July 1849, p. 107; August 1849, pp. 122–3. Xayimpi was to become notorious for his murder of the military settlers at Woburn on the outbreak of the 1850–3 war and his subsequent long evasion of imperial justice. He was eventually convicted of horse-stealing in 1857. See CA, GH 20/2/2/1 *Miscellaneous Papers Relating to British Kaffraria, 1853–58*, Maclean to Grey, 5 November 1857.

38. See Cumming, *Diary*, 9–28 November and 1–26 December 1849; see 31 July and 30 November 1850 for the marriage of Brown and Chalmers and the birth of their son.

39. This sentiment was also repeated to Renton in an encounter he had with Sandile at Thyumie at about the same time. See Cumming, *Diary*, 16 January 1851; United Presbyterian Church, *Missionary Record*, April 1852, pp. 55–8,

for a full report on this interesting encounter, in which Sandile complains how he could not trust the English, who never kept their word; how they killed the Son of God and wanted to kill him, Sandile; and how they split the Xhosa by demanding loyalty from the mission natives, concluding, "I am angry with the English. I am tired of the English on account of their bad conduct. Englishmen make promises about land and break them. They make a boundary and then take it away. I do not wish to live under the English ... I shall die fighting." The last was true, but not until 1878. There is a similar account of this meeting in George Brown, *Personal Adventures in South Africa* (London, 1855), pp. 154–5.

40. Brown, *Personal Adventures in South Africa*, pp. 75–6.

41. Ibid., pp. 200–2. For the same split view of Maqoma, see Cole, *The Cape and the Kaffirs*, pp. 174–7; and Wilmot, *A Cape Traveller's Diary, 1856*, p. 63.

42. Brown, *Personal Adventures in South Africa*, pp. 12, 40–2, 81–2, 90–2, 135.

43. Ibid., p. 146: a theme of evangelical religion that fails to figure large in most accounts.

44. For an excellent account of Old Soga see Janet Hodgson, "Soga and Dukwana: The Christian Struggle for Liberation in Mid-Nineteenth Century South Africa," *Journal of Religion in Africa* 16.3 (1986), pp. 186–208.

45. Janet Hodgson, "A Battle for Sacred Power: Christian Beginnings among the Xhosa," in Richard Elphick and Rodney Davenport, *Christianity in South Africa: A Political, Social and Cultural History* (Berkeley, 1997), p. 78; Rev. H. T. Cousins, *Tiyo Soga: The Model Kaffir Missionary* (London, 1897), p. 112. When Brownlee was reassigned in 1864, it was reported that Old Soga gave a "short speech of singular neatness ... in token of his genuine gratitude and high appreciation of the services he [Brownlee, had] rendered to the Kaffir nation." Charles Brownlee, *Reminiscinces of Kaffir Life and History* (Lovedale, 1896), pp. 74–5; Peires, *House of Phalo*, p. 108; Williams, *Umfundisi*, pp. 6–9.

46. Du Plessis, *History of Christian Missions in South Africa*, p. 363; Glasgow African Missionary Society, *Caffrarian Messenger*, April 1843, pp. 193–7; *Report of 1844*, pp. 7–15; United Presbyterian Church, *Missionary Record*, August 1848, pp. 119–20.

47. Williams, *Umfundisi*, p. 47. For the meeting between Renton and Sandile see United Presbyterian Church, *Missionary Record*, April 1852, pp. 54–8. Renton just happened to be visiting the area when he was caught up in the maelstrom. He had been sent out from Glasgow to investigate the squabbles among the local missionaries. Sandile probably wanted to seize the chance to get his side of the story of the war across to a sympathetic listener who was soon to return to Britain.

48. Soga, *The South Eastern Bantu*, pp. xi–xv.

49. Brown, *Personal Adventures*, p. 302; see also pp. 157–8, 170, 154–5, 150. In the event, Sandile did not insist that they join him, although many in fact did.

50. CWM, LMS, South Africa, *Incoming Correspondence*, Box 22, folder 1, Calderwood to Tidman, 2 March 1846; see also LMS, *Missionary Magazine*, 1847, p. 148.

6   The closing of the missionary mind

The implosion of missionary humanitarianism

Missionary culture was challenged and transformed as a result of confrontations with Xhosa culture and politics. The optimistic and hopeful missionary culture of the evangelical revival was steadily eroded, to be replaced by a volatile, pessimistic despair. The bright hopes for the Xhosa were supplanted by premonitions that became progressively dark. Slowly, unevenly, never completely, missionary culture imploded from within as the fragilities of its worldview crumpled under the realities of the encounter with the Xhosa. Missionary culture closed down from the open, engaged and observing culture that it had been when it first entered into the encounter with the Xhosa. It reformulated what it "knew" about the Xhosa, and this new "knowledge" fed into and contributed to a view of the Xhosa that was consistent with the racial essentialism that, by the 1860s, had come to dominate the wider discourse on race.

The tipping point within missionary culture in this respect in southern Africa came sometime in the late 1840s. This was the moment when the traditional humanitarian conception of a culturally based racial hierarchy gave way to the conception of racial essentialism. Until the late 1840s the humanitarian vision still remained the dominant subjectivity for missionaries in the missionary enterprise. It was the apostasy of Henry Calderwood when he joined the imperial administration that broke that spell. Although Calderwood found little sympathy from his fellow missionaries – who took some delight in what was described as his subsequent "miserable life," a life that included needing a police guard for some of the time – he was nevertheless symptomatic of a shifting mentality.[1]

This was a shift that was registered both in the provincial capital, Cape Town, and in the metropole of empire. By the late 1830s, liberal opinion in Cape Town had begun to move away from the racial discourse of universal humanitarianism. This was coincident with the rising voice of eastern Cape settler politics, whose language was aggressively anti-missionary and anti-Xhosa. In tandem, the two white segments of southern African society,

127

Boer and British, began to seek a racial alliance around whiteness, even if hostilities remained over specific issues. Nonetheless, until the late 1840s, when John Philip retired and a more open (white) politics came to the Cape, the missionary lobby was still (probably) the dominant voice in official opinion and policy-making both in the Colony and in the metropole.[2]

Furthermore, the evangelical definition of racial hierarchies was about to be displaced in Britain. In 1849, Thomas Carlyle published his notorious article "Occasional Discourse on the Nigger Question," and one year later Robert Knox's book *The Races of Man* appeared. Neither of these publications marked the first time that race-based views of history or politics had been heard. As an aside, it is worth noting that Knox had developed his interest in racial classification while serving as an Army surgeon in the eastern Cape in the war of 1819–20. He had returned home with a collection of skulls. When Knox first began to publish on different skull types in the 1820s, it was merely a curiosity. But by the late 1840s, his views were part of an increasingly powerful challenge to the ideas that racial hierarchy was cultural. The political climate began to change. By 1852 Disraeli – ever one to spot the shifting winds of opinion – was arguing that slave emancipation had been unwise. And when the eastern Cape missionary Robert Niven arrived in England in 1852, he wrote to his old friend Charles Stretch complaining that he had found it quite impossible to get a hearing in London in support of the Xhosa.[3]

The displacement of evangelical humanitarian discourse from its controlling place in British politics was a profoundly important event. This is not the place to enter into a full consideration of the shifting racial discourse in Britain over the mid-nineteenth century. But it is important to make two points. The first is a matter of less importance – that of chronology. Discussion of the shifting tides of racial discourse in Britain in the mid-nineteenth century tends to associate the shift with the Indian Rebellion of 1857 and the Morant Bay uprising in Jamaica of 1865. These were dramatic and important events which profoundly disturbed the mid-Victorian cultural, political and imperial equipoise. They both sparked important debates which exposed how race and empire were thought about in Britain. But neither event was responsible for reintroducing that discourse on race into culture and politics; it was already there, and the most these events achieved was to dramatize and further extend its appeal.

If – and this is my second point – we turn aside from chronology to ask why it was that, from the late 1840s, the racial discourse changed in this way, the role of the empire in the shifting tides of opinion in the metropole takes on a slightly different hue. The fading of one kind of cultural and political discourse and the emergence of another are complicated social, cultural and political processes. But in this case one key aspect was the implosion of missionary culture at the frontier of empire. Missionaries were obviously aware of the currents of metropolitan opinion, but, sitting out on the far frontier of empire, they were not compelled by them. What they experienced in their everyday encounters with the Xhosa led them to rethink their agenda and beliefs.

It was these experiences that caused missionary culture to implode and fatally weaken the humanitarian discourse, not only in South Africa, but in the metropole, too. Once the missionaries who were actually living out the evangelical ideology of race ceased to believe in it, or were forced to reconsider it and, as a consequence, readjust their modes of engagement with the Xhosa, how could evangelical humanitarianism retain its hold as a discourse of imperial politics? Once missionaries themselves had lost confidence in their ideology – for that is what happened, whether they surrendered to racial essentialism or not – then the idea of a universal humanity with cultural rather than biological differences itself was diminished and undermined. Once evangelical humanitarianism was drained of its vitality at the site where it was supposed to be validated, how could it serve to resist a discourse of racial essentialism?

The loss of missionary culture's intellectual moorings was not a process that happened only through the personal, individual encounters that we have discussed in the previous chapters. There were also external influences that were brought to bear on missionary culture. There were broader contexts for this story which it is now necessary to bring into the narrative. I want to move away from a single focus on the internalities of the missionary experience to place the changes in missionary culture in this broader context. And the most important external influence on the implosion of missionary culture in the eastern Cape was war.

The context of war

Until the end of the 1850s, the eastern Cape was a frontier war zone, constantly swept by war, or by rumors of war. The line of the frontier was steadily moving to the east in this period, as settlers, with the imperial state close behind them, ceaselessly pressed their domain upon the Xhosa. It had been this way since the end of the 1770s, when the Cape Colony was under the rule of the Dutch East India Company. The eastern frontier was opened in 1769, when the first white settlers reached the Sundays river about 500 miles from Cape Town. Since the Xhosa were also moving south, a competition for the land known as the Zuurveld began. In 1779 the first of nine frontier wars broke out. It inaugurated a hundred years of war between the Xhosa and the Dutch, and then, after 1806, between the Xhosa and the British, that was not to close until the final war of 1877–8.

Each war resulted in a further retreat of the Xhosa, but the expansion of imperial control over their land was erratic – and the Xhosa's full independence was not destroyed until the 1850s. Indeed, the land between Xhosaland and Natal was not colored British red until the mid-1890s.[4]

The hundred years of war that the Xhosa fought against European imperialism have not figured much in British imperial history.[5] But this period had a profound impact on the missionary community of the eastern Cape. Three times between 1834 and 1850 the missionaries were uprooted by war. Each time war broke out they watched helplessly as their missions were burned and looted. During war, all missionary work came to a halt. It was true that every time they were driven out, the missionaries returned to start again. But with each disruption, recovery was more difficult. After the 1834–5 war, the missionaries were largely back in place by the spring of 1836. After the War of the Axe, in 1846–7, it took at least a year for most missionaries to get back in business, and Brownlee was not able to return to Xhosaland until May 1849. Recovery was hardest of all after the eighth frontier war, and stretched well into the mid-1850s. There is a revealing entry in James Laing's journal from 1858, which noted how "the wars of 1846 and 1850 and the alarms regarding war in August 1856 caused me to pack up my books and papers and it is only now that in some measure I am able to rectify the disorders of the last twelve years."[6]

Each time the missionaries returned to begin again, something had been lost; each time, more reserves of evangelical optimism were bled away. Richard Birt was a London Missionary Society missionary who had arrived in the same party as Henry Calderwood. Unlike Calderwood, he did not lose his faith in missionary work. But the war of 1846 caused him to reflect that missionaries alone could not civilize the Xhosa; sterner measures were needed if they were to be adequately controlled. Indeed, the terrible truth for Birt was that "the Caffres have not been humbled by anything our force has done, and they are as unsubdued as at the commencement of hostilities ... their actual loss by war and conflict is not sufficient to remove from their minds the idea that *we* have had the worst of it."[7]

The Xhosa were right. The missionaries *had* had the worst of it. Their hopes and expectations were seriously dented. Even the most sympathetic of them usually found it impossible to stay among the Xhosa during wartime. Indeed, after the 1850–3 war there was serious debate within the Glasgow Missionary Society as to whether they *could* recover. Robert Renton, on his tour of inspection from Glasgow, thought that they would have to cease work among the Xhosa and concentrate on the Mfengu, a tribal grouping created by the British in 1834, who served as their most loyal mercenaries. In the event, the Society stayed on, but some missionaries, like Robert Niven, left never to return.[8]

Even the London Missionary Society was badly shattered by the war of 1850–3. Only a few months before the war erupted, the Society claimed that things were working well in South Africa. Conversion rates were up; cultural practices were reported to be changing; there were plenty of improvements to be made, but the belief in universal humanity remained firm. But then suddenly everything was in ruins. By October 1851 Friedrich Kayser was begging the Society not to give up the Xhosaland missions. Kayser argued that the Xhosa declaration of war of 1850 had shown that while it was true that the Xhosa had rejected the gospel, missionaries should now look to the effects of catastrophe on their consciousness. Perhaps the devastating experience of war would lead them to consider the error of their ways.[9]

Kayser's letter was revealing. Kayser was the most long-suffering of the missionaries. Perhaps he was one of the saintliest, too. He had risked his life to plead with Maqoma not to go to war in 1834. He had stayed out of the internecine squabbles between the various missionaries in the 1840s. He never abandoned his belief in a universal humanity. But this letter tells us that he no longer believed that the original missionary strategy could work. He had accepted, however unconsciously, Calderwood's formulation that the Xhosa had indeed *refused* the gospel. And although he was not prepared to go the next step and say that therefore they had no hearts, he did need to ask himself how that refusal could be reversed. His answer was catastrophe and war, a terrible answer for a man of God. But this was an answer that was to become a commonplace in the next few years.

Each war not only sapped missionary optimism; it also provided fuel for those who wanted to expose the hypocrisy and hollowness of missionary sentimentality towards indigenous races. Missionaries were left, themselves, with fewer and fewer defenses. It was in this respect that war contributed to the implosion of missionary culture.

The war of 1834–5 was particularly important in this respect. Following the devastation of the war, the first calls were heard for a politics that rested on racial hostility. Indeed, one of the first to speak this language was the Methodist missionary William Shaw, who just happened to be in London as news of the outbreak of war arrived. He penned a letter to Lord Aberdeen, Secretary of State for the Colonies, in which he defended the settlers as the victims and the Xhosa as the aggressors in the war.[10] Such views were in a distinct minority in the evangelical community. Indeed, 1835 was the highwater mark of evangelical control of colonial policy. The final triumph of abolitionism had been ordered; slavery was to come to an end in 1838. The Select Committee on Aborigines was about to pronounce a thoroughly humanitarian agenda for colonial policy. A prominent member of the humanitarian, anti-slavery faction, Lord Glenelg, was in charge of the

Colonial Office. The missionaries of the London and Glasgow missionary societies had no reason to think that they were on the losing side of history. The attitude of the London Missionary Society was that the war was an unnecessary interruption to a process of civilizing influences that was proceeding in a promising and progressive direction. They blamed the settlers and the state. Their official line was that great progress had been made over the past ten years in spreading Christianity and civilized culture. From the perspective of the Society, the impediments to the successful realization of the missionary project was the administration of frontier policy, and the absence of a system of international law to govern relations between the Xhosa chiefs and the British.[11]

The London Missionary Society, in the person of John Philip, the superintendent of its missions in southern Africa, was shocked at the harsh policies of expulsion and punishment proclaimed by the Governor, Sir Benjamin D'Urban. Philip was particularly taken aback because he had labored under the fond delusion that D'Urban was a supporter of a humanitarian frontier policy that would work to protect the Xhosa from the contaminating influences of civilization. So Philip could hardly believe his eyes when D'Urban blamed the tribes for the war, declaring them "irredeemable savages" and expelling them from Ceded Territory between the Fish and Keiskamma rivers. "I had to keep reading it [D'Urban's Proclamation] to satisfy myself that I was actually living in the nineteenth century ... [what I read] upset all my ideas and shook all my former confidences." What could explain this apparent shift in D'Urban's policy? Philip could put it down only to racism: "the Caffres have black skins ... they are irredeemable savages therefore they have to be treated as wild beasts ... They have black skins therefore they have no right any country as we wish to possess [sic] and we are the wild beasts not them."[12]

But the war of 1834–5 *strengthened* Philip's belief in universal humanity, if it also made him more pessimistic about his countrymen. When Philip asked what it was that allowed this kind of sentiment to prevail, he explained it as a result of the absence of restraint in empire, which allowed men to "gratify their evil passions." The result was that in empire, Britons sank far below the moral grade of the people they regarded as savages. Philip was not alone in these sentiments. He was deluged with reports from his agents on the eastern frontier protesting the direction of British policy and the outrages that were being committed against the Xhosa.

Thus, the war of 1834–5 tended to reinforce the assumptions of the London Missionary Society missionaries even as it caused the Methodists to re-evaluate their position. But if the London and Glasgow missionaries could absorb the war of 1834–5, their confidence was shaken by the War of the Axe, which broke out at the end of 1846. A distinct change of tone was registered in the correspondence of the London Missionary Society. There was far less protest about the war, and little critique of government policy. Indeed, the consensus among the frontier missionaries was that it was the Xhosa who were entirely to blame for the outbreak of the war. It is something of a surprise to find James Read, the pioneer missionary who had married a Khoe woman and was a steady champion of the universal humanity of mankind, also absolving the colonists and the state of responsibility. His son John even took part in the military operation. John Philip, too, had softened his hostility to the imperial state. Indeed, he supported the war precisely in the hope that it would result in bringing all the Xhosa under the protection of the state. He now saw war as necessary to introduce a benevolent, protective, paternalist imperial domination of the Xhosa.[13]

This represented a very significant shift in Philip's thinking. Previously he had seen the role of the state as a facilitator for the missionary project. The state should protect the Xhosa by keeping the riff-raff of the British Isles out of their lands. But the state should not interfere in the missionary role of bringing civilization to the heathen. This was the view he expressed in *Researches in South Africa* (1828), and it remained intact through 1835. By 1846 he had come to see the state control of the Xhosa as *necessary* to the civilizing mission of the missionaries. This was exactly the same policy that Calderwood was advocating. So it is clear that the beliefs and values of missionary culture as a whole were in motion. In which direction was this current running? Two main streams provide the answer to that question. One was to reinforce the skepticism that missionaries were learning from other aspects of the encounter about the ability of the Xhosa to receive the missionary message. The other direction was to re-evaluate their relationship to the imperial state. Let us look at those matters in turn.[14]

Ignorance, machination and deceit

In some ways the most shocking experience of war for the missionaries was the way it revealed their *ignorance*. Each time a frontier war erupted, everyone was taken by surprise. In 1834 William Chalmers left his mission in the second week of December completely unaware that war was pending. A week or so later, his mission was overrun and turned into a "place of festivities, goats being slaughtered in every direction … nor could we restrain them from their evil practices." The first rumor of war that John Cumming recorded in his diary was at the end of September 1850, with war expected to break out in October. But this moment of crisis seemed to pass. Robert Niven inquired of Charles Stretch in November 1850 if he had heard the rumors of war, and Stretch replied that they were being got up by the Grahamstown merchants who wanted to feed at the trough of government contracts. This was not so unreasonable. Rumors were a currency of politics on the frontier, and it must have been difficult to sort out what was reasonable or unreasonable. One week before the war of 1850–3 erupted, Niven and Cumming left a conference between Governor Harry Smith and the Xhosa chiefs convinced that peace would prevail.[15]

These missionaries lived literally cheek by jowl with the Xhosa. They spoke their language, they had Xhosa servants, they were surrounded by Xhosa mission people, and they were in daily contact with Xhosa chiefs. What did this tell them about the distance that remained between the British and the Xhosa after twenty years of close contact? How did they explain their failure to recognize the signs that war was approaching, or their failure to be tipped off by anyone in their circle of Xhosa acquaintances? They could only put it down to those qualities of "cunning" and "deceit" that they were increasingly coming to use to explain other aspects of their encounter with the Xhosa. As George Brown explained, "I never suspected the sincerity of the Caffres" when they continued to "assure me in the most positive terms that none of the Chiefs had any thoughts of war."[16] The mystery of the wars – the fact that missionaries had neither predicted nor observed their imminence – reinforced their growing tendency to attribute much that they did not understand to the machinations of the chiefs.

The tendency to seek explanation for missionary ignorance in the deceptions of the chiefs was closely related to their demonization that was increasingly part of the wider discourse on the Xhosa. It emanated particularly from settler politics, and began in the war of 1834–5 with the portrayal of Chief Hintsa as the secret manipulator of Xhosa unrest and theft. But the discourse of demonization fitted very well with the missionary frustrations in their dealings with the chiefs.[17]

John Ayliff, for example, who watched events in 1834–5 unfold at quite close quarters from his mission at Butterworth, was convinced of Hintsa's duplicity. Even though Hintsa had told Ayliff he would not fight, and even though he remained ostentatiously neutral, Ayliff still believed the worst of him, including that he intended to massacre the Europeans resident in his territory. Such views were quite widespread among the imperial officials on the frontier. It was widely accepted among frontier officials that the war of 1834–5 was concocted by a conspiracy of the chiefs in the summer of 1834. Conspiracy theory also explained why certain chiefs were neutral. It was believed that the chiefs adopted the strategy of allowing some to remain neutral and profess friendship to the Colony so that, in the case of a defeat, some protection could be given to the tribes. Mhala was reputed to be the originator of this idea. Thus, for Methodists and certain imperial officials, the 1834–5 war demonstrated the "duplicity of the Kaffir Chiefs," and an explanation was to hand to explain those facts – such as Hintsa's clear desire to avoid war – that did not fit the images being purveyed by the settler politicians of Xhosa hordes erupting into the Colony. "Their [chiefs'] conduct at the time was very dubious. Hintza in particular while professing attachment to the colony ... was at the same time receiving and concealing ... immense herds of cattle plundered from the Colony."[18]

By 1850 the idea that all war on the frontier was the result of the machinations of the Xhosa chiefs and the "duplicity of character" of the Xhosa was a commonplace. The implications of this analysis were expressed most fully by Calderwood, in response to a request from London for an assessment of the state of affairs in Xhosaland. He explained how the power of the chiefs was reflective of the inherent "duplicity of character" of the Xhosa as a whole. The chiefs, and those around them, he explained, were responding to the growing checks on their power by the imperial state. But they were able to play on the inherent character of the Xhosa. Freeman (the Secretary of the LMS) had asked Calderwood whether the Xhosa chiefs still felt aggrieved for the loss of their land and for having to pay fines for missing colonial cattle. Calderwood replied that naturally they remained aggrieved, because they were "thieves and murderers" who could hardly expect to be happy at being controlled.[19]

Calderwood saw the chiefs as using Xhosa culture to preserve their own power. But Richard Birt, too, had come to a similar perception of the relationship between cultural practices, chiefly power and the difficulties facing the missionary project. In commenting on the place of witchcraft in society, he burst out: "The worst part of the case is that it is done through a slavish fear of the Chief and the customs of society over powering in superstition." Birt saw the chiefs' use of cultural practices, such as witch-craft, to manipulate their tribes as the most natural thing possible. "It was not to be expected," he wrote, "that the Chiefs would give up their power and revenue without a struggle." Thus, the chiefs "got up a war party" to hold on to their own power by mobilizing the tribes "around the super-stitions of the people" to throw off the yoke of the British power. By 1851 Birt was ready to claim that now was the moment for "some one power [to] be placed above the heads of the Chiefs – [and] no power was so proper as the British." The common people, he believed, would thus be "easily won over to confide in our rule."[20]

The questions the missionaries faced as they contemplated the wreck-age of their plans from the standpoint of the eighth frontier war of 1850–3 were: How could the missionary project move forward in the face of this wall of manipulation and deceit? What was now needed to secure change? Where could support be found for the conversions of the Xhosa, which were necessary for civilization to advance? The answer to these questions led in three directions. First, it led to the growth of what we might call a catastrophic view of conversions. Second, they were led to reconsider their assumption that salvation was a *precondition* of civilization and entertain the possibility that salvation could not be realized *without* civilization. This involved rethinking the relationship between their project and the state. And third, a new mode of engagement between the missionaries and the Xhosa replaced the open, engaged and observing mode that dominated the first part of the century. This new mode expressed reduced expectations for the missionary project and a new, less hopeful view of Xhosa culture, reflecting this closing of the missionary mind.

Catastrophe and conversion

At the time of the War of the Axe (1846–7) a new sentiment began to creep into the missionary records. It is the belief that the Xhosa needed catastrophe to bring them to their senses. At one level this represented the providentialist pessimism that was inherent in evangelical thought. In the eastern Cape, however, it came to be associated with man-made catastrophe rather than with the sudden intervention of acts of God. John Cumming expressed the hope that "this present outbreak [the War of the Axe] will be the means of disposing the people in such a way as to give greater access to the benign influence of God." Ayliff felt the same way, reporting home in 1848 an expectation that ground had been cleared for a renewed and more promising round of activity. And William Shaw hoped that "we shall now have such opening as we never had before in Kaffirland." Similarly, the *Missionary Record* of the United Presbyterian Church commented how "the fury of war will, it is to be hoped, be followed by a lasting peace when the missionaries and their converts can return and when the humbled Caffres may be more disposed to receive the glad and consoling doctrines of the Gospel of Christ."[21]

But the strongest association between catastrophe and conversion was to be found in the missionary response to the cattle-killing of 1856–7. We shall have occasion to address the wider significance of the cattle-killing at a later point. Here we may merely note that it was a traumatic event in Xhosa history which represented a collective suicide by the Xhosa people. Young women prophets predicted the return of long-dead chiefs and the appearance of new people who would bring cattle and corn and help the Xhosa drive the British into the sea. I have already noted the surprising fact that the missionary reports do not record much interest in the cattle-killing. But when the cattle-killing *was* noted, it was greeted as an event that might shake the Xhosa from their cultural stupor.

The contrast with how such an event would have been observed in the private records of the missionary world twenty or even ten years before is quite astounding. In contrast, for example, to Robert Niven's 1840 pamphlet, *An Impartial Analysis of the Kaffir Character*, there was no attempt at cultural analysis. The killing was scanned through the prisms that had been ground to precision over the previous ten years, as a reflection of the way in which the "progress of the Gospel has been retarded by the malignant influence of superstition and ... the belief in their native prophets so extensively prevalent among the Kaffirs." In other words, the power of superstition and the delusions of the witchdoctors and prophets allowed them, in the words of Kayser, to "break themselves to pieces." But it was also generally agreed that this could turn out to be a good thing. As Ayliff remarked, "Perhaps after this they may be humbled and be made willing to receive the Gospel of Christ." From the opposite end of the missionary spectrum, John Forbes Cumming agreed. "The spell is now broken," he wrote to the United Presbyterian Church's *Missionary Record*. "As a nation, the Caffres declare themselves to be destroyed, and that by their own hand ... good will come out of evil ... their ancient customs will lose their hold ... and thus prepare the way for the ... reception of gospel truth."[22]

It is appropriate to reflect on Cumming's grim satisfaction. For the Xhosa, the cattle-killing was the last desperate act by their nation to escape from the maw of imperial Britain. But equally, the cattle-killing marked the interment of the humanitarian discourse. It was the final proof that the Xhosa were not reasonable. And how else were the missionaries to understand this collective act of despair by a large portion of the Xhosa people? Consider it for a moment from their perspective. How could they understand the attractions of the young female prophets, Nongqawuse and Nonkosi, to the Xhosa, when for thirty years they (the missionaries) had been preaching the light of Christianity? How could they understand that a woman like Suthu, the youngest wife of the great Xhosa chief Ngqika, could be waiting expectantly each day for her lord to return, patiently sweeping and tidying her hut so that he would find it neat and ready when he returned? Suthu had been in touch with missionaries since the 1820s; she had been a frequent attender at church services; she was known to a wide range of British missionaries and imperial officials; she was a woman of substance who had acted as regent of the tribe before Sandile was of age; she was respected and even liked by the British. And here was she, taken in by the two young girl prophets – one only nine years of age – who claimed to have spoken to the ancestors and seen them on their way to save the Xhosa people.[23]

But there was a further irony here. The missionaries turned out to be right about the cattle-killing opening the way to conversions. Following the cattle-killing, there was a new receptivity to Christian evangelizing.

By the mid-1860s a revival in native missions was in full swing. Coincidentally, an American evangelist named William Taylor launched a crusade in the area, which accomplished what had eluded the British missionaries for the past thirty years. Thousands of Xhosa were converted to Christianity. But the irony ran even deeper than that. For it was not Taylor who was doing the converting. He could not even speak Xhosa, and needed translators. It was a small group of Xhosa converts who were drawn (mainly) from the Wesleyan community and engaged by Taylor as interlocutors who did the conversion. So successful were they at translating Taylor's evangelical enthusiasm that they went out into the villages on their own and began to sign up hundreds for the Christian cause. It was the beginning of the native African church.[24]

Civilization before salvation: missionaries and the state

The evangelical revival had taught that salvation was a precondition of civilization. When Robert Niven had laid out his conception of how the Xhosa would be civilized, in his pamphlet *An Impartial Analysis of the Kaffir Character* in 1840, he had paid little attention to external, institutional forces such as education. Preaching the Gospel and salvation was the main strategy. Niven assumed that education was essentially an add-on, something that was desirable as bringing the superior culture of the West to the Xhosa and as a site to train them up to be teachers and the like. For the most part he assumed that "friendly intercourse" would suffice to point Xhosa behavior toward the civilities of the civilized world. The *example* of the missionary or the civilized white settler would be enough to persuade the Xhosa to adopt western methods of cultivation and the like. The most notable absence in Niven's conception of how the civilizing process would work, of course, was the imperial state. By the late 1840s Robert Niven was exhibiting very different priorities. He now welcomed the involvement of the state in the missionary project; indeed, he now looked to the state as a potential source of money and logistical support for missionary work.[25]

Like the other missionaries on the eastern frontier, in 1848 Niven greeted the new Governor, Sir Harry Smith, as a savior. On the face of it this was surprising. Smith was a military man who had played a leading role in D'Urban's policy of retribution against the tribes which had so horrified John Philip in 1835. But in 1848 Niven was positively ecstatic at the arrival of Smith, who had been "chosen by providence to effect change at this crucial time." Similarly, James Read, of all people, saw him as a liberator, especially when he replaced a brutal magistrate at the Kat river settlement with one more sympathetic to the Khoe settlers.

The reason for this enthusiasm from some of the most independent-minded of the missionary community was that Smith seemed about to inaugurate a regime which combined paternal control of the Xhosa by the state with missionary-led social policies and prescriptions. He had been sent out to the Cape to create British Kaffraria as a British-administered living space for the Xhosa, where the forces of civilization would be allowed to proceed, protected by the power of the state. One of the first things Smith did was to solicit missionary opinion as to what was needed to accomplish this aim. The main direction of their responses was that there was a need for institutions of learning and civilization, to be administered by them but protected and underwritten by state policy. From December 1848 the state began to hand out subsidies to various missionary educational institutions.[26]

The enthusiasm with which the missionary community greeted Smith, therefore, revealed a change of tone within missionary culture. This change involved displacing the traditional prioritizing of individual salvation as the path to civilization with the recognition that the Xhosa must be civilized first, before they would be ready to receive Christianity. Social, economic and political reform of the Xhosa was now assigned a new importance within the missionary project. Robert Niven, again, revealed this shift. In contrast to his position in 1840, for example, Niven now attached first importance to conquering "the yet unconquered ignorance and superstition and feudal attachments ... which stand between us and the consummation for Caffraria of peaceful incorporation, good citizenship and regenerative Christianity." He saw this transformation no longer as a byproduct of receiving Christ through individual salvation *but as a precondition for it.* And in this effort, the help and engagement of the imperial state were necessary. Thus, in response to Smith's call to the missionaries for policy ideas and suggestions, Niven offered him an elaborate social engineering plan for educational institutions that would be paid for by government subsidies.[27]

In tandem with this new-found interest in interventionist social reform, the discourse of political economy now began to find its way into missionary writings where it had previously been absent. A new concern with inculcating habits of industry and labor among the Xhosa began to preoccupy missionary minds. As James Laing wrote to the frontier official John Maclean, it was necessary to find ways to instill habits of "continuous labor among the natives," for they were "naturally indolent and lazy." Laing then went on to discuss which payment system best suited the Xhosa. He concluded that some form of sliding scale and piecework was most appropriate, since they needed an inducement to "throw off their natural indolence." Only once the habit of continuous labor was attained was it safe to put the Xhosa on payment by the day! Salvation had now given way to wage incentive schemes as best-practice missionary technique.[28] What caused this shift in missionary outlook from a focus on issues of individual reformation to a new interest in issues of social and economic reform? In simple terms, it was a response to their evident failure to crack the hold over the Xhosa of superstitions such as witchcraft. Combined with this was the equal failure to enlist the Xhosa political hierarchy, controlled by the chiefs, in the missionary effort. Naturally, there were still missionaries who remained committed to "the necessity of civilization following close in the train of the Gospel" (as one of them put it in response to Smith's request for ideas).[29] But one gets the sense from the sources that by the late 1840s this was increasingly anachronistic.

Thus, although missionaries like Niven recoiled in horror at Calderwood's apostasy in going to work for the imperial state, his reasons were not so far distant from currents that were flowing in missionary culture more generally. As early as 1844 the idea that the coercive power of the state should be enlisted to root out the obstacle of traditional customs had floated into Richard Birt's head. He wrote to magistrate Charles Stretch asking him for a policeman to come and make enquiries about a witchcraft smelling-out ceremony that Chief Bhotomane was currently running. He knew that Stretch had no formal power actually to intervene in such cases. But he thought that the mere hint of some interest by the state would have a good effect. *"How such things long to make one deprive the Chiefs of their power for mischief."*[30]

The new enthusiasm for a close relationship with the state thus signified more than just a change of strategy by the missionaries. It reflected a change in *mentality*. They now accepted that changing Xhosa society was not just a matter of opening hearts. It was the culture that stood in the way, both the "heathenish practices" and their political manipulation by the chiefs. Behavior must be changed more directly, therefore, even with a touch of coercion. Just after the eighth frontier war, Richard Birt expressed agreement with the idea that the Xhosa could

only be reclaimed by, first training them to civilized habits and works of art, and by constantly and progressively pointing out to them the immutable connection between cause and effect which we call Laws of Nature; bring them to a grateful and devout knowledge of the omnipotent and benevolent giver of these laws. When this truth is duly implanted in them, then, and not until then, will they be capable of being benefited by the reading of the Bible, and the preaching of the Gospel.[31]

By the 1860s it was a commonplace within missionary culture that coercion was a necessary element to bring religious and social civilization to the Xhosa. The missionary William Holden, who wrote one of the defining accounts of the Xhosa, declared that they could not be civilized without coercion and control, for they see no advantages in the "institutions and restrains of civilized society; but rather look on them with distaste and aversion as being laborious superfluities,without attraction and without enjoyment." A missionary conference in King William's Town in 1866 to discuss policy toward the Xhosa agreed on the need "to bring the natives under a stricter control, and to exact from them a more rapid conformity to the manners and customs of civilized life."[32]

The missionaries had now come round to an instinctive acceptance of one of the most persistent pathologies of colonial culture: *the habit of turning responsibility for the practices of imperial culture back on to the colonized themselves.* At the conference in King William's Town, for example, it was argued that the bigotry of the settlers was the fault of the Xhosa themselves. By this reckoning, settler racism was a function of the behavior of the Xhosa, who had failed to adopt civilized methods rapidly enough. Missionaries had given up trying to change cultural practices by preaching and voluntarism. They now supported the demands of the settlers that certain customs like polygamy and witchcraft should be legally suppressed by law.

The closing of the missionary mind

After 1850, then, the idea that the Xhosa possessed a humanity that would allow them to receive the Gospel simply through the agency of the missionary message was displaced as the central tenet of belief in missionary culture. It was replaced with the conviction that the character of Xhosa culture and society was the central obstacle to the spread of missionary civilization. Missionary culture before the 1850s was built upon the notion that what needed to be changed in Xhosa society were Xhosa hearts. But by 1850 the idea had entered missionary culture that the Xhosa had no hearts. Before 1850 a dominant theme of missionary culture was that the chiefs would provide access to Xhosa culture. But that idea too had been eroded, as the chiefs came to be seen as being at the center of the cultural resistance to the missionary project.

This is not to say that the humanitarian spirit that we have described as central to the missionary culture of the first half of the century dropped entirely out of sight. It lingered on in some places and persons. But the missionaries who have figured in our story largely go silent after mid-century.[33] Humanitarian ideology survived longest within the missionary culture of Britain itself. Just at the moment when humanitarianism no longer described the discourse on racial policy, it was more firmly attached to the image of empire within the domestic culture. A key figure in this transformation was David Livingstone.

Livingstone arrived in southern Africa in 1841. He identified himself very much with the tradition of John Philip. He condemned Calderwood bitterly, expressed admiration for the Khoe rebels of the Kat river settlement, and supported the Xhosa in the war of 1850–3. An article that he wrote in 1851 in support of the Xhosa was rejected for publication by the *British Quarterly*. In many ways Livingstone seemed set to become as much a maverick within missionary circles as James Read. Like Read, he remained a universal humanitarian in the mold of that earlier generation of missionaries. But Livingstone's career took a different turn from Read's. He never spent much time as a working missionary. His fame rested upon his role as an explorer. In fact, he turned to exploration because of a disillusionment with missionary work that was partly a function of his lack of success. Still, the way he fused commerce and Christianity in his ideology of missionary travel was not that dissimilar to the journey traced by the missionaries we have followed as they waltzed – like Livingstone – toward a closer embrace with the imperial state.[34]

The important thing about Livingstone was not what he believed, but what he represented. Once he became a public figure, he was very careful to temper what he said in public with ambiguity and restraint. He was complicit in his own transformation from a private man, who believed in the rights of the African to fight to be free of the colonizer, to the public man who was the seal of moral approval for British imperialism. Livingstone was a constructed hero. But the key to estimating his historical significance does not lie in his achievements. Rather, the key lies in the gap between these achievements and how they were represented within the domestic culture. Livingstone came to epitomize Britain's imperial missionary culture, not because of what he *did*, but because of what he was *represented* to have done. He was important because he posed a vision of British imperialism that fused moral purpose with the civilizing functions and values of commerce. He was important because he normalized missionary effort in British culture; he made missionaries into "heroes" rather than eccentric zealots. This was terribly important to British culture in Britain, but it said very little about the conditions of missionary existence in the empire itself. It was as an icon rather than as an expression of what was happening to missionary culture on the ground in the empire that Livingstone is a significant historical figure. He was a religious version of the imperial hero, and it is within that line of tradition that he should be treated.[35]

One of the most famous stories about Livingstone is his encounter with an African rain doctor. In the story, Livingstone is shown engaging and exchanging opinions with the doctor, and taking the worldview of the African seriously. It is a story that established the humanity of Livingstone and served to legitimate the principle of universal humanity that he represented. But his position in this respect was by this time eccentric. Most such encounters were not nearly so clinical on the missionary's side, nor was missionary culture any longer much interested in this kind of engagement.[36] It was deeply ironic that just at the moment when the missionary effort in Britain was being installed as the moral center of Britain's imperial identity, the original intent and assumptions of the missionary project among the Xhosa were in tatters. The pessimism and fear inherent in missionary mentality ultimately won out over the optimistic view that any human heart could receive Christian civilization. A combination of circumstances had led the missionaries to this position, but they all revolved around the evidence that the encounter with the Xhosa had not proceeded according to plan. The result was that new modes of engagement with the Xhosa were developed.

Conclusion

The ideological failure of the original missionary project left its missionaries stranded. Where were they to go intellectually? Some, like Richard Birt, found a new equilibrium of belief that enabled them to carry on with an intellectual and moral coherence. Some, like William Shaw, shifted ideologically and politically toward the settler community, and wholeheartedly embraced the settler discourse on the Xhosa. Others, like George Brown, William Shrewsbury and Henry Calderwood, gave up and moved to completely new (and presciently modern) positions. Yet others – the majority – like J. F. Cumming, or the celebrated Read family, seem to have withdrawn into various degrees of silence, accepting the limitations that surrounded their work. They were the ones who built the institutions of separate, sect-like missions existing in uneasy interaction with Xhosa Christianity.[37]

All of these intellectual positions, however, reflected to a greater or lesser degree the way that the missionary culture of the early nineteenth century closed its mind to the Xhosa. And we may complete this account of the closing of the missionary mind with two stories that nicely capture where missionary culture ultimately came to rest. In their different ways they illustrate how Xhosa culture had been transformed in missionary minds from a site of hopeful light to a site of hopeless darkness.

The first story concerns Charles Brownlee, a long-time imperial official on the frontier. Brownlee was a man who could claim to "know" the Xhosa as well as anyone in his generation. His father, John Brownlee, had been one of the first missionaries in the eastern Cape. He had traveled to Cape Town in the same boat as Robert Moffat in 1816 and had been a founder of King William's Town in 1823. Brownlee grew up close to the Xhosa; he spoke the language perfectly, and was intimately acquainted with all the leading *dramatis personae* on both sides of the frontier during the whole of this period. Governor Smith appointed him as Commissioner to Sandile's branch of the Xhosa in 1847. He served in this capacity until 1867, when he was appointed magistrate at Somerset East, following which he became the first Secretary for Native Affairs to the Cape Government in 1872. With Theophilus Shepstone in Natal, Brownlee was the first modern British "authority" on African affairs. Although he was never a formal missionary, his life had been forged in the missionary culture of the early nineteenth-century eastern Cape. As a young person he had been educated by the American missionaries in Natal, while he served as their interpreter.[38]

When he took his leave of Sandile's tribe in 1867, a day of ceremony was staged, at which numerous speeches were given by the leading Xhosa chiefs and others. The Xhosa proclaimed their regret that Brownlee was leaving, and thanked him for his guidance over the years, attributing to him the peace of the past few years and lamenting the loss of a voice that could speak for them in the circles of imperial power. These expressions of regret were probably genuine. In their dealings with the imperial state, the Xhosa found real advantage in a Commissioner who was familiar, whose foibles they knew well and whose history they had lived. But it is Brownlee's speech that interests us.[39]

Brownlee's speech dispensed with the polite formalities that one might have expected on such an occasion. Nor did it provide a comforting assessment of the progress the tribe had made under his benevolent guidance. He made no attempt to celebrate his own record of achievement. Instead, it was a diatribe, a scolding worthy of the stereotypical Victorian father. He addressed the Xhosa as "My children" and went on to provide a report card on their behavior, each chief receiving a public character assessment. The story of the Xhosa as it was recounted in his address was one of repeated obduracy. They had failed to heed his warning never to fight against the Government; they had wantonly destroyed their prosperity in the cattle-killing; they had failed to learn the lessons of morality that he had taught them; robbery and cattle-thieving were still rampant. They had learnt nothing; they had gained no wisdom: "Your customs are unchanged, so is your practice." Brownlee left them, he said, "in sadness ... because I accomplished nothing ... I leave you as I found you ... Long since have I told you that as British subjects you could not prosper while you lived in antagonism to British customs and laws ... [but] you still live as if you had never heard of a better way ... Where is this leading you? ... it leads to ruin."[40]

Brownlee's speech was a remarkable insight into the mental world of those who had spent the previous thirty years encountering the Xhosa from the standpoint of missionary culture. The speech was an open admission of failure. Brownlee confessed that the energy and work that had been put into changing and influencing the hearts, culture and behavior of the Xhosa had all been for nought. For Brownlee, as for Calderwood, we may recall, this failure was personal. He also assumed that it would be personal for them, too, as it would for a delinquent child. He believed that his word would be hard for the Xhosa to hear, but his tough-love approach required that they be said: "My words may be hard. I bequeath them to you because I love you." Brownlee's speech thus reveals an injured narcissism that is typical of imperial culture. The narcissist believes that all is centered on him or her, so Brownlee must personalize his condemnation of the Xhosa for their rejection of his wisdom. Importantly, it did not occur to Brownlee to think that this was good news to the Xhosa, that it showed the success of their attempts to evade the controls of British culture.

Furthermore, Brownlee's speech suggested the narcissism of imperial culture in another respect. Just as the narcissist generally fails to take responsibility for what happens to him or her, so Brownlee was incapable of self-reflection. In his contemplation of the failure of missionary-led cultural reform among the Xhosa, Brownlee was not led to ponder the contribution of missionary or British ideology to that result. To the contrary, responsibility for Brownlee's failure was projected back on to the Xhosa themselves, just as it was by Calderwood and Brown. The Xhosa had *refused* the wisdom and light they were offered. Since this was a failure of the Xhosa themselves, Brownlee and the others did not have to confront their own responsibility for this failure. It was the inherent character of the Xhosa themselves that had caused the missionary project to stumble. It had nothing to do with the missionaries. This was (and it remains today) the characteristic sleight of hand of imperial culture: its failure to persuade its subjects to accept imperial rule is attributed to the intractable character and culture of the colonized. This, in its turn, provides justification for the colonizers to impose and extend their rule even further.

Let us leave Charles Brownlee wallowing in his injured narcissism, and turn now to a further example of how the missionary mind had closed by the 1860s. I take it from an event in the life of John A. Chalmers, a missionary from the Glasgow Missionary Society who took up his station in the early 1860s. Chalmers was a generation younger than Brownlee, but he came from the same kind of family tradition. His father, William Chalmers, had arrived on the eastern frontier in the mid-1820s, in company with James Weir and Alexander McDiarmid, to establish mission stations at Balfour, Pirie and Burnshill. William Chalmers settled at Tyhume and began many years of intimate contact between his family and the Xhosa.[41]

John Chalmers was sent to Britain to be educated, and returned in 1863 to assist Tiyo Soga, the Xhosa missionary at the Emgwali station. Chalmers's response to his re-encounter with the Xhosa repeated a pattern we have noted among the previous generation of missionaries. His initial reports after his arrival were hopeful and upbeat. He engaged with the cultural customs of the Xhosa at close quarters and reported successful interventions and promising signs of change. Within a couple of years, however, a change had come over Chalmers. It may have been connected with the move to a new station, which took him away from Soga. Or it may have had to do with a strange and unsettling encounter he had at a funeral ceremony for Namba, a son of Maqoma, who had been treated by witch-doctors for consumption. In any case, it is evident that the strain of his persistent struggles with the "silly practices of their forefathers" was beginning to tell. He began to exhibit the characteristic signs of a missionary in emotional and intellectual crisis. He reported himself "broken hearted at the small signs of spiritual life." He regretted being "cast ... among untutored savages ... to labor amongst rude barbarians." He told how "often after my work is done I sit alone in this hut ... well nigh broken hearted at the apparent unfruitfulness of my labours." It was no wonder. He had just returned from an experience that would try all but the most self-righteous of persons.[42]

Arriving at his church one day in November 1864 he found a large congregation. His initial surprise and pleasure soon dissolved when he realized that the audience was largely drunk. They had been drinking all night, and one can only assume that they had arrived to taunt the missionary. Predictably, the service was a disaster. The audience laughed and chatted during the preliminary service, they refused to *stop* singing when the hymn was over, and insisting on smoking throughout it all. Chalmers claimed that he rescued the situation by singling out one or two of the worst offenders and severely rebuking them, so that by the end all was perfect order. But one hardly believes this. Like Calderwood's reports of his encounter with Maqoma, Chalmers's claim was more likely a rhetorical contrivance to convince the audience back home – this was written for the *Missionary Record* – that the moral superiority of the missionary would prevail over the people who were "still in darkness." And darkness is what Chalmers now found everywhere. Except, that is, in the settler community. He began to praise the settler community, and to argue how they had been much maligned, how liberal-minded they really were, and how (telling phrase) missions on the frontier "are not invested with that halo of romance which hangs around them at home." Once missionaries like Chalmers started eulogizing settlers, it is a sure sign that the foundations of their mental world were trembling.[43]

Then, a few months later, in the April of 1865, Chalmers published an article in the *King William's Town Gazette* that announced a decisive shift in his consciousness and his break with the missionary culture of his past. His article proceeded from a theory popularized by Robert Knox that the degenerate races of the world would be unable to sustain the race for life and were destined for extinction. The Xhosa race had shown by their behavior that they qualified for this fate. They were incapable of embracing the benefits that British culture had to offer. Instead, they possessed a seemingly insatiable desire for the vice that the British brought with them. He instanced the rate of drunkenness among the chiefs, bearing in mind the funeral of Namba, at which Anta and Oba, both drunk, had used the occasion to make proto-nationalist speeches about the way "we are now trampled under foot by the white man."

But it was not the white man Chalmers blamed the most for the state of the Xhosa – as John Philip and his generation would have done. The Xhosa were responsible for their own fate. Their indolent habits and sloth prevented the spread of industrious habits. They were the ones who refused to take advantage of the schooling that was offered, for example, with the result that they are "steeped in ignorance, [and] every year must witness a gradual sinking until they lose their nationality." Chalmers now joined the road that Calderwood and Brown had walked before him.[44]

By 1865 missionaries inhabited a very different mental universe from the pioneering days of the 1830s. Their confrontation with Xhosa culture had not worked out the way that was expected or predicted. Their own culture had buckled under the strains of its encounter with Xhosa culture. But it was not enough for missionaries to retreat into the closed mindset that has been described above. New structures of understanding had to be erected to replace the tattered remnant of the evangelical humanitarianism of the earlier part of the century. A new knowledge system had to be created that would enable the Xhosa to be explained, categorized and understood. Missionaries contributed significantly to this new discourse; but by the 1860s it was of interest not merely to missionaries. As the British imperial state came to play an ever-larger role in the affairs of the Xhosa, such a knowledge system was necessary for imperial culture as a whole. If the Xhosa were to be ruled by Britain, and if they were to join the roster of other "savage" peoples the British presumed to "civilize," they had to be "known." I shall therefore now turn to how the imperial knowledge system about the Xhosa was created. And in doing so this next chapter will serve as a transitional bridge that moves the narrative away from the world of missionaries and toward the world of the imperial state.

NOTES

1. CA, LG 600, *Papers Received from C. L. Stretch, Diplomatic Agent, Relating to Stock Thefts on the Frontier 1837–1844* , p. 355: "Mr. Calderwood's life was miserable after he descended from elated position of missionary to accept a paltry magistracy that his bread might be buttered thicker. So alarmed was he for his life at Alice that his residence was like a prison, with bars at his doors and windows and the head of the Police informed me that he had two policemen often to accompany him to his office. I was exceedingly pained at these facts as I always looked forward to his assuming the position of the late Dr. Philip in defending the aborigines generally in this colony." This volume is sometimes referred to as Stretch's diary, although it is not that. This entry was written much later than the dates on the title page.

2. Andrew Bank, "Losing Faith in the Civilizing Mission: The Premature Decline of Humanitarian Liberalism at the Cape, 1840–60," in Martin Daunton and Richard Halpern, *Empire and Others: British Encounters with Indigenous Peoples, 1600–1850* (Philadelphia, 1999), pp. 364–83. But see Saul Dubow, *A Commonwealth of Knowledge: Science, Sensibility and White South Africa 1820–2000* (Oxford, 2006), ch. 2, for the continuation of this type of discourse into the 1870s.

3. There is of course an enormous bibliography on this question. See Philip Curtin, *The Image of Africa: British Ideas and Action, 1780–1850* (Madison, 1964), vol. II, pp. 380–2; Christine Bolt, *Victorian Ideas of Race* (London, 1971); Douglas Lorrimer, *Victorians and Race* (Montreal, 1974); Catherine Hall, "'From Greenland's Icy Mountains … to Afric's Golden Sand': Ethnicity, Race and Nation in Mid-Century England," *Gender and History* 5.2 (Summer 1993), pp. 212–30; Nancy Stepan, *The Idea of Race in Science: Great Britain 1800–1960* (Hamden, CN, 1982); Peter Mandler, "'Race' and 'Nation' in Mid-Victorian Thought," in Richard Whatmore, Stefan Collini and Brian Young, *History, Religion and Culture: British Intellectual History 1750–1850* (Cambridge, 2000), pp. 224–43; Robert Knox, *The Races of Man* (London, 1850); William Miller Macmillan, *Bantu, Boer and Briton: The Making of the South African Native Problem* (Oxford, 1963), pp. 306–7 for the Niven assertion. Robert Knox, "Inquiry into the Origin and Characteristic Differences of the Native Races inhabiting the Extra-tropical part of Southern Africa," *Memoirs of the Wernerian Natural History Society*, vol. V (1823–5), pp. 208–10.

4. For a good introduction to the early phase of the opening of the eastern Cape frontier, see Herman Giliomee, "The Eastern Frontier, 1770–1812," in Richard Elphick and Hermann Giliomee, *The Shaping of South African Society, 1652–1840* (Middletown, CN, 1988), pp. 421–59.

5. The wars that interest us were the sixth (1834–5), seventh (1846–7) and eighth (1850–3). There is a very good account of the wars of 1812 and 1819, when the frontier of the Sundays river was breached by the British and a new frontier established, for a while, on the Fish River: see Ben Maclennan, *A Proper Degree of Terror: John Graham and the Cape's Eastern Frontier* (Johannesburg, 1986).

6. GMS, *Minutes of the Presbytery of Kaffraria*, 5 April 1836; CWM, LMS, *Report for 1849*, p. 101; *Report for 1850*, pp. 86–7; *Report for 1854*, p. 56; CWM, LMS, South Africa, *Incoming Correspondence*, Box 23, folder 1, Kayser to Tidman, 21 March 1847; Box 25, folder 2, Brownlee to Tidman, 12 March

1850; Box 29, folder 2, Birt to Thompson, 31 August 1854; Laing, *Journal*, 1 March 1858.

7. CWM, LMS, South Africa, *Incoming Correspondence*, Box 22, folder 1, Calderwood to Tidman, 2 March 1846, reporting the removal of all missionaries from Xhosaland; Box 23, folder 1, Birt to Directors, 14 April 1847.

8. See Cumming, *Diary*, 13, 6, 19 and 20 January 1850 and 21 July 1851, for the trauma and sadness of being forced to leave his mission in January 1851. They had hoped to stay on, remaining neutral, but Sandile's counselors insisted that they leave. United Presbyterian Church, *Missionary Record*, May 1851, p. 94. Niven was expelled by Governor Cathcart for supposedly meddling in imperial policy matters.

9. Joseph John Freeman, *A Tour of South Africa* (London, 1851), pp. 69, 95–8. Freeman was the secretary of the LMS and had taken an inspection tour of Mauritius and South Africa in 1849. He was critical of institutions like Bethelsdorp and of their Khoi residents, and he was concerned about the quality of conversions. But for the most part, his report endorsed the policy associated with John Philip as expressed in the latter's *Researches in South Africa* in the late 1820s; CWM, LMS, South Africa, *Incoming Correspondence*, Box 26, folder 3, Kayser to Directors, 14 October 1851.

10. Celia Sadler (compiler), *Never a Young Man: Extracts from the Letters and Journals of William Shaw* (Cape Town, 1967), pp. 93, 157–8, which note was originally a letter to Lord Aberdeen. See Clifton Crais, *White Supremacy and Black Resistance in Pre-industrial South Africa. The Making of the Colonial Order in the Eastern Cape 1790–1865* (Cambridge, 1992), pp. 128–34, for a good discussion of the shift in settler discourse from a "humanitarian" to a more racialist discourse throughout the 1820s. See also William Shaw, *The Story of My Mission in South-Eastern Africa: Comprising some Account of the European Colonists with Extended Notices of the Kaffir and Other Native Tribes* (London, 1860), p. 159; WMMS, South Africa, *Incoming Correspondence 1830–1857*, Box 3, fiche 93, Shrewsbury, Haddy and Young to Directors, 1 January 1835, and Haddy to Directors, 18 January 1835, for the private views of the Methodist missionaries of the damage the war did to good relations with the Xhosa.

11. Elizabeth Elbourne, "The Creation of 'Knowledge' about 'Aborigines' in the Early Nineteenth-Century British Empire" (Canadian Historical Association, Toronto, 2003); "The Sin of the Settler: The 1835–36 Select Committee on Aborigines and Debates over Virtue and Conquest in the Early Nineteenth-Century British White Settler Empire," *Journal of Colonialism and Colonial Studies* 4.3 (2003); Zoe Laidlaw, *Colonial Connections 1815–45: Patronage, the Information Revolution and Colonial Government* (Manchester, 2005), pp. 147–54.

12. CWM, LMS, South Africa, *Incoming Correspondence*, Box 14, folder 4, Philip to Ellis, 4 June 1835.

13. CWM, LMS, South Africa, *Incoming Correspondence*, Box 22, folder 2, Philip to Maitland, 5 November 1846; Box 23, folder 1, James Read Snr., to Directors, 23 March 1847. Freeman, *Tour of South Africa*, pp. 102–3, 206–7, 210–11, is about the only statement I can find from an LMS official which attributes the war to imperial policy and is critical of its treatment of the Xhosa. Macmillan, *Bantu, Boer and Briton*, pp. 278–305, and Andrew Ross, *John Philip 1775–1851:*

Missions, Race and Politics in South Africa (Aberdeen, 1986), are not very illuminating on this.

14. For frontier policy see John S. Galbraith, *Reluctant Empire: British Policy on the South African Frontier 1834–1854* (Berkeley, 1963), pp. 142–67. CWM, LMS, South Africa, *Incoming Correspondence*, Box 22, folder 2, Calderwood to Tildman, 13 August 1846; Andrew Porter, *Religion Versus Empire? British Protestant Missionaries and Overseas Expansion 1700–1914* (Manchester, 2004), pp. 111–13, 116–17.

15. GMS, *Minutes of the Presbytery of Kaffraria*, 28 February 1835; Cumming, *Diary*, 28 September and 26 October 1850; CWM, LMS, South Africa, *Incoming Correspondence*, Box 25, folder 4, Niven to Stretch, 8 November 1850; United Presbyterian Church, *Missionary Record*, May 1851, p. 71.

16. Brown, *Personal Adventures in South Africa*, p. 40.

17. This question is treated in Premish Lalu, "The Grammar of Domination and the Subjection of Agency: Colonial Texts and Modes of Evidence," *History and Theory*, Theme Issue 39 (2000), pp. 45–68.

18. CA, A80(2), Ayliff, *Journal 1832–50*, 17 February 1835; CA, LG 408, *Letters Received from Resident Agent Fort Peddie 1844, 1845; Fort Waterloo 1836–1837; Tambookieland 1837–1838*; undated and unsigned memorandum from 1836–7, probably by H. F. Fynn, resident agent in "Tambookieland," in the volume at pp. 215–19; Rev. William J. Shrewsbury, *The Journal and Selected Letters of Rev. William J. Shrewsbury 1826–1835*, ed. Hildegarde Fast (Johannesburg, 1994), pp. 173–6. The idea of chiefly conspiracies from now on plays an important role in the way the imperial administration explained events in Xhosaland. See Chapter 8 below.

19. CWM, LMS, South Africa, *Incoming Correspondence*, Box 25, folder 4, Calderwood to Freeman, 2 July 1850. This is a long (fifteen-page) document whose dominant theme is the absolute benignity of the frontier policy of the government and the absolute responsibility of the Xhosa for the war due to their plundering behavior and unwillingness to accept government's terms. For other missionary views that blamed the Xhosa see ibid., Box 26, folder 1, Birt to Freeman, 12 March 1851; Kayser to Freeman, 21 April 1851; Brownlee to Birt, 26 May 1851. Only James Read provided a counter-analysis: see Read to Freeman, 13 April 1851.

20. Ibid., Box 26, folder 1, Birt to Freeman, 12 March 1851.

21. Cumming, *Diary*, 27 June 1847; WMMS, *Reports for 1848*, p. 71; United Presbyterian Church, *Missionary Record*, December 1846, p. 181.

22. CWM, LMS, *Report for 1858*, p. 58: this was Friedrich Kayser's view; CWM, LMS, South Africa, *Incoming Correspondence*, Box 30, folder 2, Kayser to Directors, 7 October 1857; SPCK, *Recollections of a Visit to British Kaffraria* (London, 1866), pp. 37–8; CA, A 80 (4), Ayliff Papers, *Journal of John Ayliff, 1856–59*, 7 January 1857, for sentiments similar to Kayser's. United Presbyterian Church, *Missionary Record*, 1 September 1857, pp. 166–7. The *Missionary Record* did include a long account of the cattle-killing in May 1857, pp. 91–3.

23. United Presbyterian Church, *Missionary Record*, 1 January 1858, p. 8, as reported by Cumming.

24. Landau, "Nineteenth Century Transformations," p. 16; Johannes Du Plessis, *A History of Christian Missions in South Africa* (London, 1911), p. 29; Wallace G. Mills, "The Taylor Revival of 1866 and the Roots of African Nationalism in the Cape Colony," *Journal of Religion in Africa* 8.2 (1976), pp. 105–22.

25. Reverend R. Niven, *An Impartial Analysis of the Kaffir character in a letter from Rev. Robert Niven to Mr Stretch* (Graham's Town, 1840), pp. 16–19.

26. CA, BK 443, *Missionary Letters to the High Commissioner 1848*, Niven to Smith, 28 October 1848; Read's momentary infatuation with Smith faded when, as was usual with Smith, he failed to follow through on his promises; see CWM, LMS, South Africa, *Incoming Correspondence*, Box 23, folder 1, James Read Snr. to Tidman, 21 January 1848; Read to Philip, 4 February 1848; folder 6, Read to Tidman, 7 June 1848.

27. Niven's program of action is collected along with submissions from other missionaries in CA, BK 443, *Missionaries Letters to the High Commissioner 1848*.

28. CA, BK 90, *Missions: Correspondence Between Chief Commissioner, British Kaffraria, and Missionaries 1848–56*, Laing to Maclean, 20 December 1854, and Birt to Maclean, 6 July and 27 July 1854, for some thoughts from Richard Birt on how to inculcate market relations among the Xhosa. Such discussion of the best wage schemes was current in Britain at the time.

29. Ibid., J. C. Warner to Smith, 17 May 1848.

30. CA, GH14/2, *Papers Received from Native Tribes, Diplomatic Agents and Government Officials 1844–45*, Birt to Stretch, 14 December 1844; LG 402, *Letters Received from the Diplomatic Agent of Caffraria 1844*, Stretch to Hare, 14 January 1844, emphasis added.

31. CA, BK 90, *Missions*, Cathcart to Birt, 18 April 1854. Birt was not alone. William Impey, another Glasgow missionary, had experienced a similar kind of awakening. Ten years after his arrival at the Cape he admitted that his early hope for the salvation of the Xhosa was naive. The Xhosa were little changed, he argued. And it was necessary to take forceful action to remove the hindrances to civilizing influences. Civilization could take root only if they were uprooted from their villages and concentrated into settlements, where their communitarian culture would be removed and they would be obliged to adopt the principles of private property. In order to bring civilization and freedom to the Xhosa, it was necessary to deploy a despotic power and authority against them. GH 19/8, *Papers Connected with Sandilli, Kreli, Pato Etc. 1847*, Impey to Smith, 22 October 1850; Rev. William Impey, *Journal 1838–1847*, 10 March 1839.

32. LMS, *Missionary Magazine*, 1866, p. 226. See also Du Toit, "Cape Frontier," pp. 38–9; Rev. William C. Holden, *The Past and Future of the Kaffir Races* (Cape Town, repr. 1963), pp. 279–80, 393–407. Where the logic of this reorientation of missionary culture *could* end up was revealed by the support of the LMS for harsh, military-style Chartered Company rule over the Matebele in the 1880s; see H. Alan Cairns, *Prelude to Imperialism: British Reactions to Central African Society 1840–1890* (London, 1965), pp. 242–4.

33. The group of Presbyterian missionaries in Blantyre, Malawi, in the 1890s continued to hold to the values of universal humanitarianism, expressing the core belief that the natural capacity of Africans was not inferior to that of Europeans. But when they tried to create a multiracial community, they were

blocked by a new generation of missionaries from Britain and discredited in the same way that Samuel Crowther had been in West Africa at about the same time. Ross, "Christian Missions and the Mid-Nineteenth Century Change in Attitudes to Race: The African Experience," in Andrew Porter (ed.), *The Imperial Horizons of British Protestant Missions 1880–1914* (Grand Rapids, Michigan, 2003), pp. 85–105. The diaries of people like Cumming and Impey dry up in terms of evidence of what they were thinking and how they were interacting with the Xhosa.

34. Elizabeth Elbourne, *Blood Ground: Colonialism, Missions, and the Contest for Christianity in the Cape Colony and Britain, 1799–1853* (Kingston, Ont., 2002), pp. 311–14; Andrew Ross, *John Philip 1775–1851: Missions, Race and Politics in South Africa* (Aberdeen, 1986), p. 227; Christopher Petrusic, "Violence as Masculinity: David Livingstone's Radical Politics in the Cape Colony and the Transvaal, 1845–1852," *International History Review* 26.1 (2004), pp. 20–55; Andrew Ross, *David Livingstone: Mission and Empire* (London, 2002), pp. 69–75. Tim Jeal, *Livingstone* (New York, 1973), ch. 11; see also Felix Driver, *Geography Militant: Cultures of Exploration and Empire* (Oxford, 2000), pp. 68–89.

35. The way in which the Livingstone image was constructed is demonstrated in Dorothy Helly, *Livingstone's Legacy: Horace Waller and Victorian Myth-making* (Athens, OH, 1987); see also Ross, *David Livingstone*, ch. 8; Twells, "Children of a Larger Growth," pp. 8–9; Neil Gunson, *Messengers of Grace: Evangelical Mission in the South Seas 1797–1860* (Melbourne, 1978), p. 335.

36. David Livingstone, *Missionary Travels and Researches in South Africa* (New York, 1858), pp. 25–7. It is worth noting that Livingstone was, at least, argued to a stalement by the Tswana man, but he did not have the same reaction as Calderwood. It may be that Livingstone's medical training was important here. Another example that I have come across that represented this older style of engagement was that of D. John Fitzgerald, whom Sir George Grey recruited to set up a native hospital in King William's Town. He made a study of Xhosa traditional medical methods and treated his Xhosa counterparts more as professional colleagues than as examples of an inferior race. Of course, he was concerned to demonstrate the superiority of his medical techniques. But neither was he willing to dismiss the Xhosa methods as being of no account. He understood the distinction that was continually being confused in imperial culture between the native doctors and the so-called witchdoctors. For Fitzgerald see David Gordon, "A Sword of Empire? Medicine and Colonialism in King William's Town, Xhosaland, 1856–1891," *African Studies* 60.2 (2001), pp. 165–83. NLSA (CT), Grey Collection, MSB 223, *Miscellaneous Manuscripts*, Folder 10, "Witch Doctors, etc. Dr. Fitzgerald."

37. It was, of course, politically dangerous to be pro-Xhosa in the early 1850s, and we should never underestimate the silencing effect of the changing terms of politics. Indeed, the Reads were marginalized and discredited by the support the Kat river settlement gave to the Xhosa–Khoe alliance in the eighth frontier war. See Elbourne, *Blood Ground*, pp. 368–74, for the political trials that followed.

38. Thus see two "Addresses to the Missionary Conference," printed in Charles Brownlee, *Reminiscences of Kaffir Life and History* (Lovedale, 1896), pp. 366–94.

39. A similar lamentation from the Xhosa was heard when J. C. Warner – another longstanding figure in Xhosa–British relations – was removed from the Thembu in 1865, and for similar reasons; see Holden, *Past and Future of the Kaffir Races*, pp. 398–9.
40. See Brownlee, *Reminiscences of Kafir Life and History*, pp. 68–78, for the complete address. Illustrating its significance for missionary culture, the LMS *Missionary Magazine*, 1868, pp. 167–72, printed a full report of the meeting and speeches. His report card on each chief depended on their posture toward missionary teaching.
41. Du Plessis, *History of Christian Missions in South Africa*, pp. 184–7.
42. United Presbyterian Church, *Missionary Record*, 1 March 1862, pp. 38–9; 1 January 1863, pp. 7–11; 2 May 1864, p. 87.
43. Ibid., 1 March 1865, p. 37. It is worth noting that Chalmers did not excuse the British from their part in this story. He talks of the tendency of colonization to import the dregs of the mother country and the worst vices of the metropole. Of course, this sat uneasily with his earlier defense of the settlers. But this kind of incoherence in argument likely reflects the volatility of his mental state under the pressures of the encounter.
44. *King William's Town Gazette*, 3 April 1865. There was another fascinating context for this diatribe: it was originally published in the Xhosa language paper *Indaba*. And Chalmers must have written it in close proximity to his colleague Tiyo Soga. There is no evidence that he and Soga did not get along; indeed, Chalmers was Soga's first biographer. The outburst caused Soga much pain, however. He made a dignified reply in the *King William's Town Gazette*, 11 May 1865. See also *Cumming Correspondence*, MSB 139, Box 5, Soga to Cumming, 21 May 1865. For the discourse on the extinction of inferior races, see Patrick Brantlinger, *Dark Vanishings: Discourse on the Extinction of Primitive Races* (Ithaca, NY, 2003).

7   Creating colonial knowledge

From knowledge to ignorance

Knowledge systems are essential for empire. Agents of empire need to understand the behavior and culture of those they rule. They need maps of the terrains their subjects occupy; they need to be able to read what it is they are seeing when they gaze out at the colonized. Naturally, the knowledge systems that are used in empire seldom capture the realities of their subjects' lives. But this hardly matters, since the purpose of such systems is to legitimate the superiority that the colonizers know they enjoy. If the knowledge that the colonizers possess is to be functional in imperial culture, it must reinforce and feed the colonizers' own view of themselves and of what they are actually *doing* in their imperial role. In this chapter, I am concerned to ask how a knowledge system about the Xhosa was constructed that fulfilled those needs.[1]

Most treatments of colonial knowledge systems assume that they are commodities conjured in the metropole, packed into the baggage of the imperial traveler, and unwrapped on the first encounter with the indigenous peoples the imperialists had come to rule. But this was not so. Colonial culture had to be *created* and *constructed* out of the interaction between the metropolitan culture that the colonizers brought with them and the cultures they found at the frontier of empire. This was the foundation upon which the knowledge system of empire was built. The knowledge that was produced in empire then had to be fitted into the culture of the metropole. This process of transmission back to the metropole and its representation in metropolitan culture was a complicated one which is too large to be described here.[2]

Different knowledge systems were created for different parts of the empire, depending upon the specific local and historical circumstances under which the systems were produced. The need to construct a knowledge system about the Xhosa was triggered by the changing strategic significance of the Cape for the British empire after 1801. Little reliable knowledge existed about the interior of the Cape Colony. After *c.* 1800 a new market existed for accounts of the interior that could be used by the government and fed to the large reading public eager for travelers' accounts of exotic peoples like the Xhosa.[3]

The knowledge system that came out of this imperative at the turn of the century, however, was not coherent. It did not present a complete explanation of Xhosa culture, society and character. It presented a split and uncertain view of the Xhosa. The production of knowledge by ethnographers and missionaries about the Xhosa in the first and second decades of the nineteenth century was not yet a truly colonial knowledge system. It did not provide a logical, interlocking set of precepts which the British could use as a reference system to categorize and comprehend all aspects of Xhosa life and behavior.

By the second and third decades of the nineteenth century, missionary activity in the Cape had begun to produce a steady stream of accounts of the Xhosa that fused an ethnographic approach with the ideology of missionary culture. And as missionary culture imploded under the impact of its encounter with the Xhosa, the need for a system of knowledge that could explain this outcome was painfully obvious. By that time, also, missionaries were not the only spokespersons for British culture on the eastern frontier. White settler politics emerged after 1835 to challenge the monopoly of the missionaries over who should speak for the Cape Colony in British politics. After 1835, too, an incipient imperial bureaucracy represented the British state on the frontier. Missionaries were not the only ones who could claim to know the Xhosa. Settlers needed to assert their own identity, which they could do only partly in reference to the Xhosa "other." And the imperial administration needed a handy set of reference ideas so that it could understand the Xhosa as allies, opponents or subjects – or, indeed, all three.

From the mid-1830s, therefore, there were growing pressures to develop a knowledge system that summarized what was known about the Xhosa into fixed and comprehensible precepts. The split and open knowledge system that had prevailed in the early years of the century began to be replaced by a view of the Xhosa dominated by fixed stereotypes. By the 1850s the Xhosa were *known* to be deceitful and cunning, and inveterate thieves, and their chiefs conspiring manipulators, and their culture was *known* to be irredeemably savage. The old ethnographic studies that represented a more fluid view of Xhosa society disappeared. Their place was taken by texts that presented a description of Xhosa society, culture and character that was certified by authoritative sources: the missionaries, the settlers and the imperial administrators. These groups had stronger claims to *know* the Xhosa than ethnographic observers who wandered into Xhosaland and spent perhaps two months there before moving on.

Equally, these new "authorities" on the Xhosa were precisely the groups who needed a system that would justify and explain colonial rule.

The stereotyped images that came to describe the Xhosa by the mid-nineteenth century were *reductions* that the British employed to explain their own inability to process the knowledge they had gained by observation and interaction into something other than simplifications. It was the mark of this constructed knowledge system that it did not *need* to watch the Xhosa to know them; it did not *need* to observe them to understand their world. The travelers' accounts of the mid-century were essentially repeated endorsements of the stereotypes of this knowledge system. They revealed little about the Xhosa, and much about the British. Precisely because what was known about the Xhosa had been systematized, there remained nothing more to learn about them. The literature of observation that characterized the first phase of the encounter with the Xhosa was replaced by a literature of stereotypes. It is in that sense that the creation of a colonial knowledge system involved a transition from knowledge to ignorance.

I shall open this chapter with a discussion of the early observers of the Xhosa. Included in this group are such well-known figures as Sir John Barrow and Henry Lichtenstein, and less well-known observers like Ludwig Alberti. These people dominated the image of the Xhosa that was presented to the British public until the 1820s, when ethnographic-missionary accounts began to appear. By the end of the 1840s a literature that was more purely anectodal emerged, which dealt entirely in stereotypes. In these works the Xhosa were presented in stark and certain terms, with none of the qualifications and nuances of the earlier literature. This literature was closely associated with the emergence of settler politics in the 1830s. The growth of settler politics was a major condition for the shifting discourse about the Xhosa, and it is important to say something about how that came about.

The literature of popular discourse of mid-century was too slight and rhetorical to provide the texts of a colonial knowledge system about the Xhosa. It lacked authority, since the books tended to be produced by amateur observers who happened to find themselves in Xhosaland. They were not produced by "experts." By the 1860s, however, two texts had emerged to serve as authoritative statements of what was "known" about the Xhosa. One was the product of a frontier imperial administrator, and the other the product of a longstanding Methodist missionary. These were the two categories of Britons who had the closest contact with the Xhosa, and their observations possessed an inherent legitimacy. These texts authorized the stereotypes that had grown out of the failure of missionary culture and the "othering" tendencies of settler politics. A discussion of these texts will form the final section of the chapter.

Discourses about the Xhosa, 1800–1850

A small, steady stream of ethnographic literature and travelers' accounts of southern Africa appeared before the nineteenth century. Some of this reflected fascination with the "Hottentots" which had begun with the first contact between English sailors and the Khoesan peoples from the 1590s. Early modern characterizations of the peoples of southern Africa were dominated by negative representations. But in the eighteenth century more favorable views came to compete with the notion that southern Africa was home to the lowest and basest form of humankind. Accounts of the peoples of the interior began to appear in the early nineteenth century, including the first serious descriptions of the Xhosa. These accounts were more interesting and nuanced than is typically realized.[4]

Early descriptions of Xhosa society conveyed a detailed sense of the complexities of those peoples. Indeed, the indigenes were all over these accounts, as the authors grappled with the necessity to understand and categorize them. It was true that such writers *also* talked about the flora, fauna and topography. But these complemented the very detailed descriptions of customs and cultures. There was increasingly some sharing of material in these accounts, so that one can see how stereotypes came into being. But this body of early observer literature is characterized by descriptions of the Xhosa that are complex rather than simplified. The dominant themes of Xhosa society and culture that are presented by this literature fall under three main headings.[5]

First, they presented a balanced view of Xhosa society. Those aspects of Xhosa culture that conformed to European standards of civilization were reported, as well those aspects that were less flattering. Although there were differences of emphasis, all tended to remark, for example, on the "dignity" of the men and the "modesty" of the women. Barrow described Xhosa men as "the finest figures I ever beheld," and the women as "lively, but not impudent." It was agreed that the subordinate and commodity status of women in Xhosa society disguised the very real influence they exercised within the home. According to Henry Lichtenstein, women controlled the property of the household. Similarly, these observers were impressed with the strong sense of internal cohesion and social responsibility that marked Xhosa society. Loyalty to friends and politesse to visitors were important values for the Xhosa. It was thus possible to travel through their country with perfect security and safety. Indeed, Barrow gushed with praise as he described the personal characteristics of the Xhosa. They were

a mild, rational, and in some degree civilized people … Their rest is not disturbed by violent love, nor their minds ruffled by jealousy; they are free from those licentious appetites ... their frame is neither shaken nor enervated by the use of intoxicating liquors ... The countenance of a Kaffer is always cheerful; and the whole of his demeanour bespeaks content and peace of mind.[6]

Secondly, Xhosa cultural customs and habits were similarly presented in a balanced and nuanced way. Their polity was described as well-ordered and governed by a dense legal code, which regulated morality through its punishment of adultery, and theft through a complex system of fines. Alberti was impressed by the attention that was given to child-rearing. He described the Xhosa as honest and reliable; agreements entered into were seldom violated. But these signs of humanity and civilization were combined with darker signs. If the Xhosa were recognized to be intelligent, they also held to "gross superstition"; if they were seen to be "good natured," they were also acknowledged to plunder colonial cattle enthusiastically. If they were committed to maintaining social peace within their tribes, they were also capable of fierce warfare. If polygamy was practiced, it tended to be as much a political practice of the chiefs as a moral perversion. Infidelity, it was claimed, was rare.[7]

It was noteworthy that these early observers did not define Xhosa society solely around its cultural customs. This is important because the character of those customs was the central feature of colonial knowledge about the Xhosa as it emerged in the later part of the century. But this was not true of early travelers and observers. Such customs were not ignored. Some authors saw them as evidence that the Xhosa fell into the category of "uncivilized." But for others, including Alberti and Barrow, their cultural practices were not highlighted to categorize the Xhosa as a savage and barbarian race. Witchcraft was not treated as the nexus of evil and darkness in Xhosa society. In that respect the perspective of these early commentators formed a sharp contrast to the bias in later perceptions of Xhosa society, where witchcraft was regarded as symptomatic of the degraded state of their culture and as central to the despotism of their political system.[8]

The third characteristic of this literature is the consistently dualistic treatment of the Xhosa. The positive and the negative attributes of Xhosa society were held in tension without one overwhelming the other. This suggests the open and observing qualities these writers brought to the Xhosa. They were not concerned to build stereotypes. This dualism may be illustrated through the example of how the chiefs were described in this literature. The importance of the chiefs to missionary experience of the Xhosa has already been noted. What is impressive about early knowledge of the Xhosa is its recognition of chiefly power as conditioned and constrained.

The question of chiefly power, of course, boiled down to the question: Were they despots or were they constitutional monarchs? The tendency in the early literature was to recognize the complexities that attached to the role of chief. There was little of the simplified formulations that were to describe chiefly power later in the century. Ludwig Alberti observed that the chief combined considerable power that bestowed a formal despotism upon him. But, *in fact*, this power was restrained by popular democratic forces that contained any despotic tendencies he might display. Barrow had been sent by the British Government specifically to make contact with Ngqika. He was considerably impressed with the chief as a formidable negotiator and a statesman, who was "adored by his people." Barrow did not write very deeply about the nature of chiefly power – none of these writers did – but what he did observe was that the chief "had no power over the lives of his subjects." And Lichtenstein, who was otherwise quite critical of Barrow's view of the Xhosa, agreed in this respect with his rival. He noted how chiefs could not govern without consultation with their councils. But Lichtenstein was also the first to point out how the chief's power rested on cattle fines, which gave him a material interest in manipulating the justice system. Conspicuously absent from these accounts, however, was the charge that was later to become a central indictment of chiefly politics: that cultural customs such as witchcraft were manipulated to sustain their power.[9]

From the 1820s through the 1840s, missionary writings dominated the discourse about the Xhosa. This literature was more concerned with problems of frontier policy than with mere ethnographic description. It started from the premise of the universal humanity of cultures and peoples. But it was also concerned to balance the respective attitudes of the British and the Boers toward the Xhosa. In common with the main line of missionary thinking of the 1820s–30s, they attribute most blame to both British and Boers for the instabilities and growing violence of frontier politics. The Xhosa are seen more as victims than as perpetrators of this instability.[10]

Thus the first thing to note about this literature is that its narratives tended to move away from the open-ended observational literature of the early decades of the century. The missionary-inspired literature remained observational in the manner of people like Barrow and Lichtenstein. But prescriptive elements and a moralizing tone were added to this context. James Backhouse's narrative, for example, was shaped by the theme of "improvement." At every point he was concerned to gauge the gains that could be registered thanks to the civilizing influences of the Christian settlements and missions.[11]

A second way in which this literature departed from earlier accounts of the Xhosa was the place accorded to cultural practices. These now moved to the fore as descriptors of Xhosa society, and they highlighted the darker side of Xhosa culture. Whereas Barrow and the others had presented basically favorable descriptions of Xhosa morality, the missionary literature reversed this picture. Barrow's Xhosa women were modest and chaste; Kay's Xhosa women were immodest and unchaste, and fornication was common. Thompson's Xhosa women were drudges to the men, which marked their society as a lower order of civilization. Barrow observed that polygamy was relatively uncommon; the missionaries were obsessed with polygamy. These accounts put witchcraft at the center of social customs and began to identify it as an agent of political tyranny. The use of torture in witchcraft trials appeared in these accounts, whereas it was absent from the observations of people like Alberti, who had spent many years on the frontier. Henceforth, torture was to be a permanent part of the writ the missionaries compiled against Xhosa society. These accounts drew a view of Xhosa culture that presented it as debased. The military observer J. E. Alexander, for example, reported how any crime could be forgiven on payment of cattle fines. Thus the laws of the Xhosa were subject to the venality of the culture. The contrast with the tenor and tone employed by the initial observers could not have been sharper. From being a peacefully inclined people who fought only when they were provoked, they became a predatory nation where thievery was endemic to their character. This kind of presentation laid the intellectual footings for an essentialized racialism.[12]

In its treatment of the chiefs, however, this literature remained dualistic. In fact, the chiefs did not figure very prominently at all. When they were considered, it was still within the framework established earlier: as powerful individuals who existed within a world of political and democratic restraints. George Thompson gave most consideration to the chiefs, and his view affords a nice illustration of a time when there was still no settled, accepted interpretation of chiefly power. On the one hand, Thompson pointed out, the chiefs were absolute sovereigns, chosen by hereditary succession, who decided everything of importance. But their theoretical absolutism was seldom exercised, and, indeed, he believed that Ngqika had willingly surrendered some of his most extensive privileges. Thus "there is more freedom among the Caffers than in many countries far more advanced in civilisation." Chiefly power was constrained by a variety of checks and balances. The fear of desertion by his people was the most powerful of these, being frequently used by individuals who did not like their current chief. Furthermore, although the chief was the judge in serious criminal cases, he always referred his judgment to an assembly of counselors for their advice and consent. Punishment usually took the form of cattle fines; the severest punishments were reserved for witchcraft and sorcery cases. It should be remarked that absent from this litany was the connection that was foregrounded by later writers, between chiefly power and cultural practices such as witchcraft.[13]

This tone was also to be found in the more general literature that presented the Xhosa to the British public. Cowper Rose, for example, who spent four years in southern Africa in the 1820s, wrote how the Xhosa were not a cruel or vindictive people. He was particularly impressed with the chiefs, whom he compared to the representations of Greek and Etruscan figures. It was similarly the case with Thomas Phillips, an 1820 settler who was perhaps the most significant publicist writer about the Cape in Britain. His view of the Xhosa combined the optimism of early missionary culture with the favorable portrayals of their society that had marked the writings of the initial observers. In his *Scenes and Occurrences in Albany and Caffer-Land, South Africa*, published in 1827, for example, Phillips provided a positive account of the Xhosa that it would be impossible to elicit from a settler after 1835. The native tribes, he wrote, were a fine race, with kindly feelings and capable of appreciating the benefits of civilization.[14]

Thomas Phillips belonged, of course, to the humanitarian party that continued to dominate the discourse on racial politics throughout the 1820s and 1830s. By the end of the 1840s, however, a new kind of literature had appeared to inform the British about the Xhosa. This literature was different again from the missionary ethnographies that we have just mentioned. It was a literature that reflected the growing reaction in culture and politics against the humanitarian lobby's view of racial politics. It presented a series of personalized, anecdotal stereotypes. For just these reasons, this literature is fundamentally uninteresting. There is no author among this group to compare, for example, with Barrow's *Travels into the Interior of Southern Africa*. But it is important to note the main themes that ran through this literature, because the series of images that it purveyed was central to the colonial knowledge system that came to govern discourse about the Xhosa.[15]

The first writer to present to the British public the emerging set of stereotypes about the Xhosa was Mrs. Harriet Ward. Harriet Ward was a true nineteenth-century imperial woman. The wife of a captain in the 40th Regiment, she accompanied her husband on his posting to the eastern Cape in the late 1840s and was a witness to the War of the Axe in 1846. A representative of the quiet feminism of her generation of Victorian women, she made a small name for herself as an author. Her most successful work was the book she published after her time in the eastern Cape, *The Cape and the Kaffirs*, which drew upon her observations of the interaction between British and Xhosa. Mrs. Ward then went on to have a career as a writer of fiction. Indeed, she was one of the first writers to pioneer that new genre of juvenile literature: the boy's adventure story set in empire. She published two such books, using her Cape experiences for inspiration.[16]

Harriet Ward also made a contribution to colonial knowledge. Her account of her five years in Xhosaland is notable for several reasons. She was one of the first metropolitan writers to adopt the perspective of the settlers. And, like the representatives of settler discourse, she staked her claim to authority on expertise she had acquired during the years spent living among the Xhosa. By the same token, she used her expert authority to challenge the humanitarian discourse on the Xhosa. Her knowledge of the Xhosa, she claimed, was based on a hard-nosed observation that revealed the "real" Xhosa. This contrasted with the sentimental pieties of the humanitarian knowledge about the Xhosa that were particularly common in Britain itself. Furthermore, she presented her view of the Xhosa as the *truly* humanitarian view. She, too, wanted to bring civilization to the Xhosa, but she recognized that to do so required a clear-eyed view of their cunning and depravity.[17]

Thus her account devolved into a one-sided presentation of the Xhosa that made no pretense at balance. Her narrative is dominated by a long indictment of Xhosa life and behavior, with some sketches of prominent chiefs or their children thrown in for color. It does not pretend to be a work of ethnographic observation, but rather a justification for British dominion that draws upon her personal memories. The Xhosa are reported to be savage intruders who have no rights to the land they claim. They are predatory and treacherous, cunning and incorrigible thieves, who, contrary to the claims of earlier writers, were not in the least bit hospitable or generous, but rather cruel and unfeeling. There is one portion of her account that adequately captures the discourse that Mrs. Ward was part of and which points up the contrast with the prior discourses on the Xhosa:

It must be allowed [this good lady writes] that a Kaffir skin more resembles the hide of some powerful animal than the skin of a human being. In the early part of this war [i.e. the War of the Axe] some person procured the entire skin of a Kafir, and had it treated in the same way leather is first prepared for tanning. I am told that the texture is at least three times the thickness of a white man's and I see no reason to doubting that assertion.

And immediately following this juicy little observation, without any sense of irony, is a discussion of how the Xhosa have no sense of gratitude or generosity! Small wonder, if Mrs. Ward accurately conveys the mentality of the British interaction with the Xhosa by the time of the War of the Axe.[18]

Mrs. Ward's Xhosa was typical of the image being purveyed to the British public by the 1850s. There is no reason to drag the reader through the dull, repetitive corpus of which her book was part. It is enough to say that the unflattering features of Xhosa society that were mentioned in past accounts now moved to occupy the center of the discourse. The Xhosa were cunning and deceitful; their culture was shaped by the horrible cultural practices that missionaries had been combating for the previous twenty years. They had no religion – something Barrow, for one, was not prepared to admit – only superstition. They were indolent and unwilling to settle down. Almost the only remnant of the dualism that marked earlier accounts of the Xhosa was a subdued debate as to where they should be placed in the hierarchy of race. Were they semi-civilized, as their reasoning powers would suggest? Or had their cultural practices so dissolved any hints of civilized status they might have possessed as to drive them to the level of barbarians of the lowest class?[19]

Fortunately, we hardly need linger over that question. We have another question to address, a question that is more open to a satisfactory answer. What were the origins of this shift in the public discourse on the Xhosa? Why was there a change in the nature and quality of the "knowledge" that filled out the discourse about the Xhosa? Why did that discourse move from an open and balanced observational literature to a grab-bag of stereotypes that were repeated and fixed and closed to contrary evidence? I have already given part of the answer to that question: the implosion of missionary culture as it confronted Xhosa culture and politics, and the fracturing of the humanitarian ideology of missionary evangelicalism. But there was another factor that established its presence at the same time, which we must now address: the emergence of settler politics.

The emergence of settler discourse

Until the war of 1834–5, settler politics was not of much consequence either in Britain or in southern Africa. A few petitions that date from the 1820s bemoan the abandonment of the 1820 settlers by the British Government. Within the humanitarian discourse, settlers were viewed as a distinctly dubious asset in the mission to spread British civilization across the world. The general opinion was that they were certainly not to be trusted with the task of civilizing the Xhosa. This was why missionary politics at the Cape put so much emphasis on mission settlements for the Khoi, and on strict protection of the Xhosa from the "avaricious and covetous disposition of the colonists and their licentious conduct."[20]

The war of 1834–5, however, gave impetus to a settler discourse which challenged the dominance of the humanitarian lobby over Colonial Office policies and British public opinion. By the early 1830s the foundations for an institutionalized civic discourse existed within the settler community, particularly through the *Graham's Town Journal*. The *Journal* had been established in 1831 precisely to ensure that the settlers possessed a voice that the government would hear. Three years later Robert Godlonton took it over. Godlonton was the perfect megaphone for the settlers. He was an 1820 emigrant who by the early 1830s had made the transition from unsuccessful farmer to successful commercial agent, landowner and politician. He had been the dominant influence over the newspaper from the beginning; upon becoming full owner, he set about turning it into the voice of the settler community. Before long, its reach was felt in Cape Town and in London, where it supplied *The Times* with news from this far-flung outpost of empire. And so, for the first time, an alternative to the missionary version of southern African affairs was broadcast in the heart of empire.[21]

I am not much concerned with how loud or successful this voice was in shaping the debate on southern African matters, although that is an important question. I am more interested in the kinds of ways the settler case was presented. In projecting themselves into the political discourse, settlers were laying claim to their identity, to stating who they were. They were not staking their claim to be southern Africans; they remained tied to their status as Britishers who were making Britain overseas. Thus the roots of their discourse were almost entirely negative and reactive. They sought to express their identity by locating those enemies who stood in the way of settlers coming into their just rights and having their legitimate demands properly heard. There were three such groups of enemies: the British Government, the humanitarians, and the Xhosa.

The objection to the Government was that its frontier policy left the settlers unprotected from the depredations of the Xhosa. The first to make a full presentation of this case was William Boyce, whose *Notes on South African Affairs* was published in 1838. Boyce was an assistant to the Methodist missionary William Shaw, and had worked as an adviser to D'Urban in the 1834–5 war. His book announced the alliance that had now been forged between the Methodist missionaries and settler politics and identity. But the book attempted to make a reasoned presentation of the settlers' case using official documents around a series of "Notes" on border policies and issues. Boyce's central theme was the responsibility Government frontier policy bore for the instabilities of the region, not injustices wrought upon the Xhosa by the settlers.

Boyce was not unsympathetic to the plight of the Xhosa, however; he had none of the harshness that was to be associated with other spokespersons for the settler position. Indeed, he aligned himself with the main finding of the Select Committee on Aborigines that the greatest injustice of colonization was the appropriation of the land from indigenous

peoples. He used the discourse of humanitarianism against the humanitarians themselves, reminding his readers that it had been missionary
groups that had pressed for some of the most notable removals of Xhosa
from their land in order to make room for mission settlements for the
Khoesan. Indeed, his central criticism of Government frontier policy was
that it had presided over the expulsions of the Xhosa from these lands.
The Xhosa had good reason to be aggrieved. But so did the British
settlers, who had been lured to the eastern Cape by extravagant promises
and then abandoned by the Government and excluded from all say in
policy-making.[22]

In Boyce's analysis, the real grievances of the Xhosa were matched by
their envy at the settlers' wealth. And this revealed the incompatibility of
an independent Xhosa government and society with settler society. "The
residence of a pastoral and predatory people, under its own independent
Government, in the immediate neighbourhood of a civilized community,
has ever proved incompatible with the existence and spread of civilization," he wrote. The solution was paternal control of the Xhosa by the
British. Such control was necessary, Boyce argued, as the only way of
overcoming the resistance of the political and cultural structures of Xhosa
society to Christianizing influences. The British Government had insisted
on treating the Xhosa as independent polities. Frontier instability was the
result as the Xhosa were tempted to attack and despoil the unprotected
property of the settlers.[23]

Boyce's book contained a petition presented to the Colonial Office in
1836, titled "Case and Claims of the British Colonists of Albany."
Godlonton was one of its signatories, and the petition rehearsed what
was to become the dominant settler narrative of their early history. It
recounted how they had been dumped on the shore at Port Elizabeth in
1820 and left to fend for themselves. Their land grants were too small;
they had been unaware of the dangers they faced from "the constant
depredations of the Kaffers"; the British Government had offered them
little protection from the Xhosa. The consequence of all this was the
"irruption" of the Xhosa into the colony in December 1834, and the
displacement and murder of many settlers.

The settlers who signed this petition, however, were also concerned to
assert their status as decent British citizens. They wanted to correct their
image in England as "oppressive to the native tribes, and as factious to the
government." To this end, they laid claim to the mantle of humanitarianism, too. They had gone to southern Africa, the petition claimed, with the
highest hopes and the most benevolent intentions towards the "coloured
classes." Although this petition was noticed in the London press, and was
presented to the House of Commons by no less a personage than William

Gladstone, the Colonial Secretary dismissed their pleas with a recitation of the familiar humanitarian line on the settlers – how they were the source of frontier instability, not its victims.[24]

Settler resentment against the British Government was fueled by the frontier policy decreed by London from 1836 to the mid-1840s. This policy treated the Xhosa as an independent sovereignty and placed severe restrictions on the rights of the settlers to cross the frontier in search of stolen or missing cattle. Andries Stockenstrom, a Boer of Swedish descent, was put in charge of administering the policy, as Lieutenant Governor. Stockenstrom came under immediate attack from local settlers and from within the imperial administration. He had to defend himself against an accusation that he had been involved in a murder, and he was ultimately neutralized and forced out of the imperial administration in 1838. But the policy remained and it continued to stoke settler unrest.[25]

One of Stockenstrom's opponents in the imperial administration was John Mitford Bowker. Bowker had been suspended as a frontier official in 1838 over tensions with the Lieutenant Governor, and he soon emerged as a leading spokesperson for the settler position. Bowker had contempt for the humanitarian influence over imperial policy. He believed that the existing frontier policy created only the illusion of peace. The agents of the imperial administration tightly controlled the rights of the settlers to cross the colonial boundary in pursuit of stolen livestock, and they therefore ceded the right of the Xhosa to steal with impunity. The result was that the British Government abandoned settlers to the mercy of a "set of lawless savages." Those imperial officials who administered this policy with clear humanitarian prejudices were particularly disliked within the settler community.[26]

Bowker spoke for a growing consensus in settler society that a frontier policy based on missionary humanitarianism was flawed by its basic misreading of the Xhosa. Humanitarian attitudes towards the Xhosa, it was argued, rested on sentiment, not real knowledge or familiarity with the Africans. The claim that was being made here went to the heart of the authority of the humanitarian discourse: that it did *not* possess true knowledge about the Xhosa; by contrast, it was the settlers who were the *true* experts on the culture and politics of Xhosa society. Such an assertion was integral to the development of a settler identity and discourse. It was necessary to destroy the credibility of humanitarian claims to knowledge in order to establish the credibility and claims of a white settler colonial identity. During the 1830s, such claims were even reflected in popular culture literature, as in the 1838 play *Kaatje Kekkelbek*, which satirized the ignorance of the humanitarian about native peoples.[27]

Suspicion of the evangelical notion of the equality of mankind before God had quickly emerged among the 1820 settler classes. But in the aftermath of the war of 1834–5 this voice secured a more public influence than it had possessed before. By the mid-1830s, settler discourse was claiming superiority over the missionary discourse on the basis of better and more intimate knowledge of and experience with the Xhosa. Settler spokespersons began to deploy facts and figures to support the narrative about honest settlers surrounded by thieving tribes who were continually threatening to disrupt the civilizing work of commerce. John Centlives Chase, another leading settler spokesperson in the 1830s, published an article in the *Graham's Town Journal* in November 1839 which used statistics drawn from parliamentary Blue Books to demonstrate the failure of the frontier policy inaugurated by the "humanitarian" Colonial Secretary, Lord Glenelg.[28]

The appeal to the superior knowledge of the settlers was usually directed at a metropolitan audience. But it gained considerable credibility as missionary voices themselves began to be added to the settler case. In his 1843 sermons at the Union Chapel, Cape Town, for example, Henry Calderwood declared contempt for the sentimental tendencies of humanitarianism toward indigenous peoples. By the time he came to tell the story of his life in Xhosaland, he fully endorsed the narrative of settler politics against the British Government's buckling under the humanitarian lobby, which did not understand the true nature of the Xhosa as inveterate thieves and cunning despoilers. It became a common trope in the literature of ex-humanitarians like Calderwood that they, too, had possessed a sentimental attitude towards the "poor Xhosa" until they had learnt better from their actual experiences with the dark cunning of the people.[29]

But perhaps the most important event that allowed the settler narrative to enter the discourse on frontier policies was the support it received from the brief dominance of Sir Benjamin D'Urban and Colonel Harry Smith over the frontier during 1835 and 1836. Their response to the sixth frontier war was to create a new province – Queen Adelaide Province – where the Xhosa would be governed by a paternal imperial rule headed by Smith. From the settler standpoint, this provided a model for a proper frontier policy, and both men became heroes to the settler community. Glenelg repudiated their policy when news of it reached him several months after the fact. But in his response to Glenelg's letter of dismissal, D'Urban laid out the mantras that were to lie at the core of the settler consciousness: that the invasion by the Xhosa was completely unprovoked by settler actions, that the settlers were in reality the injured party, suffering plunder and loss of capital, and that much responsibility lay with British frontier policy, which refused to face up to the savagery of the Xhosa and refused to take the kind of coercive, reforming action that he and Smith had intended to implement in their schemes for Queen Adelaide Province as a homeland for the Xhosa under close British supervision.[30]

This was the line of argument that was being woven into the construction of a settler narrative of frontier history. The key figure in this respect was Robert Godlonton. Godlonton took the opportunity of the sixth and eighth frontier wars (1834–5 and 1850–3) to produce large, ungainly and shoddily presented accounts that laid out the settler version of British–Xhosa history and relations. In his first book (*A Narrative of the Irruption of the Kaffir Hordes Into the Eastern Province of the Cape of Good Hope 1834–1835*), Godlonton provided a political history of the frontier that indicted both the British Government and the humanitarian party, while justifying the settler position. In both tone and argument, the book is a debate with and a refutation of the humanitarian colonial policy and their reigning concepts about Xhosa society.[31]

Godlonton imported into the book the violence that was a perpetual undercurrent of settler politics. He set out to denigrate those committed to humanitarianism and to reverse the prevailing images of settlers and Xhosa. Whereas the humanitarians portrayed the settlers as the oppressors and the Xhosa as the victims, Godlonton argued the contrary case. Godlonton was fortunate in having to hand an image of African ferocity and terror that had recently been developed. This was Shaka, the creator of the Zulu kingdom who at this time was being marketed to the Cape Town authorities by a small group of Port Natal traders as the successful builder of a powerful, centralized kingdom and as the very model of a despotic and cruel African chief. Rumors were rife in the settler community that Shaka's army was attacking the Xhosa from the north, and was about to spread his *mfecane* disorder into the colony.[32]

Godlonton could not find anyone like Shaka among the Xhosa. No one categorized the Xhosa as a militaristic race, and Godlonton did not try. On the contrary, Xhosa attributes were the very reverse of manly militarism. Godlonton represented the Xhosa as dark, cunning, and with no virtue. Xhosa culture was so embedded in "disgusting and sensual vices" that it was sunk in an irredeemable "moral darkness." The absence of a death penalty in Xhosa law for all offenses except a direct attack on the chief was not in his eyes a sign of a higher civilization, but rather further evidence of "their darkness." Witchcraft, of course, reflected the strong hold of superstition, and opened the Xhosa to the manipulation of chiefs and prophets. The subordinate status of women and the dowry system amounted to a system of buying and selling of wives. The use of cattle for currency fostered their natural willingness to steal and plunder. And all this amounted to a *system* that meant that the Xhosa were "ever ripe for mischief ... their mode of living and their customs all conduce to this [and there is] ... no perception of moral rectitude to deter him from the commission of plunder."[33]

If the Xhosa were not the innocent victims they were often claimed to be, that status was attached by Godlonton to the settlers. The settlers were the victims of a sinister and crafty people who preyed on innocent and enterprising Britons, and constantly threatened the peace of the frontier. Misled by the roseate view of the Xhosa painted by the humanitarians, the British Government did not appreciate how the Xhosa were characterologically treacherous and unreliable. It was therefore impossible to base a frontier policy on concepts of trust and honor. Freed from such constraints, the Xhosa were able to run rings around the attempts of the imperial administration to bring stability to the frontier. The only policy that would work was one that allowed "no deviation from that high path of rectitude" – meaning control of the Xhosa by main force.[34]

It would be tedious to continue; the main point is clear. But a brief comparative mention of Godlonton's second book is worthwhile. This book, *A Narrative of the Kaffir War of 1850–51*, published both in London and Grahamstown in 1851, was designed to provide a pro-settler narrative of the eighth frontier war. It obviously appeared in a very different climate of opinion. By this time settler consciousness about the Xhosa was about to become the received wisdom. Thus Godlonton was able to project a more self-confident claim for the superior knowledge of the settlers on matters concerning frontier politics and the Xhosa.

Only the settlers lived close enough to the Xhosa, Godlonton claimed, really to know their nature at first hand. All the other groups – the missionaries, the imperial administration, and the home government – were liable to be misled by them, either because they were too far away or because they tended to see them through the distortions of an ideological vision. Godlonton demonstrated this by laying out a narrative about the coming of the eighth frontier war in December 1850. In this narrative, British administrators were portrayed as naive peace-lovers, "deceived by the profound craft and specious professions of the Xhosa." Only the farmers and settlers, Godlonton claimed, were not taken in by Xhosa dissembling for peace. It was true that both missionaries and administrators were taken by surprise by the war. There is very little evidence that the settlers were any better informed of Xhosa intentions than anyone else. Some of these self-same farmers who lived cheek by jowl with the Xhosa were sitting unsuspectingly at their Christmas dinners when they were murdered by their Xhosa neighbors. But Godlonton's story needed neither logical consistency nor a truth that captured the complexities of Xhosa society. The point was to establish a narrative that authorized the truth of the settler view of the Xhosa as a cunning and deceptive people.[35]

A new knowledge system

By the 1850s, then, the shifting constellation of colonial and metropolitan politics called for a new knowledge system about the Xhosa. The intellectual discourse and beliefs that the missionaries had carried with them from Britain had imploded under the weight of the encounter with the Xhosa. Settler politics and consciousness had blossomed into full flower and now revolved around the appetite of eastern separatists to carve a separate colony out of the frontier zone which would include British Kaffraria.[36] The settler critique of both missionary culture and the policies of the imperial state tapped into a dark view of the Xhosa that even missionaries were unable now to resist. Finally, there was the imperial state, which was increasingly set upon a course of enforcing its rule over the Xhosa. Thus, an authoritative view of Xhosa society was needed that was consistent with all these developments.

The result was that the discourses of the first half of the century that competed to capture what the Xhosa were *really* like were reconciled. The fog of befuddlement within missionary culture as to how to understand the Xhosa refusal of conversion could now be blown away. A unitary and coherent explanation for Xhosa behavior, culture and character emerged. I have already alluded to the appearance in popular literature of this new view of the Xhosa. I want now to return to a fuller contemplation of that new knowledge system in two texts that provided an *authoritative* statement of what British culture had decided it *knew* about the Xhosa. There are two reasons why it is important to return to this matter.

The first is that the knowledge system that emerged in the mid-century marked the introduction of a kind of discourse that was to become a common feature of the empire in Africa. It was a discourse of expertise, produced by specialists who spoke with authority because of their long association with and study of the natives. Although it was settler political discourse that established this criterion of credibility, the experts who became authorities on the Xhosa often had missionary connections. They were experts who claimed to offer complete guides to the Xhosa and their society and were not at all reluctant to offer prescriptions across a wide range of issues. They claimed a wide mastery of all aspects of native society, not merely the moral and religious. This kind of literature of expertise is new to the empire, in southern Africa at least. But it was the first of a long lineage of British expertise on Africa.

The second reason why it is worth deconstructing this knowledge system is that it was not simply an intellectual construct that fixed the Xhosa in certain categories for British imperialism. Imperial knowledge systems did more than just the intellectual work of empire. They were also instruments that *enabled* British rule. They were providing a *culture of rule for the*

British. A knowledge system was necessary to allow the British to explain to themselves why they were justified in ruling the Xhosa, and why they were justified, ultimately, in destroying the Xhosa's own civic culture. There were two founding documents in the literature of expertise on the Xhosa. The first was a *Compendium of Kafir Laws and Customs*, compiled in 1858 by John Maclean, the Chief Commissioner in British Kaffraria. It was intended as a handbook to guide resident magistrates through what was known about Xhosa cultural customs, history, government and law. It was the first such reference book in the African empire. It remained in use into the twentieth century and was reprinted as late as 1906. Two of the three major contributors were longstanding missionaries on the frontier, and the third was Charles Brownlee, who was already regarded as the most qualified expert on the Xhosa. This book may be taken to represent official thinking about the Xhosa in the 1850s.

The second book was a much larger production, intended for a more general reading public: William C. Holden's *The Past and Future of the Kaffir Races*, published in 1866. Holden had been a Wesleyan missionary in Natal for about twenty years, and his book addressed the "Kaffirs" as a whole, not merely the Xhosa. His book purported to provide a complete account of the history, customs and manners of the natives between Port Elizabeth and Natal, along with policy prescriptions for their "improvement." Holden had long been interested in compiling and systematizing knowledge about Britain's southern African subjects. He had published one of the first histories of Natal in 1855, and he claimed that the manuscript for *The Past and Future of the Kaffir Races* had been put together in the late 1840s, but that its publication had been delayed. If this is so, we may take Holden's book to be representative of missionary circles' thinking on the Xhosa by mid-century.

Holden's book became the standard work on the Xhosa and Zulu in the mid-nineteenth century. In nearly 500 pages, it distilled all that needed to be known about the natives of the eastern seaboard of southern Africa; so much so that when Anthony Trollope came "a-trolloping" around South Africa on one of his empire jaunts in 1878, everything that he saw and observed about the Xhosa was derived from the knowledge system detailed by Holden. There was virtually nothing that Trollope regurgitated for the British public about the Xhosa that was not in Holden's book. Holden's status as the first synthetic interpreter of the Xhosa was attested by the next generation of experts, when they came to rework what was "known" about the indigenes in order to produce another knowledge system more suited to the era in which they lived.[37]

The knowledge system presented by Maclean's compilation and Holden's treatise may be discussed under four headings: their portrayal of Xhosa society as urbane, yet also as dark and cunning; their assertions that the Xhosa were characterologically closed to the spread of civilizing influences by persuasion; their argument that this characterological flaw was locked in by the linkage between superstitious cultural practices and the political structures of chiefly power; and their agreement that coercion was therefore a necessary strategy for bringing civilization to the Xhosa.

Both books drained the complexity and sophistication out of the societies they described. This was done by arguing that the elements of urbanity that they identified in Xhosa society were ultimately deployed to serve dark ends. There was nothing simple or straightforward about the Xhosa society that was portrayed by Maclean's contributors and Holden. The elaborate network of codes and rituals and the intricate set of legal forms that governed Xhosa civil society were recognized by both Maclean and Holden. Yet, unlike earlier observers, these authors were not befuddled or confused by that complexity and sophistication. No traces of the dualism that ran through the accounts of people like Alberti or Barrow remain in their accounts. Holden and Maclean were in no doubt that the "good" parts of Xhosa society were merely instruments of its darkness. Let us take the example of the legal system of the Xhosa as it was presented in the Maclean *Compendium*. It was a reflection of how important the law was in Xhosa society that each of the essays in the Maclean compilation addressed Xhosa law. The essay by J. C. Warner, sometime missionary, was the most extensive. Warner was currently the diplomatic agent with the Thembu; he had lived among them for some twenty years, and, like Brownlee, was one of the first generation of African "experts" in British service.

Warner described the civil and criminal legal system of the Xhosa in great detail. Punishments were graduated according the seriousness of the offense, and consisted largely of fines rather than corporal punishment. There were prohibitions against acts – rape and abortion, for example – that surely received his approval, although he remarked how the "seduction of virgins" was not a crime. Other things went conspicuously unmentioned in his account, including the absence of capital punishment. But the Xhosa legal system provided for most of the same kind of eventualities that were to be found in the British system. Indeed, Warner could not but be impressed by the legal system. It was a fully formed entity, and it successfully maintained social peace and order.[38]

The success of the Xhosa legal system, he noted, lay in the way it operated on the principle of collective responsibility. Fines and other punishments were the responsibility of the kraal or clan. But this implied another feature of the legal system, which was the way it operated through debate and discussion. There were no lawyers among the Xhosa; every man (women were excluded, it would seem) was a lawyer. Cases could be brought by any plaintiff. A party representing the plaintiff would arrive at the residence of the defendant to announce the bringing of a complaint. There was no system of examination. The accused had to prove his innocence rather than have his guilt proved. The plaintiff's party and the defendant's party confronted one another through an elaborate ritual of conversation and discussion before the actual case commenced. The consequence was that discussion could go on and on. Legal arguments were often prolonged for several days as each side endeavored to convince the other. The process was a verbal tug of war in which "the Socratic method of debate appears in all its perfection, both parties being equally versed in it." If this exhaustive argument produced no consensual resolution, appeals were made all the way up to the chief and his *ampakati* (his counsel, composed of senior men of the tribe), where an equally elaborate set of codes and arguments would occur, but where the law of precedent was very much in evidence in the final decision. In sum, the legal procedures emphasized conflict resolution through debate.[39]

What did Warner and his cohorts make of this? On the one hand, there was much to admire; on the other hand, it was a system that defied the prejudices of imperial culture. The British frequently remarked how skilled the Xhosa were in argumentation. The missionaries encountered this very skill in the interrogation of their beliefs by the Xhosa. The imperial state was treated to the same behavior in its negotiations with the Xhosa. So the British did not approach this quality of Xhosa character with positive experiences in mind. To the contrary, Xhosa ability to contest and argue was used to impede and block the progress of British culture. Consequently, in the eyes of Maclean's authorities, a characteristic of the legal system which operated on the basis of debate and argument must perforce conceal something much more sinister. Because the Xhosa practice of disputation was not structured by rules of evidence or cross-examination, any question could be asked and any rhetorical device could be employed by the plaintiff and defendant if they thought it would enhance their case. There was no such offense as perjury; there were no judicial oaths. From the British perspective the result was that the system of law endorsed and authorized systematic lying. It meant that "defendant, plaintiff, witnesses are *allowed to tell as many lies as they like in order to make the best of their case.*" Thus, the legal system both embodied and reinforced the idea that the Xhosa were incorrigible liars.[40]

From their actual descriptions of the Xhosa legal system, however, it would have been quite possible for these authorities to have reached very different conclusions. They could easily have concluded that it was a legal system that was highly functional for the Xhosa. The Xhosa had no written records and kept track of decisions or processes by oral tradition. A system that rested entirely upon speaking was a practical necessity; memory and current rhetoric were the prime instruments of legal argumentation. The British could have admitted that there were things about the system they did not like – the failure to distinguish between various kinds of homicide, for example, or the different definitions of theft that obtained in the Xhosa system.[41] But this was not the kind of anomaly they focused on, nor was this the line of criticism they mounted.

The British played a more tortuous, subtle and, in its way, devilishly brilliant game with the "knowledge" that they had gathered about the qualities of the Xhosa legal system. They identified certain qualities that seemed to be virtues and turned them inside out, arguing that their appearance was a mere disguise. Debate was, after all, the basis of the British legal system, just as it was for the Xhosa. Unlike in Britain, however, Xhosa debate went on until the matter was resolved by the withdrawal of one party or the emergence of a consensus. This was a system that all in the community had access to; and it was a system that secured social cohesion and peace. It was not a class-based system of justice. Yet, Maclean and his collaborators argued, it only *seemed* to be like that; it was not really that at all. It was *really* a system that ran on lies and deceit and cunning. It was a system in which victory went to those who had the most of those qualities. And this provided an explanation for the characterological evasiveness, cunning and habit of lying that the British pinned on the Xhosa. Thus the skills in argumentation of the Xhosa were explained by the deficient working of their legal system, and what could have been interpreted as a virtuous quality was turned into a sign of their savagery.[42]

And this helped the British understand the second defining characteristic of the Xhosa that the colonial knowledge system now considered proved: that they were characterologically closed to the persuasive influences of civilization. Warner drew directly upon the experience of missionary pessimism when he argued that the Xhosa had something more than the "*ordinary* darkness and corruption of the human heart." "Ordinary" darkness was common to all human hearts. The British had it, just as the Xhosa had it. But the Xhosa had something extra. They had an additional coating of sinfulness that lay beneath this common or garden kind. Where was this located? Warner described it as flowing from the "system of superstition" which provided a thick covering of protection for the Xhosa against the light of Christianity. The missionary effort would fail for as long as it was unable to recognize this, and Xhosa conversions themselves would be very shallow, as, indeed, we have seen that they were.[43]

Holden offered a slightly different variant on this theme, but he too believed that the Xhosa were characterologically incapable of being persuaded of the benefits of Christian civilization. His explanation was more secular, however. The "Kaffir mind," he claimed, knew no restraint, and without restraint civilized society was impossible. Thus, "in the mind of the native there is the absence of the only element or principle upon which the civilizer can fairly work." Holden attempted to fuse this essentializing argument with the remnants of evangelical humanitarianism that formed the milieu of his youth. It is worth noting this conjunction because it provides a nice little example of how the conceptions of evangelical humanitarianism from the early part of the century were transformed into the more essentialized racism of the later part of the century.[44]

Holden argued that peoples were divided into three categories: those who were able to yield to moral suasion and thus could step on to the elevator of civilization; those who had to be "beaten and weakened before they could enter upon an improving elevating process"; and those who were doomed to extinction by their obdurate resistance to civilization. He put the Xhosa into the second category, of those who needed to be whipped on to the road of civilizational improvement. This status was no disgrace, he noted, because this was where the British had been until the Romans beat civilized values into them. In this backhanded tribute, Holden was able to fuse a culturalist view of racial hierarchy with the essentialist argument that the Xhosa possessed inbuilt characterological deficits. It was still possible to imagine the Xhosa progressing beyond the rung on the cultural ladder of civilization that they presently occupied.[45]

It is worth interrupting this argument about the essential character traits of the Xhosa for a moment to notice one particular aspect of the morphology of the Xhosa that Holden and the others presented. And that was the way they infantalized the Xhosa. One of the curious aspects of the British treatment of the Xhosa is that they *were never genderized*. They were never masculinized like the Sikhs or Zulu. And this was in spite of the fact that the Xhosa were more formidable and persistent military opponents than the Zulu. But they tended to fight guerrilla campaigns rather than employ the set-piece tactics of the Zulu armies. This was a more effective military response to the British Army, but it also the confirmed the British view that they were as cunning, deceitful and evasive in the qualities of martial spirit as they were in so many other ways. By the same token, however, they could not be treated as feminine because the male qualities of bearing and dignity and intellect were inescapably in evidence. So they were never feminized in the manner of the Bengalis. Thus the imperial category that best fit them was that of the infant arrested at a childhood level of civilizational maturity.[46]

Infantalization of the colonial subject is a familiar strategy of imperial culture.[47] But the use of the metaphor of childhood was not common in the early years of the encounter with the Xhosa. For the first thirty years or forty years of the century, missionary culture was not committed to the idea of explaining the Xhosa through the category of the child. It became a popular discourse only at mid-century. And to illustrate this we may track its emergence in one local context in the changing educational regime at Lovedale Institution in the early 1860s.[48]

Lovedale had been founded in 1840 as an educational symbol of the missionary culture's belief in the universal humanity of man. It was originally designed to provide the same education to both white and black boys. The idea was that both would be trained in the classical arts of the British upper classes. Greek and Latin were at the core of the curriculum. And for the next twenty years or so this remained the guiding philosophy of the school under its original founder and leader, William Govan. Some things did change over that period. White boys and black boys ate at separate tables, and a girls' school was added sometime in the late 1840s. But when James Stewart joined the staff in 1864, things really began to change.

Stewart had been sent out with specific instructions to move the school away from Govan's original vision of training up a cadre of classically educated Xhosa. It was a sign of how far the original missionary idealism had been eroded that this bastion of the Glasgow Missionary Society was destined to be turned into a place where the "practical arts" were to be taught to the Xhosa, and the highest professional level that they were expected to reach would be that of elementary school teacher for their own sort. It took Stewart quite a while to wrest control of the school away from the aging Govan. But in 1870 Govan retired and the Stewart era began in earnest.

The assumption that the Xhosa should be trained only for the lesser crafts and lower-level professions was an expression of the idea that they were developmentally at the level of childhood. Under Stewart this became a key metaphor for explaining the philosophy of Lovedale Institution and the knowledge of the Xhosa that underpinned it. The idea of infancy was fundamental to Stewart's conception of Xhosa civilization. For Stewart, the notion of educational equality between black and white was obviated by the fact that the Xhosa had only recently started on the path to civilization. How could they possibly absorb the wisdom of the British, who had been at that game for 2,000 years? It was possible, of course, to believe that infancy really was just a temporary phase which would quickly pass into adolescence and then adulthood. But the problem (and advantage) with that metaphor was that only the parent got to judge

when the stage of childhood had matured into adulthood. And the difficulty was that the signifiers of Xhosa culture that marked it as a
lower-level culture were increasingly regarded as inherent and ingrained.
By the 1880s, therefore, the metaphor of infancy had hardened into a
perpetual description of the African. When Stewart addressed the
Lovedale Literary Society in 1884 with the question "What single thing
have you done as a race which the world will preserve, [and] who first
utilized steam and perfected the steam engine?" we can see that a fully
fledged, self-contained and self-confirming knowledge system was in
place.[49]

Still, as the Victorians knew well, children could be both innocent and
evil. The metaphor of childhood fitted the Xhosa well in this respect, too.
Ungoverned and licentious behavior was a central characteristic of Xhosa
cultural practices. Evil was close to the surface of Xhosa society through
the cultural practices that were ingrained in their society. And of all those
cultural practices that epitomized evil, witchcraft was the most repulsively
fascinating.[50]

Like most commentators, Holden (to return to our main theme) was
obsessed with witchcraft. He came back to it again and again. He provided
full and complete details of the various rites, rituals and gruesome punishments that surrounded the practice of witchcraft. For the British, witchcraft was emblematic of the degeneracy and darkness of Xhosa culture. It
enabled things to be explained about the Xhosa that otherwise would
remain mysterious and enigmatic. The cattle-killing of the later 1850s,
for example, could be comfortingly explained by the hold of superstition
over the culture. Most centrally, witchcraft was emblematic of the close
connection that existed between the cultural practices of the Xhosa and
their political institutions.[51] Witchcraft was believed to be one of the
methods by which the chiefs and their allies among the witchdoctors
manipulated and controlled tribal politics. Witchcraft was one of the few
crimes that was punishable by death, and all the property of the witch went
to the chief. Thus, for the British it was fairly simple and obvious: "the
Chiefs find this a very convenient and powerful state engine to support
their power, and enable them to remove individuals whom they would
otherwise find great difficulty in getting rid of."[52]

But the colonial knowledge system could not shake itself free of the
inherent contradictions that this model of witchcraft contained.
Witchcraft was seen as a joint product of Satan and of chiefly manipulation. But what was the relative weight of both? What was the degree of
Satanic power and deceptive manipulation at play in witchcraft? How
much did the chief and witchdoctors themselves believe in the process?
Did they deceive themselves entirely, or just partially? Were they all party

to the deceptions? These kinds of questions sat uneasily on the minds of those like Holden, who admitted that "there is no doubt but that these priests are to a considerable extent deceived themselves as well as the deceivers of others ... [but that] in addition to self-deception, they have often to revert to every kind of jugglery in order effectually to impose upon others and maintain their craft."[53]

What were the conclusions about the direction of British policy that could be drawn from this knowledge about the Xhosa? The logic of the analysis of the Xhosa pointed only one way: toward coercion. The careful discussion of Xhosa culture, institutions and polity led to only one conclusion. They had shown themselves resolutely resistant to "moral suasion and religious influence" as the means to improvement. Only one way was left open: "the sword must first – not *exterminate* them, but – break them up as tribes and destroy their political existence." Holden agreed: "they will probably be broken and humbled by the sword before they are raised and elevated by the Gospel." Once this had been done, they would be "set free from the shackles by which they are bound, civilisation and Christianity will no doubt make rapid progress among them, for they are a noble race, no wise deficient in mental capacity," and well worth the benevolent attention of the British empire. So here was the central policy recommendation this knowledge system bequeathed to imperial culture: to destroy the Xhosa in order to set them free.[54]

If the sword of civilization was necessary before conversion could be realized, that sword could be wielded only by the state. And a long list of "improvements" was included in Holden's account. All groups on the frontier – the missionaries, the settlers and the state – had their appointed roles. But the state had to take the lead. Among those improvements were the destruction of their cultural practices and the obliteration of their system of government. The political power of the chiefs had to be eliminated with the same thoroughness as witchcraft had to be prohibited.[55]

There was an ironic twist to the intellectual apparatus supporting this notion, however. The prescription of coercion was required *because* the Xhosa were *children*. For Holden they were "children in knowledge" in the bodies of adults. Herein lay the reasons for Britain's difficulties with the Xhosa. Although they were men and women, there was a disjunction between their minds and their bodies. It would be a violation of the laws of nature to treat them as adults. It would be the equivalent of handing authority in a family over to the children: "no family could be thus well governed." The state had to provide the necessary parental authority. Children needed to be governed and they should therefore "be placed under a regimen at least as severe as that of the children in civilized countries."

I have arrived at the conclusion that, while there cannot and ought not to be any slavery, serfdom or vassalage, there ought to be a course of obligation imposed, by which these wild sons of nature – capricious, idle, and ignorant, the victims of their own passions, and often guilty of the most revolting crimes – should have the power of evil checked and brought under healthy and powerful restraint.[56]

What did Holden mean by this? He meant that the Xhosa had to be coerced into the civilization by work. Work would make them free. They must be dragooned into forming a labor supply for the Colony. "The white needs labour to enable him to carry out his projects." The state would have to oversee this; it would exercise tight control over the labor supply in each kraal, keeping careful tabs on who was available for work, and what kind of work they could best give. A huge imperial bureaucracy was imagined to oversee this putative gulag, which would also contain properly run institutions of education so that "the arts of life as well as the habits of industry" would be formed. And all of this would lead to a happy ending. The end result was the lifting up of the Xhosa to a civilized state. All would finally be right. The old universal humanitarianism of evangelical culture was *still* valid. "The black races," Holden intoned, "are fully capable of self-government, and of rising to the highest state in the civil and ecclesiastical world." There was nothing in their racial state that prevented them from becoming British. All they had to do was to cease to be Xhosa.[57]

Let us leave the Reverend Holden reveling in his imperial dreams. For the Xhosa his schemes had already provided the stuff of nightmares. Holden's voice was the voice of the liberal imperialist, the voice that transformed the definition of humanitarianism from an idealist vision about the brotherhood of man into a dream that offered despotism and coercion as the route to freedom. This was the face of the mid-nineteenth-century empire.

Conclusion

Many events compete for the honor of the crucial moment when the discourse of racial essentialism triumphed over the discourse of evangelical humanitarianism. I like a moment in the spring of 1865, when the newly formed Anthropological Society of London debated whether Africans could be civilized through the efforts of missionaries. Although victory in the culture war between these two different discourses had, in fact, been settled sometime before, the exchanges in the Anthropological Society revealed the decay into which missionary humanitarian discourse had fallen.

The debate was opened when Winwood Reade, an explorer of West Africa and an aspiring "expert" on African affairs, delivered a scathing denunciation of the failures of the British missionary effort. In the audience sat Bishop John Colenso, fresh from Natal and in the midst of his own controversy around the Pentateuch, and Richard Burton, fresh from his own explorations. Reade's paper was hardly a piece of serious scholarly reasoning; it possessed more the quality of a polemical diatribe. But it mercilessly identified the failures of the missionary effort in Africa. Reade pilloried the missionary effort as a "wretched bubble," challenged the idea that British Christianity could ever "flourish on a savage soil," slandered missionaries as charlatans, and denigrated their converts as being "prostitutes" if they were women and "thieves" if they were men. His most resonant criticism was one that was hard to refute: that few converts had been made and that cultures of superstition continued to reign supreme. Reade's solution was to advocate the forceful introduction of civilization through imperial domination. After savage customs had been repressed, missionaries could be set loose to convert the Africans. In the debate that followed, a missionary from the Gabon futilely attempted a refutation; Richard Burton applauded Reade's analysis and the meeting overwhelmingly expressed its support.[58]

At subsequent meetings of the Anthropological Society, missionaries tried vainly to mount a defense of their efforts. They offered statistics and case studies. But their attempts to build a reasoned argument were dismissed by Burton and others, who claimed to be the experts who really "knew" Africa. Eventually, Colenso was moved to intervene. In May he delivered a long, powerfully argued paper in reply. But although Colenso's response was coherent and rational, at its core lay its admission of Reade's case: that the missionaries had failed. Colenso attributed this to the complexities of the task and to the problem of settler oppression rather than to the intrinsic inability of Africans to hear the word of God – which was the thrust of Reade's and Burton's assault. But Colenso was in no position to stem the tide running against the idea of a universal humanitarianism. Colenso was on his own path to intellectual oblivion in British culture. Indeed, he was in Britain at this moment to try to rescue his intellectual reputation. His heretical biblical scholarship was only one reason why his reputation was in jeopardy. He was also under attack because of his attempt to democratize knowledge by integrating African culture and civilizations into the strategies of evangelization. Colenso's attempt to revitalize missionary culture at the Anthropological Society fell on deaf ears and remained a historical curiosity from a man increasingly the subject of squibs and ridicule.[59]

The story of the debate within the London Anthropological Society and the dismissal of Colenso as a crank and heretic were distant echoes of the new knowledge system about colonial subjects that had been constructed in empire. This new knowledge system filled the vacuum created by the implosion of missionary culture. In its southern African version, it provided clear answers about what the Xhosa were really like. But it was a knowledge system that was closed rather than open, that sought distance from the Xhosa rather than engagement, and that looked at the Xhosa through distorting lenses rather than through opened eyes. As a knowledge system, it possessed the paradoxical quality of retreating into *ignorance* while at the same time purporting to present good data as knowledge about the Xhosa. Indeed, this ignorance was to be the main critique launched against it at the end of the nineteenth century, when a new kind of knowledge system began to be constructed around anthropological methods.[60]

NOTES

1. There are many studies on knowledge systems more generally. I have found the following books useful. It will be a familiar list. Bernard Cohn, *Colonialism and its Forms of Knowledge: The British in India* (Princeton, 1996); Mark Harrison, *Climates and Constitutions: Health, Race, Environment and British Imperialism in India* (New Dehli, 1999); Anne Stoler, *Carnal Knowledge and Imperial Power: Race and the Intimate in Colonial Rule* (Berkeley, 2002); Homi Bhaba, *The Location of Culture* (London, 1994); Mary Louise Pratt, *Imperial Eyes: Travel Writing and Tranculturation* (London, 1992); Edward Said, *Orientalism* (New York, 1979); Fred Cooper and Anne Stoler, *Tensions of Empire: Colonial Cultures in a Bourgeois World* (Berkeley, CA, 1997).
2. Peter Hulme's pioneering *Colonial Encounters: Europe and the Native Caribbean 1497–1797* (London, 1986) and Pratt, *Imperial Eyes*, and most who have followed them, have taken the perspective critiqued here. For a different, and very intelligent, approach to this question, see Pramod K. Nayar, "Marvelous Excess: English Travel Writing and India, 1608–1727," *Journal of British Studies* 44.2 (2005), pp. 213–38. Nayar has a very good sense of how the different phases in the creation of knowledge systems reflect different historical conditions and imperatives. We have noted how the various generations of LMS missionaries seemingly had each time to "learn" anew that, for example, the chiefs were going to be slippery to deal with. I suspect that this pattern of learning and relearning was characteristic of imperial encounters from the early modern period to the last third or so of the nineteenth century. After that, changes in methods and modes of cultural communication and knowledge transmission change so dramatically that the whole process of knowledge creation was fundamentally altered.
3. Thus the best-known published work of this genre, Sir John Barrow, *Travels into the Interior of Southern Africa in the Years 1797 and 1798*, 2 vols. (London, 1801).
4. The subject of pre-modern representations of the Khoesan has been treated very thoroughly by Linda E. Merins, *Envisioning the Worst: Representations of the*

"Hottentot" in Early Modern England (Cranbury, NJ, 2001). For Xhosaland, see Robin Derricourt, "Early European Travelers in the Transkei and Ciskei," *African Studies* 35.3 (1976), pp. 273–91. Pratt, in *Imperial Eyes*, pp. 38–68, argues, for southern Africa, that the indigenes disappeared from travel accounts between the mid-eighteenth century and the early nineteenth. Tim Youngs, *Travellers in Africa: British Travelogues 1850–1900* (Manchester, 1994), is disappointingly narrow in its focus and very ahistorical in its treatment of the interaction of metropolitan culture and indigenous cultures.

5. The works that I have consulted for this section include Ludwig Alberti's *Account of the Tribal Life and Customs of the Xhosa in 1807* (Cape Town, 1968) (originally available only in German, but Alberti was a longstanding official of the Dutch administration, he was known to Brownlee, and his views may be taken as both authoritative on the Xhosa and as reflecting a stream of thought about them); Barrow, *Travels into the Interior of Southern Africa*; Henry Lichtenstein, *Travels in Southern Africa in the Years 1803, 1804, 1805, and 1806* (London, 1812); C. I. Latrobe, *Journal of a Visit to South Africa, in 1815 and 1816* (London, 1818); William J. Burchell, *Travels in the Interior of Southern Africa*, 2 vols. (London, 1822); and John Campbell, *Travels in South Africa Undertaken at the Request of the Missionary Society* (Andover, 1816).

6. Alberti, *Account of the Tribal Life and Customs of the Xhosa*, pp. 35–6, 59–67, 70–7, 85; Barrow, *Travels into the Interior of Southern Africa*, vol. I, pp. 166–9; Lichtenstein, *Travels in Southern Africa*, pp. 309, 326–7, 301; Burchell, *Travels in the Interior of Southern Africa*, vol. I, p. 268.

7. Alberti, *Account of the Tribal Life and Customs of the Xhosa*, pp. 36–9; Lichtenstein, *Travels in Southern Africa*, pp. 301, 340; Barrow, *Travels into the Interior of Southern Africa*, vol. I, pp. 206–7. And, indeed, the Xhosa gained a reputation among the British for being far too lenient with their children – something that Victorian England tried to avoid.

8. Alberti, *Account of the Tribal Life and Customs of the Xhosa*, pp. 49–52; Barrow, *Travels into the Interior of Southern Africa*, vol. I, p. 216; Lichtenstein, *Travels in Southern Africa*, p. 270. Lichtenstein consciously set himself against Barrow, and emphasized more the dark side of Xhosa life. But even he conforms to the general pattern described here.

9. Alberti, *Account of the Tribal Life and Customs of the Xhosa*, pp. 81–2; Barrow, *Travels into the Interior of Southern Africa*, vol. I, pp. 198–207; Lichtenstein, *Travels in Southern Africa*, p. 353; Campbell, *Travels in South Africa*, pp. 352–4.

10. The books I have used for this style of representation of the Xhosa include Stephen Kay, *Travels and Researches in Caffraria: Describing the Character, Customs, and Moral Condition of the Tribes Inhabiting that Portion of Southern Africa* (London, 1833); James Backhouse, *A Narrative of a Visit to The Mauritius and South Africa* (London, 1844); Andrew Steedman, *Wanderings and Adventures in the Interior of Southern Africa*, 2 vols. (London, 1835); Robert Moffat, *Missionary Labours and Scenes in Southern Africa* (London, 1842); James Edward Alexander, *Narrative of a Voyage of Observation among the Colonies of Western Africa*, vol. I (London, 1837); and George Thompson, *Travels and Adventures in Southern Africa*, 2 vols. (London, 1829). There are

many additional books in this genre, but I have confined myself to those that directly address the Xhosa.

11. Backhouse, *Narrative of a Visit*, pp. 129, 196–7; Kay, *Travels and Researches*, pp. 18–19, 241–66, 497.

12. Kay, *Travels and Researches*, pp. 157, 1990; Steedman, *Wanderings and Adventures*, vol. I, pp. 37–42, 45–6, 136–7, 231, 240, 261–2; vol. II, pp. 136–42; Backhouse, *Narrative of a Visit*, pp. 230–1, 243–6; Moffat, *Missionary Labours*, p. 24; Alexander, *Narrative of a Voyage*, vol. I, pp. 374, 383–405; Thompson, *Travels and Adventures*, vol. I, pp. 162–3, 167–9.

13. Steedman, *Wanderings and Adventures*, vol. I, pp. 136–7; Backhouse, *Narrative of a Visit*, p. 235; Thompson, *Travels and Adventures*, vol. II, pp. 201–3.

14. Cowper Rose, *Four Years in South Africa* (London, 1829), pp. 74, 197–9. He spoke of the naturally good manners and "easy graceful attitudes and mild eyes" that chiefs possessed until they were angered. [Thomas Phillips,] *Scenes and Occurrences in Albany and Caffer-Land, South Africa* (London, 1827), pp. ix–xi. His descriptions became more ambiguous when he described the specifics of, for example, Ngqika's court. But it is generally accurate to characterize this account as being sympathetic to the Xhosa and within the humanitarian discourse. Thomas Pringle, another 1820 settler, who returned to Britain and became Secretary of the Aborigines Protection Society, also wrote long, idyllic descriptions of the interior of the Cape in prose and poetry; see his *African Sketches* (London, 1835).

15. The authors I have chosen to focus on in the following paragraphs are Harriet Ward, *The Cape and the Kaffirs: A Diary of Five Years' Residence in Kaffirland*, 3rd edn. (London, 1851) (there was an earlier edition of Harriet Ward's book with the different title of *Five Years in Kaffirland: With Sketches of the Late War in that Country to the Conclusion of the Peace: Written on the Spot* [London, 1848]; the British Library copy of this edition seems to be missing); Reverend Francis Fleming, *Kaffraria and its Inhabitants* (London, 1853); Alfred W. Cole, *The Cape and the Kaffirs: Or, Notes of Five Years' Residence in South Africa* (London, 1852); Robert Wilmot, *A Cape Traveller's Diary, 1856* (London, 1857); Thornley Smith, *South Africa Delineated* (London, 1850).

16. Harriet Ward gets a mention in J. S. Bratton, "Of England, Home and Duty: The Image of England in Victorian and Edwardian Juvenile Fiction," in John Mackenzie (ed.), *Imperialism and Popular Culture* (Manchester, 1986), pp. 86, who cites Ward's book *Hardy and Hunter* (London, 1858). But there is an earlier one, even more of a penny dreadful, titled *Jasper Lyle: A Tale of Kaffirland* (London, 1851). This book was reprinted as late as 1879. *The Cape and the Kaffirs* was also intended as an emigration manual. In the early 1850s there was an attempt to sell the Cape to would-be British emigrants as an alternative to Australia or North America. See also Malvern van Wyk Smith, "'What the waves were always saying': Dombey and Sons and Textual Ripples on an African Shore," in Wendy S. Jackson (ed.), *Dickens and the Children of Empire* (London, 2000), pp. 148–9. See also Leigh Dale, "Imperial Traveler, Colonial Observer: Humanity and Difference in *Five Years in Kaffirland*," in Helen Gilbert and Anna Johnston (eds.), *In Transit: Text, Travel and Empire* (New York, 2002), pp. 85–101.

17. Dale, "Imperial Traveler," pp. 87–9, 92–3, 95–7.

18. Harriet Ward, *The Cape and the Kaffirs* (London, 1851), pp. 26, 30–2, 65–9, 77, 98–100, 168; the passage cited is from p. 165. Where did she get such an idea if not from practices that were not unknown on the frontier?

19. Fleming, *Kaffraria and its Inhabitants*, pp. 15–17, 91–3; Cole, *The Cape and the Kaffirs*, pp. 126–7, 185–92; Wilmot, *Cape Traveller's Diary*, pp. 53, 57–9; Smith, *South Africa Delineated*, pp. 32, 80–2, 87, 90–1.

20. Barrow, *Travels into the Interior of Southern Africa*, p. 111. In this section I am concerned only with settler discourse of the eastern Cape. At this period, it was distinct from the settler discourses elsewhere in southern Africa, and perhaps it was a more complicated construct. In Natal, for example, the labor question dominated the public discourse of the settlers. See Keletso E. Atkins, *The Moon is Dead: Give Us Our Money! The Cultural Origins of an African Work Ethic: Natal 1843–1900* (Portsmouth, NH, 1993). Until the later 1830s, Cape Town interests controlled access to policy-makers in London. Aside from Philip, with his connections to the Buxtons and others, commercial interests were represented in London by the Cape of Good Hope Trade Society, founded in 1825 and concerned mainly with tariff questions. But the trade society was used by the eastern Cape settlers after 1835 with some success.

21. On the settler discourse across the British empire in the southern hemisphere, see Alan Lester, "British Settler Discourse and the Circuits of Empire," *History Workshop Journal* 54 (2002), pp. 25–48; and Lester, "Humanitarians and White Settlers in the Nineteenth Century," in Norman Etherington (ed.), *The Oxford History of the British Empire Companion Series*, vol. V: *Missions and Empire* (Oxford, 2005), pp. 86–106. Zoë Laidlaw, *Colonial Connections*, pp. 155–9. On Godlonton, see for example Basil Le Cordeur, *The Politics of Eastern Cape Separatism 1820–1854* (Cape Town, 1981), pp. 64–5. He was not much liked in most missionary circles; see for example Rev. William Govan, *Memoirs of the Missionary Career of Reverend James Laing* (Glasgow, 1875), p. 37. Stephen Kay, *A Succinct Statement of the Kaffer's Case* (London, 1837), p. 3.

22. William Boyce, *Notes on South African Affairs* (repr. Cape Town, 1971), pp. 2–27.

23. Ibid., pp. 49–71, 72–106. For the border policy of this period, see John S. Galbraith, *Reluctant Empire: British Policy on the South African Frontier 1834–1854* (Berkeley, 1963), pp 116–67.

24. Boyce, *Notes on South African Affairs*, pp. 196–215. Similar petitions were presented in 1835 and 1836 to King William IV and Lord Glenelg; see William Shaw, *The Story of My Mission in South-Eastern Africa: Comprising Some Account of the European Colonists with Extended Notices of the Kaffir and Other Native Tribes* (London, 1860), pp. 162–6. Glenelg argued that the state of the colony could hardly be worse, "owing in great degree to the aggression of British subjects on the Aboriginal inhabitants, and their endeavours to extend their territory in this quarter for selfish and interested purposes."

25. See Timothy Keegan, *Colonial South Africa and the Origins of the Racial Order* (Cape Town, 1996), pp. 196–208, for a useful survey. On Stockenstrom particularly, see J. L. Dracopoli, *Sir Andries Stockenstrom: The Origins of Racial Conflict in South Africa 1792–1864* (Cape Town, 1969). [Andries

Stockenstrom,] *The Autobiography of the Late Sir Andries Stockenstrom*, 2 vols. (1887; repr. Cape Town, 1964), vol. II, pp. 94–209. For a study of humanitarian influence on frontier policy see J. G. Pretorius, *The British Humanitarians and the Cape Eastern Frontier 1834–36* (Pretoria, 1988).

26. John Mitford Bowker, *Speeches, Letters and Selections from the Important Papers of the Late John Mitford Bowker* (Cape Town, repr. 1962), esp. pp. 88–9, 100–6, 111–25. There was considerable tension within the frontier administration at this point, with some officials strongly supporting the Glenelg–Stockenstrom approach and others opposing it. Charles Stretch was the leading "humanitarian" frontier official.

27. Lester, "British Settler Discourse," and Alan Lester, "The Margins of Order: Strategies of Segregation on the Eastern Cape Frontier 1806–1850," *Journal of Southern African Studies* 23.4 (1997), pp. 635–53. Elizabeth Elbourne, "The Sin of the Settler: The 1835–36 Settler Committee on Aborigines and Debates over Virtue and Conquest in the Early Nineteenth-Century British White Settler Empire," *Journal of Colonialism and Colonial Studies* 4.3 (2003); and Elbourne, "The Creation of 'Knowledge' about 'Aborigines' in the Early Nineteenth-Century British Empire," Canadian Historical Association, 2003.

28. John Cumming noted as soon as he arrived on the frontier how sensitive his white congregants were to any suggestion that they had bad attitudes towards the Xhosa; Cumming, *Diary*, 4 December 1840 and 18 July 1851, for how a group of English people would not come to his prayer meeting, "either despising religion or myself because I was a missionary to their enemies." Chase's article was published in the *Journal* of 7 November 1839. I saw the clipping in CA, BK 113, *Kaffir Depredations 1850–1865*.

29. Henry Calderwood, *Prayer: The Christian's Stronghold and Means of Triumph* (Cape Town, 1842), p. 88. "I have no sympathy with those sentimental philanthropists who seem to think and speak as though colonization were in all cases almost an unmingled evil to the native tribes. It is not the case. There may be and are many evils connected with colonization. These cannot be entirely avoided." Henry Calderwood, *Caffres and Caffre Missions* (London, 1858), p. 49; George Brown, *Personal Adventures in South Africa* (London, 1855), p. vi.

30. NLSA (CT), MSB 142, *D'Urban–Smith Correspondence. Letters between Smith and D'Urban re. Queen Adelaide Province*, D'Urban to Glenelg, 8 June 1836. He cited the numbers of farms destroyed by the Xhosa as 450, along with 4,000 horses and 100,000 cattle. D'Urban was *persona non grata* with the Colonial Office from this point on, it would seem. Bowker wrote to him in 1846 when he was visiting London, asking if he could use his contacts in Whitehall to get access for the settler voice on frontier policy, but D'Urban responded: "I hope I have not been altogether useless, although Downing Street has been imperviously closed to me from my arrival in England." See Bowker, *Speeches, Letters and Selections*, pp. 274–5.

31. It is interesting to note that an attempt in 1844 to create a public celebration and certification of the settler historical narrative constructed by Godlonton ended in disaster, as class lines and division asserted themselves to override

the attempt to unite around "whiteness." This was to be the first of several planned meetings of celebration in Port Elizabeth and Bathurst. But "rowdyness and boisterous" violence led by the proletarian Thomas Stubbs upset the meeting. Stubbs objected to the triumphalist view of settler history that Godlonton presented. A later meeting was organized, with entry by ticket only to ensure the exclusion of the less respectable elements. The usual elements of the settler narrative were trotted out at this meeting: their sturdy empire-building virtue, their benevolence towards the Xhosa, their victim status as subject to Xhosa violence. For this episode see Robert Ross, *Status and Respectability in the Cape Colony, 1750–1870: A Tragedy of Manners* (Cambridge, 1999), pp. 63–6; Robert Godlonton, *Memorials of the British Settlers of South Africa* (Grahamstown, 1844), pp. 38–45.

32. Robert Godlonton, *A Narrative of the Irruption of the Kaffir Hordes into the Eastern Province of the Cape of Good Hope, 1834–35* (Graham's Town, 1836), pp. 6–7, 106–7. The spokespersons for the humanitarian view were regarded either as naive philanthropists or as motivated by anti-settler bile. In his lexicon of villains, Thomas Pringle and John Philip were at the top of the list. For the construction of the Shaka image and Fynn, see Julie Pridmore, "Beyond the 'Natal Frontier'? H. F. Fynn's Cape Career 1834–1852," *Journal of Natal and Zulu History* 16 (1996), pp. 31–67; Jeff Guy, "Shaka KaSenzangakhona – A Reassessment," *Journal of Natal and Zulu History* 16, (1996), pp. 1–29; Carolyn Hamilton, *Terrific Majesty: The Powers of Shaka Zulu and the Limits of Historical Invention* (Cape Town and Johannesburg, 1998), esp. ch. 1. For an example of Shaka imagery in this respect, see the memoirs of William Shaw, *The Story of My Mission in South-Eastern Africa: Comprising Some Account of the European Colonists with Extended Notices of the Kaffir and Other Native Tribes* (London, 1860), p. 437; George Thompson, *Travels and Adventures in South Africa*, vol. I, p. 173.

33. Godlonton, *Narrative of the Irruption*, pp. 170, 215–23, 226–7.

34. Ibid., pp. 20–3, 32.

35. Robert Godlonton and Edward Irving, *A Narrative of the Kaffir War of 1850–51* (London and Grahamstown, 1851), pp. 22–3, 113–18, 180–5. For an example of the idea of expertise attached to settler discourse, see Cole, *The Cape and the Kaffirs*, pp. 150–1.

36. An issue that reinforced their need to secure access to London. See Basil Le Cordeur, *The Politics of Eastern Cape Separatism 1820–1854* (Cape Town, 1981).

37. Although Holden's book included the Zulu within its purview, it is possible to select out the parts that apply to the Xhosa alone, and I have concentrated on them. Anthony Trollope, *South Africa*, 2 vols. (London, 1878). The phrase "a-trolloping" was a Jamaican play on Trollope's name that came from his trip there in 1859; see Catherine Hall, *Civilising Subjects: Colony and Metropole in the English Imagination 1830–1867* (Oxford, 2002), p. 210. It meant "travelling commentators who knew not what they saw." George Theal and Dudley Kidd were the leading representatives of the next generation of experts. Their knowledge systems reflected the discourse of anthropology. George Theal, *Kaffir Folk Lore: A Collection of Traditional Tales Common Among the People*

Living on the Eastern Border of the Cape Colony (London, 1886), Dudley Kidd, *Kaffir Socialism* (London, 1908). Kidd paid tribute to Holden as a reliable observer in *The Essential Kaffir* (London, 1925), p. 425. Charles Brownlee's *Reminiscences of Kaffir Life and History* (Lovedale, 1896) could also qualify as a statement similar to Holden's. In its conception and attitudes, it belongs to the same worldview. But it was not published until 1896.

38. J. C. Warner in John Maclean, *A Compendium of Kafir Laws and Customs* (Mount Coke, 1858), pp. 62–3. There were provisions for marriage, divorce, injury to property, inheritance, and theft.

39. Ibid., pp. 39–44, 60–1. Warner noted how during the debate "every proof is attempted to be invalidated; objection meets objection … each disputant endeavouring … to throw the burden of answering on his opponent." This Xhosa procedure was the roots of the claim of the annoyed British that the Xhosa were great lawyers.

40. Ibid, pp. 60–1. Holden's treatment of the legal system is surprisingly short, but generally follows this same line; see his *Past and Future of the Kaffir Races*, pp. 332–40.

41. Maclean, *Compendium of Kafir Laws and Customs*, pp. 67–9, for Warner and theft.

42. John Henderson Soga, *The Ama-Xosa: Life and Customs* (Lovedale, 1932), pp. 42–4. In spite of its complex levels of administration, which were characterized by openness and consultation between the various elements, this system was argued to foster and support crime and predatory habits precisely because those self-same habits did not allow a "uniform administration of justice." See Holden, *Past and Future of the Kaffir Races*, p. 331.

43. Maclean, *Compendium of Kafir Laws and Customs*, pp. 79–80.

44. Holden, *Past and Future of the Kaffir Races*, pp. 279–80.

45. Ibid., p. 390. This, of course, was the intellectual trick that liberalism effected to endorse empire.

46. For the Zulu see Dan Wylie, "Language and Assassination: Cultural Negations in White Writers' Portrayal of Shaka and the Zulu," and Carolyn Hamilton, "'The character and objects of Chaka': A Reconsideration of the Making of Shaka as Mfecane Motor," in Carolyn Hamilton (ed.), *The Mfecane Aftermath: Reconstructive Debates in Southern African History* (Johannesburg, 1995). Hamilton also addresses this issue in her *Terrific Majesty*. For a contemporary example of the threat that the fierceness of the Zulu was believed to pose to missionary presence, see CA, A80(2), Ayliff Papers, *Journal 1832–50*, 18 June 1833. For the Bengali, see Mrinalini Sinha, *The "Effeminate" Bengali and the "Manly" Englishman* (Manchester, 1995).

47. See Ashis Nandy, *Intimate Enemy: Loss and Recovery of Self Under Colonialism* (Dehli, 1983), pp. 12–15, 56, 66; Nicholas Thomas, *Colonialism's Culture: Anthropology, Travel and Government* (Princeton, 1994), pp. 133–6. One reason for the appeal of this category was that it could be used with ease by paternalists like Sir Harry Smith or liberals like Sir George Grey. It allowed the hierarchy and distinctions between imperial culture and the culture of the indigenes to be explained and maintained. Most of the literature has focused on the way the colonialist infantilizes the colonized. But what also needs to be

considered is the way empire reduces the colonialist to childlike behavior. It is not possible to explore this idea fully here; but it could be explored through the dependence of the early colonizers, in particular, upon the indigenes for their sustenance and guidance, which we have had occasion to mention earlier. We may also see evidence of it in the behavior of Sir Harry Smith towards the Xhosa. When they behaved as he wished and respectfully, he was benign and forthcoming and enthusiastic about his successes. When they failed to follow his prescriptions, he turned vicious and cruel, as well as self-doubting.

48. Anti-slavery humanitarianism rested on the notion that slaves were also men and women. David Bogue's lectures at Gosport specifically warned against infantalizing the people being converted because if they were "taught as children you make them children, but teaching them as men and endeavouring to lead them to act as men you make them men." This was ambiguous, but it clearly tends toward the idea that even if they were "children" when the missionaries encountered them, they were capable of rapidly transcending that limitation. CWM, *Home Odds*, Box 25, in the lecture titled "Behaviour of missionaries to different classes of people." See also, CWM, LMS, *South Africa Journals, 1816–1824*, f. 60, Evan Evans 1816–1817, 5 April 1816.

49. For Lovedale, see Michael Ashley, "African Education and Society in the Nineteenth Century Eastern Cape," in Christopher Saunders and Robin Derricourt, *Beyond the Cape Frontier: Studies in the History of the Transkei and Ciskei* (London, 1974), pp. 199–212; Govan, *Memoirs of ... Laing*, pp. 116, 154–7; James Wells, *Life of James Stewart* (London, 1907); Leon de Kock, *Civilizing Barbarians: Missionary Narrative and African Textual Response in Nineteenth-Century South Africa* (Johannesburg, 1996), pp. 89–94.

50. Thus, for example, circumcision rites and similar ceremonies for young girls involved rites of sexual initiation that authorized at an early age the promiscuous behavior that was believed to characterize Xhosa society. Maclean, *Compendium of Kafir Laws and Customs*, pp. 100–5, for circumcision and its related customs.

51. See chs. 11–14 in Holden, which all revolve around this issue, and pp. 292–5 for the cattle-killing as originating in witchcraft. Brownlee also subscribed to this view at one point, although he later revised his view of the matter; see Brownlee, *Reminiscences of Kaffir Life and History*, pp. 240–61 for accounts of witchcraft, and pp. 395–8 for a letter to Maclean which attributes the cattle-killing to witchcraft.

52. Witchcraft was a weapon in tribal politics. It tended to reflect conflict and tension within the tribes. It had its own place within the legal system. In spite of the lurid descriptions that dominated British conceptions of the practice, it by no means always ended in some poor soul being eaten alive by swarms of hungry ants. It was possible to escape death and indeed to be proved not guilty of a witchcraft allegation. Colonial observers also tended to confuse the different categories of witches, diviners and rainmakers and lump them all together as witchdoctors practicing Satanic rites. Warner in Maclean, *Compendium of Kafir Laws and Customs*, pp. 81–91, 94–5; Holden, *Past and Future of the Kaffir Races*, pp. 294–5.

53. Holden, *Past and Future of the Kaffir Races*, pp. 316–17, 287, 294.

54. Maclean, *Compendium of Kafir Laws and Customs*, p. 112; Holden, *Past and Future of the Kafir Races*, pp 390–91.

55. Holden, *Past and Future of the Kaffir Races*, pp. 417–62.

56. Ibid, pp. 423–5.

57. Ibid., pp. 432–64, 468–72. This statement, of course, provides a nice example of the way a liberal view of empire's mission sat upon the reality of despotism and coercion.

58. Anthropological Society of London, *Anthropological Review*, March 1865, pp. clviii–clxxxiii. For Reade, who was quite celebrated at the time, though forgotten today, see Felix Driver, *Geography Militant: Cultures of Exploration and Empire* (Oxford, 2001), ch. 5. For Colenso and this episode, see Jeff Guy, *The Heretic: A Study of the Life of John William Colenso 1814–1883* (Pietermaritzburg, 1983), pp. 75–80.

59. *Anthropological Review*, May 1865, pp. ccxlviii–cclxxxii. British historians have neglected Colenso. It is significant that the most important work on him has been done by the South African scholar Jeff Guy. It should not be forgotten that it was Matthew Arnold who led the intellectual charge to discredit Colenso, directing particular attention to Colenso's desire to democratize knowledge by engaging in serious dialogue with Africans. See Jeff Guy, "Class, Imperialism and Literary Criticism: William Ngidi, John Colenso and Matthew Arnold," *Journal of Southern African Studies* 23.2 (1997), pp. 219–41. The quip by Disraeli about Zulus defeating our generals and converting our bishops is well known, but that was from the late 1870s. At the time, the squibs were more pointed; this one, for example: "A Bishop there was of Natal / Who had a Zulu for a Pal. / Said the native, 'Look here, / Ain't the Pentateuch queer?' / Which converted my Lord of Natal."

60. See e.g. Theal, *Kaffir Folklore*, p. 210.

q

Missionaries

Fig. 1. Reverend Henry Calderwood

Fig. 2. Reverend William Shaw

Fig. 3. Reverend Richard Birt

Xhosa chiefs

Fig. 4. Sandile

Fig. 5. Sandile and his counselors

Fig. 6. Maqoma

Fig. 7. Xhoxho

Fig. 8. Meeting between Governor Janssens and Chief Ngqika, 1803

Fig. 9. Meeting with Xhosa chiefs at Charles Brownlee's residence

Fig. 10. Sir Harry Smith

Fig. 11. George Grey

Fig. 12. Charles Lennox Stretch, frontier official

Fig. 13. Lt. General Sir George Pomeroy Colley

Fig. 14. Maqoma and his wife at Robben Island

Fig. 15. Chiefs at Robben Island

Fig. 16. Mhala, Maqoma and Xhoxho

Fig. 17. Nongqawuse and Nonkosi

8   Meetings, ceremonies and display

Displaying imperial power

In May 1792 two sailors were killed on the beach at Waimea, one of the Hawaiian Islands. They were members of a supply ship that was sailing between Australia and an expedition to the northwest coast of North America led by Sir George Vancouver. In all likelihood the men had been killed because the Hawaiians associated them with a recent massacre committed by members of a visiting American ship. The hapless victims had no knowledge of these events, and thus, to the European mind, their deaths were meaningless attacks that demonstrated the unknowable depths of Hawaiian savagery. As such, Sir George Vancouver determined that they could hardly go unnoticed. He set sail for Hawaii, and after elaborate and prolonged negotiations the local authorities selected two men as the murderers. Vancouver insisted that they be ritually tried using the ceremony of British justice, but that they be executed by the Hawaiians themselves. Dependent upon the cooperation of the local chiefs, Vancouver could not verify the guilt or innocence of the men, and in fact they were almost certainly innocent. Still, that was hardly the point. Vancouver wanted to serve notice of the limitless reach of the British empire. And so, Greg Dening tells us, as the sentences on the victims were announced Vancouver deployed some of the theatrics of rule that he knew from home – hushed silence, ponderous tones, military precision.[1]

Nearly forty years later a similar episode took place near Fort Willshire on the banks of the Keiskamma river. Two soldiers had been murdered, and the British demanded that the perpetrators be handed over. Two men were identified and examined by Chief Dushane, who ascertained their guilt in the presence of Samuel Young, the Methodist missionary. They were then transferred to the Colony, and tried in a British court. Like Vancouver, the British authorities on the frontier were anxious to ensure that British justice was seen to be carried out by the Xhosa chiefs. The murderers were handed over the Ngqika for *him* to try them in public, and, when found guilty, execute them. And so it was: "they underwent a short trial in the presence of British officers, and after the confirmation of the sentence, preparations were made for putting them to death."

The execution itself attracted quite a crowd. The leading Xhosa chiefs were there; people trekked out from Grahamstown to witness the event; extra troops were dispatched, whether to provide an audience or to overawe the people is not clear. There was a clutch of the Methodist men of God. William Shrewsbury, Samuel Young and William Shaw were all there. The spiritual punishment of the culprits was not ignored. They were not permitted to sleep. Shrewsbury spent the whole night with them in prayer and exhortation, urging them to repent and convert before they met eternity. Nor were they allowed to die quietly. At the execution, the sermon praised the sentence of death as not only demanded by British justice, but also reflecting God's justice, which was so much better than Xhosa justice, which punished murder only by cattle fines.[2]

What do these two events have in common? They are small vignettes of how an empire rules before it has declared itself an empire; of the methods of command it uses before it has developed a fully elaborated *system* of rule and authority. Such moments occur when an imperial presence is hovering around the edges of an indigenous society but is not yet committed to a formal empire or is unsure how to implement an imperial rule. Making the imperial presence felt was a considerable problem for empire in the days before it had established an apparatus of administration or established procedures of rule. It was a familiar problem for the British, who had faced it in Ireland in the seventeenth century, and in North America in its dealing with the first peoples of that continent.[3]

For the first four decades of British contact with the Xhosa, a fixed uncertainty governed relations between the British state and the Xhosa. There were certain continuing themes, of course, such as the perpetual friction around the issue of stock and cattle theft. But the imperial state did not decide to extend its rule over Xhosaland until 1848, when British Kaffraria was created. And even after 1848 not *all* of Xhosa territory was claimed, although Britain asserted the right to monitor events. Thus, the British imperial administration did not possess direct lines of authority into the tribes until the mid-1850s. For most of our period, therefore, Xhosaland may be considered part of Britain's informal empire, even though it is not what most historians would think of when they consider informal empire.

But informal empire needed rules and modes of engagement; it needed a culture of imperial dominion and techniques of imperial rule. Even at the frontier of empire, the imperial state needed to fashion strategies that deployed its power. Xhosaland is an example of the methods and techniques that could be used to rule a people who were clearly regarded by the

British as in need of suzerain guidance and direction, but who, for a variety of reasons, were not yet incorporated into the empire's system of rule and control. This is the topic I want to address in this chapter. How did the imperial state impose its presence and will on the Xhosa before it proclaimed them subjects? What strategies, what culture, did it develop to project its authority and legitimacy?[4]

The modes and styles of personal rule

When the sixth frontier war of 1834–5 sputtered to an end in the (southern) winter of 1835, the military commander, Colonel Harry Smith, and the Governor, Sir Benjamin D'Urban, faced the problem of preserving the peace. Since the war had been unanticipated, and policy instructions from London took up to six months to arrive, this was a classic "man on the spot" moment in imperial history. They devised an audacious scheme to settle frontier instability permanently. They proposed to create a new territory between the Kei and Fish rivers, to be called Queen Adelaide Province. The Xhosa tribes would be settled here under British supervision. Smith would be the day-to-day administrator, and he would preside over a program of anglicization of the Xhosa. The intent was to remake the Xhosa into facsimiles of English people. It was an overt and open attempt to colonize minds and bodies rather than land and spaces. This area is better known to modern ears as the Ciskei, one of the notorious homelands of the apartheid regime in South Africa.

After the war of 1835, therefore, the first attempt was made to bring the Xhosa within the umbra of British authority. The peace treaties that were signed in September made the Xhosa into subjects of Great Britain, and allowed the British to regulate their living spaces. The chiefs put themselves under the protection of English law, promised to obey the Governor, and in return received his protection. Missionaries were to have right of access to the territory, and diplomatic agents were appointed to regulate tribal customs and guide them along the path of civilized behavior. Even when Queen Adelaide Province was dismantled a year later, much of the apparatus of British presence remained – the diplomatic agents, for example – and the claims to regulate Xhosa settlement and movement were never surrendered.[5]

This remarkable episode is little known to imperial historiography. But it was the origins of Britain's African empire. It was the first attempt by the British to impose a system of imperial rule over a large body of independent Africans. By any standards the project was extraordinary. It was an unintended laboratory for the British to try out strategies of rule over Africans. As such, it is deserving of some attention. And the same is true of the man who was at the center of these events, whose self-appointed task it was to turn the Xhosa into black English. Who was Colonel Harry Smith, that he should have been called to be the first British proconsul of her black African empire?[6]

Smith was a member of the network of Peninsular War veterans deployed by the Duke of Wellington across the empire in various commands. After many years of service largely outside of Britain – service which included the role of intelligence officer during the war of 1812, and helping to eat Dolly Madison's unfinished dinner in the White House – Smith was appointed Military Secretary to the Cape in 1828. He stayed there for about ten years, serving as Frontier Commandant during the sixth frontier war. He then moved to India, where he was knighted in 1843 for service in the Sind war. His name was made when he led the force that broke the power of the Sikh army a year later. His reward was appointment as Governor of the Cape Colony in 1847. His second tour of duty at the Cape began in triumph and ended in disaster. He was sent out to bring peace to the frontier by reviving his own plan for a supervised homeland for the Xhosa. But with the coming of the eighth frontier war in 1850, Smith's career unraveled and he was recalled in 1852 to be put out to pasture in command of the Western District at Plymouth.

Smith has been treated by historians as something between a nonentity and a buffoon. Even academic treatments of his career portray him as if he was too outrageous to be taken seriously. It is true that his behavior tended to attract attention. Smith had more than the touch of the psychopath about him. He was a blustering bully with an enormous (and fragile) ego and a flawed ability to read political fortunes, and was subject to erratic and sudden mood swings. In the Cape he was known for his outbursts of foul language, showering abuse one moment and offering kindnesses the next. He was attentive to his troops, sent the wounded dainties from his table, and quite possibly was addicted to laudanum. Such attributes hardly disqualify him from embodying key qualities of imperial culture; they may, in fact, mirror some of its fundamental essence.[7]

Smith deserves serious consideration. The styles and the methods of rule that he tried out in Queen Adelaide Province and British Kaffraria prefigured how the British empire would present itself to Africans. He infantilized the Xhosa and acted the paternalist towards them. Like all true paternalists, he believed that personal influence and contact could work to effect civilizing change. But he also recognized that imperial rule needed the trappings of ceremonial authority. In Queen Adelaide Province and British Kaffraria, "traditions" and ceremonies were invented to express and facilitate imperial might. This was forty or fifty years before the British appropriated the Indian Durbar as a site of imperial assemblage.

It was in this remote part of empire, too, that the first "District Commissioners" were to be found in the resident agents that Smith left behind with the tribes in 1836. And it was from the experience of these resident agents in the obscurity of the Cape bush, rather than the shimmering deserts of northern Nigeria, that indirect rule in Africa was first imagined. Finally, although Smith's ambition to remake Xhosa society in Queen Adelaide Province and British Kaffraria ultimately came to grief, his program was picked up by Sir George Grey in the 1850s with very different results. Smith was something more than the free-booting, bungling joke he has typically been made out to be.[8]

Queen Adelaide Province and British Kaffraria were boldly conceived schemes of social engineering. But they were also products of their time. In particular they paralleled the ambitions of missionary culture. Although in 1835 Smith and D'Urban were viewed with suspicion by most missionaries, the stated aim of Queen Adelaide Province rested on the assumption that it was cultural difference that separated the Xhosa from the British. If models of British civil society could insinuate British subjectivities among them, the Xhosa would rapidly progress up the ladder of civilization. The Harry Smith model of imperial governance shared common themes with missionary culture. Indeed, there were several moments in the first months of the Queen Adelaide project when Smith pondered the nature of Xhosa intelligence using the language of the humanitarian. Smith formed a more sophisticated estimation of Xhosa character and culture than some of his actions might lead us to believe. "It is with some astonishment I have listened to their arguments, their just, clear and concise mode of reasoning," he wrote amid a long description of the power of the Xhosa mind. Thus Smith was convinced that a combination of paternal pressure from well-meaning and right-minded Englishmen would soon lead the Xhosa to the "honest habits of a civilised life."[9]

But Smith's vision was deeply schizoid. Accompanying this humanitarian perspective was the coercive, bullying racist. At more or less the same time as he was writing in humanitarian mode, he confessed to D'Urban that he saw the Xhosa as "savages ... whose extermination would be a blessing." Then, drawing back into the humanitarian register, he went on to say that "my study and exertions should be for their reformation, improvement and consequence happiness." This split personality is not simply a reflection of the psychopathology of Harry Smith. This range of behavior and perspective mirrored imperial culture as a whole as it confronted the Xhosa and other complicated native cultures.[10]

Harry Smith's ambition for Queen Adelaide Province and then British Kaffraria was the ambition of empire in microcosm. He wanted to bring peace and security to the province by sprinkling military forts throughout.

In this he represented the coercions of empire. He wanted to introduce energetic clergy, but not those who were too fanatical, to teach the habits of industry, and he wanted to establish schools of industry. In these ways, he represented the ideal of the paternal civilizing mission. He wanted to convert the chiefs and petty chiefs into a British governing hierarchy, dispensing law and order. And in this way he reflected the ideal of enlisting the political and social authority of traditional authority in the service of empire.[11]

Imperial paternalism rested on the belief that historical time could be foreshortened by the active personal intervention of civilized Britons. Smith epitomized this assumption. Within days of declaring his plan for Queen Adelaide Province, he was ready to confirm that the wheel of history had begun to turn for the Xhosa. He wrote to D'Urban in September 1835 that, using legal coercion and human persuasion, he expected soon to convert "a savage and vexatious enemy into peaceable and useful subjects." In November 1835 he appointed a hierarchy of chiefs as magistrates who were to administer a mixture of Xhosa and British law under his supervision. The lesser chiefs were made Justices of the Peace; each kraal headman was responsible for administering the law in his kraal. By January 1836 Smith claimed there were already significant signs of cultural progress. He reported seeing flourishing gardens on the land that he had given them, clergymen working among them, and signs that they had already awakened to the virtues of living under British laws administered by their own magistrate chiefs. The Xhosa obligingly fed his dreams, for when he asked the assembled multitudes if they all wanted to be Englishmen, they all answered "Yes," and he congratulated them: "You have chosen well," he intoned.[12]

Xhosa behavior tended to reinforce Smith's illusions about the reach of his own personal power. He was accustomed to hearing chiefs tell him how happy, contented and loyal they were.[13] Chiefs made public statements that tended to affirm Smith's own presentation of events. On 22 September 1835, for example, Siyolo, Gazala and Mhala all came to express their gratitude to him. He responded by giving them clothes and other presents and making a little speech about controlling crime. Five days later Mhala publicly urged obeisance to Smith, profusely thanking him publicly for his help, asking solicitously (or obsequiously?) about the schools of industry that Smith had grandiously promised he would bring them, and agreeing with Smith that the Xhosa were an ignorant people, and that they needed instruction in the arts of industry and agriculture. Mhala was repeating back to Smith the latter's own policy aspirations. But Smith read it as confirming the success of his policy of personal rule. He seems not to have realized that he was encountering Xhosa politeness, evasion and their habit of negotiating the terms of the encounter with the British. One imagines Mhala smiling with sly satisfaction at the good results of his dissembling.[14]

A few months later, Mhala suffered a backsliding. Mhala was testing the limits of Smith's tolerance. He failed to turn up when summoned – a favorite demonstration of Mhala's insolence. He had acted beyond his authority as one of Smith's magistrates and collected fines of cattle for his own account. Smith decided on a showdown. He gathered the chiefs together, stripped Mhala of his magistrate's medal, deprived him of some cattle, and demanded an explanation. In response, Mhala did public penance and apologized. Having secured a public confession, of sorts, Smith made him retake his magistrate's oath of office and returned the medal. Smith did more than just reinstate Mhala; he also returned the cattle that he had fined him. Smith intended his behavior to convey the power of imperial paternalism. It is hard to believe that Smith's conduct in this episode had the effect that he intended. More likely it was seen by the Xhosa as yet another form of negotiation.[15]

In this and in other ways Smith wanted to see around him the small signs of wonder that his scheme was in fact working. A mere three months after the province had been established, Smith reported excitedly to D'Urban the goodwill and cooperation of the chiefs. They were well on their way to being converted to English ways, he claimed. He was particularly pleased with Maqoma – "one of the finest Kafirs I have to deal with." Smith was particularly impressed that the Xhosa began to call him *Inkosi Enkulu*, or Great Chief.[16] Indeed, he decided to adopt the title as his very own, thinking that it served to legitimate his power by drawing from Xhosa culture and history. The term is a Xhosa (and Zulu) phrase which is commonly used as a term of respect, often to an older, more senior man. It is unlikely that it had quite the symbolic significance that Smith seems to have assumed. Nor was Smith the first official to utter the phrase in imperial conversation. But Smith does seem to have been the first Governor actually to claim this title for himself. And the term was most closely associated with his rule in both Queen Adelaide Province and British Kaffraria. After the outbreak of the 1850–3 war, its usage faded quite quickly.[17]

Smith was not only the generous, if mercurial, paternalist. He was also the harsh disciplinarian and an expert practitioner in the darker arts of paternal persuasion. Indeed, the project of Queen Adelaide Province itself was juxtaposed directly with the devastation that Smith and D'Urban had wrought on Xhosaland in the first half of 1835. At the same moment when Smith was writing to D'Urban about the days he was devoting to learning the ways of the Xhosa and working to "bring them to the blessings of religion and morality," he was also burning their huts. But this was precisely the point. What good was paternal guidance without the iron fist of coercion? As Smith explained to D'Urban, "2700 huts are occasionally destroyed in one week, thereby blending persuasion with coercion."[18]

Violence and humiliation were integral to the style of paternal rule that Smith practiced. But here too, Sir Harry Smith was firmly in the mainstream of imperial experience. Humiliation is not a category that gets much play in imperial historiography. Certain notorious episodes such as the "crawling order" in India in 1919 are well known. But humiliation, like violence, was not an aberrant, occasional strategy of British rule. It was persistent and always available. Smith made full use of it against the chiefs in public settings during his time as *Enkosi Inkulu* of Queen Adelaide Province. Both Mhala and Maqoma were subject to his rages when he believed they were stepping out of line. It was an important part of Smith's strategy that this humiliation be done in public, so that the shame would be the more strongly felt, and then he could forgive more readily. After one such humiliation of Maqoma, Smith ostentatiously forgave him, claiming that he told him: "You are now more in need of me than ever. I will therefore try you once more and if you deceive me I will make you the most degraded of my children." After this, Smith felt that he had cemented his relationship with Maqoma, just as Calderwood, it will be recalled, felt that good had come out of his own particular confrontation with the chief.[19]

Humiliation easily shades over into violence, however, and violence was always liable to erupt from Harry Smith's volatile personality. In this respect, there is an even more remarkable episode involving Smith and Maqoma that needs to be recorded. It occurred a decade or so later in December 1847, when Lieutenant Colonel Sir Harry Smith, Governor of the Cape Colony, arrived at Port Elizabeth to begin a tour of inspection of the new colony of British Kaffraria. Upon his disembarkation, Smith spotted Maqoma in the crowd. Maqoma had moved to Port Elizabeth with his family a year or so before, partly to avoid further entanglement in the War of the Axe. His life there had not been particularly chiefly. He was reported to be living with a few retainers in pretty lowly circumstances. He was also in one of his bouts of drinking heavily. In any case, he was no threat to anyone.[20]

Given his past history with Smith, which had not been all bad, Maqoma might have expected at least a polite reunion at Port Elizabeth when he wandered to the town to observe the arrival of the new Governor. If so, he was to be sorely disabused. The exact sequence of what happened next is not precisely clear, but the main outlines of the story are not in dispute. All authorities agree that Smith called Maqoma forward, seemingly to shake his hand. But he pulled his sword out of its scabbard, instead, as if to attack the unarmed chief. As Maqoma shrank back, the crowd of mainly white settlers roared its approval. One version has it that Smith then knocked Maqoma to the ground, put his foot on his neck and yelled a few choice phrases, such as "You are a dog ... This is to teach you that I have come hither to teach Kaffirland that I am Chief and master here and in this way I shall treat the enemies of the Queen." Other versions claim that this foot-stomping incident happened a little later, when Smith had summoned the chief to his hotel room, where he was upbraided for "his treachery and folly" for having taken part in the recent war.[21]

In actual fact, it hardly matters whether Maqoma's neck was a footrest for Smith in public or in private. The story soon became common gossip on the frontier, and went into the local folklore, where it became a perfect example of the kind of colonial reasoning that blamed the colonized for the actions of the colonizer. Methodist missionary John Ayliff wrote a letter to the *Frontier Times* in 1851 blaming Maqoma himself for Smith's violation of his dignity. It was Maqoma's character that was responsible, Ayliff explained. Such a man in Europe would have been brought to "condign punishment ["the Gallows" has been crossed out in the original] long since." It was an episode that went into Xhosa lore also, although with a slightly different twist. Needless to say, it is not to be found in any imperial historiography. What is one to make of an imperial Governor, a representative of the Crown, behaving like a common hooligan? No wonder that both Smith and D'Urban have been written out of imperial historiography. What would they do to its categories?[22]

But if violent behavior was integral to the paternal rule of Harry Smith, so too were strategies of persuasion, negotiation and communication. Smith was aware of the need of imperial culture to persuade its subjects of the legitimacy and justice of its rule. And to do this, it was necessary to seek means of political communication that would establish a "language" of political rule to convince the Xhosa to accept Harry Smith, or any other imperial administrator. Ultimately this was the point of Smith's claiming chiefly status: it was a way of Smith establishing "a mutual confidence as well as a mutual understanding [so that] all parties so lately at war have joined in amity." For this purpose, public ceremonial and display were essential.[23]

Sites of encounter, sites of ceremony

Until the mid-1850s the most important site of official business between the British and the Xhosa was the public meeting. Negotiations occurred, agreements were reached and treaties signed in public view. Thus, the public meeting assumed a central importance for the display of both British and Xhosa power and presence. It was where imperial purpose, intention and ideology were on display. Equally, it was where the Xhosa reception and response to that presence could be gauged. In these meetings, then, we can see something of the dynamics of personal rule, of the ceremony and show, and of the negotiating styles that were characteristic of the British and the Xhosa at this particular moment.

Although the practice of holding public meetings to negotiate the domain of the imperial state was peculiar neither to southern Africa nor to the British, the war of 1834–5 marked its emergence as a central strategy of imperial culture in southern Africa.[24] A series of five meetings between September 1835 and the beginning of January 1836 negotiated an end to the war and the arrangements for the creation of Queen Adelaide Province. It is important to note that the British seem to have treated these meetings as effective surrenders by the Xhosa, which gave them the right to make demands and changes as they wished. But it is far from clear that this was how the Xhosa understood them. Indeed, the British found themselves negotiating quite hard with this "defeated" enemy, although there is no formal recognition of this fact in the British records.

Such miscommunication went to the very heart of the treaties. By the middle of August 1835 the British had received clear intimations that the Xhosa wished to bring the war to an end. This was typical of the way the Xhosa made peace; they just stopped fighting when they felt the point had been made, or enough had been gained or lost. This was the cultural antithesis of the British way of war. And the Xhosa surely had enough experience of the British by now to know that they fought by very different principles. Perhaps it was this that led Maqoma to tell the emissary from D'Urban on 15 August that " they wished to place themselves under the Governor's feet; we wish to be his children, his soldiers." D'Urban took this literally. But this ignored the fact that he was relying on a report that itself had been translated. And it ignored the possibility, too, that Maqoma was dissembling, telling the British what he thought they wanted to hear, or speaking in a language of exaggerated politeness and subservience.[25]

In any case, even reading the British record of the process of peace negotiations, it is clear that there was hard and continual bargaining that bore little resemblance to unconditional surrender. In negotiations over where the various chiefs and tribes would settle, for example, Smith and D'Urban yielded quite a lot. They retreated from their intention to drive the Xhosa across the River Kie, setting the Keiskamma as the new boundary of the Colony. This was quite a concession, since the land between the Keiskamma and the Kei was the heart of Xhosaland; it contained the Great Place of Ngqika and of Ndlambe, and it was within striking distance for Maqoma of his old land on the Kat river, from which he had been expelled in 1827. They relented in their original plan for Maqoma and granted him his request for a specific piece of land on the Keiskamma. And in January 1836 Smith readjusted the land concessions even further on receiving a report from the Commissioners he had appointed.[26]

Such concessions were significant reflections that the British faced certain limitations, even if they refused to admit them. They had abandoned their intention to push the Xhosa across the Kie, for example, because they were unable to dislodge Maqoma from the Amatolas mountains. Indeed, it seems likely that the idea of Queen Adelaide Province itself came out of the recognition that a military stalemate had been reached. But from the Xhosa standpoint this fed the perception that everything remained negotiable. Smith complained to D'Urban about dealing with "these fickle, vacillating Kafirs ... for no sooner is one matter settled than a new one arises." It may very well have been this, too, that explains the behavior of the chiefs at the great public ceremonies that were mounted to announce to the tribes that a new agreement had been reached. On the one hand, there was the performance of servility, and on the other there was evidence of evasion. Both these patterns were to become very familiar to the British over the next fifteen years.[27]

The great meetings were opportunities for the British to demonstrate their raw power through the well-practiced arts of ceremony and display.[28] The meeting of 17 November 1835 was opened with a cannonade to announce the "approach of the Great Chief (myself)." While a band played "God Save the King," Smith seated himself before the assembled chiefs and their counselors and called on God to bless the proceedings. The band then played the hymn "Glory be to Thee, O God." The chiefs were then sworn in as British magistrates. Each one was dressed in a blue serge suit for the occasion, received a seal of office, took an oath of allegiance to the King and was subjected to a bullying tirade from Smith. Assuming the rights of a Xhosa chief, Smith brought the theater of the law into the occasion. He ostentatiously commuted the death sentence on a man convicted of stealing, and distributed the criminal's cattle to various chiefs. He settled a boundary dispute between Maqoma and Bhurhu (one of Sarhili's chiefs) and "thundered out an order ... that all redress had to be by ordinary course of the law." Smith was satisfied that he had conducted one of the "greatest meetings that was ever held in Kafirland," which, he promised D'Urban, would have "a very extraordinary effect."[29]

Theatrical display was an important part of Smith's conduct of these meetings because it substituted for an established set of codes within which imperial relations could be conducted. Smith recognized the need to invent ritual and symbols that would invoke the magic of imperial rule. He developed stage props to help impress the Xhosa with his ceremony. Among these were his "magic wands," large sticks topped with various knobs depending on the status of the officer. The native police carried a stick with a brass knob. At headquarters, "I had a very long stick with a large knob which was always held by my Gold Stick [an official post that he invented] when I was in council or upon trials … And when I seized the stick, held it myself, and gave a decisive order, that was formal and irrevocable. For when once I had decided, no power could induce me to swerve from that decision."[30]

Similarly, in 1847, when Smith had returned as Governor, his talent for theatrical performance was again on full display. At a meeting of the chiefs and their counselors on 23 December, called to announce his conditions for ending the war, Smith adapted two sergeants' halberds for his performance. Held ceremoniously in his hands, one was sharpened at the end to represent the stick of war, and the other, topped with a brass knob, was his baton of peace. Each chief had to come forward and touch the stick they chose – for war, or for peace. Several hundred troops were assembled around the circle of chiefs, their counselors and a large number of their people. It was not surprising, therefore, that they all – "most cheerfully" he reported to Earl Grey – chose the wand of peace. At the end, Smith took the staff of war and hurled it to the ground, declaring an end to war and demanding three cheers for peace.[31]

Foot-kissing was one of Smith's favorite signs of obedience and submission. It was reported that on his return to Kaffraria as Governor in 1847, the road from Fort Cox to Fort Willshire was lined with Xhosa who were so happy at the return of "their old and kind friend and benefactor" that they ran alongside his horse, kissing his foot and proclaiming their enthusiasm for peace.[32] Whether or not that was so, Smith was clearly taken with the appropriate symbolism of the act because, after the Proclamation declaring the establishment of British Kaffraria on 18 December 1847, he not only shook each chief's hand, "never having previously done so," but also had them come forward "to kiss the Governor's foot in token of absolute submission, and deep humility for their past aggressions upon the Colony and hostility to the British government." It was reported that Phato was so eager to ingratiate himself that he kissed not only the point of Smith's boot, but also the sole and heel! And, as one disconcerted missionary noted sourly in his diary, "this farce being ended" Smith dramatically tore up copies of the frontier treaties that had formed the centerpieces of British policy with the Xhosa since 1836, and declared that now that they were all subjects of the Queen, there would be no more treaties.[33]

But Smith had not yet done with public meetings. After his triumphal tour across the new colony of British Kaffraria, a great meeting was called for 7 January 1848, at which he announced his program for the reconstruction of Xhosa society. A full ceremonial was mounted for this meeting. In all, 2,000 persons attended. Troops were drawn up in two lines, and the Governor with his staff rode to the front while the national anthem played; a prayer by the Reverend Henry Dugmore opened the meeting. The gathering was intended to register the public consent of the chiefs to the program that Smith had prepared for the new province. Smith's address is worth noting because it was a clear statement of the ideology of personal rule and of the kind of language that he believed would be effective in persuading the Xhosa to accept that rule.[34]

Smith referred to the Xhosa as "my people and if good, again, my children." He told them they were now subjects of the Queen, with only one paramount chief (himself); he reminded them that he had returned because they had failed to learn to become Englishmen and he was now going to teach them again. After making each chief swear a loyalty oath, he explained his intentions for British Kaffraria, which were largely a reprise of the program he had declared for Queen Adelaide Province in 1835. The chiefs had to promise to obey the commands of *Inkosi Enkulu* and to ensure that their people complied with imperial rule. Witchcraft was to be abolished, as was the practice of buying and selling wives. Murder was to cease; those who robbed from the Colony were to be punished. Children were to be sent to school "to learn the habits of industry and knowledge which make Englishmen well, good, happy and clothed." And on the anniversary of this day, "one fat ox" was to be presented as symbolic of the land held by grant of Her Majesty.[35]

They would now become English, and British Kaffraria would become the Home Counties of southern Africa. Towns and villages would be laid out in districts, named Kent, Surrey and Sussex. Their lands would be properly surveyed and marked in a book he would keep. He was going to teach them to labor and become industrious; he would provide traders to teach them the finer points of commerce, and missionaries to teach them the virtues of reading, writing and clothing. Smith impressed upon his listeners the importance of attending to the missionaries and even becoming missionaries themselves, and if they did, he was going to build them houses and make gardens and "give you money every year to teach others."

Their conduct would be marked in (another) book each year, and if they earned a "good" through proper behavior he would provide them with plows and tools for their fields and gardens. Good conduct and work were inseparable in Smith's vision. If they learnt to "work as we do," they would get richer and he would be good to them. But "idle and bad conduct will bring on you" the confiscation of land and property. Surveillance was implicit in this reformation: "I will watch over you." And indeed, Smith did not exaggerate. One of the first acts of the new imperial administration was to conduct a census of Xhosaland – this was, after all, the first age of statistics. The ambition of this census mirrored the megalomaniac ambitions of Sir Harry Smith. It was quite remarkable in the precision of its categories. Not only did it aim to capture in figures every horse and cow – which, had it done so, would have been of tremendous value in controlling the problem of theft – but every widow and married and unmarried woman in the province also.[36]

In the final analysis it was the force of his own personality that Smith relied upon for ensuring the security of imperial rule. And in the efficacy of this volatile and widely recognized weapon, the victor of the Aliwal had no doubts at all. "I *will* make you good," he proclaimed, as he launched into an escalating crescendo of admonishment of those he described (quite unself-consciously as) "his children." He described his distress at coming back after eleven years and finding that their conduct had gone from bad to worse, year by year. He recounted his unhappiness at seeing them miserable, wretched and "eaten up" because they had "dared to make war! *You dare to make war!!* You dare to attack our wagons [referring to a wagon train attacked by the Xhosa on the outbreak of war]. See what I will do if you ever dare to touch a wagon or the oxen belonging to it." And in a forensic display of the power of imperial magic, he pointed with his "magic wand" to a wagon parked some way off. The wagon exploded, which, he warned them, was what would happen to them if they misbehaved. He announced the formation of a native police force and the appointment of Colonel George Mackinnon as Chief Commissioner. He then closed the proceedings by ordering them all to shout "Peace, Peace, Peace" which, he claimed, they "echoed in a tremendous roar."

In spite of the fact that it often seems to make him seem like something out of a Gilbert and Sullivan satire, Smith's behavior revealed many of the traits of mainstream imperial culture: its tendency to optimism and belief that it could foreshorten the historical process, its faith in the power of personal presence and influence, and its confidence in the efficacy of paternal methods. Like imperial culture generally, there was much that Smith did not see about the Xhosa. And there was much that he did not *know* that he did not see. But Smith did understand the need to try to create the conditions for consent, too. His antics and his invented rituals were designed to establish a language of communication and persuasion.

His roaring and the like at the great meetings were not simply attempts to shock and awe the Xhosa into accepting imperial rule. They were also shaped by his appropriation of what he believed to be Xhosa symbols and cultural practices in the effort to communicate and persuade. His frequent recourse to "magic" was a way of demonstrating the superior power of British magic over Xhosa magic, thinking as he did that magic was a key category of understanding for the Xhosa. When he pointed his "magic wand" towards a wagon to explode it at the meeting of 23 December 1847, he believed that they were much impressed with this display of his supernatural power.

Similarly, we may see his use of theatrical props, like his wands of war and peace and his adoption of the title *Inkosi Enkulu*, as attempts to establish intercultural means of communication. Smith was original in this respect; there is little evidence that other governors tried to invent tradition in this way. And his ceremonies pre-dated by two decades the famous Durbars that the British "invented" in India after the Mutiny. Like the Durbars, Smith's inventions were hybrid creations of the colonial encounter. Just as the Durbars were rooted in Indian culture, so Smith claimed that his rituals and ceremonies included adaptations from the Xhosa society itself.[37]

Indeed, Smith anticipated this would give them authorizing force. As he explained to Benjamin D'Urban in 1836, "I have renewed an old practice among them: a long cane with a cat's tail on the top, for which I have substituted a brass knob. A Chief sends this and sticks it in the kraal, making a demand; the man of the kraal brings it with him; no other person dare touch it. I have a long one *behind me* in Council." It was similarly the case with foot-kissing. The chiefs had voluntarily kissed his feet, he claimed, in pursuance of old Xhosa custom, and had easily understood his claims to be paramount chief, since this accorded with their own schemes of government.[38]

Smith's claims were regarded with scarcely disguised amusement in some quarters. But he was not, in fact, a pure fantasist in this respect. His sticks did have a place in Xhosa custom. It was the tradition, when war threatened, for the paramount chief to send out official messengers, who were called "tails" (*imi-sili* in Xhosa) because their insignia of office was an ox tail. It was their job to warn all the heads of clans that war was imminent. Presumably, their messages carried some authority and instructions. But it would have been contrary to Xhosa governance for the paramount chief to claim the absolute obedience that, Smith argued, accompanied the symbol of the stick.[39]

Likewise, he commonly described himself as delivering his "word" at the great meetings. In this, too, he was reaching out to the language of

Xhosa society and politics. In Xhosa society the "word" was the equivalent of the official statement or authoritative opinion. Once the "word" of the Xhosa ruler was conveyed, obedience was expected to be total. And although Smith failed to recognize that in Xhosa politics the "word" was not the pronouncement of the chief, but the product of a system of advice and counseling offered to the chief by his *ampakati*, he was seeking a language that was part of the common vocabulary of imperial communication with the Xhosa.[40]

But it was not only the language and cultural symbols of Xhosa society that Smith wanted to enlist in support of imperial rule. Like any other system of imperial authority, personal rule needed *structures* to maintain its presence and continuity. Smith recognized from the beginning in 1835 that he needed to enlist the support of the chiefs. Indeed, like the missionaries, it was always imagined that the chiefs would be the channel of communication and authority to the tribes. We shall return to that theme in the next chapter. But obviously, the chiefs alone were not enough. Like-minded Britons needed to be recruited to bring personal influence and supervision to bear on the chiefs and tribes so that personal rule could operate at a truly personal level. Thus, to continue the work of personal rule it was necessary to create the beginnings of an imperial bureaucracy. As his legacy in Queen Adelaide Province, Smith left behind the first cadre of imperial administrators in Africa, known initially as resident agents.

The resident agents

Resident agents were appointed to sit with particular tribes and to cultivate strong relationships with the chiefs. They were part diplomatic representative (since, after the dissolution of Queen Adelaide Province, the fiction was maintained that the Xhosa were independent polities), part civilizing agent (since their job was to continue to push the Xhosa along the path of civilization by working against superstitious practices), part legal officer (since they were to administer Xhosa law and British law for certain offenses like murder or witchcraft), and part participant observer (since their job was to surveil and understand the Xhosa). The best-known were from missionary families. Others were from Army backgrounds. Some were from 1820 settler families, and were close to settler culture. With the establishment of British Kaffraria, their titles changed to Commissioner, and the Agent-General to whom they reported was replaced by a Chief Commissioner, responsible to the High Commissioner, who was always the Governor of the Cape. After about 1850 they were referred to as resident magistrates, reflecting their increasingly legal authority.[41]

Resident agents were the face of the British state to the Xhosa. Like the missionaries, they developed close personal relationships with the Xhosa chiefs. Some, like Charles Stretch, saw themselves as spokespersons for the interests of the tribes. But Stretch was an unusually "humanitarian" imperial officer. For their part, the chiefs saw the resident agents as potentially useful channels of communication with the imperial state. We have seen how Sandile and other chiefs were genuinely sorry to see Brownlee leave in 1863. Brownlee had tried to modify the harsh policy dictated by Governor Grey in the late 1850s. But Sandile had known Brownlee from his youth. Brownlee had been present at his circumcision ceremony. But this intimacy only heightened the ambiguity that was built into the relationship between the chiefs and the agents over the extent of their authority over the tribes.[42]

The difficulty consisted in the fact that personal rule also meant indirect rule. Harry Smith's attempt to use the chiefs as the magistracy that would bring British law and eventually British cultural standards to the Xhosa installed the principle of indirect rule at the heart of personal rule. The idea that the chiefs would be enlisted in the imperial project was henceforth an unchanging part of the British state's relationship with the Xhosa. The treaties that ended the sixth frontier war in 1835 protected Xhosa law and custom, except in the cases of murder, theft and witchcraft. All other areas of Xhosa law were to remain untouched. And this distinction between good and bad Xhosa laws, with the British intervening only in the latter, was repeated when British Kaffraria was created in 1847.[43]

Resident agents were to exercise an osmotic civilizing influence on the chiefs. As D'Urban explained in his instructions to Bowker in 1835, he was to be at once the "magistrate, the monitor, the arbitrator among these peoples," and their "general protector."[44] But what did this mean? Its general nature meant that resident agents were left to make their own judgments about most matters. It proved impossible for resident agents to steer clear of traditional justice and customs because the boundary between such practices and the British civilizing mission was hardly clear-cut. Indeed, Harry Smith, at some of his great meetings, had told the chiefs that they could no longer levy fines as an excuse to dispossess people of cattle. Yet it was not clear how extensive this injunction was, so cattle continued to be used as fines, and indeed the resident agents were soon involved in arbitrating such cases.

The impossibility of drawing clear lines between Xhosa customary law and imperial policy is illustrated in one case of November 1836. A complaint had been laid by Jan Tzatzoe against another chief, Siyolo, for forcible seizure of cattle. But was this theft? On being summoned, Siyolo argued that it was not theft, because he had taken the cattle from someone who, before the war, had been his subject, and who owed him a fine for not reporting the bewitching of one of his counselors, who had subsequently died. When the local resident agent insisted that he had no right to take the law into his own hands, and ordered him to restore the cattle, Siyolo refused, claiming that they had been told that "we could administer our laws as before." The agent was stumped by this Xhosa chief quoting back to him the British policy of indirect rule. He could only protest to the Agent-General that this was what happened when it was undecided "whether British laws or the Kaffir laws are to have prevalence on this side of the Keiskamma."[45]

This was the dilemma that the resident agents frequently confronted. It was hard to know when they should bring British ideas of justice to bear, and when they should act as the arbiter for the proper application of Xhosa laws. Much depended on the personality and predisposition of the resident agent. Certain agents, like Theophilus Shepstone, clearly saw themselves as acting to enforce Xhosa law. In one case, for example, Shepstone ordered that a man who had sought refuge at Fort Peddie from a witchcraft accusation was not to be given up. But the authority for this was not the British abhorrence of witchcraft prosecutions. Rather, it was Xhosa custom, which stated that "in such cases if a man succeeds in entering the boundaries of another tribe with his property he cannot be followed by force and it remains optional with the Chief of such tribe … to give him up or not upon hearing the circumstances of the case."[46]

Other resident agents were willing to push the line of their authority further. But this usually involved them in matching their role to Xhosa law and custom. John Maclean, for example, was quite willing to adjudicate in Xhosa marriage disputes. In 1849 Maclean awarded cattle to a wife who had left her husband when he married another woman, on the grounds that the Governor's "word" had forbidden the buying and selling of wives. Although this might seem like an imposition of British custom and morality, in fact it was an application of Xhosa law. The woman was reclaiming her bride-wealth, which the husband was trying to keep; Xhosa law allowed for this to be returned to the wife if the husband was responsible for the breakup of the marriage.[47]

Similarly, Maclean was frequently engaged in settling intertribal disputes. In May 1850, he dealt with Mhala over the chief's seizure of some cattle from a member of his own tribe. The issue was important because it involved questions of chiefly authority. The case had begun in July 1849, when Mhala seized four head of cattle from one of Siwani's tribe. (Siwani was Mhala's nephew.) A complaint was lodged with Maclean. Mhala explained that he had seized the cattle as a fine because the man in question, named Roxo in the records, had disobeyed an order carried by his *imi-sili*. This was his right as a chief under Xhosa law. The case was aggravated by the fact that Roxo had killed several of the animals in defiance of the chief's order. Such an act was considered a serious crime among the Xhosa because it was a deliberate challenge to chiefly authority. Mhala kept the remaining cattle to demonstrate his authority, "for unless his people see that he has the power of carrying out certain cases under the authority of the Commissioner he will lose all power of co-operating with the Government." One can easily imagine Mhala's delight in making this argument. Maclean had to agree. And he turned the case over to Mhala to handle.

But a few months later Maclean had to confess that he had been deceived by Mhala as to the facts of the case. He moved to revoke the award of cattle to the chief, but had to threaten armed force in order to get Mhala to accede. This case is interesting because it stands as an illustration of how the resident magistrates could get tangled in very complex issues of Xhosa law that were not easily clarified. It is also an example of the way agents could be manipulated by the chiefs for their own ends. Mhala was using Maclean's authority to legitimate his administration of Xhosa justice, whatever the merits of the particular case. And, knowing Mhala, it is quite possible that he saw it as a way also of pushing the boundary between imperial justice and Xhosa justice a bit further away from him.[48]

The limits of the resident agent's authority was a source of constant frustration to the more activist among them. In 1839 Shepstone wrote to Henry Hudson of the difficulties he had in protecting the Mfengu from the hostility of the Xhosa.[49] Witchcraft accusations were used in the struggles between the two groups, and Shepstone pointed out that "had the resident agent any authority over these people which would enable him at once to put a stop to the proceeding … and inflict a punishment on offenders all collision with the Kafirs on this score would be avoided." He continued: "I have constantly been obliged to exercise an authority which I do not possess but which I have thought it my duty to take the responsibility of assuming in order to enable the Fingo Chiefs to accomplish the enforcement of their necessary decisions among their own people." He therefore requested instructions on how far he should intervene in order to support a chief who was engaged in a dispute with a witchdoctor from another tribe.[50]

Shepstone's request for instructions in this case did not go unanswered. But it was a reply that referred only to the particular case. There was no simple policy formulation that could determine when a particular case fell within the sphere of Xhosa law, or when it fell within the sphere in which Smith had decreed the British would adjudicate. Like the other resident agents, Shepstone was constantly faced with having to make judgment calls on this and other issues that reflected the ambiguities and contradictions that resulted from their position as agents rather than as magistrates. In October 1839 Shepstone found himself mediating in a witchcraft dispute between a chief and a Mfengu witchdoctor who had failed to give the chief satisfactory service! The problem was that the Mfengu were under British protection at Fort Peddie, but under Xhosa law the witchdoctor could have been put to death if it could be proved that he had deliberately set out to harm the chief. A couple of months later, another case involving a complex cast of characters, including Mhala and his translator – who was a deserter from the Cape Mounted Rifles! – threatened to erupt into conflict. It was at this point that Shepstone wrote to Hudson of his frustrations regarding his lack of authority over the tribes.[51]

Shepstone later became famous for his policy of indirect rule as Secretary for Native Affairs in Natal, where he gained a reputation as a champion of preserving native tradition and custom and allowing the chiefs to exercise their authority. His policy in Natal was born out of his long experience with the Xhosa on the eastern frontier. In Natal he resolved the problem of the power of the resident agent by acting himself as a true *Inkosi Enkulu* and exercising the kind of control over the tribes that Harry Smith could only fantasize about. Shepstone always retained the final authority on decisions, in a way that had not been possible in Xhosaland. He built up a cadre of dependent chiefs, some of whom he appointed to that position, and a variety of ceremonies and traditions that went along with this dependence. Indirect rule as formulated by Shepstone was direct rule in disguise, since he assumed the power to disallow any decision by chiefs of whom he disapproved.[52]

It was clearly important for the resident agents to work with and through the chiefs. And when the treaty system of frontier control was working at its best, from 1836 to the early 1840s, the partnership of chief and resident agent did a lot to maintain the peace. As agent with Sandile, Charles Stretch met with the chief more or less every week, and they worked effectively together, apprehending thieves and quieting down a commotion with Maqoma when he was involved in some drunken affray. In cases like this, a good personal relationship was all important. In the spring of 1846 Maclean was trying to dampen the growing tension on the frontier by working with well-disposed chiefs such as Mqhayi.[53]

But if they were to do the work of bringing the practices of British civilization to the Xhosa, resident agents needed the chiefs. They were dependent on the chiefs to arrive at mutually agreeable decisions and to see that those decisions were carried out. Since the chiefs were not formal dependants of the imperial administration, and possessed political and cultural resources of their own, the relationship was inherently conflictual and could quickly deteriorate. A few months after working with Stretch to quiet Maqoma, for example, Sandile himself became agitated about the construction of new military posts on his land. Maclean's spies reported a series of meetings between the chiefs, with Sandile's orders to "be ready" to repel an expected invasion by the British.[54]

The British might see the resident agent as a benign influence, as a domestic missionary who sometimes moonlighted as a policeman. But for the Xhosa he was a representative of the British state, and, like the missionary, he represented an alternative system of power and authority. When the chiefs looked back from 1846 over the previous decade, they saw unmistakable signs that their power had been compromised by the policies of the British state. But the chiefs were past masters at political maneuvering, or else they would not have been chiefs. So they could hardly be expected to sit still and wait for their power to disappear.

British Kaffraria 1848–1850 and the failure of personal rule

By the mid-1840s the system that had been created in 1836, of monitoring the Xhosa through treaty obligations and the presence of resident agents, had fallen into disrepute. There was little evidence that the agents were moving Xhosa culture toward the nirvana of British civilization. Indeed, there were reports that traditional cultural practices that the British thought had been abolished were being revived. Furthermore, the frontier remained unstable and the political voice of the settler community was noisily protesting the continuing problem of stock theft. The result was the adoption from 1844 of a more aggressive frontier policy by the British and renewed suspicions of the imperial state by the Xhosa. This began a slide to war, and when the seventh frontier war broke out in March 1846 it reflected the breakdown of a system that had been designed to bring peace to the frontier through diplomatic negotiation.[55]

The war itself was conducted with a singular lack of enthusiasm – the Boers were induced to join the British effort only with the greatest difficulty. As was usual in these little colonial wars, the British claims of success were hardly matched by Xhosa recognition of failure. In London, the military stalemate led to a rethinking of frontier policy. There was a considerable debate within the Colonial Office as to how to create a frontier policy that would preserve the peace, satisfy the settlers' need for protection, and work to civilize the Xhosa. The Colonial Office accepted that the treaty system had broken down. But what kind of system could take its place? Their answer was to return to the precedent of Queen

Adelaide Province and establish sovereignty over the land between the Fish and the Kei where the Xhosa tribes could be contained in the interests of imperial control. It was to be known as British Kaffraria.

Much was carried over from Smith and D'Urban's original creation of Queen Adelaide Province in 1835–6. The tribes were put under British protection but were to be governed through the chiefs according to their own laws and customs. The colony was to be administered directly by the Governor of the Cape, thus protecting the Xhosa from the pressures of settler politics. All of this was decided before Sir Harry Smith was appointed to replace the short-lived governorship of Sir Henry Pottinger at the end of 1847. But Smith defined the enterprise more ambitiously than the Colonial Office had in mind. He treated the tribes as British subjects, although the legal status of their citizenship remained ambiguous. Similarly, he extended the powers of the resident agents, now called Commissioners. In his instructions to George Mackinnon – appointed by Smith to be Chief Commissioner of British Kaffraria – the chiefs were to act under the supervision of the British magistrates. Furthermore, the magistrates were able to receive appeals against the decisions of the chiefs on all matters, including tribal law.[56]

The same audacious vision of remaking the Xhosa into good Englishmen was Smith's declared objective for British Kaffraria. He consulted with Henry Calderwood and other missionaries and presented a bold blueprint that would settle the disorderly frontier and bring civilization to the Xhosa. He planned a series of villages with mixed populations of Europeans, Christianized Khoi and reformed Xhosa and Mfengu. British Kaffraria was to be an intermediate zone between civilization and barbarism. Its conception combined the remnants of evangelical humanitarianism with the military exigencies of frontier defense. A wave of enthusiasm for Smith's schemes lapped to the very top of the imperial hierarchy. The Queen herself read Smith's report on British Kaffraria and strongly approved of the measures he proposed to extend "civilisation and Christianity."[57]

Some of these dreams did become reality. Military villages were established where ex-soldiers tilled the soil as armed farmers and served as a trip wire of defence in the event of another Xhosa invasion. But the social engineering optimism of the scheme was doomed from the start. Sir Harry Smith soon returned to Cape Town, where he became preoccupied with growing demands for representative government. Smith's attention span was never great at the best of times. For the next couple of years he seems to have forgotten all about British Kaffraria.[58]

Still, between 1848 and the end of 1850 Smith had some reason to feel that the great experiment was working. The frontier remained in a state of unaccustomed tranquility. The numbers of troops on the frontier were reduced, so that by 1850 only about 1,700 remained. From the British side there was a general sense that the frontier had stabilized. Among the informed observers of the frontier only Sir Andries Stockenstrom uttered jeremiads on the policy. Stockenstrom was now in retirement, but he was still a voice to be heard. As early as August 1849 he notified the Colonial Office that the Xhosa were not happy with British Kaffraria. Indeed, he warned they were planning another war. Stockenstrom, however, could be dismissed as a cranky old man.[59]

Nobody in the imperial administration saw the war of 1850–3 coming. But by the summer of 1850 the first worrying signs began to surface. There was an upturn in the theft of horses; guns were being purchased and assegais being forged; Xhosa workers in the Colony began to desert from their employers and drift back home. Most ominously, a new prophet appeared among the Xhosa. This was Mlanjeni, a young man of about eighteen years, who began preaching a mix of Christian and traditional Xhosa beliefs about the need for the Xhosa to purify themselves in preparation for great events. This should have raised a red flag to the British. Similar prophets in the past had presaged war. And although some observers made this connection, their initial reaction was one of puzzled bemusement at this man-boy who urged the Xhosa to give up witchcraft, made vague mutterings about praying to the sun, and urged them to get rid of all the *ubuthi* (evil substance) that surrounded them.[60]

Maclean decided to keep an eye on Mlanjeni, and his imperial spies were soon buzzing around. It was reported that large meetings had been held at Mlanjeni's kraal. So Maclean ordered Mlanjeni and his father to appear before him. When they failed to turn up, he sent some police, who found Mlanjeni so weak and emaciated that he had to be carried out of his kraal. This was a time of drought and famine in Xhosaland; cattle were dying, the hard land was resisting the plow. It was possible that the millenarian movement was a response to economic hardship. But to be on the safe side Maclean personally supervised the destruction of the prophet's hut and the fifty anti-witchcraft poles Mlanjeni had planted around it, and ordered him to be removed to Mqhayi's kraal, where Maclean could keep an eye on him.

Maclean's initial instinct was to view Mlanjeni as a "maniac who styles himself a prophet" and to dismiss the notion that any subversion was involved. As an imperial administrator, Maclean's first thought had to be: Is a rebellion brewing here? But his immediate second thought was: How could that be, when all the outward signs suggest that things are going so well? To think of rebellion was out of the question, since the "mild and just Government" of the past three years had "gained the confidence of the people."[61]

A month later, Mlanjeni had returned to his kraal, had re-erected his hut and his "witchcraft poles," and was resuming his prophetic meetings. When Maclean spoke to Mqhayi about it, the chief was calmly reassuring. Mlanjeni was doing a lot of good, Maclean was told. After all, he was actually preaching what the English had so often told them: that there must be no witchcraft or murder. Mqhayi was dissembling. This was not the first time he had fed Maclean disinformation.[62] The British were constantly having to fight their way through a fog of "knowledge" that in fact only exposed their "ignorance." By the beginning of October, Maclean felt the first prickles of alarm. From his spies he knew that Sandile, Mhala, Anta and Sarhili had met with Mlanjeni. Mhala had refused to attend a meeting with Maclean, claiming illness, which Maclean knew was false. His lead spy had even urged that Brownlee not be given the secret information that he was feeding to Maclean, since "if Brownlee knows it, Sandili will know it" (an interesting sidelight on the consequences of close relationships between the commissioners and the chiefs).[63]

Maclean decided to hold a meeting with the chiefs on 5 October. The meeting calmed his concerns and confirmed the official line that the beneficence of British rule in British Kaffraria was sufficient protection against the dangerous currents that were flowing. He was led to this assurance by a private conversation with a minor Chief named Toise. In this conversation Toise gave Maclean the analysis of what was happening that became the British explanation for the outbreak of war. It was also the message that Maclean, Mackinnon and Smith, sitting in Cape Town, *wanted* to hear: that the Xhosa subjects were contented with British rule, and that the disaffection was a conspiracy whipped up by disgruntled chiefs.

It is a deep irony, yet a lesson of the first importance, that what was to become the dominant British view of the origins of the 1850 war – that it was a conspiracy of chiefs – originated (or at least was validated) by Xhosa sources themselves. This is a very nice example of the way colonial knowledge can be produced in a circular fashion, originating *from* the colonized, getting filtered through the deluded ideology of what the colonizers *want* to believe, and then becoming fixed as "truth" in the system of colonial understanding. Toise delivered a wholesale litany that confirmed what Maclean already believed. Toise explained that Mlanjeni was being used by the chiefs, that he was their instrument to regain the power that they were losing over the common people by the beneficent administration of the British, that the common people *wanted* the custody of the imperial administration, and that they were in favor of British Kaffraria, precisely because it protected them from being "eaten up" by the chiefs. Maclean quoted Toise as saying that all the common people "see that they are happier under the government than under the chiefs."[64]

At about the same time Brownlee also held a meeting with another set of chiefs to reassure them about recent troop movements. The chiefs responded in their usual, politely misleading way. They denied their associations with Mlanjeni, denied that they contemplated war, and assured Brownlee of their loyalty to Government. Like Smith, Brownlee was convinced of the beneficial effects of his admonitions. He noted how his talk with them had won over their initial suspicions. Personal rule had worked again. It did not seem to occur to him that their good spirits could have been the result of his disclosures about the troop movements rather than their internalization of his message.[65]

It is hard to escape the conclusion that Maclean was being fed a steady stream of disinformation with the object of keeping him off balance. The Xhosa knew that Maclean's main informant, Toise, was a government spy. On at least one occasion Toise was deliberately given information to ratchet up the tension in the British camp. There is other evidence that suggests how incompletely the British understood Xhosa deportment over these months. The chiefs began to exhibit erratic behavior and demeanor towards imperial officers. Some chiefs would avoid meetings, for example, but then profusely proclaimed their loyalty. Others protested violently when the commissioners made legal awards of cattle that went against them, but then appeared the next day to make due obeisance.[66]

The fog of ignorance that enveloped British responses to the Xhosa was revealed when Sir Harry Smith attempted to act as a true *Inkosi Enkulu* and depose Sandile as chief of the Rharhabe Xhosa at the end of October. He proposed to put the Commissioner Charles Brownlee in his place. The immediate excuse that Smith gave for his action was that Sandile had refused an order to meet with him in the middle of October. But the real reason was Sandile's supposed role in plotting against the imperial government. The removal of chiefs had no precedent in Xhosa law; chiefs were not usually deposed. They were abandoned by their people if they fell out of favor. Still, as we have seen, all the (mis)information reaching Smith led him to believe that Sandile's people had indeed "left" him in terms of loyalty. Maclean and the others were repeating the line that the ordinary people had transferred their allegiance to the imperial administration in gratitude for the protection it provided against the tyrannies of the chiefs. These inventions were being repeated all the way to London.[67]

The important thing about this absurd piece of hubris – which Smith had probably picked up in India – was the way Sandile's displacement was received by the Xhosa. There seemed to be an acceptance by the other chiefs that Smith had due cause to depose Sandile. On 29 October some of the leading chiefs gathered to receive this news, and all expressed their dismay at Sandile's behavior in refusing to meet with Smith. And a few days later, a similar meeting was called to get the chiefs' reaction to Smith's deposition of Sandile. Again the general response of the chiefs was to nod their heads in noncommittal agreement. Mhala, for example, thanked Maclean for the news and agreed that Smith had done as he thought best. Others agreed that Sandile had only himself to blame.[68]

Brownlee held another meeting on 2 November. About 350 Xhosa notables were present. At this gathering a group of chiefs asked to speak with him in private and deputed Bhotomane to speak for them. Brownlee should have realized from the tone of this meeting – even as it is reported in the official documents – that all was not well. But subtlety is not a property of imperial culture, and Brownlee failed to spot the reservations that were expressed about Smith's actions. Perhaps he was fooled into thinking that the reservations reflected weakness. The chiefs apologized for Sandile's behavior but explained it as a function of his fear of the Governor. Bhotomane begged for mercy on Sandile's behalf, hinting darkly that others were more to blame than the young chief. Brownlee, however, was not listening. He responded brusquely that "Sandile's offence consisted in believing liars [presumably Mlanjeni] rather than the Governor, and that I had most urgently warned him of the consequences." Brownlee was satisfied that this meeting showed how things were now in a "satisfactory condition."[69]

When Smith heard this, he took it to mean that his actions were having the desired effect. He failed to realize that even pro-government chiefs were offering only lukewarm protestations of support. Others, like Maqoma, were conspicuously absent. Indeed, Maqoma does not seem to have been much in the mind of the imperial administration at this point. He hardly featured in their attempts to understand what was going on. This was a serious error, and a dramatic example of their ignorance of the state of affairs among the Xhosa. While British attention was focused on Sandile, Maqoma was assiduously working away to stitch together an alliance between the two leading black groups in southern Africa, the Xhosa and the Khoi, that would confront the British with their most serious military challenge there. The British had written Maqoma off as a has-been. When he appeared on the scene toward the very end of this period of "negotiation," in front of several thousand warriors, to meet with Smith on 19 December and ask for his old land back, Smith screamed at him that he was a "drunken beast." This was a profound misreading. Maqoma had stopped drinking and had started organizing. His formidable talents were now turned to political and military planning. Maqoma was to lead the first black nationalist revolt against the British in the history of its empire in Africa.[70]

So, until the very end of this phony peace, Smith was feeding the Colonial Office his deluded line on the state of the frontier; a line that was fed to him from the Xhosa themselves. It was a line that confirmed his own knowledge system about the Xhosa and that bolstered his own belief in the power of his personal rule. His actions had been well received, he assured London. Sandile's own mother and four of his counselors all agreed that he had merited "the degradation which I had inflicted [on him, and] ... even 'thanked' me for my having spared his life." They were agreed that Sandile was not worthy to be a chief, and they were grateful to Smith for "having given them the 'word' of peace, and having declared that I would continue to protect them from oppression."[71]

The last of the great meetings, 19 December 1850

Smith now produced his trump card. He would hold a large meeting, on the model of those of 1835, 1836, 1847 and 1848, at which he had settled wars and issued policy proclamations. He would once again exercise the strategy of personal power and presence as an instrument of imperial rule. He would roar at the Xhosa, play the role of their *Inkosi Enkulu* and Great Father, reduce them to subservience by his imperial presence, issue a proclamation that would contain the concession of replacing Brownlee with a Xhosa as Regent, and settle things in British Kaffraria once and for all. Little did he know that he was to experience the burial of the policy of personal rule. The meeting of the Xhosa chiefs and their followers was called for 19 December 1850. We happen to have a full transcript of this meeting. It is worth our attention for several reasons.

In the first place, it is a rare case of a close look at the interaction between the highest levels of the imperial administration and indigenous peoples. In particular, it is a nice little example of truth being spoken to those in power. There must be few instances where the Governor of a Crown Colony is spoken to in the manner recorded at this meeting. Certainly, subsequent Governors made sure that they did not expose themselves to such ridicule as Smith was to experience.

Secondly, this meeting revealed the extent to which it was Xhosa truth that was driving the imperial relationship. It is a record of the intelligence possessed by the Xhosa, and one that exposes the huge gulf that always exists in imperial culture between the apparatus of imperial power and the response of the imperial subjects, between what the imperial power *thinks* it knows about those it rules and the extent of its true ignorance: thus the necessity for imperial culture to make up stories about the nature of its rule.

And finally, the meeting marked the end of the experiment of governing the Xhosa through the culture of personal rule, through a culture that blended codes of paternalism with indirect rule and knit them together with the power of personal relationships. Indeed, it was the last time an appeal to this kind of culture of rule was to be made in Xhosaland. As a result of the war that followed the meeting, a new culture of rule had to be devised for British Kaffraria.[72]

Smith opened the meeting – which was attended by 3,000 persons – by reading a long proclamation that laid out the claims of imperial legitimacy. It sought to establish a basis for common dialogue by tying their meeting place to past events in their relationship. They met, he pointed out, at the same spot where peace had been made in 1836, near the burial place of Ngqika, whose "dying words [to his sons] was [*sic*] ... ever keep peace with the English." He sought to persuade the gathering that it was Sandile who was the source of the troubles they now faced, that he had betrayed the trust Smith had placed in him. He reminded them that Sandile had not been punished after the war of 1846, but Sandile had shown himself to be deceitful and unworthy of that trust. He had begun to listen to evil counselors and to undermine the "system by which I rule you and which *all the people* ... tell me renders them happy and secure." So "their father" had returned, but this time with troops, and more on the way.

Now Smith switched into another familiar imperial guise: the stern paternalist who possesses the capacity for violence and humiliation. He announced that he was not going to kill the rebellious chiefs – ignoring the truth, it would seem, that none had yet rebelled. He would let them live in peace. But he hinted at how both the settlers and the Mfengu were eagerly waiting to be unleashed upon them. He demanded that Sandile and Anta be handed over, that all the outstanding fines be paid, that weapons be surrendered, and that all who were dissatisfied with his rule leave the country; and if the "bad men" did not go, he would drive them out. He denied rumors that he wished to do away with the chiefs; he just wanted them to do their duty as agents of indirect rule. Here he slipped in the concession about appointing a Xhosa successor to Sandile. He told them to choose between remaining British subjects and leaving the country never to return. And, finally, he asked them to consult together after this meeting and to let him know what they recommended.

It was at this point that things began to go wrong for Smith. A dialogue ensued for all to see. To read the transcript is like reading a clever legal cross-examination interspersed with statements of supplication. The lawyers, however, are the chiefs; Governor Sir Harry Smith is the defendant. The full qualities of Xhosa lawyer-like evasion and sly insolence were on display. Their rhetoric ranged seamlessly between a deferential ingratiation that teetered on fawning obsequiousness, and a sudden rearing back into a prickly assertiveness. Smith was pulled from pillar to post. By the time they had finished with him, Smith's attempt to persuade, coerce and overawe the Xhosa into accepting his authority was in tatters. Had the encounters of empire been decided in a school debating society, or a British court room, the empire in South Africa would have packed its bags on that cloudy day in December and slunk away.

Maqoma was the first of the chiefs to respond. Smith had called on him, and one can only imagine that Maqoma had been waiting eagerly for this moment since his humiliation by Smith in December 1847. Maqoma began as they all were to begin. He thanked Smith for coming and for bringing them "the news." This was a familiar opening by the Xhosa. It reflected Xhosa politeness and Xhosa evasion, since sometimes it was all that was said. Equally, it could be the introduction to the sly insolence that the Xhosa practiced so deftly. Maqoma went on: "I have had an opportunity of speaking with the English, it is very satisfactory. I know now how I am to go. I do not like this confusion." In the light of Maqoma's forthcoming role as the foremost guerrilla leader, it is hard not to read this as announcing to all that the way to war had now been cleared by Smith's pronouncements. But in a delicious irony, Smith seemed to think that Maqoma was agreeing with him, and said that he did not like confusion either.

Maqoma then changed direction entirely and asked Smith: "Why did I lose my country so?" Maqoma was referring here to his expulsion in 1829 from his "traditional" homelands of the Kat river area. This was the defining event of Maqoma's political life. He never ceased to harbor deep bitterness about his exclusion and about the brutal manner in which it had been undertaken.[73] But Smith refused to be drawn into speaking of the past. So Maqoma fell back on the question that had been posed at all the previous meetings: If Smith wanted peace, why had he brought so many troops with him? Smith's reply was always the same blend of bluster and nonsensical reasoning – which presumably was why he was being interrogated. The troops were there, he answered, "to show I have the power of putting down rebellion .... I bring the troops to protect the good from the bad."

And so it went on. All the leading chiefs spoke, and the pattern was the same. Smith was thanked and then he was provoked. His peaceable intentions were recognized; he was assured that the Xhosa were a peace-loving people who did not want war and who knew they could not withstand the English. But why, they wondered, did he bring so many soldiers with him? Some tried other tactics, such as appealing to his self-proclaimed humanity to ask for mercy for Sandile, or declaring that he could do what he liked with Sandile.

The dialogue with Tola may serve as an example. Tola thanked Smith for coming and stated how ashamed of themselves they were, "for it is hardly a month since we met you at King William's Town; there you told us we were at peace; if you say all is peace, there is peace." And then came the challenging conclusion: "Then why are we called here today?"

To which Smith replied: "Because Sandilli and Anta have been trying to excite a rebellion."

But Tola wanted to know, "What has Sandilli done?"

Smith – getting flustered – "Why has he not done all? Did he not bring on the last war and then desert you? ... Has he not disobeyed my orders?"

But Tola, again, wanted to know, "What has caused the excitement you spoke of?"

Smith replied: "Sandilli's conduct. But this is not war, it is rebellion. I see all the people happy and the cattle in their kraals. I come here to see the people sit happy. I come here to throw Sandilli away, and I have thrown him away."

Having won the cross-examination, Tola ended: "I thank you for the people."

Then it was the turn of Xhoxho, younger brother of Maqoma and disliked by the colonial administration for his reputed cattle-thieving. Xhoxho thanked Smith for coming, repeating that they were his children and how "yours is a good word that you brought." Then, without skipping a beat, "Why have you brought so many soldiers?"

Smith: "Because you dispute my word."

Xhoxho: "How will you catch Sandilli?"

Smith: "That is my business. Money is a good thing. Give up Sandilli and Anta; they are rebels and traitors, false to you."

Xhoxho, in a calculated act of insolence: "I say no more. No person can ever say I take cattle. Toise told Anta not to come."

This last was a marvelous insult. Toise, of course, was the pro-government chief, used by the imperial administration as a spy. Xhoxho was announcing to Smith that the Xhosa too had their sources of intelligence and knew all about Toise's activities.[74]

It was no surprise, perhaps, that following this series of deliberate insults, Smith's patience snapped. He began to rant about how bad Sandile was, and how he, Smith, had brought the troops to act and not to talk; and he warned them that they should not "make me an angry Governor, not ... make me once more Colonel Smith in the bush" – a reference to the ravages of his command in the 1834–5 war. And then the meeting ended in a short exchange that could have been scripted for the theater.

Sandile's mother, Suthu, announced that she wanted to speak. We have met Suthu several times in this narrative. She was highly respected by both the Xhosa and the British. She was the great wife of Nqgika. She had been a great beauty in her youth. She was also a pretty smart politician. On Ngqika's death in 1829, Suthu had become regent of the Rharhabe Xhosa before Sandile was of age. She survived a witchcraft accusation in 1842. And she had long experience in dealing with the British. She had often served as an interlocutor between the tribes and the British officials and missionaries. More than once she had appeared as the contrite mother trying to protect her wayward son from the wrath of the authorities.[75]

Her comments were short, sharp and revealing. She announced that she wanted to speak of Sandile. But instead she publicly subverted Smith's reading of Xhosa politics and used the authority of her age and position to support the renegade Xhoxho, undermine the government satrap, Toise, and legitimate the rebellious chief Anta, who at this moment was Sandile's closest counselor and ally. "Toise told Anta not to come [to the meeting]," she claimed.

Smith responded: "That is a lie of Anta's. Anta is a great liar."

And then delivering the rhetorical *coup de grâce*, Suthu replied, "Why believe his word more than Toise's?"

Smith's authority had clearly worn very thin. Although by this time others had lost faith in Smith's magic powers, he refused to recognize the way things were drifting. The calm insolence of the Xhosa chiefs was explained within the week. On Christmas Eve a coordinated attack across all of British Kaffraria was launched by the Xhosa. The military villages of Auckland and Woburn, which Smith had established, were targets of a ferocious attack. The men were murdered and the women and children sent packing. The Chief Commissioner, Colonel George Mackinnon, escorting a large wagon train, was ambushed in the Boomah Pass and over 100 supply wagons were destroyed.

Most humiliating of all, Smith himself was besieged in Fort Hare, cut off from the rest of his command and reliant on Xhosa messengers to communicate with his military commanders. He eventually escaped by blacking his face, as if he were a Cape Coloured, and riding hell for leather through hostile country to King William's Town. Small wonder that his handwriting was uncharacteristically shaky and scrawling as he sat down to inform the Colonial Office on 26 December 1850 that the situation in British Kaffraria was critical and that all his exertions to "improve their moral and social conditions" had proved of no avail. "No people can evince more determined, reckless and savage hostility, than do the Kafirs at this moment."[76]

In truth, of course, the Xhosa were to be no match for the British in *their* savage hostility. But the fact remained that the British, and Smith in particular, had been caught seriously off guard. And Smith continued to reel under the unraveling of his system of imperial rule. Why did the

Xhosa reject his rule? he asked rhetorically in letter to Lord Henry Somerset. "I have no reply. They have all been treated with parental care, and every measure prudence or foresight or judgement can suggest adopted for their improvement. The outbreak has astonished me and everyone." But he was to get another shock a few weeks later, when half the Cape Mounted Rifles deserted with their arms and military expertise and joined the Xhosa rebels.[77]

The Xhosa showed themselves to be effective guerrilla fighters, entangling the British in the dense brush of the Waterkloof. The British, hampered by the terrain, and by commissariat and transport inefficiencies, took a long time to establish their technical mastery over the struggle. Indeed, for the next two and a half years the British faced the most serious rebellion ever in southern Africa. Xhosa resistance was worn down by the development of classic counter-guerrilla tactics. Under the leadership of Lieutenant Colonel William Eyre, a system of light cavalry patrols was instituted, operating out of a ring of forts around the Xhosa fastness of the Amatolas mountains. Xhosa supply routes were disrupted, kraals were burned, inhabitants murdered, atrocities casually committed, cattle killed in huge numbers, corn pits destroyed. But it took two years to get to that point. In the meantime, Smith's career was ruined by his failures either to prevent the war or to bring it to a speedy conclusion. He was recalled in 1852. Maqoma had his revenge.[78]

Conclusion

The failure of Smith's policy of personal rule, with its utopian expectations that British "civilization" could be force-fed into Xhosa culture, was not surprising. It shared the same fragilities as the assumptions of missionary culture; in particular, the assumption that Xhosa culture and institutions and politicians would be of little account in this encounter, or would willingly cooperate with its goals and aspirations. This failure had not been registered earlier because Queen Adelaide Province did not last long enough for those weaknesses to become apparent. Still, the collapse of the policy of personal rule meant that a new kind of policy needed to be devised to rule the Xhosa. The question of what that policy should be was delayed for several years while Britain fought the eighth frontier war. Once that war was declared to be over, in March 1853, the question of how to rule the Xhosa emerged again. For various reasons, it was not until the governorship of Sir George Grey in 1855 that the attention of the imperial administration was decisively turned again to address that question. When the Grey system was put in place, however, two central elements linked it back into continuity with the system of personal rule. It resolved the question of whose authority should prevail within Xhosa society: the chief's or the imperial state's? And it reduced ceremony and display from their central role as a place where consent for rule was secured, to their "modern" role, where it is truly ceremonial display and not a direct instrument of rule.

NOTES

1. Dening, *The Death of William Gooch*, pp. 38–43, for this fascinating story.
2. For various accounts of this event, see WMMS, South Africa, *Incoming Correspondence 1825–30*, Box 2, fiche 64, Young to Secretaries, 21 April 1829; Rev. William J. Shrewsbury, *The Journal and Selected Letters of Rev. William J. Shrewsbury 1826–1835*, ed. Hildegarde First (Johannesburg, 1994), pp. 97–8. This was not the first time such an event had been staged to bring Xhosa murderers to justice. We have the account of a similar episode in 1822; see Donovan Williams, *When Races Meet: The Life and Times of William Ritchie Thomson, Glasgow Society Missionary, Government Agent and Dutch Reformed Church Minister 1794–1891* (Johannesburg, 1967), p. 52. John Brownlee delivered the address on the law of murder on that occasion.
3. Jane H. Ohlmeyer, "A Laboratory for Empire? Early Modern Ireland and English Imperialism," in Kevin Kenny (ed.), *Oxford History of the British Empire*, vol. III: *Companion Series Ireland and the British Empire* (Oxford, 2004), pp. 1–25. Nicholas Canny, "England's New World and the Old," in Nicholas Canny (ed.), *The Origins of Empire* (Oxford, 1998), pp. 157–8. The footprint of the British state was probably lighter in West Africa than in Xhosaland in this period. It was concerned mainly to regulate the slave trade and was content to let merchants provide the apparatus of rule. See Philip Curtin, *The Image of Africa: British Ideas and Action, 1780–1850* (Madison, 1964), vol. II, pp. 289–317.
4. The best parallel for British–Xhosa relations at this time is British–Maori relations. See, for example, James Belich, *The Victorian Interpretation of Racial Conflict: The Maori, the British and the New Zealand Wars* (Montreal and Kingston, Ont., 1989). Raewyn Dalziel, "Southern Islands: New Zealand and Polynesia," in Andrew Porter (ed.), *The Oxford History of the British Empire*, vol. III: *The Nineteenth Century* (Oxford, 1999), pp. 578–88.
5. John S. Galbraith, *Reluctant Empire: British Policy on the South African Frontier 1834–1854* (Bearkeley, 1963), p. 117; CA, GH 34/5, *Sir Benjamin D'Urban, Eastern Frontier Letter Book*, pp. 79–81 (henceforth *D'Urban Letter Book*).
6. Alan Lester is one of the few British historians to notice and treat this episode. See Lester, *Imperial Networks*, ch. 4; Keegan, *Colonial South Africa and the Origins of the Racial Order* (Cape Town, 1996), pp. 147–50; Noel Mostert, *Frontiers: The Epic Story of South Africa's Creation and the Tragedy of the Xhosa People* (London, 1992), pp. 759–60, 764–75. Exactly how the scheme was concocted is not clear. Smith seems to have been the main initiator, and certainly the styles and methods of rule that he devised were his.

7. There are two biographies of Smith, both thorough enough, but not very interpretive: Joseph H. Lehmann, *Remember You Are An Englishman* (London, 1977), and A.L Harrington, *Sir Harry Smith: Bungling Hero* (Cape Town, 1980). Christopher Saunders and Iain Smith, "South Africa, 1795–1910," in Porter, *Oxford History of the British Empire*, vol. III: *The Nineteenth Century*, p. 601. For his volatility, see Charles Brownlee, *Reminiscences of Kaffir Life and History* (Lovedale, 1896), pp. 4–5; and Captain A.L. Balfour, *Journal of Arthur L. Balfour During a Tour of Army Duty in South Africa 1835–36*, MSS 11890–1, Townley Hall Papers, National Library of Ireland, Dublin, entries for 11 April and 12 May 1835. Balfour was Smith's ADC. For laudanum, which he was taking twice a day in 1836, see CA, Acc. 519, *Sir Benjamin D'Urban Papers*, vol. V, ff. 12–15, Smith to D'Urban, 1 September 1836.

8. Indirect rule came in different forms, of course, which I will not try to distinguish here. Current historiography pays little attention to it. There are very few references in Porter, *Oxford History of the British Empire*, vol. III: *The Nineteenth Century*, pp. 196, 468, 682. Judith Brown and William Roger Louis (eds.), *The Oxford History of the British Empire*, vol. IV: *The Twentieth Century* (Oxford, 200), pp. 237–43, 247–51, has more. It is treated entirely as an administrative issue, with no attention to its social or political contexts or implications except in reference to its relationship to independence movements. See also Ronald Hyam, *Britain's Imperial Century 1815–1914: A Study of Empire and Expansion*, 3rd. edn. (Basingstoke, 2002), pp. 269, 309–10. Some historians have realized the importance of the eastern Cape for indirect rule; see Norman Etherington, *The Great Treks: The Transformation of Southern Africa, 1815–1854* (Harlow, 2001), p. 234; Margery Perham, "A Re-Statement of Indirect Rule," *Africa: Journal of the International African Institute* 7.3 (1934), pp. 321–34. Perham, of course, argued that Lugard's administration of indirect rule was the most effective version, not that it was the only one. Still, the eastern Cape origins of the strategy have not been much noticed.

9. For these themes see, CA, GH 34/7, *Letter Book of Sir Harry Smith*, Smith to Durban, 16 August 1835; 6 October, 17 November 1835 (Xhosa character); 10 January 1836 (negotiations); CA, Acc. 519, *D'Urban Papers*, vol. V, ff. 31–7, "Minutes of a conversation between Colonel Smith and Guanca [?] the Great Counselor of Macomo," for a fascinating transcript of a negotiating session as preparatory to the treaty of 17 September. Smith later used Guanca as an informant.

10. CA, GH 34/7, *Letter Book of Sir Harry Smith*, Smith to D'Urban, 27 September and 6 October 1835, for examples of his thinking his way through these issues. Harry Smith deserves serious treatment, therefore, because his madness embodies the madness of empire.

11. Ibid., Smith to D'Urban, 22 and 27 September 1835, for his plans in this regard. It is interesting to note that his desire to avoid "fanatical preachers" accorded closely with Maqoma's desire, stated to Smith, for "teachers" who were not dogmatic but "who will teach the Xhosa how to be useful to each other." One suspects that Smith got this idea from Maqoma.

12. Ibid., Smith to D'Urban, 17 November 1835.
13. Ibid., Smith to Durban, 28 January 1838, for example, where it is recorded how they "had never been so happy, or [their] people either"; how they wanted him to "scold us and protect us; we wish to do right"; how they were "at your [D'Urban's] feet [to do] ... all you desire."
14. Ibid., Smith to D'Urban, 22 and 27 September 1835.
15. NLSA (CT), MSB 142, *D'Urban–Smith Correspondence*, Smith to D'Urban, 26 March 1836.
16. Ibid., Smith to D'Urban, 1 and 24 March; D'Urban to Smith, 25 March 1836; CA, GH 34/7, *Letter Book of Sir Harry Smith*, Smith to D'Urban, 27 October and 25 and 30 November 1835; 26 January 1836. Like the missionaries, Smith was always on the lookout for those small signs that his methods of paternal control were civilizing the Xhosa. Smith first used the *Inkosi Enkulu* title in a letter to D'Urban in June 1836. NLSA (CT), MSB, 142, *D'Urban–Smith Correspondence*, Smith to D'Urban, 4 June 1836. He was not the first colonial official to use it. Colonel John Graham had done so in conversation with Chief Ndlambe in 1817 when he referred to the Governor who had sent him on his mission. Others, like Grey, occasionally used it when they wished to make the point about his power. Ben Maclennan, *A Proper Degree of Terror: John Graham and the Cape's Eastern Frontier* (Johannesburg, 1986), p. 107; CA, GH 8/24, Cathcart to Maclean, 29 March 1854. CA, BK 140, *Kaffir Chiefs and Counselors*, Maclean to Mhala, 26 June 1857; GH 8/27, Maclean to the Gclecka chief, 24 October 1855, referring to Grey as *Inkosi Enkulu*. It was used in 1860 to describe Prince Alfred on his visit to Kaffraria.
17. Smith's assumption of the role of Great Chief was also a reflection of the different political forms that emerged to mediate relations between imperialist and indigene. Communities of mixed-race groups such as the Griqua, headed by Adam Kok and his family, emerged as artificial quasi-statelets which stood somewhere between a traditional African tribe and a fully formed nation state. In this social and political context, the possibility of white men assuming a chieftainship over the native peoples was not outside the realm of political thinking. Indeed, there were some celebrated cases in our period where this did happen. A scheme was floated in the later 1850s to install Theophilus Shepstone, the Secretary of Native Affairs in Natal, as chief of an independent Zulu kingdom. This idea received serious discussion all the way up to Downing Street. Shepstone surely got the idea from the time of his service under Smith twenty years earlier. On the Griqua and Shepstone, see Robert Ross, *Adam Kok's Griquas: A Study in the Development of Stratification in South Africa* (New York, 1976); Karel Schoeman, *Griqua Records: The Philippolis Captaincy, 1825–1861* (Cape Town, 1996); Jeff Guy, *The Destruction of the Zulu Kingdom: The Civil War in Zululand 1879–1884* (Pietermaritzburg, 1994), pp. 72–5, 84–6; Hamilton, *Terrific Majesty*, p. 75; Ruth E. Gordon, *Shepstone: The Role of the Family in the History of South Africa 1820–1900* (Cape Town, 1968), p. 176. There are other examples of Englishmen setting themselves up as chiefs.

Cetshwayo recognized an Englishman named John Dunn as one of the chiefs of a sub-tribe of the Zulu nation. And there was a very interesting case in the 1850s in Pondoland which involved the son of the missionary William Shaw. See Timothy J. Stapleton, *Faku: Rulership and Colonialism in the Mpondo Kingdom (c. 1780–1867)* (Waterloo, Ont., 2001), pp. 98–102.

18. CA, Acc 519, *D'Urban Papers*, ff. 53–67, D'Urban to Smith, 17 September 1835, "Notes upon the treaties of the 17th. September 1835 … shewing the grounds upon which they are to be framed and the prospects which they may be expected to realize." Smith's thoughts are minuted on the dispatch, presumably for a reply.

19. On humiliation and violence see, for example, Urvashi Butulia, "Legacies of Departure: Decolonization, Nation-making and Gender," and Josh McCullock, "Empire and Violence, 1900–1939," in Philippa Levine, *Gender and Empire* (Oxford, 2004), pp. 203–19 and 220–39; Mark Cocker, *Rivers of Blood, Rivers of Gold* (London, 1998); Diane Kirkby and Catherine Coleborne, *Law, History, Colonialism: The Reach of Empire* (Manchester, 2001); and Ann Laura Stoler, "'In Cold Blood': Hierarchies of Credibility and the Politics of Colonial Narrative," *Representations* 37 (1992), pp. 151–89. Violence is a constant background in Elizabeth Elbourne, *Blood Ground: Colonialism, Missions, and the Contest for Christianity in the Cape Colony and Britain, 1799–1853* (Kingston, Ont., 2002). Caroline Elkins, *Imperial Reckoning: The Untold Story of Britain's Gulag in Kenya* (New York, 2005); David Anderson, *The Histories of the Hanged: The Dirty War in Kenya and the End of Empire* (New York, 2005). NLSA (CT), MSB 142, *D'Urban–Smith Correspondence*, Smith to D'Urban, 26 March and 1 May 1836. For another occasion see *Letter Book of Sir Harry Smith*, Smith to D'Urban, 10 November 1835, when he combined humiliation of Maqoma with a grand gesture of paternal forgiveness, thus fusing both the strategies of paternalism to condemn and pardon at the same time.

20. Stapleton, *Maqoma*, p. 145, although he had by no means lost his wits. See CA, GH 22/2, *High Commissioner, Miscellaneous Papers, 1847–48*, for a report on a conversation with Rev. Passmore, 10 December 1847, in which he gives a very cogent critique of the unreliability of the British and the volatilities of frontier policy.

21. Stapleton, *Maqoma*, p. 145; George McCall Theal, *History of South Africa* (Cape Town, repr., 1964), vol. VII, p. 55. The report in *The Graham's Town Journal*, 18 December 1848, does not record the hotel room incident. John Henderson Soga, *The South Eastern Bantu* (Johannesburg, 1930), p. 176; Harriet Ward, *The Cape and the Kaffirs* (London, 1851), p. 214.

22. In Ayliff's account a long list of Maqoma's characterological flaws, such as his polygamy, justified his treatment. CA, A80(3), *Journal of Reverend John Ayliff 1850–51*, 14 May 1851; CA, BK 83, *Reports of Resident Magistrate with Pato 1858*, Report from Vigne, 8 February 1858, which states that Chief Phato and his counselors, in considering the strategies of their Resident Magistrate to establish a police force loyal to himself, "said that they would never wait for

me to put my 'foot on their necks.'" This incident in 1847 seems to have gone entirely unmarked in metropolitan politics. Violence and humiliation were integral strategies that were embedded in imperial culture at all levels. We could note a similar incident in 1873 when Theophilus Shepstone framed the Hlubi chieftain Langalibalele for a crime that Shepstone himself had concocted, and then paraded him through Pietermaritzburg in chains as a punishment. Shepstone was *the* recognized expert in "native policy" for the mid-nineteenth century. But the British were experts at framing chiefs, and we shall return to this theme later in this book. For Shepstone see Guy, *Heretic*, pp. 195–207; Stapleton, *Maqoma*, pp. 187–90.

23. CA, GH 34/7, *Letter Book of Sir Harry Smith*, Smith to D'Urban, 10 January 1836.
24. It had been used with the North American Indians, and Dutch governors, too, had made the arduous trek to the frontier during particularly troubled times. See Fred Anderson, *Crucible of War: The Seven Years War and the Fate of Empire in British North America 1754–1766* (New York, 2001), p. 39, for the tradition of meetings as a site of negotiation with North American Indians.
25. CA, GH 34/5, *D'Urban Letter Book*, pp. 79–81, which are his instructions to the Warden.
26. CA, GH 34/7, *Letter Book of Sir Harry Smith 1835–36*, Smith to D'Urban, 27 September 1835, 10 January 1836. My account of the meetings over this period are taken largely from this source.
27. CA, GH 34/7, *Letter Book of Sir Harry Smith*, Smith to D'Urban, "Most Private," 1 and 27 September 1835.
28. There are suggestions that the Xhosa, too, were able to mount impressive displays of their own. In the preamble to the negotiations of 1835, when various British officers were wandering around the countryside trying to deliver a message from D'Urban to the Xhosa chiefs, one of the British delegations suddenly found itself in front of "four thousand well armed warriors and another twelve hundred mounted men who came up in a disciplined compact body so as to form about two-thirds of a crescent while the mounted men completed the crescent with the chiefs in the centre. When the officer in charge walked to greet the chiefs he was saluted by a shout from the whole body." Captain Arthur L. Balfour, *Reply to "The Wrongs of the Kafir Nation" by Justus* (unpublished MS, Townley Hall Papers, 10, 268, National Library of Ireland Dublin), f. 24.
29. CA, GH 34/7, *Letter Book of Sir Harry Smith*, Smith to D'Urban, 17 November 1835.
30. Sir Harry Smith, *The Autobiography of … Sir Harry Smith*, ed. G.C. Moore Smith, vol. II (London, 1902), p. 78. This was clearly not true, a fact of which the Xhosa must have been well aware. But it is important not to be blinded to the significance of these symbols in the culture of rule Smith was practicing by the bluster that he possessed in great proportion.
31. Robert Godlonton, *A Narrative of the Irruption of the Kaffir Hardes into the Eastern Province of the Cape of Good Hope, 1834–35* (Graham's Town, 1836); the account of the meetings of 23 December 1847 is in NA CO 48/279; Smith, *Autobiography*, pp. 229–31; Alan Lester, *Imperial Networks: Creating Identies in Nineteenth-Century South Africa and Britain* (London, 2001), pp. 149–53. I have noted additional information that I have included from other sources.

For the 1847 war see Basil Le Cordeur and Christopher Saunders, *The War of the Axe* (Johannesburg, 1981).

32. *The Graham's Town Journal*, 1 January 1848; the expression of their hope to return home – i.e. to have their old lands restored to them – perhaps the key part of this report.

33. John F. Cumming, *Diaries*, entry for December 1847.

34. The following account of this meeting is taken mainly from Smith's dispatch in NA CO 48/283.

35. This list of demands in itself deserves more comment than can be made here. Suffice it to note that it was the first time that all Xhosa land was declared to be the property of the British Government.

36. CA, CO 6155, *Census of the Gaika and Tslambie Districts 1848*. It was compiled by Charles Brownlee.

37. For which, of course, see Bernard Cohn, "Representing Authority in Victorian India," in Eric Hobsbawm and Terence Ranger (eds.), *The Invention of Tradition* (Cambridge, 1983), pp. 166–7, 196–9. It is possible that Smith's natural bent toward seeking cross-cultural symbols of communication was a product of his long service in the empire, and particularly in India, where such crossings were integral to the British experience.

38. NLSA (CT), MSB 142, *D'Urban–Smith Correspondence*, Smith to D'Urban, 23 March 1836; CO 48/283.

39. John Henderson Soga, *The Ama-Xhosa: Life and Customs* (Lovedale, 1932), p. 65; see Henry Lichtenstein, *Travels in Southern Africa in the Years 1803, 1804, 1805, and 1806* (London, 1812), and Sir John Barrow, *Travels into the Interior of Southern Africa in the Years 1797 and 1798* (London, 1801), for sticks in Xhosa custom; J. B. Peires, *The House of Phalo: A History of the Xhosa People in the Days of Their Independence* (Johannesburg, 1981), p. 114.

40. It may have carried over from the early missionary contact, when each side put much effort into understanding the other's religious perspective – or lack thereof. Janet Hodgson, "A Battle for Sacred Power: Christian Beginnings Among the Xhosa," in Richard Elphick and Rodney Davenport, *Christianity in South Africa: A Political, Social and Cultural History* (Berkeley, 1997), p. 70; for a similar use of the "word" by Calderwood in a meeting with Sandile see CAD, GH 8/46, *Letters of Reverend H. Calderwood*, 17 March 1847.

41. Charles Brownlee and Theophilus and George Shepstone were from missionary families; Charles Stretch and Rawston were from the Army; John Bowker and Richard Southey from 1820 settler families.

42. Stretch was reprimanded for being too supportive of Maqoma in a dispute with the imperial government; see CA, LG 403, *Letters Received from the Diplomatic Agent of Caffraria (Stretch) 1843–46*, Hudson to Stretch, 19 October 1843.

43. CA, GH 8/45, *Letters of Captain Maclean*, Maclean to Woosnam, 2 April 1847, for Maclean's address to Sandile and other chiefs, that "they would be allowed to retain whatever might be good and desirable of their own laws and customs under the guidance of their respective chiefs, but that all objectionable portions would be peremptorily abolished and to carry this out the Government would make provision for a rigid system of surveillance over the whole."

44. CA, GH 19/4, *Border Tribes Treaties, Miscellaneous Papers 1834–1845*, ff. 256–8, "Confidential Instructions to John Bowker," 23 November 1835. Stretch and Southey received similar instructions that also stipulated that, except for murder and theft, all other cases were to be left to the domestic authorities of the tribe.

45. By the end of November, Siyolo had still failed to restore the cattle. CA, LG 408, *Letters received from the Resident Agent at Fort Peddie etc.*, Rawston to Hudson, 1 and 22 November 1836.

46. Similarly, Charles Stretch refused to intervene regarding the children of a mission native who had died and whose uncle was now insisting on his rights to adopt the children, as laid down by Xhosa law. The missionaries wanted him to block the uncle's right to adoption. Stretch refused to intervene because Xhosa laws asserted the claims of such guardians on the death of a parent. For these see CA, GH 14/3, *Papers Received from Native Tribes, Diplomatic Agents and Government Officials, 1845*, Shepstone Report, 13 March 1845; Govan to Stretch, April 1845 (no day date); 14 May 1845; GH 14/2, *Papers Received from Native Tribes, Diplomatic Agents, and Government Officials, 1844–45*, Stretch to Montague (secretary to Governor), 23 December 1844.

47. CA, BK 435, *Letters from the Hlambie Commissioner*, 1849, Maclean to Mackinnon, 3 September 1849. Maclean also adjudicated in adultery cases using Xhosa law; see BK 74, *Letterbook of the Tslambie Commissioner 1849–52*, Maclean to Mackinnon, 25 June 1850. My thanks to Robert Ross for information on this case.

48. "Being aware of Umhala's duplicity," Maclean wrote to Mackinnon, "I have always taken the precaution of having witnesses at all conferences held with him." CA, BK 435, *Letters from the Hlambie Commissioner to the Chief Commissioner*, 1849, Maclean to Mackinnon, 11 July 1849; BK 74, *Letterbook of the Tslambie Commissioner*, 1848–52, Maclean to Mackinnon, 3 March and 16 May 1850.

49. The Mfengu, whom the British called Fingoes, were Xhosa whom the British had taken into their protection in 1835, ostensibly to rescue them from the tyranny of Hintsa. Henceforth, they were regarded as a "tribe" and as the most loyal supporters of the British on the frontier. They formed mercenary companies for the British in all the subsequent frontier wars. There is some historical controversy around their real identity, however. See Keegan, *Colonial South Africa*, pp. 145–7. Probably the best study of the Mfengu is Alan Webster, "Unmasking the Fingo: The War of 1835 Revisited," in Carolyn Hamilton (ed.), *The Mfecane Aftermath: Reconstructive Debates in Southern African History* (Johannesburg, 1995), pp. 241–76, who argues that they were essentially created by the British out of Xhosa collaborators during the 1834–5 war. See also Richard Moyer, "The Mfengu, Self-Defence and the Cape Frontier Wars," in Christopher Saunders and Robin Derricourt (eds.), *Beyond the Cape Frontier* (London, 1974), pp. 101–26.

50. CA, LG 406, *Letters Received from the Resident Agent at Fort Peddie 1837–1838, 1839–1840, 1841–1844*, Shepstone to Hudson, 24 December 1839.

51. Ibid., Report from Shepstone, 31 October 1839; Shepstone to Hudson, 24 December 1839.

52. To remind the reader: Shepstone had served as Smith's interpreter in 1835, and was appointed as resident agent at Fort Peddie in 1838, where he remained until 1846, when he was sent to Natal. As the leading practitioner of indirect rule, fifty years before Frederick Lugard, Shepstone should occupy a larger place in imperial historiography than he currently does. The scholarship on Shepstone is variable. The best includes Keletso E. Atkins, *The Moon is Dead: Give Us Our Money! The Cultural Origins of an African Work Ethic: Natal 1843–1900* (Portsmouth, NH, 1993), pp. 115–16; and Norman Etherington, "The 'Shepstone System' in the Colony of Natal and Beyond the Borders," in Andrew Duminy and Bill Guest (eds.), *Natal and Zululand from Earliest Times to 1910* (Pietermaritzburg, 1989), pp. 170–92. For an older work, see C. J. Uys, *In the Era of Shepstone: Being a Study of British Expansion in South Africa 1842–1877* (Lovedale, 1933). Thomas McClendon, "The Man who Would Be Inkosi: Civilizing Missions in Shepstone's Early Career," *Journal of Southern African Studies* 30.2 (2004), pp. 339–58.

53. CA, LG 404, *Letters Received from the Diplomatic Agent at Fort Peddie*, 1846; *Butterworth 1841–43*, Fynn to Hudson, 8 December 1837; GH 14/4, *Papers Received from Native Tribes, Diplomatic Agents and Government Officials*, 1845, Stretch Report, 13 July 1845; CA, GH 14/7, *Papers Received from Native Tribes* ... 1846–8, Blackmore to Maclean, 20 February 1846; Maclean Report to Agent General, 24 February 1846; Maclean Report to Agent General, 4 March 1846; Maclean Report to Agent General, 10 March 1846. Note that Mhala was also somehow involved in this fracas and acted with his usual insolence toward the imperial administration, refusing to attend a meeting with Maclean and the Agent General, but then turning up a day late with a large body of followers. At about this time, Maclean wrote his short biographies of the chiefs, later incorporated into his *Compendium of Kafir Laws and Customs* and referred to Mhala as the most intelligent of the chiefs. Mqhayi was Mhala's brother, but was regarded as being of "weak intellect." Maclean to Agent General, 24 July 1846. Maclean and Mqhayi worked together to discipline Mqhayi's nephew Siwani, who had assaulted a trader. Mqhayi agreed to discipline Siwani, but he also took the opportunity to point out to Maclean that Government policy had progressively eroded the authority of the chiefs over matters where his word had previously been law. It is interesting to note that after the war of 1846 Siwani became a pro-British chief.

54. This reflected a newly aggressive British frontier policy which was a lead-up to the War of the Axe in 1846. For this see George McCall Theal, *History of South Africa* (Cape Town, repr., 1964), VI, pp. 260–1; CA, GH 14/6, *Papers Received from Native Tribes* ... 1845–6, Stretch Reports, 21 and 28, January 1846; Maclean Report, 29 January 1846; Report of Meeting with Stretch, Lt. Gov. Hare, Hudson and Sandile, 4 February 1846. In an interesting example of the historical memory of the Xhosa (as compared with the absence of any historical memory in imperial culture), it was reported to Stretch by Suthu that the new military post of Fort Victoria had stirred memories among the Xhosa of Fort Willshire 1824, which the Governor assured Ngqika would be his strength, but "it turned out to be his enemy and his country was taken. This is the thing we remember."

55. When Lord Glenelg dissolved Queen Adelaide's Province in July 1836, he ordered new treaties to be negotiated that would treat the Xhosa as sovereign nations and govern frontier relations. These treaties were hated by the settler faction as being pro-Xhosa because they imposed strict conditions on commando raids into Xhosa territory. But some informed observers felt that they did work well enough, and that it was the "pro-Xhosa" element of the treaties that fueled the pressure for their abrogation by Governor Maitland in 1844. For the treaty system until 1844 see CA, LG 600, *Papers received from C. L. Stretch, Diplomatic Agent, Relating to Stock Losses on the Frontier 1837–1844*, pp. 2–5, 352–5, for how the frontier treaties worked well and how they were, therefore, the target of the "Grahamstown clique." George McCall Theal, *History of South Africa*, vol. VI (Cape Town, repr., 1964), pp. 254–64, provides, of course, a settler and colonial interpretation of the run-up to the 1846 war. Keegan, *Colonial South Africa*, pp. 215–17, is a convenient summary of the tangled events that led up to the 1846–7 war, and of the shoddy way it was prosecuted. See also Anthonie Eduard Du Toit, "The Cape Frontier: A Study of Native Policy with Special Reference to the years 1847–1866" (DPhil thesis, University of Pretoria, 1949), pp. 38–9; and Basil Le Cordeur and Christopher Saunders, *The War of the Axe* (Johannesburg, 1981).

56. See Du Toit, "Cape Frontiers," pp. 31–5, 43–5, 55–8; Keegan, *Colonial South Africa*, pp. 217–19; Galbraith, *Reluctant Empire*, pp. 212–16. The land east of the Kei (the Transkei) was now called Independent Kaffraria, where the paramount of the Xhosa, Sarhili, lived. Britain did not have any formal claims to this part of Xhosaland, and it was not annexed by the Cape Colony, which now had achieved self-government, until the 1880s. It was not untouched by the British presence, being subject to frequent raids and interventions.

57. GH 23/18, *General Dispatches: Letters from the Governor to the Colonial Secretary, London*, 1847–9, Smith to Grey, 1 January 1848, detailing his policy for British Kaffraria; Du Toit, "Cape Frontiers," pp. 69–72; BK 426, *Letters from the High Commissioner*, 1848–9, Grey to Smith, 14 April 1849.

58. For these developments see H.J. Mandelbrote, "Constitutional Development, 1834–1858," in A.P. Newton, E.A. Benians and Eric A. Walker (eds.), *The Cambridge History of the British Empire*, vol. VIII: *South Africa, Rhodesia and The Protectorates* (Cambridge, 1936), pp. 359–90.

59. Du Toit, "Cape Frontiers," pp. 86–101.

60. J.B. Peires, *The Dead Will Arise: Nongqawuse and the Great Xhosa Cattle-Killing Movement of 1856–7* (Johannesburg, London, and Bloomington, IN, 1989), pp. 1–4.

61. CA BK 436, *Letters from the Hlambie Commissioner to the Chief Commissioner*, 1850, Maclean to Mackinnon, 26 and 29 August 1850. He reported to Mackinnon his absolute confidence that the Kaffir Police were very popular among the ordinary people and would continue to serve loyally, even "without the incitement to plunder which might if necessary be held out to them if their services were more actively required than at present." When the war broke out, the native police deserted in large numbers.

62. Ibid., 27 September 1850, where he contradicts a report that Maclean had received from one of his spies, and repeats his claim that Mlanjeni was doing

good work at a time when Maclean had firm information that Sandile and others had been meeting with Mlanjeni to discuss the anti-British implications of his prophecies.

63. Ibid., Maclean to Mackinnon, 26 and 27 September; 2, 4 and 21 October 1850.

64. Ibid., Maclean to Mackinnon, 11 October 1850. Maclean wrote: "I venture to state that the system at present in operation has so effectually convinced the people that they are enjoying the protection of a just and mild government that there is no chance of their wishing to return to the control of the chiefs."

65. CA, BK 440, *Letters of the Gaika Commissioner to the Chief Commissioner*, Brownlee to Mackinnon, 11 October 1850. He told them, for example, that the commander of frontier forces was away, which clearly lessened the likelihood of a surprise British attack.

66. Ibid., Maclean to Mackinnon, 28 November 1850.

67. NA, CO 48/309, *Dispatches from Governor, Sir Harry Smith, to Secretary Grey, November–December 1850*, 26 November 1850, for Smith's account of his deposition of Sandile and the tranquil state of the frontier. The Colonial Office had other sources of information, however – mainly the settler press, which led Merivale to minute on this dispatch how "you will see from the enclosed number of the Cape *Frontier Times* that the state of the frontier does not appear to be so satisfactory as is represented in this dispatch." Which suggests that London could be better informed, or more realistic, about the realities of the frontier than those actually on the site.

68. CA, BK 436, *Letters from the Hlambie Commissioner, 1850*, "Reply of the Hlambie Chiefs on Hearing the Governor's 'Word' Relative to the Conduct of Sandili in not appearing before His Excellency and the Consequences Thereof." "Reply of the Chiefs to the Proclamation of His Excellency the High Commissioner on Deposing the Gaika Chief Sandili from his rank as Chief."

69. CO 48/309, Brownlee to Smith, 2 November 1850.

70. Stapleton, *Maqoma*, pp. 151–3; Elbourne, *Blood Ground*, pp. 362–4.

71. NA, CO 48/309, *Dispatches from Governor, Sir Harry Smith, to Secretary Grey*, November–December 1850, Smith to Grey, 6 November 1850. In the same dispatch he announced that he had "thrown away" Mlanjeni, judging it wiser to allow him to dwindle into obscurity rather than to apprehend him. One can understand Smith's misreadings. From the end of November the British were faced with a growing collection of contradictory signs about Xhosa intentions. At meetings in December, the deposition of Sandile seemed to be accepted by the other chiefs. But the Commissioners with the tribes were also reporting on growing unrest. Loyal chiefs were beginning to suggest more clearly to the British the possibility of war. There were reports that the Xhosa chiefs were slaughtering cattle as a prelude to war. Smith decided to go to the frontier to bring the Xhosa to their senses.

72. This account of the meeting is drawn from the verbatim report in *The Graham's Town Journal*, 28 December 1850, and from Theal, *History of South Africa*, vol. VII, p. 93; CO 48/309. There is a short account of it in John F. Cumming, *Diary*, 19 December 1850, who remarks on Smith's bombastic style.

73. Even Smith recognized the justice of Maqoma's complaints about his treatment on that occasion; see CA, GH 34/7, *Letterbook of Sir Harry Smith 1836–37*, Smith to D'Urban, 11 September 1835, 28 January 1836.

74. There is ample documentation on Toise's role as a government informer, which was to continue well into the 1850s. See, for example, CA, GH 8/45, *Captain Maclean's Letters* 23 September 1847. Toise was not the only informer, of course, that the British used; but my sense is that after the late 1840s the practice of surveillance by spies became more systematic and common.

75. For descriptions of Suthu see Charles J.F. Bunbury, *Journal of a Residence at the Cape of Good Hope* (repr. New York, 1969), p. 159; CWM, *LMS Correspondence*, Kayser to Directors, 7 October 1845; NA CO 48/309 for his dispatch of 6 November where Smith reported that "Sutu, Sandilli's mother, thanked me particularly for my lenience and observed that great was her sorrow to feel that her son was not worthy to be a Chief." Suthu's prestige and importance derived from the fact that in Xhosa society the mother of the chief was always accorded great prestige and occupied a place as major adviser and counselor to her son once he became chief.

76. Smith to Grey 26 December 1850, CO 48/309; *LMS Correspondence*, Read Snr. to Freeman, 13 April 1851.

77. NA, WO 135/2, *Sir Harry Smith, Field Letter Book 1851*, Smith to Somerset, 13 February and 15 March 1851. For the Xhosa–Khoi alliance in this war, the first example of black unity against whites in southern Africa, see Elbourne, *Blood Ground*.

78. For good accounts of the war, see Mostert, *Frontiers*, pp. 1014–60; Peires, *Dead Will Arise*, pp. 12–29. Colonel C.E. Calwell, in *Small Wars: Their Principles and Practice*, 3rd edn. (1906; repr. Lincoln, NE, 1996), pp. 27, 33, 103, 130, 135, 148, 454, for some observations on this war. Smith was found employment as Commander of the Western District in Britain, but was passed over for service in the Crimean War. There was a brief revival of interest in Smith around the time of the South African War of 1899–1902, which afforded the opportunity for his nephew, G.C. Moore Smith, a Cambridge don, to publish his autobiography: Sir Harry Smith, *The Autobiography of Lieutenant-General Sir Harry Smith, Baronet of Aliwal on the Sutlej* (London, 1901). His memory lives on, of course, in various town names in South Africa, such as Harrismith and Ladysmith.

9   Empire as democracy: the imperial state and the chiefs

The problem of the chiefs

How does empire gain access to the people it seeks to rule? How is the orbit of empire extended to engage the culture and politics of its subject peoples? There is no simple solution to how that may be done. The key, however, lies in the relationship between the imperial state and the political elites of the indigenes. From the opening days of contact between the British and the Xhosa, the importance of the Xhosa chiefs was recognized. Only the chiefs could grant the imperial state access to Xhosa society. Thus the problem of establishing imperial rule devolved into a problem of the relationship between the imperial state and the chiefs. It is this story that is the focus of this chapter.

It is not a pretty story. There is a view to be found in histories of the British empire that Britain was rather good with native elites. Indirect rule was Britain's secret in this respect. How else could 900 white civil servants and 70,000 soldiers rule 250 million Indians in the Raj if not by making strategic alliances with traditional other elites in the subcontinent? But there was precious little respect from the British for the Xhosa elites. When indirect rule was established in Kaffraria it was built upon the ruins of Xhosa civil society and the humiliating degradation of the chiefs. These men were not even granted the moment of celebrity that Cetshwayo, the Zulu king, experienced in the summer of 1882 when he visited London to try to save his kingdom and was lionized by society.[1]

A bleak end game awaited the Xhosa chiefs in their encounter with the imperial state. When we enter the story, at the opening of the second decade of the nineteenth century, the chiefs stood as heads of independent tribes. When our narrative closes, around the early 1860s, Xhosa civil society was devastated and subdued. As lung sickness and the millenarian cattle-killing culled out their herds, the imperial state launched an offensive which destroyed the social and political authority of the chiefs. It was an attack that had been in the minds of various officials since the days of Queen Adelaide Province. The collective fates of the chiefs were starkly

233

simple. Some were killed; some were sent to Robben Island. Those who remained were reduced to satraps of the government, vulnerable to the slightest whim of the imperial administration. By the late 1850s all of the chiefs had been reduced to various states of penury and humiliating dependence upon imperial officers.[2]

This chapter tracks the relationship between the chiefs and the state until the end of the eighth frontier war in 1853. The dramatic denouement of the 1850s will be addressed in the next chapter. I separate these parts to simplify the narrative. But the story was not straightforward. The relationship between the state and the Xhosa chiefs was ambiguous and contradictory. Both sought gains and advantages from the other. The lines of interest were shifting and were not preordained. However much the imperial state needed the assistance of the chiefs in its project of imperial reformation, it could never bring itself to trust them. The chiefs saw opportunities as well as dangers in a relationship with this new polity that lurked on the frontier of Xhosaland. They sought to maximize the promise of additional power that a relationship with the imperial state could bestow. But they found the state a capricious and arbitrary partner. Consequently, their collaborations were always conducted in an atmosphere of mistrust, fear and evasion.

I shall begin with the war of 1850–3. And I want to focus particularly on how the origins and causes of the war were explained by the administrators of British Kaffraria to themselves and to their colleagues in the Cape and London. I start here because this was the moment when a consensus view of Xhosa politics and of the chiefs' place within Xhosa civil society emerged within the imperial state. The eighth frontier war provided clear proof to the state that the chiefs were at the center of a politics of conspiracy and manipulation. But in order to understand where this narrative explanation for the breakdown of British Kaffraria came from, it is necessary to track the history of the engagement between the Xhosa chieftains and the imperial state over the previous half-century. Thus, after discussing the British explanation for the war of 1850–3, I shall move backward in time to contextualize that explanation within the historical patterns of the encounter between the state and the Xhosa chiefs.

What were the factors that governed the relationship between the chiefs and the imperial state from the 1820s? Imperial policy toward the Xhosa seemed to twist and turn between engagement and separation. But up to 1850 it was precisely this capricious volatility that provided its enduring consistency. The Xhosa chiefs quickly recognized that the imperial state was a partner with the temper of a sociopath. In one iteration, the policy of the state would be rendered benign; in another iteration, it would turn vicious and vengeful. In one person, the state might appear cooperative and even likable; in another person, the state would act like a mad dog. Why was the policy of the imperial state so volatile?

I shall explain this volatility as a function of the uncertainties within imperial culture as to how the chiefs should be categorized. We have noted the divided views on the character of chiefly power. Were they despots or constitutional monarchs? Most informed imperial administrators knew that the Xhosa chiefs approximated more to constitutional monarchs than to despots. But this admission contradicted the unstated aim of imperial policy from the mid-1830s: to undermine the chiefs' power and authority in the pursuit of imperial control. It was not until this tension had been resolved within imperial culture that it could confidently proceed to confront Xhosa society and chiefly power.

My final topic, therefore, will be to describe how an ideology emerged to resolve that tension. This ideology ascribed to the chiefs the role of tyrants while ascribing to the imperial state the role of democratic liberator. Chiefs were presented as committed to obstructing the imperial state from delivering the tribes from cultural and spiritual darkness. In this ideology, then, it is imperial culture that was a democratizing force, and the chiefs who were agents of tyranny.

At the conclusion of this chapter, I shall return again to the eighth frontier war. This war solved the ideological problem of how to regard the chiefs. But it did not solve the political problem of the chiefs' relationship to the imperial state; it was an insufficient victory for the British to reduce the chiefs into reliable agents of indirect rule. Or rather, the chiefs did not *feel* it as a defeat. The scene was set, therefore, for the next and final act in this drama: the advent of Britain's premier liberal imperialist, Sir George Grey.

Explaining the war of 1850–3

As far as British opinion was concerned, the war of 1850–3 was the least contentious of all the frontier wars. It was virtually unanimously agreed that the Xhosa were the source of this conflict. The problem the war posed for the British lay more in its shrouded origins. Neither the imperial administration nor the missionaries saw it coming. Even when they began to pick up hints of a stirring war spirit, they were reluctant to read the logic of their senses. How was this failure of knowledge to be explained? What was the alibi for the ignorance of the imperial administration? This problem was solved by a conviction that the war was a product of a conspiracy of chiefs who had orchestrated the war as a desperate attempt to halt the loss of their own power in the face of a beneficent and democratizing imperial presence. In other words, the war was seen as an effort to impede and obstruct the mission of imperial culture to free their people from the chiefs' tyrannical grasp.[3]

Indeed, *this explanation was prepared by imperial administrators before war actually erupted.* At the end of August 1850, various Commissioners, sensing some activity, tried to assess whether the tribes were coordinating their moves. John Maclean made the argument that the increasing restiveness was among the great chiefs who "see clearly that their power is passing away." Two months later, he wrote to the Chief Commissioner, George Mackinnon, that there was a chiefs' conspiracy brewing to grab back the power that the imperial administration was prising from their grasp. But Maclean claimed that this was a conspiracy confined to the senior chiefs. The petty chiefs, like the ordinary people, appreciated the protections the imperial state provided. Maclean did not believe that the people would respond to the machinations of the conspirators, because "there is no chance of their wishing to return to the control of their chiefs."[4]

Once the war broke out, these views were recycled around the imperial administration as it struggled to understand what had happened. In August 1851 George Mackinnon reviewed the policy before the war for Sir Harry Smith. Mackinnon's career was on the line. He was responsible for administering Smith's policy in British Kaffraria and his ruminations contained more than a morsel of self-justification. Nevertheless, his storyline was consistent with all the others I have encountered. It was not the system of government that was at fault; the people were happy and "there is less injustice and more real liberty than ever before." The "power of the British government is exercised for restraint only upon that which is evil." Mackinnon's conclusion was that the imperial government had exercised too little force. It had not deployed enough coercion to allow for the liberation of the ordinary people from their oppressors within Xhosa society. More imperial force would have provided the space to allow the people to forget their bad old ways, and they "would have soon looked wholly to us and not to their Chiefs." Thus Mackinnon circled back to the problem of the chiefs as obstacles to the benign effects of the imperial presence. They were the obstacles to their people's receiving the liberal benefits that empire had to offer.[5]

This was a view that was repeated again and again in all sectors of the imperial project, and it is not particularly helpful to assess the truths behind these claims. Like all invented narratives, this one contained more than a grain of truth. It was to be expected that the chiefs would conspire to combat the British; indeed, it would have been remarkable if they had not. But when the uprising came, it was impressive precisely for its breadth and depth of support from both Xhosa and Khoesan. Whatever else it was, the war was also a popular uprising. What is interesting about the imperial interpretation of the war of 1850–3 as a conspiracy of tyrannical chiefs is how it was paralleled by the projection of British imperialism as the conduit of democratic liberation. How did such a view develop?[6]

The state and the chiefs: the ambiguities of an imperial relationship

The story of the relationship between the Xhosa chiefs and the British state was, from one perspective, the story of colonial uncertainty. The British did not have a clearly formulated policy towards the Xhosa chiefs until fairly late in the relationship. It was only with the policies of Sir George Grey in the 1850s that the relationship between the state and the chiefs was bureaucratized into a formal pattern. Similarly, for their part, the Xhosa chiefs saw the imperial state as presenting a series of possibilities. The imperial state contained both opportunities for their aggrandisement as well as threats to their power. So the starting point for any understanding of the relationship between the state and the chiefs is to appreciate that it was at all levels complex and ambiguous.

Thus, the chiefs spent as much time collaborating with their resident magistrate as they did resisting and evading him – and sometimes the line between the two poles was itself unclear. Even those chiefs most distrusted by the imperial administration were entangled in a mutual and collaborative relationship with the state through their association with the resident magistrate. In early 1842, for example, Shepstone put a lot of time and effort into working with Seyolo, Gazala and Mhala to gain their cooperation in putting a stop to cattle-thieving. He had more success with the first two, but even Mhala was willing to bestir himself to some extent. Although Mhala tried to evade any decision he did not like, he recognized that he could use the state to his advantage. In the early 1840s he called in a Mfengu witchdoctor to perform a ceremony that would improve his standing with the imperial authorities.[7]

Even a chief such as Xhoxho, who was detested by the imperial administrators for his "low cunning" and his reputation as an inveterate horse thief, was not always at odds with the imperial administration. Xhoxho is a nice illustration of the complexity of the chiefs' entanglements with the state. Calderwood found him a slippery and troublesome character. But Xhoxho cooperated quite well with Charles Brownlee in the 1850s, and he was the beneficiary of largesse from Sir George Grey, who provided him with agricultural implements and cut a water course for him in order to encourage him to settle down as an arable farmer rather than being a pastoral wanderer. But Xhoxho's loyalties were always contingent, and he died fighting in the final stand of the Xhosa against British imperialism in the war of 1878–9.[8]

At the other end of the spectrum from Mhala and Xhoxho stood chiefs who sought to build an enduring alliance with the imperial state. Apart from those like Toise – Maclean's lead spy – who owed their position entirely to the state, such chiefs were usually those attached to missionary culture. Khama is the best example of this style. Khama was the most consistently pro-British chief on the frontier. He was the son of Chungwa, chief of the Gqunukhwebe branch of the Xhosa. Although his father had been shot by the British in 1812, Khama was the one Xhosa chief of his generation the British could claim as a consistent and sincere convert to Christianity. By the 1850s, Khama was a model citizen, a promising example of Xhosa modernity. He was a budding entrepreneur, a friend of local Dutch and British farmers, and the owner of a small wagon business. Yet what did this get him? His "tribe" was a hollow pretense; he had few followers. And when he had the temerity to drag his feet in implementing the Grey system of indirect rule in the later 1850s, he was rudely told to get in line or face the consequences.[9]

But that was not all. Even Khama was subject to the kind of humiliation and harassment that was meted out to chiefs like Maqoma. In June 1857 he was staying with a prominent frontier family, the Bowkers, after attending the opening of a new missionary school in the presence of the Governor. He was about to leave for Grahamstown to get his wagon painted when he was rudely accosted by a patrol of the Frontier Armed and Mounted Police, led by their Commandant, Walter Currie. Khama was threatened with arrest for a supposedly incorrectly filled-out pass. He was confined to the Bowkers' house while his magistrate was contacted and the bureaucratic error – for such it was – corrected. Only the protection and protests of the Bowkers saved him from being carted off to jail. Walter Currie was later to be knighted for his services to empire, and he is buried in a place of honor in Grahamstown Cathedral. He could hardly have been ignorant of Khama's position and status.[10]

As this little episode suggests, the imperial state was a fickle and volatile creature. It was impossible to escape contact with the state. But the chiefs could not assess their exposure to the dangers that came from such contact. This pattern was set from the very beginning of serious contact between the imperial state and the chiefs when Ngqika, chief of the Rharhabe branch of the Xhosa, came to meet Governor Charles, Lord Somerset, at the Kei river on 2 April 1817. This meeting was the first between a British Governor and a Xhosa chief, and its purpose was to strike an agreement that would bring stability to the frontier.

Both men had come to the meeting with their own agendas. Ngqika was concerned to enlist British help in his current intertribal struggle with his uncle, Ndlambe. Somerset had selected *him* precisely because he was losing that power struggle. Somerset hoped that he would be able to use Ngqika as the enforcer of a peaceful frontier, recognizing that he would have to build up his power to do that. For his part Ngqika made it quite clear to Somerset that although he did have claims to be *primus inter pares* of the Xhosa chiefs, he was not recognized as such by most of them, and, in any case, he did not have the power to enforce his authority.

Somerset, however, refused to acknowledge this. He intended to treat Ngqika if he were a sovereign, and the other chiefs were to work through him. Ngqika would be responsible for tribal movement across the frontier. This was a very large order which he could not fulfill. But it announced the policy of creating dependency of the chiefs upon the imperial state. Naturally enough, Ngqika's role of enforcer for the imperial state aroused the hostility of other Xhosa. After his defeat by Ndlambe at the battle of Amalinde (1818), he turned to the British to prop up his tottering throne. Ngqika now owed everything to the British. His reward was further abuse. After the war of 1819–20 the British took a goodly portion of his land and pushed the frontier of Xhosaland back another 50 miles to the Keiskamma river. The loss of his "traditional" lands brought no security either. The British refused to support him against *mfecane* raids in the late 1820s. In short, since he had first reluctantly met with a British Governor in 1817, his independence and power had degenerated.

As if in tandem, Ngqika's personality went into decline also. When John Barrow described him at the turn of the century, he highlighted his dignity as a commander and man. Thirty years later, other visitors found him overwhelmed by "English vices," addicted to the alcohol from which he died, and willing to prostitute his wives for brandy. Naturally, such an end confirmed for the British the ultimate depravity of the Xhosa character. Sympathetic observers at the time more realistically attributed his decline to his treatment at the hands of the imperial state.[11]

Ngqika was at least allowed to die in peace by the British in 1829. On his deathbed he warned his sons (Maqoma among them) not to oppose the British. This was a suitably rueful legacy for him to pass on to his children. It was a warning that was also absorbed into the memory of imperial culture. British administrators would use it as a stock reminder when they needed to contrast the "wisdom" of Ngqika to the foolishness of his sons. Shamelessness is a standard quality of imperial culture, and it showed no embarrassment in using Ngqika as a symbol of the wisdom of Xhosa cooperation with the imperial state.[12]

The story of Hintsa in the 1830s is a further example of vulnerabilities to which the chiefs were exposed. In his case the end game was fatal. During the war of 1834–5 the British chose to award him the same power they had foisted on Ngqika, asserting that he possessed a paramount status over the other branches of the Xhosa which gave him dominion over all the other chiefs. It was true that Hintsa possessed better claims than Ngqika to be the Xhosa paramount, because he was a direct descendant of Phalo, the recognized founder of the Xhosa nation in the mid-eighteenth century. Still, this did not carry the authority that would permit him to dole out instructions and orders to the other chiefs.

This was exactly what Sir Benjamin D'Urban and Colonel Harry Smith demanded, however, when they insisted that he order the tribes to deliver up 40,000 head of cattle as an indemnity to end the war. Both D'Urban and Smith purveyed the notion that Hintsa was the *éminence grise* behind the federation of chiefs who were fighting the war. Hintsa was seen as the conspiring chief who cunningly led the Xhosa into war while pretending to be disengaged himself. In fact, Hintsa was not a combatant in the sixth frontier war. It was undoubtedly true that his territory was used as a refuge for the cattle of those Xhosa chiefs who were fighting. Lodging cattle from neighboring tribes was a common Xhosa courtesy, as well as being a wartime strategy. For D'Urban and Smith, this was enough to establish his complicity in the war.[13]

So Hintsa was lured into the British camp at the end of April 1835 under the pretext of negotiating an end to hostilities. Once in the camp, he was forcibly detained and subjected to crude tactics of disorientation. There were moments of generous treatment by Smith, who on one occasion reprimanded his ADC for not making Hintsa coffee. But a bugler was ordered to play reveille every ten minutes outside Hintsa's tent at night. D'Urban threatened to string him up. It is not surprising that Hintsa seems to have made some sort of agreement with these gentlemen about returning cattle. On 30 April peace was declared with much fanfare.[14]

But Hintsa was not released. He continued to be held hostage pending the arrival of the cattle. By 10 May none had arrived, and Hintsa was sent out with Smith on a patrol to try to persuade the other chiefs to deliver the cattle. Hintsa was a desperate and resourceful man. He proceeded to lead Smith a merry chase, taking him to one place after another without ever encountering the sub-chiefs he was supposed to find – although groups of Xhosa were always in view, monitoring the movements of the patrol. On 12 May, Hintsa made a dash for freedom. He was chased by Smith and several others. Wounded, Hintsa at some point dismounted or fell off his horse, perhaps to scramble down into a ravine and hide. George Southey, commander of the scouts, and Captain Balfour, Smith's ADC, came upon him hiding behind a rock with an assegai in his hand, reportedly calling to surrender. Southey shot him in the head. His body was subsequently mutilated.[15]

This incident caused a tremendous scandal within the walls of the Colonial Office. When the Colonial Secretary, Lord Glenelg, heard about it, he was outraged. Glenelg was an evangelical who genuinely wanted to bring humanitarian policies to bear in dealings with other races. He insisted on a commission of inquiry into the affair. For a while Harry Smith feared for the future of his career. But the commission sat at Grahamstown, far from the prying eyes of British politicians; it was composed of junior army officers who were not about to challenge their superiors, and was open to the most blatant manipulation and interference from Smith, who actually sat on the sidelines as it took evidence, shouting out advice and admonitions to the witnesses. And the evidence was fixed, anyway. Captain Balfour's evidence was at odds with his private diary entries, and George Southey simply refused to answer the key questions.[16]

Hintsa's death was excused by the reasons that the British had invented to blame him for the war in the first place, and additional justifications were conjured up to make the case watertight. Thus, in the narrative that was developed both by imperial officials and settler apologists, *it was Hintsa's character that became the issue*, not his death. In official correspondence, it was remarked by Harry Smith that Hintsa deserved death because he was guilty of three murders himself: one man, who had interrupted his love-making was stabbed, a wife had her brains bashed out, and his brother was tied to wild horses and torn apart. These were probably pure inventions. But Hintsa's attempt to escape was the most serviceable item of all for the narrative that was now constructed around his death. Here was clear evidence of his perfidy, cunning and cowardice. In what came to serve as the official view of Hintsa, it was declared that he was a cowardly ingrate who "planned ... to [lead] an officer [Harry Smith] who had greeted him with distinguished kindness ... into a situation of such difficulty and embarrassment [that is, escaping, and embarrassing Smith professionally] as would ensure his destruction." But "he fell victim to his own perfidy."[17]

I would like the reader to pause for a moment here and reflect on this claim. It is a remarkable piece of reasoning. But it is a typical example of *colonial* reasoning, whose purpose is to produce a narrative that will authorize imperial culture. The central claim is that the victim (Hintsa) was responsible for all the bad things that happened to him and to others. Hintsa's character warranted his fate, and his attempt to destroy the career of Harry Smith by escaping is claimed as the reason for his murder. Hintsa's fate was also useful as a warning to threaten other chiefs in the future. And at appropriate moments in the next twenty years or so, imperial officials reminded the Xhosa of Hintsa's fate. Here is John Maclean, writing to Sarhili (Hintsa's son) in 1847:

> As to what Kreli [the British name for Sarhili] some time ago conveyed about the death of his father Hintza, if Hintza had been true and faithful and not shown himself treacherous he would have been quite safe with the English, but he broke his faith and proved treacherous and was leading the troops into a snare. Let Kreli lay aside injustice and false dealing and prove himself honest and just and he will have nothing to fear from the white men.[18]

Spies, informers and surveillance

Empire without surveillance is unthinkable. Indeed, the quality of information provided by surveillance is directly related to the efficacy of imperial rule. The recruitment of a network of informants in Xhosaland occurred as the imperial state began to take serious interest in the place. The chiefs were the main targets of surveillance, as they were also often the main sources of information. Compared to India, the apparatus of surveillance in British Kaffraria was pretty rudimentary. There was no network of sophisticated imperial bureaucrats administering the place, only the individual resident magistrate or Commissioner, who, until fairly late, were without any reliable police force. It was very much up to the individual Commissioner or magistrate to develop his own networks of informants and spies. Missionaries, of course, were the most commonly used source of information for the imperial state. Still, missionaries were not exactly secret informers, and by the 1840s Charles Brownlee and his fellow Commissioners were already on the lookout to recruit likely candidates for their growing networks.

Brownlee, for example, forged a relationship with a man he called Go. Brownlee first encountered Go in January 1849. At that point he was a "wild and desperate Kaffir ... a notorious thief who has figured no less than four times in the Returns of Colonial property reported stolen." Brownlee's newly formed "Kaffir Police" had been hard on Go's trail for some time. After escaping from their clutches three times, the Police ultimately captured him and he threw himself on Brownlee's mercy. Go impressed Brownlee, who immediately saw that his "knowledge of thefts could be useful to the Government." Brownlee wanted to avoid a trial, therefore. Since British Kaffraria was in a legal limbo, the High Commissioner could do what he liked, so, taking advantage of "our peculiar [legal] position in British Kaffraria," Go was offered the choice of a pardon if he would work as an informant for Brownlee.[19]

Go turned out to be a good investment. He became a consistent and loyal informer and agent for the Commissioner. Among other services,

Go helped Brownlee track down and bring other thieves to trial; he was Brownlee's constant companion whenever he traveled among the Xhosa; he gave him advance warning of a plot to kidnap him in 1852. Naturally, this was a mutually beneficial relationship. Brownlee acted as Go's benefactor and protector. After the eighth frontier war, he set Go up as a policeman, granted him some land and arranged for a line of credit for him to buy sheep. Go rapidly became a wealthy man, marrying the daughter of a powerful chief, and by 1877 he was the proud owner of two farms.[20]

All good imperial officers had their informants who allowed them some sort of access into local society. When Captain John Maclean was appointed Commissioner to the Ndlambe in 1847, he already had some experience of spy networks. His first official report was an assessment of the characters and personalities of the chiefs under his supervision. He had been watching Phato for some time, writing in March 1846 that he was "a designing and false Chief and I have spies from this settlement watching Pato's movements and will not fail to report anything suspicious." During the war of 1846–7 his network was heavily used to report on Mhala, Tzatzoe and others.[21]

In September 1847 a new name appears in Maclean's correspondence as an informant. This was the minor chief, Toise, whom we have met before. Toise had recently surrendered (the War of the Axe was dragging on) and was working to ingratiate himself into Maclean's services. At the beginning of September Maclean noted that Toise "has again come forward as openly and honestly as I think any Kafir under existing circumstances can be expected – he informs me confidentially to warn the government not to place any trust in the professions of any Kaffir Chief." Maclean rapidly gained confidence in Toise, and Toise expeditiously made his commitment to serving Maclean. Within the month he was carrying out his first assignment for Maclean and reporting on a meeting of chiefs convened to discuss the treatment of Sandile by the government.[22]

Toise continued to serve as informant throughout the war of 1850–53. On one occasion he was captured by rebels from the Cape Mounted Rifles, and only the intervention of Sandile saved his life. He continued to serve his imperial masters well into the 1850s. Toise was the best kind of informant. As a cousin of Mhala, he was close to the centers of power and knew all the main players on the Xhosa side. Spies and informants were frequently drawn from such circles. Maclean attempted to recruit Delima, Phato's son, for example. He also used a nephew of Mhala in 1852 to watch his uncle's movements. And John Cox Gawler, Grey's enforcer with Mhala, did the same soon after his appointment as magistrate in late 1855.[23]

Surveillance was a constant activity, of course. No chief was exempt, and even in times of relative calm, vigilant resident agents like Shepstone and Maclean wanted to know what was going on. Even after the Xhosa accepted peace in 1853, Brownlee sent out spies to find out what the chiefs were really doing, because they were dragging their feet implementing the conditions of the peace. At times of tension particular efforts were made to watch and monitor comings and goings. Very close tabs were kept on internal tribal politics during the cattle-killing. Informants were sent to meet with Mhlakaza and report back.[24]

But the network of informers and spies did not go unnoticed by the chiefs. They knew that they were being watched, and it is likely that they knew who the watchers were. Sometimes they even let the imperial state know that they knew. Toise was very quickly rumbled by the Xhosa as the eyes and ears of the government. His position as chief was regarded by the other Xhosa as resting solely on the support of the imperial government, even though he claimed to be holding the inheritance as a Regent for the rightful heir. Similarly, there is a nice moment caught by the records when Sarhili let his diplomatic agent W. D. Fynn know that he knew everything about Fynn's efforts to collect information.[25]

The response of the chiefs to the imperial state

Chiefs were not pristine innocents. They were tough and wily politicians who stayed in power by working hard to maintain the support of their people and by coping with the divisions and complexities of intra-tribal rivalries and politics. The appearance of the British imperial state on the frontier of the Cape in the second decade of the century merely added one more element to a regional politics that was already increasingly unstable and insecure. But it soon became clear that the destabilizing power of the British imperial state and its settler appendages was far beyond that of any of the other players in the politics of the region. It was the war of 1811–12 that demonstrated, for example, the sheer ruthlessness of the British methods of war. And from that point onwards, the Xhosa knew they were dealing with a terrible force.

Xhosa chiefs were eager to seek a *modus vivendi* with the imperial state. They were willing to collaborate and cooperate to keep the frontier stable. They were willing to entertain the silly rituals and forms that Harry Smith devised. They were even willing to put up with the land dispossession they experienced and accept the practical necessity of following the imperial state's delineations of their boundaries. But they were not prepared to willingly sell their independence. They struggled continually to prevent the bonds of imperial control strangling them; at every point they sought to maximize their sphere of autonomy both for themselves and for their tribes. It was in that struggle that their nobility and their tragedy lay.

The Xhosa chiefs greeted the imperial state with intelligence, perception and *sense of history*. In 1835, for example, Maqoma recorded for James Clark (a missionary associated with Friedrich Kayser) the arbitrary dispossession that the Xhosa had experienced only in his lifetime, ending with the most recent demand that they move across the Thyumie river. He noted that his father Ngqika had refused to join an alliance with the Boers against the British (he was referring to the Slachterneks rebellion of 1815), but his reward was to lose half of his country by being expelled from the Fish river. And he asked the central question: "When shall my people get rest? ... We do no injury to the Colony, and yet I remain under the foot of the English. I would beg the favour of your enquiring at the Government for me the reason of all these things."[26]

One of the ironies of Maqoma's critique was that it was hardly news to the imperial administration. At exactly the same time that this untutored chief was cataloguing the Xhosa complaints to James Clark, various bureaucrats in London were openly admitting the Xhosa case. An internal Colonial Office memorandum pointed to the way the volatilities of frontier policy unsettled the Xhosa. Land was taken away from them, which they were then allowed to reoccupy, before being expelled again. This contradictory behavior could only "have the most injurious effects on the minds of the Kaffers." Similarly, the failure to develop a consistent policy had made it impossible for them "to know by what rules they were to be governed, [and] has oppressed and exasperated them by the suffering which it has so frequently inflicted upon them."[27]

Nor was Maqoma the only perceptive chief. A year or so after Maqoma made his statement to James Clark, Mhala met with Andries Stockenstrom to inaugurate the latest frontier policy. Mhala expressed his skepticism whether it would last. He pointed out that the chiefs "did not know how to make treaties with the English, as no sooner was a treaty made than the Governor went away and another came and made a new one, and upset all the others had done before him." A few years later Maclean received a bitter retort from Mqhayi that although the Government wanted the chiefs to maintain law and order, its policies undermined that authority. Indeed, "government are alone to blame for all the trouble in the land." The chiefs could not possibly serve both their tribes and the imperial master.[28]

Fourteen years later, Mhala revealed the same prescience. It was December 1850, and the Xhosa chiefs were planning their offensive against the British. It is an interesting report because it makes explicit the harsh alternatives that faced them as they confronted the relentless power of the British imperial state. Mhala was in conversation with Phato, who was warning him against going to war. Phato reminded Mhala that his (Phato's) family had never recovered from the last war. "The English," he said, "can go everywhere." Mhala agreed, but pointed out that it was important to assist Sandile, or else

I ask you where will you get assistance when the English turn on you, for don't you see that the English don't wish to fight all the Chiefs together? I see clearly that they will deprive us all of our Chieftainships one after another. I would not care if the English took all of Sandili's cattle, but when I saw Smith attempt to seize Sandili, then every Chief should fight.[29]

How, then, can we capture the dominant themes of the chiefs' response to the imperial state? This generation of chiefs reacted to the imperial state with the combined responses of fear and evasion. The shock of Colonel John Graham's ruthless strategy during the war of 1811–12 planted these instincts in the minds of the Xhosa chiefs. Ngqika had good reason for his deep reluctance to meet with Somerset in 1817. The fate of Chungwa – shot on his sickbed – must have been fresh in his mind. He feared that Somerset was really coming to take revenge on a recent murder of a settler. Somerset's envoy, Major Fraser, had to work very hard to persuade Ngqika that he would be safe. Until the last moment, the chief was reluctant. When he spotted the 300 troops lined up for the meeting on the other side of the Kat river, he almost had to be dragged across. Once it was over, Ngqika scampered off as fast as he could, without waiting to eat the meal Somerset had provided for him. Maqoma and other future chiefs were also present at this meeting, and it is unlikely that Ngqika's apprehension went unnoticed by them.[30]

A wary fear constantly hovered in the minds of the chiefs as they dealt with the British. They were always aware that they could suddenly be struck down. As the direct heir to Ngqika's title, Sandile was acutely conscious of this danger. Sandile had good reason to be sensitive. He had himself experienced a typical piece of British treachery. Induced by Henry, Lord Somerset (son of Lord Charles), to accompany Captain Bisset for negotiations to end the War of the Axe, he found himself arrested and clapped in Grahamstown jail for several weeks. From then on he was "afraid to place myself in the power of the English." Little wonder that Sandile continued to refer back to the fate of Hintsa. His refusal to meet Smith in November 1850 (which led to Smith's deposition of him as Rharhabe chief) was due to fear for his safety rather than to disrespect. In August 1853, Sandile explained his reluctance to meet Governor Cathcart at a military post, by referring to the fate of Hintsa and others. In 1860 he was unexpectedly invited to accompany Prince Alfred back to Cape Town as part of a ceremonial delegation that Grey had put together. Fearing that he would end up as a guest of Her Majesty at Robben Island, he refused to go. He was persuaded only when the Reverend Tiyo Soga agreed to accompany him as a guarantor of his safety.[31]

The historical record provides ample justification for the fear of the chiefs. But this fed into a bind that trapped both British and Xhosa. Xhosa historical memory led them to be very wary and evasive around the British. Procrastination was, thus, a key strategy of the Xhosa chiefs for dealing with the British demands. It was a natural response to the arbitrary and volatile character of frontier policy and British actions. It was a sensible strategy of "wait and see," allowing time to reveal whether a particular initiative would burn itself out or change into something else.

From the British side, Xhosa evasion and procrastination, however, did not seem reasonable at all. They could hardly be expected to see themselves as capricious, changeable and cruel. Indeed, Xhosa evasion provided proof to the British of the inherent cunning and deceit of the Xhosa. For the British, evasiveness could be easily reduced to an essential character of the Xhosa, not a product of a historical encounter that the British had a large hand in shaping. The Xhosa had good reason for *their* take on British policy. But there were also reasons that lay within the imperial state that explain why British policy on the frontier was changeable and unstable. And we must now examine the roots of that volatility.

The roots of volatility in British policy

There is a strong tradition in the historiography of British imperialism that argues how policy was ultimately made by the "man on the spot." In the early nineteenth century, when communication was a protracted matter of months, the influence of *anyone* was bound to be weak in such a far-flung piece of the empire as the eastern Cape. Even Cape Town was a long way away in the 1830s and 1840s. Sir Harry Smith was the first Governor to benefit from the technology of the steamship, which enabled him to arrive on the frontier in a matter of days. The reach of the Colonial Office extended as far as Grahamstown in only the most general sense. For most of the time, the eastern Cape was not a bright line on the radar screen of the Colonial Office. And when it was, the priorities that London had identified would be diluted and undermined by the time they were laid upon the Xhosa. The handling of frontier affairs by Sir Benjamin D'Urban, and then by his successor, Governor Napier, from 1835 to 1844, illustrate the turnabout that often occurred between London and the eastern frontier. Both had been sent out by "humanitarian" administrations in London with the expectation that they would pursue humanitarian frontier policies. Both ended up instituting harsher policies than London wanted, in

D'Urban's case so harsh that he was made to suffer the extreme displeasure of dismissal.

Shifts in frontier policy reflected the tensions within the various locales and levels of the imperial administration. The complaint of the chiefs that one policy followed another with each change of Governor had some justice. But beyond all the rational elements that explained changing frontier policies, the capricious behavior of the imperial state reflected the cultural and psychological processes of the encounter. In order to understand the interaction between the chiefs and the imperial state, we need to look below the surface of policy swings associated with one Governor or another to see the continuities that rippled through the culture of the imperial administration. And we need to ask such questions as: How were the chiefs seen by the imperial state? What was the understanding of the chiefs as political actors and potential allies?

A deep polarity ran through the way the chiefs were understood in imperial culture. We have already seen how commentary on Xhosa society throughout the first half of the century was unable to decide whether the chiefs were constitutional sovereigns or agents of despotism and tyranny. The volatility of imperial policy mirrored the ambiguity and uncertainty at the deepest level of the imperial culture itself as to how it should regard the chiefs.

Just as there are moments in the missionary record when we can see the missionaries struggling to bring their cognitive senses into line with their intellectual beliefs, so there are similar moments among the resident agents of the imperial administration. At one moment, the agents think that they have "got it" in terms of understanding what the chiefs are up to. At another, they are thrown into confusion by some move or development that they do not understand, or have not seen coming. There is a particularly nice example of this from the journal of John Bowker, one of the first of the resident agents. It is an especially relevant example because, as we have seen, Bowker was to become a prominent spokesperson for the hardline settler position on the Xhosa.

In August 1837 Bowker wrote to his superior of an attack by some of Seyolo's people on the local Mfengu. The chief's claim was that the Mfengu had stolen some of his tribe's cattle and he was merely acting to get them back. Bowker was present at an episode in this saga when a Mfengu chief was stabbed, and his initial assessment of this event was that Seyolo was unable to prevent the violence. About 500 Xhosa were present, and "I believe Seyolo did his best to restrain them, but he should not have brought them, for I at that moment saw how little power a Chief has over his people when collected for mischief." But *one day* later, he revised his opinion on this matter, perhaps because the affray continued in full view of his very house. "Although yesterday," he wrote, "I mentioned that the Chiefs used their endeavours to restrain the people – yet – after due consideration I have every reason to conclude that they shewed that disposition in my sights merely to delude me, their object was the destruction of the Fingo settlement at Fort Peddie."

What was it that led him to radically shift his view on this fundamental matter in the course of one day? It is not clear. What is clear is that he was struggling to understand the nature of Xhosa kingship, for he returned to it again and again over the next few weeks. Ultimately, Hudson, his superior, expressed some impatience with Bowker's dithering as to whether the Xhosa chiefs were acting properly or improperly. These tergiversations, Hudson minuted on a letter of 22 August, were "most perplexing and disturbing" because they left unsettled precisely the most important point; that is, whether the Xhosa chief acted as a restraining force or not in the attempt to kill the Fingo chief. If this question could be decided, then the larger question whether the chiefs were at the mercy of the people's will or whether they were in control of what the people did, would be answered – at least according to British logic. Bowker was thus forced to get off the fence. And at the end of August he attributed his reversal of opinion to information that suggested that "no sooner had I left the Kafirs [at the scene of the original attack] to return to the post than Seyolo, Stock etc. joined with and assisted their people in driving off the Fingo cattle." So there it was; evidence of the cunning and deception of the chiefs. They had led him to believe that they were at the mercy of the common people. But when his back was turned they demonstrated that, in fact, they were the ringleaders of the common people's attack on the Fingo.[32]

But did this conclusion follow from the conviction of hard fact, or was it the result of the need to bring these facts into alignment with other things that he also *knew*? I want to draw attention to the point that was suggested at the outset of Bowker's attempt to understand this episode. Bowker clearly indicated a recognition that the chief's power was indeed constrained by tribal politics. Bowker was not alone in this recognition. There is plenty of evidence in the record of the imperial state to illustrate that its administrators understood that chiefly power was closer to that of constitutional monarchs than it was to feudal despots. There were many occasions when resident agents and others encountered the realities of tribal politics, when chiefs needed to consult their *ampakati*, or to work to maintain the support of their people. In other words, what was rediscovered by social anthropologists from the early twentieth century and repeatedly confirmed subsequently, that chiefs were subject to democratic constraints, was *also* known to the imperial administration of this period and place. The fact that it did not form the basis for the consensus view of

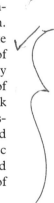

the chiefs in the imperial mind had nothing to do with the "facts." *It had more to do with the cultural and ideological needs of imperial culture.*

Thus, in 1843 Charles Stretch lamented the fact that Maqoma could not enforce a legitimate demand from other chiefs to compensate them for thirty-odd cattle that his people had stolen. Similarly, it was clearly recognized by the imperial administration that Tzatzoe and Khama had lost their power in the traditional way a chief lost his power: by his people packing up and transferring their loyalty to another chief. Part of the problem here was precisely that the imperial administration was intent on using those divisions within tribes to divide and rule. Still, the larger lessons did not escape their gaze. Theophilus Shepstone had to deal with continual tension between Mhala and Gazela in the mid-1840s, when Gazela was being harassed and threatened by Mhala and appealed to Shepstone for protection. The tension stemmed from Gazela's attempt to secure his independence from Mhala by aligning himself with the imperial administration. But it was clearly recognized by Shepstone, and by the missionaries from the Berlin Missionary Society who were advising Gazela, that he had lost the support of most of his people when he transferred his loyalty to Christian and British culture. Thus he was entirely dependent on the imperial state for support, as was Tzatzoe also by this time.[33]

We have seen how, from the very beginning of the imperial state's involvement with the Xhosa, there was an intention to use the chiefs to transmit imperial policy to the tribes. But from the days of Harry Smith and Benjamin D'Urban onwards, there was another aspect of British policy towards the chiefs which was not so explicit and which on the face of it stood in contradiction to the notion of ruling through the chiefs. When Smith addressed the Xhosa chiefs on 7 January 1836, announcing the creation of Queen Adelaide Province and describing the system of government he intended to introduce, he laid out three major themes. The first stated that the Xhosa would continue to be ruled by their chiefs; the second was that magistrates would use British law to advise the chiefs and instill the habits of British culture. But the third element to Smith's scheme was less comforting to the chiefs, and it surely did not escape their sharp ears. One of the great benefits of English law, Smith explained, was that the weak were protected from the tyranny of the strong. As British subjects, the people would be protected from tyranny, and their property would be safe from the system of fines that the chiefs imposed as payment for their administration of Xhosa law. Since the chiefs were now to be deprived of the revenue that they had in the past secured from administering their law, they would be compensated by receiving salaries from the state as payment for their magisterial work. Thus the circle was closed.

The chiefs would become dispensers of English justice and British standards of civilization, the Xhosa would be weaned away from their culture, and the traditional power of the chiefs would be transferred to the legitimating authority of the imperial state.[34]

Undermining the power of the chiefs while using them to accomplish imperial rule had been the clear-eyed purpose of Smith and D'Urban from the outset. The moment peace was declared in September 1835, Smith and D'Urban were writing to each other about the intention of their policy in Queen Adelaide Province to undermine the "system of clanship [which] ... will be at once broken up; and its spirit and feeling will be rapidly subdued and forgotten as the power of the Chiefs will be seen to have ceased and passed away." Smith expected this process to be gradual and silent, so that the chiefs would "find before they are aware of it, their supreme power dissipated and divided and themselves reduced to the more wholesome position of subordinate magistrates (or Field Cornets) acting under prescribed rules and limits." He was aware of the delicate line being walked here. He did not want the chiefs to be "startled in the outset ... Hence it is important to go on gently ... and in due time and when all is ready the laws will assist their own sway and be efficiently felt when they can no longer be resisted or evaded."[35]

Smith and D'Urban were not alone in giving thought to how to remove the obstacles the chiefs posed to imperial rule. An unsigned document in the Cape Archives written about the same time laid out the ur-text of imperial policy towards the chiefs for the next twenty years. The memo argued that the political power of the Xhosa chiefs rested upon their control of the justice system. The chiefs collected cattle fines which were used to enrich their followers. They manipulated cultural practices like witchcraft which, in turn, produced legal cases to adjudicate. The more witchcraft there was, the more cattle fines they could impose, and the more cattle booty could be distributed to the chiefs' followers. In other words, chiefly power and popularity depended upon these superstitions and the legion opportunities for chiefs to manipulate them to this end.

How was this connection between chiefly power and control over cultural customs to be broken? The law, our policy-maker argued, was of little use in this respect. Anticipating arguments that were to become a core part of colonial knowledge twenty years later, it was pointed out that the civil law was not effective against cultural practices like witchcraft. These practices were not susceptible to the kind of rational display of evidence that was the foundational principle of European civil law. In addition, the law offered the Xhosa "so many opportunities to escape punishment [and this] ... to an illiterate Kaffir is a stimulus to the renewal of the crime." In short, Xhosa cunning and deceit would enable them to manipulate the fair operation of

British law successfully in order to evade its application. The best solution to this problem was martial law, which "appears better calculated to govern a people like the Kafir than that of the Civil Law while their internal government remains unaltered."[36]

Thus, even at the very beginning of the British attempts to rule the Xhosa by the indirect rule of the resident agents, the project was seen to be jeopardized by the manipulative cunning of the chiefs and the behavioral DNA of the Xhosa. Even before imperial rule was constructed, the reasoning was available to afford a moral justification for coercive intervention in the internal authority structure of the tribes. The chiefs were naturally expected to be evasive, deceitful and cunning because their very political power depended on their control of evil superstitions like witchcraft. Imperial policy should aim to sever the hold of those dark practices and bring the light of civilization to the tribes. But it could only do so by breaking the power of the Chiefs, and in so doing it would do the work of democratic liberation.

The claim of British policy that was articulated in this memo and by Smith and D'Urban was that *in displacing the power of the chiefs, it was releasing the people from the oppressions of the chiefs and bringing democracy and freedom to the Xhosa.* This claim was to become a central justification for British imperial rule in Xhosaland over the next twenty years. It served as a key rhetorical device and as a self-delusion to allow imperial culture to combine imperial coercion with the traditional values of British liberalism.

The expectation at the beginning was that the chiefs would enter into this bargain and accept the diminution of their power. Indeed, by accepting the mandate of the imperial state to be magistrates, and by receiving the material gifts that the state had to offer, the chiefs were partially complicit in this Faustian bargain. By the spring of 1836, Smith was writing to D'Urban that all was going swimmingly. The people were happy with this development, and the chiefs, too, were accepting of it, he avowed. Smith's claim was echoed by the resident agents (or perhaps it derived from them in the first place). In a letter to Hougham Hudson, John Bowker wrote how the chiefs saw the advantage in the loss of their power to impose various exactions on their people because of the greater security that it brought to the frontier, and therefore the less they would be pressured by the Colony. For their part, the people, "seeing they can live in security will be less liable to be imposed upon [by the chiefs] when they wish to make them their instruments of mischief. Knowing the British government preserves them from the arbitrary power of their Chiefs which they formerly were in constant dread of they will not be easily persuaded to rise up against it." This piece of colonial reasoning illustrated how a key aspect of imperial ideology became firmly established as truth. In addition, in making the claim for the liberating mission of empire, Bowker drew upon the existing discourse that categorized the chiefs as despots. Displacing the tyranny of the cultural practices that the chiefs exercised was both morally right and the duty of empire.[37]

There was, however, the problem of the chiefs themselves. More cautious voices warned of the necessity to proceed carefully. Captain T. Rawston, another resident agent, warned Hudson against revealing the hidden purpose of policy too soon, since the imperial administration still needed the chiefs' assistance in administering justice and controlling the tribes. He advised making considerable allowance for their "hitherto state of perfect freedom and independence" and continuing to allow them profits from their fines. D'Urban himself echoed this call to caution. He advised Smith to be more wary. The ultimate goal of weakening the chiefs' authority remained the same, but he predicted trouble once the chiefs spotted what was happening: "as they perceive the power gliding out of their grasp, then they should resort to an outbreak in the hope of recovery in the tumult. It behooves us to have our eyes open and our post alert and our combinations preconceived."[38]

Had the chiefs been privy to this correspondence, their worst fears would have been amply confirmed. There was a duality to imperial policy that consisted of two logically incompatible aims. On the one hand, the imperial state wanted to secure the loyalty of the chiefs to assist in the implementation of its policies. On the other, it sought to undermine the authority and power of the chiefs. It was this duality that was the root cause of the volatility and the arbitrariness with which the imperial state treated the chiefs. There were times when imperial administrators were honest enough to admit this. During the prologue to the war of 1850–3, at a time when the imperial administration was increasingly aware that events were slipping out of their control, George Mackinnon posed the question directly of how to assure the loyalty of the chiefs while undermining their authority. Writing to Smith, Mackinnon admitted that he had believed that the gifts that he presented to the chiefs in an annual ceremony would be enough to secure their assent. But he saw now that he was mistaken, and his suggested solution was to put the chiefs on a stipend. It was not possible to implement this in October 1850, but it was exactly the solution that George Grey was to introduce in 1856.[39]

We are now in a position to understand more fully where the view of the chiefs as cunning and deceitful conspirators came from. It was a product of the policy aspiration of imperial culture itself. It was a projection by the imperial administration of its own objectives and aims. *The explanation of the chiefs as cunning conspirators was a reflection of the imperial mind itself.* A theme of conspiracy ran through imperial policy toward the Xhosa chiefs, even if it was not consistently and deliberately pursued. Imperial policy was, from the beginning of its engagement with the Xhosa, a conspiracy, which was sometimes kept secret from the chiefs, and sometimes hinted at in the democratic rhetoric of speeches in the ceremonies of display. It was a conspiracy to deceive and trap the chiefs in a dynamic that would lead to their own demise.

The bland cynicism of imperial policy should not surprise us, of course. I wish to make a rather different point. And that is how the conspiratorial intent of imperial policy described exactly the quality that was attributed to the chiefs themselves when it was necessary to explain the failures of imperial policy. When, in late 1850, imperial administrators wondered out loud how the Xhosa could possibly have rejected the benevolent governance of Britain, they could answer that question only by dredging up reasons that described *their* behavior and intent. The importance of the rhetoric of conspiracy in Britain's relationship to the Xhosa is that it is a rather neat example of the reversal that is inherent in colonial reasoning and endemic in the culture of imperial rule: *the practice of projecting on to the indigenes the actual habits of the colonizer.*

The ideology of imperial democracy

Imperial culture, then, was faced with two problems in constructing its beliefs about the chiefs. First, it had to reconcile the contradiction between its policy of enlisting the chiefs in its mission, and its desire to erode the foundations of their tribal authority. Second, it then had to confront the politics of the chiefs' responses; responses that included attempts to find areas of accommodation, but which also featured attempts to evade the grasp of the imperial presence. The evasiveness of the Xhosa was most troubling to the imperial state, for this suggested a rejection of the self-proclaimed benignity of imperial rule. How was the state to explain the refusal of the chiefs to accept the benevolence of its leadership? It needed to explain to itself – as well as to its public in the metropole – why, in the vocabulary of Sir Harry Smith, "his children" persisted in being "bad" and refused to follow the script that had been devised for them.

The answer that it found to these disjunctures and dilemmas was to mark the chiefs as despots, and imperial control as liberating. The chiefs conspired to keep their people mired in a superstitious culture in order to prevent the liberation of their people by Christian and British culture. It was the mission, therefore, of the imperial state to bring democracy to the tribes by breaking the power of the chiefs. The various contradictions within imperial policy could be reconciled and stabilized only if the civil authority of the Xhosa could be seen as dominated by morally corrupt chiefs who manipulated traditional cultural practices in order to maintain their power, and for whom the democratizing mission of the imperial state posed a fatal challenge.

The problem was that at the frontier of empire the contradictions and tensions within this ideology were sharply exposed. Imperial administrators were subjected to experiences that directly contradicted the reasoning that underlay their policies. If the chiefs were despots, then it was possible to believe that empire carried the promise of freedom. But if they were not despots, and subject to the constraints of civic practices and institutions, then how were attempts to displace their authority to be justified by imperial officers? How were such tensions within imperial culture to be contained? For as long as there was uncertainty and debate within the imperial discourse as to the exact character of chiefly authority, the hold of imperial policy and ideology would be unstable. And we can see this tussle in the mind of one frontier imperial administrator in particular: Captain, later Colonel, John Maclean.

Maclean was the single most important imperial administrator on the eastern Cape frontier during our period. He was first appointed to replace Theophilus Shepstone as resident agent at Fort Peddie in December 1845. In late 1852 he was promoted to Chief Commissioner of British Kaffraria to replace George Mackinnon. He remained in that post until 1864, when he was given a knighthood and shuffled off to Natal in preparation for the absorption of British Kaffraria into the Cape Colony. Maclean was an important policy-maker and a tough bureaucratic survivor. He came to know the Xhosa chiefs on a personal level, and from the moment he first encountered them he correctly perceived the complexities of their position. In March 1846, for example, he wrote how "the Chief is dependent upon the good will of the people [and] he finds it necessary to a certain extent to court popularity." The rule of the chiefs, Maclean went on, "is in reality the rule of his Counselors, therefore the general opinion that the Chief holds despotic sway is erroneous." A year later, in an assessment of each of the leading chiefs, he echoed the same sentiments And he was repeating the same assessments to Sir George Grey in the mid-1850s, and when he published his handbook for imperial administrators in British Kaffraria in 1858.[40]

Maclean was a steady supporter of the idea of ruling through the chief; an early practitioner of indirect rule. But Maclean was also committed to undermining their power. In 1847 he wrote of his plans to recruit native police only from those "who have openly cast off the allegiance of their Chiefs." Using these police he actively practiced a policy of "divide and rule" within the tribes under his supervision. Similarly, Maclean did not allow his knowledge of the constraints on chiefly power to colour his judgment of chiefly action. He chose not to understand the chiefs as political beings seeking to balance a variety of competing pressures and interests. Rather, he chose to understand them as shifty, moral reprobates who could not be trusted and must be viewed with profound suspicion. Maclean attributed difficulties with the chiefs to their low moral character rather than to the political milieu they inhabited.[41]

The inherent tension between the competing views of the chiefs could easily tip over, therefore, into a view that demonized their role in the perpetuation of uncivilized and barbaric practices. It was easy for chiefly power to become theorized as the main obstacle to the progress of imperial civilization. We have seen how, by the mid-1840s, missionaries were beginning to argue the necessity of removing the despotic power of the chiefs. By the time he joined the imperial administration, Henry Calderwood was convinced that the cultural practices that the British found so loathsome were directly linked into the system of chiefly authority. For Calderwood, this meant that the structures of political authority served as "the effectual check to all advance on the part of the people and is regarded by the Chiefs and leading men as one of the chief means of subjecting the body of the people to their own mischievous designs." Thus, in explaining to his superiors why it was difficult to secure evidence of crimes committed by notorious and known cattle-rustlers, he attributed it to the duplicitous behavior of the chiefs and the tyranny they exercised over the tribes. "It is almost impossible to get at such evidence in such cases …The people have felt themselves so exposed to the vengeance of the Chief that the cases are very rare indeed in which any will venture to give evidence against them." The conclusion Calderwood drew was that such practices "cannot be tolerated if British authority is to be paramount."[42]

Calderwood was right, although it was to be a few years before his prescription was realized. By the war of 1850–3, the intellectual pieces were in place for imperial culture to explain to itself why the policies of the past had failed. When it was articulated, that explanation boiled down to the juncture between the cultural practices of the Xhosa that resisted Christianization and the structures of civic and political authority of the chiefs. Imperial rule would thus be emancipatory in two respects. It would lift the pall of savage and barbaric culture from the tribes and open the way for the bright light of British civilization. It would also free the tribes from the despotism of their chiefs, and bring them the benefits of democracy. One problem remained, however. The British needed the chiefs to help them rule. And the previous few years had shown the dilemma that this presented. The chiefs were prepared to enter into a relationship with the British state, but they found it impossible to establish a trust relationship with the imperial administration. How was that conundrum to be resolved?

Conclusion: the failure of the eighth frontier war

The challenge of how to fit together British rule and chiefly power was not resolved by the war of 1850–3. The war failed to settle the problem of the chiefs. Although the British declared the war a victory, it was at best a partial victory. Nevertheless, it was a horrible war. The British had to resort to scorched earth policies and other atrocities to wear the Xhosa down. Over 16,000 Xhosa died, countless numbers of cattle were destroyed, kraals were demolished and corn supplies destroyed. Still, in spite of the devastation that British methods of warfare wrought, the Xhosa were not decisively defeated.[43]

The military could not understand why this war could not be won. At the top of the military command there was deep puzzlement that continual sweeps through the enemy strongholds failed to bring any resolution. By the beginning of 1852, Sir Harry Smith had willy-nilly discovered the strategy for gaining the advantage in guerrilla warfare. He set Lieutenant Colonel William Eyre loose on the crops and gardens of the Xhosa in a desperate attempt to destroy their means of subsistence, and he constructed a series of military outposts in the Amatola mountains from which lightly armed patrols constantly swept the territory. Although the frontier wars always featured British destruction of crops and kraals, the innovation introduced by Smith and Eyre was the systematic and coordinated devastation of fields and gardens. Eyre has a claim to be one of the founders of anti-guerrilla warfare in the British Army.[44]

Smith's replacement, Lieutenant General Sir George Cathcart, continued these tactics, although he did not get on well with Eyre. But he did bring new supplies and reinforcements in an attempt to turn the tide by the sheer weight of resources. Nevertheless, Cathcart had no more success than Smith. He was foolish enough to launch an expedition against the Basotho kingdom in an attempt to intercept the aid they were providing to Maqoma. Here was another strategy that prefigured the counter-insurgency campaigns of the twentieth century – going after the sources of support. But Cathcart fared no better than his twentieth-century successors. He was defeated by the Basotho king Mosheshoe at Berea in January 1853. Naturally, this was not admitted in official dispatches, so metropolitan culture was spared from absorbing this "no end of a lesson" fifty years before Kipling trumpeted the thought. But at the company level it was confessed that the Xhosa "must know how anxious we are to make peace."

By February 1853, rumors were rife among the officers that Cathcart was tired of this fruitless war and wanted to get home to the grouse-shooting. He was reported as constantly trying to make peace, using as his excuse that he had been sent out to make peace and clean up Harry Smith's mess and not to make war. Both sides had an interest in calling a halt to the conflict.

Although it was clear that the British could not win this war, it was equally clear that neither could the Xhosa. But the British could keep it up indefinitely if necessary.[45]   .

The conditions that were laid out for the Xhosa were not regarded as very severe. Sandile, for example, was required to surrender only 100 stand of arms. The chiefs were told by Cathcart that they would be allowed to govern the people according to their own laws. It was true that there was the usual displacement from their existing lands. They were pushed back over the Keiskamma and Tyhume rivers, and they lost the Amatolas, whose craggy heights and heavily forested kloofs had been a major strategic asset for the Xhosa in all the previous wars. They were allowed to remain east of King William's Town. But these losses and restrictions were mitigated by the British intention to retain British Kaffraria as a site of imperial social engineering which would be off limits to white settlement. Not surprisingly, the Xhosa did not behave as a defeated enemy. The leading chiefs were reported as looking hale and hearty at the peace meeting of 15 March 1853. Nor were they particularly subdued about the conditions of peace. There were persistent complaints from Sandile and Maqoma that the land assigned to them was neither their traditional land nor large enough. Maqoma continued to press for the return of his old land around the Kat river, as he would to the end of his days. Things had evidently not changed since Harry Smith was faced with the same kinds of demands in 1847.[46]

A year after Cathcart and Sandile met in the Yellow Woods to declare an end to the fighting, spies, missionaries and informers were reporting attempts to create a confederacy between the Xhosa and the Mfengu against the British. This was potentially serious, because there was traditional enmity between these groups, which the British fostered by posing as the protectors of the Mfengu. The Mfengu had been alienated by reports that the Cape Parliament was contemplating a further displacement of their locations. Their unease had been reinforced by attacks on their cultural customs by the superintendent of the Mfengu Fort Beaufort location. Calderwood was sent in to investigate, and he received the usual blank denials from Sandile, although Mhala admitted to taking a Mfengu wife, a sign that something was up. By November, Maclean was declaring the scare over, although a month later Grey was writing to London that he fully expected another war. December was always a month when imperial antennae scanned the horizon, because it was the favorite month for the Xhosa to launch their attacks. In December 1854, rumors abounded about armed men moving around the Crown Reserve and into the Amatolas. Neither Maclean nor Brownlee could figure out what was going on. Eighteen months after the end of the war, the old rhythms of frontier instability had reasserted themselves.[47]

After March 1853 there was a return also to the *status quo ante* in the relationship between the imperial state and the chiefs. Contentious land issues continued to occupy a good portion of the Commissioners' attention, as did the difficulties of knowing when to intervene and when not to intervene in the traditional cultural practices of the tribe. Cathcart clearly recognized that there were more lessons for the British to take from the war than there were for the Xhosa. Like every Governor, he was led to chew on the intractable problem of ruling the Xhosa. Just before he left the Cape he wrote a long memorandum to Maclean, laying out his conclusions that ruling through the traditional authority structure of the tribes was the only way the imperial state could hope to cope with the Xhosa. This was not a piece of original thinking about imperial governance. Indeed, there was nothing in it that had not been said before. Still, it was an interesting document, for three reasons.

In the first place, it reflected the now conventional analysis of chiefly power as feudal and repressive and as needing to be undermined and replaced. It demonstrated how firmly this view was now part of imperial culture. But, in the second place, Cathcart developed the principle of indirect rule more precisely and more clearly than before. He accepted what was now also conventional wisdom, that "the only safe way to govern is through the Chiefs," but he wanted to be sure that they were given the space and latitude to do this. He believed that it was impossible and unwise to "attempt suddenly to anglicize his whole system of government." The chief should be held responsible "as a vassal of the Crown for the good conduct of his people, [to] allow him for the present to govern his Clansmen according to accustomed Kafrarian usage." To this end it was necessary to treat the chiefs with respect, "not with pompous displays of authority, but by frequent personal interviews so as to gain their confidence and esteem and convince them that Her Majesty desires to be their friend and that Her Agents are commissioned to be their advisers and protectors as well as their controllers." Cathcart wanted imperial administration to turn its back on the humiliation and infantilization that were part of the practices of imperial policy. He noted particularly that "we must not destroy the self-respect of these chiefs or degrade them in the eyes of their dependencies."[48]

Finally, however, this document suggested that the war had solved very little in terms of resolving the inherent ambiguity between the chiefs and the imperial state. Indeed, the very fact that explicit assertions of internal independence were made here and elsewhere was a reflection of how incompletely the Xhosa chiefs had been coerced into submission. The lesson that Cathcart took from his time as Governor was that a long-term process of civilizing influences was necessary to displace their power. In 1854 this policy was about to become orthodoxy. Leading imperial administrators like Maclean and Brownlee were very sympathetic to Cathcart's formulation of policy. The Letters Patent for British Kaffraria that were issued at the same time as Cathcart's memo restated the policy of allowing traditional Xhosa customs to continue if they were not repugnant to civilized humanity – which was exactly the formulation D'Urban and Smith had presented twenty years earlier. They also reasserted the intention of the state not to interfere with the authority system and power of the chiefs. The chiefs took note of all this, remembered it for future reference, and presumably were somewhat buoyed. If implemented, such a policy would represent the best possible arrangement of their ambiguous and reciprocal relationship with the imperial state. But neither Cathcart, the imperial administrators, nor the Xhosa had reckoned with the imminent arrival of Sir George Grey, who stepped ashore at Cape Town on 4 December 1854. His ideas were very different indeed.[49]

NOTES

1. The ornamentalism that, David Cannadine has argued, marked imperial social relations is not in evidence here; see his *Ornamentalism: How the British Saw Their Empire* (Oxford, 2001). Cetshwayo's celebrity did not save him from being stripped of the trappings of a sovereign monarch, hunted by British-supported adversaries in a civil war, and ultimately reduced to begging protection from a mean-spirited, small-minded imperial agent named Melmoth Osborne, who is remembered still with hatred in Zululand. Jeff Guy, *The Destruction of the Zulu Kingdom: The Civil War in Zululand 1879–1884* (Pietermaritzburg, 1994), pp. 183–204. See also Neil Parsons, *King Khama, Emperor Joe and the Great White Queen: Victorian Britain thorugh African Eyes* (Chicago, 1998), for a study of other celebrity chiefs.
2. Of the leading chiefs of the era, only Sarhili, the Gceleka chief and formal paramount of the Xhosa, who was the son of Hintsa, managed to escape the grip of the imperial maw. He resided across the Kei in "Independent Kaffraria," but he was not entirely free from the anger of the imperial state; see p. 341. Sandile, chief of the Rharhabe branch of the Xhosa people, bobbed and weaved around the tentacles of the imperial monster, leading in some ways a charmed life until his luck ran out in the last of the frontier wars, 1877–8, when he was killed by Mfengu mercenaries.
3. It certainly became the established interpretation of the war in southern African historiography, see George McCall Theal, *History of South Africa* (Cape Town, repr., 1964), vol. III, pp. 90–3.
4. CA, BK 436, *Letters from the Hlambie Commissioner, 1850*, Maclean to Mackinnon, 29 August 1850, 11 October 1850; BK 371, *Letters from the Chief Commissioner British Kaffraria to the High Commissioner, 1848–1853*, Mackinnon to Smith, 21 October 1850; Anthonic Eduard Du Toit, "The Cape Frontier: A Study of Native Policy with Special Reference to the Years 1847–1866" (DPhil thesis, University of Pretoria, 1949), pp. 103–4.

5. CA, BK 371, *Letters from the Chief Commissioner*, Mackinnon to Smith, 9 August 1851.

6. For this view of the war expressed by missionaries, see CWM, LMS, *Africa, Odds*, Box 9, Brownlee Letters, Brownlow to Tidman, 6 September 1851; CA, A 80 (3), *Ayliff, Journal 1850–51*, pp. 13–18; Robert Godlonton and Edward Irving, *Narrative of the Kaffir War 1850, 1851, 1852* (Cape Town, 1852), pp. 9–11. Note that the only exception to this chorus were the Scottish Presbyterians. But they had very little voice in public discussion, either in South Africa – where they were viewed with deep suspicion – or in Britain itself. See *United Presbyterian Church Magazine*, May 1851, p. 7.

7. CA, LG 404, *Letters Received from the Resident Agent at Fort Peddie, 1841–44*, Shepstone to Hudson, 17 August 1842 and 14 May 1843, for Khama wanting the state to arbitrate between himself and Phato regarding territory. See BK 435, *Letters from Hlambie Commissioner to Chief Commissioner, 1849*, Maclean to Mackinnon, 16 July, 24 August and 25 September 1849, for Mhala cooperating in returning cattle; Maclean to Mackinnon, 11 July 1849; for other examples of cooperation see 24 August, 16 July and 25 September 1849; BK 74, *Letter book of the Tslambi Commissioner, 1849–52*, Maclean to Mackinnon, 3 March and 16 May 1850. LG 407, *Letters ... Fort Peddie 1841–44*, Shulsheift to Shepstone, 20 April 1843.

8. Xhoxho was the chief whose wounding sparked the 1834–5 war. Charles Brownlee devoted a whole chapter to Xhoxho in his *Reminiscences of Kaffir Life and History* (Lovedale, 1896), pp. 320–8. Calderwood regarded him as the archetype of Xhosa duplicity; see CA, GH 8/46, *Letters of Reverend Henry Calderwood*, Calderwood to Woosman, 24 April 1849; GH 8/26, *Chief Commissioner, British Kaffraria,1854*, Maclean to Grey, 2 June 1855; GH 8/35, *Despatches of the Chief Commissioner of British Kaffraria, 1858*, 5 April 1858; GH 8/50, *Demi-Official Letters from British Kaffraria, 1857–58*, Maclean to Grey, 18 December 1857. At the moment of his death, however, Xhoxho's son Herbert, who had been educated at Sir George Grey's school for the sons of chiefs at Zonnebloem, was a member of the emergent black professional classes, working as a teacher at King William's Town; NLSA (CT), *Grey Collection, African Chiefs*, MSB 223, 5, f. 4.

9. See CA, BK 86, *Reports of the Special Magistrate with Kama 1856–58*, Report of Frederick Reeve, 5 June 1857. Note that Reeve supported Khama who complained to the imperial administration. And earlier, the case of Chief Botman provided a similar example of a loyal chief who was actually jailed for an offense although he was not only entirely innocent, but endeavoring to assist the authorities apprehend the culprit. For these see CA, LG 402, *Letters Received from the Diplomatic Agent in Caffraria 1844*, Birt to Borcherds, 4 July; Stretch to Hudson, 4 and 28 July 1844; Borcherds to Civil Commissioner of Albany, Grahamstown, 28 June 1844.

10. See *Reports of the Special Magistrate with Kama 1856–58*, 5 June 1857.

11. Andrew Steedman, *Wanderings and Adventures in the Interior of Southern Africa* (London, 1835), vol. I, pp. 72–3; Charles J. F. Bunbury, *Journal of a Residence at the Cape of Good Hope* (repr. New York, 1969), p. 169; Justus [Beverley Mackenzie], *The Wrongs of the Caffre Nation* (London, 1837), p. 111; Cowper

Rose, *Four Years in South Africa* (London, 1829), pp. 94–5. CA, GH 34/4A, *Letterbook of the Private Secretary to the Lieutenant Governor*, Maj. Gen. Richard Bourke to Sir Richard Plaskett, 16 September 1827. Note that the accusation that Ngqika prostituted his wives seems to have been a common imperial trope employed against the chiefs at this time. Maqoma was accused of exactly the same behavior in 1851.

12. At the gathering of the chiefs called to explain future British policy on 7 January 1836, Smith paid tribute to the person who (he claimed) first suggested they place themselves under the protection of Britain and then reminded them: "Did not your Great Father Gaika on his death-bed assemble his sons around him, and ... tell them to hold fast the word of peace with the English?" Their failure to heed this testament had landed them where they were today, Smith claimed. See the whole report of that meeting by Smith in CA, Acc. 519, *D'Urban Papers*, vol. IV, ff. 8–22; Captain Arthur L. Balfour, *Reply to "The Wrongs of the Kafir Nation"* by Justus (unpublished MS, Townley Hall Papers, 10, 268, National Library of Ireland, Dublin), f. 26; CWM, LMS, *South Africa, Journals 1824–1892*, Box 4, f. 104, J. Brownlee Journal, 30 December 1830, for Ngqika's deathbed warning.

13. But, for the British, this merely proved that he *was* the puppet-master behind the screen. He was "known to be the instigator of war," D'Urban wrote, thus "war on him was justified." NLSA (CT), MSB 142, *D'Urban–Smith Correspondence*, D'Urban to Smith, 17 April 1836.

14. CA, GH 19/4 *Border Treaties, Miscellaneous Papers 1834–45*, ff. 799–809, for a memo describing the events leading up to Hintsa's arrival in D'Urban's camp, which lays out the British case against Hintsa. Note that the young Theophilus Shepstone was the interpreter. For the most athoritative account of his stay in the British camp see NLSA (CT), MSB 16, 1 (3), *Cesar Andrews' Field Diary, 1835*. Transcription of original.

15. An enormous amount has been written about this incident in South African historiography, in part because of the political significance that came to be invested in Hintsa and his generation of Xhosa leaders. Hintsa's body was mutilated and his head removed. Just after the change of regime in southern Africa, the head was reputedly found and, as with the body of Saartje Baartman – the famed "Hottentot Venus" – the demand for its restitution became a momentary political issue. It need hardly be said that this episode is virtually unknown to British imperial historiography. For a sample of the literature on Hintsa, see Jay Naidoo, *Tracking Down Historical Myths: Eight South African Cases* (Johannesburg, 1989). The one source that gives the most authoritative account of his death, by an eyewitness, remains largely unused, and that is Captain Arthur L. Balfour, *Journal of Arthur L. Balfour During a Tour of Army Duty in South Africa 1835–6*, which is MSS 11890–1, Townley Hall Papers, National Library of Ireland, Dublin. Southey was a member of a family of 1820 settlers later prominent in the politics of South Africa; see Alexander Wilmot, *The Life and Times of Sir Richard Southey* (London, 1904).

16. NA CO 537/145, *Supplementary Correspondence, Cape of Good Hope 1834–1838*, Glenelg to D'Urban, 30 December 1835, for the reaction of the Colonial Secretary. It is a remarkable statement of the humanitarian position on the

treatment of indigenes and a scathing condemnation of D'Urban's and Smith's whole way of proceeding. This was the dispatch that ordered the dissolution of Queen Adelaide Province. NA, CO 48/185, *Report of the Court of Inquiry into the Death of Hintza*, for the transcript of the Court of Inquiry. For Smith's plans to subvert the Inquiry see NLSA (CT), MSB 142, *D'Urban–Smith Correspondence*, Smith to D'Urban, 17 April 1836. Balfour, *Journal*, MS 11890, 12 May 1835, where Southey is recorded as having shot Hintsa; compare his testimony on p. 76 of the *Report of the Court of Inquiry*, where he denies seeing Southey shoot Hintsa.

17. On the way the Hintsa story was constructed to serve the purposes of colonial ideology, see Premish Lalu, "The Grammar of Domination and the Subjection of Agency: Colonial Texts and Modes of Evidence," *History and Theory*, Theme Issue 39 (2000), pp. 45–68; Robert Godlonton, *A Narrative of the Irruption of the Kaffir Hordes into the Eastern Province of the Cape of Good Hope, 1834–35* (Graham's Town, 1836), p. 170; Smith was able to include this version of the death of Hintsa in the record of the Court of Inquiry into the death of Hintsa; see NA CO 48/18, pp. 37–65.

18. CA, BK 437, *Letters from the Hlambie Commissioner to the Chief Commissioner, 1851,* 10 January 1851; GH 8/45, *Letters of Captain Maclean 1847*, Maclean to Kreli [Sarhili], 2 January 1847.

19. CA, BK 371, *Letters from the Chief Commissioner, British Kaffraria, to the High Commissioner, 1848–53,* Mackinnon to Smith, 25 January 1849; BK 425, *Letters from the High Commissioner, 1848,* Smith to Mackinnon, 29 January 1849; GH 14/48, *Letters from the Chief Commissioner, British Kaffraria, 1848–1849,* Mackinnon to High Commissioner, 21 January 1849; Brownlee to Mackinnon, 19 January 1849; Brownlee to HC, 21 January 1849. As these letters indicate, the recruitment of Go was a matter of discussion at the highest levels of the administration.

20. CA, GH 8/29, *Chief Commissioner, British Kaffraria, 1856,* Brownlee to Maclean, 20 October 1856; this relationship is similar to those of Shepstone and Goza and of Merriman and Goliath/Mhalakza. Brownlee turned the story of Go into a Victorian morality tale in his *Reminiscences of Kaffir Life and History,* pp. 269–302.

21. For Maclean's spies in 1847 see CA, GH 14/7, *Papers Received from Native Tribes, Diplomatic Agents and Government Officials 1846–48,* Maclean to Hudson, 31 March 1846; GH 8/45, *Captain Maclean's Letters 1847,* Maclean to Woosnam, 14 March and 16 April 1847.

22. CA, GH 8/45, *Captain Maclean's Letters,* 9 and 23 September 1847.

23. For more on Toise see CA, BK 436, *Letters from the Hlambie Commissioner to the Chief Commissioner, 1850,* Maclean to Mackinnon, 27 September and 1, 4 and 11 October 1850. BK 74, *Letter Book of the Tslambi Commissioner, 1849–52,* Maclean to Mackinnon, 22 July 1852; GH 8/29, *Chief Commissioner, British Kaffraria, 1856,* Brownlee to Maclean, 29 June 1856, for the recruitment of another nephew of Mhala. There is a report from the spring of 1856 which described the planning for a new combination of chiefs with Maqoma at its center, and this information even reached the Colonial Office; see NA, DO119/1, *British Kaffraria, High Commissioner's Miscellaneous Correspondence,* Report of Toise, 24 April 1856.

24. For this paragraph see CA, GH 8/29, *Chief Commissioner, British Kaffraria, 1856*, Maclean, "Secret Information," 4 July 1856; BK 436, *Letters from the Hlambie Commissioner*, Maclean to Mackinnon, 22 September 1850, for the report on Umlanjeni; BK 371, *Letters from the Chief Commissioner, British Kaffraria, to the High Commissioner, 1848–53*, Maclean to Cathcart, 30 August 1853; BK 69, *Reports from the Gaika Commissioner 1853–56*, has useful material from Charles Brownlee that illustrates the same theme.

25. CA, LG 683, *Unnumbered Letters Received from the Diplomatic Agent with Faku's Tribe, 1851; Kreli's Tribe 1851–52*, Fynn to Garvock, 4 April 1851; BK 435, *Letters from Hlambie Commissioner to Chief Commissioner 1849*, Toise to Maclean, 22 September 1849; Anta to Maclean, 2 October 1849; Toise to Maclean, 12 October 1849.

26. NA, CO 58/165, *Dispatches Relating to the Kafir Irruption 1835*, Maqoma to James Clark, 18 November 1835, pp. 170–1: "My father was always the best friend to the English Government although he was a loser by them."

27. NA CO 48/165, *Dispatches Relating to the Kafir Irruption*. pp. 26–35. This memo was part of the development of the Glenelg–Stockenstrom attempt to create a frontier policy that would recognize the independence of the Xhosa and afford them some protection from the relentless expansion of the settlers.

28. Norman Etherington, *The Great Treks: The Transformation of Southern Africa, 1815–1854* (Harlow, 2001), p. 317; CA, GH 14/7, *Papers Received from Native Tribes, Diplomatic Agents and Government Officials*, Maclean to Hudson, 24 February 1846. Mqhayi claimed: "I tell you I will never come right again" – referring to his internal authority over his tribe. And he wanted the government to find him a place in the colony just for himself and his family to remove him from this dilemma.

29. CA, BK 436, *Letters from Hlambie Commissioner to the Chief Commissioner 1850*, Maclean to Mackinnon, 15 December 1850. Mhala had a similar conversation in January 1851 with Mqhayi and Siwani, whom he reproved for "sitting still" in the war. Mhala asked what good it would do them. "Was not Hintza killed for sitting still? Where is Mqhayi's greatness now? … Has not Smith taken our charmed sticks from us and broken them? Arise, let us fight, let us die together upon one ridge." BK 437, *Letters from Hlambie Commissioner to the Chief Commissioner 1851*, Maclean to Mackinnon, 10 January 1851.

30. NA, CO 48/33, *Cape of Good Hope, 1817, Lord Charles Somerset Correspondence*, Minutes of the Conference, 2 April 1817.

31. John Henderson Soga, *The South Eastern Bantu* (Johannesburg, 1930), pp. 226–7; Harriet Ward, *The Cape and the Kaffirs* (London, 1851), p. 195; NA CO 48/309, *Dispatches from Governor, Sir Harry Smith, to Secretary Grey*, Brownlee letter 2 November 1850; CA, BK 374, *Schedules of Documents submitted to His Excellency the High Commissioner*, 23 August 1853, copy of a statement Sandile made to Charles Brownlee; GH 8/25 *Chief Commissioner, British Kaffraria 1854*, Brownlee to Maclean, 2 September 1854, explaining Sandile's evasiveness; *United Presbyterian Magazine*, March 1861, p. 43.

32. CA, LG 405, *Letters Received from the Resident Agent at Fort Cox, Fort Peddie 1836–38*, Bowker to Hudson, 2 and 3 August 1837; LG 406, *Letters Received from the Resident Agent at Fort Peddie 1837–38*, Bowker to Hudson, 22 and

29 August 1837. For another example of this phenomenon of volatile understanding of what they saw among the Xhosa, see the account of the first few
months of W. D. Fynn's posting to Sarhili, in LG 404, *Letters Received from the
Diplomatic Agent at Fort Peddie, 1846; Fort Butterworth 1841–43, 1846*, Fynn to
Hudson, 21 March and 8 December 1837, 19 March 1838. Although the title
of this volume places it in the 1840s, in fact it contains the correspondence of
Fynn to Hudson from 1837 to 1842.

33. CA, LG 401, *Letters Received from the Diplomatic Agent of Caffraria, November
1843–December 1843*, Stretch to Hudson, 12 October, 12, 23 and 26 December
1843; LG 407, *Letters Received from the Resident Agent at Fort Peddie 1841–44*,
Shepstone to Hudson, 6 September 1841, 10, 22, 23 and 25 April 1843;
Schulshieft to Shepstone, 6, 20 and 23 April 1843; Gasela's statement,
23 April 1843, shows that he endorsed the view of chiefly power as being
dependent on the support of his people. It was with good reason, then, that
when John Maclean put together his guide to Xhosa laws, it gave recognition
to the fact that the chiefs were not despots, but closer to constitutional
monarchs, surrounded by a tradition of law and advice-giving and constrained ultimately by the ability of their people to pack up and leave them.
See John Maclean, *Compendium of Kafir Laws and Customs*, (Mount Coke,
1858), pp. 23–20, 38–42.

34. Smith's address to the chiefs is in CA, Acc. 519, *D'Urban Papers*, Smith to
D'Urban, 7 Janury 1836, ff. 8–22.

35. CA, Acc. 519, *D'Urban Papers 1836*, D'Urban to Smith, 30 September 1835.

36. CA, LG 420, *Kaffir Papers 1836–1837*, an unnumbered and miscellaneous
collection of letters from official individuals on a variety of topics. This
memo, which is unsigned and undated, is to be found at pp. 141–4.

37. CA, LG 405, *Letters Received from the Resident Agent at Fort Cox, Fort Peddie,
1836–38*, Bowker to Hudson, 10 May 1836.

38. CA, LG 408, *Letters Received from the Resident Agent at Fort Peddie, 1844–45;
Fort Waterloo, 1836–37; Tambookieland 1837–38*, Rawston to Hudson, 4 May
1836; NLSA (CT), MSB 142, *D'Urban–Smith Correspondence*, D'Urban to
Smith, 15 March 1836; CA, GH34/7, *Letter Book of Sir Harry Smith*,
28 January, 12 February 1836.

39. CA, BK 371, *Letters from the Chief Commissioner, British Kaffraria, to the High
Commissioner 1848–53*, Mackinnon to Smith, 20 October 1850.

40. CA, GH 14/7, *Papers Received from Native Tribes, Diplomatic Agents and
Government Officials 1846–48*, document from Maclean, undated, surveying
the T'Slambie District and the chiefs. Note that a version of this survey was
repeated by Maclean in his *Compendium of Kafir Laws and Customs*, pp. 131–9.

41. CA, BK 74, *Letter Book of the Tslambi Commissioner 1849–52*, Maclean to
Mackinnon, 16 May 1850; GH 8/25, *Chief Commissioner, British Kaffraria,
1854, 1854*, Maclean to Grey, 3 November 1855; GH 8/45, *Letters of Captain
Maclean*, Maclean to Pottinger, 16 April and 16 October 1847 for suspicion and
testing of Tzatzoe. He trusted none of the chiefs, even broken-down wrecks
like Jan Tzatzoe, and spied on them all.

42. CA, GH 8/46, *Letters of the Reverend Henry Calderwood*, Calderwood to
Woosnam, 21 and 24 April 1847.

43. The best account of the war is in Noel Mostert, *Frontiers: The Epic Story of South Africa's Creation and the Tragedy of the Xhosa People* (London, 1992), pp. 1015–60; but see also J. B. Peires, *The Dead Will Arise: Nongqawuse and the Great Xhosa Cattle-Killing Movement of 1856–7* (Johannesburg, London, and Bloomington, IN, 1989), p. 25, for atrocities.

44. Peires, *Dead Will Arise*, pp. 21–25; Sir George Cathcart, *Correspondence of Lieut.-General The Hon. Sir George Cathcart. K.C.B. Relative to His Military Operations in Kaffraria, Until the Termination of the Kafir War, and to His Measures for the Future Maintenance of Peace on That Frontier, and the Protection and Welfare of the People of South Africa*, 2nd edn. (London, 1857), pp. 8–11, for puzzlement over how to bring the war to issue. The first attempt to theorize such wars was E. L. Callwell, *Small Wars: Their Principles and Practice* (London, 1896).

45. For a good view of the campaign of this war from the ordinary soldier's point of view, see Africanea Collection, Rhodes House Library, Lumley Graham, *Journal*, 5, 8 and 22 January, 11 and 25 February and 15 March 1853, and the fairly extensive literature published as autobiography later. See, for example, James McKay, *Reminiscences of the Last Kafir War* (1871; repr. Cape Town, 1970); W. R. King, *Campaigning in Kaffir-Land* (London, 1855); Louise King-Hall (ed.), *Sea Saga: Being the Naval Diaries of Four Generations of the King-Hall Family* (London, 1935).

46. CA, GH 8/28, *Chief Commissioner, British Kaffraria, 1856*, Maclean to Grey, 15 March 1856. GH 8/24, *British Kaffraria, Miscellaneous, Sir George Clerk 1853–1854*, for land settlements. There were about 1,200 whites in British Kaffraria in September 1853.

47. NA, CO 897/1, *Papers on the Kaffir War 1851–52*, confidential paper titled "Apprehended Confederacy of Native Tribes on the Frontier of the Cape"; and in the same volume, Governor Sir George Grey to Colonial Secretary Sir George Grey, 19 December 1854, pp. 115–17, Grey to Grey, 22 December 1854, pp. 24–8; GH 19/8, *Papers re. Sandili*, Maclean to Liddle, 21 November 1854.

48. CA, GH 8/24, *British Kaffraria, Miscellaneous, Sir George Clerk 1853–1854*, Cathcart to Maclean, 29 March 1854.

49. CA, GH 8/28, *Chief Commissioner, British Kaffraria 1856*, Maclean to Grey, 15 February 1856, citing the Letters Patent of 7 March 1854. Cathcart had been called back for service in the Crimean War, in which he perished.

10 Empire and liberalism: the creation of the Grey system

Sir George Grey in history

The Cape Colony had never known a governor like Sir George Grey. He was the first modern imperial administrator the colony was to experience. Although he would not have been out of place in the twentieth-century empire, Grey was very much a man of the nineteenth century. He had become an imperial hero as a young man, when he led several successful explorations of the Australian outback. He served as Governor of South Australia in the early 1840s, before moving on to New Zealand, where he introduced responsible government and fought the first Maori war. His career had begun in Ireland, but it was made in the new and farthest reaches of the empire. He combined military credentials with the strengths of an experienced imperial bureaucrat. He was rigid, outwardly self-confident, yet inwardly somewhat insecure and paranoid. He was able and intelligent and subject to moods of depression and doubt. He combined a firm intellectual grasp of policy details with an absolute clarity of vision for the ends of his policy. But his supreme strength was the necessary force of will to push his objectives through the obstructionism of those below him and the nervous uncertainties from those above. These attributes were undoubtedly assisted by the fact that Grey was an accomplished, self-righteous liar.

Grey was also a universal humanitarian. It was this that made him a perfect representative of the liberalism of the nineteenth-century empire. He did not believe that the Australian aborigine, the New Zealand Maori or the South African Xhosa was intrinsically inferior to the white man. He believed their mental capacity was quite as great as that of the European. Indeed, to his credit, he took a deep interest in the peoples he was assigned to rule. Grey collected the artifacts and studied the ethnography of the native societies he ruled. He was the only Governor to learn Xhosa. He wrote a handbook of native Australian dialect and a scholarly study of Polynesian society, although his material was actually produced by a Maori historian whom Grey had hired.[1]

Grey was a quintessential representative of how nineteenth-century liberalism reconciled itself to the building of empire. He believed that native African and Australasian cultures were antithetical to enlightened progress. He did not believe they would change naturally, or that it was possible to wait for this to happen. To awaken the sleeping capacities of such peoples, a program of social, political and cultural intervention was necessary. Grey's rhetoric and discourse were consistent with the move in evangelical humanitarian ideology away from the idea that civilization would follow conversion and toward the idea that civilization had to be introduced first, using the coercive power of the state. It was natural, therefore, that Grey was a favorite of the humanitarian lobby in London. But in both New Zealand and especially in South Africa, his policy exposed the dark side of British liberalism. Grey was a bold practitioner of legal lynching and violent methods. Grey sat astride the central fault line of liberalism's intellectual contradiction when confronted with empire. He had no compunction about using the methods of despotism to bring liberal freedoms to the people of empire. Grey personified what the empire did to Victorian liberalism; how it forced it inside out, to become the very reverse of itself.[2]

When he arrived at the Cape in November 1854, Grey was at the top of his game. He came with a history of success in New Zealand. He had shown the Maoris the steel of force and brought them to an equitable and peaceful reconciliation with the New Zealand colonists. It was with this perception of Grey that the Colonial Office sent him off to the Cape with a mandate to bring a lasting stability to British Kaffraria. In response to his importuning that this would cost money, the government of Lord John Russell stuffed his pockets with a special subsidy of £45,000 to do it. His promise was that he would turn British Kaffraria into a very model of how Britain could civilize savage races. It must be said of Grey that he was as good as his word.[3]

Grey has figured very large in the historiography of New Zealand. He has a presence in South African historiography. But this exemplar of the mid-nineteenth-century liberal empire is virtually invisible in the imperial historiography. Why this should be is something of a mystery. Perhaps it has something to do with the fact that Grey ultimately found colonial society more to his liking than the metropole. From the time of his arrival in Australia in the late 1830s he spent most of his life in the southern hemisphere; so it was not surprising that after his second stint as Governor of New Zealand from 1861 to 1868 he stayed on to have a distinguished provincial political career. It is impossible to say what imperial historiography thinks of Sir George Grey. He is hardly to be glimpsed in the new standard works on empire. The last original consideration of his career,

Rutherford's *Sir George Grey*, was published as long ago as 1961, and that by a New Zealand historian. In many ways this is a fine piece of scholarship. But its treatment of Grey's policy in British Kaffraria serves as an example of how easy it is to write the underside of empire out of its history.[4]

Rutherford's calm and measured account of Sir George Grey's inter-action with the Xhosa sanitized the story. Rutherford recognized that Grey's policy towards the Xhosa was driven by the desire to destroy the power of the chiefs. Yet his summary of all this contrasts with the violence of the actual historical story. Silence and denial ran through his account: silence about the tragic denouement for the Xhosa in the final days of their independence, and denial about the chaos and brutality that were the natural partners of Grey's policies. For Rutherford, the chiefs were "unruly" and deserved to be "punished." When Rutherford came to sum up Grey's governorship in the Cape, the weight of attention rests on the difficulties of Grey's relations with the Colonial Office: how the long-suffering Colonial Office finally lost patience with Grey's lies and deceit and forced him out. All these matters are discussed in an honest and serious manner that contrasts sharply with the shroud of silence that is cast over the human cost to the Xhosa and their leaders of their encounter with Grey.[5]

Rutherford's choice of emphasis in this conclusion is almost entirely misplaced. Grey's relations with the Colonial Office are of little significance as a historical problem and are of interest to no one except Grey and the Colonial Office. What Grey did to the Xhosa is of far greater historical moment. Yet this matter receives precisely one paragraph of attention in Rutherford's conclusion. And what a paragraph it is! Rutherford begins by disowning Grey's "native policy" as being "founded on certain basic mis-conceptions which were common at that time." Yet he quickly moves on to exculpation. Ultimately, Rutherford claims, Grey had no alternative but to take forceful measures against the Xhosa. "There was never much prospect of his winning the confidence of the Chiefs, [and so] any solution would have had to be imposed authoritatively from above." What follows is in contradistinction to all the evidence presented earlier. In any case, Rutherford continues, Grey's authoritative imposition was a fairly trivial affair. "His coercion did not go beyond a demonstration of force, a few somewhat irregular armed police expeditions, and a rather free use of martial law. [Furthermore,] His handling of the cattle-killing crisis was technically superb." And in the final analysis his policy was regarded as a success. "It was only the Kafirs who disliked it, and some of them derived some benefits from it." Indeed.[6]

These few sentences serve to deny and silence one of the great atrocities of empire. In this way was recorded the story of the gutting of the customary authority and political power of the Xhosa chiefs, and the final destruction of the independence of the Xhosa nation. Rutherford skated over the punitive raids into Independent Kaffraria by the Frontier Armed and Mounted Police in a hunt for Sarhili, son of the murdered Hintza. The narrative ignored the tens of thousands of Xhosas who were in effect deported into the Colony. The destitution and starvation that ran through that blighted land in 1858 was similarly ignored. Rutherford's account was silent on the legal persecution of the chiefs, and on the reduction of British Kaffraria to a labor reserve for the Colony, with many of the chiefs being sent into domestic service or to public works labor themselves. And in all of this Rutherford blames the Xhosa for the destitution and despair that marked their society!

More recently, it is true, the story of Sir George Grey and the destruction of the Xhosa chiefs has been told in a way that departs radically from the interpretation of Rutherford. In his book *The Dead will Arise*, J. B. Peires demonstrated how the cattle-killing delusion that swept over Xhosland in 1856–7 was used by Grey as the perfect opportunity to target the chiefs for political destruction. He exposed the brutal methods that Grey's magistrates used to split the tribes, bring recalcitrant chiefs to their knees, and create the correct conditions for true indirect rule in British Kaffraria. So, if the story of the cattle-killing and the expansion of British rule has been told so thoroughly and so well before, what would be the reason to bother telling it again?[7]

There are several reasons why it is worth revisiting. The first has to do with historiography. For Peires, the cattle-killing was the central moment in nineteenth-century Xhosa history. It marked the end of their independence and the reduction of their society to an appendage of British imperialism. In the memory of Xhosa society the cattle-killing occupies the same place that World War I did for twentieth-century Britain. That memory is a constant theme of modern Xhosa culture. As late as 1927 there were live disputes and political fault lines in Sarhili's old tribe as to who bore the responsibility for the advice he received during the cattle-killing that led him to grant credence to the prophecies. In more recent times, Zakes Mda, the South African novelist, framed his novel *The Heart of Redness* around the way the events and divisions between the believers and unbelievers in the prophecies of the mid-1850s continued to resonate in Xhosa society. The Xhosa came to view the cattle-killing as a plot by Grey, assisted by the missionaries, to clear the land for the British and the German legionnaires that Grey wanted to settle in British Kaffraria as a military-settler protective barrier.[8]

Sir George Grey is therefore more alive to Xhosa memory than he is to British. I wish to claim both Grey and the cattle-killing for British imperial history. Imperial historiography has tended to ignore this nasty little episode of empire. It is appropriate to try to remedy this silence. For the deeds and actions that undid the chiefs and gutted civil society in British Kaffraria were done by upstanding Victorian gentlemen. They were exemplars of the culture of Britain's *liberal* empire. And as such, they need to be brought into the full light of history.

The cattle-killing is a complicated historical phenomenon. There is considerable disagreement among South African historians as to its exact significance. But it seems best to see it as a combination of a prophylactic veterinary strategy that got entangled with the internal politics of the tribes and cultural traditions about resurrection and redemption. Thus the killing of cattle began as a thoroughly sensible response to the lung sickness that began to infect Xhosa herds from 1855. This was not the first time that lung disease had ravaged the herds. But it was the most serious to date and was a consequence of increased European contact. Almost from the beginning, however, millenarian prophecies were associated with the cattle-killing. This, too, was not unprecedented. In the past, when tensions with the British were rising, prophets had appeared urging the Xhosa to kill their cattle as part of a national cleansing necessary for war. In the mid-1850s, as in previous episodes, these prophecies were a curious amalgam of Christian imagery and traditional Xhosa belief. The Xhosa were urged to redeem their wickedness by rejecting witchcraft. They were promised that their ancestors would arise to lead them to salvation from the British. In 1856–8, however, the cattle-killing reinforced the destruction of herds through lung disease and played into the political divisions that were a permanent part of Xhosa politics.[9]

My concern, however, is less with these matters and more to see the cattle-killing as an episode in the encounter between the British and the Xhosa since the 1820s. Sir George Grey was a central figure in this story. But he was also playing a walk-on part on a stage that had been under construction since the 1820s. The cattle-killing and the destruction of the chiefs was the climax to a history that began in the 1820s. Grey brought to fruition a project that had been lurking within the imagination of imperial culture since Smith and D'Urban created Queen Adelaide Province in 1835–6. The Xhosa cast of characters for this final act had been assembled in the 1820s. All of those who were to play leading or bit parts in the drama of the cattle-killing and the destruction of the chiefs had known the British since the 1820s. Mhala, Maqoma, Sandili, Sarhili, Phato, Kama, Tzatzoe, Soga, Kobe Kongo – all of them had interacted with the British from the very first days of its encounter with the Xhosa. They were the children of Ngqika, Ndlambe and Hintsa. They had spent the previous thirty years or so trying to figure out how to cope with the imperial state. They were now about to confront the leading representative of Britain's liberal empire. They were to discover that there was no coping to be done.

In addition, Grey's policies in British Kaffraria rested on ground that had been prepared over the previous twenty years. Little of what Grey wanted to do was new. Most of the policies he brought with him had been laid out by earlier imperial administrators or missionaries. There was a consensus around the need to socially engineer a moral reformation of Xhosa society. There was a similar agreement that the power of the chiefs was the prime obstacle to both this and the advance of imperial power. The expectation of Sir Harry Smith that he could replace the traditional content of chiefly authority with the ideology of British civilization was consonant with Grey's aspirations. The difference was that Grey succeeded where Smith failed. He did so for a variety of reasons. But most of all he succeeded because circumstances allowed him to launch a serious assault on the chiefs. Smith had aimed to seduce, coopt and overawe with his bombast. Grey used weapons that were handed to him – principally starvation – and ruthlessly deployed a few of his own, including the majesty of the law.

Grey visits the frontier

Grey was sent out to the Cape Colony by a government committed to fiscal and social conservatism at home and in the empire. Grey's mandate was to follow the policy that Cathcart had left in place. Peace was to be kept on the frontier, and there were to be no more costly adventures such as had been seen in the previous few years. Grey had no intention of abiding by his instructions. As early as 1841 he had formulated his credo regarding indigenous peoples in a memorandum he sent to London from Australia. His experience with the Maori qualified him as an expert in handling natives. He believed in the necessity of coercive intervention in their cultures and customs in order to free them from the stultifying restraints of their traditions. He believed in the democratizing mission of empire. He believed in the necessity of white settlers living among the indigenes to transmit the values of civilized society. And he believed in using the power of the state to engineer the essential social and moral reformation to move these peoples toward this imperial nirvana. He arrived in Cape Town knowing what needed to be done.[10]

That is not the same, however, as knowing exactly how it was to be done, or exactly when it was to be done. Almost the first thing Grey did after his arrival was to travel up to the frontier to see British Kaffraria for himself. When he got there he found the groundwork already prepared for his schemes. The missionaries were primed to welcome the helping hand of the state. There were plenty of supplications, therefore, for the seed corn of Grey's £40,000, and he scattered it liberally around. He funded Anglican schools in Mhala's and Sandile's tribes. He give money to Richard Birt for a girls' boarding school, and to Lovedale to support a new industrial arts curriculum there. He awarded £900 for an industrial school in the Fingo location. He funded the establishment of the Heald Town industrial school by the Methodist missionaries.

Nor did Grey confine himself to supporting educational institutions. He put state money into agricultural improvement. Grants of plows and the cutting of water courses now became the business of the government rather than the work of individual missionaries. Naturally enough, the chiefs responded eagerly and greedily to this new-found source of largesse. Brownlee and Maclean were inundated with requests for support. More ominously, Grey started schemes of employment on public works. He directed Maclean to begin to hire labor to cut roads. The dual aim was to provide easy military access and to demonstrate to the Xhosa the practical advantages of wage labor. By the end of the year he was trumpeting to the Colonial Office his cleverness in using the Xhosa themselves to conquer their own country. He was fortunate in his time, of course. An ever-enlarging supply of ready labor was available as lung sickness among the cattle made its way across British Kaffraria. The Xhosa response to the lung sickness was eminently sensible: they killed their herds in an attempt to stop the infection. But this also caused economic hardship, and so more and more males were freed up for wage labor on government schemes or in the Colony itself. Xhosa society had begun to be hollowed out long before cattle-killing turned from a prophylactic veterinary strategy to the politics of delusion.[11]

Grey left British Kaffraria encouraged and buoyed. On his return to Cape Town, he wrote to Maclean about his scheme for settling military pensioners around King William's Town as the first stage of leavening Xhosaland with white colonists. This signaled the first clear move away from the policy that British Kaffraria should be a homeland for the Xhosa alone. In his first major speech to the new Cape Parliament in March 1855 he announced his plans to remake British Kaffraria in the image of British civilization through schemes of social and political reformation. He employed the rhetoric of Christian duty and imperial commitment. It was stirring stuff. What was not explicit, but what was certainly percolating in Grey's mind, was the intention to subordinate the chiefs to the authority of the imperial state.[12]

These plans, however, were laid bare in a confidential communication to his Chief Commissioner in British Kaffraria, John Maclean. He wrote to Maclean on 26 July 1855 of the opportunity the lung sickness epidemic presented to expand British control in British Kaffraria. The more cattle that were killed, the more the currency of chiefly power would be under-mined. Since cattle were the main source of fines and other payments to the chiefs, the killing will "remove the advantages which the Chiefs and Counsellors derived from this barbarous mode of administering justice and present a most favourable opportunity for introducing a new system for the administration of justice." He then outlined to Maclean a specific series of bold, indeed radical, proposals. He intended to expand the numbers of magistrates currently serving with the Xhosa. He wanted to put the chiefs and counselors on the imperial payroll, paying each a salary for defined duties. He proposed to reinforce the judicial role of the magistrates, who would sit with the chiefs as adviser and assessor. Fines would be monetized, and they would be paid to the government, not the chiefs. Magistrates would move around the country assigned to them, encouraging modern agricultural techniques and the methods of industry and generally promoting civilization.[13]

Exactly what Maclean knew about this before it arrived on his desk in dusty King William's Town is not clear. But his initial response was extremely negative. Maclean was unnerved by the radical implications of the scheme. He saw that it threatened to decisively disrupt the way relations with the chiefs had been conducted over the previous twenty years. It is unlikely that this memo was the first inkling Maclean had of what Grey had in mind. But if that was so, it makes his frank and discouraging response on 4 August even more interesting as illustrating the considerable opposition Grey faced from the imperial administration. Maclean scathingly critiqued the proposal as the "work of theorists in Cape Town" who had no knowl-edge of the frontier. He suggested that the scheme was doomed to failure because it would alienate the chiefs and perhaps drive them to war. He was particularly doubtful of Grey's scheme to increase the power of the magis-trates so that they would be supreme over the chiefs.[14]

Maclean's doubts were well placed. Grey's scheme rested upon a series of false assumptions about the nature of chiefly power. It reduced the problem of chiefly authority to a simple perception that reflected exactly in broad and crude outline the understanding of chiefly power that had emerged over the past twenty years. He attributed the insecurity of the frontier to the arbitrary power they possessed, and the way they secured power and wealth in their tribes through the system of fines they imposed as part of their judicial administration of traditional law. He argued that this meant that no man's property was secure from seizure by the chiefs and that a culture of theft was therefore built in to the structure of chiefly power. Once the chiefs were put on a salary, the system of fines would be made redundant and the root cause of instability on the frontier would be removed. From this, everything would follow. Property would be more secure, a stimulus would be given to industry, and the creation of a revenue stream would be stimulated.

There was not much in this analysis that was new to frontier officials like Maclean. Indeed, it presented a view of the chiefs they themselves had propagated. But Maclean's first concern was that Grey's schemes would upset the way things were done on the frontier. As we have seen, the imperial administration was complicit in traditional Xhosa cultural arrangements. Not only had they previously supported the chiefs' administration of justice; they had also trafficked in cattle currency themselves, levying and demanding fines in cattle. Relations between the frontier officials and the chiefs had settled into a kind of mutually comforting pattern of intimacy in which each side basically understood the moves the other made and the rules of behavior governing their conduct. Thus, for both the chiefs and the frontier officials like Maclean, it was the imperial state at the regional level (i.e. Cape Town) that was the destabilizing factor.

But Grey was a master of moving sideways toward his objective. In his response to Maclean – which came in the form of a conversation on a second trip to the frontier in September – he denied any intention of radically departing from the system of rule already in place. Maclean must have misunderstood, he averred. He asserted his intention that the magistrates only act as advisers to the chiefs and that the will of the chief should prevail in the event of difference. His expectation was exactly the same as that of Smith and D'Urban when they had appointed the first resident magistrates in 1836: "that talented and honorable European gentleman being in constant contact with the Chiefs will exercise a great improving role and gain an influence over them which in the course of time will induce them to adopt our customs and laws in place of their own, which the system I propose to introduce will gradually undermine." And he announced that he intended the first two magistrates to be John Cox Gawler and Frederick Reeve. Gawler was to be posted to Mhala's tribe, and Reeve to Maqoma's.[15]

How are we to understand this curious little spat between Grey and Maclean? I think it suggests three conclusions. The first is that there was genuine disagreement within the imperial bureaucracy on how to move in regard to the chiefs. Some saw the opportunities presented by the lung sickness quite early; others took longer to come around to the view that it provided a golden opportunity to strike a decisive blow against chiefly power. Administrators like Maclean and Brownlee were burdened by their knowledge of the past and came fairly late to Grey's view. They were aware that the Xhosa chiefs had not been decisively defeated in 1853, and were not now behaving like a defeated people. In November 1854, Maclean wrote to the secretary to the government in Cape Town of a projected Xhosa–Fingo alliance. This was a common fear of the frontier officials. Frontier officials like Maclean knew that dealing with the chiefs and tribes was in practice a matter of continual negotiation and navigation through uncertain territories. They had seen Governors come and go; they had heard schemes like Grey's before. But the practice of day-to-day relations with the chiefs had changed little. They were committed to a system that had become familiar, whereas Grey was an outsider who knew what he knew from "theory."[16]

The second conclusion is that this episode was a classic example of Grey's bureaucratic insinuation. There is little doubt that Maclean's original reading was correct. Grey intended to use the decimation of the cattle herds through the lung disease to attack the structure of chiefly power. But Grey's original letter was so cautiously phrased as to ensure deniability – a reflex of the skilled bureaucratic manipulator. And deny Maclean's reading is what Grey did. In the communication of September he disingenuously assured Maclean that he was mistaken. Yet the subtext was a dogged adherence to his program. Grey continued to pull back from any suggestion of a radical move when it suited him, even as his plans pressed ahead. Similarly, he assured Brownlee – another skeptic – that he would be the lead magistrate in the scheme, and that only once a new working relationship with Sandile had been established would the scheme be extended to the other chiefs. In fact, Grey probably had no intention of so proceeding. In their attempts to put the brakes on Grey's schemes, poor Maclean and Brownlee were easily outmaneuvered by the vastly more experienced Grey.[17]

But third, and most interestingly, Maclean's opposition also reflected a deeper psychological tension within Maclean himself about the intellectual assumptions of Grey's program. Maclean knew very well that to present the chiefs as all-powerful manipulators of tribal politics was false. But Maclean himself had fostered and encouraged this analysis of chiefly power. His surveillance system was constantly scanning for evidence of the chiefs as conspirators; and he also explained the culture of superstition in the tribes as the product of chiefly manipulation. The tension between this view of the chiefs and the (more accurate) one that saw them as subject to democratic constraints was built into the psychology of imperial administrators. Only an outsider like Grey was exempt from that tension; hence his ability to hold a confident rectitude and clear-sighted determination. For Maclean it was more complicated. On the one hand, the assumptions of the Grey scheme about the nature of chiefly power were the assumptions that Maclean used every day as an imperial administrator. They were the discourse of imperial culture.

But, on the other hand, Maclean also knew better. He had an intimate relationship with these men; he worked with them as collaborators as well as opponents, and he could observe the way they operated within the context of tribal politics. Somewhere in his brain was the knowledge that these assumptions were not the whole story. Like Brownlee, he had spent too long in Kaffraria not to have seen the constraints on chiefly power. Therefore, his ability to hold what was now the emerging conventional wisdom of imperial culture regarding the chiefs was unstable. His resistance to Grey's scheme surely reflected that instability. It was this tension between Maclean's commitment to the ideology of chiefly power that imperial culture had invented over the years, and his own knowledge that it was at best a series of half-truths, that lay at the base of his hesitations when it came to Grey's scheme. But since Grey's policy objectives also reflected the logic of imperial rule since 1835, a logic that Maclean himself was obviously fully committed to, he could not long resist Grey's logic. His resistance soon crumbled, as did the reservations of Brownlee.

The Grey system was irresistible also because of the continuities it possessed with prior imperial policy since the days of Smith and D'Urban. The idea that magistrates would sit with the chiefs and guide them in the direction of British standards of justice on certain issues, leaving other matters to customary law, was exactly what Harry Smith had in mind in 1835–6. The expectation that they would act as beacons spreading civilized light over the culture of the tribes was also standard utopian imperial ideology. Similarly, the idea of putting the chiefs on salaries had been around from the beginning. Even Grey's aspiration – which he carefully kept out of any correspondence – to make the magistrate the final authority over the chief was not divergent from earlier aspirations. The principle of intervening in traditional custom only when it involved matters repugnant to "civilized" standards (such as murder and rape) had in practice been subject entirely to local circumstances. Grey was proposing to end this indeterminacy by establishing once and for all the undivided authority of the resident magistrates.[18]

The chiefs instantly recognized Grey's scheme as a threat. They correctly spotted the key element of originality in the plan – its promise to install a more penetrating imperial bureaucracy deep into the culture and polity of the tribes. Grey proposed to regularize the appointments of the magistrates and to standardize their responsibilities and powers.

Persuading the chiefs

The first task therefore was to get the chiefs to agree to go on the imperial payroll and to receive the magistrates. A concerted effort to achieve this began in September 1855 and ran through the early months of 1856. As was always the case when the chiefs dealt with the imperial state, the pull of mutual interest exerted itself. Grey met with Sandile in September and told him of his intention to put him and the other chiefs on salary, and Sandile welcomed this news. Brownlee then met with Maqoma and Sandile and gave them the news about the magistrate. Neither seemed to realize that salaries were to replace their control over fines. Sandile urged that his lesser chiefs also be given salaries, otherwise they would be a tax on his income. The control over salaries was to be a flashpoint of conflict in the system, yet at first Sandile positively welcomed it.

Sandile's behavior could have been predicted. Although Grey seems to have deliberately left certain things unsaid in his meeting with the chief in September, we should not assume that Sandile was blind to where things were tending. His preferred strategy was to embrace the initiatives of the imperial state and then wait for its pressure to slacken off. In this way, Sandile had long succeeded in evading the full weight of imperial power and in preserving a degree of independence throughout the twists and turns of frontier policies. Maqoma was more reserved and noncommittal. He was playing his traditional part, too, as the most serious potential opponent of the British. It was not surprising, therefore, that by October Brownlee was looking at Maqoma as the key to the successful introduction of the system. At all events, by the middle of October it was clear that all was not to be plain sailing, and Brownlee was soon warning against pushing the chiefs too hard.[19]

Brownlee had flagged the growing unease of the chiefs at a meeting with Sandile, Maqoma, Fynn and Xhoxho and their various counselors in October. Brownlee explained that henceforth the chiefs would become salaried servants of the state. They would cease to collect cattle fines; they would be subject to the supervision of the magistrates; and various schemes of social reform would instill industrious habits into their people. After he had finished, the objections began to be heard. The chiefs remained silent. It to fell to Old Soga, Sandile's senior counselor, to lay out the arguments against the system. His speech is worth noting as the voice of the subaltern addressing the hypocrisies and manipulations of the imperial state. Soga saw right through Grey's intention. It suggested how well the Xhosa *knew* imperial culture. Soga objected to the measure

as breaking down the customs of the Kaffirs, depriving the Chiefs of the concessions which Sir George Cathcart had made to them of governing their people according to their own laws, and what the Chiefs' counsellors would secure from salaries would not be equal to what they now had as a source of revenue. It was also asked why the Governor wished to change the present system, who had complained of it and if he could change what Sir George Cathcart had conceded to them why can he not change what the former Governors had done with regard to land and restore their country to them?

Brownlee engaged the metaphors of children and paternal kindness to repeat Grey's lies, which he may have believed: that the "Governor would do nothing by force, that his only desire was to teach the people and to convince them by kindness," and he extolled at length the advantage to the chiefs of a regular salary. Sandile began to backtrack on his earlier commitment. He objected to the loss of chiefs' rights over their cattle fines and announced he could make no answer until he had consulted with other chiefs.[20]

It is perhaps useful to pause here a moment to remark on Soga's appeal to the policies of Cathcart. We have noted earlier how Cathcart's parting shot as Governor was a memo that recommended that British policy allow the chiefs to retain their traditional authority to administer Xhosa customary law. Cathcart was drawing upon his frustrating experience in first trying to defeat the Xhosa and then trying to negotiate with them. By the beginning of 1856, Grey was to realize how strongly the Xhosa chiefs believed in this commitment, and that it posed a serious obstacle to the rapid implementation of his system. And so he requested a history of the issue from Maclean. Until this moment, Grey had given no indication that he was aware of the matter. Assuming that he was not being disingenuous (a big assumption to make about Sir George Grey), this meant that he had not read the files, had not received full briefings from Maclean and others, or had paid no attention to the warnings. We know that Maclean had expressed his doubts about Grey's policy, and it is hard to believe that in conversation with Grey he had not elaborated on the arguments of his memo of September 1855. My own interpretation, therefore, is that Grey was not initially interested in listening to Maclean on this issue. He had, after all, come to southern Africa with a policy already in his head. Grey was only acting out the tendency of imperial culture to ignore history in pursuit of its will.

One can imagine the quiet pleasure Maclean took in giving Grey this history lesson. In a long memo of 15 February 1856 he took Grey through the various commitments made to the chiefs that they would be allowed to govern themselves. The most recent commitments began with Smith in January 1851, when, besieged on all sides, he was desperately trying to stem the rush to rebellion and to contain the spread of the uprising. It had been repeated subsequently to individual chiefs, particularly Mhala and Phato. *Significantly, it was these two chiefs who were to be the strongest resisters to Grey's scheme.* Cathcart had reiterated the pledge at his first meeting with the chiefs in October 1852, when he, too, was becoming eager to end the war. And during the negotiations in March 1853, which brought hostilities to an end, he had "formally stated to them [the chiefs] that henceforth the Chiefs should be allowed to govern their people according to their own laws." That same principle was encoded in the Letters Patent for British Kaffraria that were issued on 7 March 1854, which repeated the familiar formula that there would be no interference with Xhosa customs except in those repugnant to civilized humanity. Surely Grey was aware of all this? So Maclean concluded that neither he nor Brownlee entertained the slightest doubt "but that the same is held by every Chief in Kaffirland as an acknowledged principle of our rule over them." Indeed, he claimed, in the years since the end of the last war, some chiefs had begun to test where the boundaries of their power lay by putting people to death for witchcraft, something the British had always claimed lay outside their realm of tolerance.[21]

This history, Maclean pointed out, was the well-grounded basis of Soga's objections. The Xhosa were accustomed to the capricious arbitrariness of the imperial state, and they surely sensed that Grey's purpose was to rip to shreds the principle of cultural autonomy for the Xhosa. Nevertheless, by December some progress had been made in getting the chiefs to agree to become salaried by the state and to accept magistrates. Since September 1855 Brownlee and Maclean spent much of their time working to persuade the chiefs to accept the system. The chiefs maintained a united front, deferring to Sandile. Sandile, in his turn, told Brownlee he would make no decision until he had consulted the chiefs! This was the familiar style of chiefly negotiation: deferring to the senior chief while the senior chief deferred to consultation with the others. It was reminiscent of Ngqika and Hintsa's dealings with the first missionaries in the 1820s. It must have infuriated imperial administrators.[22]

In the effort to crack the united front of the chiefs, the ceremony of the public meeting was employed to convey a sense of consultation and inevitability. Maclean was reluctant to revive this method of personal rule. But Brownlee advised Maclean that it was the only way to communicate effectively and to secure the chiefs' consent. Passing the issues around to the individual chiefs would never secure an answer, he reported; each would wait on all the others. Thus a meeting with the Ndlambe chiefs was held at Fort Murray on 24 October 1855. It seemed to secure the essential breakthrough. Thirty thousand were reported as being present, including such leading pro-government chiefs as Khama and Jan Tzatzoe, Siwani and Phato. They asked for an adjournment so that they could consult Mhala. But they met again with Maclean on 30 October and reported that he still refused to commit. At this point Toise, Siwani and Tzatzoe accepted unconditionally. Khama, the one truly Christian chief, still refused to commit. On 3 November a joint meeting of the Ndlambe and Ngqika branches of the Xhosa was held, at which the official announcement of the policy was made. At this meeting, the objections raised in October were repeated. The difficulty resolved itself into the presence of European magistrates and the removal from the chiefs' authority of the right to fine.

Maclean explained to Grey that the latter issue was so deeply entrenched in the customary rights of the chiefs that he felt it best to try to compromise on that point, and so he had agreed that the customary fining system should remain in place.[23]

On the face of it, this was quite a concession. In the actual event, it turned out to count for little. Aggressive magistrates rode roughshod over the agreement, which was, in any case, verbal only. But at the time it served to break the logjam of a united opposition. Following this meeting, it was announced that Khama and Phato were willing to accept the scheme. In the middle of November it was announced that Mhala had sent word that he agreed to the proposal. Sandile, ever the cautious and evasive chieftain, held out until December, and it seems that he did so partly to negotiate an assurance that Brownlee would continue to be his magistrate. Once this was assured, on 11 December, he gave in.

This provided Grey with the essential endorsement of the senior Xhosa chieftain. It caused Maqoma to explode:

Does Sandili fully understand what he is about to do? Hitherto we have been British subjects in name, henceforth we shall be subjects in truth. Is Sandili prepared to meet [meaning agree to the measures proposed by] the Governor at all times and in all places? Once he has received the Governors' money he must no longer talk of his fears, but must obey in everything … Let Sandili well consider what he is doing, let him not be tempted by the money and afterwards become a liar to the Government.[24]

As was his habit, Maqoma had put his finger exactly on the issue.

Maclean immediately reported to Grey that Maqoma remained the only one to hold out. But this turned out to be not quite true. The Xhosa ability to duck and dive in their dealings with the imperial state continued to plague the imperial administration. As soon as it seemed that an agreement had been secured, reservations began to pop up again. Suddenly Mhala and Phato and even Khama began to assert their right to object to the choice of magistrate appointed to their tribes. Khama wanted a magistrate who spoke the Xhosa language, because he did not trust the interpreters. Within a week of Maclean's telling Grey that Mhala had agreed, he was writing back that Mhala was objecting to the appointment of John Cox Gawler to his tribe. Maclean wrote asking for instructions, warning that if the chiefs were to secure "the selection of those officers … themselves [it] may be made the means of neutralizing His Excellency's intentions." Grey replied that Maclean was to press ahead with the appointment of the magistrates anyway. He was to tell Khama that he could not choose which magistrate was assigned to him. But he advised Maclean to select somebody who was agreeable to him anyway. Ever the brilliant tactician, Grey was bending with the wind, because Maclean was quite right about Xhosa intentions. One of the Xhosa styles of dealing with the imperial state was precisely to allow its initiatives to be smothered in their embrace. The prerogative of the imperial administration to choose the magistrate and to define his duties had been naturally assumed by Grey. Now, suddenly, it had become a matter for negotiation.[25]

This foot-dragging continued for some months. Khama agreed to accept a magistrate on Grey's terms in January 1856, and Maclean assured him he would appoint someone worthy of his confidence. Khama's reserve was significant. Khama had a long history of accommodation with the imperial state. He could be presumed to know a thing or two about its ways, and he was reported to be actively spreading the story that "the whole scheme is a mere trick to allure the Chiefs and that the real object is to do away with Chieftainship and to make the Kaffirs as subservient as the Fingoes." This was exactly right, of course. But Maclean recommended withholding his pension of £20 per year as punishment for speaking this truth! Maqoma continued to wriggle, seemingly with a view to exploring the possibility of returning to his old lands in the Amatolas, now in the Crown Reserve. Maqoma engaged in his typical style of negotiating: saying one thing to Brownlee, another to Sandile and yet a third thing to Maclean, all in the hope of finding and exploiting divisions and differences. Maqoma finally gave up this attempt to seek an escape hatch in April 1856, when T. J. Lucas was installed as magistrate to both Maqoma and Botman. But this merely moved the struggle to a new level.[26]

A decision was made to make the installation of Lucas a ceremonial event. Brownlee attended to announce that he was passing the care of Maqoma's tribe to Lucas, who was then introduced by John Ayliff, the Methodist missionary. But Maqoma spoilt the display. He interrupted Ayliff to point out that when he accepted the Governor's scheme, he also made it known that he wanted his own land in return (the land, again the land, from which he had been expelled). He wanted now to know the Governor's answer to that condition. When Ayliff responded that Maqoma knew the answer, the chief paused and then opened a new line of argument. "Will the magistrate represent our wishes to the government?" he asked, meaning: will the magistrate be a representative of the tribe to the government? Ayliff replied that he would, but that he would report through Maclean. Maqoma then welcomed the magistrate with a speech that was clearly designed to express his expectation that the magistrate would transmit the wishes of the tribe to the imperial administration. Maqoma stated that the magistrate must "submit our requests at all times to the Governor ... and get us more land." And when Ayliff intervened to warn Maqoma that only reasonable requests would be transmitted, Maqoma replied that "he must ask, ask and never tire and never say 'the Governor has refused I cannot ask again,' He must continue to ask. Our friends by perseverance in forwarding applications in former times got back land for us."[27]

Once again, the slipperiness of the Xhosa chiefs was revealed. Accepting the magistrate merely opened a new front in the ongoing negotiation with the imperial state, one which attempted to establish the precedent of the magistrate as representative of the tribe to the government, rather than as the conduit for government *orders* to the tribe. But Maqoma was not to lead this particular struggle. Indeed, although the British could not know it, his glory days were over. He remained the most feared chief in Xhosaland. But he was a spent force. The mantle of Maqoma now passed to Mhala. It was Mhala who fought the critical battle against the usurpation of the chief's authority. And in the early months of 1856 Mhala conducted a final campaign to undermine Grey's scheme.

Since his appointment to Mhala's tribe by Grey in November 1855, John Cox Gawler had been cooling his heels at Mhala's kraal while the chief continued to bombard Maclean with requests that he appoint Richard Tainton as his magistrate. In this struggle of wills, final victory was to come only a year or so later. As the imperial administration well knew, Mhala the "wild cat" was an expert at feigning and evading. At a meeting with Maclean on 13 January 1856, Mhala told him that although he had originally wanted to choose his own magistrate, he now saw that Major Gawler was a "gentleman in every way worthy of confidence and one that would do me justice." He therefore was willing to accept Gawler as "his friend and adviser."

But before Maclean could sigh with relief, a new issue was presented to him. Since the Governor had chosen the magistrate, Mhala wanted to choose the interpreter. He did not know Maclean's appointment – J. Warner – and he wanted William Shepstone. But Shepstone was Maclean's interpreter. Surely Mhala was goading Maclean! Facing Maclean's demurral, he then changed tack and tried to negotiate a salary equivalent to Phato's. He alluded to the fact that he was, after all, the head of the Ndlambe chiefs and, like Phato, had given a good account of himself in the late war. Again, this piece of insolence was studied. Mhala was regarded by the imperial administration of having played both sides during the war. Formally neutral, in fact he provided refuge for the warring tribes' cattle, in return for a sizeable cut for himself. Maclean had had enough; he stopped him there and warned him "not to enter the subject of the last war."[28]

It was just at this moment that one of two young girls, out frightening birds from their uncle's crops, had the first of her many visions. She saw two strangers, one of whom turned out to be her uncle's dead brother. They told her that the day was coming when the dead would arise and return to come to the aid of the Xhosa. But all the cattle must be slaughtered and all cultivation must cease in order to prepare the way for the new people. She immediately told her uncle, Mhlakaza, who became the interlocutor between those with the visions and the tribal authorities. He immediately passed the news on to Sarhili. The great Xhosa cattle-killing was about to begin.[29]

The cattle-killing and colonial knowledge

Nongqawuse (for that was her name) was not the first prophet to advocate killing cattle. As early as October 1855, five prophets were noted as operating in Khama's territory, predicting that the chief would abandon Christianity and that the white people would be destroyed by God's wrath for "putting to death his son." The Xhosa would then become the chosen race. Prophets were preaching a similar message in Mhala's, Stock's and Siwani's tribes. But the movement did not become a national obsession for the Xhosa until the early months of 1856. It reached its height at the beginning of 1858 as the date approached in February that was prophesied for the return of the dead ancestors. When this date passed without incident, faith in the movement cracked, and throughout that year destitution and starvation stalked the land and the Xhosa people were reduced to imperial servitude. It was precisely in this period, when the cattle-killing craze dominated Xhosa politics, that the frontier magistrates charged with implementing Grey's system did their work.[30]

The cattle-killing and the degradation of Xhosa political authority were intimately entwined. But even before the prophecies became the dominant political ideology within the tribes, we have seen how the possibility of using the cattle-killing to political advantage had lodged itself in Grey's calculating mind. Once the killings moved from a prophylaxis against lung disease to political prophecy, it was in Grey's interest that the "believers" (as the pro-cattle-killing faction in the tribes were called) should be encouraged. Grey ordered that their salaries were not to be stopped, and "in a few months we shall be in a position which will enable us to command and enforce obedience." Contrary to the public statements that were made about the venality of those chiefs who fostered the delusions of the prophets, Grey wanted to keep the believers in the cattle-killing in positions of power in the tribes. The reason was obvious: it would continue to destroy the national wealth of the Xhosa nation, and it would continue the splits and divisions within the tribes. We hardly need to establish the Machiavellian credentials of the esteemed Governor. But let us just note the following: when it came time to try the chiefs in the courts, it was exactly their commitment to the cattle-killing as a way of mobilizing the tribes against the British that appeared on their charge sheet.[31]

The idea that a chiefly conspiracy lay behind the cattle-killing was central to the legal case that the imperial state built against the chiefs in 1858. But the imperial administration had to work hard to convince itself that a conspiracy really was at the root of the cattle-killing. It required quite a stretch of the imperial imagination to convince *itself* that the mass delusion that prescribed killing cattle was a chiefly plot designed to lead to war. We need to take a moment to understand this because it provides a rich example of how imperial culture constructs ideological justifications for its rule. And we are fortunate to have some correspondence between Brownlee, Maclean and Grey which reveals how their ideological knowledge that the cattle-killing was a chiefs' conspiracy was reconciled with their cognitive knowledge that contradicted this claim. I will begin with two letters, both written on 26 August 1856. One letter is from Brownlee to Maclean and the other is from Maclean to Grey. Maclean's letter to Grey was likely written in the light of Brownlee's letter to him. Let us look first at the letter from Brownlee to Maclean.

As the senior administrator on the frontier in terms of service, Brownlee had the longest association with the Xhosa. He was reluctant to endorse the idea that there was in fact a chiefly plot. But he admitted that he had no other explanation of how to read the signs of events in Xhosaland. "To all appearance it would seem that Kreili [Sarhili] was the mover and Umhlakaza [Mhlakaza] the tool, but without even the most indirect evidence I should regret to bring this charge against Krieli." Brownlee was skeptical of the official line on the cattle-killing, doubting whether the chiefs could have "brought the people to this pass" and preferring to believe that it was a movement of the common people. Similarly, he doubted whether a coalition involving Moshesh (the Swazi king) was being assembled to plan "an aggressive move on the white man, though appearances may favour that conclusion."

This was the reflective Brownlee speaking: the Brownlee who could see the hesitations and uncertainties among the chiefs on whether to take the prophecies seriously or not; the Brownlee who knew that chiefly power was constrained by popular sentiment. But the same letter also contains another Brownlee, who is prepared to go some way to admitting the official version of events. Thus he agreed that this was a time of danger, although he could not bring himself to think war likely. Still, he was prepared to admit that theoretically "there may be a deep and well laid scheme I am not in a position to deny and that the Chiefs are the unseen movers in it I would not venture to dispute."[32]

Here is a neat example of the instability of colonial knowledge and of its effort to reconcile incompatible positions. All the things that Brownlee was skeptical about were exactly the elements of the case that was to be constructed by the imperial state when it accused the chiefs of conspiring to foment the cattle-killing. Brownlee doubted whether a plot was being hatched, whether Moshesh was involved, and whether Sarhili was a manipulator of the prophecies; he saw the cattle-killing as a movement of the common people – as the Xhosa equivalent of the "poor deluded followers of Joanna Southcott." Yet at the same time he could not decisively reject the imperial story that was being constructed around these events. Thus we see how two opposed views could be held at the same time; how the case against the chiefs was being constructed out of contrary and opposite facts.

If this was true of such a level-headed and relatively independent imperial agent as Brownlee, it was even more the case with John Maclean. On the same day that Maclean received this letter from Brownlee – the day we can regard the chiefs' plot as coming into being in the imperial mind – Maclean wrote a letter to Grey that was both reflective of Brownlee's mixed message and in direct contradiction to it. It is a letter that serves to illustrate the mental effort it took people like Maclean to fit their cognitive appreciation of the complexities of chiefly power with the ideological need to explain chiefly actions in a way that justified imperial culture's attitude toward them.

On the one hand, Maclean announced to Grey that "everything bears a peaceful and tranquil aspect" in British Kaffraria. On the other hand, such tranquility was surely deceptive, because

I am more convinced than ever that Moshesh is doing his utmost to carry out an organised system of combination and also that Kreli [i.e. Sarhili] has participated in the scheme. As to the other Chiefs there is as yet nothing to shew that they are cognizant of the plot [to encourage their followers to kill cattle using the arguments of the women prophets], although I have no doubt in my mind that Sandili, Umhala and Pato have been consulted.

Maclean, however, had to address the logical problem that always confronted the imperial administration when it tried to argue that the chiefs used superstitious cultural practices: how could the chiefs *know* that the prophecies were humbug, but continue to fool all of the people all of the time into believing them? Maclean tried to deal with this contradiction without actually confronting it. He proposed a distinction between the lesser chiefs and those like Mhala and Sandile who were plotting to combine and use the people's superstitions against the British. The lesser chiefs, he argued, "will no doubt listen to the prophet because they are not one whit less ignorant or less superstitious than any other

Kaffir ... and it does not follow that he or they disbelieve in these superstitions."[33]

Maclean continued to have doubts about how to regard the cattle-killing. Was it not enough to explain it simply as delusion? he asked in a memo to Grey in March 1857. After reviewing all the evidence, he concluded somewhat uneasily that although "many of the points adduced [as to the conspiracy theory] carry little weight when taken singly yet it appears on a general review that some are not to be explained on the supposition of a mere fanatical delusion, while all agree that superstition was made use of to attain a political result."[34] It was clearly not enough just to explain it as a function of superstition; the cattle-killing had to have a political dimension for it to be comprehensible to the imperial administration. Although Maclean continued to be hesitant about Grey's desire to use the cattle-killing as the excuse for a full-scale assault on the chiefs, he laid to rest any doubts he had about the conspiratorial interpretation of the movement. Indeed, ultimately he could not resist this conclusion. Like all the other imperial administrators, he was a firm believer that the chiefs used traditional cultural superstitions as weapons of their political power.[35] Thus, at the end of September 1857 Maclean sent a detailed "Report on the Chiefs" to Grey which marked Maclean's complete acceptance of the official interpretation of the cattle-killing and must have been music to Grey's ears. It confirmed that Mhala was at the center of a plot, that he used witchcraft beliefs to manipulate and intimidate his people; that the leading prophet in his tribe was controlled by one of Mhala's closest counselors, and that therefore "the prophetess in Umhala's country had not merely their origins in the superstitious excitement then prevalent, but were designedly raised up and placed there by some external agency."[36]

The intellectual anxiety caused by the effort to explain the obvious anomalies in the argument of a chiefs' plot to mobilize their people against the British was not confined to Brownlee or Maclean. It extended throughout the imperial administration. Henry Barrington, the newly appointed Attorney-General of British Kaffraria, and a lawyer who was to play a key role in framing the indictments against the chiefs, may be seen performing the same kind of game of self-persuasion as Maclean and Brownlee. In a letter of 20 June 1857 to Maclean, Barrington admitted that "I think the Chiefs must have a sort of a belief in the prophet though they know it is a got up affair. Their uneducated minds are too weak to reject the imposture though they are aware it is one; and one of their own getting up – as a great liar at least believes his own lies." In this letter we can see how both the image of the Xhosa as inherent liars and the image of the chiefs as manipulators were employed by Barrington to reconcile the obvious contradictions of the chiefs as at one and the same time believers in cultural superstitions and as cynical manipulators of those practices for political aims.[37]

The idea of a chiefly plot was now part of common belief about the Xhosa. Henry Calderwood expressed the conventional view when he labeled it as the most extensive combination ever entered into against the white man in southern Africa. This was a deep exaggeration. But the reason that a national suicide could be seen as a dastardly *threat* to imperial power flowed from the narcissism that is inherent in imperial culture. Exactly how a collective suicide of the Xhosa people was supposed to result in a mass offensive against the whites and the British government required quite a convoluted explanation. The killing of livestock, Calderwood argued, would force the people into the Colony in overwhelming numbers, where presumably these destitute and property-less, malnourished people would rise up and overwhelm the well-armed and well-fed whites with murder and destruction.[38]

Was the idea of a chiefs' conspiracy true? The belief that chiefs manipulated cultural practices and conspiracies both against their own people and against the British was by this time a key tenet of imperial culture. But imperial culture did not simply invent its image of the Xhosa out of what it wanted to see. It got some things right. And surely among those things was the attempts of the chiefs to coordinate and create alliances against the British. In other words, British ideas about chiefly plots were not *simply* a projection of their own plotting against the chiefs. The believing chiefs were in touch with one another and were desperately hoping that the prophecies would come true, because they would then drive the British into the sea. But just as often, what the British interpreted as meetings to conspire were attempts by the chiefs to assess the credibility of the prophecies, attempts to understand the meaning of the rumors and beliefs that were flying around. A stream of counselors and advisers flowed toward Sarhili's territory to talk to the prophets and experience the visions for themselves. Mhala sent three commissions to Sarhili to observe the visions of the prophets in clear attempts to assess the truth of the predictions that the new people were on their way to rescue the Xhosa from the British. After the last one, he was reported as being as puzzled as ever and still not sure what to believe.[39]

For our purposes, however, whether the chiefs were plotting or not hardly matters. Whenever the British saw meetings and frequent contact between the chiefs, they smelt conspiracy. The British had learned to be constantly on the lookout for certain signs of trouble on the frontier. Cattle-killing was associated with previous outbreaks of violence. Throughout 1855 and 1856 the correspondence of the imperial administrators was dotted with rumors that confederations of chiefs were being built, or that prophets were abroad predicting the coming end of white rule, or that an invasion by the Russians to aid the Xhosa was imminent. These were all taken seriously because the imperial administrators knew that they were often symptoms of pending conflict. Prophets always appeared just before wars.[40]

So the imperial administrators watched the spread of the cattle-killing with a mixture of anticipation and alarm. The information they received from their spies and informers tended to confirm their already deep suspicions of the chiefs. Ironically, one of these informers was Mjuza, a son of Nxele, the prophet and Xhosa Christian who led the Ndlambe against the British in 1819 and who was sent to Robben Island for his insolence. Another was the firebrand of 1850, Anta, who by now was firmly in the government camp. Anta's land had been little affected by the lung sickness and so he was not a believer in the prophecies. But he kept his magistrate, Frederick Robertson, well informed with the kind of information that Robertson and Maclean wanted to hear: that Sarhili was ready to start a war with the British. These highly placed informants demonstrated the degree to which the Xhosa tribes were split by the cattle-killing, and no imperial officer could ignore the political advantages that this opened up.[41]

Conspiracy then was central to the way the British viewed the cattle-killing. But it was not only the chiefs who fell within its net. Conspiracy was necessary for imperial culture to explain the prophets, too. And here they engaged their understanding of witchcraft as a tool whereby the chiefs manipulated politics in the tribes. The imperial imagination constructed the prophets as tools of the chiefs, and much effort was to be expended in drawing the lines of connection between them that would satisfy British legal sensibilities.

Maclean referred to the appearance of prophets in Mhala's tribe as an opening of the "Umhlakaza Central Office, where prophetesses like Umhalakaza's [sic] niece [Nongqawuse] saw and had communications with the underground people." The leading prophet in this case was a nine-year-old girl by the name of Nonkosi. Gawler had her in for questioning on 15 October, and Maclean saw her a few days later. The style of this interrogation was to listen to the girl's story and then to interpret it for her. After she had spoken, Maclean reminded her that the chiefs had now admitted that the sightings of the dead people were all a deception – which was not true – and that therefore she had no need to fear speaking the truth. At which point she began to tell the story that Maclean wanted: that Kwitchi, a counselor of Mhala, had told her to say that she had seen the dead people and their cows and had even visited their home beneath the river.[42]

This confession was the breakthrough in securing Xhosa authentication for what was already an article of belief in imperial culture. And it was the initial justification for the legal offensive that was about to be launched against the errant chiefs. But it was not the last confession. There continued to be an obsessive fascination with the case of the prophets. Well into 1858, Gawler was tracking down other prophets and prophetesses and re-interrogating Kwitchi as if to assure himself that what he believed about the chiefs' conspiracy was true. And in April, he brought in the big prize of all – Nonqgawuse – to confirm what he already knew, that Mhlakaza, her uncle, and the lead prophet for interpreting the visions of Nonqgawuse and her sister, was in fact merely a tool of Sarhili and the other chiefs. The ground had been laid for the legal offensive against the chiefs.[43]

Conclusion

The purpose of this collection of confessions was as much ideological as it was legal. They were necessary to validate the understanding that the imperial administration had of the cattle-killing. For this view of the chiefs as despots who cunningly manipulated superstition was inherently unstable. The hesitancies and ambivalences that we have noted in Maclean and Brownlee surely reflected how hard they had to work mentally to reconcile what they needed to believe ideologically with the qualifications of that ideology that their knowledge and senses revealed. Confessions like that of Kwitchi and Nonkosi were important because they brought authenticity to the dominant tendency in this understanding of the chiefs. They validated what imperial culture wanted to know about the chiefs.

The cattle-killing, then, provided a suitable climactic to the developing view of the chiefs within imperial culture. For the British it was a supreme example of chiefs as conspiratorial manipulators of the superstitions of the Xhosa. How else were they to hold together the understanding of chiefly power and politics that they had developed? The flaws in their case against the chiefs were several. It contained a logic that was contrary to historical experience: that the threat of starvation would lead the Xhosa to fight. It contained contradictory reasoning: that the chiefs both were believers in superstition and that they were not believers but manipulators of superstition. It was paranoid, seeing conspiracy everywhere, when in fact the cattle-killing caused deep division within the tribes. It misread the search for understanding of the prophecies by the chiefs as evidence of their machinations.

But all of this dissonance had ultimately to be swept aside. Understanding the chiefs in this light was vital to the ability of the imperial administrators to carry out the task that Grey had set them. They needed such a justification for the brutal work that was involved in the implementation of the Grey system and for the perversions of British notions of justice that were contained in the coming trials of the chiefs.

NOTES

1. James Belich, *Making Peoples. A History of the New Zealanders: From the Polynesian Settlement to the End of the Nineteenth Century* (Honolulu, 1996), pp. 109, 192; Sir George Grey, *Polynesian Mythology and Ancient Traditional History of the New Zealand Race* (London, 1855); Grey, *A Vocabulary of the Dialects of South Western Australia* (London, 1840); James Cameron, *The Library of Sir George Grey* (London, 1858).

2. For a good discussion of the contradictions within liberal political thought on empire, see Uday Mehta, *Liberalism and Empire: A Study in Nineteenth-Century British Liberal Thought* (Chicago, 1999); and for a classic study of the application of liberal principles to imperial policy see Ranajit Guha, *A Rule of Property for Bengal: An Essay on the Idea of Permanent Settlement*, 2nd edn. (Durham, NC, 1996).

3. We now know that his political and military victories were largely inventions, carefully presented to London in order to bolster his reputation and ensure the continued funding of his policies. For Grey's misrepresentations in New Zealand see James Belich, *The Victorian Interpretation of Racial Conflict: The Maori, the British and the New Zealand Wars* (Montreal and Kingston, Ont., 1986), pp. 58–70, 123–5, 211. J. B. Peires, "The Late Great Plot: The Official Delusion Concerning the Xhosa Cattle Killing, 1856–57," *History in Africa*, 12 (1985), pp. 258–9, for an example in South Africa regarding relations with Moshoeshoe.

4. There are a few inconsequential references in Andrew Porter (ed.), *The Oxford History of the British Empire*, vol. III: *The Nineteenth Century* (Oxford, 1999), pp. 177, 212, 213, 583–6, 591, 602. J. Rutherford, *Sir George Grey KCB 1812–1898: A Study in Colonial Government* (London, 1961) remains the standard work. The most recent biography is by Edmund Bohan, *To be a Hero: A Biography of Sir George Grey 1812–1898* (Auckland, 1998), but it adds nothing to Rutherford. See also W. P. Morrell, *British Colonial Policy in the Mid-Victorian Age: South Africa, New Zealand and the West Indies* (Oxford, 1969), pp. 64–93, for Grey at the Cape. For an important assessment of his career which emphasizes the importance of his Irish origins for his attitude towards empire, see Leigh Dale, "George Grey in Ireland: Narrative and Network," in David Lambert and Alan Lester, *Colonial Lives across the British Empire: Imperial Careering in the Long Nineteenth Century* (Cambridge, 2006), pp. 145–75.

5. Rutherford, *Sir George Grey*, pp. 330–80, for the whole period, pp. 436–8 for the summation.

6. Ibid., pp. 436–8.

7. J. B. Peires, *The Dead Will Arise: Nongqawuse and the Great Xhosa Cattle-Killing Movement of 1856–7* (Johannesburg, London, and Bloomington, IN, 1989), especially chs. 3–7.

8. John Henderson Soga, *The Ama-Xhosa: Life and Customs* (Lovedale, 1932), pp. 103–4; Peires, *Dead Will Arise*, pp. 122–3.

9. For some of the debate around the cattle-killing see the following essays by Peires, "Late Great Plot"; "'Soft' Believers and 'Hard' Believers in the Xhosa Cattle Killing," *Journal of African History* 27 (1986), pp. 443–61; "The Central Beliefs of the Xhosa Cattle Killing," *Journal of African History* 28 (1987),

pp. 43–63; and "Suicide or Genocide? Xhosa Perceptions of the Nonqwawuse Catastrophe," *Radical History Review* 47.7 (1990), pp. 47–57. Peires's interpretation has been challenged by Timothy Stapleton, who sees it as a lower-class rebellion against a weakened Xhosa aristocracy. My own view lies much closer to that of Peires. Stapleton is right to point to the importance of cattle in the economy of the Xhosa, but in my view exaggerates the extent to which chiefly power had been degraded already by 1856. See Timothy Stapleton, "They No Longer Care for their Chiefs: A New Look at the Xhosa Cattle Killing of 1856–1857," *International Journal of African Historical Studies* 24.2 (1991), pp. 383–92. Peires's view of Xhosa history has also been critiqued from a feminist perspective by Helen Bradford in a most interesting article, "Framing African Women: Visionaries in Southern Africa and Their Photographic Afterlife, 1850–2004," *Kronos: Journal of Cape History* 30 (2004), pp. 70–93. See also Sheila Boniface Davis, "Raising the Dead: The Xhosa Cattle-Killing and the Mhlakaza–Goliat Delusion," *Journal of Southern Africa Studies* 33.1 (2007), pp. 19–41.

10. Peires, *Dead Will Arise*, pp. 48–50; Parliamentary Papers, *Correspondence Respecting the Colonization of New Zealand* 1841, [311] pp. 43–7. It was rumored that Grey had sent advice from New Zealand on how to handle the Xhosa – advice which Cathcart had dismissed as impractical.

11. CA, GH 8/26, *Chief Commissioner, British Kaffraria, 1855*, Maclean to Grey, 2 June 1855; Shaw to Maclean, 3 April 1855; GH 30/4, *Letter Book of Chief Commissioner, British Kaffraria, 1852–58*, Grey to Maclean, 23 June 1855; Anthonie Eduard Du Toit, "The Cape Frontier: A study of Native Policy with Special Reference to the Years 1847–1866" (DPhil thesis, University of Preteria, 1949), pp. 61–3.

12. CA, GH 8/26, *Chief Commissioner, British Kaffraria, 1855*, Grey To Maclean, 28 April 1855; Peires, *Dead Will Arise*, pp. 56–7; Parliamentary Papers, *Papers Relative to the State of Kaffir Tribes*, 1854–1855, vol. XXXVIII [cd. 1969] for his speech to the Cape Parliament.

13. CA, GH 30/4, *Letter Book of Chief Commissioner, British Kaffraria, 1852–58*, Grey to Maclean, 26 July 1855.

14. CA, BK 10, *Lieutenant Governor, Miscellaneous Dispatches 1852–64*, Grey to Maclean, 26 July 1855; Maclean to Grey, 4 August 1855; Report of conversation of 11 September 1855 between Maclean and Grey.

15. CA, GH 30/4 *Letterbook of Chief Commissioner 1855*, Grey to Maclean, 17 September 1855; BK 10, *Lieutenant Governor, Miscellaneous Dispatches, 1852–64*, Report of conversation between Grey and Maclean, 11 September 1855.

16. CA, GH 19/8, *Papers Connected with Sandilli, Kreli, Pato Etc., 1847*, Maclean to Liddle, 21 November 1854; BK 8/24, *British Kaffraria Miscellaneous, Sir George Clerk 1853–1854*, Report from "Melele" (one of Maclean's spies), 28 July 1855. For the evolution of Brownlee's view, see, for example, BK 70, *Reports of Gaika Commissioner 1854–56, 1858, 1860–61*, Brownlee to Maclean, 4 March, 11 May, and 6, 11, 22 and 25 August 1856. By contrast, M. B. Shaw accepted the Grey line earlier; GH 8/26, *Chief Commissioner, British Kaffraria, 1856*, Shaw to Maclean, 3 April 1856. As late as December 1856, Maclean was urging Grey to exercise caution in using the cattle-killing to government

advantage; see GH 8/30, *Chief Commissioner, British Kaffraria, Dispatches from Maclean, 1856*, Maclean to Grey, 18 December 1856.

17. CA, BK 140, *Kaffir Chiefs, Counsellors, and Headmen Allowances and Pensions*, Grey to Maclean, 18 December 1855; Brownlee to Maclean 25 and 26 December 1855.

18. NLSA (CT), MSB 142, *D'Urban–Smith Correspondence*, Smith to D'Urban, 6 April 1836; CA, BK 371, *Letters from the Chief Commissioner, British Kaffraria, to the High Commissioner, 1848–53*, Mackinnon to Smith, 9 August 1851; BK 140, *Letters from Kaffir Chiefs*, memo from Cathcart to Siwani, 29 April, 3 May and 26 August 1852; Du Toit, Cape Frontier, pp. 28–30.

19. CA, GH 8/27, *Dispatches, Chief Commissioner, British Kaffraria, 1855*, reports from Brownlee of 17 and 27 September 1855.

20. Zakes Mda, *The Heart of Redness* (Oxford, 2000); CA, GH 8/27, *Chief Commissioner, British Kaffraria, 1855*, Brownlee to Maclean, 9 October 1855.

21. CA, GH 8/28, *Dispatches, Chief Commissioner, British Kaffraria, 1856*, Maclean to Grey, 15 February 1856; BK 140, *Kaffir Chiefs, Counsellors, Headmen*, Letters Patent for British Kaffraria, 7 March 1854.

22. Ibid., Brownlee to Maclean, 18 October 1855.

23. This was the last time such assemblies were to be gathered for the purpose of negotiation in the old style that we discussed in Chapter 7 above.

24. CA, GH 8/27, *Dispatches, Chief Commissioner, British Kaffraria, 1855*, Brownlee to Maclean, 6 December 1855.

25. Ibid., Maclean to Grey, 24 October, 3 November and 12 December 1855; Maclean memo, 16 November 1855; Maclean to Grey, 23 November 1855; BK 140, *Kaffir Chiefs, Counsellors and Headmen*, Grey to Maclean, 24 December 1855; Maclean to Grey, 3 January 1856. Maclean clearly tried to ease the passage of the Grey system by making appointments where he could that would meet the approval of the chief; see Maclean to Liddle, 21 January 1856, on the appointment of Maximilian Kayser as interpreter for Maqoma.

26. CA, BK 140, *Kaffir Chiefs, Counsellors and Headmen*, Grey to Maclean, 24 December 1855, 3 and 4 January 1856; Brownlee to Maclean, 21, 30 and 31 January 1856 for Maqoma; George McCall Theal, *History of South Africa* (Cape Town, repr., 1964), vol. V, p. 298.

27. CA, GH 8/28, *Dispatches, Chief Commissioner, British Kaffraria, 1856*, Maclean to Grey, 21 April 1856. The same display was repeated when the party moved on to Botman's kraal. Botman wanted to know why the government had not given him a piece of land separate from Sandile's.

28. CA, BK140, *Kaffir Chiefs, Counsellors and Headmen*, Maclean to Grey, 4 and 20 January 1856.

29. Peires, *Dead Will Arise*, pp. 78–9.

30. CA, GH 8/28, *Dispatches, Chief Commissioner, British Kaffraria, 1856*, Brownlee to Maclean, 11 May 1856; Peires, *Dead Will Arise*, p. 166. As was usual in these cases, the Xhosa were urged to abandon their witchcraft beliefs. What was new was evidence that the Xhosa were aware of wider world events. Thus all agreed that the Russians would come to the Xhosa's assistance as part of their struggle against the British in the Crimea.

31. CA, GH 8/30, *Chief Commissioner, British Kaffraria, Despatches from Maclean, 1856*, Grey to Maclean, 18 December 1856; this was a minute on a dispatch from Maclean urging caution.

32. CA, GH 20/2/1, *Miscellaneous Papers Relating to British Kaffraria, 1853–58*, Brownlee to Maclean, 25 August 1856.

33. CA, GH 8/49, *Demi-Official Letters, British Kaffraria, 1854–56*, Maclean to Grey, 25 August 1856.

34. CA, BK373, *Letter Book, High Commissioner, British Kaffraria, 1854–63*, Maclean to Grey, 25 March 1857.

35. Maclean was getting reports from his subordinates that fed the same interpretation; see CA, BK 85, *Reports of Special Magistrate with Anta's Tribe 1856–65*, Lucas to Maclean, 29 November 1856, for how "hitherto the chiefs have not allowed the people to have a voice in the matter [of the cattle-killing] ... I am of the opinion that the chiefs are trying to postpone a meeting [of counselors] until the sowing season is over; their object would then be gained. But the people are getting clamourous about not sowing." See also Lucas to Maclean, 7 January 1857, on how the chiefs were manipulating the people through the prophets.

36. CA, GH 8/50, *Demi-Official Correspondence, British Kaffraria 1857–58*, Maclean to Grey, 30 September 1857. And see BK 373, *Letter Book, High Commissioner, British Kaffraria, 1854–63*, Maclean to Grey 20 and 25 November 1857, for his repetition of the official line on the cattle-killing as a chiefly plot. The most likely explanation for this shift is that this was the moment when all the strands of imperial policy were coming together. Gawler had successfully split Mhala's tribe with his right-hand son Smith as the new breakaway chief. Mhala was trying to surrender. Most important of all, Maqoma had been arrested without sparking any protest of challenge from the other chiefs. Maclean's self-confidence was expressed in other ways too. He stopped arguing for a cautious policy regarding the prosecution of Maqoma, and ended his resistance to charging him with murder.

37. CA, BK 14, *President, Criminal Court Proceedings, British Kaffraria, 1856–60*, Barrington to Maclean, 20 June 1857.

38. Henry Calderwood, *Caffres and Caffre Missions* (London, 1858), pp. 212–13. Calderwood was not the only one to engage in this mental contortion. The more liberal-minded missionary, James Laing of Lovedale, also repeated the conventional view that the cattle-killing was a chiefly manipulation of superstition and delusion. Rev. William Govan, *Memorials of the Missionary Career of Reverend James Laing* (Glasgow, 1875), pp. 180–4.

39. CA, A793, *Letter Book of John Gawler*, 7 September, 14 and 31 October, and 22 November 1856. Peires believes that the idea of a chiefs' plot was an invention of the imperial administration. Peires, *Dead Will Arise*, pp. 219–21; "The Late Great Plot," pp. 257–8.

40. CA, GH 8/26, *Chief Commissioner, British Kaffraria, Letters and other material to Maclean*, Brownlee to Maclean, 11 May 1856; GH 8/24, *British Kaffraria Miscellaneous, Sir George Clerk 1853–1854*, information received from "Melele," 28 July1855; BK 70, *Reports from the Gaika Commissioner*, Brownlee to Maclean, 4 March and 11 May 1856.

41. CA, GH 30/4, *Chief Commissioner, British Kaffraria, Despatches from Maclean, 1856,* Maclean to Grey, 12 November 1856; Robertson to Maclean, 23 November 1856.

42. CA, GH 8/48, *Letters from Native Chiefs, Residents, Eastern Frontier, 1856–60,* Maclean, memo of 30 September 1857. The account of the interrogation is in GH 8/33, *Dispatches from the Chief Commissioner of British Kaffraria, 1856,* Examination of Nonkosi before the Chief Commissioner, 23 October 1857. See below, pp. 319–20, for the rest of this story.

43. CA, GH 8/34, *Dispatches of Chief Commissioner, British Kaffraria, 1858,* Maclean to Grey, 4 March 1858; GH 8/35, *Despatches of Chief Commissioner, British Kaffraria, April–August 1858,* 12 April 1858, Examination of Nonqause by Gawler.

11   The destruction of the Xhosa chiefs

The dramatis personae

From April 1856 through to the Christmas of 1858 the Xhosa chiefs faced a two-pronged challenge to their political authority. One was from the cattle-killing that erupted with force over the months following Nongqawuse's sightings. The other was the increasingly relentless pressure from the imperial administration to turn them into imperial civil servants. These challenges to chiefly authority were mutually reinforcing. The cattle-killing split the tribes into believers and non-believers, dividing and weakening them. Sir George Grey and his officers worked hard to exploit that division and to create new ones. The end result was the final act in a scenario that the imperial state had imagined, sometimes dimly, sometimes with clarity, since the mid-1830s: the erosion of the traditional power of the chiefs and their transformation into reliable pipelines for the transmission of imperial authority and culture. For the generation of chiefs who had first encountered the British as young men in the second decade of the nineteenth century, this fate marked the nadir of their struggle to retain a sphere of independence and autonomy for Xhosa politics.

I shall tell this story standing where the pressures of the cattle-killing and the imperial state impinged most sharply on the chiefly authority of the Xhosa. The crucial battle between the chiefs and the Grey system centered around two chiefs – Mhala and Phato. These chiefs were at different places on the spectrum of relationships of the chiefs to the imperial state. Vanquishing Mhala meant subjugating the most dangerous leader in British Kaffraria. Subordinating Phato meant delivering a lesson to the loyal chiefs, such as Khama and Tzatzoe. Mhala's story was the more dramatic. Mhala had been a source of trouble from the first moment that the British encountered him. He had largely stayed out of the wars. But this merely added to the British belief that he was the very epitome of Xhosa cunning and deceit. Another way of putting this, however, was to admit that Mhala was a supremely adept politician. Like all the chiefs, his relationship with the British was suffused with ambiguity. Two of his sons were named after British officers. His right-hand son was named Smith in honor of Sir Harry, and his great son was named Mackinnon, after the hapless Chief Commissioner of British Kaffraria. By 1857, however, the clever dance that had always kept Mhala just beyond the grip of the imperial state had reached its final set.

Phato's history could not have been more different. We know much less about Phato than we do Mhala. But the key thing about his history with the British is that he had moved from being an overt opponent to being one of the most useful allies the British possessed in Xhosaland. It is not clear exactly why. Two factors were probably operative. First, he came from a lineage with a strong British connection. His brothers, Khama and Kobus, were closely associated with missionary culture. Second, he had learnt through personal experience the price of fighting the British. For the British, Phato's value lay in the land his people occupied. It sat astride the key routes between King William's Town, the capital of British Kaffraria, the port of East London to the east, and Grahamstown to the south. In the war of 1850–3 he had protected these crucial lifelines. Needless to say, that did not save him when it came time for the imperial administration to impose the Grey system on his tribe.

In their different ways, these two chiefs resisted the encroaching grip of the imperial state for a year or so before they crumbled under its pressure. They each faced aggressive resident magistrates. Mhala's magistrate was Major John Gawler. Gawler was a true child of empire. His family had been entwined in empire networks for a century. A great-grandfather had staggered up the path from Fuller's Cove to the Plains of Abraham with Wolfe in 1759 to win Quebec for the British empire. A grandfather had died helping to secure Mysore for the British. His father had served in the Peninsular War and then a brief term as Governor of South Australia in 1838, before being recalled under a cloud of financial scandal. He was replaced by a man who may have contributed to the scandal in the first place. That man was George Grey.[1]

It is possible that the son, John Cox Gawler, had feelings of resentment about what had happened to his father. Certainly, Gawler failed to observe the usual courtesy of thanking Grey for his appointment as resident magistrate. Yet there is no evidence of a sour relationship; indeed, more than once Grey conveyed his strong appreciation of Cox's work. As well he might. Gawler carried in his blood the family tradition of loyal service in the cause of empire. He saw action with the 73rd Regiment in the counter-insurgency campaign of Lieutenant Colonel William Eyre during the eighth frontier war, an appropriate apprenticeship for the work he was to do in Mhala's tribe. He had served a brief stint as Field Adjutant in

Natal before being picked out for service as one of the new magistrates entrusted to implement the Grey system in British Kaffraria. We might note that after southern Africa, he transferred to India where he was part of an expedition against Sikkim in 1861, and returned briefly to Grahamstown as Military Secretary before being completing his service to empire by being appointed in 1872 to the sinecure of Keeper of the Crown Jewels at the Tower of London.[2]

Gawler had a full and exciting life, ending up in a position of status and respectability. He was not without intellect. He published a book on military tactics and pamphlets on Zionism. But, as J. B. Peires remarks, he wrote not one word about his engagement with Xhosa polities and society. When we know the story of his destruction of Mhala's authority and his role in the legal framing of other chiefs, we can understand why. The brutality of his methods raised eyebrows even within the imperial administration. The magistrate with Maqoma, Captain Frederick Reeve, complained about the violent behavior of Gawler's police. The venerable missionary Friedrich Kayser protested to Gawler about his brutal interrogations of witnesses, only to have a sjambok shaken in his face. One doubts whether Gawler was ashamed of his behavior. In later life he wrote lengthy treatises on how the British empire was God's choice as successor to Ancient Israel. So presumably the ends justified the means. But it is the *silence* that is worth noting. Empire in Britain was not the same as empire in the empire. And silence was one way of ensuring that the two were not confused.[3]

Phato's magistrate was Herbert Vigne. He was appointed to Phato's tribe in the beginning of 1856. Apart from his work as Grey's agent, Vigne is a shadowy figure. He did not have the successful career that Gawler achieved. Indeed, there were doubts about him from the very beginning, which may have involved his class status. He was not very well connected socially, and he first appears in the historical record seeking an appointment in British Kaffraria. Grey wrote to Maclean that "Mr. Vigne might be placed with Pato [sic] as he would then be under your own immediate observation." In his appointment letter to Vigne, Maclean makes it clear that in the event that he was found unsuitable, the government reserved the right to dispense with his services forthwith.[4]

In many ways, however, Vigne was most suitable, and for a while a successful career on this edge of empire beckoned. He brought Phato into line with British policy. He raised a local "Kaffir" police troop, suborned Phato's authority and began to move the tribe into British-administered "villages." His methods rivaled Gawler's in their roughness. Certainly, the Xhosa were unfavorably impressed, and by February 1858 there were reports that Vigne was regarded as worse than

Gawler. There was some talk about a plot to assassinate him. He played a role second only to Gawler's in the campaign against the chiefs, and for his service he was promoted as Commissioner of the Crown Reserve section of British Kaffraria in 1859.[5]

Then a sexual scandal hit Herbert Vigne, and his career unraveled. It began in March 1860, when Maclean received an anonymous letter accusing Vigne of being " a gross sensualist" who concealed "his career as a libertine under the portrait of an eminently virtuous man ... as guardian to two girls given to his safe keeping by Pato's wife Noxina, one being the daughter of Pato, the other of Stock." Both fathers were currently serving prison terms, thanks largely to the exertions of Herbert Vigne. What made it worse was that one of the girls had been made pregnant by Vigne, who had arranged for the girl to be married to one of his policemen, so that he could plausibly deny his own connection with her. Maclean sat on the accusation when it first arrived and waited until September before passing it along to Grey. When Grey received notice of Vigne's transgressions, he was outraged and demanded his immediate dismissal if the claims of the anonymous letter turned out to be correct. Vigne was confronted with the charges and admitted his guilt, although he offered inventive excuses – such as that he was not sleeping with both girls at the same time – and pleaded that "there are so many extenuating circumstances," which he offered to explain to Grey in person. These appeals fell on deaf ears, and Vigne was dismissed, at which point he disappears from the historical record.[6]

These, then, were two Victorian gentlemen who built the empire on the Cape's eastern frontier. Their types seldom grace the pages of imperial history. But that silence should not shield their achievement; after all, they were among the men who frequented the underside of the empire of liberal Britain to do its dirty work.

Mhala and Gawler

There were two strategies that the Grey system used to erode the authority of the chief. The first was for the magistrate to insert himself into the authority structure of the tribe and to demonstrate that there could be no structure of authority in the tribe independent of the state. The second strategy was to exploit the tribal divisions opened by the cattle-killing by creating new factions that defied the authority of the chief. John Cox Gawler was an enthusiastic and expert practitioner of both maneuvers.[7]

Gawler's opening gambit was to usurp the authority of Mhala over crime in the tribe. Mhala had not moved aggressively enough for Gawler's taste to seek out the culprits who had stolen some guns from a distant Mfengu kraal. Gawler's claim was that the case was a test of the principle of equal justice – a British legal principle that the chiefs were now to apply. The Mfengu, Gawler argued, deserved as much protection as the Xhosa, and it was the chief's responsibility to uphold the principle of equal treatment before the law. For Mhala, however, things were more complicated. It was not even clear that the kraal in question was really part of his tribe. His authority was under challenge from a variety of sources. Both Sandile and Maqoma claimed allegiances of people living in Mhala's territory, and there were constant jurisdictional disputes about who actually had authority over these persons. There were persistent rumors that Sandile had designs on Mhala's chieftainship. And, finally, the Mfengu were hardly loyal members of Mhala's clan. They had been created as a tribe by the British in 1834–5 and were regarded, not unfairly, as "government people."

None of this resonated much with Gawler except to demonstrate that Mhala was refusing to administer justice without regard to property or persons. Mhala's refusal to act against the known thieves was, according to Gawler, motivated by his desire "to gain popularity with his people by screening them from our law." When Gawler made it clear that he was going to go after the thieves by himself, Mhala asked him if he would share the cattle that Gawler would collect from the kraal as a fine for shielding the culprits! For Gawler, here was further proof of the venal character of chiefly authority.[8]

Gawler set off with a large party of men as the sword of justice. Once the party reached the kraal, Gawler soon lost control of the situation. One of the thieves resisted arrest and was fired upon. Gawler's troop quickly scattered, a little too quickly, one senses, and this soon turned into a headlong retreat. At first only two people from the kraal resisted Gawler's party. But as the melée mounted, more joined them and soon there were fifteen or so armed men chasing Gawler's group – who were unarmed – across the veldt. The cattle that had been collected as fines ran loose and were recaptured by the thieves. Gawler had to shoot his way out of the fray, accompanied by one of Mhala's sons, who never left his side.[9]

Gawler was not put off by this setback, however, and a few days later he launched another offensive against Mhala. This involved the distribution of government money to the headmen. Was the money to be given to the chief, who could then distribute it as he wished, or was the resident magistrate to determine who among the headmen got the monthly payments? It was Grey's intention that the magistrate should decide who was worthy of the supplement, although the chief could advise and suggest. But there had been confusion about this from the start. Charles Brownlee had given the first salary payment to Sandile for him to distribute among his headmen. Gawler himself had made an initial distribution of money to Mhala because he was without a translator to explain to him who was who in the tribe. Knowing that this was against government policy, Gawler made the next distribution to headmen of his own choosing. This was the occasion for the first major confrontation with Mhala, who marched up to Gawler's hut with 100 followers, claiming that they had all come for their money. Gawler successfully faced Mhala down on this occasion. This may have been because he had already made progress in splitting the tribe. Several sub-chiefs came to visit him after the meeting to tell him how much they disapproved of Mhala's confrontational tactics. Gawler smoothly told them that "the government did not want them to be at Mhala's mercy" with regard to the money. They went away, "perfectly satisfied." But Gawler may also have been helped in this instance by Mhala himself. And I want to take note of the little vignette that followed this episode, since it provides a further example of the way imperial culture worked to justify itself.

The sub-chiefs were not the only one to revisit Gawler. Mhala also appeared the next day in an attempt to patch things up. Gawler at first refused his approach, declining to shake his hand. But after a while things warmed between them, and they spent the next two or three hours roasting and eating mealies like a couple of old buddies. What brought them together in this way? They were bonded by the ambiguous reciprocity between the chiefs and the magistrates which neither Gawler nor Mhala could escape. And there was also a secret they shared that was a consequence of a subterfuge into which Mhala had drawn Gawler.

At the first distribution of money – which, it will be recalled, Gawler had made entirely to Mhala – the chief asked Gawler to hold some money back. Mhala explained that if it was known that he had more, then he would certainly be asked for it and "it would be impolite to refuse." This was consistent with Xhosa custom, in which gift-giving was a strong cultural practice. But for Gawler the request was a godsend. As he pointed out to Maclean, it gave him "a little secret to hold over Mhala" that could be used to discredit Mhala with his counselors. Indeed, Gawler's knowledge allowed him to interpret Mhala's behavior in a way that confirmed the ideological view of the Xhosa chiefs within imperial culture. Mhala's behavior in the public confrontation the previous day – "his daring to get so violent" – was "one among many proofs I have of the faith Kaffers place in an Englishman's word," since disclosure by Gawler of their little secret would disgrace him in front of his people. Equally, Mhala's willingness to act on this assurance and behave the way he did was evidence of his own duplicity and cunning. So Gawler was at an advantage on both counts. He was affirmed in the superiority of his value system over the Xhosa's, and by threatening to expose the secret he secured a rhetorical and strategic advantage over the chief.[10]

There were other occasions, too, when Gawler forcefully inserted himself into the authority structure of the tribe. But he achieved only limited results. For the best part of a year Mhala managed to stave off Gawler's energetic offensive against his authority. Ultimately, however, the pressure from Gawler combined with the challenge that Mhala faced from the cattle-killing delusion to sweep away his authority and destroy his tribe.[11]

The prophecies about the coming of new people to save the Xhosa from the British were as much a problem for Mhala as for Gawler. On the one hand, the prophecies divided the tribe between the believers and the non-believers. By the same token, however, the prophecies might offer a way to escape the vortex that was threatening to swallow up the chief. What was Mhala to make of the prophecies? Were they to be believed? Such prophecies were always hovering beneath the surface of Xhosa culture in its dealings with the British; during times of war, they broke through to become part of the political discourse. They had been part of Mhala's cultural experience stretching back to the wars of 1811–12 and 1819–20. It would be perfectly natural for him to take such prophecies seriously, especially as they held out the promise of a definitive answer to the problem of the British.

Mhala sent two commissions, headed by his sons, to assess the reports that the new people had been sighted. If the prophecies were accurate that heroic ancestors like Nxele, or Mhala's father Ndlambe, would return to help them drive the British back into the sea, then it was worth defying Gawler and following the prophets' orders to kill cattle and not to plant corn. In Mhala's mind the dismissive attitude of the British to the prophecies was surely less credible than the fantastic claims of the prophetesses to have seen the ancestors and replacement cattle waiting to come out of the sea. *Why should Mhala believe anything that Gawler, Maclean or Grey told him?* Had he not spent the last twenty years listening to the equally fantastic notions of the missionaries about a God in the sky and a place called heaven which could be seen only when he was dead? What was more believable? That or the insights of some of his own people?[12]

But the cattle-killing posed a real political problem for the chiefs. Tribal units were always fragile coalitions; they were always liable to be fractured through discontent with the existing chief or by the rivalries between chiefs for claims over land and people. The cattle-killing added a new element of divisiveness to tribal politics. Mhala's tribe was particularly susceptible to divisions. Mhala's claims to the chieftainship were not straightforward. He was not the rightful heir to Ndlambe's place and there were doubts regarding his legitimacy. He had established himself as chief through a combination of rough political infighting and sheer talent. It was probably a tribe that was hard to hold together. It was, therefore, an obvious target for Grey's machinations through his agent, Gawler.

Gawler's efforts to use the cattle-killing to split the tribe and undermine Mhala's authority had been ongoing from the latter part of 1856. In October 1856 Gawler attended a meeting of Mhala and his counselors where the credibility of the prophecies was discussed. Gawler challenged the reports from Sarhili that he (Sarhili) had actually seen the new people. Interestingly enough, Gawler did not dismiss the whole idea of new people being sighted, but questioned whether Sarhili's evidence could withstand interrogation. After all, he had only glimpsed the new people from a long distance, and could not tell whether they were black or white. "Is this the kind of words on which you destroy your property?" he asked. Sarhili's messenger retorted (with a black nationalist tone) that if they believed "this Englishman you are no Kaffirs: who are you?" When Mhala spoke, he typically made some enigmatic remark about only "believing what one saw with one's own eyes." Gawler seems to have lost that debate. Although he left feeling that Mhala would continue to cultivate his fields, a few days later he learnt that that was not the case and that another commission had been sent off to try to ferret out the truth about the prophecies.[13]

Such information spurred Gawler on to drive a wedge in the tribe between the believers and the non-believers. In October and November 1856 he and Mhala had a contretemps about Gawler's relationship with a counselor who was a non-believer and whom Mhala was trying to eliminate through a witchcraft accusation. Gawler warned him that if anything happened to the counselor he would stop Mhala's pay and that of the other counselors too. Through the end of the year the balance of power in the tribe swung back and forth. Gawler confessed to being befuddled by what was going on, and his confusion probably reflected the genuinely unstable state of opinion within the tribe. Mhala was tacking back and forth between the believers and non-believers in the tribe. He was anxiously seeking signs that the prophecies were credible. At the same time he was trying to escape from Gawler's relentless pressure. He was reported to have killed some of his own cattle, and at the end of November 1856 he sent another commission to Mhlakaza. A week later he was telling Gawler that he would in fact plant the corn.[14]

As the year turned, the political situation in the tribe began to clarify. Mhala moved more decisively to the side of the believers, and was reported to be killing two or three cattle a day in January 1857. Gawler reported to Maclean with a new sense of optimism that the divisions in the tribe could be worked to the government's advantage. Gawler had good reason for optimism.[15] By the end of January 1857 the chief never slept at home; he had men posted throughout the territory to warn him of the approach of troops; he sent his son on another trip to mouth of the River Gxarha (a small stream east of the Kei), where the new people were supposed to be waiting. The climax of this wriggling came on 16 and 17 February 1857, which was when the new people were supposed to appear. When this failed to happen, the believers were thrown into despair. An orgy of cattle-killing had preceded this date, and hardly any corn had been sown. Starvation stared the Xhosa in the face. At this point Mhala began to thrash wildly around, desperate to find a way out of the gathering crisis. By 24 February, recognizing that the prophecies would not be realized, he told Gawler that he wanted to send a message to Grey, admitting his mistake and asking for help with starvation. But he still had not given up all hope of the prophecies. Four days later he sent another son to Mhlakaza for instructions, and himself visited the prophetess in his tribe.[16]

Power in the tribe now tilted away from the believers. Mhala vainly tried to reassert his authority. The property and persons of the unbelievers in the tribe were attacked. Mhala refused to protect them, so they appealed to Gawler. He had about thirty tribal police at his disposal, but it was not enough, and their loyalties were suspect. So he requested some troops, whose presence would give the unbelievers the confidence to "make a revolution against Umhala."[17] By the end of February, the unbelievers had been brought together by Gawler and agreed to remove themselves from Mhala's authority and to concentrate together in a different location. Gawler then set about dealing with the logistics of such a move. About 120 people were involved, and they were to form the core of a new tribe under British sponsorship and with the protection of two companies of British infantry. He proposed to dispense with the existing counselors except those who were "well disposed." Among the latter were Mhala's close relatives Smith and Mdayi, who would receive an appropriate rate of pay. Typically enough in such British schemes, Gawler foresaw retaining Mhala himself "as a dummy" if it was thought desirable![18]

It was just at this moment that the final confrontation between Mhala and Gawler occurred. Gawler described the event in detail in his *Letter Book*. If reported correctly by Gawler, it is a fascinating description of a crucial moment in the establishment of British dominion. Exactly what it was that led Gawler to be present at a large meeting of Mhala's counselors on 16 March 1857 is not clear. But Gawler was no stranger to these meetings, and it is easy to imagine why Mhala chose this moment to vent his outrage on Gawler. He shrewdly chose the question of how Gawler was using the distribution of government money to undermine traditional tribal authority and to portray Gawler as deceitful and dishon-est. He pointed out that the initial distribution of government money had been left to Mhala's discretion. But now Gawler was distributing it directly, bypassing Mhala, and what was even worse, deciding to whom it should go. Mhala seems to have tried to set Gawler up, at least rhetori-cally, because he skillfully drew him into a lawyerly cross-examination in which Gawler was led to concede that he had initially paid the money to Mhala; at which point Mhala exclaimed: "You see my friends, he's acknowledged when I got it straight from Maclean I got it all-all-all." Gawler then made a significant admission: "Why should I not give it among my friends after our differences and the way your friends behaved?" But Mhala considered that he had won the exchange. He launched into a rhetorical crescendo that reflected not merely the frus-trations of this particular occasion, but the eloquent cry of a Xhosa chief watching his patrimony disappear in front of his eyes. It is worth quoting in full:

But Umhala then jumped in shouting out, "That's all I want ... no more. He's said it – did your hear? He pays his own friends. He takes my money ... tell the Governor he pays his own friends. Where's the kraal of H'lambie [Ndlambe, Mhala's father]? Nowhere. Here's his child – that's all – True I was not born the great son but I made myself greater. Where's H'lambie? Gone. Where's his house? Gone. You've destroyed it (vehemently) killed it – it's nowhere – gone. Be off you; tell the Governor Gawler has ruined the houses of H'lambie!!" and the old gentle-man sank back with bright staring eyes and gasping for breath.[19]

But it was already too late to stop the growing division in the tribe. As soon as Gawler returned to his hut he was besieged by some of Mhala's counselors urging him not to take the chief's attack seriously, and excus-ing it as a product of drink. A day later Mhala wandered sheepishly up to Gawler's house, attempting to make light of the quarrel as what "great men" did, and that "I ought to forget it." More ominously, Gawler was visited by a group of non-believers who urged him to implement his plan to move them to a new location soon because Mhala was getting ready to take their cattle and distribute it to his supporters. Gawler thus felt good about the day's work, concluding that "there never was a better oppor-tunity of breaking Umhala's influence and bringing forward young Kaffirland."[20]

The reference to "young Kaffirland" was Gawler's way of signaling that he had successfully suborned at least two of Mhala's sons. Gawler had successfully appealed to the ambitions of some of Mhala's family, who saw the opportunity to set themselves up as separate chiefdoms. Indeed, he had built a network of informants out of the non-believing members of

Mhala's family and his counselors. Through this network of spies, he was able to keep close tabs on virtually every move that Mhala made. He was aware of the trips to Sarhili, and what was reported back; he was aware of the witch trials, and even turned up at one of them; he was aware of the divisions within Mhala's counselors when some ordered their people to cultivate corn and others ordered the opposite; and he was aware of the attempts to subvert the loyalty of the Kaffir police. These people were to be the core group of the new, pro-government tribe.[21]

Following the climactic confrontation in March 1857, Gawler put his plans into action. In the middle of April, Gawler gathered the 200 non-believers and their families who were willing to move, and settled them at a place called Ichabo. By June, others were beginning to drift in, some from Mhala's tribe who had tried to sit out the turmoil, and some from other tribes, including a cousin of Phato. These men were rewarded with their government shilling, although in their case it was £3 per month. These gyrations continued throughout the year; Mhala did not surrender to his fate easily. In June 1857 he made a futile attempt to revive the old issue of magistrates serving at the will of the chief, and demanded from Maclean that Gawler be removed. Maclean, of course, brushed this off with contempt. At the same time he was reported to have asked Toise for money. At the beginning of August he tried another tack, expressing remorse for believing the prophecies and requesting a trader who would help revive the economy of the tribe. He accused Gawler of burning some of his kraals (which Gawler denied) and again requested another magistrate – this time on the ground that Gawler had left him to join the breakaway members of Mhala's tribe. By the beginning of September it was almost all over. He signaled to Gawler that he wanted to submit, promising to be "the policeman of the government," admitting his mistake in following the prophets, claiming, "I was deceived by that talk ... But now I have yielded in truth and I am cultivating. I have yielded." But even now Mhala continued to live up to his reputation of a cunning wildcat. One day after this submission, he was reported to be plotting an attack on Mjuza, one of Gawler's headmen and a leader of the breakaway tribe that Gawler had created.[22]

By October 1857 Gawler claimed that all but one of Mhala's wives had abandoned him, seeking the magistrate's protection, and nine months later Gawler's tribe had moved again to the banks of the Bashee river, where they formed a nice example of what the Grey system was meant to accomplish. The tribe was distributed in eight villages, under various pro-government chiefs including Siwani and Mdayi. Difficulties plagued the enterprise, however. Siwani lost support because of his overly enthusiastic embrace of the British cause, and had got into a rivalry with his brother Mackinnon. There was conflict between the resident magistrates. Herbert Vigne, Phato's magistrate, was reported to be offering the pick of Phato's country and the same pay to all who would leave Gawler and put themselves forward as Phato's headmen, guarding the essential British roadways in the region! Nor was support for Mhala completely dead. There were continuing hopes for his return. At the beginning of 1859 a rumor went around that Governor Grey had discovered that Mhala had been wrongly convicted in the trial that Gawler had arranged for him. The story went that Grey had learnt that Gawler had framed the evidence against Mhala. This was a claim that was not so far from the truth. On learning this, so the tale continued, Grey was so furious that he freed Mhala, and condemned Gawler to be hanged for not taking care of Mhala. Of course, this was only wishful thinking. The reality was Shakespearean. It was Grey who was the puppet-master in the framing and trial of Mhala.[23]

The story about Mhala's wrong conviction was dutifully reported to the British by Gawler's spy, Mjuza, son of the prophet Nxele. The British got good value from Mjuza. He continued to spy for them. He was used by Gawler to arrest and interrogate some of the lesser prophets that floated around in Nongqawuse's shadow. He was sent to arrest the leading prophetess herself, but she had already fled across the Bashee. Mjuza noted in his report that "the Kaffirs have an idea that being the son of Lynx [Nxele] . . . I am capable of detecting any deception." So Nxele's witchcraft turned out to be of advantage to the British after all. It was Mjuza who led them to Mhala when they were looking to arrest him and put him on trial.[24]

But it will be no surprise to learn that Mjuza was not always treated so well by the British. One year after he had been appointed as headman of Village No. 5 on the Bashee, his land was under attack from one of the new white settlers that Grey had allowed into British Kaffraria. Gawler had noted earlier that this was good and bountiful land, so it was not surprising that the covetous eyes of a "Mr. Scholtz" should settle on Mjuza's village. Sholtz may very well have seen an opportunity created by another outbreak of lung disease. Nevertheless, Mjuza soon began to feel the pressure to move. Gawler was away on a punitive expedition against Sarhili. The acting special magistrate (who happened to be a son of Freidrich Kayser) was in no mood to support Mjuza. Various inducements were held out to him, such as exemption from taxation and the promise of a gift of money. Scholtz and his two brothers twice went to the village and tried to induce the Xhosa to move. When this failed to have the desired effect, threats were brandished. There are a series of dignified, but somewhat pathetic, statements from Mjuza in the records protesting against his treatment, pointing out that he had been put there by the Governor "because the other Kafirs would kill me on account of my apprehending the Chief Umhala," begging to be allowed to keep his gardens, and putting himself entirely at the government's disposal. How it all ended is not clear. But it seems to have turned out all right for Mjuza. As late as 1865, the records describe him still feeding information to Gawler – who by this time was back in southern Africa after his spell in India. In that same year he had apparently become the very model of Xhosa modernity:

He now lives at the Tshabo, between Ft. Murray and Berlin, and has arrived at that point of civilization where the iron plough supersedes the old Dutch plough. Umjusa [sic] cultivates his grounds upon scientific principles. He keeps two iron ploughs going, and is particularly anxious to try a few sheep on his land. He has a notion, too, that transport riding is a profitable business, and he came to see Colonel Gawler with a view to getting a little assistance for putting his very practical ideas into effect.[25]

Phato and Vigne

Phato had never been an important chief like Maqoma or Mhala. But he was popular with his tribe and had given the British good service in the recent frontier war by guarding the road between King William's Town and the port of East London. In the mid-1850s, Phato would have to count among those Xhosa chiefs who had made their peace with the British. This makes his resistance to the Grey system even more significant. But it is a story that we can tell more rapidly than the story of Mhala, in part because the records are less revealing.

Phato's importance to the Grey system was strategic. He sat astride the key transportation and communication networks between British Kaffraria and the Colony, which was also one of the major routes along which stolen cattle were driven. It was Phato's job, therefore, to supervise and control the headmen of the various kraals who would be responsible for tracking the spoor of stolen cattle and turning the culprits over to the "Kaffir Police." Herbert Vigne's job after his arrival at Phato's Great Place in the April of 1856 was to ensure that the system of tribal authority was turned to those purposes.

In spite of Phato's reputation as a friendly chief, this was to be no easy task. In the latter part of 1856 there were complaints both from the imperial administration and from Vigne that Phato had ceased to trace cattle spoors. The issue was serious enough for the Chief Commissioner, John Maclean, to intervene. He met privately with Phato on 26 September and laid out the imperial demands. He detailed the number of robberies that had taken place on the East London road, warned him that a war spirit was rising among white settlers on the east bank of the Keiskamma, and denied that the government wanted his land, but threatened to introduce white settlers if his people misbehaved, and announced that there would be eight police stations along the road. It must have all seemed so sensible to Maclean. He had detailed knowledge of specific cases of cattle theft. All he wanted was for Phato to exercise control over "his people" in order to ward off continuing tension with the white farmers in the Colony who were panting to be allowed to break out into British Kaffraria anyway.

It is not hard to imagine how such reasoning was read by Phato. Here was the velvet-gloved hypocrisy of the imperial state at its most self-righteous, assuming in its demands (even though Maclean knew better) that Phato could issue an order and have it instantly obeyed. Still, at the subsequent public meeting with his counselors, Phato played his assigned role. He loudly asserted his commitment to the government and his intention to remain at peace. He demanded that the counselors tighten up control over tracking down thieves and report them to him for punishment. The counselors played their role too, with their usual measure of sly civility. "Of course," they all chorused in support of Phato's admonitions. Phato was thanked for speaking and was told how it was good to hear what he had said. The people must listen to him and turn in thieves even if they were family members. Delima, the great son, endorsed his father's claim that "there must be no war." But always there was the ambiguity that the British saw as reflecting the inherent, essential evasiveness of the Xhosa. Thus, here is Xosa, one of Photo's headmen: "You have said you serve the Government. After you have expressed your opinion … no one will differ from you." And Valentyne, another headman: "your tribe always has been known to pay great attention to what the Government wants."[26]

Whether Maclean and Vigne understood what this ambiguity betokened is uncertain. But it marked the opening shots in the campaign by the imperial administration to transform the chiefs into the police agents of the empire. Throughout the last quarter of 1856, Vigne endeavored to pressure Phato and his counselors to live up to their sentiments of agreement at the conference of 26 September. Vigne wanted 75 headmen appointed; Phato and his counselors would only agree to 29 and refused to commit themselves to supporting those appointments until they saw who they were. There was quibbling about what kinds of persons to appoint, and whether certain areas that Vigne claimed were under Phato's control really did contain his people. When Vigne complained to Phato at the end of October about the delays in appointing headmen, Phato replied that it was because there was not much support in his tribe for the new responsibilities that were being placed upon the headmen – in other words, there was resistance to the Grey system.[27]

The struggle around these issues went on for about a year, more or less the length of time it took to subdue Mhala. It was a struggle that ended only when the imperial state decided to bring into play the panoply of British law. Along the way, there was the usual combination of mixed signals that we have come to expect of the relationship between the chiefs and the imperial state. In February 1857, Vigne reported that Phato was in low spirits. Like many of the chiefs, he was an uncertain supporter of the prophets. Once the time for fulfillment of prophecies passed, he began to lose heart. He was being deserted by many of the non-believers; he was contrite about his earlier support of the killing; he had borrowed money from Vigne to feed his children; he was anxious to divorce himself from any association with Mhala and promised not to join any war council that Mhala might call; he admitted that he and his tribe had been lax in protecting the government's interest, and he pledged himself to work hard to make amends. He was frantic lest Vigne stop his salary.[28]

This, of course, is just what Vigne wanted to keep Phato in line. Whether or not it was successful in getting Phato to exert himself more energetically as the policeman of the imperial state in this part of British Kaffraria is not clear. What is clear is that the struggle for control over tribal authority continued. In April 1857 Vigne reported on a conversation he had with Delima, Phato's great son. In his account of the conversation, Vigne claimed that Delima had come to Vigne with an offer: for an increase in pay, he would police the road to King William's Town! Vigne was himself desperate enough to show some results for all his efforts to take this offer seriously and to defend the notion to Maclean. Vigne had come to realize that suborning the chiefs was not to be achieved simply by coercive intervention. The existing authority structure could be enlisted into the service of the imperial system more effectively if it could be persuasively coopted. And this implied using the prevailing conventions of civic authority. Thus Delima's proposal was attractive. As Vigne described it to Maclean, he could not just go in and appoint the 70-odd headmen without respecting existing tribal customs and hierarchy. He pointed out that "the influential men of the tribe living near the [East London] road will not be ordered about by men far beneath them in rank, even though they are in the pay of the Government, whereas if these men have charge of the road under Delima every other man on its whole length will be compelled by Kafir law and custom to obey their behest."[29]

But who was recruiting whom? Was Delima proposing to Vigne that he become the government agent for this part of the territory? And if so, what was his motive? Was it to do some deal with the imperial state, separate from his father? Or was he doing this as part of some deep-laid scheme concocted by his father? What we do know is that by September 1857

Vigne was actively trying to recruit Delima as an alternative to Phato. Like Gawler, Vigne was working to exploit the divisions within the tribe occasioned by the cattle-killing. He reported trying to convince Delima that it was his duty to government and to his own people "to assist me in any way he could even although he should in some instances act without consulting his father." Delima was purportedly willing to so act if Vigne would produce more money. Two days later, Vigne reported that Delima was preparing to move in with him, presumably for his own protection and as an overt sign of his commitment to the government side. That same day, however, Phato came to Vigne in a state of contrition. He claimed that in spite of their quarreling, he was determined to live amicably with Vigne.[30]

For Vigne, as for Gawler, the experience of dealing with the Xhosa must have seemed a never-ending series of false dawns. One month after this seemingly successful effort to wear down Phato's resistance and install a putative successor in his son, Vigne was again recording the obstacles he faced in trying to appropriate the authority structure of the tribe for the support of empire. Vigne found that bullying Phato or trying to buy the loyalty of the headmen and counselors just did not work. They took the money, established a police force of sorts to track spoor, but still remained beyond Vigne's control. Vigne had no way of knowing to what extent the headmen were carrying out their imperial duties, or how far Phato was orchestrating their tepid response to the Grey system.

Vigne poured out his frustrations in long letter to Maclean, which was a remarkable confession of how ineffective his campaign to control the tribe had been. He complained of the obstacles that Phato had thrown in the way of the system from the beginning, and of the dishonesty and duplicity of the counselors. He found that they pulled the wool over his eyes all the time, "beguiling me [by telling me] … any long plausible rigmarole story – exculpatory of themselves and friends and which they were too well aware I was unable to disprove." He had no independent means of checking these stories about thieves captured or escaped, or patrols undertaken along the road, because he found his own police force acting as spies for the counselors and backing them up "in their lies – of all this I am daily gathering fresh proof."

Inevitably, he was led to the Gawler solution: to create a body of picked men whom he controlled to contain the robberies which the counselors had failed to curb. This was now working, he claimed, although he had to winnow out from the force the informants Phato had planted. But this experience had led him to what we might call a "Calderwood moment" when the scales fell from his eyes about the way the chiefs controlled all things in their tribes. It was the chief who was the thief master-general, manipulating a network of felons and disguising it all through guile and deception. His own police, he reported, had provided him with "such information [as] has opened my eyes to the complicity of the Great Chiefs themselves ... everything was either hid from me or so altered or added to that all hope of tracing out the perpetrators for any act was lost and the only person caught by me was one whom Captain Fielding arrested some 12 months ago."[31]

Vigne's strategy of going around Phato and creating his own policing system began to bear results in controlling cattle theft. It was a sure sign that Vigne's efforts to subborn Phato's authority were meeting with some success that a plot was hatched against his life. This was reminiscent of the assassination plots against Shepstone in the same place over fourteen years before. Phato was reported as saying that he was not going to wait for Vigne to put his foot on his neck – in a direct reference to the notorious episode between Harry Smith and Maqoma. By March 1858, however, Phato's tribe had been decapitated. Phato and his sons were removed into the custody of the British legal system. The traditional authority of the chiefs had been replaced by an authority system that was tied entirely to the imperial system. Maclean wrote to Vigne on 15 March that it was Grey's intention to move the people of Phato's tribe to Jali's country, to the southwest of King William's Town. If they were unwilling so to uproot themselves, Vigne was instructed to eject them by force. Almost as an afterthought, he was told to inform Chief Jali of these new tenants on his lands and "secure his cooperation." Three days later, Vigne was ordered to send armed police to clear the "Gulee bush and arrest all found in it" and to move the people he had separated from Mhala's tribe into villages as soon as possible. By May 1858, Phato was in custody at the Cape, and the only problem that he now posed was whether or not his stipend should be paid to his great wife, Noxina, who was living with Herbert Vigne![32]

NOTES

1. J. B. Peires, *The Dead Will Arise: Nongqawuse and the Great Xhosa Cattle-Killing Movement of 1856–7* (Johannesburg, London, and Bloomington, IN, 1989), pp. 187–9; J. Rutherford, *Sir George Grey KCB 1812–1898: A Study in Colonial Government* (London, 1961), pp. 24–6.

2. For expressions of Grey's appreciation, see CA, BK 140, *Kaffir Chiefs, Counsellors and Headmen*, Grey to Maclean, 4 January 1856; BK 147, *Miscellaneous Letter Book of Chief Commissioner, British Kaffraria, 1858*, Maclean to Gawler, 3 October 1858. Peires, *Dead Will Arise*, pp. 188, 332. For his account of the Sikkim expedition, which also contains some early theorizing on guerrilla warfare, see John Cox Gawler, *Sikkim: With Hints on Mountain and Jungle Warfare* (London, 1873). He became a supporter of the idea that the British empire should be seen as God's successor to Ancient Israel,

and published several pro-Zionist tracts. See his *Dan, the Pioneer of Israel* (London, 1880), and *Our Scythian Ancestors identified with Israel* (London, 1875).

3. Peires, *Dead Will Arise*, p. 213; CA, BK 81, *Letters from Major Gawler, Resident Magistrate with Umhala 1856–59*, 10 December 1857, where Gawler airily dismisses these complaints with the response that there was no property to plunder, and all his police took was a gun and assegai.

4. CA, BK 1, *Dispatches of the High Commissioner, British Kaffraria, 1847–1856*, Grey to Maclean, 13 March 1856; Maclean to Vigne, 26 March 1856.

5. CA, BK 83, *Reports of Resident Magistrate with Pato, 1856–62*, 8 February 1858.

6. The record of this business is to be found (appropriately) scattered unsystematically across different groups of records. Although in itself it is a sordid little affair, it is worth noting that I have come across only one other similar case in British Kaffraria. In contrast to the encounter with the Khoi, there seems to have been relatively little crossing of sexual boundaries between the British and the Xhosa. See CA, GH 8/43, *Unbound Letters*, Anonymous to Maclean, 10 March 1860; Vigne to Maclean, 18 August 1860; Tainton to Maclean, 23 August 1860; Vigne to Maclean, 24 August 1860; Maclean to Grey, 30 September 1860; Maclean to Vigne, 15 October 1860; Vigne to Maclean, 23 October 1860; Maclean to Vigne, 25 October 1860; Vigne to Maclean, 27 October 1860; GH 8/50, *Demi-Official Letter British Kaffraria 1857–58*, Maclean to Grey, 3 May 1858, for Pato's great wife, Noxina, living with Mr. Vigne. GH 30/5, Travers (Grey's secretary in Cape Town) to Maclean, 6 October 1860. Ironically, Grey had just gone through a sexual crisis of his own in the summer of 1860. On their way back to Cape Town from London, Lady Grey had a serious flirtation with Admiral Keppel. For the next thirty-seven years Sir George and Lady Grey lived separate lives; see Rutherford, *Sir George Grey*, p. 428.

7. CA, BK 140, *Kaffir Chiefs, Counselors and Headmen. Pensions and Allowances 1852–62*, Maclean to Grey, 20 January 1856. In this latter respect, the British adopted the traditional Xhosa method of rejecting a chief's authority by deserting the tribe.

8. CA, BK 81, *Letters from Major Gawler, Resident Magistrate with Umhala 1856–59*, Gawler to Maclean, 19 April 1856.

9. Peires, *Dead Will Arise*, pp. 192–3; CA, GH 8/28, *Chief Commissioner, British Kaffraria, 1856*, Gawler to Maclean, 19 April 1856; and BK 81, *Letters from Major Gawler, Resident Magistrate with Umhala*, Gawler to Maclean, 19 April 1856.

10. The above is taken from CA, BK 81, *Letters from Major Gawler, Resident Magistrate with Umhala*, Gawler to Maclean, 24 April 1856.

11. For Gawler's failure to enforce a fine on some of the men involved in the fracas recounted earlier, see CA, BK 81, *Letters from Major Gawler*, Gawler to Maclean, 13 May 1856. Mhala continued to challenge Gawler on the question of the payment of money, for example, so that quarrels between the two were quite frequent throughout 1856; see GH 8/29, *Chief Commissioner, British Kaffraria, 1856*, Gawler to Maclean, 14 August 1856.

12. CA, GH 8/50, *Demi-Official Letters, British Kaffraria, 1857–58*, Gawler to Maclean, 14 October and 20 November 1856. In October 1856 Mhala was reported to have sent a message (which was as much an enquiry as a statement) to Mhalakaza: "the English tell us to cultivate and not to kill our cattle but how can we obey them when they have taken and killed our chiefs Hintsa, Seyolo etc. and we have done them no harm?"

13. *Contra* Jean and John Camaroff, *Of Revelation and Revolution: Christianity, Colonialism and Consciousness in South Africa*, vol. I (Chicago, 1991), this incident provides a clear example of the British failing to control the Xhosa through controlling the discourse. CA, A793, *Gawler Letter Book*, 1 and 7 October 1856. At one point Mhala urged Gawler to send a white man to observe the new people because the prophet "would not deceive a white man"; entry of 26 November.

14. CA, BK 81, *Letters from Gawler*, Gawler to Maclean, 20 November and 4 December 1856.

15. CA, A 793, *Gawler Letter Book*, 20, 22 and 23 November 1856; GH 8/30, *Chief Commissioner, British Kaffraria, Dispatches from Maclean 1856*, Maclean to Grey, 8 December 1856 and 26 January 1857. GH 8/50, *Demi-Official Letters, British Kaffraria 1857–58*, Gawler to Maclean, 31 October and 2 November 1856. The division in Mhala's tribe between the believers and the non-believers probably followed broadly generational lines.

16. CA, BK 81, *Letters from Gawler*, Gawler to Maclean, 26 January and 18, 24 and 28 February 1857.

17. CA, GH 8/31, *Dispatches from Chief Commissioner, British Kaffraria 1857*, Gawler to Maclean, 15 March 1857.

18. For Gawler's planning for this secession, see "Proposal for creating a revolution in Umhala's country aiding the well disposed and bringing all under control," CA, BK 81, *Letters from Gawler*, 28 February and 1, 14 and 19 March 1857; GH 8/30, *Dispatches, Chief Commissioner British Kaffraria 1856*, 8 and 15 December 1856.

19. CA, A 793, *Gawler Letter Book*, 16 March 1857.

20. Ibid., 21 March 1857.

21. Ibid., 7, 14, 24 and 29 October 1856. Gawler, of course, was not alone in keeping a close watch on the chiefs. Sandile was continually watched. His communications with Sarhili were the object of particular interest. Like Mhala, he put great effort into trying to assess whether the prophecies were real or not. See BK 10, *Lieutenant Governor, Miscellaneous Dispatches 1852–1864*, Maclean to Grey, 19 January and 5 November 1857, and Brownlee to Maclean, 15 November 1855, for information on his attitude to the Grey system.

22. CA, BK 81 *Letters from Gawler*, Gawler to Maclean, 10 September 1857; GH 8/32, *Dispatches from Chief Commissioner, British Kaffraria, 1857*, Maclean to Grey, 1 June, 6 August and 9 September 1857; BK 140, *Kaffir Chiefs, Counselors and Headmen*, Gawler to Maclean, 9 September 1857; GH 8/50, *Demi-Official Letters, British Kaffrari, 1857*, Maclean to Grey, 10 September 1857.

23. For Gawler's people, as the new tribe was known, see CA, GH 8/35, *Dispatches from Chief Commissioner of British Kaffraria 1858*, Gawler to Maclean, 3 June

1858; Gawler to Maclean, 29 May 1858; Maclean to Grey, 1 September 1858; A 793, *Gawler Letter Book*, 30 May 1858 and 31 August 1858. For the rumor regarding Mhala and Gawler, see GH 8/37, *Dispatches from the Chief Commissioner for British Kaffraria 1859*, Dispatch of 10 Februry 1859.

24. CA, GH 8/34, *Dispatches of Chief Commissioner, British Kaffraria, 1858*, 4 March 1858; BK 11, *Dispatches between Resident Secretary and Lt. Governor*, 18 March 1859, statement of Umjuza to W. B. Chalmers. In March 1859 Mjuza reported on the dissatisfaction among the Mfengu, who were also being resettled into villages and who were talking of fighting all the way to Cape Town if necessary.

25. CA, BK 81, *Letters from Major Gawler, Resident Magistrate with Umhala, 1856–59*, 11 February 1859; *King William's Town Gazette*, 17 April 1865.

26. CA, BK 140, *Kaffir Chiefs, Counselors and Headmen*, 26 September 1856, "Brief Sketch of a Conversation between the Chief Commissioner and Pato," and "Minutes of a Meeting at Pato's Great Place."

27. Ibid., "Report of a Meeting with Pato for the purpose of appointing headmen," 2 October 1856; "Conference with Phato and Counselors," 23 October 1856; Vigne to Maclean, 26 November 1856.

28. CA, BK 83, *Reports of Resident Magistrate with Pato 1856–62*, Vigne to Maclean, 23 February 1857.

29. Ibid., Vigne to Maclean, 7 April 1857.

30. Ibid., Vigne to Maclean, 2 and 4 September 1857. Phato had lived in Maclean's back room during much of the 1850–3 war when he protected the East London road.

31. CA, GH 8/33, *Dispatches from Chief Commissioner of British Kaffraria, October–December 1857*, Vigne to Maclean, 3 October 1857. Note that this strategy was contrary to what Maclean and Grey had intended for Phato's tribe. They wanted indirect rule on the cheap, whereby the existing officers of the tribe – the counselors and headmen – would appoint local police under their authority. In a strict sense, Vigne was acting outside the policy by adopting the Gawler solution of a police force that was directly under his control. And there was some question regarding the expenses that were incurred because of this. But he seems to have convinced both Maclean and Grey that it was a necessary contravention of instructions, Grey having told him (presumably on one of his visits to the frontier) that "so long as the spirit of his scheme was adhered to I had carte blanche to adopt any modification suitable to the occasion." And in a dispatch to Grey of 19 October 1857, Maclean recommended that Vigne be allowed to continue as he was doing. A regular "Kaffir Police" as well as a white-dominated Frontier Armed Mounted Police were also in the process of formation at this time.

32. These movements were part of the settlement of the Xhosa into controlled villages. CA, GH 8/34, *Dispatches of Chief Commissioner, British Kaffraria 1858*, Maclean to Grey, 4 March 1858; BK 83, *Reports of Resident Magistrate with Pato, 1856–62*, Vigne to Maclean, 8 February 1858. BK 407, *Miscellaneous Letter Book of Chief Commissioner, British Kaffraria, 1858*, Maclean to Vigne, 13 and 18 March 1858; GH 8/50, *Demi-Official Letters, British Kaffraria 1857–58*, Maclean to Grey, 3 May 1858.

12   The trials of the chiefs

The uses of law in Empire

In the Cape spring of 1857, the consequences of the cattle-killing approached their devastating climax. British Kaffraria, and Independent Kaffraria too, were being emptied of people. Those who were not starving were streaming into the colony, if they could walk, to find work; some were choosing to die rather than leave. British Kaffraria was being transformed into a labor pool for the eastern Cape. The chiefs were reduced to beggary. It was just at this moment that the imperial state fired its final salvo at the tattered remains of chiefly power. The British legal system was trundled into play to scoop up most of the prominent chiefs in the province, try them, convict them, and sentence them to varying terms on Robben Island.

I wish to highlight the trials as an example of the relationship between empire and justice. This is no small matter. The law, after all, lay at the heart of Britain's identity as a *liberal* empire, as an empire of freedom. And one of the key defenses of the British empire hereafter was that it introduced the British judicial system to large parts of the world and embedded the virtues of due process, habeas corpus and the like where they were unknown. But before the advantages of British justice could be realized in British Kaffraria, it first had to turn into the reverse of itself. Whether this was a typical pattern is too big a question to be addressed here. But certainly in this part of the empire, British justice worked through travesties of its procedures to complete and legitimate the destruction that had been wrought by the likes of Major Gawler and Herbert Vigne. How were the transgressions of the law reconciled in the minds of imperial administrators? How did Sir George Grey, the epitome of mid-Victorian Britain's liberal empire, justify to himself his deliberate perversion of the law to destroy the Xhosa chiefs? What intellectual work did he have to do within his own head to reconcile the tensions that followed from his use of the law to complete his political end?[1]

Between the (southern hemisphere) springs of 1857 and 1858 about a dozen of the leading chiefs of British Kaffraria were prosecuted, convicted

316

and transported to Robben Island. This season of trials was bookended by the prosecution of the two chiefs who had been the most effective and determined leaders of the anti-British opposition since the 1830s. Maqoma was brought to trial in November 1857 and Mhala was tried in September 1858. In between, the lesser lights were dealt with. Phato and two of his sons were sentenced in the first half of 1858, as were long-standing opponents of the British such as Xayimpi, the man the British claimed had led the killing of the male military settlers at Woburn on Christmas Eve, 1850, at the opening of the eighth frontier war.

Only those chiefs who were firmly committed to the British, such as Khama, escaped the prosecutorial reach of the imperial state. But a history of attachment to the British was no guaranteed protection. Jan Tzatzoe only just escaped being caught in the imperial dragnet. Phato's son Delima was arrested in November on a long list of charges that included a murder, dating back six months. A few months before, Vigne had been trying to recruit him as an imperial informer and as the British candidate to replace his father as tribal chief. Sandile, as usual, managed to pick his way deli-cately between the landmines of Xhosa and imperial politics. And although his performance during the cattle-killing mirrored that of the other chiefs – waxing hot and cold on whether he should kill or not, sending messengers to Sarhili to test the word of Nongqawuse – the imperial administration gave no serious thought to including him in their sweep. This probably reflected their sense that they needed some figure of authority to implement their version of indirect rule. In many respects Sandile was a spent force.[2]

Constructing the cases

From the middle of 1857, the imperial administration was on the lookout for anything that could be used to mount a legal prosecution of the chiefs. Grey had let it be known that he was most "anxious that the Chiefs should be shewn that they are no longer to … rob and murder with impunity." Grey's leading henchman in British Kaffraria, John Cox Gawler, was the center of such activity. The murder of Fusani, one of Gawler's spies, in early 1857 gave Gawler the opening he needed. Gawler immediately began to build a case against Maqoma for this murder, starting from the belief that Fusani was murdered in revenge for some unspecified infor-mation he had given to Gawler. Fusani was currently attached to Maqoma's tribe. A raid had been launched on Fusani's kraal driving off some cattle and also resulting in Fusani's death. Using evidence from Fusani's sons, who secured it in turn from one of Fusani's counselors, in August 1857 Gawler arrested the supposed murderers, one of whom belonged to Mhala's tribe, while the other belonged to Maqoma's.[3]

The evidence at this trial pointing to Maqoma's involvement was inconsequential. One of the murderers turned state's evidence and testified that Maqoma had sent the patrol out specifically to murder Fusani. This assertion was weakened by other evidence that was presented. Fusani had struck the first blow, throwing an assegai at one of the attackers, who had responded with somewhat more accuracy to kill him. It was also testified that Maqoma had ordered only that Fusani should be "eaten up" – that is, his cattle seized – not that he should be killed. Maqoma's defense rested on the prerogatives of his chiefly authority – a commodity that was precisely at stake here. He claimed that the patrol had been sent to punish Fusani because of his involvement in a murder. If this was the case, Xhosa law gave Maqoma the right to exact punishment from Fusani in the form of a cattle fine. The death of Fusani was an accident of that event, and not an intended result.[4]

Was this enough to charge Maqoma with murder? Maclean felt it was not. Gawler had been pressing Maclean to arrest Maqoma on this charge since May. But Maclean, ever cautious, had resisted doing this without Grey's permission because "no proof could be produced of his participation in Fusani's murder." And with some wavering back and forth he held this position until the end of September, when he acceded to the request to proceed against Maqoma. What caused Maclean to change his mind?

Maqoma had been arrested at the end of August on a pass charge that carried with it one year's hard labor. Maclean suddenly found his courage because this arrest had passed off without arousing much notice among the Xhosa. "He is in our power without trouble or any risk of an excitement being raised as might have been some time ago had he been taken here." So Maclean concluded that "a trip to the Western Districts [i.e. Robben Island] would be of much service to Macoma and be a good warning to others."[5]

Between August and November, Maclean carefully put the pieces in place to prosecute Maqoma. And the success of Maqoma's detention encouraged Maclean to collect evidence against the other chiefs. By October, the process of building cases was in full swing. Although the chiefs were all charged with some counts of receiving stolen goods, it was not this charge that occupied the attention of the imperial witch finders. They focused entirely upon the charge of conspiracy between the chiefs and the prophets. Maclean now dropped all the reservations about the quality of the evidence he had previously expressed about Maqoma and participated fully in the development of the case that indicted the chiefs for using the prophets to raise a rebellion against British rule. It was to prove this argument that Maclean, Gawler and Barrington directed their efforts. The leading prophet, Nongqawuse, was somewhere with Sarhili, and

Mhlakaza was likewise unavailable because he had died of starvation. Maclean and Gawler therefore focused on the way the conspiracy worked in Mhala's tribe.[6]

This meant bringing the child prophet Nonkosi in for interrogation and getting her to implicate her uncle Kwitchi, Mhala's counselor. Nonkosi was nine years old. It took Maclean and Gawler three days to get what they wanted out of her. They needed evidence to soften up Kwitchi, who had served as Nonkosi's minder. Nonkosi had lived under his care and, they believed, was coached by him on the instructions, ultimately, of Mhala. It is hard to know exactly what tactics Maclean and Gawler used to get Nonkosi to say what they wanted. Maclean described her as an intelligent and self-possessed child who knew a lot, but also knew how to keep silent. Until 25 October, Nonkosi "persisted in a repetition of her misrepresentations." But she then broke, and admitted that Kwitchi had coached her in what to say, that he had acted the part of Mlanjeni coming out of the water, and that he had alternatively bribed her with money and threatened her with strangling if she told anyone the truth. The ground was now laid to use this evidence against Kwitchi.[7]

Kwitchi tried to evade interrogation; he twice escaped from custody. But his grilling began on 12 November and two days later it was complete. There is much that is mysterious about this investigation. Kwitchi was a counselor to Mhala. It is also possible that he was an informant for Gawler. At one point in the interrogation Kwitchi mentioned his service for Gawler, but Gawler cut him off and told him: "I did not want to hear about his conscientious scruples I wanted to know why Umhala liked 'Nonkosi' talk and who told her all this nonsense." Gawler alternatively threatened and prompted him. Kwitchi broke fairly easily, and soon made a full statement that he had fed Nonkosi information on Mhala's instructions. Kwitchi gave Gawler everything he wanted: that Mhala and Sarhili were in communication; that "the object was war"; that all the chiefs were involved, including Toise, Khama, Siwani and Mhala's own son Smith; but that these were all dupes of Mhala, and "Umhala and I were the only ones in on the secret." When Kwitchi told Mhala that he did not believe that either cattle or people were to rise out of the sea, Mhala replied, "He was not hoping for *that*, it was only a plan for driving the English out of the country and for taking possession of their country."[8]

So there it was; the evidence was in place now that confirmed what the imperial administration already knew. The cattle-killing *was* a conspiracy in which Mhala had played a leading role. Kwitchi was the Crown's best witness. As Mhala's counselor, he had a lot of information that could be used in the case that was being built against this chief. Kwitchi continued to be questioned into January 1858. Indeed, Barrington was not convinced that there was enough demonstrable evidence, and there was some debate between the officials over how best to use the evidence that Kwitchi could provide. Barrington, being a lawyer, was aware, as he put it, that "the case against Umhala is not likely to be supported by much evidence and will therefore only be justified by political necessity, not prudence." Maclean wrote to Grey in the middle of December that Barrington had not yet discovered enough demonstrable evidence to pin the conspiracy on Mhala. This was precisely the problem, of course. There was insufficient evidence to make that case, which anyway was full of logical holes. But Gawler was pushing Barrington to make haste, so that he could sweep up the rest of the chiefs. By mid-December Phato and Xhoxho were already in jail on charges of having received stolen horses. And Delima, Tola, Mate and Stock were the next targets, Gawler arguing that arresting them would make the case even bigger.[9]

There is no doubt that Gawler was carrying out Grey's wishes. Maclean and Barrington felt obliged to turn up the heat on the interrogation of Kwitchi. Barrington subjected the witchdoctor to three more interrogations sometime in the early part of January, and during the last two he secured the breakthrough he felt was necessary. How he did this is not clear; there is no record, of course, of any physical compulsion, but that cannot be ruled out. Unsurprisingly, the threat that he too could fall into the judicial net of the imperial state was used; and this in itself may have been effective. Kwitchi had resisted for several months before succumbing to administration pressure. By the middle of January Barrington was proclaiming that Kwitchi now "appeared to have made up his mind to say all he knows in connection with the war plans of the Chiefs. That matter seems to have been fully confessed now."

There remained only one other area where Kwitchi was required to deliver testimony: the robberies that Mhala had ordered. Barrington promised that if he came through on that evidence, "the Governor will not punish him for his misdeed therein and I have told him to consider the matter over in his mind." For his part, of course, Kwitchi was concerned about his safety after turning Queen's evidence. "He hopes what he has said will not be published, for he feels sure the Chiefs will kill him. I told him the Governor will take his own course on that, but that he would be protected." But Kwitchi provided Barrington with what he wanted, detailing the role that Mhala and Phato had played in orchestrating the sightings of the "new people" reported by Nonkosi, and in the murder of non-believers. He offered four other witnesses whom Gawler could bring in to verify these crimes.[10]

In the meantime, the trial of Maqoma had taken place. He sat in the dock with eight other members of his tribe. He was charged with inciting the theft of Fusani's cattle, with knowingly receiving the stolen stock, and with involvement in the murder of the chief. The trial set the pattern for those that were to follow. It was a military tribunal, composed of Army officers and resident magistrates. There were no defense counsels. The imperial officers were judges, prosecutors and juries. These tribunals were not regular courts of law, but specially created under the martial law that still operated in British Kaffraria, and the supreme authority of the High Commissioner over all aspects of government in the colony. The police-man Gawler was also the prosecutor, as he was to be in Phato's and Delima's trials. Two of those charged turned Queen's evidence and had the charges against them withdrawn. All defendants pleaded not guilty to murder charges and guilty to the charges of theft. In truth the trial was a farce. It was never claimed that Maqoma ordered the murder of Fusani. The evidence that he did was third-hand, and that evidence came from those who had turned state's evidence. No one actually saw Fusani die; only one witness could attest to his being wounded. Indeed, there was no body. It was five months before a body, or rather a skull, was produced. And it was Gawler who testified that the skull was that of Fusani, on the basis of the teeth that Gawler had seen so often when he had paid him his monthly retainer: "Fusani had a habit of showing his teeth in conversation."

Gawler's speculation, repeated at the trial, was that Maqoma had ordered Fusani to be killed because he passed information about stolen cattle and had told Gawler where they were quartered. When the police went to arrest the thief, he resisted and was shot dead. Gawler believed that Maqoma ordered the raid on Fusani's kraal and his death in revenge. About three days before his disappearance, Fusani came to Gawler in fear because it had become known that he was the informer. It was at this point in the trial that Maqoma made his only substantive intervention. Maqoma had maintained silence throughout all the evidence. He had no counsel. But now he chose to cross-examine Gawler. And even though the tran-script of the trial is mysteriously garbled at this point, Maqoma's sharp mind comes through. The point of his cross-examination brought out the admission that Gawler knew nothing about the cattle theft except what had come from Fusani. And since Fusani was dead, there could be no corroboration.

This intervention suggests that, even without the benefit of the English language, Maqoma understood well the finer points of English legal procedure. His silence during the trial may have reflected resignation that his fate was sealed anyway, or contempt, or both. Only one witness that he called in his defense turned up, and, indeed, there was hardly a government case to answer. He did admit that he had sent the patrol to

Fusani. He could hardly do anything else; all the other defendants had testified that they assumed as much. But he claimed, in effect, that he was asserting his rights under Xhosa law to punish Fusani by taking a fine of cattle for his role in the death of the man killed by Gawler's police. Henry Barrington assured Maclean and Grey that this was a fair trial, claiming that "the Court even aided them in suggesting defence which they readily availed themselves of." But there is no evidence of this in the transcript. Referring to the failure of the defendants to offer cross-examination of witnesses Barrington noted that he did not think it likely that any cross-examination "would have improved the prisoners cases directly."[11]

It is hard to see how Barrington could square this with his conscience. Even this court could not bring itself to bring in a verdict of murder against Maqoma. He and his compatriots were sentenced on the basis of the stock theft. But for this he was convicted of three capital charges of receiving stolen goods, and sentenced to death. This gave Grey complete freedom to do what he wanted, and, in his infinite mercy, he commuted that sentence to twenty years in prison, adding the pious gratuity that although Maqoma was found not guilty of murder, he was morally responsible for inspiring it. Moral inspiration was of course a crime unknown to English law. If it had been, Sir George Grey could have been hanged many times over.[12]

Once Maqoma had been disposed of, the state was encouraged to move against the others. A spate of trials followed in the early part of 1858, the most important of which was that of Phato and his sons Mate and Delima, followed by Mhala's in September. We do not need to follow in great detail the course of these trials. They essentially repeated the pattern set by Maqoma's. There were three kinds of charges brought against the chiefs: stock theft, murder (in the case of Delima) and conspiracy to wage war (Mhala). It would be wrong to take the formal charges too seriously. They were often poorly drawn, there was little direct fit between the evidence and the verdict, and the trials were rife with constitutional improprieties. Phato's case suggests the raggedly farcical nature of this enterprise.

He was charged with knowingly receiving stolen horses. Unfortunately, the government's case fell apart the moment the court proceedings began. Phato's brother, Khama, came to his rescue. Khama announced that he had arrested the thief. And what was worse, Herbert Vigne, for reasons that are mystifying, gave some evidence at the trial that supported Phato's claim not to have known that the horses had been stolen. This embarrassing turn of events makes one wonder what Gawler and Maclean had been doing for the past few months. Had they not reported to Grey their confidence about the cases they were assembling? Faced with this admission, the court had no choice but to find Phato and his son Mpafa (or

Mpassa) not guilty. This could not be allowed, however. Acting on Grey's orders Maclean contended that the verdict did not fit the evidence and ordered the court to reassemble and reconsider. This they duly did, and obediently reversed their findings. Phato and his son were packed off to the Cape for five years.[13]

The original verdict on Phato was delivered by a stacked court. How, then, was this extraordinary reversal of its "not guilty" verdict squared in the minds of the participants? We know what arguments Henry Barrington used to coach Maclean to justify his intervention in the work of the special criminal tribunal. This fragment of evidence reveals an *imperial state of mind*, an example of how the psychology of imperial culture works. Barrington employed a style of reasoning that is endemic to imperial culture. It involved turning the facts of a situation inside out, to make them point to exactly the opposite conclusion that common sense and the rule of logic would suggest. Such reversals were necessary when some fundamental transgression of cultural values and beliefs had to be enacted. They were vital to allow the work of imperial rule to continue undisturbed, and to persuade those who were carrying it out that they were doing the right thing.

Barrington pointed out that there was a conflict between the verdict and the evidence. It was not a conflict such as you, the reader, might imagine. The conflict was not between the charge and the evidence as it was presented. The conflict that Barrington saw was rather one between the evidence of Phato and the evidence of the owner of the stolen horses. Phato had testified that the horses in question had been in his possession for four years, and the owner testified that they had been stolen three years before. Thus, the central question was: whom was the court to believe? The court had initially chosen to believe Phato and his son. The weight of the evidence supported that verdict. Khama had arrested the thief. Even Herbert Vigne had testified that Phato did not know that the horse was stolen. Barrington argued, however, that the conflict of evidence was really between Phato and the supposed owner of the horse, a man called Whitfield. If Phato's defense was accepted, Whitfield must have given false evidence regarding the time of the theft. And if this were the case, then nothing that Whitfield said should be believed at all. "Yet the court believed this witness when he swears the horse is his, and believes Phato when he says the horse had been his four years." Barrington found the court's logic flawed, therefore, because it was "preferring to believe the assertions of such people as a Kafir Chief's witness and Kafir prisoners to the sworn testimony in a court of justice of Christians whose characters ... are unimpeachable." What it came down to, then, for Barrington, was that it was impossible to believe both Phato and Khama even though the weight of the evidence and testimony pointed precisely in that direction.[14]

Mhala was brought to trial in September 1858. He and two others were charged with two offenses. The first was that of receiving stolen cattle, and the second was that of devising a war against the Queen. He was found guilty on both charges, although his codefendants were acquitted of the "treason" charge. His sentence was to be transported for life, which gave Grey the chance again to demonstrate his humanity by reducing it to five years. The main witnesses against him were Mjuza and Gawler, who used the evidence gained from Kwitchi and Nonkosi to make the treason charge stick. As in the previous cases, the presentations of the trial are their least interesting aspect. A great deal of extraneous detail was laboriously offered and solemnly recorded. Most of it was window-dressing and failed to speak to the charges at issue. Much of Gawler's testimony, for example, was taken up with the details of Mhala's capture. There was the same gap between evidence and verdict. In the case of the cattle theft, for example, the best that could be presented was that some remains of oxen with the same color skin as those that had been stolen were found 100 yards from Mhala's hiding place.

The most noteworthy part of the record was Mhala's defense, a sad and even pathetic document. Unlike the other chiefs, Mhala chose to make a statement. He succeeded only in confirming the government's case. He denied involvement in the crimes he was charged with, but admitted that he had participated in the cattle-killing, explaining that it was because he had wanted to see his mother and father again. This was certainly true. Virtually the sole possession found on him when Gawler's police tracked him down was a bundle of his father Ndlambe's old assegais. He admitted that he had "sinned against the government," pleaded forgiveness and begged not to be sent to "distant places." But it was all in vain. This "most cunning and subtle of the Chiefs," in Maclean's words, had at last been delivered to the tender mercies of the law. Justice must be seen to be done. Mhala was led in chains to the boat that was to transport him to Cape Town. At the quayside, a rope was dropped from a crane as if to string him up. On board the ship he was much frightened by the waves that crashed against the side of the ship, letting out three "dreadful yells" before sinking to a morose and wistful gaze at the land he thought he would never see again.[15]

Law and empire: constitutional dissonances

The main theme that ran through these trials was a sharp disconnect between evidence and verdict, and the naked use of "law" to remove the Xhosa chiefs from their patrimony. Legal procedures in empire always posed serious challenges to the self-image of the British as a nation of law.

This was a problem that was familiar to the British, although the variance between the ideal of the law in the British imagination and its practice in the case of British Kaffraria must be quite unusual. These trials exposed clear departures from constitutional principles and procedures. How were these violations received by the imperial administration, and how were they explained and justified? By what means, in other words, does imperial culture reconcile the contradiction between its claims to possess civilized principles and the reality that those principles must be transgressed in the service of empire?[16]

As early as April 1857, the machination to legally hang the chiefs was launched. Henry Barrington sent a memo to Grey titled "Trial and Sentencing of Kaffir Prisoners." Its purpose was to provide a rationale for the violations of rules of evidence, and other standard procedures of English law, that would be necessary in trials of the chiefs in British Kaffraria. A regular court might be forced to acquit the Xhosa, Barrington claimed. His reasoning was that the kind of evidence the British were likely to produce would tend to point to acquittal. And this was made more likely by the inherent tendency of the Xhosa to lie even under oath. Barrington therefore proposed that "the ends of justice could be met" by the special magistrate's summoning military officers to form a court, "first however satisfying himself by a short preliminary examination of a reasonable ground" for trial. Then the usual process would take place, witnesses presenting testimony all under the presidency of a special magistrate. There was no provision for a defense counsel, although prisoners would be allowed to make a defense. The special magistrate would pronounce sentence according to a schedule of punishments that he provided, and the Chief Commissioner would order execution of sentence or modify it.[17]

This was an attempt to mesh the procedures of British law, the peculiar constitutional position of British Kaffraria and the perceived need to compensate for Xhosa cunning and deceit into a system that would ensure the punishment of chiefs already known to be guilty. Barrington may have solved the procedural question, but there remained the difficulty of how to prove their guilt and preserve intact the idea of British justice. For aside from the problems of evidence, there were issues that went to the very heart of the constitutional processes that British rule was supposed to embody. These objections were identified by the Attorney General of the Cape Colony, William Porter, to whom the trials were referred for legal opinion before passing to Sir George Grey to confirm or alter the sentences.[18]

In the case of Mhala, Porter noted the gap between the evidence and the verdict as regards stolen oxen, and the mistreatment of the evidence by Gawler, who had returned to their supposed owners two oxen that had supposedly been stolen. Thus no evidence remained. This alone, Porter pointed out, would be enough to disallow the evidence in a British court. In Mhala's case there were even more serious questions of constitutional principle at stake. Mhala had been tried on what was loosely referred to as a treason charge. Yet the statute under which he was arraigned – a statute that referred to making war against the Queen – could not extend to British Kaffraria. It had been passed after British Kaffraria came into existence and the statute had not specified that British Kaffraria fell under its scope. Constitutionally, therefore, it was not possible to convict Mhala for "treason." In addition, the charge was defective in its substance. The indictment had been drawn up by Maclean, who was not a lawyer. It did not claim that Mhala and his codefendants were subjects of the Crown and were thus liable to prosecution for "treason."[19]

We should pause here to note that Porter was introducing an issue that was cloaked in uncertainty. It was not clear that the Xhosa in British Kaffraria were legally British subjects at all. Although Porter did not spend much time on this issue, it continued to nag at the imperial administration. Thus Barrington sent a memo to Maclean a year later in which he admitted that Mhala was not strictly a British subject. The problem went back to the way British Kaffraria had been constituted in 1847. It had been declared a British territory by Smith, who also announced that its residents were British subjects. An oath to the Queen was taken and they were brought under British martial law. But there was nothing in the proclamation of 1847 which made the Xhosa British subjects. At the great meeting of 23 December 1847, Smith had verbally declared them to be such. Barrington knew that this was not enough in law, and he excused the indictment of Mhala as being "not a formal indictment [but] framed so as best to suit the circumstances and the case." And he concluded by admitting that this was a political trial in which the public good had to prevail over the rules of evidence.[20]

Underlying the principal constitutional problems with the trials was the larger issue of the constitutionality of British Kaffraria itself. Harry Smith had issued a proclamation and asserted the Crown's title over the land and people as if he possessed the authority by virtue of his governorship. Yet Porter and others doubted whether the Crown alone had the right to make the people of a territory British subjects; and if it had, a Governor certainly did not. These reservations were quite widely known within the imperial administration at the Cape and within the circles of policy-making power in London. There was concern that if this became the subject of widespread public discussion, embarrassing questions would be raised in Parliament.

British Kaffraria was an unconstitutional entity. It had been proclaimed in an irregular way and governed without Parliamentary approval, and neither Smith nor Grey had taken the necessary steps to remedy these inconsistencies. Sir George Grey was fully aware of all this. There is a memo in his papers explaining it. He was quite conscious, therefore, of the weak constitutional and principled grounds upon which his whole policy rested. This was surely in his mind when he came to justify his elimination of the chiefs – a justification that, as we shall see, mixed the pious self-righteousness of the paternalistic liberal with the formal severity of the duty-bound, even-handed executor of "the law."[21]

Beyond these large constitutional issues, however, there were other, more mundane difficulties that Attorney-General William Porter felt obliged to bring to Grey's attention. He pointed out that Maclean's indictment of Mhala was unclear with regard to the exact charge against the chief. Was it treason or inciting hostilities? In either case, the conclusion did not follow. Porter went to the heart of the government's case against the chiefs and exploded its logic. Porter blew the whistle on the whole conspiracy theory when he examined the evidence that was presented in the trial of Mhala. In his commentary on the case, he pointed out that the evidence of the trial suggested the opposite of what it was taken to mean. The evidence that was gathered to support the idea that Mhala was the puppet-master of the prophecies in his tribe *in fact suggested the opposite*. The testimony of Kwitchi and Nonkosi tended to point more to the conclusion that Mhala had been their dupe, not the reverse; that he had believed the prophecies. The idea that he conspired to propagate these ideas as a way of uniting his people against the British was not believable. Although there may have been reasons of state to remove Mhala, there was no case that he was making plans for war, only a case that he believed in natural and supernatural causes that he hoped would expel the English. Porter admitted that all this might have made his removal desirable, but "I would prefer to have it on those grounds rather than using the law improperly or defective evidence."[22]

This commentary on Mhala's trial transcript left the government's case in tatters. It amounted to the claim that Mhala was being punished for believing that people could rise from the dead. How was Sir George Grey to receive it? He did what we would expect. He rejected his Attorney-General's opinion and went ahead to confirm all the sentences, altering them as he saw fit. What is of interest is the reasoning process that he used to justify his cloaking of his political objective within the formalities and logic of British law. The glaring gap between the evidence on the one hand, and the sentence and Grey's actions on it on the other, required some explanation from the Governor. It was always possible that he might be called to account for his actions publicly. But there was, I suspect, an even more powerful reason why Grey needed to explain why he was going to reject the cold legal logic of Porter. It was necessary for Grey to keep intact the *intellectual* coherence of what he was doing. He needed to persuade himself that he was doing the right thing when he railroaded these chiefs, violated the basic canons of British legal procedure, and thereby transgressed the cultural notions of British civilized superiority and "fairness" that he himself embodied.

Grey's response to the dilemma Porter had presented is a neat little example of how mid-nineteenth-century Britain reconciled its liberalism with the realities of empire. As the leading liberal imperialist of the nineteenth century, Grey is a prize specimen for observing how this procedure was navigated in the here and now of imperial administration. He accomplished the trick by a combination of moralizing platitudes, by resort to a thinly veiled utilitarian argument about the greater good taking precedence over legal procedure, and by the assertion that the guilt of the accused was established anyway, in spite of all the disjunctures and contradictions in the evidence. He then satisfied his conscience by reducing all the sentences delivered by the special courts in British Kaffraria. Let us follow Sir George Grey on his logical journey in the cases of Phato and Mhala.

To begin with Phato. Grey justified Phato's trial by employing a common trick of imperial reasoning. He turned the issue away from the procedure of the trial and the evidence and toward the behavior of Phato himself. He explained that Phato had fallen under the influence of bad sons like Delima. Maclean, Herbert Vigne and even Sir George Grey himself had all attempted to win him over to the imperial side by kindness and persuasion. But Phato had refused those outstretched hands and supported the party which plunged the country into war. This then became for Grey the basis for Phato's trial and ultimate conviction: "the offence for which he was tried and convicted was therefore not an ordinary one, and it might also have led to ulterior very serious consequences [*sic*], to the peace of the country and the safety of its inhabitants."

The objections to the procedure of the court Grey dismissed as a "technical informality," and he set himself up as the arbiter of fundamental legal procedure. If he believed that those infractions had in fact prevented the defendants from presenting their defense or showing their innocence, he "would have at once given the Prisoners the benefit of this informality and ordered them to be discharged." But the argument he made is dominated by non sequiturs and tortured logic:

Kaffraria is still in so unsettled a state. The Crown has such difficulty in constituting Courts there, in having prosecutions properly conducted, in compelling the attendance of witnesses and in many other similar respects is in such an unusual position … with all these disadvantages militating against the prosecution and apprehension of prisoners on one hand. The native on the other hand can claim every technical advantage which would be awarded to a British subject in a regularly constituted Court established in a country in a state settled. This perfect system shall undoubtedly be introduced as soon as possible into Kaffraria, but at present it cannot in all cases be acted upon. Nor would the natives themselves understand why parties undoubtedly guilty of an offence and whose guilt had been proved should be now let free as if innocent on account of a technicality which would be quite beyond their comprehension.

Thus, he wrote, "I feel it therefore my duty" that Phato and his sons be sentenced to five years. Phato was saved the rigors of Robben Island, however. He was allowed to serve his sentence at Somerset Hospital in Cape Town.[23]

All things considered, Phato probably considered himself lucky. The Somerset Hospital – which still stands today in Cape Town – was located in Greenpoint, facing the sea, and he was given the run of the grounds. Mhala and the others were not so fortunate. But the reasoning process that Grey employed in favor of Mhala's treatment possessed the same elements of circular self-justification wrapped up in liberal pieties and sentiments. Grey started by establishing Mhala as an object of pity: he was a fugitive, his tribe had been dispersed, he had no means of support. And however much he may have deserved this fate, it was not possible to see this "powerful Chief reduced to abject misery without feeling great pity for him." Thus, Grey averred that to treat or punish him as a "low and ordinary thief … would have the appearance of almost insulting misfortune." One contemplates this passage with a breathless astonishment. The audacity of the formulation is incredible. It was Grey's policy which had brought Mhala to this state. And insult is added to this injury by Grey's hypocritical pretense that he was not going to humiliate this great chief by treating him (as he was in fact being treated) as a common criminal. The purpose of Grey's formulation was rhetorical and self-justifying: to lay the ground for the vindication of his subsequent decisions.

He went on to claim that Mhala's crime was that of wishing to expel Europeans from southern Africa. And then followed the most astounding move of all. If, Grey remarked, proof of this crime had been wanting, it would have been necessary to remove him from the country for the offense of receiving stolen goods. But, fortunately, Grey was convinced of his guilt on this serious charge and, therefore, as evidence of his humanity and pity, he was willing to overlook the stolen-goods charges and punish him only for the (non-existent) offense of trying to expel Europeans!

The problem for Grey, however, was that Porter had already undermined all of these claims. He had noted how the evidence of conspiracy with Nonkosi and Kwitchi did not fit the finding, how the charge of conspiracy to wage war on the Queen had no statutory basis, and how the charges were improperly drawn. Grey ignored all of this. He claimed that he found the evidence of Kwitchi and Nonkosi persuasive. Although he gave no argument in support of this claim, Sir George Grey had taken his stand on a strong ground. His reasoning was convergent with the view of the chiefs that was dominant within imperial culture: that they were conspiratorial manipulators of superstitious practices. This was a view that would be instantly understood by all who considered the matter. It was one that possessed far greater credibility than the legal parsing of William Porter. Thus Grey concluded with a flourish of self-righteous piety. Having considered everything, he regretfully differed from his Attorney-General, and so "I must of course do my duty." But in the light of Porter's reservations, Grey will exercise his clemency and reduce Mhala's sentence from fourteen years to five! Grey's genius consisted in framing issues with a thick coating of liberal sentiment and reason that effectively disguised their hypocrisy and feeble foundations of fact.[24]

Conclusion

And so the long struggle to reconcile the chiefs to British rule was finally achieved, using the procedures and methods of liberalism. The chiefs' authority had been eroded and they had been legally lynched. It was the law that had accomplished this task. Most of the chiefs were soon allowed to return from the harsh environment of Robben Island to the eastern Cape. But their lives were now closely regulated by the local administration. And when they arrived back home they found themselves confined to small plots of land, prohibited from gathering their tribe around them again, and generally reduced to the status of dependent pensioners of the government. Their status had decisively changed. But a small event that followed Phato's return suggested how the empire would still have to work hard to maintain its rule over the Xhosa chiefs.[25]

When Phato returned back to the eastern Cape he was immediately taken to an interview with John Maclean. The first issue Phato raised with Maclean was the possibility of his being allocated a location where he could reconstitute his tribe. Maclean must have felt that this was *déjà vu* all over again. He began to explain patiently that the governor's pardon of Phato was conditional precisely upon his *not* receiving such consideration. The most Phato could hope for was a small plot of land for his own use and that of his immediate family. It was explained that

Sir George Grey wished Pato to be taken care of and treated kindly. That the Chief Commissioner's own wish is to be kind to Pato and to take care of him. That Pato would be fed and well cared for by the Government, that he would receive his pension and sufficient land for cultivation for himself and his family, but that would continue only so long as Pato behaved himself well and made no attempt to establish for himself a Chieftainship and gather his tribe around him.

Phato replied that he did not want to be a chief, only to ensure that his people had their own location, even if it was separate from his piece of land. At this point it dawned upon Maclean that the time Phato had spent in Cape Town – and in the comfortable quarters of Somerset Hospital at that – had done no good. He was still trying to bargain over the conditions of his subordination. Maclean began to get more heated. He told him "that there was no use in again talking over the matter which he had so fully explained, that if Pato did not wish to return to Cape Town he must give up all idea of receiving a location for his people."

At this, Phato seemed to cease arguing. He replied that he would be perfectly satisfied if the government gave him land for himself and family. But he did not give up completely. Maclean asked him if he wanted to think over which piece of land he would like. He replied, seemingly totally compliant, that he did not care; he would take what the Chief Commissioner gave him. But "he asked if he would not be allowed to have even a few of his people located near him." The Chief Commissioner answered that, after the explanation given, he did not understand how Phato could continue to talk like this. The government had firmly decided that his people should never be together and that – showing just a hint of cold steel – "if Phato misunderstands this and wishes to live in peace ... he must not renew the subject again." And Maclean pointedly reminded him that he was an old man who could not expect to live much longer. It was better that he live out his days in as much comfort as he could. At this point Phato submitted to his fate, and he disappears from our history.[26]

NOTES

1. The story of the legal victimization of the Xhosa chiefs has been told before, most vividly by J. B. Peires in, *The Dead will Arise: Nongqawuse and the Great Xhosa Cattle-Killing Movement of 1856–7* (Johannesburg, London, and Bloomington, IN, 1989), pp. 226–37. British law is among the gifts of empire that Niall Ferguson highlights in *Empire: The Rise and Demise of the British World Order and the Lessons for Global Power* (New York, 2002), p. xxv. The law is nowhere featured in *The Oxford History of the British Empire*. But see Diane Kirkby and Catherine Colebourne, *Law, History, Colonialism: The Reach of Empire* (Manchester, 2001). It should be noted that at the same time as the Xhosa chiefs were being subjected to the rigors of British law, a similar but even more egregious course of treatment was being meted out to the sons, grandsons and other relatives of Bahadur Shah Zafar II, the last Mughal Emperor, in India. See William Dalyrmple, *The Last Mughal: The Fall of a Dynasty: Delhi, 1857* (New York, 2006), pp. 363–402.
2. Anthonie Eduard Du Toit, "The Cape Frontier: A Study of Native Policy with Special Reference to the Years 1847–1866" (DPhil thesis, University of Pretoria, 1949), p. 184; on Delima see CA, BK 10, *Lieutenant Governor,*

Miscellaneous Dispatches 1852–64, Maclean to Grey, 5 November 1857; BK 83, *Special Magistrate with Macoma and Botman 1856–57*, for the attempt to recruit him as a spy. It is not clear whether Delima was always loyal to Phato or whether he did contemplate going over to the British side.

3.   CA, A 793, *Gawler Letter Book*, 16 and 30 July 1857. BK 406, *Miscellaneous Letter Book of the Chief Commissioner of British Kaffraria 1856–57*, Maclean to Barrington, 15 September 1857.

4   CA, BK 406, *Miscellaneous Letter Book of the Chief Commissioner*, 25 August 1857; BK, 82, *Special Magistrate with Macoma and Botman 1856–57*, Lucas to Maclean, 18 July, 8, 25, 12 and 31 August and 3 September 1857; Gawler to Maclean, 25 and 36 August 1857.

5.   CA, GH 8/50, *Demi-Official Letters, British Kaffraria 1857–58*, Maclean to Grey, 31 August and 3 and 24 September 1857. Note how in Maclean's letter the arrest precedes the collection of evidence.

6.   Ibid., Maclean to Grey, 29 October 1857; Maclean to Bates, 26 October 1857, for his laying of the legal groundwork.

7.   We do not know what techniques of interrogation they used. But they did remind Nonkosi of her parents' death, and they used the untrue claim that "now the chiefs had admitted it was all deception she should therefore speak the truth now having nothing to fear." This was said sometime between 23 and 26 October 1857, long before the trials had taken place at which such claims were presented. And those claims were never admitted by the chiefs. CA, GH 8/33, *Dispatches from the Chief Commissioner, British Kaffraria, October–December 1857*, 23 October 1857, Examination of Nonkosi; GH 8/50, *Demi-Official Letters, British Kaffraria 1857–58*, Maclean to Grey, 26 October 1857.

8.   CA, GH 8/33, *Dispatches from the Chief Commissioner … October–December 1857*, Gawler to Maclean, "Interrogation of Kwtichi," 12 November 1857; Examination of Kwitchi by Maclean, 12, 13 and 14 November 1857.

9.   CA, GH 8/48, *Letters from Native chiefs, Residents, Eastern Frontier, 1856–60*, Report on the chiefs by Maclean, 30 September 1857; GH 8/50, *Demi-Official Letters 1857–58*, Maclean to Grey, 18 December; Barrington to Maclean, 12 December 1857; Gawler to Maclean, 25 December 1857.

10. CA, GH 8/50, *Demi-Official Letters 1857–58*, Barrington to Maclean, 19 January 1858; GH 20/2/1, *Miscellaneous Papers Relating to British Kaffraria 1853–58*, Barrington to Maclean, 19 January 1858.

11. This account is taken from CA, GH 8/33, *Dispatches from the Chief Commissioner*, Maclean to Grey, 3 December 1857. See also Timothy Stapleton, *Maqoma: Xhosa Resistance to Colonial Advance 1798–1873* (Johannesburg, 1994), pp. 189–90; Peires, *Dead Will Arise*, pp. 228–9.

12. Peires, *Dead Will Arise*, p. 229.

13. Ibid., p. 231; CA, GH 8/34, Maclean to Grey, 18 January 1858; GH 8/34, *Dispatches of the Chief Commissioner*, Maclean to Grey, 8 March.

14. CA, BK 14, *President, Criminal Court Commission 1856–60*, Barrington to Maclean, 27 February 1858. Barrington's specialty seems to have been offering readings of evidence that did not conform to the facts. Thus, in the trial of Delima, Phato's son, in April 1858, he argued that the court should have

found him guilty of murder even though they had no direct evidence, and had reduced the charge to manslaughter. See BK 140, *Kaffir Chiefs, Counsellors, and Headmen*, Barrington's comment on the trial of Delima, 27 April 1858.

15. Peires, *Dead Will Arise*, p. 237. The transcript of the trial of Mhala is to be found in CA, GH 8/36, *Dispatches of the Chief Commissioner of British Kaffraria*, 23 September 1858.

16. The tone of the administration in British Kaffraria is captured by Gawler's announcement to the presiding judge at Maqoma's trial that, as instructed, he would be at Fort Hare as the prosecuting officer for "the trial of that savage villain Maqoma and his gang." But, he was hasten to add, "not as I go prejudiced against him in this particular instance but the numerous charges you have sent against him ... [mean] he will be a fortunate fellow to clear away." CA, GH 8/50, *Demi-Official Letters, 1857–58*, Gawler to Pickney, 8 November 1857; see Peires, *Dead Will Arise*, pp. 223–4; Bernard Cohn, *Colonialism and its Forms of Knowledge: The British in India* (Princeton, 1996), ch. 3; Sudipta Sen, *Distant Sovereignty: National Imperialism and the Origins of British India* (London, 2002), for these issues.

17. CA, BK 14, *President, Criminal Court Commission, British Kaffraria, 1856–60*, Barrington to Maclean, 24 April 1857, "Trial and Sentencing of Kaffir Prisoners." We noted in Chapter 6 how Xhosa lying was seen by the British as intrinsic to their own legal system.

18. CA, BK 109, *British Kaffraria, Government Ordinances 1847–66*, Ordinances of 1861. Porter pointed out regarding the case of Phato's trial that it discredited British law and standing for the court to return one verdict, to be told by John Maclean that they were wrong, and then to reassemble and obediently reverse their first finding. GH 8/34, *Dispatches of the Chief Commissioner, British Kaffraria, 1858*, dispatch of 8 March 1858, comment of Porter on the transcript.

19. This and the following few paragraphs are taken from Porter's commentary on Mhala's trial in CA, GH 8/36, *Dispatches of the Chief Commissioner, British Kaffraria, September–December 1858*, September–December 1858, 23 September and 4 November 1858.

20. CA, GH 8/38, *Dispatches of the Chief Commissioner, British Kaffraria, April–June 1859*, Barrington to Maclean, 1 June 1859. Mhala's subject status was uncertain; the subject status of Bahadur Shah Zafar II, the Mughal Emperor, was unambiguous. He was certainly not a British subject. His trial opened on 27 January 1858. Dalrymple, *Last Mughal*, pp. 399–402.

21. NLSA (CT), Grey Collection, *Miscellaneous Manuscripts*, MSB 223.8, f. 25, "Memo from H. Sewell," 1852. For the delicacy of the constitutional position in British Kaffraria, see a letter from Grey's successor as Governor to the Duke of Newcastle in 1863, which admitted that the powers of the High Commissioner were completely unconstitutional, but that this should be concealed for fear of raising questions in Parliament which might end in impeding the ability of the Governor and High Commissioner to govern British Kaffraria effectively. The problem was a complicated, technical matter which had effectively resulted in the constitutional position of the province

being left undefined. Both Cathcart and Grey preferred to keep it that way, since it allowed them to do more or less what they liked. See Foreign Office Library, *Private Correspondence of Sir Philip Wodehouse*, Wodehouse to Newcastle, 20 August 1863, where this remarkable admission occurs: "No one knows or can tell what they [the High Commissioner's powers] really are – but ... black and white have come to believe that on our frontiers he can do just what he pleases – and I would earnestly dissuade Your Grace from taking any step calculated to overthrow that belief. The Law Officers of the Crown hold that the Queen does not possess the power to give me the powers I claim to exercise – that I quite admit. But it does not follow that because the Queen cannot give them, I cannot assume and exercise them." For a discussion of the constitutional irregularities of British Kaffraria as a colony, see John Benyon, *Proconsul and Paramountcy in South Africa: The High Commission, British Supremacy and the Sub-Continent* (Pietermaritzburg, 1980), pp. 53–9, 62–6.

22. CA, GH 8/36, *Dispatches of the Chief Commissioner, British Kaffraria, 1858*, Porter's memo on Mhala's trial.

23. CA, GH 8/34, *Dispatches of the Chief Commissioner, British Kaffraria, 1858*, Grey's memo on the "Proceedings in the Trial of Pato and Sons," dispatch of 8 March 1858.

24. The previous few paragraphs come from Grey's summary enclosed in the dispatch on the "Trial of Mhala" in CA, GH 8/36, *Dispatches of the Chief Commissioner, British Kaffraria, September–December 1858*, 23 September 1858.

25. For some details of the return of chiefs from prison, see CA, BK 9, *Letters Received, Colonial Secretary, Cape Town 1856–66*, Rawston to Secy Govt., 23 December 1863, Maskem to Rawstone, 11 December 1863; Fielding to Hudson, cc. Somerset, 26 November 1863.

26. CA, GH 8/42, *Dispatches of the Chief Commissioner, British Kaffraria, 1860*, Maclean to Grey, 11 October 1860.

13   Postscript: endings and beginnings

A new phase of Xhosa history

The Grey system of civil authority and the cattle-killing inaugurated a new phase in Xhosa history. It was a phase that has received scant attention from historians of southern Africa. Little is known about the civil and political forms that were to be found in Xhosa society in the period *c.* 1860–*c.* 1880. Xhosa history does not get much notice until the end of the nineteenth century, when the first glimmerings of modern African nationalism heave into view. This relative neglect is quite understandable. After the discovery of diamonds at Kimberly, new centers of gravity opened for southern African history. The eastern Cape frontier lost its place as the driving force of imperial policy. After 1870 the stakes for Britain in southern Africa assumed a much larger profile in the minds of imperial policy-makers. It is appropriate, therefore, that this study conclude with the combined trauma of the cattle-killing and the successful implementation of the Grey system of imperial authority. But if there were new departures after *c.* 1860 in Xhosa history and in Xhosa–British relations, there were also continuities. I think it important, then, to close this book with a brief discussion of these endings and beginnings.

In the first place, and fundamentally, the landscape of Xhosaland changed after the cattle-killing. The land was stripped of its wealth and of its people. This material destruction matched the political ruin that Grey had visited upon Xhosa society. Societies that undergo such ruin also demonstrate an amazing resilience, however, and recovery soon appeared. But recovery was accompanied by commercial capitalist relations, to mark a truly new stage in historical experience for the Xhosa.

My second theme addresses the *limits* to the supremacy of the British over the Xhosa. British supremacy was unchallenged after the Grey system and the cattle-killing; nevertheless, it continued to be problematic. The old politics of the imperial encounter were brought to an end. But there was no final resolution to the problems of imperial rule. Once Xhosa society showed signs of physical recovery, political recovery followed close behind. The same issues that had plagued British relations with the Xhosa before the late 1850s returned to irritate the imperial overseers by the early 1860s. The context of these frictions was very different; but they were a reminder that the imperial project remained incomplete.

The establishment of an undoubted British supremacy, however, allowed the British to develop new ways of representing the imperial relationship. This is my third theme. One of the more curious consequences of this era in southern Africa was the invention of the Royal Tour. In 1860, Prince Alfred, Queen Victoria's second son, visited southern Africa. Such visits could occur only once the colonies had reached a certain level of sophistication and pacification. The tour of Prince Alfred suggested that imperial relationships were shifting in several ways. It presented an opportunity to invent new ceremonials to describe the relationship between the British and the Xhosa. The Royal Tour was one substitute for the public meeting that had been the traditional site where British–Xhosa relations had been negotiated. Such public gatherings now became purely symbolic events which expressed the hierarchy of imperial authority. When business had to be done, it was conducted through the channels of the imperial bureaucracy, not in the open space of the mass assembly.

And, finally, there is a fourth theme I believe it is important to address. Indeed, this theme is perhaps the most important of all, for it suggests the way continuity and change were entwined in the historical process. By the end of the nineteenth century, the first stirrings of a nationalist opposition to British and white rule in southern Africa began to ripple through the eastern Cape. These stirrings possessed direct links and connections to the history of encounter we have tracked in the course of this book, and they are, therefore, an appropriate theme with which it should close.

The changed landscape of Xhosaland

A few simple facts tell the story of how Xhosa society was crippled by the cattle-killing. A virtual depopulation of large areas of British and Independent Kaffraria followed the delusion. Around 40,000 people starved. Another 20,000 moved into the Cape Colony to avoid that fate by becoming agricultural and domestic laborers. The result was that the population of British Kaffraria declined by two thirds by the middle part of 1858, from 105,000 to around 37,000. For individual tribes, the effect was dramatic. Sandile's location, the largest of the Rharhabe Xhosa, lost about half of its people as a result of the killing. By the opening months of 1858, Phato's tribe had been reduced by about 90 percent of its members. The remnants of his tribe subsequently moved to live with his brother Khama, whose tribe was described in 1860 as a collection of refugees from other locations.[1]

The wealth of the Xhosa, of course, also disappeared. Over 400,000 cattle had been slain in the delusional distress that had gripped the tribes. A new phase in the movement of peoples was also inaugurated. It was driven partly by deliberate British policy and partly by the desperate search for survival and subsistence. Gawler's resettlement of part of Mhala's tribe has already been noted. But that was only the tip of an iceberg. Sarhili and his people were deprived of their longstanding land around Butterworth and pushed further east to the other side of the Mbashe river. This was the work of Gawler and Major Pomeroy Colley of Majuba Hill fame. Mfengu were moved from the colony into the vacuum previously occupied by the Gcaleka in order to form a band of loyal settlement on the eastern bank of the Kei. British tactics for border control still contained strong elements of van Reibeeck's hedge strategy, creating a protective line of settlements that would shield the colony's farmers from the incursions of the Xhosa. This was the intent behind the military colonist-farmers that Grey brought in from Britain's German Legion and settled around King William's Town. Grey expected that such strategies would discourage the Xhosa from returning.

The personal suffering and indignity that were involved in this massive disruption is not sufficiently captured by these bald statements and statistics. An example of this grim process survives in a story that Charles Brownlee recounted in his autobiography. It is a story that reveals the destitution that affected the Xhosa but also illustrates just how their indigenous hierarchy was diminished by the cattle-killing and the British response to it. It is a story, also, that captures the extent to which the disruption and devastation were forced by colonial policy. The cattle-killing was used to drive home a labor discipline and policy that had been sought since Ordinance 50 of 1828 had made modern wage labor the official policy of the imperial state in the Cape.[2]

Brownlee's story concerned a petty chief, Qola, who came to him for relief from starvation. After about eight days, Brownlee told him that he had to leave with a labor draft that he had put together to go to work in the Cape Colony. This was a major part of the work of the resident magistrates in 1858. Brownlee wanted to pack Qola off to the colony. But Qola had other ideas, and he told Brownlee that he was a chief, that he had never been in service, and he was afraid of the treatment he would receive if he went as a servant to a farmer in the colony. He even offered to work for Brownlee, since it was no shame for one chief to serve another chief. Brownlee was having none of it. And so Qola returned to his kraal to see if he could salvage anything from the pits the Xhosa used to store corn.

When he returned to Brownlee weak and emaciated, Brownlee again fed him and told him to join the next labor draft. But Qola again disappeared, only to be found by Brownlee two weeks later by the side of the road, his dead body rolled up in a blanket. "The poor fellow, it appeared, had gone home again, and stayed too long."[3]

As this little story suggests, a new political economy was one consequence of the aftermath of the Grey system. Indeed, this aspect of Xhosa history has been fairly well documented. The expansion of market relations was the defining theme of the new economy of Xhosaland. This was true in terms of labor employment and in terms of the modes of production. From the moment he arrived at the Cape, Grey had wanted to bring the Xhosa more fully into modern labor relations. But his various plans to do this, such as using Xhosa labor in road-building and other civil engineering projects in British Kaffraria, had achieved singularly little success until the cattle-killing provided the necessary incentive. There was a significant revolution in the way labor was used, both within Xhosaland and beyond. British Kaffraria became a labor reserve for the colony, something that had been a gleam in the eyes of settlers for a long time. But this was true also within British Kaffraria itself, as white farms expanded and black agricultural wage labor expanded with them.[4]

This economic revolution extended way beyond labor utilization. Western goods and technology now made decisive inroads into Xhosa society. By the middle 1860s, the kaross had been replaced by Witney blankets as the general item of dress for the Xhosa. Similarly, at long last, the missionary campaign to change the means of production and the gender division of labor began to bear fruit. The metal plow and hoe – also made in Britain, of course – replaced the wooden spade. Watercourses began to be cut, and there was the usual competition between the chiefs to see who could benefit most from the largesse offered by the imperial state. At the same time, market and political forces encouraged the expansion of a British conception of domestic division of labor. The men began to move out from tending the cows in the kraals and replace the women in the fields. When these kinds of changes were combined with the social engineering scheme of Grey to concentrate the Xhosa into organized villages, the structure of life was entirely changed. One small indicator of this was the way commuting from the village to work in the fields now became a common feature of Xhosa life. Some journeys of this sort involved 6–8 miles of walking each day.[5]

The structure of land tenure and ownership also changed. The main theme was the expansion of individual ownership. Different types of landholding were introduced which were designed to encourage the creation of peasant proprietors, presumably in an attempt to break up collective tribal loyalties. By the mid-1860s Africans were being granted freehold plots of 20 acres in size in British Kaffraria. In the Crown Reserve, land was still held under customary tribal tenure, with allocations decided by the chiefs and headmen. While there were some moves here to create a southern African peasant class, which has been much written about, the most significant change in landholding was far less favorable for the original occupants.[6]

More than once the British had given an assurance that they had no designs on Xhosa land in British Kaffraria. But it had always been Grey's intention to open up the province to white settlers. (His speech to the Cape Parliament in March 1855 had stated this aim.) As was usual with Grey, the language of liberal piety cloaked this land-grab. He portrayed it as a measure that would push forward the civilizing mission. Whites of a superior morality would be introduced where they could form small islands of civilization and provide the prototype of a multiracial society. In fact, nothing of the sort was in prospect.

The first large-scale introduction of whites was the importation of the German Legion in early 1856. More than 2,000 Germans who had fought for the British during the Crimean War were settled as armed farmers along the border, on an axis from Stutterheim to East London. The scheme was hardly a stunning success. The settlers were dumped down and left to fend for themselves; few of them were able to make their way in farming. Only 300 of the legionnaires had wives (although Grey and the Colonial Office thoughtfully recruited about 800 Irish workhouse girls to come out as wives). There was much drunkenness, rape of Xhosa women, and even murder of one another, but especially of Xhosa. By September 1858, this colonization effort was falling apart. The legionnaires were such a disruptive presence that they had become a real problem and embarrassment, even to Grey. The Colonial Office was beginning to ask questions, so Grey had the majority of them shipped off to help fight against the rebels in India, where they disappear from our history.[7]

This was only the beginning of a white influx. By the end of 1857, 200 farms of 1,500 acres had been assigned between East London and King William's Town Road in Phato's old country. By the middle part of 1858, about 2,000 square miles had been distributed to white farmers, and in 1859 a further 300 farm grants were made. Regulations were also passed allowing natives to purchase small plots of land. Grey explained to Maclean how the purpose was to create a society "in which the two races live together in a state of happiness and contentment." Such a thing could not happen all the time "the coloured population are subjected to their own chiefs." He had hoped that the sale of land in British Kaffraria would finance British immigration on the model of New

Zealand. But this did not happen. British Kaffraria attracted those who were not making a go of it in the Cape Colony – not exactly the types to provide the kind of uplifting white moral presence for the Xhosa that Grey advertised.[8]

The ease with which Grey could implement this transfer of ownership of land reflected how British power ran unchallenged throughout Xhosaland. The early return of some of the chiefs from Robben Island demonstrated the confidence of the imperial administration. By the middle of the 1860s all the chiefs except Maqoma, Xhoxho and Siyolo had been returned. A pathetic letter from Delima captures the stripped-down state of the chiefs' status and power. On his return from Robben Island he found himself entirely dependent on the charity of his family and a few friends. He hoped that the government would continue his allowance, and promised "to be a faithful subject to the Queen." Even his Resident Magistrate urged favorable consideration of his claim for an allowance, explaining how he had not been used to working in his early life and now found it "difficult to obtain a living particularly as he has no entitled place of abode."[9]

An ordinance of December 1862 epitomized the degree of control over Xhosa life that the imperial administration could now anticipate. It greatly extended the reach of the pass laws, and gave the Governor absolute authority to control all movement by the Xhosa. The mere receipt of a letter was enough to trigger the enforcement of this law, and violation was punishable by up to seven years imprisonment. A couple of years' later it was proposed to expand the jurisdiction of the resident magistrates into areas of civil and native law not previously under their jurisdiction. They were to be given summary power to remove squatters, to issue passes for the driving of cattle, to supervise the marriage customs of native law, and to punish natives who could not prove their innocence of cattle theft when spoors of stolen cattle were found near their kraals – thus reversing the basic provision in British law of the presumption of innocence.[10]

These ordinances were thought to be necessary in order to guard against any possible revival of chiefly power following the return of most of the chiefs from Robben Island. In some part of the official mind, Mhala and Phato were still feared for the trouble they could create. Maclean sought to perpetuate the despotic powers of Kaffrarian government. But from the mid-1860s a new age was dawning as plans were made to regularize the constitutional position of British Kaffraria by incorporating the province into the Cape Colony.[11]

Now that the chiefs had been effectively neutered, of course, it was quite safe to parade such constitutional niceties. In any case, by this time there were plenty of ways of exercising raw British power. Notable among these was the Frontier Armed Mounted Police, created by Cathcart in 1853. The FAMP came into its own during the cattle-killing, when Grey used it to push the Gcaleka Xhosa back from the Kei. This campaign inaugurated the use of the FAMP as an institutionalization of the commando system. Rumors of war continued to erupt on the frontier from the early 1860s. The imperial administration continued to imagine that dire plots were coursing through Xhosa minds – and who could blame them if they were? Sarhili was typically fingered as the instigator of such schemes, and the head of the Gcaleka Xhosa now became the latest of the chiefs to be demonized by the British as the source of instability on the frontier. One such scare in 1864 led to the mobilization of a regiment of the regular army and panic in the frontier towns. Although this rumor turned out to be the invention of a spy, it served to justify a raid into Sarhili's territory. The Transkei remained nominally independent until 1872. But it nevertheless remained vulnerable to the slash-and-burn raids of the Frontier Armed Mounted Police.[12]

After the impact of the cattle-killing and the Grey system of governance, therefore, British power was unrestrained. This meant that the social engineering policies that Grey favored could be more easily implemented. The aspiration to re-engineer Xhosa society had always been present in the British Kaffrarian project. Putting the Xhosa into supervised villages was an idea that had been around since the late 1840s. After the war of 1850–3, a Native Improvement Board was set up and was particularly active among the Mfengu. But Grey was different from previous governors. He was persistent and bureaucratically effective. And he had money, or was prepared to spend it even if he did not have it.[13] From the beginning of his governorship, Grey's intended to implement an extensive social engineering program that would include public works, hospitals, institutions of education and other institutions designed to win the Xhosa to Christianity and civilisation. These dreams could be executed only after the devastation of the tribes in the mid-1850s. The major result of Grey's effort in this regard was the implementation of his village system, something that had long been talked about, but which Grey was now able to push through.[14]

The resettlement of the Xhosa into villages was achieved through a combination of voluntary and coercive methods. Gawler split Mhala's tribe and separated the non-believers of the cattle-killing prophecies into a separate community – known as "Gawler's people" – on the Idutwya river. The movement of Anta, Oba and Khama's people into villages was more voluntary, although it was not accomplished without some pressure from the magistrates. Richard Birt wrote home to the Directors of the London Missionary Society in 1860 describing how the natives had been "rendered more accessible by the compulsory regulation of the Government for them to reside in large villages instead of being in separate kraals." But it is equally clear that the scheme soon ran into resistance, even from loyal chiefs, who had to be pressed and pushed by their resident magistrates to hurry the work along. Maclean sent a circular to the resident magistrates in April 1860 reminding them of the necessity of concentrating the native villages in their districts into settlements of up to 200 huts. But the resident magistrate with Khama wrote apologetically to Maclean of his woes in trying to persuade this Christian chief to comply with the Governor's wishes.

I have pointed out the limits of all the villages so they will be as concentrated as I can insist upon . . . to have put them into straight lines would have necessitated the removal of every hut in the location which I consider would have created such opposition that we should have found we were going too fast and trying what we cannot carry out . . . I could not persuade them that there could be any sense in straight lines. I could not personally superintend the building of the huts and Kraals, nor could I with my police do anything if the whole location was opposed to a measure. I therefore trust you will be satisfied with what I have done, which is in fact more than I a month since anticipated such was the opposition to any move.[15]

Just how typical this was is not clear. The disruptions of the cattle-killing and the political persecutions of Sir George Grey had left the Xhosa vulnerable to this kind of interventionist social engineering. But the prostration of the Xhosa did not last. And as demographic renewal appeared, so, too, did suggestions of a political and social revitalization. Once again, the British administration was to be perturbed in ways that were reminiscent of the past. The altered landscape of Xhosaland did not mean an end to the problems of imperial rule.

Continuities: problems of imperial rule

By the end of the 1850s the British had finally decided *how* to rule the Xhosa. The central obstacle to British rule – the presence of independent chieftainships – had been removed. A new era dawned in which the balance of power tilted decisively to a permanent British domain. But there remained strong continuities with the past rgarding how that power was realized. And we need briefly to note the ways in which this was so.

A dense network of imperial administrators covered Xhosaland, and their lines of responsibility and authority were clearly defined. But the tussle between the authority of the resident magistrates and traditional Xhosa law and custom continued. How to decide on which side of the line a particular "crime" or action lay remained murky. J. C. Warner, the Thembu magistrate, grappled with the same kinds of conflicts over traditional Xhosa law as his predecessors in the 1830s. Was he permitted, he wondered, to use British law against a rainmaker? Or did that fall outside of his province? And since the resident magistrate depended on the chief to administer the tribe, his authority was more tightly entwined with the authority of the chief than it had been before. In one instance Warner found himself administering Xhosa law to compensate some wrongly accused thieves in order to maintain the credibility of his own authority system.[16]

Warner's experience led him to favor a greater use of traditional Xhosa law because it simplified the relationship with the imperial state. Indirect rule, again! In the early 1860s he reported that the pro-British Thembu disliked being subject to British law. Indeed, there was a strong sentiment among the Thembu to move beyond the colonial boundary in order to escape the benefits of British law. Warner saw advantages in such a move. The Thembu would still be under the control of the imperial government, but would be free to administer their own law. It was also more effective to use Xhosa law to control crimes that had an impact on the border security of the colony. Warner used the customary structures of authority to find and punish stock thieves, even though this also involved honoring the Xhosa custom of cutting the chief in on a share of the recovered stock. If such cases were to be tried in colonial courts, the accused would often escape because of "the absence of that kind of evidence required by our Courts." So here we have a post-Grey magistrate bolstering imperial rule by a wholesale adoption of Xhosa culture and law![17]

In addition, issues began to reappear which suggest that a *lack of imperial control* continued to plague the British administration. By the early 1860s a revival of chiefly power was beginning to make life difficult again for the imperial administration. It posed nothing like the threat of the past. But it was a reminder that there was no closure to imperial social and political relations. In spite of the powers of the cattle-killing delusion and the willpower of Sir George Grey, the tension between indigenous culture and imperial authority had not been settled once and for all. What was interesting about this phase of the struggle was that it centered on tribes that had traditionally been friendly to the British.

Perhaps this was hardly surprising. These groups had been the beneficiaries of the British-led breakup of the offending tribes. They had been both enlarged and destabilized by the incorporation of large numbers of strangers into their ranks. Khama, the Christian Xhosa, began to cause difficulties, as did the previously pro-British Thembu, whom Warner supervised. Khama got into a classic authority struggle with his resident magistrate over the limits of his authority to administer justice. Khama wanted to convene a court under his jurisdiction to administer dowry cases. The imperial administration objected because (they claimed) it encouraged the sale of wives and divorce. More significantly, it allowed Khama to perpetuate one of the traditional sources of chiefly power – a commission on any cattle fines that he might impose. This tussle went on for several years. Khama complained that the magistrate was trying to depose him from his chieftainship, and the magistrate complained that Khama was (among other things) restricting the access of preachers other than Wesleyans to his tribe.[18]

Warner feared that the Thembu posed a potential threat to British rule. Even though the power of the chiefs had been diminished and Xhosa power broken up, "yet I fear it is still much more formidable than is generally supposed." They required constant monitoring and surveillance, for they chafed under the yoke of colonial rule, and "if a favourable opportunity were to present itself, they would no doubt make the attempt to break loose from its constraints." Only a small minority "are really and truly well affected towards us." A few months after this report, Warner thought he detected signs of boldness and insolence that suggested a political recovery from the starvation and famine of the cattle-killing.[19]

The habit of the imperial administration to move the tribes about to suit changing needs of land utilization continued, and it was now easier to accomplish. But in other respects, the same resistance and stubbornness were likely to recur. In the mid-1860s Warner was having trouble relocating some Mfengu groups, and so Walter Currie and his Frontier Police were dispatched to "help some 12000 Fingoes from the neighbourhood of [Fort] Beaufort where they are so greatly crowded." And a year later Sandile was being pressured to move across the Kei into Sarhili's country. He refused, and the government decided not to press the point for fear of war.[20]

War was probably not a serious threat at this point. But the fear of war and the ease with which rumors of war spread around the eastern Cape revealed a continuity of another sort. Even at the peak of its actual power in Xhosaland, imperial culture could not shake itself free of its paranoid fears. These fears were rooted in the reality that (to paraphrase Ranajit Guha) the imperialist is never really "at home in Empire." However far the independent tribes were pushed away to make room for white settlement, and however effectively the organs of Xhosa social and civic life were disemboweled, the imperial mind was always haunted by the fear that the weak were about to recover their strength. Not long after Sir George Grey had returned to New Zealand, the old frontier paranoia revived to take its natural place at the center of imperial culture. In the middle of 1861 Warner believed that an anti-colonial confederation was again being put in place with the pretext of attacking the Thembu, but in fact it was intended "to be a combination against *us.*" Here was a reprise of the analysis of the cattle-killing as a chiefs' conspiracy.

The end of the great meeting; the beginnings of the Royal Tour

Among the many attributes that Sir George Grey possessed was the trait of the bureaucrat. Grey wanted to do away with the big public meeting as the place where the British and the Xhosa formalized their settlements; he preferred to meet in private. On each of his trips to the frontier, he met privately only with Sandile. He did not meet once with the chiefs and people in a great assembly. He was the first Governor who did not observe this nicety. And although this was not remarked much on at the time, Maqoma, with his usual prescience, seems to have realized what it implied.

Maqoma wrote to a letter to Grey in April 1856 in which he listed various complaints about the Grey system. Among those complaints was the Governor's refusal to hear the chiefs' objections to the Grey system in person. Grey had insisted that they put their thoughts in writing. But, as Maqoma pointed out, he also failed to answer their letters. Grey was far too wily an administrator to be caught replying. He was not about to be drawn into negotiating in the way the Xhosa had drawn in previous governors. He intended to formalize and bureaucratize Xhosa–British relations. He did not want to allow the Xhosa to believe that they could *negotiate* the conditions of their subordination through the great assembly. So he responded to Maqoma through Maclean. He told Maclean to instruct Maqoma that his letter should have been sent through proper channels (i.e. to Maclean) rather than directly to Grey. And, he wanted to know, with just a hint of menacing irritation, who had penned the letter for Maqoma?[21]

By the time this little episode had occurred, the other imperial administrators had by and large got the message that the great meeting was out of fashion. The meetings that had governed British–Xhosa relations since Somerset met with Ngqika came to an end in October and November 1855, when the Grey system was announced to the chiefs. What Grey had in mind was a system of command and control that would operate through the personnel of the High Commissioner, the Chief Commissioner, the tribal Commissioners like Brownlee, and the resident magistrates. The chiefs would be at the tail end of this bureaucratic food chain, responsive (if not responsible) to the resident magistrates. The advantage of this was that it would avoid the hazards of misunderstanding, and it left little room for Xhosa evasion.[22]

Sir George Grey recognized the importance of ceremony in securing imperial authority, however. But it was not the kind of antics of display that Sir Harry Smith had seen fit to invent. Grey's conception of imperial ceremonial employed more abiding symbols of imperial hierarchy and authority. Sir George Grey brought the symbolic authority of the Royal Family into legitimizing the imperial relationship. And in doing so he invented the Royal Tour.

It would seem that this occurred largely by happenstance. Sir George Grey was in London during the latter part of 1859. While there he lobbied to have Edward, Prince of Wales, visit Cape Town to lay the foundation stone of the new harbor that was planned for the city. But Grey was fobbed off with the second stringer of the Royal Family, Alfred, while Edward was sent to open the Victoria Bridge across the St. Lawrence river in Canada. It might be argued that Alfred's was the more significant visit, since it was purely an empire trip, whereas Edward went on a goodwill trip to the USA. In addition, a major focus of Alfred's visit was to allow the indigenous peoples of southern Africa to express their loyalty to the imperial hierarchy. The visit was judged to be so successful that it was closely followed by further trips to India and Australia. The phenomenon of the Royal Tour had begun.[23]

Alfred arrived in Cape Town on 14 July 1860 and stayed until October. He did all the kinds of things that royalty were to do in the empire over the next hundred years. In Cape Town he laid a foundation stone to the harbor; he opened the South African Library; he attended Grey's new college for the children of Xhosa chiefs at Zonnebloem; and he was greeted by a Cape Malay delegation. He attended a large fete and fair at Greenpoint, just outside the city center, and he traveled. He visited Kaffraria, Natal, Swaziland and the Orange Free State. He inaugurated the game safari, and he massacred an enormous amount of wildlife. The visit was also an opportunity to mobilize a white South African imperial identity. The good citizens of King William's Town took the opportunity to establish a Volunteer Corps on the model of those currently popular in Britain itself. Alfred graciously consented to become its first Colonel-in-Chief. He met the great Sotho king Mosheshoe, and the Boer President, Brand. Shepstone introduced him to Zulu life in Natal, and Grey and Brownlee shepherded him around territory that only a few years before had been contested land. The visit was royal theater of the first order. But it was also imperial theater, orchestrated by the likes of Sir George Grey. It was an example of the new kind of meeting, whose purpose was to parade the symbols of imperial hierarchy before the subjects of empire and allow them the opportunity to display their loyalty to the imperial system.[24]

The visit of Prince Alfred illustrated the different power equation that now existed in the British–Xhosa relationship. The fact that Alfred could visit Kaffraria at all was cogent testimony to the pacification that had occurred over the past three years. The visit served to normalize the atrocities that had preceded Alfred's royal progress, and invented a version of history that authenticated imperial rule. It was remarked how

the first part of the road [from Grahamstown to King William's Town] threads the woody defiles by which the Ecca Pass is descended, a spot once an impregnable fastness of Kafir marauders, now one of the most inviting districts in the Eastern Province, infested by no more formidable spoiler than the geological student or the devotee of the picturesque.

Similarly, the greeting Alfred received from Mfengu in British Kaffraria was used to explain the origins of the Mfengu as refugees from Xhosa oppression who had been saved and protected by the British. The destruction of Hintsa was explained as a function of his tyranny towards the Mfengu, and his death likewise was explained a result of his own treachery in the face of the honest treatment he had received from D'Urban and Smith. Empire as a liberating, democratic experience was affirmed.[25]

The visit was carefully orchestrated to demonstrate the loyalty and identification with empire of its subject peoples. In addition to the usual parades, decorative arches and military maneuvers, the array of diverse ethnic communities in southern Africa was paraded before the Prince. The Cape Malay delegations that were presented to Alfred delivered a congratulatory address in Arabic. Loyal greetings were offered from Xhosa youths, presumably from some of the educational institutions that Grey sponsored. Cultural ceremonies were invented and constructed specifically for inclusion in this display of imperial culture.[26]

The visit was used as an opportunity to associate African culture with imperial loyalty. At Grahamstown a large gathering was held at Oatlands estate, currently the home of Walter Currie, commander of the FAMP. Given the military associations with the place, it was appropriate that the Xhosa part of this gathering should be an assegai-throwing contest. The winning assegai was then presented to Alfred. A few miles away, in the rather different milieu of Healdtown – one of Grey's favored educational institutions – Alfred sat among the congregants while the Reverend William Impey preached a sermon in Xhosa. A similar pattern was followed at Lovedale, where he observed inter-racial classes. On his rides throughout British Kaffraria, the Prince was "followed by crowds of shouting Kafirs ... in [an] excess of enthusiastic joy and pressing eagerly for a full sight of Inkosi Inkulu."[27]

A little later, when passing through the Thembu country, a wild display was organized that was captured by the still camera. A large group of tribesmen charged down a hill to greet Alfred, yelling war cries and waving spears. They came to within 40 yards of the royal party before suddenly stopping and shouting a deafening yell of welcome "in the most enthusiastic Kafir style." There is a picture of Alfred, a slight young boy, with Grey at his side, awkwardly reviewing a mass of black warriors. Grey then gave a speech in which he urged the Thembu to continue their loyal behavior, and ordered a ceremonial bullock to be slaughtered for each of the tribes that were represented. Various chiefs were presented, including some with a history of opposition to the British.[28]

An encounter with Sandile was surely a contrived piece of ceremonial theater. Leaving the German Legion village of Stutterheim, the Prince's party was joined by Sandile and a large number of his followers who had come to pay homage to the royal traveler. It was reported that Sandile and his party were hard to separate from the Prince, and, "had it not been for the cold... would have run alongside the carriage with the intention of accompanying him to Queens Town." It was arranged that Sandile should go to Port Elizabeth and from there travel with Alfred to Natal, and then on to Cape Town. Sandile, it will be recalled, was somewhat nervous of this trip, which surely had been planned by Grey and Brownlee precisely for its ceremonial purpose. Accompanied by the Reverend Tiyo Soga as his protector, Sandile (along with several other Xhosa Christians) was taken to Cape Town to be duly impressed with the modernizing power of the British empire.

In Cape Town, Sandile presented an address to "the young great Chief" that was described as a "farewell salutation." It could hardly have been written by Sandile; it must have been composed by Grey. The document was a public, official recognition of the capitulation of the Xhosa. It was a humiliating recitation by the leading chieftain in British Kaffraria of the imperial version of the recent history of the Xhosa. It was an endorsement of the official discourse of imperial culture as a liberating force whose benefits were now fully accepted by the Xhosa. And it attained special force for the British by being presented in Cape Town, the capital of the colony and the site of official imperial ceremonial. Surely this is one of the first instances of what was to become a common feature of imperial ceremonial: the public use of the traditional indigenous hierarchy in the service of endorsing and legitimizing imperial hierarchy. It is a neat piece of the ornamentalism of indirect rule. But it is also a document which expresses the smug conceit of the imperial power in manipulating its subjects to embrace and celebrate their own dispossession.

The time is near when great Chief you must depart form this land and leave us. Your great kindness has brought me where no Kaffir ever came of his own free will ... The way through which we have passed on the mighty sea is known only to us as having been travelled by those of us who had committed some offence. But now we have passed through the sea as your friends and ... our hearts are overcome ... We think of ourselves from this time as the loyal and dutiful subjects of your royal Mother; we shall take care that our great and good Chief Sir George Grey complains nothing about us in time to come. Our present position and circumstances brought about by our mad resistance to the authority and power of the English people has been a great warning to the other tribes in South Africa and it is now our determination that our loyal and faithful service to your Royal Mother shall be an example for the imitation of those tribes. [And, it goes on] when you are there [at home] and think of your wanderings through this far off land remember that in Kafir land too there are hearts that from time to time think and speak of you with love.[29]

Among the signatories were some of the most famous names of Xhosaland, whose lives had been entwined with British imperial culture for the past forty years: Tyala, Festiri Maqoma, Dukwana, and Tiyo Soga, who, unlike the others, signed his name.

Alfred then moved on to Natal, where he encountered the Zulu, who were already assuming their place within the British imagination as the archetype of African peoples. The events that were mounted for Alfred in Natal sprang largely from the scheming and fertile mind of Theophilus Shepstone, and were directed by him, his brothers and sons. Like Grey, Shepstone was a founding father of imperial ceremonial. He understood fully the importance of adapting native cultural customs and ceremonial to the purposes of imperial culture. And in this case we have a clear account of how an African ceremonial was invented to serve the purpose of imperial culture.[30]

Shepstone ordered the chiefs near to Maritzburg to hold themselves in readiness to attend on the Prince. They were to perform a dance of homage in full war costume, but their assegais were to be left behind. The native dress that they donned, however, was designed by Shepstone's chief henchman, Ngoza. Ngoza normally wore European clothing, but for this occasion he dressed himself in ostrich feathers and monkey tails. Similarly, the ceremonial dances that were to greet Alfred were invented especially for the visit. The authentic dances and performances that would normally have been used for such an occasion would occupy too much time. Indeed, the *preliminary* part of the traditional ceremony would have taken over two hours. So the chiefs were told to deliver the short version that would involve "a few congratulatory sentences ... to be presented in common for all clans." The 2,000 "warriors" who had gathered on the outskirts of Maritzburg "were directed to take up their positions in a semicircle below the flagstaff, so that on the arrival of the Prince, the salute might be given at once."

Ngoza had gathered representatives of tribes that had been devastated by Shaka and Dingaan and were now "sheltered under the aegis of British colonization." Ngoza himself had been installed by Shepstone as the chief of the remnants of about twenty such dislocated tribes. Most of the chiefs in the area controlled by the British were Shepstone's satraps, whom he could pass off as loyal native subjects. And they played their appointed part. Shepstone read a congratulatory address which it was claimed the chiefs had agreed on. It had the same quality of obsequious loyalty – of false ornamentalism – as the speech that Grey had constructed for Sandile. It thanked the Queen for making them a united people and for entrusting her young son to their care for a short while, and it assured her that "she has black subjects as well as white who will fight for her." Ngoza advanced with "his" tribe and they did a little dance of homage. This was followed in turn by the dances of tribute, and a " considerable amount of time was thus unavoidably occupied." After about an hour, Alfred and his party left while the dance was still in progress.[31]

The intention of the ceremonials that were constructed around Alfred's visit was to authenticate the legitimacy of imperial rule. They were designed to radiate a set of values that imperial culture wished to project about itself. The theme of a unified commitment to the imperial ideal by the diverse subjects of empire ran through the events of Alfred's sojourn in southern Africa. But Grey added an extra touch of imperial benevolence. He used the occasion to demonstrate the merciful nature of British rule. When Alfred visited Somerset Hospital he encountered Phato; Grey took the opportunity to make the compassionate gesture of ordering his early release. Similarly, in British Kaffraria, Alfred met Hintsa's widow, Numsa, the mother of Sarhili. She was allowed to present a petition to Alfred requesting that she be permitted to return from an exile Maclean had imposed upon her. As part of this petition, she repudiated her son's support of the cattle-killing and noted the price of his apostasy: "the tribes of my son are broken and he is a wanderer in the mountains which over-look the land of his father." The government had refused an earlier request from Numsa. But this was too good an opportunity to turn down, and Grey used it to demonstrate the generosity of imperial mercy. Alfred, surely coached in this by Grey, played his role as the royal favor-giver. He responded to the petition by declaring that he would be pleased to use his influence in her favor and that he wished her remaining years to be spent in happiness and peace. But Grey had already written to Maclean to check that these acts of royal beneficence would be all right with him! And so it was done.[32]

The ceremonies and pageantry that marked the visit of Prince Alfred to the Cape Colony introduced a new element to imperial culture. They were qualitatively different from the demonstrations of display that were performed by Sir Harry Smith at an earlier stage of British Kaffrarian history. Both types of ceremonies were designed to make public displays of the legitimacy of imperial rule, and both appropriated elements of indigenous culture as a means of communicating and reinforcing that legitimacy. But in the contrivances of Grey and Shepstone around Alfred's visit, we can observe something more complicated and more subtle than the crude displays of Sir Harry Smith. Grey and Shepstone were inventing a tradition of ceremonial that, for the first time, employed the most visible symbol of the imperial hierarchy – the Royal Family. In a sense, they were importing the royal ceremonial of the metropole and adapting it to local traditions. Around such a framework a whole system of cultural symbolism and ceremonial could be built, as, indeed, it was in the adaptation of the Indian Durbar for imperial purposes from the 1870s. Alfred's visit to southern Africa in 1860, therefore, was a small beginning for a pageant that was to occupy a central role in the panoply of imperial culture in the coming century.[33]

Looking forward: continuity and change

Finally, I want to close this study with a story and a summary which will serve to link the Xhosa past to the South African future. Both the story and the summary carry Xhosa politics into the early twentieth century, and they address the way continuities and change in history are bound together in a web of interconnection. They focus on the Xhosa side of the story that I have recounted in this book, rather than on the British side. And it is right that this should be so; for it was to the Xhosa, not to British imperial culture, that the future belonged.

The story concerns Maqoma, the Xhosa chief who has figured so large in this book. Maqoma was not as fortunate as his fellow chief, Phato. Sir George Grey did not dole out a royal pardon for him. He spent eleven years in the harsh environment of Robben Island. In this, as in so many other ways, Maqoma was a pioneer and a forerunner of the Xhosa leaders of the mid-twentieth century. Unlike Nelson Mandela, Oliver Tambo and the rest, however, Maqoma was largely forgotten, especially by the British sitting a mile or so across Table Bay. When Maqoma returned to the eastern Cape in September 1869, it was as if to a foreign land. British Kaffraria had disappeared; its irregular constitutional and legal status had been resolved by its absorption into the Cape Colony in 1866. Maqoma's tribe had been scattered. One of his sons had moved in with Jan Tzatzoe; Namba, his favorite son, had lived with Anta before succumbing to consumption in 1862; Tini was the most successful in western terms, but he was a minor son in Xhosa terms. He lived quietly near Fort Beaufort and owned two farms. Another son, George, had been taken to Zonnenbloem by Grey and then on to Nuneaton, of all places, to be educated. His eldest son ruled a sad fragment of about a hundred souls. And that was all that was left of Maqoma's once mighty Chiefship. The colonial government dictated that Maqoma should live near Sandile, whom he despised.[34]

Maqoma at this time was about seventy-two years old. But he had lost none of his ability to fascinate the British. They continued to lust after the one thing they could not possess: his soul. On his return from Robben Island, the London Missionary Society missionary Richard Birt observed Maqoma's homecoming. Birt noted how the old chief was received with joy and respect by the Christian people of the settlement. He noted, too, how Maqoma seemed to prefer their company, shunning those of the heathen people. "His conversation was so Christianlike; he began to exhibit a deep interest in religious services," which he allowed to be held daily in his house. Christian Xhosa from other stations came to visit and went away awed by the "wonderful change in the old man." He claimed that he wanted a chapel built next to his hut and also near to Birt himself.

A tremor of hope fluttered in Birt's breast. Was this the moment that missionaries had been waiting for since Friedrich Kayser first settled near Maqoma in the 1820s? Was the rock that had dashed the faith of Henry Calderwood about to crumble? Birt hurriedly consulted with Tiyo Soga. Soga spent two days conversing with Maqoma. They both recognized "him as one on whom the Spirit of God had wrought the great change." Birt felt that he was now fit "for church fellowship, [and] I spoke with him about making a public profession to Christianity which resulted in him being proposed to the Church." Maqoma was still the big prize that the missionaries sought. If he could be claimed for God, who knew what might follow? At the very least, it would justify all the efforts that had been made, with so few results, by the missionaries of the evangelical generation.[35]

Alas, the old chief escaped them again. A short while after Birt had conferred with Maqoma about joining the Christian community, the real reason for Maqoma's demeanor emerged, although Birt did not recognize it. The hopes and dreams that Maqoma had possessed since the 1820s still beat within *his* breast. *He wanted his old land back*, and he embarked on a campaign to get it. He visited the Civil Commissioner in King William's Town and came back with stories of promises made. He began quietly to gather his old supporters around him – thus, perhaps, the trail of visitors that Birt remarked upon. Rumors began to circulate within the white settler community that he was headed to the Amatolas clutching a promise from the Governor. The imperial administration stirred uneasily. They had trouble keeping up with Maqoma. He moved from one place to the next with a fluctuating body of followers. What he intended was a mystery. Birt thought that he had lost his mind to "a mania on the subject of land." Birt was wrong about Maqoma's mind; he was right about the land. Maqoma's consistent political objective, to which all else was subordinated, was to recover the land of the Kat river from which he had been expelled in the 1820s. Like another Xhosa a century later, Maqoma never took his eyes off the main prize. Unlike Nelson Mandela, however, Maqoma's prize was not to be redeemed. The imperial administration finally decided to act. In November 1871 he was picked up on a pass charge. They hustled the old man away, surrounded by twelve heavily armed Frontier Armed Mounted Police, using a side entrance of the Grahamstown jail so as not to provoke attention. Maqoma was still capable of arousing the fear of the imperial administration.

Once again the law was put to its useful purpose. It was a brand of British law that we have come to know well in this book. It was not one that most Britons would own to, however. There was no charge. Indeed, there could not be, for it had never been decided that Maqoma was a British subject. Nevertheless, he was accused of violating the terms of his release. Those terms had never been published, nor had they been specified. And when one bold Cape legislator had the temerity to raise this question in the Parliament, he was subjected to the warm refutation that awaited all such honest colonial liberals. On the orders of the Governor, Maqoma was returned to Robben Island. There he remained until his death on that cold and awful island in September 1873. His tomb is unknown. He lies somewhere in an unmarked grave, a victim of the British empire.[36]

Maqoma did not live long enough to see the rest of the Xhosa century. Had he done so, he would surely have perished in the last eruption of the war that the Xhosa had been fighting against European encroachment for the past century. This war, known to South African history as the war of the Ngcayecibi, grew out of a struggle between Sarhili's Gcaleka Xhosa and the Mfengu in 1877–8. It is the least-known of the frontier wars, perhaps because it was overshadowed by the imminent disaster of Isandlwana. Unlike the earlier frontier wars, the ninth presented little challenge to British dominion. Yet it was the bloodiest of all the wars. The deaths totalled over 3,600 Xhosa, 145 black troops, and 60 whites, including Richard Tainton, a resident magistrate, whom Mhala had wanted as his translator in 1856. The war was followed by another phase of population removal; one half of Sandile's people were forcibly relocated to the Cape as indentured labor. Sarhili escaped across the Bashe to go into exile in a remote part of Pondoland, where he died.[37]

This war stood at the crossroads between the world of British Kaffraria and the world of modern South Africa. Sandile died in this war. Sandile had spent his life trying to evade the smothering grip of the imperial state, never fully committing himself to opposition, reluctantly fighting when forced to by internal Xhosa politics and external British pressures. At the end, however, Sandile came to the defense of his paramount Sarhili. He was killed by Mfengu mercenaries in a skirmish near King William's Town in May 1878. With him died his counselor, "Old Soga," the patriarch of one of the leading families of Xhosaland. Tiyo's father had opposed the war, but he was committed to following his chief, as were other names from an earlier time who also perished in this war, like Siyolo and Tyhali.

It was not only the older generation who fought. Some of the sons also took to arms. Most revealingly, they included those who had been singled out for anglicization, like Gonye Sandile, known to the English as Edmund. Edmund had attended Zonnebloem, but he ended up breaking stones on Robben Island for a decade. So, too, did Tini Maqoma, who tried to return home to his farm in the Waterkloof, when he was arrested. Dukwana, the son of Ntsikana (the "good" prophet of the early part of the century), also fought in this last war. So did the sons of the "wild cat" Mhala. Two of his sons had fled east to Sarhili's country following the cattle-killing. But one, Nathaniel Mhala, had been selected by Grey for a western education. Nathaniel attended Bishops Court School and then Zonnebloem. He had been baptized into the Anglican church and in the 1860s had spent some time at St. Augustine's, Canterbury, Kent. At the time of the 1877–8 war, he had attained white-collar status, and was working as a court official in King William's Town. While he did not actually fight in the war, there was good reason to think that he passed information to the rebels. He was later charged with high treason, but acquitted.[38]

The last reminders of old Xhosaland, of Queen Adelaide Province, of British Kaffraria, died in the war of the Ngcayecibi. But the participation of those who held such famous names as Mhala and Sandile and Maqoma illustrates the strong continuities at this moment of transition. Just three year after this last frontier war, a new kind of Xhosa politics emerged in the eastern Cape. This was a politics that focused on electoral organization, encouraged the growth of black associational life, sought alliances with liberal white politicians, and that mobilized the small numbers of black voters to secure political leverage. After 1880, modern politics came to the Xhosa. Among its taproots were the educational institutions of Kaffraria that the missionaries had established and Grey had fostered. Lovedale and Healdtown produced the graduates who formed the Native Educational Association in 1880. Its first president was an African teacher, ironically named "John Gawler." The first political association was formed in 1882.

A few year later, Nathaniel Mhala, William Kobe Ntsikana (grandson of the prophet) and the sons of Tiyo Soga were to be found in another political enterprise. They were among the original founders of the South African National Congress in 1891, the antecedent of the present-day African National Congress. The history of British Kaffraria had come full circle. The dynamic that Sir Harry Smith and the rest put into motion ended in places that they could never have imagined. It is not wishful thinking to imagine that Maqoma would not have been surprised.[39]

For the Xhosa understand that history is a living thing. This is why the days of the cattle-killing, of Sir George Grey, and chiefs like Sandile, continue to crop up in their praise poems, in their oral tradition, and also in Xhosa novels. Indeed, the famous Xhosa novelist, A. C. Jordan, was a direct descendant of one of the bit players who appear in this book: Robert Balfour, an early follower of Ntsikana, and a worker at the Chumie mission with Robert Bennie in the 1820s and in other places afterward. Small wonder that Jordan's novels are redolent of the struggle between the intrusive forces of change and modernization and the ways of tradition.

By contrast, the events we have described are far away from the British. I would be willing to bet that not one British historian in a thousand has heard the name Sandile or Maqoma. Only a few more will recognize the name of Sir George Grey. Yet the Xhosa know the name of George Grey well. To this day they blame him for the disaster of the cattle-killing. In their tradition, the events of the cattle-killing were orchestrated by George Grey precisely in order that the Xhosa might be destroyed. They remember Charles Brownlee, too. Sandile's praise poem says of Brownlee that he was not to be trusted; he favored the Germans and he wanted to herd Sandile as one drives a herd of cattle. How many British historians have heard of Brownlee? Yet he was one of the men who built their empire.[40]

It is ironic, perhaps, that the Xhosa remember Sir George Grey and Charles Brownlee far better than these men are remembered among British historians. But it is not surprising. It is not simply that the history of empire as it was lived on the ground, at the frontier, remains a very small part of imperial historiography. It is, more profoundly, that the practices of denial, of silence, of forgetting, are deeply ingrained in the history of Britain, and particularly in the history of its empire. It is only recently, for example, that the sordid and violent history of the end of empire has begun to challenge the roseate images of a peaceful and timely "sunset" with its "graceful exit." If historians have good reason to draw a veil over the nastiness of Britain's exit from empire, how much more reason do they have to assume a silence about what went on in places like British Kaffraria? Who would want to claim John Cox Gawler as an imperial hero? Far better to leave Pomeroy Colley dying heroically on Majuba Hill in the First Boer War, 1881, than to know him for shooting Chief Tola and his young sons in the bush of the Transkei and then hanging their bodies from a tree by the roadside for the vultures to pick apart. We *know* that Colley committed atrocities on this expedition because John Maclean admitted that he did. There is, however, a cute story that Colley's dying words at Majuba Hill were the same words that Tola uttered in 1858 when he was about to be taken and killed. Perhaps Colley was haunted by the atrocities that were committed by his command in the Transkeian expedition of early 1858.[41]

And so it has been with British Kaffraria and the Xhosa. Indeed, when I started this project, I made it a practice to ask my colleagues: "Have you ever heard of British Kaffraria?" I cannot recall that any had. A few, mostly of the older generation, recalled the "Kaffir wars" from distant and now anachronistic school history lessons. Yet most British historians of my generation grew up with a full awareness of the empire. Indeed, one of my own first political memories was a conversation about the Mau Mau. And I developed an interest in history in the first place by reading about "deeds that won the empire." But the empire we grew up with was not only an empire in terminal decline; it was also an empire *as it was known in Britain*. Historians need to appreciate more fully how that empire was an artifice, a fiction, a creation from events that were filtered and silenced and denied to produce a version of empire that fitted the cultural expectations and aspirations of the British themselves. This was not the empire that the Xhosa knew. Neither was it the empire that other dispossessed peoples knew. In this book, I have tried to reclaim a small slice of that other empire for British history.

NOTES

1. CA, GH 8/40, *Dispatches Chief Commissioner, British Kaffraria, January–April 1860*, Maclean to Grey, 23 March 1860: "All newcomers are however registered and compelled to reside in the existing native villages under paid headmen." The details of devastation are taken from J. B. Peires, *The Dead Will Arise: Nongqawuse and the Great Xhosa Cattle-Killing Movement of 1856–7* (Johannesburg, London, and Bloomington, IN, 1989), pp. 243, 248–9, 266, 288–90; Leonard Thompson, *History of South Africa*, (3rd edn. New Haven, 2001), pp. 79–80; T. R. H. Davenport, *South Africa: A Modern History*, 4th edn. (Toronto, 1991), pp. 121–13; Anthonie Eduard Du Toit, "The Cape Frontier: A study of Native Policy with special Reference to the years 1847–1866" (DPhil thesis, University of Preteria, 1949), p. 475. It was an indication of the relative rapidity of recovery from the physical destruction suffered that Sandile's location had recovered its population strength by December 1861 and grew again by 50 percent by 1864.

2. For Ordinance 50 see Clifton Crais, *White Supremacy and Black Resistance in Pre-Industrial South Africa: The Making of the Colonial Order in the Eastern Cape, 1770–1865* (Cambridge, 1992), pp. 58–61, 73–79; William Miller Macmillan, *Bantu, Boer and Briton: The Making of the South African Native Problem*, rev. edn. (Oxford, 1963) pp. 16–18, 20–1.

3. Charles Brownlee, *Reminiscences of Kaffir Life and History* (Lovedale, 1896), pp. 167–8. Creating Xhosaland as a labor reserve for the Cape Colony was so important to Grey's schemes that an attempt to set up charity aid to the Xhosa was bureaucratically harried and publicly savaged precisely because it conflicted with Grey's intention to use the cattle-killing to drive the principles of wage labor even more deeply into Xhosa culture. See J. B. Peires, "Sir George Grey versus the Kaffir Relief Committee," *Journal of Southern African Studies* 10.2 (1984), pp. 145–69.

4. Du Toit, p. 433. CA, BK 71, *Report from Commissioner to the Gaika People 1855–1858*, Brownlee to Maclean, 21 January 1857, for some further examples of this theme. But in this respect as in so many other enterprises of the imperial state, Grey found support among some of the chiefs who were eager to get what *they* could out of his plans. Thus Tyala "expressed great satisfaction with His Excellency's public works, saying he hoped they would be carried on extensively through the whole land, that the Gaikas would thus become attached to their present country and forget their old land." Even the anti-British chief Tola was eager to participate in the labor scheme. Xhoxho also was seeking help from Grey's civil engineering project at the same time, asking for a watercourse. See GH 8/26, *Chief Commissioner, British Kaffraria, 1854*, Maclean to Grey, 2 June 1855.

5. The changes in the economy and social relations have been the most thoroughly investigated of those that took place in Xhosaland following the Grey system and the cattle-killing. See Les Switzer, *Power and Resistance in an African Society: The Ciskei Xhosa and the Making of South Africa* (Madison, WI, 1993), pp. 86–96; Colin Bundy, *The Rise and Fall of the South African Peasantry*, 2nd edn. (Cape Town and Johannesburg, 1988), pp. 51–60. CA, GH 8/26, *Chief Commissioner, British Kaffraria, 1854*, Maclean to Grey, 2 June 1855.

6. Du Toit, "Cape Frontier", pp. 479–80; Bundy, *Rise and Fall of the South African Peasantry*; Charles van Onselen, *The Seed is Mine: The Life of Kas Maine, a South African Sharecropper 1894–1985* (New York, 1996).

7. See Du Toit, "The Cape Frontier," pp. 192, 207–10; J. Rutherford, *Sir George Grey KCB 1812–1898: A Study in Colonial Government* (London, 1961), pp. 350–2, 359–61, 391–4; Dr. J. F. Schwar and Dr. R. W. Jardine (eds.), *The Letters and Journal of Gustav Steinbart, II: The Journal 28 February 1857 – 1 August 1858* (Port Elizabeth, 1974); see CA, BK 41, *Irish Female Settlers 1857–58*, for the details of the scheme to import 2,000 Irish workhouse girls.

8. Du Toit, *Cape Frontier*, pp. 192, 210, 315; Peires, *Dead Shall Arise*, pp. 287–8; CA, GH 30/5, *Letter Book of the Chief Commissioner 1858–1860*, Grey to Maclean, 14 July 1858; GH 8/38, *Dispatches of Chief Commissioner, British Kaffraria April 1859–June 1860*, has material on the settlement of white farmers in British Kaffraria. See Penelope Silva (ed.), *The Albany Journals of Thomas Shone* (Grahamstown, 1992), for one such settler's experiences and the

marginal economic life he led. Shone could hardly have been the kind of
settler Grey had in mind to provide an example of the moral superiority of
white civilization. He was perpetually on the verge of bankruptcy, battled
alcoholism, was jailed several times, was continually fighting with his children, had an on-and-off affair with a neighbor's wife (the husband being
away) and sired two illegitimate children with the woman. He did end his
life a reformed Christian, however.

9. CA, BK 68, *Civil Commissioner and Resident Magistrate, King William's Town
   1853–1866*, 19 October 1865, R. Taylor. About the same time, on Mhala's
   return from prison, he was settled on a piece of land belonging to the Peelton
   mission, having been told he could not go to the land that he wanted to
   occupy. See the report from R. Fielding, special magistrate with Umhala, to
   R. Taylor, 26 July 1865.
10. CA, BK 12, *Attorney General of British Kaffraria 1858–1863*, Draft Ordinance
    of 9 December 1862 and Draft Ordinance of 1863, no day/month.
11. Du Toit, "Cape Frontier," pp. 297–302. The Colonial Office and the
    Governor, now Sir Philip Wodehouse, were reluctant to promulgate official
    ordinances that conflicted so openly with the rhetoric of British constitution-
    alism and its legal processes of law that were supposed to mark the character of
    the British empire.
12. Ibid., pp. 311–12, 318–19, 320–1, 330–6; CA, GH 8/37, *Dispatches of Chief
    Commissioner British Kaffraria, January–March 1859*, 10 March 1859, Colley
    to Maclean; LG 411, *Letters Received from the Tambookie Agent 1858–1863*,
    Warner to Hudson, 21 July 1861.
13. CA, BK 90, *Missions: Correspondence between the Chief Commissioner, British
    Kaffraria, and Missionaries 1848–1856*, Laing to Maclean, 20 December 1854,
    as an example; GH 23/18, *General Despatches: Letters from the Governor to the
    Colonial Secretary, London 1847–1849*, Sir Harry Smith to Earl Grey, 1 January
    1848. Du Toit, "Cape Frontier," pp. 64–70, 408–9. CA, CO 6155, *Census of
    the Gaika and Tslambie Districts 1848*; Du Toit, "Cape Frontier," pp. 64–6.
    Impey letter to be found in CA, GH 19/8, *Papers Connected with Sandilli, Kreli,
    Pato Etc. 1847.*
14. Du Toit, "Cape Frontier," pp. 408–9.
15. CA, BK 82, *Reports of Resident Magistrate with Kama, 1859–61*, Miller to
    Maclean, 1 June 1860. For the village system see also GH 8/37, *Dispatches of
    Chief Commissioner, British Kaffraria, January–March, 1859*, dispatch of
    27 January 1859; GH 8/41, *Dispatches of Chief Commissioner, British
    Kaffraria, May–August 1860*, circular from Maclean, 25 April 1846;
    Brownlee to Maclean, 25 June 1860; Du Toit, "Cape Frontier," p. 188; GH
    8/34, *Dispatches of Chief Commissioner, British Kaffraria, 1858*, Maclean to
    Grey, 4 March 1858; CWM, LMS, South Africa, *Incoming Correspondence*,
    Box 32, folder 1, Birt to Directors, 22 May 1860.
16. CA, LG 411, *Letters Received from the Tambookie Agent, 1858–1863*, Warner to
    Southey, 25 January, 8 June and 30 August 1858; Warner to Hudson, 27 May
    1861.
17. Ibid., Warner to Southey, 19 March 1860; Warner to Carlisle, 24 February
    1861. There are two letters of this last date which deal with this issue, and they

are interesting examples of the way in which indirect rule worked at the local level and of the persistence of the kinds of difficulties that traditionally had marked the resident magistrate's existence. The problem of the Thembu, however, was quite complicated, because they were formally within the colonial boundary – being in the Crown reserve – and thus liable to colonial law. But for reasons that are not quite clear, the Attorney-General insisted that they not be dealt with by colonial law. And the Cape Parliament would not pass legislation regularizing the situation. Legally, therefore, Warner was constantly acting in an illegal manner and was constantly afraid of falling foul of the legal authorities of the Cape. It was so absurd that at one point Grey recommended to him that if this happened he should take himself off to British Kaffraria proper to avoid the clutches of the colonial judges. After 1864 this situation resolved itself because the Thembu did move into the Transkei, and Warner and other resident magistrates moved with them. But this only increased the ambiguities regarding how they were to interact with the Xhosa, since the Transkei was not formally part of the British empire. See Du Toit, "Cape Frontier," pp. 260, 380.

18. CA, BK 87, *Reports of Resident Magistrate with Kama, 1859–61*, 28 July 1860; BK 88, *Report of Resident Magistrate with Kama, 1862–66*, 30 August 1862, 2 December 1864.

19. CA, LG 411, *Letters received from the Tambookie Agent*, Warner to Carlisle, 15 October 1860 and 24 and 26 February 1861. Warner, it will be recalled, was one of the authorities Maclean used in his *Compendium of Kaffir Laws and Customs* (Mount Coke, 1858), and he had lived among the Thembu for twenty years, yet he confessed that they remained largely unknown to him. In 1860 he ruminated on how they were "still a formidable and compact people" in spite of the damage the cattle-killing had done to "their ability to do us mischief or resist imperial authority."

20. Foreign Office Library, *Private Correspondence of Sir Philip Wodehouse*, Wodehouse to Edmund Wodehouse, 5 July 1864; Wodehouse to Cardwell, 12 July 1865. For the Sandile issue and the rumors of war, see *King William's Town Gazette*, 20 and 23 March; 3 and 17 April, and 4 May 1865. There was a clash between some Thembu and the FAMP.

21. CA, BK 140, *Kaffir Chiefs, Counsellors and Headmen: Pensions and Allowances 1852–1862*, Maqoma and Botman to Grey, 27 April 1856 (Botman was the British name for Bhotomane, a senior chief who was closely associated with Maqoma); Grey to Maclean, 15 May 1856.

22. CA, GH 8/27, *Dispatches of the Chief Commissioner, British Kaffraria, 1855*, Maclean to Grey, 3 November 1855.

23. Rutherford, *Sir George Grey*, pp. 406–28. For Edward's tour of North America, see Ian Radforth, *Royal Spectacle: The 1860 Visit of the Prince of Wales to Canada and the United States* (Toronto, 2004). The St. Lawrence Bridge and the Cape Town breakwater were the two largest civil engineering projects in the empire to date. My student Charles Reed is currently completing a doctoral dissertation on the early years of the Royal Tour, which will tell us much about the beginnings of this imperial ceremonial.

24. Alfred's visit was captured in one of the first picture books to commemorate such a empire ceremonial. See [Saul Solomon, comp.,] *The Progress of Prince*

Alfred Through the Cape Colony, British Kaffraria, The Orange Free State and Port Natal in the Year 1860 (Cape Town, 1861). It is not clear whether it was published in Britain, or how widely available it was there.

25. Ibid., pp. 48–53.
26. Ibid., pp. 15, 60–1, 107–8. Cultural practices were unveiled in order to be incorporated into imperial culture. Cape Malays publicly performed for the first time a ceremonial that was usually conducted "at night in secret." It was described in suitably sensational terms as involving "dervish like dances . . . [with the dancers] working themselves up into a frenzy until they have a glow of ecstasy which is positively evil. The fury of fanaticism seems kindled in each lurid eye." Yet this piece of exotic orientalism was devoid of danger, and was conducted in the "most perfect order with no police around."
27. Ibid., pp. 43, 54–5.
28. Ibid., p. 66.
29. Ibid., pp. 63; CA, GH 8/48, *Letters from Native Chiefs, Residents, Eastern Frontier 1856–1860*, 18 September 1860.
30. Ceremonials were an important instrument of Shepstone's rule in Natal. He invented and orchestrated a ceremony for Cetshwayo in 1861 that recognized him as the heir to the crown of Zululand. And then he presided over the chief's formal coronation in 1873. For Shepstone and the installation and coronation of Cetshwayo see Carolyn Hamilton, *Terrific Majesty: The Powers of Shaku Zulu and the Limits of Historical Invention* (Cape Town and Johannesburg, 1998), pp. 75–81; and C. J. [Cornelius Janse] Uys, *In the Era of Shepstone: Being a Study of British Expansion in South Africa 1842–1877* (Lovedale, 1933), pp. 64, 83–4. But the coronation of Cetshwayo by Shepstone was solely for European eyes, to legitimate British claims to suzerainty over Zululand. There was another coronation ceremony, out of sight of the Europeans, which represented the official Zulu investiture.
31. This account is drawn from a paper by R. J. Mann, "The Gathering of the Native Clans," to be found in the NLSA (CT), Grey Collection, MSB 223, *Miscellaneous Manuscripts*, f. 18. Ngoza was an almost entirely "created" Zulu chief. But he came to represent how Zulus were presented to the British public through the photographs of him in various types of dress that were almost entirely invented. On this see the very important article by Jeff Guy, "'A paralysis of perspective': Image and Text in the Creation of an African Chief," *South African Historical Journal* 47 (2002), pp. 51–74.
32. CA, GH 30/5, *Letter Book of the Chief Commissioner, British Kaffraria, 1858–1860*, Grey to Maclean, 2 August 1860; GH 8/42, *Dispatches of the Chief Commissioner, British Kaffraria, 1860*, Maclean to Grey, 22 September 1860; GH 8/48, *Letters from Native Chiefs*, "Petition from Numsa to Prince Alfred," n.d.
33. David Cannadine, "The Context, Performance and Meaning of Ritual: The British Monarchy and the 'Invention of Tradition', *c.* 1820–1977," and Bernard S. Cohn, "Representing Authority in Victorian India," in Eric Hobsbawm and Terence Ranger (eds.), *The Invention of Tradition* (Cambridge, 1983), pp. 101–64, 165–210. Terence Ranger's essay in that volume, "The Invention of Tradition in Colonial Africa," pp. 211–62, focuses

on the twentieth century. See also William Kuhn, *Democratic Royalism: The Transformation of the British Monarchy, 1861–1914* (Basingstoke, 1996).

34. Timothy Stapleton, *Maqoma: Xhosa Resistance to Colonial Advance 1798–1873* (Johannesburg, 1994), pp. 200–2; NLSA (CT), MSB 223, 5, Grey Collection, *African Chiefs*, f. 7, Letter from George Maqoma, 1 October 1860, ironically enough congratulating Grey on the success of the Alfred tour. Thus the relationship between the chiefs and the imperial state continued to be rent by ambiguity and paradox.

35. CWM, LMS, *South Africa Reports*, Report from Birt to LMS Directors for 1870.

36. Stapleton, *Maqoma*, pp. 202–6.

37. Switzer, *Power and Resistance*, pp. 73–4; T. R. H. Davenport, *South Africa: A Modern History*, 4th edn. (Toronto, 1991), pp. 124–25; Noel Mostert, *Frontiers: The Epic Story of South Africa's Creation and the Tragedy of the Xhosa People* (London, 1992), pp. 1249–53.

38. C. C. Saunders, "Through an African's Eyes: The Diary of Nathaniel Umhala," *Quarterly Bulletin of the South African Library* 34 (1979–80), pp. 24–38.

39. Switzer, *Power and Resistance*, pp. 139–55, 160–2. There is a good case for including Tiyo Soga as a bridging figure between the world of our history and modern Xhosa nationalism. We have noted how he founded a famous dynasty of black southern African professionals and academics. His last testament to his sons possessed a nationalistic message. He urged them to identify themselves as black in spite of their racially mixed parentage and to be proud of their Xhosa heritage and origins. See Donovan Williams, *The Journal and Selected Writings of Tiyo Soga* (Cape Town, 1983). Soga also was a precursor of black religious leaders who from the late 1860s succeeded where the missionaries had failed in implanting Christianity among the Xhosa. See Wallace G. Mills, "The Taylor Revival of 1866 and the Roots of African Nationalism in the Cape Colony," *Journal of Religion in Africa* 8 (1976), pp. 105–22. For a clear statement of the new Xhosa politics that emerges in the 1880s, see the debate about electoral politics in the Xhosa newspaper *Isigidimi samaXhosa*, cited by Isabel Hofmeyr, *The Portable Bunyan: A Transnational History of The Pilgrim's Progress* (Princeton, 2004), pp. 128–9.

40. For the themes of this paragraph see Jeff Opland, "Praise Poems as Historical Sources," in Christopher Saunders and Robin Derricourt (eds.), *Beyond the Cape Frontier: Studies in the History of the Transkei and Ciskei* (London, 1974), pp. 1–38; Opland, "Nineteenth Century Xhosa Literature," *Kronos: A Journal of Cape History* 30 (2004), pp. 22–46; Nongenile Masithathu Zenani, *The World and the Word: Tales and Observations from the Xhosa Oral Tradition* (Madison, WI, 1992); Zakes Mda, *The Heart of Redness* (Oxford, 2000); and A. C. Jordan, *The Wrath of the Ancestors* (Johannesburg and Cape Town, 1980).

41. For important revisionist books about the end of empire, see Caroline Elkins, *Imperial Reckoning: The Untold Story of Britain's Gulag in Kenya* (New York, 2005); and David Anderson, *Histories of the Hanged: The Dirty War in Kenya and the End of Empire* (New York, 2005). For Colley using

the same words as he was abandoned by his men on Majuba Hill as Tola had as he was cornered by Colley's patrol: "Oh, my men, do not run, follow me," see Lieutenant-General Sir William F. Butler, *The Life of Pomeroy-Colley, K. C. S. I., C. B., C. M. G., 1835–1881* (London, 1899), pp. 49–50. CA, GH 8/50, *Demi-Official Letters, British Kaffraria 1857–58*, "Statement by one of Colley's Police," 22 December 1858; and see Maclean to Grey, 18 April 1858, admitting that the Transkeian expedition led by Gawler and Colley had committed acts "of a most unpleasant nature." They were pursuing Tola to try to arrest him for trial with the other chiefs.

Note on sources

The primary and secondary sources that I have drawn upon for this book are fully documented in the footnotes, and there is no compelling need to repeat them in a traditional bibliography. But readers may find it useful to have a brief account of the character of the principal manuscript collections that I have used in this book, since much of my narrative is dependent upon stories that I collected from these archives.

One of my intentions in researching this book was to go to the empire to write the history of the British imperial experience. In doing so, I stumbled upon the enormous riches of the imperial archive in South Africa. The most important collections I used in this respect were those of the Western Province Cape Archive Service, which are housed in the old Roeland Street prison in Cape Town. (The actual name of this depository has changed over time. For convenience I refer to it as the Cape Archive.) A better use for this sturdy old prison building would be hard to imagine. The Cape Archives are extraordinarily rich, and they are well known to South African historians. They are fairly well organized. There are helpful finding aids, and some digitization. But the vagaries of their various classification categories – which have changed over time – have caused records to be grouped in ways that make it very difficult to track stories from their beginning to their end. Much of the material came to me in the form of fragments. I found myself coming in on the middle of a story, for example, with no obvious way of finding anything relating to its beginning or ending. To some extent this was true of all the manuscript records I consulted for this book. But in the case of the government documents there was no necessary logic governing the distribution of material in the various record groups that I describe below.

The holdings in the Cape Archives that interested me were records of the early imperial administration. As an early practitioner of "history from the bottom up," I wanted to look at those records that could bring me close to the "on the ground" experience of the imperial encounter. For this reason I decided at the beginning not to rely upon the published selections of this imperial archive that had found their way into the bound volumes of the Parliamentary Papers. Even though the volumes published by Parliament do include some of the kinds of material that I was interested in viewing, I did not want to be at the mercy of the bureaucratic screening that was inevitably practiced by the imperial administration.[1] This meant that much of my research was conducted in the old-fashioned way: promising-sounding volumes of bound records were called up and leafed through. I was seldom disappointed. Only a small minority of these large books were entirely empty of interest. There were three main record groups that I found most useful.

The first record group – I mention them not necessarily in order of importance – was the Lieutenant Governor's series, known as the LG series. The records in this grouping are much broader than that name implies; indeed, there was a Lieutenant Governor of the eastern province for only a few years of the period covered by this book. The series comprises mainly papers from the key officials – the resident agents, the diplomatic agents and the magistrates who resided with the tribes in the 1830s and 1840s at the time that the Xhosa were formally regarded as independent sovereignties, before British Kaffraria itself was created.

The second, much larger, group was the GH series. These were officially named the Government House records and they include all the official and "demi-official" correspondence that was channeled between the eastern Cape and Cape Town. This record group was particularly useful for my purposes for tracking the exchange of information and policy between the Chief Commissioner of British Kaffraria and the Governor in Cape Town, who was also the High Commissioner of British Kaffraria. But, as described above, these records were not exclusively confined to one level of the imperial administration. Thus, although this record group contained the correspondence between the Chief Commissioner in British Kaffraria and the Governor, it also included records of exchanges between the resident agents with the tribes and the Chief Commissioner. More normally, however, such records were to be found in the third group of records that I used.

This group was the BK series, which are the records of British Kaffraria from its inception in late 1847 to its demise in 1866. This is a large collection, consisting of over 400 bound volumes. It contains all the records generated by the British Kaffrarian administration, and I was particularly interested in the files of the correspondence and reports of the magistrates placed with certain chiefs and tribes that were typically submitted to the Chief Commissioner. These records complemented the records of the LG and GH series in giving the closest access to the encounter between the British imperial administration and the Xhosa.

Missionary collections were the second indispensable set of records that were used to construct the stories told in this book. They are much better known, of course, than the records of the Cape Archives. The papers of the London Missionary Society, housed in the Council of World Missions archive at the School of Oriental and African Studies (SOAS) in the University of London, were the single most important non-official manuscript collection that I consulted. These records are well organized and divided into various self-explanatory categories, such as the Journals that the missionaries were required to keep, summarizing their activities for the home authorities. As with the official governmental records, my interest in these records lay in what they revealed about the content and dynamics of the encounter. And for this, they were of most interest in the period of the initial encounter, when missionaries were eager to note in close detail their experiences and observations. As I have explained, this period lasted into the 1840s, before missionary culture was overcome by stereotypes that constricted and confined how the Xhosa were seen.

In addition to the LMS archives, however, SOAS contains microcard copies of the papers of the Wesleyan Methodist Missionary Society. These records are similar in content to the LMS records, although they are less extensive and harder to use, because of their microfilm format, which causes many of the individual papers to be virtually illegible. As a collection, I also found that they tailed off in value from the end of the 1830s, when the quality of information diminishes greatly.

The National Archives, formerly the Public Record Office, was of limited use for this book, since I was not generally interested in the flows of policy debate or how issues were handled in Cape Town and London. Thus I did not see the need to go through the main Cape Colony series, CO 48, in a systematic way. Indeed, it is doubtful whether such a task would be feasible, since these records are currently available only on microfilm. But the National Archives do hold some individual gems, such as the Field Diary of Sir Harry Smith for 1851 (WO 135/2), when he was deep in fighting the eighth frontier war, or the official transcript of the Court of Inquiry into the Death of Hintza (CO 48/185).

A variety of other collections were used, some of which are seldom if ever used by imperial historians. These included various missionary papers at the Cory Library in Rhodes University. Among the holdings at this archive are individual missionary papers and journals, and most notably the extremely interesting minute book of the Glasgow Missionary Society Presbytery for Caffraria for several years in the 1840s. Such records must lie scattered throughout the archives of the old empire. Likewise, in the Cape Archives is the Letter Book of Captain John Gawler for 1856–7, which records in close detail his struggle for power with Mhala the Ndlambe chief. This record was drawn to my attention by Clifton Crais, who has used it himself. It is a wonderful example of a record that allows us to observe the process of empire-building on the ground. Similarly, the papers of officials like Sir Harry Smith, Sir Benjamin D'Urban and Sir George Grey, which are held in both the Cape Archives and the Cape Town branch of the National Library of South Africa, were essential for a close look at the dynamics of imperial culture in the policy-making realm.

NOTE

1. The most important of the Parliamentary Papers for this topic are the following: *Correspondence Between Lord Glenelg and Governor D'Urban*, 1837 (503), vol. XLIII; *Correspondence with the Governor of the Cape of Good Hope relative to the state of the Kafir Tribes on the Eastern Frontier of the Colony*, 1847 [786], vol. XXXVIII; *Correspondence with the Governor...Colony*, 1847–8 [912], vol. XLIII; *Correspondence with the Governor...Colony*, 1847–8 [969], vol. XLIII; *Correspondence with the Governor...Colony*, 1849 [1056], vol. XXXVI; *Correspondence with the Governor...Colony*, 1850 [1288], vol. XXXVIII; *Correspondence with the Governor...Relative to the State of the Kafir Tribes and the Recent Outbreak on the Eastern Frontier of the Colony*, 1851 [1334, 1352, 1380], vol. XXXVIII; *Kafir Tribes: Copies and Extracts of Correspondence relative to the Kafir Tribes between the years 1837 and 1845*, 1851 [424], vol. XXXVIII; *Correspondence with the Governor...Colony*, 1852 [1428], vol. XXXIII; *Correspondence with the Governor...Colony*, 1852–3 [1635], vol. LXVI; *Further Papers Relative to the State of the Kaffir Tribes*, 1854–5 [1969], vol. XXXVIII; *Further Papers...Tribes*, 1856 [2096], vol. XLII; *Further Papers...Tribes*, 1857 [2202], vol. X; *Further Papers...Tribes*, 1857–8 [2352], vol. XL.

Index